BANKING AND BILLS OF EXCHANGE

THE CANADIAN LAW

OF

BANKS AND BANKING

THE CLEARING HOUSE,

CURRENCY,

DOMINION NOTES,

BILLS, NOTES, CHEQUES

AND OTHER

NEGOTIABLE INSTRUMENTS

BY

JOHN DELATRE FALCONBRIDGE, M.A., LL.B.

OF OSGOODE HALL, BARRISTER-AT-LAW

TORONTO :

CANADA LAW BOOK COMPANY, LIMITED

1907

.

.

.

,

PREFACE.

The book which I am venturing to commit to the kindly consideration of the bankers and the members of my own profession in the Dominion consists primarily of an exposition of the Bank Act and the Bills of Exchange Act, recently re-enacted as Chapters 29 and 119 of the Revised Statutes of Canada, 1906.

The former Act has established a system of banking which differs in many respects from that prevailing either in England or in the United States. The Act contains provisions in regard to the incorporation, organization and existence of chartered banks with important but carefully limited lending powers and other privileges, and in regard to the security afforded by the banks to the public.

Since 1901 no commentary on the Bank Act has been published and the cases on the subject which have been reported during the last six years are both numerous and important.

In connection with the Bank Act, I have not neglected to discuss the general relation of banker and customer and the body of law merchant which governs that relation, but the limits of time and space have restricted my discussion of them to a moderate length. The Act affects such relation to a comparatively small extent, and the standard English text books contain an exposition of the law more in detail than it has been possible to include in a book of the somewhat wide range of this one.

In the course of the second part of the book, I have had frequent occasion to acknowledge my indebtedness to Chalmers on Bills of Exchange. The fact that the English Act was drafted by the author of that work and that the provisions of the Act were for the most part his deductions from the cases which he cites as illustrations gives his work a peculiar importance. I have, therefore, made a free use of Chalmers' illustrations. In doing so I am following the example of previous commentators on the Canadian Act.

Both the Bank Act and the Bills of Exchange Act are also illustrated by the leading Canadian cases. Inasmuch, however, as the Bills of Exchange Act is a codifying Act and has made plain many matters which before were obscure, or has given statutory sanction to many propositions which formerly required to be supported by the citation of reported cases, I have not hesitated to omit a reference to cases where I considered that their citation would increase the size of the book without adding materially to its usefulness.

Both the statutes above mentioned have undergone great changes in form in the revision of 1906. Whenever an alteration in wording or arrangement is not obviously immaterial, I have in the notes drawn attention to the change. By virtue of the Revised Statutes of Canada, 1906, Act, if upon any point the provisions of the Revised Statutes are not in effect the same as those of the Acts for which they are substituted, the provisions of the Revised Statutes prevail as respects all transactions, matters and things subsequent to the time when the Revised Statutes take effect, that is, on, from and after the 31st of January, 1907.

One result of the revision of the Bills of Exchange Act is that, while before the revision its sections corresponded almost exactly with those of the English Act and only a few important differences had to be borne in mind, now the arrangement and section-numbering of the Canadian and the English Acts are so different that an English text book no longer affords a convenient guide to the Canadian Act.

It gives me pleasure to acknowledge my obligation to Mr. Arthur Whyte Anglin, Barrister-at-law, who was so kind as to read the manuscript of the first half of the book and who made numerous valuable suggestions which I was glad to adopt. The responsibility for the final form of the text is, however, mine alone. I am indebted to my father for the affectionate care with which he read the whole book in proof form. The proof was also read, and the table of cases prepared, by Mr. R. B. Lowndes.

J. D. F.

Toronto, April, 1907.

TABLE OF CONTENTS.

PREFACE.   v
LIST OF ABBREVIATIONS   ix
TABLE OF CASES.   xi

BOOK I.

BANKING AND THE BANK ACT.

CHAPTER.   PAGE.
 1. Review of Banking Legislation.   1
 2. Usage and the Law Merchant.   21
 3. The Bank Act: Short Title and Interpretation.   30
 4. Application of the Act.   36
 5. Incorporation and Organization of Banks.   40
 6. Internal Regulations.   48
 7. Capital Stock.   70
 8. Shares and Calls.   75
 9. Transfer and Transmission of Shares.   87
10. Shares Subject to Trusts.   98
11. Annual Statement and Inspection.   104
12. Dividends.   108
13. Cash Reserves.   112
14. The Issue and Circulation of Notes.   114
15. Business and Powers of a Bank.   130
16. Warehouse Receipts, etc., as Collateral Security.   164
17. Interest and Collection and Agency Fees.   204
18. Deposits and the Current Account.   209
19. The Purchase of the Assets of a Bank.   223
20. Returns by a Bank.   229
21. Payments to the Minister upon Winding-Up.   234
22. The Curator.   237
23. By-laws of the Canadian Bankers' Association.   241
24. Insolvency of a Bank.   246
25. Offences and Penalties.   259
26. Schedules to the Bank Act.   280
27. The Canadian Bankers' Association.   287
28. The Clearing House.   293
29. Currency and Dominion Notes.   306

BOOK II.

NEGOTIABLE INSTRUMENTS AND THE BILLS OF EXCHANGE ACT.

30. Negotiable Instruments........................... 321
31. Introduction to the Bills of Exchange Act........... 331
32. Bills of Exchange Act: Short Title and Interpretation.. 341

PART I.

33. Bills of Exchange Act: General Provisions........... 348

PART II.

BILLS OF EXCHANGE.

34. Form of Bill and Interpretation.................... 362
35. Acceptance and Interpretation..................... 405
36. Delivery and Oral Evidence....................... 418
37. Computation of Time, Non-juridical Days and Days of
        Grace...................................... 423
38. Capacity and Authority of Parties................. 428
39. Consideration.................................. 447
40. Negotiation of Bills............................. 462
41. Presentment for Acceptance....................... 484
42. Presentment for Payment......................... 495
43. Dishonour..................................... 509
44. Protest....................................... 536
45. Liabilities of Parties............................ 547
46. Discharge of Bill............................... 573
47. Acceptance and Payment for Honour................ 588
48. Lost Instruments............................... 594
49. Bill in a Set.................................. 596
50. Conflict of Laws............................... 598

PART III.

51. Cheques on a Bank.............................. 608
52. Crossed Cheques................................ 619

PART IV.

53. Promissory Notes............................... 629
54. Schedule to the Bills of Exchange Act.............. 641

INDEX....................................... 653

LIST OF ABBREVIATIONS

(OMITTING THE USUAL ABBREVIATIONS OF ENGLISH REPORTS.)

A.R. ....Ontario Appeal Reports.
Allen ....Allen's New Brunswick Reports.
Am.R...........American Reports.

Barb ....Barbour's New York Supreme Court Reports.
B.C.R. ....British Columbia Reports.

Can. Crim. Cases...Canadian Criminal Cases.
Can. Ex. C.R......Exchequer Court of Canada Reports.
Can. L.R........Canadian Law Review.
C.C.............Civil Code of Lower Canada.
Chalmers ....Chalmers on Bills of Exchange, 6th ed. 1903.
Chipman........Chipman's New Brunswick Reports.
C.L.T. ....Canadian Law Times.
Com. L.R.......Commercial Law Reports (Canada).
Com. Ca. ....Commercial Cases (English).
Conn............Connecticut Reports
C.P.............Upper Canada Common Pleas Reports.
Cush. ....Cushing's Massachusetts Reports.

Draper. ....Draper's Upper Canada King's Bench Reports.

East. L.R. ....Eastern Law Reports.

G. and O. ....Geldert and Oxley's Nova Scotia Reports.
Girouard ....Girouard on Bills and Notes (1891).
Gr. ....Grant's Upper Canada Chancery Reports.

Han...........Hannay's New Brunswick Reports.
Harv. L.R. ......Harvard Law Review.

Journal C.B.A. ...Journal of the Canadian Bankers' Association.

Kerr...........Kerr's New Brunswick Reports.

L.C.J............Lower Canada Jurist.
L.C.R. ....Lower Canada Reports.
L.N. ....Legal News (Québec).
L.Q.R...........Law Quarterly Review.

Man. R. ....Manitoba Reports.
Mason..........United States Circuit Court Reports.
Mass ....Massachusetts Reports.
M.L.R., S.C. .....Montreal Law Reports, Superior Court.
McCreary ....United States Circuit Court Reports.
McLean ....United States Circuit Court Reports.

N.B. Eq. Cas.. ...New Brunswick Equity Cases.
N.B.R. ....New Brunswick Reports.
N.S.D. ....Nova Scotia Decisions.

B—BANK ACT.

N.S.R. . . . . Nova Scotia Reports.
N.S.W.R. . . . . New South Wales Reports.
N.Y. . . . . New York Reports.

O.L.R. . . . . Ontario Law Reports (since 1900).
O.R. . . . . Ontario Reports (before 1901).
O.S. . . . . Upper Canada Queen's Bench Reports, Old Series.
O.W.R. . . . . Ontario Weekly Reporter.

P.R. . . . . Ontario Practice Reports.
Pugs. . . . . Pugsley's New Brunswick Reports.

Q.L.R. . . . . Quebec Law Reports.
Q.R., Q.B. . . . . . . Quebec Reports, Queen's Bench.
Q.R., K.B. . . . . . . Quebec Reports, King's Bench.
Q.R., S.C. . . . . . . Quebec Reports, Superior Court.

R.C. . . . . English Ruling Cases.
R.L. . . . . Revue Légale (Quebec).
Rev. de Leg. . . . . Revue de Législation (Quebec).
R.J.R.Q. . . . . . . Rapports Judiciaires Revisés de Québec.
R. and G. . . . . . . Russell and Geldert's Nova Scotia Reports.
R.R. . . . . English Revised Reports.

S.C.Cas. . . . . Supreme Court Cases.
S.C.R. . . . . Supreme Court of Canada Reports.

Terr. L.R. . . . . . . Territories Law Reports.

U.C.R. . . . . Upper Canada Reports (Queen's Bench).
U.S. . . . . Reports of the Supreme Court of the United States.

Wend. . . . . Wendell's New York Reports.
West. L.R. . . . . . Western Law Reports.

TABLE OF CASES CITED.

Abbott v. Fraser, 343
Abbott v. Wurtele, 587
Aberaman Ironworks, Re; Peek's case, 81
Abrey v. Crux, 415, 421, 581
Adams v. Bank of Montreal, 48, 206
Adams v. Thomas, 421
Adelphi Co., Re; Best's case, 81
Agra Bank's claim; Re European Bank, 215, 219
Agra and Masterman's Bank, Re, 322, 323
Agra Bank v. Leighton, 460
Alcock v. Smith, 477, 479, 601, 602
Alderson v. Langdale, 584
Aldous v. Cornwall, 587
Alexander v. Burchfield, 506, 615, 616
Alexander v. Simpson, 66
Alexander v. Sizer, 445, 446
Alexander v. Thomas, 369
Allen v. Edmundson, 499, 519, 520
Allen v. Kemble, 599
Allen v. Mawson, 632
Allen v. Ont. & Rainy River, 43, 48
Allen v. Sea, 388
Alliance Bank v. Carey, 599
Alliance Bank v. Kearsley, 561
Allison v. McDonald, 554
Alma Spinning Co., In re; Bottomly's case, 42
Alsager v. Close, 419
Amazon v. Quebec, 477
Amner v. Clark, 387
Amory v. Merryweather, 478
Anderson v. Weston, 480
Angers v. Dillon, 364, 369
Archer v. Bamford, 460
Archer v. Bank of England, 472
Armfield v. Allport, 396
Armour v. Gates, 446
Armstrong v. Buchanan, 195
Armstrong v. Christiani, 521
Armstrong v. Merchants, 83
Arnold v. Cheque Bank, 416, 432
Arsell v. Baker, 574
Ashbury v. Riche, 48
Ashpitel v. Bryan, 377
Ashworth v. Munn, 75
Asiatic Banking Corporation, Re; Royal Bank of India's case, 142
Asprey v. Levy, 566
Athill, Re, 141

Atkins v. Wardle, 408
Atkinson v. Hawdon, 584
Attenborough v. Clarke, 451
Attenborough v. Mackenzie, 481, 575
Attorney-General v. Jewish Colon. Assocn., 80
Atty.-Genl. v. Pratt, 549
Atty.-Genl. for Ont. v. Atty.-Genl. for Canada, 489
Atty.-Genl. for Ont. v. Hamilton Street Ry., 392
Atty.-Genl. v. Newman, 78, 79, 210
Attwood v. Griffin, 586
Attwood v. Munnings, 442, 443
Atwood v. Crowdie, 451
Auldjo v. McDougall, 350, 374
Awde v. Dixon, 400, 455
Ayers v. South Australian Banking Co., 146
Ayr v. Wallace, 559
Ayrey v. Fearnsides, 366

Backhouse v. Charlton, 618
Bailey v. Bidwell, 459
Bailey v. Bodenham, 518
Bailey v. Jellett, 215
Bailey v. Jephcott, 220, 618
Bailey v. Porter, 500, 521
Baillie v. Dickson, 527
Bain v. Gregory, 522
Bain v. Torrance, 139
Baines' case; Re Central Bank, 82, 89, 256
Baker v. Birch, 505
Bank of Africa v. Salisbury, 150
Bank of America v. Copland, 607
Bank of Australasia v. Breillat, 131, 562
Bank of Brazil, Ex parte; Re English Bank, 568, 592
Bank of B. N. A. v. Bossuyt, 206, 207
Bank of B. N. A. v. Browne, 40
Bank of B. N. A. v. Clarkson, 34, 180
Bank of B. N. A. v. Gibson, 368
Bank of Commerce v. Jenkins, 63
Bank of England v. Parsons, 99
Bank of England v. Vagliano, 212, 342, 375, 377, 381
Bank of Hamilton v. Donaldson, 157

Bank of Hamilton v. Halstead, 198, 199
Bank of Hamilton v. Noye, 168, 175, 198
Bank of Hamilton v. Shepherd, 198
Bank of Hindustan v. Alison, 81
Bank of Liverpool v. Bigelow, 90
Bank of Montreal v. De Latre, 446
Bank of Montreal v. Hartman, 206
Bank of Montreal v. Henderson, 87
Bank of Montreal v. Little, 217
Bank of Montreal v. Sweeny, 143
Bank of Montreal v. Thomas, 548
Bank of Montreal's Claim; Re Chatham Banner Co., 106
Bank of N. S. W. v. Campbell, 159
Bank of N. S. W. v. Goulburn, 220
Bank of N. S. W. v. Owston, 62
Bank of Ontario, Re, 92
Bank of Ottawa v. Harty, 440
Bank of Scotland v. Dominion Bank, 133
Bank of Syria, In re, 58
Bank of Toronto v. Cobourg Ry. Co., 328
Bank of Toronto v. Dickinson, 219
Bank of Toronto v. Hamilton, 441
Bank of Toronto v. Lambe, 31, 77
Bank of Toronto v. Perkins, 146, 156
Bank of Toronto v. St. Lawrence, 343
Bank of Upper Canada v. Baldwin, 106
Bank of Upper Canada v. Bradshaw, 64
Bank of Upper Canada v. Killaly, 158
Bank of Upper Canada v. Scott, 159
Bank of Upper Canada v. Turcotte, 504
Bank of Van Diemen's Land v. Bank of Victoria, 133, 417, 491
Banner v. Johnston, 368
Banque d'Hochelaga's case; Re Commercial Bank, 585, 586, 612
Banque d'Hochelaga v. Merchant's Bank, 175
Banque de St. Hyacinthe v. Sarrazin, 207
Banque Jacques-Cartier v. Gagnon, 527, 560
Banque Jacques-Cartier v. Lalonde, 350
Banque Jacques-Cartier v. Lescard, 350, 398
Banque Jacques-Cartier v. Limoilou, 611, 612, 613, 614, 615
Banque Jacques-Cartier v. The Queen, 330
Banque Jacques-Cartier v. Strachan, 595
Banque Molson v. Cooke, 350
Banque Nationale v. City Bank, 63
Banque Nationale v. Martel, 540
Banque Nationale v. Merchants Bank, 293, 298
Banque Populaire v. Cavé, 569
Banque Provinciale v. Arnoldi, 586
Banque Provinciale v. Charbonneau, 64
Barber v. Richards, 450
Barclay, Ex parte, 577
Barkwell's claim; Re Commercial Bank of Manitoba, 217
Barnard, Re; Edwards v. Barnard, 407
Barned's Bank, Re, 211
Barrington, Re, 465
Barss v. Bank of N.S., 88
Barthe v. Armstrong, 470
Bartlett v. Benson, 470
Bartrum v. Caddy, 575
Barwick v. English Joint Stock Bank, 62
Bateman v. Mid Wales Railway Co., 429
Bathgate v. Merchants Bank, 146
Bavins v. London & S. W. Bank, 364
Baxendale v. Bennett, 398, 399, 419, 582
Beaudry v. Laflamme, 631
Beaumont v. Greathead, 575, 634
Bechervaise v. Lewis, 452
Bechuanaland v. London, 328
Beecham v. Smith, 634
Beeching v. Gower, 390, 500
Beeman v. Duck, 551, 552
Begbie v. Levi, 393
Belfast v. Doherty, 459
Bell v. Lord Ingestre, 420
Bellamy v. Majoribanks, 619
Bellemare v. Gray, 461
Belshaw v. Bush, 574
Beltz v. Molsons Bank, 585
Benallack v. Bank of B. N. A., 207
Bennett v. O'Meara, 162
Bentham Mills, Re, 93
Berridge v. Fitzgerald, 514, 526
Berry v. Alderman, 459
Besant v. Cross, 421
Best's case; Re Adelphi Co., 81
Bignold, Ex parte, 505

Billing v. Devaux, 549
Bird, Ex parte, 572
Birkbeck v. Johnston, 143
Birmingham Bank, Ex parte, 349
Bishop v. Chitty, 506
Bishop v. Young, 639
Black v. Homersham, 109
Black v. Strickland, 471
Blackie v. Pidding, 595
Blackman v. Lehman, 386
Blackwood v. The Queen, 78
Blanckenhagen v. Blundell, 371
Blane, Ex parte; Re Hallett & Co., 215
Bloomenthal v. Ford, 72
Bobbett v. Pinkett, 625
Boddington v. Schlencker, 293
Boehm v. Garcias, 409
Bolton v. Dugdale, 366
Bond v. Barrow, 110
Borland's Trustee v. Steel, 76
Boschoek v. Fuke, 56, 61, 66
Bottomly's case; Re Alma Spinning Co., 42
Boultbee v. Gzowski, 89, 256
Boulton v. Jones, 367
Boulton v. Langmuir, 585
Bounsall v. Harrison, 480
Bowes, Re, 151
Bowes v. Holland, 452
Bowes v. Howe, 505
Boyd v. Bank of N. B., 99
Boyd v. Nasmith, 609, 610, 612, 614
Boys, Re, 420
Boyse, Re, 368
Bradford Banking Co. v. Briggs, 151
Bradlaugh v. De Rin, 601
Braithwaite v. Gardiner, 551
Brandao v. Barrett, 22 23, 151, 152, 329
Brandon's case; Re Marseilles Extension Co., 602
Bray v. Hadwen, 517, 523, 524
Brett v. Levett, 532
Brewery Assets Corp., In re; Truman's case, 80
Bridges v. Berry, 515
Bridgewater v. Murphy, 442
British Columbia v. Ellis, 399
Britton v. Milsom, 532
Bromage v. Lloyd, 416, 420
Bromage v. Vaughan, 522
Brook v. Hook, 433
Brooke v. Bank of Upper Canada, 248
Brooks v. Elkins, 631
Brooks v. Mitchell, 479, 636

Brown's case; In re Metropolitan, etc., Co., 56
Brown v. Holland, 408, 421
Brown v. Langley, 422
Brown v. Toronto General Trusts, 213
Browne v. Commercial Bank, 133
Bryant v. Eastman, 467
Bryant v. Quebec Bank, 442
Buck v. Robson, 547
Buckley v. Jackson, 472
Bullard v. Bell, 324
Bullion v. Cartwright, 460
Bult v. Morrell, 406
Burchfield v. Moore, 571, 583, 584, 585
Burdon v. Benton, 450
Burgh v. Legge, 532
Burland v. Earle, 50, 69, 109, 113
Burmester v. Barron, 527
Burnett v. Monaghan, 505
Burnham v. Watts, 367
Burton v. Goffin, 399, 504
Bush v. Fry, 177
Butler v. Crips, 370
Buxton v. Jones, 501

Calderwood's case; Re Provincial Grocers, 81
Callow v. Lawrence, 471, 578
Cambefort v. Chapman, 515
Campbell v. French, 426
Campbell v. Hodgson, 421
Campbell v. McKay, 446
Cameron v. Kerr, 156
Cameron v. Perrin, 174
Canada Paper Co. v. Gazette, 446, 638
Canada Shipping Co.'s case; Re Central Bank, 200
Canadian Bank of Commerce v. McDonald, 146, 207
Canadian Bank of Commerce v. Perram, 558, 559
Canadian Tin Plate Co., Re; Morton's case, 81*
Capital & Counties Bank v. Gordon, 134, 139
Carew's Estate Act, Re, 199
Carew v. Duckworth, 532, 533
Cariss v. Tattersall, 584
Carlon v. Kenealy, 383, 394
Carlos v. Fancourt, 368, 369
Carnegie v. Federal Bank, 148, 154
Carrique v. Beatty, 557, 583, 585
Carstairs v. Bates, 140
Carter v. Flower, 533

Carter v. White, 402, 496
Carvick v. Vickery, 466
Cassidy v. Mansfield, 522
Castrique v. Bernabo, 492, 510, 512
Castrique v. Buttigieg, 403, 564
Castrique v. Imrie, 582
Caunt v. Thompson, 534
Cawley & Co., Re, 83
Central Bank v. Garland, 153
Central Bank & Hogg, Re, 249
Central Bank and the Winding-up Act, Re, 248
Central Bank, Re, 254
Central Bank, Re; Baines' case, 82, 89, 256
Central Bank, Re; Canada Shipping Co.'s case, 200
Central Bank, Re; Home Savings & Loan Co.'s case, 90, 102
Central Bank, Re; Morton and Block's claims, 210, 216
Central Bank, Re; Nasmith's and Baines' cases, 82, 89, 90, 148
Central Bank, Re; Wells & Mc-Murchy's case, 258
Chalmers v. Lanion, 478
Chamberlain v. Young, 370, 375, 399
Chambers v. Miller, 212
Chapman v. Cottrell, 604
Chapman v. Keane, 525
Chard v. Fox, 522
Charlebois v. Montreal, 365
Charles v. Blackwell, 432, 436, 437
Charnley v. Grundy, 595
Chartered Bank v. Dickson,
Chatham Banner Co., Re; Bank of Montreal's claim, 106
Chatterton v. London & County Bank, 213
Chawcour v. Salter, 23
Cheshire Banking Co., Re; Duff's Executor's case, 103
Chesney v. St. John, 364, 633
Ching v. Jeffrey, 478
Chorlton v. Lings, 344
Citizens' Bank v. New Orleans, 549
City Bank v. Barrow, 177
City Bank v. Cheney, 446
City Bank v. Rowan, 381
City Discount Co. v. McLean, 214
Clarke, In re, 76
Clarke v. London County Bank, 627
Clarke v. Sharpe, 526
Clarkson v. Lawson, 457
Clayton's case, Devaynes v. Noble, 213, 215

Clayton v. Gosling, 386
Clearahue v. Morris, 394
Clench v. Consolidated Bank, 220
Clifford v. Parker, 584
Clipperton v. Spettique, 566
Clode v. Bayley, 523
Clutton v. Attenborough, 375, 378, 419
Cochrane v. Caie, 367
Cockburn v. Sylvester, 172
Cockburn v. Johnston, 566
Cocks v. Masterman, 441
Codd v. Lewis, 358
Cohen v. Hale, 617
Cole v. North Western Bank, 177
Colehan v. Cook, 386
Collen v. Wright, 89, 444
Collinson v. Lister, 455
Collott v. Haigh, 453
Colonial Bank v. Cady, 144
Colonial Bank v. Marshall, 441
Colonial Bank v. Whinney, 87, 89
Colquhoun v. Brooks, 77
Commercial Bank, Re, 570
Commercial Bank, Re; Banque d'Hochelaga's case, 585, 586, 612
Commercial Bank v. Bissett, 638
Commercial Bank of Manitoba, Re, 254
Commercial Bank of Manitoba, Re; Barkwell's claim, 217
Commercial Bank v. Bank of Upper Canada, 156, 157
Commercial Bank v. Cotton, 204
Commercial Bank v. Morrison, 420, 455, 468
Commercial Bank v. Weller, 520
Commercial National Bank v. Corcoran, 33
Confederation Life v. Howard, 327
Confederation Life v. Labatt, 196
Conflans v. Parker, 329
Conn v. Smith, 202
Conova v. Earl, 466
Cook v. Dodds, 357, 634
Cook v. Lister, 533, 574, 576, 579
Cook v. Royal Canadian Bank, 150, 151
Cook v. Wright, 448
Cooper v. Blacklock, 442
Cooper v. Meyer, 551
Cooper v. Waldegrave, 604
Cordery v. Colville, 532
Cornes v. Taylor, 507
Cosgrave v. Boyle, 528
Costa Rica v. Forwood, 54
Cote, Ex parte, 415, 416

Coté v. Lemieux, 392
Counsell v. Livingstone, 519, 521
County of Gloucester Bank v. Rudry, 49
Coward v. Hughes, 448
Cowie v. Sterling, 371
Cox v. Troy, 415
Craig v. Benjamin, 360
Cranley v. Hillary, 507
Crawley's case; Re Peruvian Railway Co., 81
Crears v. Hunter, 448
Creelman v. Stewart, 448
Creighton v. Halifax Banking Co., 562
Cripps v. Davis, 574
Croft v. Hamlin, 637
Crombie v. Overholtzer, 393
Crosse v. Smith, 501, 519
Crossley v. Ham, 480
Crouch v. Credit Foncier, 321, 328, 351, 483
Crouse v. Park, 394
Crowe v. Clay, 507, 594
Crowfoot v. Gurney, 366
Crutchley v. Mann, 399
Cullerne v. London & Suburban, 54
Cumming v. Shand, 132
Cunard v. Symon-Kaye, 637
Cundy v. Marriott, 584
Cunliffe Brooks v. Blackburn, 211
Cunnington v. Peterson, 583
Currie v. Misa, 447, 448, 456, 515
Cushing v. Dupuy, 86, 182
Cutts v. Perkins, 549

Da Costa v. Cole, 395
Dasylva v. Dufour, 631
Davidson v. Cooper, 583
Davis v. Bowsher, 151
Davis v. Clarke, 406
Davis v. Dunn, 385
Davis v. Isaacs, 599
Davis v. Jones, 389
Davison, Re, 634
Dawkes v. Lord Deloraine, 368
Day v. Nix, 460
De Bernales v. Fuller, 132, 547
De Fries Critten v. Chemical National Bank, 213
De la Chaumette v. Bank of England, 456
De la Torre v. Barclay, 581
De Serres v. Enard, 611
De Sola v. Ascher, 631
De Tastet v. Baring, 570
Deacon v. Stodhart, 575

Decroix v. Meyer, 373, 383, 412, 587
Deep sea Fishery Co.'s claim; Re Fenwick, 514
Deering v. Hayden, 504
Demers v. Rousseau, 512
Denham & Co., In re, 55, 107
Denton v. Peters, 415, 420
Derry v. Peek, 444
Des Rosiers v. Montreal, 329
Désy v. Daly, 631
Devaynes v. Noble, Clayton's case, 214
Deverges v. Sandeman, 153
Dickenson v. Clemow, 448
Dickenson v. Valpy, 562
Dillon v. Rimmer, 577
Dixon v. Kennaway, 72
Dombroski v. Laliberté, 421
Dominion Bank v. Davidson, 173
Dominion Bank v. Ewing, 433
Dominion Bank v. Kennedy, 219
Dominion Bank v. Oliver, 157, 198
Dominion Bank v. Wiggins, 364
Don v. Lippman, 599
Donald v. Suckling, 151, 153
Donnelly v. Hall, 189
Donogh v. Gillespie, 134
Dooley v. Ryarson, 369
Dovey v. Cory, 55, 111, 273
Down v. Halling, 479
Drain v. Harvey, 421
Drake v. Bank of Toronto, 204
Drapeau v. Pominville, 389
Drury v. Macauley, 364
Duchaine v. Maguire, 369
Duck v. Tower, 49
Duff's Executor's case; Re Cheshire Banking Co., 103
Dumont v. Aubert, 90
Duncan & Co., Re, 211
Duncan v. North & South Wales Bank, 507, 553, 564, 578
Dunn v. Allen, 366
Duthie v. Essery, 482, 557
Dutton v. Marsh, 446

East v. Smith, 514, 518, 522
East of England Banking Co., Re, 211
Easton v. London, etc., Bank, 324
Eastwood v. Bain, 444
Eastwood v. Kenyon, 448
Edelstein v. Schuler, 23, 327
Edgar v. Magee, 511
Edge v. Bumford, 464
Edie v. East India Co., 383, 469
Edis v. Bury, 632

Edmunds v. Bushell, 561
Edwards, Ex parte, 433
Edwards v. Barnard; Re Barnard, 407
Edwards v. Dick, 461
Edwards v. Hall, 75
Edwards v. Vere, 211
Edwards v. Walters, 581
Elder v. Kelly, 564
Elford v. Teed, 499
Elliott v. Beech, 386
Ellison v. Collingridge, 363
Elsam v. Denny, 578
Emard v. Marcille, 560
Embiricos v. Anglo Austrian Bank, 600, 602
Emerson v. Erwin, 421
English Bank, Re; Ex parte Bank of Brazil, 568, 592
Ernest v. Loma, 68
Esdaile v. Sowerby, 505
Essex Land & Timber Co., Re; Trout's case, 156
European Bank, Re, 451
European Bank Re; Agra Bank's claim, 215, 219
European Bank, Re; Ex parte Oriental Bank, 478, 576
Evans v. Cramlington, 471
Everard v. Watson, 520, 521
Ewin v. Lancaster, 422, 554
Ewing, In re, 76
Ewing v. Cameron, 358
Ewing v. Dominion Bank, 434
Exchange Bank v. Fletcher, 146, 148
Exchange Bank v. Quebec Bank, 472
Exchange Bank v. Reg., 257

Fairchild v. Ferguson, 445
Fairclough v. Pavia, 470, 478
Faith v. Richmond, 561
Fanshawe v. Peat, 413, 587
Farley v. Turner, 210
Farmer v. Ellis, 459
Farmers' Bank v. Dominion Coal Co., 459
Farquhar, Ex parte; Re Land Securities Co., 140
Farquhar v. Southey, 587
Farquharson v. King, 178
Federal Bank v. Northwood, 562
Fenwick, Re; Deep Sea Fishery Co.'s claim, 514
Ferris v. Bond, 634
Fielder v. Marshall, 372, 632
Fielding v. Corry, 139, 524
Fine Art v. Union Bank, 329

Firbanks v. Humphreys, 444
Firth v. Brooks, 616
Forth v. Thrush, 520, 523
Fisher v. Calvert, 368
Fisher v. Meehan, 566
Fitch v. Jones, 459
Fitch v. Kelly, 501, 586
Fleckner v. Bank of the U.S., 140
Fleming v. Bank of New Zealand, 211, 212
Flour City Bank v. Connery, 459
Foakes v. Beer, 574
Foley v. Hill, 210
Forbes v. Marshall, 561
Ford v. Auger, 398
Ford v. Beech, 574
Forget v. Ostigny, 26
Forman v. Jacob, 560
Forman v. Wright, 460
Forster v. Mackreth, 351, 390, 391
Forsythe v. Bank of Nova Scotia, 253
Forward v. Thompson, 372
Foss v. Harbottle, 49
Foster v. Bank of London, 107
Foster v. Dawber, 580, 581
Foster v. Jolly, 421
Foster v. McKinnon, 350
Foster v. New Trinidad, 110
Foster v. Parker, 533
France v. Clark, 400, 402
Francis v. Bruce; Re George, 581
Franklin v. Bank of England, 99
Fraser v. Bank of Toronto, 190
Fraser v. McLeod, 560
Freakley v. Fox, 580
Freeman v. Cook, 435
Fuller v. Smith, 572
Fullerton v. Chapman, 368
Furse v. Sharwood, 520

Gaden v. Newfoundland Savings Bank, 134, 612. 613
Gale v. Walsh, 536
Galloway's case; Re Pakenham Pork Packing Co., 82
Garden v. Bruce, 599
Garden, Gully, etc. v. McLister, 84
Gardner v. Walsh, 585, 635
Garland v. Jacomb, 562
Garner v. Hayes, 370
Garrard v. Lewis, 396, 401, 587
Garrett v. McKewan, 139
Gaskin v. Davis, 394
Gauthier v. Reinhardt, 457
Gay v. Lander, 633

Geary v. Physic, 349
General Estate Co., Re, 324, 328
General South American Co., Re, 548, 567
George, Re; Francis v. Bruce, 581
George v. Surrey, 349
Geralopulo v. Wieler, 540, 591
Gibb v. Mather, 496, 500, 585, 639
Gibbs v. Dominion Bank, 196, 202
Gibbs v. Fremont, 563, 604
Giblin v. McMullen, 136, 137
Gibson, Ex parte, 386
Gibson v. Barton, 276
Gibson v. Coates, 458
Giles v. Bourne, 389
Gillespie, Re; Ex parte Robarts, 570
Gillies v. Commercial Bank, 158, 214
Gillin v. Cutler, 367
Giraldi v. Banque Jacques-Cartier, 220
Girvin v. Burke, 360
Glasscock v. Balls, 574, 636
Glengoil v. Pilkington, 26
Goggerley v. Cuthbert, 419
Going v. Barwick, 367
Goldie v. Harper, 460
Golding v. Waterhouse, 363, 370, 632
Goldsmid v. Hampton, 410
Gomersall, Re, 140, 349, 391
Goodall v. Dolley, 531
Goodall v. Polhill, 523, 593
Goodfallow, Re, 193
Goodman v. Harvey, 480
Goodwin v. Robarts, 22, 23, 24, 324, 327, 328, 329, 336, 354, 383, 548, 610
Gordon v. London, etc., Bank, 449, 627, 628
Gorgier v. Mievell, 328
Gosman, Re, 211
Goss v. Nelson, 386
Gosselin v. Ontario Bank, 35, 168
Gould v. Coombs, 631
Goupy v. Harden, 403
Grant v. Banque Nationale, 157, 162
Grant v. De Costa, 390
Gravelle v. Beaudoin, 26
Graves v. American Bank, 432
Graves v. Key, 478, 574
Gray v. Johnston, 219, 220
Gray v. Milner, 372
Gray v. Raper, 446
Gray v. Seckham, 451
Gray v. Worden, 367, 631

Great Northern Works, In re; Ex parte Kennedy, 42
Great Western v. London & County Bank, 131, 626, 627
Grieve v. Molsons Bank, 63
Griffin, Re, 217
Griffin v. Judson, 358
Griffin v. Weatherby, 368, 548
Guepratte v. Young, 601
Gunn's case; In re, Universal Banking Corp., 80
Gunn v. McPherson, 453, 482
Gurney v. Evans, 560
Gurney v. Womersley, 572
Guy v. Paré, 357

Hagarty v. Squier, 446
Haggart Bros. Manfg. Co., In re; Peaker & Reunion's case, 80
Halbot v. Lens, 444
Hall v. Hatch, 212
Hall v. Merrick, 633
Hall v. Prittie, 369, 547
Hallett & Co., Re, 140
Hallett & Co., Re, Ex parte Blane, 215
Hallett's Estate, Re; Knatchbull v. Hallett, 215
Halstead v. Skelton, 414, 506, 507
Halsted v. Bank of Hamilton, 182, 186, 199
Hamelin v. Bruck, 583, 586
Hamilton v. Jones, 446
Hamilton v. Spottiswoode, 365
Hannum v. McRea, 106
Hansard v. Robinson, 507, 594
Hanscombe v. Cotton, 401
Harben v. Phillips, 66, 68
Hardoon v. Belilos, 101, 102
Hardy v. Veasey, 107
Hare v. Henty, 616
Hargrave v. Clouston, 71
Harmer v. Steele, 550, 573, 575, 579
Harpham v. Child, 522
Harris' case; Re Imperial Land Co., 81, 82
Harris v. Commercial Bank, 190
Harris v. Cordingly, 210
Harris v. Parker, 298, 500
Harrison v. Dickson, 568
Harrison v. Ruscoe, 518, 520, 525
Harrold v. Plenty, 152
Harrop v. Fisher, 350, 464, 465
Hart v. McDougall, 515
Hartga v. Bank of England, 99
Harvey v. Bank of Hamilton, 382
Hatch v. Searles, 400, 402

Hatch v. Trayes, 389
Hately v. Elliott, 364
Hattersley, Ex parte, 23
Haussoulier v. Hartsinck, 368
Hawkins v. Cardy, 466
Hawley v. Beverley, 566
Hay v. Ayling, 461
Hay v. Burke, 527
Hayward, Ex parte, 410
Hays v. David, 396
Hebb's case; In re Nat. Savings Bank Assoc., 80
Heilbut v. Nevill, 466, 562
Henderson's case, 148, 256
Henderson v. Bank of Hamilton, 211
Heneker v. Bank of Montreal, 79
Herdman v. Wheeler, 400, 401, 419, 455, 464
Hertslet v. Oatway, 215
Heylin v. Adamson, 498, 629, 636
Heywood v. Pickering, 502, 518, 616
Highmore v. Primrose, 389
Hill v. Halford, 368
Hill v. Heap, 504, 505
Hill v. Lewis, 557
Hill v. Wilson, 421, 448
Hindhaugh v. Blakey, 408, 409
Hine v. Allely, 501
Hinton v. Bank of Montreal, 343, 434
Hirsche v. Sims, 54
Hirschfield v. Smith, 395, 585, 586, 605, 606
Hirschman v. Budd, 585
Hitchcock v. Edwards, 391
Hoare v. Cazenove, 590
Hogarth v. Latham, 400
Hogarth v. Wherley, 351
Hogg v. Marsh, 386
Hogg v. Skeen, 460
Holdsworth v. Hunter, 371
Hollender v. Ffoulkes, 511
Holmes v. Jacques, 371, 374
Holmes v. Kidd, 478
Holt v. Carmichael, 189
Home Life v. Walsh, 460
Hooker v. Leslie, 604
Hooper v. Treffry, 460
Hooper v. Williams, 633
Hopkinson v. Forster, 546, 610
Hopley v. Dufresne, 504
Horne v. Rouquette, 524, 525, 604, 605, 606
Houlditch v. Carty, 522
Houliston v. Parsons, 393
Housego v. Cowne, 520, 521

Household Fire v. Grant, 81
Howard v. Goddard, 520
Howell v. Brethour, 443
Howell v. McFarlane, 190
Hubbard v. Jackson, 481
Huber v. Steiner, 599
Hughes v. Rees, 76
Humberstone v. Chase, 99
Humble v. Mitchell, 76
Husband v. Davis, 218
Hutton v. Federal Bank, 207

Ianson v. Paxton, 356, 566
Imperial v. Coleman, 54
Imperial Bank v. Bank of Hamilton, 298, 441, 584
Imperial Bank v. Farmers' Trading Co., 434
Imperial Bank v. Hull, 172, 174
Imperial Hydro Hotel v. Hampson, 66
Imperial Land Co., Re; Harris' case, 81, 82
Imperial Loan v. Stone, 429
Indian Zoedone Co., In re, 68
Ingham v. Primrose, 419, 455, 582
Inglis v. Robertson, 172
Inkiel v. Laforest, 396
Innes v. Stephenson, 218
International Contract Co., Re; Levita's case, 81
Irvine v. Union Bank, 48
Irwin v. Bank of Montreal, 139, 221

Jackson v. Hudson, 406, 556
Jackson v. Turquand, 81
Jacobs v. Morris, 443
Jeffries v. Austin, 420
Jeffryes v. Agra Bank, 151
Jenkins v. Coomber, 456, 558, 559
Jenks v. Doran, 431, 432
Jenner's case; In re Percy, etc., Co., 56
Jenney v. Herle, 368
Jennings v. Napanee, 510
Jennings v. Roberts, 522
Jeune v. Ward, 409
Johnson v. Lyttle, 84
Johnson v. Martin, 360, 361
Johnson v. Roberts, 215
Johnston's claim; Re United Service Co., 136
Johnston v. Windle, 432
Jones v. Broadhurst, 481, 507, 550, 578
Jones v. Dickinson, 599
Jones v. England, 638

Jones v. Gordon, 115, 348, 349, 391, 449, 456, 458
Jones v. Imperial Bank, 130
Jones v. Ryde, 571
Jones v. Simpson, 366
Jonmenjoy v. Watson, 443
Julian v. Shobrooke, 412
Jury v. Barker, 364, 422

Keane v. Beard, 613
Kearney v. Kerich, 392
Kearney v. West Grenada Co., 596
Keith v. Burke, 531
Kelner v. Baxter, 443
Kendal v. Wood, 440
Kennedy, Ex parte; Re Great Northern Works, 42
Kennedy v. Adams, 366
Kennedy v. Thomas, 510, 511, 512
Kent v. Communante des Soeurs de Charité, 254
Keirzkowski v. Dorion, 207
Kilsby v. Williams, 212
Kimbro v. Bullit, 562
King, The,
(All cases in which the King is Plaintiff are indexed under the letter R.).
King v. Bickley, 521
King v. Hoare, 634
King v. Smith, 562
King v. Zimmerman, 595
Kingston, Ex parte, 220
Kinnear v. Goddard, 501
Kirk v. Blurton, 561
Kirkwood v. Carroll, 364, 631
Kirkwood v. Smith, 364
Kleinwort v. Comptoir d'Escompte, 627
Knatchbull v. Hallett, Re Hallett's Estate, 215
Knight v. Clements, 584
Knill v. Williams, 586
Kymar v. Laurie, 132

La Forest v. Babineau, 631
Lacave v. Credit Lyonnais, 627
Lafitte v. Slatter, 533
Laing v. Campbell, 214
Lambe v. Manuel, 78
Lancaster, Ex parte, 68
Land Credit Co., Re, 443
Land Credit Co., Re; Ex parte Overend, 352
Land Securities Co., Re; Ex parte Farquhar, 140
Lane v. Dungannon, 547

Langlois, Re, 146
Langtry v. Union Bank, 137
Laprès v. Masse, 461
Larocque v. Franklin Co. Bank, 278
Latter v. White, 416
Latouche v. Latouche, 448
Laws v. Rand, 615
Le Lievre v. Gould, 444
Leadbitter v. Farrow, 445, 555
Leather Manufacturers' Bank v. Morgan, 213
Lebel v. Tucker, 387, 563, 601
Lee v. Bank of B. N. A., 217
Leeds & County Bank v. Walker, 115, 583, 586
Leeds Estate v. Shepherd, 55
Leese v. Martin, 151
Leftley v. Mills, 384
Legare v. Arcand, 613, 616
Leggatt v. Brown, 461
Legislation respg. Abstention from Labour on Sunday, Re, 392
Leprohon v. Ottawa, 77
Leroux v. Brown, 599, 601
Letellier v. Cantin, 421
Levita's case; Re International Contract Co., 81
Lewis v. Lyster, 577
Lewis v. Parker, 480
Lewis v. Reilly, 562
Lickbarrow v. Mason, 22, 23
Lindley v. Lacey, 422
Lindus v. Bradwell, 350, 406, 560
Litman v. Montreal City, etc., Savings Bank, 134
Little v. Slackford, 365
Llado v. Morgan, 174, 184, 193
Lloyd v. Ashby, 408
Lloyd v. Howard, 478
Lloyd v. Sigourney, 472, 473
Lloyd v. Welsley, 473
Lockridge v. Lacey, 383
Lomas v. Bradshaw, 450
London Bank v. Simmons, 456
London, etc., Bank, In re; Wright's case, 66
London & Canadian v. Duggan, 143
London & County Banking Co. v. Groome, 479, 480
London & County Bank v. London & River Plate Bank, 143, 328, 448, 456
London & County Bank v. Ratcliff, 151
London & Globe Finance Corporation, 151

London & River Plate Bank v. Bank of Liverpool, 441
London & S. W. Bank v. Wentworth, 552
London & Southern Land Co., In re, 45
London & Tubbs' Contract, Re, 274
London City, etc., Bank v. Gordon, 134, 139, 389
London, etc., Bank v. Maguire, 603
London Financial v. Kelk, 55, 140
London Joint Stock Bank v. Simmons, 143, 178
London Life v. Molsons Bank, 376, 378, 380
Long v. Moore, 585
Lord v. Hall, 350
Loring v. Davis. 91
Lovell v. Hill, 363
Low v. Bouverie, 444
Lowenthal, Ex parte, 521, 536
Lubbock v. British Bank, 110
Lumley v. Musgrave, 577
Lyon v. Maxwell, 575
Lysaght v. Bryant, 417, 520, 525

MacArthur v. MacDowell, 478
McArthur v. McMillan, 214
Macbeth v. North & South Wales Bank, 376. 379. 380
McBride v. Gore Insurance Co., 172
McCall v. Taylor, 410
McCall v. Wolff, 189, 190
McCarthy v. Phelps, 504
McConnell v. Wilkins, 562
McCorkill v. Barrabe, 462
McDiarmid v. Hughes, 161
McDonald v. Elliott, 511
McDonald v. Rankin, 54
McDonald v. Smaill, 446
Macdonald v. Whitefield, 356, 422, 468. 565, 566
McDonell v. Bank of Upper Canada, 149
MacDougall v. Gardiner, 50
McEntire v. Potter. 329, 576
McFatridge v. Williston. 504
McGillivray v. Keefer. 448
McGregor v. Bishop, 460
McGregor v. Daly. 371
McGubbin v. Stephen. 631
McInnes v. Milton, 401
McKain and Canadian Birkbeck, Re, 88
McKay v. Fee. 568
Mackay v. Commercial Bank, 62
Mackay v. Judkins, 529

McKenzie v. British Linen Co., 433, 435
McKenzie v. Montreal, 324, 329
MacKersy v. Ramsay, 139
Maclae v. Sutherland, 635
McLaurin v. Seguin, 532
McLean v. Clydesdale Banking Co., 449, 456, 609, 617
McLean v. Shields, 412
McLeod v. Carman, 562
Macleod v. Snee, 368
McManus v. Bark, 422
McNeil v. Cullen, 421
McNichol v. Pinch, 186
McPherson v. Johnston, 372
McQuarrie v. Brand, 422
McQueen v. McIntyre, 585
McQueen v. McQueen, 394
McVity v. Trenmouth, 511
Madden v. Cox, 408, 446
Maguire v. Dodd, 420
Mahoney v. East Holyford, 48, 430
Maillard v. Page, 422
Mair v. McLean, 459
Mallory's case; In re Publishers' Syndicate, 80
Mander v. Royal Canadian Bank, 217
Mare v. Charles, 632
Margrett, Ex parte; Re Soltykoff, 429
Maritime Bank v. Receiver-General of N.B., 257
Maritime Bank v. Reg., 257
Maritime Bank v. Robinson, 248
Maritime Bank v. Troop, 248
Marseilles Co.. Re, 363
Marseilles Extension Co., Re; Smallpage's and Brandon's cases, 602
Martin v. Morgan, 440
Marzetti v. Williams. 211, 212
Mason v. Bradley. 585
Mason v. Great Western Railway, 171, 193
Mason v. Ramsay. 407
Massey v. Perrin, 386
Massey Manufacturing Co., In re, 71
Masson v. Merchants' Bank, 196
Master v. Miller. 583
Masters v. Baretto, 633. 637
Mather v. Maidatone, 459
Matthews v. Williams, 627
Mathiessen v. London & County Bank. 626
May v. Chapman, 457

Mayer v. Jadis, 470
Mayo's, Lady, case, 99
Mead v. Young, 432
Mecca, The, 214
Mellersh v. Rippen, 522
Mellish v. Rawdon, 487
Melville v. Bedell, 367
Menier v. Hooper's Telegraph Works, 50
Merchants Bank v. Cunningham, 560
Merchants Bank v. Darveau, 145
Merchants Bank v. Henderson, 638
Merchants Bank v. Lucas, 435
Merchants Bank v. Macdougall, 358
Merchants Bank v. McNutt, 527
Merchants Bank v. Smith, 174, 175, 180, 181
Merchants Bank v. Stirling, 585
Merchants Bank v. Suter, 200
Merchants Bank v. United Empire Club, 564
Merchants National Bank v. McLaughlin, 189
Merriam v. Wolcott, 572
Metcalfe v. Richardson, 521
Metropolitan, etc., Co., In re; Brown's case, 56
Meyer v. Decroix, 373
Michie v. Erie & Huron, 43
Miers v. Brown, 514
Miller v. Race, 22, 115
Miller v. Thomson, 388
Milloy v. Kerr, 169, 170
Mills v. Barber, 459
Misa v. Currie, 141, 448
Mitchell v. Glasgow Bank, 91
Moffatt v. Edwards, 394
Moffatt v. Merchants Bank, 156
Molineaux v. London, 56
Molleur v. Loupret, 276
Molsons Bank v. Beaudry, 184, 185
Molsons Bank v. Carscaden, 145
Molsons Bank v. Cooke, 350
Molsons Bank v. Cooper, 142
Molsons Bank v. Kennedy, 147
Molsons Bank v. McDonald, 157
Montague v. Perkins, 396, 401
Monteith, Re, 169, 170
Montreal v. Robert, 154
Moodie v. Rowatt, 371
Moore v. Scott, 510
Morley v. Culverwell, 575
Morris v. Bethell, 351, 434
Morris v. Union Bank, 72
Morris v. Walker, 481
Morrison v. Buchanan, 489

Morton's case; Re Canadian Tin Plate Co., 81
Mosely v. Koffyfontein, 72
Moshier v. Keenan, 178
Mozley v. Alston, 49
Muir v. Cameron, 453
Muir v. City of Glasgow Bank, 103
Munger v. Shannon, 368, 547
Munro v. Cox, 371, 472
Munroe v. Bordier, 450
Murray v. East India, 382
Murrow v. Stuart, 472
Mutford v. Walcott, 410
Mutton v. Peat, 215
Muttyloll v. Dent, 419
Mutual Safety v. Porter, 375, 399
Myers v. Perigal, 75

Nash v. De Freville, 579, 580
Nasmith's case; Re Central Bank, 82, 90, 148
Natal Co.'s case, Re, 328
National Bank v. Johnson, 140
National Bank v. Silke, 373, 611
National Bank of Australasia v. Cherry, 146, 157
Nat. Savings Bank Assn., In re; Hebb's case, 80
Neelon v. Thorold, 48
Neilson v. James, 91
Nelson v. Pellatt, 80
New Chile Gold Mining Co., Re, 84
New London v. Neale, 421
Newhorn v. Lawrence, 364
Newman, George, & Co., In re, 61
Newton, Ex parte, 451
Nicholls v. Diamond, 407
Nicholson v. Revill, 634
Nickle v. Douglas, 76, 77
Nicholson v. Revill, 586
Noad v. Bauchard, 577
Noble v. Forgrave, 357, 634
North Simcoe Ry. Co. v. Toronto, 43
North Sydney v. Greener, 43, 46
North-West v. Beatty, 69
North-West v. Walsh, 72
North-Western v. Jarvis, 366, 604
North-Western Bank v. Poynter, 172
Novelli v. Rossi, 582
Nowton v. Roach, 503, 504

O'Donohue v. Swain, 460
Oatway, Re; Hertslet v. Oatway, 215
Ockerman v. Blacklock, 368
Odell v. Cormack, 407

Ogden v. Benas, 432
Ogilvie v. West Australian, 435
Okell v. Charles, 407
Ontario Bank v. Burke, 358
Ontario Bank v. Chaplin, 258
Ontario Bank v. McArthur, 412
Ontario Bank v. O'Reilly, 170
Ontario Bank v. Routhier, 215
Ontario Bank v. Young, 419
Ontario Marine v. Ireland, 83
Ooregum v. Roper, 72
Oridge v. Sherborne, 394, 424
Oriental Bank, Ex parte; Re European Bank, 455, 477, 478
Oriental Commercial Bank, Re; Ex parte European Bank, 576
Oriental v. Overend, 452, 453, 554, 577
Orr v. Union Bank, 432
Orton v. Brett, 595
Ottos Kopje Diamond Mines, Re, 88
Oulds v. Harrison, 477
Outhwaite v. Luntley, 585
Overend, Re; Ex parte Swan, 453, 477, 593
Overend, Ex parte; Re Land Credit Co., 352
Overend Gurney & Co., Ex parte, 49
Overend v. Oriental, 422
Owen v. Von Uster, 407

Page v. Austin, 81
Pakenham Pork Packing Co., Re; Galloway's case, 82
Palmer v. McLennan, 631
Palmer v. Pratt, 369
Panton and The Cramp Steel Co., Re, 88
Parker v. Gordon, 499
Parker v. McQuesten, 275
Parr v. Jewell, 478
Parsons v Hart, 24
Parsons v. Queen Insurance Co., 172
Partridge v. Bank of England, 329, 354
Pasmore v. North, 391, 396
Patience v. Townley, 502
Patterson v. Turner, 80
Patton v. Fov, 40
Patton v. Melville, 371
Paul v. Joel, 520, 521
Peace v. Hirst. 451
Peacock v. Purssell. 515
Peaker v. Reunion's case; In re Haggert Bros. Mfg. Co., 80
Pearson v. Garret, 369

Peek's case; Re Aberaman Iron-works, 81
Peele v. Robinson, 446
Pegg v. Howbett, 482
Pellatt's case; Re Richmond Hill Hotel Co., 81
Pelletier v. Brosseau, 544
Penkivil v. Connell, 635
Pennington v. Crossley, 416
Penny v. Innes, 557
Penrose v. Martyr, 407
Pentz v. Stanton, 555
People's Loan v. Grant, 206, 568
Percy, etc., Co., In re; Jenner's case. 56
Perreault v. Merchants Bank, 134, 211
Perring v. Hone, 586
Perry v. Barnett, 24, 91
Perth v. McGregor, 369
Peruvian Railway Co., Re, 429
Peruvian Railway Co., Re; Crawley's case, 81
Peruvian Railways Co. v. Thames, etc., Co., 352
Petit v. Benson, 413
Peto v. Reynolds, 372
Petry v. Caisse d'Economie, 143
Pettis v. Kellogg, 190
Peuchin v. Imperial Bank, 196
Phillips v. Astling, 503
Phillips v. im Thurn, 377, 551, 552, 591
Philpot v. Briant, 498, 550
Phipps v. Tanner, 395
Phipson v. Kellner, 532
Pickard v. Sears, 551
Picker v. London & County Bank, 327
Pier v. Heinrichschoffer, 502
Pierce v. Cate, 505
Pillow v. Lespérance, 595
Pinard v. Klockman, 596
Pinder v. Cronkhite, 574
Plimley v. Westley, 382
Polhill v. Walter, 443, 444
Pollard v. Herries, 390, 395, 500
Pollard v. Ogden, 578
Pollard v. Vinton, 35
Pooley v. Brown, 571
Pooley v. Driver, 560
Popple v. Sylvester. 568
Portalis v. Tetley, 178
Porteous v. Reynar. 101
Potters v. Taylor, 412
Potts v. Reed, 472
Powell, Ex parte, 23

Powell v. Bank of Upper Canada, 190
Prange, Ex parte, 520
Pratt v. MacDougall, 560
Préfontaine v. Grenier, 27, 272, 274
Prehn v. Royal Bank, 548
Prentice v. Consolidated Bank, 196
Prescott v. Flinn, 351, 551
Price v. Taylor, 386
Prideaux v. Criddle, 502, 518, 616
Prince v. Oriental Bank, 138, 139, 297, 523, 547, 582
Provincial Grocers, Re; Calderwood's case, 81
Publishers' Syndicate, In re; Mallory's case, 80
Purdom v. Ontario Loan, 69

The Queen. (All cases in which Her late Majesty Queen Victoria was Plaintiff are indexed under the letter R.).
Quebec Bank v. Miller, 408
Quinlan v. Gordon, 206, 207
Quirt v. The Queen, 246

R. v. Badger, 274
R. v. Bank of Montreal, 134, 212, 213, 298, 440, 502
R. v. Bank of Nova Scotia, 257
R. v. Bank of Upper Canada, 69
R. v. Bartlett, 371
R. v. Bowerman, 365
R. v. Buntin, 277
R. v. Cockburn, 273
R. v. Cormack, 632
R. v. Cotté, 276
R. v. Elliott, 395
R. v. Harper, 365
R. v. Hincks, 275
R. v. Lovitt, 78, 273
R. v. Pearce, 344
R. v. Randall, 375
R. v. Ritson, 391
R. v. Senior, 274
R. v. Tolson, 274
R. v. Take, 365
R. v. Weir, 276
R. v. Wimbledon, 65
Rabey v. Gilbert, 531
Radford v. Merchants Bank, 147
Rainforth v. Keith, 89, 144
Ralli v. Dennistoun, 582
Ramchurn Mullick v. Luckmeechund Radikissen, 485, 487, 506, 609
Ramsgate v. Monteflore, 80, 81

Ramuz v. Crowe, 594
Ranken v. Alfaro, 548
Raper v. Birkbeck, 587
Raphael v. Bank of England, 115, 450, 455, 459
Raphael v. McFarlane, 143
Rayner, Ex parte, 555
Redfern v. Rosenthal, 478
Redmayne v. Burton, 416
Reed, Ex parte, 578
Reid v. Furnivall, 141
Reid v. Rigby, 442
Reinhardt v. Shirley, 455
Rennie v. Quebec Bank, 145, 149, 155
Renwick v. Tighe, 529
Reynolds v. Chettle, 298, 500
Reynolds v. Doyle, 566
Reynolds v. Wheeler, 356, 566
Rhodes v. Starnes, 275
Ricard v. Banque Nationale, 429
Rice v. Bowker, 500, 505
Rice v. Stearns, 403, 472
Richards, Re, 416, 420
Richards v. Bank of B. N. A., 214
Richards v. Bank of N.S., 63
Richards v. Bowes, 512
Richards v. Frankum, 465
Richards v. Home Assurance, 81
Richards v. Richards, 421
Richardson v. Alpena, 189
Richer v. Voyer, 216
Richmond Hill Hotel Co., Re; Pellatt's case, 81
Riddell v. Bank of Upper Canada, 151
Ridout v. Manning, 339
Ritchie v. Can. Bank of Commerce, 207
Ritchie v. Vermillion, 56
Robarts, Ex parte, 355, 567, 570
Robarts v. Tucker, 132, 210, 212, 431, 432, 576
Roberts v. Bethell, 396, 411
Robey v. Ollier, 548
Robertson v. Kensington, 468
Robertson v. Banque d'Hochelaga, 84, 252
Robertson v. Sheward, 63
Robinson v. C. P. R., 343
Robinson v. Hawksford, 615
Robinson v. Mann, 559
Robinson v. Mollett, 24
Robinson v. Reynolds, 460
Roffey v. Greenwell, 386
Rogers v. Whiteley, 618
Rogerson v. Ladbrooke, 618

Rolin v. Steward, 548
Rolland v. Caisse d'Economie, 146
Rooney v. Stanton, 109
Rose v. Scott, 189
Rose v. Sims, 447
Rose-Belford Co. v. Bank of Montreal, 614
Rosher v. Kieran, 518
Ross v. Conger, 190
Ross v. McKindsay, 358
Ross v. Tyson, 141
Rossin v. McCarty, 401
Rothschild v. Corney, 479
Rothschild v. Currie, 502, 530, 605
Rouquette v. Overman, 140, 503, 553, 599, 605, 607
Rouse v. Bradford, 214, 554
Rowe v. Tipper, 517
Rowe v. Young, 413, 493, 550
Royal Bank v. Tottenham, 391
Royal Bank of India's case; Re Asiatic Bkg. Corp., 142
Royal British Bank v. Turquand, 49
Royal Canadian Bank v. Miller, 174, 180
Royal Canadian Bank v. Cummer, 156
Royal Canadian Bank v. Ross, 147, 165, 166, 201
Royal Canadian Bank v. Shaw, 206
Royal Canadian Bank v. Wilson, 561
Ruben v. Great Fingall, 48
Ruff v. Webb, 349, 365
Rumball v. Metropolitan Bank, 143
Russell v. Phillips, 409, 413
Russell v. Wells, 369
Ryan v. Bank of Montreal, 552
Ryan v. McConnell, 141
Ryan v. McKerrall, 448, 449

Saderquist v. Ontario Bank, 217
St. John v. Rykert, 206, 568
St. Stephen Ry. Co. v. Black, 366
Salmon v. Webb, 422
Samuel v. Fairgrieve, 360
Sanders v. St. Helen's Smelting Co., 604
Sands v. Clarke, 505
Sanford v. Ross, 401
Saul v. Jones, 500, 504, 585
Saunderson v. Piper, 395
Savaria v. Paquette, 514
Sawyer v. Wisewell, 457
Scard v. Jackson, 402

Scholfield v. Londesborough, 440, 584
Schoolbred v. Clarke, 246
Schroder's case, 474
Schultz v. Astley, 382
Scott v. Godfrey, 24
Scott v. Lifford, 450, 453
Segsworth v. Meriden, 189
Serle v. Norton, 609
Seymour v. Pickett, 214
Sharp v. Bailey, 533
Sharpe, In re, 54
Shaw v. Crawford, 141
Shediac Boot Co., Re, 145
Sheffield v. London Joint Stock Bank, 143
Shelton v. Braithwaite, 530
Sherry, Re, 215
Shields v. Bank of Ireland, 220
Shillito v. Theed, 461
Shropshire v. The Queen, 101
Shuttleworth v. Stephens, 372
Sibree v. Tripp, 574
Sichel v. Borch, 416
Siffkin v. Walker, 555
Simmonds v. Taylor, 586, 619
Simpson v. Henning, 634
Simpson v. Molsons Bank, 99, 100, 101
Sims v. Bond, 211
Simson v. Ingham, 214
Sinclair v. Robson, 511, 512
Slater v. Laboree, 559
Sleigh v. Sleigh, 453, 533, 566
Smallpage's case; Re Marseilles Extension Co., 602
Smith v. Bank of N.S., 79, 88
Smith v. Bellamy, 388, 503
Smith v. Braine, 459
Smith v. Clarke, 374
Smith v. Gordon, 581
Smith v. Johnson, 430, 562
Smith v. Kendall, 424
Smith v. McClure, 383
Smith v. Mercer, 440
Smith v. Merchants Bank, 174, 175
Smith v. Mullett, 517
Smith v. Mundy, 416
Smith v. Nightingale, 366
Smith v. Richardson, 482
Smith v. Rogers, 144
Smith v. Smith, 448
Smith v. Union Bank, 620, 625
Smith v. Vertue, 409, 412, 507, 550
Smith v. Walkerville, 89, 143, 144
Smith, Knight & Co., Re; Weston's case, 88

Snowball, Ex parte, 455
Soares v. Glyn, 374
Société Générale v. Metropolitan Bank, 597
Société Générale v. Walker, 144, 398
Solarte v. Palmer, 520
Solomons v. Bank of England, 115
Soltykoff, Re; Ex parte Margrett, 429
Southall v. Rigg, 448
Southam v. Ranton, 358
Sovereen Co. v. Whitside, 58
Sovereign Bank v. Gordon, 374, 470
Soward v. Palmer, 515
Spaulding v. Evans, 371
Stagg v. Elliott, 443
Standard Bank v. Dunham, 563
Starkey v. Bank of England, 89, 444
Stayner v. Howatt, 533
Steacy v. Stayner, 566
Steele v. McKinley, 405, 406, 409, 556, 558, 559, 566, 588
Steinhoff v. Merchants Bank, 133, 139, 523
Stenning, Re; Wood v. Stenning, 215
Stewart v. Kennett, 518
Stockman v. Parr, 522
Stockton Malleable Iron Co., Re, 150
Stoke v. Taylor, 344
Story v. McKay, 604
Straker v. Graham, 487
Stuart v. Bowman, 26
Studdy v. Beesty, 517, 529, 530
Sturdy v. Henderson, 427
Succession Duty Act, Re. 210
Suffell v. Bank of England, 115, 585, 586
Susé v. Pompe, 564, 568, 569, 570
Sutherland v. Patterson, 633
Sutton v. English, 56
Sutton v. Toomer, 584, 586
Swaisland v. Davidson, 455
Swan, Ex parte; Re Overend Gurney & Co., 453, 477, 478, 593
Swan v. North British, 324, 398
Sweeting v. Halse, 582

Tassel v. Cooper, 107
Tatam v. Haslar, 348, 458, 459
Tatum v. Catomore, 584
Taylor v. Currie, 364, 422
Taylor v. Dobbins, 349
Tennant v. Union Bank, 86, 170, 171, 177, 181, 182, 187, 210

Terry v. Parker, 504
Tessier v. Caillé, 595
Thackray v. Blackett, 594
Thicknesse v. Bromilow, 562
Third National Bank v. Cosby, 366
Thrikell, Re, 190
Thomas v. Fenton, 575
Thomas v. Smith, 215
Thompson v. Advocate-General, 79
Thompson v. Bank of N.S., 62
Thompson v. Clydesdale Bank, 143
Thompson v. Cotterell, 522
Thompson v. Molsons Bank, 196
Thompson v. Quirk, 190
Thomson v. Huggins, 370
Thorne v. Smith, 634
Thorold v. Imperial Bank, 434
Tidmarsh v. Grover, 585
Todd v. Union Bank, 212
Tootell, Ex parte, 369
Toronto v. Toronto Ry. Co., 511
Toronto Brewing Co. v. Blake, 42
Toronto General Trusts v. Central Ontario, 154, 196
Torrance v. Bank of B. N. A., 548, 577
Towers v. African Tug Co., 50
Traders Bank v. Brown, 173
Traders Bank v. Goodfallow, 193
Trentell v. Barandon. 473
Triggs v. Newnham, 499
Trimble v. Hill, 511
Trimble v. Miller, 632
Trimby v. Vingnier, 601
Trout's case; Re Essex Land & Timber Co., 156
Truman v. Clare, 368
Trueman v. Loder, 560
Trunkfield v. Proctor, 549, 608
Trust & Loan v. Gauthier, 28
Trusts & Guarantee v. Abbott Mitchell, 49
Turner v. Crane, 367
Turner v. Leach, 514, 518, 531
Turner v. Samson, 504, 533
Twogood, Ex parte, 420
Twycross v. Dreyfus, 329

Union Bank v. Bulmer, 562
Union Bank v. Elliott, 141
Union Bank v. McKilligan, 500, 528
Union Bank v. Spinney, 193
Union Bank of Australia v. Murray-Aynsley, 220
United Service Co., Re; Johnston's claim, 136

Universal Banking Corporation, In
  re; Gunn's case, 80
Usher v. Dauncey, 391, 402, 618

Vagliano v. Bank of England, 377
  378
Vallée v. Talbot, 566
Vance v. Lowther, 585
Venables v. Baring, 328
Verner v. General, etc., Trust, 110
Viale v. Michael, 520, 522
Vidal v. Ford, 421
Vincent v. Horlock, 470, 555
Vinden v. Hughes, 375, 376, 378,
  379, 380

Walker v. Hamilton, 548, 567
Walker v. Macdonald, 374, 467
Wallace v. Souther, 366, 374
Wallbridge v. Beckett, 457
Walsh v. Union Bank, 90
Walter v. Cubley, 585
Walter v. James, 575
Walton v. Mascall, 496, 507, 514,
  515, 637
Ward, Lord, v. Oxford Ry. Co., 502
Waring, Ex parte, 210
Warner v. Symon-Kaye, 638
Warren v. Haigh, 478
Warrington v. Early, 394, 586
Warwick v. Nairn, 460
Warwick v. Rogers, 293, 297, 582
Watkins v. Maule, 464
Watson v. Evans, 371, 467
Watson v. Harvey, 560
Watson v. Russell, 419, 450, 456
Watts v. Christie, 214
Webb v. Derbyshire, 210
Webb v. Herne Bay Commrs., 326,
  327
Wedlake v. Hurley, 473
Wegersloffe v. Keene, 413
Wells v. Hopkins, 460
Wells v. McCarthy, 560
Wells & McMurchy's case; Re Cen-
  tral Bank, 258
Wentworth, County of, v. Smith,
  210
West v. Bown, 373
West London v. Kitson, 444
Westloh v. Brown, 586
Weston's case; Re Smith, Knight &
  Co., 88
Whatley v. Tricker, 581
Wharton v. Wright, 520

Wheatley v. Smithers, 562
Whistler v. Forster, 456, 460, 462
Whitaker, Re, 410
White v. North, 631
Whitehead v. Walker, 477, 478, 492,
  512
Whiting v. Hovey, 190
Whitlock v. Underwood, 384
Whittaker, Re, 448
Wilcox v. Wilcox, 26
Wilde v. Keep, 560
Wilder v. Wolf, 618
Wilders v. Stevens, 453, 481
Wilkins v. Jadis, 498, 499
Wilkinson v. Johnson, 471, 582
Wilkinson v. Simson, 599
Wilkinson v. Unwin, 482
Wilks v. Hornby, 453
Willans v. Ayres, 388, 570
Willey v. Snyder, 189
Williams, Re, 151
Williams v. Bayley, 433
Williams v. Germaine, 590
Williams v. James, 578
Williams v. Shadbot, 473
Willis v. Bank of England, 455
Willis v. Barrett, 374, 467
Wilson v. Barthrop, 555
Wilson v. Brown, 562
Wilson v. Holmes, 473
Wilson v. Hotchkiss, 62
Wilson v. Kerr, 189
Wilson v. Manes, 274
Wilson v. Pringle, 520, 528
Windham Bank v. Morton, 502
Windsor v. Commercial Bank, 31
Wirth v. Austin, 504, 533
Wisconsin v. Bank of B. N. A., 24
Wiseman v. Easton, 562
Wismer v. Wismer, 420
Wood v. Stenning, 215
Woodcock v. Houldsworth, 529
Woodruffe v. Moore, 512
Woodward v. Pell, 507, 574
Worley v. Harrison, 394
Wright's case; In re London, etc.,
  Bank, 66
Wright v. Wright, 448
Wyld, Ex parte, 592
Wylde v. Wetmore, 487
Wynne v. Raikes, 410
Wyoming, State of, Syndicate, In
  re, 66

Yates, Ex parte, 465, 557
Yates v. Dalton, 562

Yates v. Evans, 364
Yates v. Nash, 371
Yates v. Terry, 618
Yglesias v. River Plate Bank, 515, 582
York Tramways v. Willows, 45

Yorkshire Banking Co. v. Beatson, 560, 561, 563
Young, Re, 274
Young v. Fluke, 568
Young v. Glover, 409, 465
Young v. Macnider, 26, 325, 329, 478

BOOK I.

BANKING AND THE BANK ACT.

CHAPTER I.

REVIEW OF BANKING LEGISLATION.

The statutory banking law of Canada, notwithstanding the important changes which have taken place since 1867, is, in the main, the result of the continuation and development of the policy of the statutes relating to the subject of banking in force in Upper and Lower Canada at the time of the confederation of the provinces. It may therefore be useful to refer to some of the statutes of the late province of Canada as an aid to the understanding of the present Bank Act, and then to review briefly the banking legislation of Parliament since the formation of the Dominion.

Legislation of 1841.

The earliest legislation to which reference need be made is that of 1841. Prior to that date a number of banks were in operation, with power to issue bank notes under individual charters granted by the legislatures of Upper and Lower Canada before the Union of 1840. Some of them were at this time asking for power to increase their capital. At its first session the legislature of the united province rejected a proposal made by Lord Sydenham to establish a provincial bank of issue, and as a fiscal measure, partly in lieu of the rejected proposal, imposed upon the bank notes issued and circulating in the province a duty of one per cent. per annum calculated on the average monthly circulation as shewn by semi-annual statements furnished to the Receiver-General (4 & 5 Vict. c. 29). A Select Committee on Banking and Currency reported in favour of adopting some uniform system of banking in the province, and of granting the request of the banks for an increase in capital subject to certain restrictions, most of which had been recommended in a circular despatch dated the 4th of May, 1840, issued under the signature of Lord John Russell, Principal Secretary of State for the Colonies.

By chapter 99 of the same session the banks previously chartered by either of the provinces were authorized to carry on their business throughout the new province.

Acts were also passed in the same year and in 1842 renewing until 1862 the charters of various banks, and authorizing certain increases of capital. Although each of these acts referred to only a single bank, they all contained the restrictions recommended by the Select Committee, so that an approach was thus made to a general banking act.

In 1846 another circular despatch, dated 30th May of that year, was issued by the Colonial Office containing a series of "Revised Regulations" which were recommended to be introduced into any bills for the incorporation of banking companies in the colonies. These regulations, with the restrictions recommended by the select committee of 1841, formed the basis of the subsequent general banking legislation.

Legislation of 1850.

A general act of 1850 (13 & 14 Vict. c. 22) authorized the chartered banks to take, hold and dispose of mortgages of real and personal property by way of additional security for debts contracted to them in the course of their business and conferred certain ancillary rights upon the banks in regard to property mortgaged to them, etc.

The same year was marked by the passing of the "Act to establish Freedom of Banking" (13 & 14 Vict. c. 21). This act forbade the issue of circulating notes under the value of five shillings. Notes for five shillings or over might be issued, as theretofore, by the chartered banks, but not by other persons except as specially authorized by the act. The most significant feature of the act was the liberty it gave to individuals or general partners to establish banks, and to persons to form joint stock companies to carry on the business of banking, each with a single office in one place, and with a minimum capital of £25,000. Banking institutions under this act were permitted to issue registered notes secured by, and to an amount not exceeding, a deposit of provincial securities with the Receiver-General. These notes were exempted from the payment of the one per cent. tax levied upon the circulation of the chartered banks. The chartered banks were at liberty to surrender their rights of issuing notes against assets and to obtain registered notes against deposits of securities.

In 1851 an amendment was passed requiring monthly instead of semi-annual returns from the "free banks" (14 & 15 Vict. c. 69). In the same year an act was passed "to encourage the chartered banks to adopt, as far as conveniently practicable, the principles of the general banking act in regard to the securing of the redemption of their bank notes" (14 & 15 Vict. c. 70), and a further act was passed for the same purpose in 1853 (16 Vict. c. 62). The chartered banks, as a rule, rejected the encouragement offered by the legislation just referred to, as their own system of note issue gave greater opportunity for banking profit. Not many new banks were established under the provisions of the Free Banking Act, and those that did not cease to do business subsequently applied for and obtained charters. The act was finally repealed by the Provincial Note Act of 1866 (29 & 30 Vict. c. 10). In the meantime most of the existing chartered banks had obtained by statute further additions to their capital.

In 1858 penalties and forfeiture for usury were abolished. In 1859 another act of general application to the chartered banks was passed, being the first step in the legislation permitting banks to take warehouse receipts and bills of lading as security for advances. In the latter year a select committee of the legislature was struck, and in the evidence reported by this committee and chiefly obtained from the leading bankers, there was much pointed criticism of the existing banking system. No general legislation, however, resulted at this time, and in the years from 1858 to 1866 a number of new charters were granted subject to the general regulations and restrictions referred to above.

Dominion Act of 1867.

By section 91 of the British North America Act, 1867, exclusive legislative authority was given to the Parliament of the new Dominion of Canada created by the act in regard to:—

(14) Currency and coinage.
(15) Banking, incorporation of banks and the issue of paper money.
(16) Saving Banks.
(18) Bills of exchange and promissory notes.
(19) Interest.
(20) Legal tender.

"An Act respecting Banks" (31 Vict. c. 11) passed in the session of 1867-1868 was the earliest statute on the subject of banking enacted under this authority. It was merely a temporary measure, to expire at the end of the first session of Parliament after the 1st of January, 1870. It extended to the whole Dominion the powers of banks previously incorporated by any of the four provinces. In other respects it was mainly a re-enactment for the Dominion of the general banking legislation previously in force in the Province of Canada.

Chapter 46 of the same session, being "an Act to enable Banks in any part of Canada to use notes of the Dominion instead of issuing notes of their own," was likewise an extension to the Dominion of the Provincial Note Act of 1866. The latter act had authorized the government under the authority of the Governor-in-Council to issue not more than $8,000,000 of provincial notes payable on demand in specie at Toronto or Montreal, as they might be dated, and made such notes legal tender at places other than the offices in these cities. It also contained provisions offering inducements to the existing banks to surrender their note circulation, and to take up the issue and redemption of provincial notes, $3,000,000 of the above note issue being authorized for this purpose.

In the event, however, the chartered banks, with the exception of the Bank of Montreal, proved unwilling to reduce their resources by the retirement of their notes from circulation. This bank, owing to the fact that the government was largely indebted to it, was able advantageously to withdraw its notes from circulation, replace them by notes of the province, and set off the amount of such notes against the government's indebtedness.

By the act of 1868 the $8,000,000 worth of provincial notes prepared in 1866, and the $5,000,000 thereof in circulation in 1868, were declared to be Dominion notes redeemable at Montreal, Toronto, Halifax and St. John.

In 1869 a number of bank charters which were about to expire were extended until the end of the first session of Parliament next after the 1st of January, 1870.

By these measures time was gained to consider the important problem of creating one uniform system of currency and banking for the Dominion, applicable to all banks, both those to be incorporated in the future, and those which had originally come into existence or were doing business under charters granted by the Provinces of Canada, Nova Scotia and New Brunswick or, (as in the case of the Bank of British North America) under Royal charter.

Discussion preliminary to the Act of 1870.

In the interval between 1867 and 1870 the question of the future banking policy of the Dominion was much discussed, the chief interest being concentrated on the question of the character of the note issue. A select committee of the Senate in 1868 made a report deprecating the taking possession of the note issue by the Government, but recommending the issue of a paper currency by the banks based on the deposit of government securities, if the financial requirements of the government demanded such an expedient. The representatives of the bankers were heard by a select committee of the House of Commons in the same year, and the case against a bond secured circulation was fully argued. Nevertheless in 1869 the Hon. John Rose, Minister of Finance, proposed a banking scheme upon the model of the National Banking System of the United States, the unsecured circulation of the banks to be gradually retired after 1871. The measure was, however, temporarily withdrawn in view of the opposition which displayed itself, and before the next session of Parliament Mr. Rose had resigned, and Sir Francis Hincks had become Minister of Finance.

After a conference with the leading bankers, the new Minister on the 1st of March, 1870, brought down to the House of Commons a series of resolutions on banking and currency, which emphasized the need for a uniform banking law, and contained a number of recommendations. The most significant features of the recommendations were the issue of bank notes not secured by deposit of securities, the necessity for the security afforded by a large paid up capital, the surrender by the banks of the right to issue notes under $4, the management of the circulation of Dominion notes directly by the government instead of by the Bank of Montreal and an increase in the issue of such notes and the holding by the banks of 50 per cent. of their cash reserves in Dominion notes.

Bank Act of 1870.

The Statute 33 Vict. c. 11, an ''Act respecting Banks and Banking'' 1870, embodied the resolutions of Sir Francis Hincks. It enacted that in any act establishing a new bank or renewing the charter of any existing bank a number of restrictions should be incorporated, certain exceptions being granted in the case of the Bank of British North America and La Banque du Peuple in order to conform to the peculiarities of their respective charters.

These provisions were practically re-enacted by the Act of 1871 presently to be referred to.

The monopoly of issuing notes for circulation was assured to the banks by imposing on private or unauthorized issue a fine of $400. Previous legislation in conflict with the new act was repealed and the ''Act respecting Banks'' of 1868, was extended to the end of the session of 1872.

The act also contained provisions for the extension by letters patent of the charters of existing banks until the end of the session of Parliament next after the 1st of January, 1881, and no longer, and subject to the other provisions of the act.

Bank Act of 1871.

Only in one instance, however, was a charter renewed under the Act of 1870, bankers having expressed themselves in favour of having parliamentary charters. The government therefore determined to embody in one general banking act, not only the provisions of the Act of 1870, but also the general provisions respecting what might be termed the internal regulation of banks. The statute drafted in accordance with this purpose was passed with very slight discussion in either house, and on the 14th of April, 1871, received the royal assent. This statute was the first general law under which the banks really operated, and may be regarded as practically the first Bank Act of the Dominion.

By this act (34 Vict. c. 5) the charters or acts of incorporation, and amendments thereof, of the several banks enumerated in the schedule were continued as to their incorporation, the amount of their capital stock, the amount of each share of such stock, and the chief place of business of each bank, respectively, until the 1st of July, 1881, subject to the right of any such bank to increase its capital stock in the manner provided for by the act. In other respects the charters became subject to the provisions of the act from the 1st of July, 1871, until the end of the then next session of Parliament, after which, it was provided, the act should form and be the charters of the said banks respectively until the 1st of July, 1881, and the provisions thereof should apply to each of them respectively, and their charters as existing at the time of the act should be repealed, except only as to the matters for which the said charters were as above provided continued until the said 1st of July, 1881. It was also enacted that the provisions of the act should apply to any bank to be thereafter incorporated, (either at the then present session or at any future session), whether the act should be specially mentioned in its act of incorporation or not. Any act incorporating any bank thereafter was to declare the capital stock of such new bank, the amount of each share, the name of the bank, and the place where its chief office should be situate. The Acts of 1867 and 1870 were also repealed.

A large part of the act was devoted to the re-enactment and consolidation of legislation previously in force. One important change was the provision requiring a bank, before issuing notes or commencing the business of banking, to have $500,000 of capital stock *bonâ fide* subscribed and $100,000 *bonâ fide* paid up, a further sum of $100,000 to be paid up within two years from the commencement of business (sec. 7). Another important change was the authority given to shareholders, at any annual general meeting or any general meeting specially called for the purpose, to increase the capital of the bank.

The bank was empowered to open branches or agencies, and offices of discount and deposit, and transact business at any place or places in the Dominion.

Of the other provisions of the act which were made generally applicable to the banks as above stated and which illustrate the policy of the act, particularly as regards the security afforded to the public, the more important may be summarized as follows:

Sec. 8. Amount of notes intended for circulation issued by the bank and outstanding at any time not to exceed the amount of the bank's unimpaired paid-up capital, and no note to be for less than $4.

Sec. 9. Notes of the bank to be received in payment at par at any of its offices, but the bank not to be bound to redeem them in specie or Dominion notes at any place other than where they are made payable, the chief seat of business of the bank always to be the place or one of the places of payment.

Sec. 10. Paid up capital not to be impaired by any dividend or bonus; directors knowingly and wilfully concurring in any impairment to be individually liable for the amount thereof as a debt due to the bank. Loss of paid-up capital to be made good by calls upon unpaid stock, such loss and calls to be mentioned in the next return to the government. All net profits to be applied to make good loss, if capital impaired.

Sec. 11. No division of profits by way of dividends or bonus, or both, or in any way, exceeding 8 per cent. per annum to be paid unless, after paying the same and deducting all bad and doubtful debts, the bank shall have a rest or reserve fund equal to at least 20 per cent. of its paid-up capital.

Sec. 12. Certified lists of shareholders with their respective additions, residences, and holdings of stock, to be laid before Parliament annually.

Sec. 13. Monthly returns of assets and liabilities to be made to the government in the form prescribed by the act, signed by the chief officers of the bank.

Sec. 14. The bank to hold, as nearly as may be practical, one-half, and never less than one-third, of its cash reserve in Dominion notes.

Sec. 15. A bank to which this act is applicable to be exempt from the tax on the average amount of its notes in circulation and from the obligation to hold any of its capital in government or other debentures.

Sec. 27. Each shareholder to have one vote for each share held by him for at least 30 days before the time of shareholders' meeting.

Sec. 28. Shareholders to have power to regulate by by-law certain matters incident to the management and administration of the bank, including the qualification and the number of the directors, (to be not less than 5 nor more than 10), and the quorum thereof, the time and manner of electing directors and filling vacancies in the board of directors. No director to hold less than $3,000 of the stock of the bank, when the paid-up capital thereof is one million dollars or less, nor less than $4,000 when such capital is between one million and three millions, nor less than $5,000 when such capital exceeds three millions. Directors to be elected annually by the shareholders.

Sec. 39. The bank to have power to acquire and hold real and immovable estate for its actual use and occupation, and the management of its business.

Sec. 40. The bank not to lend money upon the security mortgage or hypothecation of any lands or tenements or of any ships or other vessels, or upon the security or pledge of its own shares, or of any goods, wares or merchandise, except as authorized by the act, or to deal in the buying and selling or bartering of goods, wares or merchandise, or to be engaged in any trade whatever, except as a dealer in gold and silver bullion, bills of exchange, discounting of promissory notes and negotiable securities, and in such trade generally as appertains to the business of banking.

Sec. 41. The bank empowered to take, hold, and dispose of mortgages upon personal as well as real property, by way of additional security for debts contracted to the bank in the course of its business.

Sec. 51. The bank not to make loans or grant discounts on the security of its own stock, but to have a privileged lien for any overdue debt on the shares and unpaid dividends of the debtor, and to have the right to decline to allow any transfer of the shares of the debtor until such debt is paid, and, if such debt is not paid when due, to realize on the shares after due notice. The bank entitled to acquire and hold as collateral security for any advance by or debt to the bank, etc., the shares of the capital stock of any other bank, the bonds or debentures of municipal or other corporations, or Dominion, provincial, British or foreign public securities.

Sec. 52. The bank not to be liable to any penalty or forfeiture for usury, but no rate of interest or discount exceeding 7 per cent. to be recoverable by the bank.

Sec. 57. Suspension by the bank of payment of any of its liabilities as they accrue, in specie or Dominion notes, if it continues for ninety days, to constitute the bank insolvent and operate a forfeiture of its charter so far as regards the issue or reissue of notes and other banking operations, the charter to remain in force for purpose of winding up only.

Sec. 58. In the event of the property and assets of the bank becoming insufficient to pay its debts and liabilities, the shareholders to be liable for the deficiency to an amount equal to the amount of their respective shares, over and above any amount not paid up on such shares. In the event of suspension of payment by the bank of any of its liabilities for six months, the directors to make calls on shareholders without waiting for the collection of any debts due to it or the sale of any of its assets or property, such calls to be made at intervals of 30 days, each call not to exceed 20 per cent. on each share. Additional liability of directors not to be affected by this section.

Sec. 59. Shareholders who have transferred their shares or registered the transfer thereof within one month before the commencement of the suspension of payment by the bank to be liable to calls under sec. 58, saving their recourse against the transferees.

Secs. 60 *et seq.* Offences and penalties.

Sec. 68. No private person or party, except a chartered bank, to issue or re-issue, make, draw, or indorse, any bill, bond, note, cheque, or other instrument intended to circulate as money, or to be used as a substitute for money, for any amount whatever under a penalty of $400.

Sec. 70. The bank to be subject to such provisions of any general or special winding-up act to be passed by Parliament as may be declared to apply to banks.

Sec. 71. The bank to be subject to any general provisions respecting banks which Parliament may deem necessary for the public interest.

Secs. 72 *et seq.* Special provisions as to certain banks.

Between 1871 *and* 1880.

In 1873 the form of the monthly return was expanded (36 Vict. c. 43), and in 1875 was amended by requiring a statement of the direct and indirect liabilities of the directors to the bank, (38 Vict. c. 17).

The same Act of 1875 forbade a bank, either directly or indirectly, to purchase or deal in any share or shares of the capital stock of the bank, except where it should be necessary "to realize upon any such share or shares held by the bank as security for any pre-existing and matured debt.''

In 1876 a general insolvent act was applied to banks with modifications (39 Vict. c. 31).

In 1879 the clause permitting banks to make loans upon shares in other chartered banks was repealed (42 Vict. c. 45), and banks were required to number their shares, all contracts for the sale of bank stock being required to specify the number of the shares to be transferred.

Revision of Bank Act in 1880.

Bank charters under the Act of 1871 being due to expire on the 1st of July, 1881, Sir Leonard Tilley, Minister of Finance, in the session of 1880, brought down a bill which became law without much debate (43 Vict. c. 22).

By this statute the charters of the thirty-four banks, which were then in operation, were continued to the 1st of July, 1891, and those of four others until the completion of their liquidation. The principal amendments of the law made by the act were the following:

Sec. 2. No person holding stock as executor, administrator, guardian or trustee of or for any person named in the books of the bank as being so represented by him or her to be personally liable as a stockholder, but the estate or funds in his or her hands, or the person for whom the trust is, to be liable.

Sec. 3. The proportion of cash reserves to be held in Dominion notes never to be less than 40 per cent. (instead of one-third as in the Act of 1871).

Sec. 4. A new and expanded form of monthly return substituted, the Minister of Finance to have power to call for special returns from any particular bank, whenever in his judgment the same are necessary in order to a full and complete knowledge of its condition.

Sec. 6. No bank to hold any real or immovable property howsoever acquired, except such as shall be required for its own use, for any period exceeding seven years from the date of the acquisition thereof.

Sec. 8. The bank forbidden to lend money on the stock of any other bank, as well as on its own, and the lien of a bank on its own shares extended to cover any "debt or liability for a debt," instead of any "overdue debt," to the bank.

Sec. 10. After the first day of July 1880 any person, firm or company assuming or using the title of "Bank" without being authorized so to do by this act or by the Act of 1871, or by some other act in force in that behalf, to be guilty of a misdemeanour.

Sec. 12. After the 1st of July, 1881,

1. The payment of the notes issued by the bank and intended for circulation, then outstanding, to be the first charge upon the assets of the bank in case of its insolvency.

2. No bank note for a sum less than $5, or for any sum not being a multiple of $5, to be issued or re-issued by the bank.

3. Any bank making any payment to make the same up to $50, at the request of the payee, in Dominion notes for $1, or $2 each.

4. Proxies to vote at a shareholders' meeting to be made or renewed within three years next preceding the time of such meeting.

Perhaps the most notable feature of the legislation of 1880 was the attempt to give greater security to the paper currency by conferring upon the holder of an insolvent bank's note a prior claim on the assets of such bank. The clause to give effect to this was objected to in the House of Commons on the ground that it was likely to increase the danger of runs from depositors anxious to convert their claims into privileged liens. This had also been the view of Sir Francis Hincks in 1870. Now, however, the proposal had the strong support of the bankers of the country. For them the privilege of note circulation was a source of easy and considerable profit. To the people it gave an elastic currency, increased sources of discount, and, through the system of branch banks promoted by it, widespread and accessible banking facilities. The scheme, already proposed before 1870, to remodel the Canadian banking system on the plan of the National Banking System of the United States was again mooted in 1880, but was energetically and successfully opposed by the bankers. A plan was also proposed for the establishment of a government bank inspection or for the appointment of an auditor by the shareholders. The bankers argued, however, that it was impossible for a government inspector or an auditor properly to inspect a Canadian bank on account of its many branches and the multiplicity and variety of the commercial paper in its assets. Many persons, they said, would make deposits upon the faith of an official report which would be more or less illusory. It was better, in their opinion, to rely on the careful organization of the bank, the vigilance of the directors, and the inspection by trained men of its own staff travelling from branch to branch and reporting to the general manager.

In the bill which he introduced the Minister gave effect to the representations of the bankers on all points.

Between 1880 *and* 1890.

In 1883 (by 46 Vict. c. 20) various money penalties were provided for contraventions of the Bank Act, the penalty of charter forfeiture having proved insufficient because of the government's unwillingness to punish transgression by a penalty of such excessive severity.

The unauthorized use of the title ''Banking Company,'' ''Banking House,'' ''Banking Association,'' ''Banking Institution'' or ''Banking Agency,'' was made a misdemeanour unless the words ''not incorporated'' were added to the title.

In 1886 the Bank Act of 1871 and amending acts were consolidated as chapter 120 of the Revised Statutes of Canada.

Two winding-up acts in part affecting banks were passed in this decade, namely, in 1882, an Act respecting Insolvent Banks, etc. (45 Vict. c. 23), consolidated as R.S.C. 1886, c. 129 (''The Winding-up Act''), and in 1889 the Winding-up Amendment Act.

Revision of Bank Act in 1890.

Before the time had arrived for the next decennial revision and renewal of charters, several defects in the banking law had become patent.

1. The prior lien given by the Act of 1880 to holders of notes of an insolvent bank made final payment in full almost certain, but failed to enable the holders of such notes to realize them at par immediately after the suspension. The discount and the delay were in some cases considerable.

2. The operation of the Statutes of Limitations upon the outstanding notes of an insolvent bank unjustly injured holders who were ignorant or unmindful of the necessity of presenting

notes for payment. The notes of a bank were never entirely redeemed before the limitation came into effect.

3. Under the existing system bank notes did not circulate at par in localities remote from the office where they were payable or in localities whose trade centre was different from that of the bank whence they were issued. The evil became aggravated as closer relations were established between different banks of the Dominion and a larger number of notes were circulated at a distance.

4. The security of a large paid-up capital was not sufficiently attained by the existing law which required $100,000 of capital to be paid up before a new bank should commence business.

Early in 1890 the views of the principal bankers on these and other points were presented to the Minister of Finance, (the Hon. Geo. E. Foster), and subsequently to the assembled members of Sir John A. Macdonald's cabinet. The question of requiring a bank to hold a fixed proportion of its debts in specie and Dominion notes was discussed; but, owing to the strong opposition of the bankers, the proposal to this end made by the government was abandoned.

In March, 1890, Mr. Foster proposed to the House of Commons a bill to amend the banking law. This was the subject in committee of the whole of a protracted and instructive debate, remarkable alike for its dispassionate tone and for the conspicuous legal ability brought to bear upon the questions at issue.

By the act as finally passed (53 Vict. c. 31), the four points above noted as defects in the banking law were dealt with as follows:

1. By sec. 53 the prior lien in favour of the holders of notes outstanding at the time of the suspension of a bank was preserved and was also extended to cover interest thereon. By sec. 54 provision was made for the establishment of a Bank Circulation Redemption Fund for the payment of the notes of any insolvent bank (with interest at 6 per cent. per annum from the day of suspension until such payment) in the event of the failure on the part of such bank to pay within two months from the suspension all its notes which should be presented. Such fund was to be contributed to by all the banks, each to deposit with the Minister of Finance in two instalments a sufficient sum to

make the total contribution of each bank equal to 5 per cent. of the average amount of its notes in circulation during the twelve months prior to the day fixed for payment of the second instalment, i.e., the 15th of July, 1893. The details of the scheme, including the provisions for replacing payments made out of the fund, need not be further referred to here as they are set out in the present Revised Statute.

The plan of a bond-secured system of note issue received in 1890 little support, in or out of Parliament, as compared with that which it received in 1880.

2. Moneys payable by the liquidator of an insolvent bank to shareholders and depositors which should remain unclaimed for three years, or until the completion of the winding up, were required to be paid to the Minister of Finance to be held by him subject to the claims of persons other than the bank. The liquidator was similarly required to pay to the Minister a sum equal to the amount of the notes of the bank intended for circulation and then outstanding (sec. 88, sub-sec. 4 and 5). The debts of a solvent bank were also exempted from the Statute of Limitations.

3. Each bank was required to make the arrangements necessary to insure the circulation at par in every part of Canada of all notes issued or re-issued by it and intended for circulation, including the establishment of agencies for the redemption and payment of its notes at the chief city of each province and at such other places as should be from time to time designated by the Treasury Board (sec. 55).

4. New banks were required before commencing business to obtain *bonâ fide* subscriptions to the extent of $500,000, of which $250,000 should be temporarily deposited with the Minister of Finance.

The bill, as originally introduced in the House of Commons, also provided for a system of compulsory audit by auditors appointed by the shareholders, the report of such auditors and their audit of the directors' report to be lodged with the Minister of Finance. The audit scheme was, however, successfully opposed in Parliament, as that of a government inspection had been by the bankers in 1880, on the ground that it would be absolutely impossible for any inspector or auditor to make a reliable estimate of the assets of the bank. He could not, for instance, ascertain the real value of the customers' paper discounted by a bank, which forms the greatest portion of its assets. In the United States it is not so difficult for an inspector to form some idea, even though an imperfect one, of the assets of one bank without branches. But even in that country it has sometimes happened that optimistic reports have been issued by the government inspectors in regard to banks which have shortly afterwards closed their doors. Under the Canadian branch system it would be a physical impossibility for an inspector to value all the assets of a large bank, or, (unless an army of inspectors inspected the head office and every branch of a bank at the same hour of the same day), even to trace or count the cash. A compulsory audit, it was argued, would only be illusory and deceive the public. This provision of the bill was struck out.

In addition to the changes above noted the whole Bank Act was revised and re-enacted. The more important of the other changes made by the act may be very briefly summed up, as they have been re-enacted in the present Revised Statute.

The payment of any amount due to the government of Canada in trust or otherwise was made the second charge on the assets of an insolvent bank and that of any amount due to the government of any of the provinces a third charge (sec. 53). This was a partial re-enactment of the Crown priority existing at common law.

Directors required to hold *paid-up* stock to qualify (sec 19).

Only a majority of the directors required to be British subjects (sec. 19).

Shareholders permitted to reduce as well as increase the capital stock, both increase and reduction however to be subject to the approval of the Treasury Board (secs. 26 and 28).

The amount of reserve required after division of profits exceeding 8 per cent. raised from 20 to 30 per cent. (sec. 49).

The bank forbidden to pledge, assign or hypothecate its notes, and no advance or loan made on the security of the notes of a bank to be recoverable from the bank or its assets (sec. 52).

A bank making any payment to make the same in Dominion notes at the request of the payee up to $100, instead of $50 as required by the Act of 1880 (sec. 57).

Making of false returns or wilful concurrence therein made an offence (sec. 99). Provision as to receiving deposits from persons otherwise unable to contract (sec. 84).

The period required for the registration of stock to be made before suspension, in order to exempt the transferor from liability, increased from 30 to 60 days (sec. 86).

The use of the titles "bank," "banking house" made an offence whether or not the expression "not incorporated" be added (sec. 100).

Persons committing an offence against the act to be liable to a fine not exceeding $1,000 and imprisonment not exceeding five years or both (sec. 101).

Penalties against circulation in excess of paid-up capital increased in severity (sec. 51, sub-sec. 3).

Finally the charters of 36 banks were continued, subject to certain contigencies, until the 1st of July, 1901, provision was made for bringing the Merchants Bank of Prince Edward Island under the operation of the act, some special features of La Banque du Peuple were again confirmed, and the two banks working under royal charter, the Bank of British North America and the Bank of British Columbia, were, except as to a few provisions, subjected to the act.

Between 1890 and 1900.

In 1899 an act was passed permitting a bank to issue and re-issue at any office or agency of the bank in any British colony or possession other than Canada, notes for one pound sterling each or for any multiple of such sum, subject to certain restrictions (62-63 Vict. c. 47).

Apart from this there was no amendment of the Bank Act of 1890 until the decennial renewal of charters in 1900. In the last mentioned year, the Hon. W. F. Fielding, the present Minister of Finance, introduced a bill to amend the Bank Act, which became law with but little modification.

Amending Act of 1900.

By the Bank Act Amendment Act, 1900, (63-64 Vict. c. 26), the charters of 34 banks then in operation were continued until the 1st of July, 1911, subject to certain contingencies (sec. 6), and the charters of La Banque du Peuple, La Banque Ville Marie, and the Commercial Bank of Manitoba, which were in process of liquidation, were also continued for the purpose of liquidation only (sec. 5).

2—BANK ACT.

To all banks, except as otherwise provided, the Bank Act and the amendments of 1899 and 1900 were made applicable.

The charters of the Bank of British North America and of the Bank of British Columbia remained in force subject to the act to the extent specified therein.

By the act of 1900 a number of amendments were also made to the general banking law, of which the more important are the following:

In addition to the statement already required to be submitted by the outgoing directors at the annual meeting, directors to submit to the shareholders such further statements of the affairs of the bank (other than statements with reference to the account of any person dealing with the bank), as the shareholders require by by-law passed at the annual or a special general meeting (sec. 9).

A bank not to issue notes during any period of suspension of payment of its liabilities, and in the event of a bank's resuming business without the consent in writing of the curator provided for in the act, it shall not issue notes again until authorized by the Treasury Board. Prohibition enforced by penalties (sec. 10).

Notes of a suspended bank to bear interest at 5 per cent. instead of at 6 per cent. (sec. 11).

Notes of a suspended bank which are paid out of the Bank Circulation Redemption Fund in excess of the credit of such bank in the fund to bear interest at 3 per cent. until the fund is recouped out of the assets of the bank (sec. 13).

Treasury Board empowered to extend the period for holding real or immovable property acquired by the bank for a further period of five years. Provisions for forfeiture in case of a bank's holding such property for a longer period (sec. 14).

If a person dies having a deposit with a bank not exceeding $500, the production to the bank and deposit with it of an authentic notarial copy of the will of such person or an authenticated copy of the probate of the will or letters of administration to be sufficient authority to the directors for paying such deposit in accordance with such probate, etc. (sec. 20).

Provision empowering the bank to purchase the assets of any other bank and setting out the conditions on which such a purchase may be made, the procedure which must be observed, etc., (secs. 33 to 44, as amended by c. 27 of the same session).

The bank to make an annual return to the Minister of Finance of all drafts or bills of exchange issued and remaining unpaid for over five years, under penalties for failure to make the same (sec. 21).

In the event of suspension of payment by a bank, a curator to be appointed by the "Canadian Bankers' Association" to supervise the affairs of such bank. Provisions as to the curator's powers, duties and remuneration (secs. 24 to 29). Further by-laws, rules and regulations to be made by the said Association, subject to the approval of the Treasury Board, not only on the subject of the curator's powers, duties and remuneration, but also as to, (1) the supervision of the making of the notes of the banks which are intended for circulation and the delivery thereof to the banks; (2) the inspection of the disposition made by the banks of such notes; (3) the destruction of notes of the banks, etc., (secs. 30 to 32).

By another statute of the same year the Canadian Bankers' Association was incorporated, among its powers being that of establishing clearing houses for banks, and of making rules and regulations in regard to them (63-64 Vict. c. 93).

Revised Statutes of Canada, 1906.

In 1906 the Bank Act, 1890, and amending acts were consolidated as c. 29 of the Revised Statutes of Canada, 1906. In the revision the arrangement of the sections has been considerably altered, and many sections have been divided into new sub-sections, and some have been re-drafted. In one or two instances it is not clear that the revisers have not effected some unintentional legislation.

Warehouse Receipts and Bills of Lading.

As noted above, the Act of 1859 was the beginning of the legislation permitting banks to take warehouse receipts and bills of lading as security for advances. By various statutes in subsequent years this privilege was very much amplified. Especially in 1890, important modifications were made in the rights of the banks in regard to this kind of security. As the legislative history of these rights is necessary to a perfect understanding of the reported cases, it has seemed more convenient to review the previous legislation under the sections of the present act which relate to this branch of the subject. The reader is therefore referred to chapter XVI, *infra*.

Authorities.

The principal authorities for the foregoing, are, of course, the original statutes, and the reports of parliamentary proceedings. In the writing of the chapter, use has also been made of Dr. R. M. Breckenridge's "Canadian Banking System, 1817-1890," published in Volume II. of the Journal of the Canadian Bankers' Association at pages 105 *et seq.*, and reviewed in Volume III. at page 100. Another valuable contribution to the history of Canadian Banking is Professor Adam Shortt's History of Canadian Currency, Banking and Exchange (not yet completed), published in instalments, the first of which appeared in Volume V. of the Journal. Reference may be had especially to Volume XII. at page 265, for a discussion of the critical period of 1870-1871 when, under the direction of Sir Francis Hincks, the general banking policy of the government was definitely settled, and to Volume XIV. at page 7, for an account of the revision of 1880.

An instructive discussion of the practical working of the Canadian banking system is contained in a paper by Mr. B. E. Walker, now President of the Canadian Bank of Commerce, read before the Congress of Bankers and Financiers at Chicago in 1893, published in Volume I. of the same journal, page 1, and reprinted as an introduction to Maclaren on Banking, (second edition, 1901). See also a similar paper read at a meeting of the New York State Bankers' Association, held at Saratoga in 1895, and at other meetings of bankers, published in Volume XII. of the Journal, at page 233.

Mr. Walker has also published a useful "History of Banking in Canada," (reprinted, 1899, from "A History of Banking in all Nations," by permission of the publishers, the Journal of Commerce and Commercial Bulletin, New York).

CHAPTER II.

USAGE AND THE LAW MERCHANT.

Formerly the law merchant or custom of merchants was not a part of the Common Law of England as it is now, but a concurrent and co-existent law. Its early history is obscure; cf. Blackburn on Sales, 8th ed., p. 317, and see an article by A. T. Carter in 17 L.Q.R. 232 (1901). *Law merchant formerly not part of the Common Law.*

Apparently this *lex mercatoria* comprised, in addition to a body of maritime law of international character, a definite body of customary mercantile law recognized both in England and on the Continent of Europe, and slightly affected perhaps by local variations. In England this mercantile law was administered in local and popular courts of *mercatores* and *marinarii*, these being the two classes of persons whom it concerned. Edward I. was particularly solicitous for the foreign merchant in endeavouring to give him the speedy justice which he demanded, and constituted the King in Council the final court of appeal in mercantile disputes. The Statute of the Staple (27 Edw. III., st. 2), is an epitome of the royal policy in this respect. Subsequently the Admiralty Court with some success struggled to usurp the jurisdiction, and the local mercantile courts fell into desuetude. The common law courts in turn destroyed the admiralty jurisdiction by issuing prohibitions wherever a maritime contract had not actually been made or goods had not actually been supplied on the high seas, and, in order to withdraw a suit from the courts of admiralty, permitting the use of the fiction that a contract really made at sea was made at the Royal Exchange. The administration of the mercantile law in the common law courts was, however, most unsatisfactory, owing doubtless to the fact that this branch of the law had never been made the subject of professional study. But for Lord Mansfield, the merchants, dissatisfied with the illiberal policy of the common law courts, might have resorted to the courts of chancery, whose doctrines and practice were in many respects similar to their own. That great judge employed his learning and his genius, "not only in doing justice to the parties litigating before him, but in settling with precision and *Early History.*

upon sound principles, general rules afterwards to be quoted
and recognized as governing all similar cases'' (Lickbarrow v.
Mason, 1787, 2 T.R. 63). He may truly be said to be the founder
of the commercial law of England.

Law merchant not stereotyped. The law merchant is not fixed and stereotyped, but is capable
of being expanded and enlarged so as to meet the wants and
requirements of trade in the varying circumstances of commerce.
It is neither more nor less than the usages of merchants and
traders in the different departments of trade, ratified by the
decisions of courts of law, which, upon such usages being proved
before them, have adopted them as settled law with a view to
the interests of trade and the public convenience. The court
proceeded herein on the well-known principle of law that, with
reference to transactions in the different departments of trade,
courts of law, in giving effect to the contracts and dealings of
the parties, will assume that the latter have dealt with one another on the footing of any custom or usage prevailing generally
in the particular department. By this process, what before was
usage only, unsanctioned by legal decision, has become engrafted
upon, or incorporated into, the common law, and may thus be
said to form part of it. ''When a general usage has been judicially ascertained and established,'' says Lord Campbell in
Brandao v. Barnett, 1846, 12 Cl. & F. at p. 805, 3 R.C. at p.
606, ''it becomes a part of the law merchant, which courts of
justice are bound to know and recognize'' (Goodwin v. Robarts,
1875, L.R. 10 Ex. 337, 346, S.C. 1 App. Cas. 476).

Examples. Thus when goldsmiths' or bankers' notes came into general
use, Lord Mansfield and the Court of King's Bench had no
difficulty in holding that the property in such notes passed by
delivery on the ground that they ''are treated as money, as cash,
in the ordinary course and transaction of business, by the general consent of mankind, which gives them the credit and currency of money, to all intents and purposes'' (Miller v. Race,
1758, 1 Burr. at p. 457, 3 R.C. at p. 63.

In Goodwin v. Robarts, *supra*, at p. 351, Cockburn, C.J.
notices another very remarkable instance of the efficacy of
usage. It is notorious, he says, that with the exception of the
Bank of England, the system of banking has recently undergone an entire change. Instead of the banker issuing his own
notes in return for the money of the customer deposited with
him, he gives credit in account to the depositor, and leaves it

to the latter to draw upon him, to bearer or order, by what is
now called a cheque.   Upon this state of things the general
course of dealing between bankers and their customers has attached incidents previously unknown, and these by the decisions
of the courts have become fixed law.   Thus, while an ordinary
drawee, although in possession of funds of the drawer, is not
bound to accept, unless by his own agreement or consent, the
banker, if he has funds, is bound to pay on presentation of a
cheque on demand.   Even admission of funds is not sufficient
to bind an ordinary drawee, while it is sufficient with a banker;
and money deposited with a banker is not only money lent, but
the banker is bound to repay it when called for by the draft of
the customer.   Besides this, a custom has grown up among
bankers themselves of marking cheques as good for the purposes
of clearance, by which they become bound to one another.

Bills of lading may also be referred to as an instance of the
manner in which general mercantile usage may give effect to a
writing which without it would not have had that effect at common law.   It is from mercantile usage as proved in evidence, and
ratified by judicial decision in the great case of Lickbarrow v.
Mason, 1787, 2 T.R. 63, that the efficacy of bills of lading to pass
the property in goods is derived.

Again in Brandao v. Barnett, *supra,* judicial notice was
taken of the usage of trade by which bankers are entitled to a
general lien on the securities of customers in their hands.

The greater or less time during which a custom has prevailed Evidence of
may be material in determining how far it has generally pre- usage.
vailed, but if it is once shewn to be universal, it is none the less
entitled to prevail because it may not have formed part of the
law merchant as previously recognized and adopted by the
courts (Goodwin v. Robarts, *supra*).

A mercantile custom may be so frequently proved in courts
of law that the courts will take judicial notice of it, and it becomes part of the law merchant.   It would entail useless expense
in such a case to require parties to prove by a large number of
witnesses a custom which has been proved over and again.   But
if the reported cases do not clearly establish a custom it must
be proved by evidence as on a question of fact (Ex parte Powell,
1875, 1 Ch. D. 501 at p. 506; Ex parte Hattersley, 1878, 8 Ch.
D. 601; Chawcour v. Salter, 1881, 18 Ch.D. 30 at p. 50; Edelstein v. Schuler, [1902] 2 K.B. 144 at p. 155).   Evidence to

establish a custom must relate to the mercantile usage of the place where the obligation is undertaken (Wisconsin v. Bank of B.N.A., 1861, 21 U.C.R. 284), and is to be performed.

Mercantile usage, however extensive, should not be allowed to prevail if contrary to positive law, including in the latter such usages as, having been made the subject of legal decision, and having been sanctioned and adopted by the courts, have become, by such adoption, part of the common law (Goodwin v. Robarts, *supra*).

Must be general and reasonable. A custom to be binding must be not merely general, but also reasonable (Perry v. Barnett, 1885, 15 Q.B.D. 388, and cases cited).

A local custom is not usually binding against a person not proved to have been acquainted with it (Robinson v. Mollett, 1875, L.R. 7 H.L. 802; Scott v. Godfrey, [1901] 2 K.B. 726, 734).

A trade custom, in order to be binding upon the public generally, must be shewn to be known to all persons whose interests required them to have knowledge of its existence, and in any case, the terms of a bill of lading, inconsistent with and repugnant to the custom of a port, must prevail against such custom (Parsons v. Hart, 1900, 30 S.C.R. 473).

Law merchant introduced into Canada as part of the Common Law. The law merchant as part of the common law of England, prevails in all the provinces of Canada except Quebec, subject to modification by any statutes enacted by competent authority subsequent to the introduction of the common law into such province.

Date of introduction of English Law. Resort must be had to the law of England as introduced on the following dates: in Nova Scotia and New Brunswick probably as of the 3rd of October, 1758; in Prince Edward Island as of the 7th of October, 1763; in Ontario as of the 15th of October, 1792; in Manitoba as of the 15th of July, 1870; in Alberta, Saskatchewan and the North-West Territories, for matters arising prior to the 2nd of June, 1886, as of the 2nd of May, 1670, and for matters arising since the 2nd of June 1886, as of the 15th of July, 1870; in British Columbia, as of the 19th of October, 1858. See Maclaren on Bills, etc., 3rd ed. 1904, pp. 6 *et seq.*

Usually, however, the precise date of the introduction of the common law becomes material only when there is a question whether some English statute is in force in a province.

In Quebec the common law of France and the Custom of Paris, as modified by laws and ordinances prior to 1663, were introduced by the edict of that year creating the Supreme Council of Quebec. The ordinances prior to this date had not made many important changes in the private law, but several of the *"grandes ordonnances"* of Louis XIV. have a particular importance for the student of commercial law. The earliest of these ordinances was that of 1667 on Civil Procedure, which was duly registered at Quebec. The subsequent ordinances of 1673 (*sur le commerce*) and of 1681 (*sur la marine*) on the contrary were never registered with the Supreme Council or its successor the Superior Council, and it has been the subject of keen controversy in the province of Quebec whether, because of their non-registration, they were ever in force there. The contention that the ordinances have never been in force in the province has received, to some extent, the sanction of judicial decision, and is supported by the most recent writer who deals with the question (Walton, Scope and Interpretation of the Civil Code, Montreal, 1907). Nevertheless, it appears clear that most of the great ordinances, although not registered at Quebec, were in fact cited and followed by the tribunals of New France. The two opposing views are summed up and the authorities referred to by Lemieux, who comes to the conclusion that the ordinances in question belonged to that class of general laws applicable to the whole kingdom of France which did not require registration in the local *parlements* (Les Origines du Droit Franco-Canadien, Montreal, 1901).

Whether the ordinances of 1673 and 1681 were technically in force in Quebec or not, their character was such that they might, for the most part, be followed as laying down rules of private law of universal application and authority, and they were in fact much relied upon by Lord Mansfield (1756-1788) and the other English judges who erected the structure of modern maritime and commercial law (Walton, pp. 139-140).

In addition to the ordinances published in France and afterwards registered at Quebec, the law of the province was altered from time to time by *arrêts* and *règlements* of the Council of Quebec itself and by ordinances of the governors and of the intendants of French Canada.

Whether, after the cession of Canada to Great Britain, English civil law was imposed upon the province by the Proclama-

Quebec commercial law.

The Quebec Act.

tion of 1763 is one of the most disputed questions in the history of the country, but by the Quebec Act, 1774, the general body of Quebec civil law including the commercial law was re-established as the rule for decision in all matters of controversy relative to property and civil rights (see Stuart v. Bowman, 1853, 3 L.C.R. 309, 3 R.J.R.Q. 228, 268; Wilcox v. Wilcox, 1857, 8 L.C.R. 34).

Notwithstanding the legislation of the century following the Cession, the Custom of Paris continued to be the fundamental law of the province, until in 1866 it was embodied with the statutory law of civil rights and property in the Civil Code of Lower Canada.

Subsequent changes.

Nevertheless some important changes were made by statute in the commercial law of the province during this period. The most notable enactments were the ordinance of the Legislative Council introducing in 1785 the English law of evidence in commercial matters, and the provincial statute 10 & 11 Vict. c. 31, in effect bringing into force the 17th section of the Statute of Frauds.

Still more important modifications have been effected by the practice of the courts. The commerce of the country was always mainly in the hands of the English-speaking part of the community and trade was carried on almost exclusively with England, the United States and the other provinces. It was natural, therefore, that the decisions of English judges on commercial law should come to be treated by Quebec courts with a high degree of deference, and this was all the more natural when it was found that there was great similarity between the English and French systems by reason of their common origin in the custom of merchants.

English authorities cited.

The result seems to be that although English decisions may not necessarily be binding authorities in Quebec on the ground that the commercial law of Quebec, as a general rule, is the French law (Gravelle v. Beaudoin, 1863, 7 L.C.J. 289, 11 R.J. R.Q. 221; Young v. Macnider, 1895, 25 S.C.R. at p. 283), yet the practice of the judges has been to consider English decisions as well as French (as *e.g.* in Young v. Macnider, 25 S.C.R. at pp. 277 and 278, and in the court below, Q.R. 3 Q.B. 539; Glengoil v. Pilkington, 1897, 28 S.C.R. 146; Forget v. Ostigny, [1895] A.C. 318, Q.R. 4 Q.B. 118).

In the recent case of Préfontaine v. Grenier, 1906, Q.R. 15 K.B. 143, involving the liability of a bank president for negligence, many English cases were cited. The members of the Judicial Committee, in affirming the judgment of the Quebec court, said that they thought that, in the absence of any legislation in force in Quebec inconsistent with the law as acted upon in England, and in the absence of any evidence of custom and course of business to the contrary, the Court of King's Bench was right in accepting the English rulings, because they were based, not upon any special rule of English law, nor upon any circumstances of a local character, but upon the broadest considerations of the nature of the position and exigencies of business: [1907] A.C. 110.

Propositions based upon the common law of England will Common not, however, always be applicable to the province of Quebec, Law not and in a number of instances in the course of this book, atten-applicable to tion will be drawn to differences between the law of that pro-Quebec. vince and that of the rest of the Dominion. It is manifest that a bank must in many cases enter into contracts, and both incur and have the benefit of obligations, governed by the civil law of a particular province.

Generally speaking, matters of provincial law, especially provincial statute law, are not within the scope of the book.

The following are, perhaps, the most salient general differences between the English and Quebec law in respect to matters which most frequently concern a bank.

(1) In Quebec the hypothecary system of the Roman law Hypothe-prevails. Under English law a mortgage is a conveyance of cary system. the mortgaged land to the mortgagee. The mortgagor retains only an equitable title known as the equity of redemption. The legal title passes to the mortgagee, who on default may take proceedings to foreclose. In Quebec the mortgagor merely hypothecates or charges the land in favour of the mortgagee in effect acknowledging the indebtedness as a personal obligation, but retaining the title in himself. On default the mortgagee may recover judgment on the obligation and bring the property to sale at the hands of the sheriff, and is entitled to be paid the amount of the hypothec as a preferred claim out of the proceeds of the sale.

(2) The Quebec law on the subject of married women is Married also peculiar. Unless husband and wife have made a contract women.

before marriage, they are held by the law to be in community, which means that a partnership is deemed to be established between them, each member being entitled to a half interest.

The husband is regarded as the head of the community or as the managing partner of the firm, and may deal with the property according to his own discretion.

Ante-nuptial contracts are quite usual and almost any form of settlement may be made, and a woman's private estate secured to her thereby. Even where such a contract exists, a married woman is subject to a legal disability which does not prevail in the other provinces. As a rule, she requires the authorization of her husband in all business transactions. A wife's mortgage of her separate property is void both as to the debt contracted and as to the disposition if it is in any way for her husband's purposes. Ignorance on the part of the lender that the money was borrowed for the husband's purposes is of no avail and the burden is on him to prove that it was not so borrowed (Trust & Loan v. Gauthier [1904] A.C. 94). In the other provinces, speaking generally, a married woman is capable of dealing with, and contracting in respect to, her property.

Interdicts.

(3) Another class of persons who are under disability to contract is that of "interdicts" that is persons who are placed under restrictions by the court on account of prodigality, drunkenness, etc., and who cannot contract without the assistance of curators appointed by the court on the advice of a family council.

Notarial system.

(4) In Quebec, as in France and other countries under the Civil Law, the notarial system prevails. The notary is an important personage. He is not, as in the other provinces, a mere verifier of documents and protester of bills, possessed of a seal and a signature, but is a member of a separate branch of the legal profession. Certain deeds must be signed before a notary, such as deeds of mortgage or hypothec, deeds of donation, marriage contracts, etc. The original deed signed by the parties is retained by the notary, and remains in his office until his death, when it is transferred to the public archives. What are known as "authentic copies" may be issued by the notary, certified by him under his seal of office, and these copies are admitted to proof in court and are sufficient for the purpose of registration in the province.

The "Lectures on the Bank Act" by A. Rives-Hall, now in course of publication in the Journal of the Canadian Bankers' Association (beginning in Vol. XIII., p. 237) and the introductory address by R. D. McGibbon, K.C. (*ibid.* p. 230) may usefully be consulted with special reference to Quebec law. Dr. Walton's treatise on the Scope and Interpretation of the Civil Code will be found particularly valuable in regard to the extent to which English decisions are applicable to the province of Quebec.

CHAPTER III.

THE BANK ACT: SHORT TITLE AND INTERPRETATION.

Upon even a casual perusal of the Bank Act, it will be obvious that the banking legislation of the Dominion leaves untouched in many respects the great body of the law merchant. The review of that legislation contained in Chapter I. shews that the efforts of Parliament have been mainly directed to the perfecting of the banking system so far as concerns the existence of the banks as corporations with special powers and privileges, and the security afforded by them to the public. The general relation of banker and customer and the rights and liabilities arising therefrom are only incidentally affected. Nevertheless the general banking law is so far affected by the Bank Act that it seems impossible to treat the general subject of banking law in any order other than that followed by the act without such an elaborate system of cross references as would unduly tax the patience of the reader. I have therefore endeavoured to discuss different phases of banking law in connection with particular sections of the act which deal with cognate subjects, although this course will necessarily involve a treatment of the whole subject without much regard to logical sequence.

REVISED STATUTES OF CANADA.

CHAPTER 29.

An Act respecting Banks and Banking.

SHORT TITLE.

title. 1. This Act may be cited as the Bank Act. 53 V., c. 31, s. 1.

For a review of the chief changes in the general banking legislation of the Dominion leading up to the present act, the reader is referred to Chapter I.

Powers of Dominion and Province in regard to Banks.

By reason of its power to legislate with regard to ''direct taxation within the province in order to the raising of a revenue for provincial purposes'' under clause 2 of sec. 92 of the British North America Act, 1867, a provincial legislature may impose a tax upon banks which carry on business within the province, varying in amount with their paid-up capital and with the number of their offices, whether or not their principal place of business is within the province (Bank of Toronto v. Lambe, 1887, 12 App. Cas. 575). It has been held in New Brunswick that a provincial legislature may impose a tax on the Dominion notes held by a bank in the province as part of its cash reserve under sec. 60 (Windsor v. Commercial Bank, 1882, 3 Cart. 377, 3 Russ. & Geld. 420).

As to the other questions of legislative power arising under the enactments of the Dominion Parliament in this Act, see notes to sec. 36 (Succession duty on shares and deposits), sec. 88 (Security for advances) and sec. 125 (Insolvency).

INTERPRETATION.

2. In this Act, unless the context otherwise requires,— Definitions:

(a) 'bank' means any bank to which this Act applies; 'Bank.'

(b) 'Minister' means the Minister of Finance and Receiver 'Minister.' General;

(c) 'Association' means the Canadian Bankers' Associa- 'Association.' tion, incorporated by the Act passed in the session held in the sixty-third and sixty-fourth years of Her late Majesty's reign, chapter ninety-three, intituled *An Act to incorporate the Canadian Bankers' Association;*

(d) 'curator' means any person appointed under the author- 'Curator.' ity of this Act by the Canadian Bankers' Association to supervise the affairs of any bank which has suspended payment in specie or Dominion notes of any of its liabilities as they accrue;

(e) 'Circulation Fund' means the fund heretofore estab- 'Circulation lished and continued by the authority of this Act under Fund.' the name of the Bank Circulation Redemption Fund;

(f) 'goods, wares and merchandise' includes, in addition to the things usually understood thereby, timber, deals, boards, staves, saw-logs and other lumber, petroleum, crude oil, and all agricultural produce and other articles of commerce;

(g) 'warehouse receipt'

(i) means any receipt given by any person for any goods, wares or merchandise in his actual visible and continued possession as bailee thereof in good faith and not as of his own property, and

(ii) includes receipts, given by any person who is the owner or keeper of a harbour, cove, pond, wharf, yard, warehouse, shed, storehouse or other place for the storage of goods, wares or merchandise, for goods, wares and merchandise delivered to him as bailee, and actually in the place or in one or more of the places owned or kept by him, whether such person is engaged in other business or not, and

(iii) includes also receipts given by any person in charge of logs or timber in transit from timber limits or other lands to the place of destination of such logs or timber;

(h) 'bill of lading' includes all receipts for goods, wares or merchandise, accompanied by an undertaking to transport the same from the place where they were received to some other place, by any mode of carriage whatever, whether by land or water, or partly by land and partly by water;

(i) 'manufacturer' includes manufacturers of logs, timber or lumber, maltsters, distillers, brewers, refiners and producers of petroleum, tanners, curers, packers, canners of meat, pork, fish, fruit or vegetables, and any person who produces by hand, art, process or mechanical means any goods, wares or merchandise;

(*j*) 'president' does not include an honorary president;

2. Where by this Act any public notice is required to be given the notice shall, unless otherwise specified, be given by advertisement,—

- (*a*) in one or more newspapers published at the place where the head office of the bank is situate; and,
- (*b*) in the *Canada Gazette.* 53 V., c. 31, ss. 2, 54 and 102; 63-64 V., c. 26, ss. 3 and 24; 4-5 E. VII., c. 4, s. 4.

(*a*) "*bank.*"

The banks to which this act applies are specified in secs. 3, 4, 5 and 6. The act does not apply to a foreign corporation (Commercial National Bank v. Corcoran, 1884, 6 O.R. 527). By sec. 156, every person assuming or using the title "bank," "banking company," etc., without being authorized so to do by this act, or by some other act in force in that behalf, is guilty of an offence against this act.

As to what is a bank in regard to its business and powers, see Chapter XIV., *infra.*

A bank for the purpose of the Bills of Exchange Act means an incorporated bank or savings bank carrying on business in Canada (see sec. 2 (*c*) of that act, *infra*).

(*b*) "*Minister.*"

The Minister of Finance and Receiver-General is frequently referred to in the act. He is also chairman of the Treasury Board, which exercises important functions under the act. See secs. 15 to 17, 33, 35, 67, 68 and 132. By the Act respecting the Department of Finance and the Treasury Board, the Board consists of the Minister of Finance and Receiver-General, and any five of the Ministers belonging to the King's Privy Council for Canada, to be nominated from time to time by the Governor-in-Council; the Board acts as a committee of the Privy Council on all matters relating to finance, revenue and expenditure, or public accounts, which are referred to it by the Council, or to which the Board thinks it necessary to call the attention of the Council, and has power to require from any public department, board or officer, or other person or party bound by law to furnish the same to the government, any account, return, statement, document or information which the Board deems requisite for the due performance of its duties.

(d) *"Association."*

The Act of incorporation of the Canadian Bankers' Association is printed in Chapter XXVII., *infra*.

(d) *"Curator."*

See sec. 117, Chapter XXI., *infra*.

(e) *"Circulation Fund."*

See sec. 64, *infra*.

(f) *Goods, Wares and Merchandise.*

See notes to sec. 76.

This expression is used also in secs. 86-91.

(g) *"Warehouse Receipt."*

(h) *"Bill of Lading."*

See notes to sec. 86.

A warehouse receipt is in some respects like a bill of lading. Each is a receipt or acknowledgment that the goods of one person have been received by another, but the legal effects of these documents at common law were very different. A bill of lading, being an acknowledgment by a carrier that goods had been received for carriage, was an instrument well-known to commerce, and by the custom of merchants peculiar incidents were attached to it, the most important of which was that upon its transfer the property in the goods mentioned in it passed to the transferee. A warehouse receipt on the contrary has not by custom any peculiar incidents attached to it, and its mere transfer did not pass to the transferee the property in the goods (Bank of British North America v. Clarkson, 1869, 19 C.P. at p. 188).

Bills of Lading and Factors Acts.
In England the Bills of Lading Act and the Factors Acts have largely extended the effect of bills of lading, and the rights of the holders of them. The former act confers upon the consignee of goods named in a bill of lading, and an endorsee of a bill of lading to whom the property in the goods pass upon or by reason of such consignment or endorsement the same rights of suit, and subjects him to the same liability, as if the contract contained in the bill of lading had been made with himself. The latter acts are intended to afford security to persons dealing

with factors or agents entrusted with the possession of goods, or Sec. 2. of the documents of title to goods. These or similar acts are in force in various parts of Canada, and like the subject of bills of lading generally are matters of provincial law; cf., however, R.S.C. c. 118.

The Bank Act does, however, deal with the subject of ware- Collateral house receipts and bills of lading (as defined in this section) security. to the extent of giving the banker special privileges in regard to taking such documents as collateral security. See secs. 86 *et seq.* The question of the power of Parliament to enact the provisions in question is discussed in the notes to sec. 88.

A bill of lading is not negotiable in the special sense that a Bill of bill of exchange may be negotiable (cf. Chapter XXX., *infra*). lading not a The mere honest possession of a bill of lading endorsed in blank, negotiable instrument. or upon which the goods are made deliverable to bearer, is not such a title to the goods as the like possession of a bill of exchange would be to the money promised to be paid by the acceptor. *The endorsement of a bill of lading gives no better right to the goods than the endorser himself had* (except in cases where an agent entrusted with it may transfer it to a *bonâ fide* holder under the Factors Acts), so that if the owner should lose or have stolen from him a bill of lading endorsed in blank, the finder or the thief could confer no title upon an innocent third person. But the title of *bonâ fide* third persons will prevail against the seller who has actually transferred the bill of lading to the buyer, although he may have been induced by the buyer's fraud to do so, because a transfer obtained by fraud is only voidable, not void. Benjamin on Sales, 5th ed. 1906, p. 919. Pollard v. Vinton, 1881, 105 U.S. at p. 8.

The absence of the endorsement of a bill of lading by the Absence of consignee therein named is notice of an outstanding interest in endorse- the goods represented by the bill, and places a person who is ment. asked to make an advance upon the security of the bill upon enquiry. The mere manual possession of the bill does not enable the possessor to make a pledge except subject to the rights of the consignee. (Gosselin v. Ontario Bank, 1905, 36 S.C.R. 406).

(*i*) *"Manufacturer."*
See notes to sec. 88.

(*j*) *"President."*
See secs. 24 and 28.

CHAPTER IV.

APPLICATION OF THE ACT.

General.

To what banks this Act applies. **3.** The provisions of this Act apply to the several banks enumerated in schedule A to this Act, and to every bank incorporated after the first day of January, one thousand nine hundred and five, whether this Act is specially mentioned in its Act of incorporation or not, but not to any other bank, except as hereinafter specially provided. 53 V., c. 31, s. 3.

The first 27 banks named in Schedule A. to the present act were included in Schedule A. to the Bank Act, 1890, and obtained the usual ten years' extension of their charters under the Act of 1900. The last seven banks named in Schedule A. have commenced business since 1900.

La Banque Provinciale du Canada was formerly named La Banque Jacques Cartier (63-64 Vict. c. 102), and the Royal Bank of Canada was formerly named the Merchants Bank of Halifax (63-64 Vict. c. 103).

The Bank of British North America is specially provided for by sec. 6.

Banks incorporated prior to 1st of January, 1905. The following banks not included in Schedule A. to the present Bank Act and incorporated prior to the 1st of January, 1905, have since that date obtained extensions of time for obtaining the certificate required by secs. 14 and 16.

1. Citizens Bank of Canada, incorporated by 3 Edw. VII., c. 106, time extended by 5 Edw. VII., c. 81 and 6 Edw. VII., c. 81.

2. Farmers Bank of Canada, incorporated by 4 Edw. VII., c. 77, time extended by 5 Edw. VII., c. 92 and by 6 Edw. VII., c. 94.

Banks incorporated since 1st of January, 1905. Since the 1st of January, 1905, acts have been passed incorporating the following banks not included in Schedule A. to the present Bank Act:

1. Monarch Bank of Canada, incorporated by 5 Edw. VII., c. 125, time extended by 6 Edw. VII., c. 127. Sec. 3.

2. Chartered Bank of London & Canada, incorporated by 6 Edw. VII., c. 80.

3. Colonial Bank of Canada, incorporated by 6 Edw. VII., c. 83.

In October, 1906, the directors of the Ontario Bank, in con- Ontario sideration of the assumption of its liabilities by the Bank of Bank. Montreal, made over most of its assets to the latter bank. Subsequently a curator was appointed by the Canadian Bankers' Association and a petition for a winding-up order was presented, but not pressed. The corporate existence of the Ontario Bank would not appear to be affected.

In January, 1907, the shareholders of the Peoples Bank of Peoples New Brunswick approved of the sale of the bank's assets to the Bank of Bank of Montreal. N. B.

4. The charters or Acts of incorporation, and any Acts in Bank char- amendment thereof, of the several banks enumerated in schedule ters contin- A to this Act are continued in force until the first day of July, 1st, 1911, as one thousand nine hundred and eleven, so far as regards, as to particulars. each of such banks,—

(a) the incorporation and corporate name;

(b) the amount of the authorized capital stock;

(c) the amount of each share of such stock; and,

(d) the chief place of business;

subject to the right of each of such banks to increase or reduce its authorized capital stock in the manner hereinafter provided.

2. As to all other particulars this Act shall form and be the As to other charter of each of the said banks until the first day of July, one particulars. thousand nine hundred and eleven.

3. Nothing in this section shall be deemed to continue in Forfeited force any charter or Act of incorporation, if, or in so far as it or void charters not is, under the terms thereof, or under the terms of this Act or of continued. any other Act passed or to be passed, forfeited or rendered void by reason of the non-performance of the conditions of such

Sec. 4.   charter or Act of incorporation, or by reason of insolvency, or for any other reason. 63-64 V., c. 26, s. 6.

The date mentioned in this section, the first day of July, 1911, is the date set for the expiration of the charters of all the banks included in Schedule A. at the decennial renewal of 1900; see review of legislation in Chapter I., *supra*.

The section does not apply to the Bank of B.N.A. (sec. 6).

The right of a bank to increase or reduce its authorized capital stock is provided for by secs. 33 and 35.

Banks in course of winding-up.

Act continues to apply for purposes of winding-up.   **5.** The provisions of this Act shall continue to apply to the banks named in schedule A to the Bank Act, passed in the fifty-third year of Her late Majesty's reign, chapter thirty-one, and not named in schedule A to this Act, but only in so far as may be necessary to wind up the business of the said banks respectively; and the charters or Acts of incorporation of the said banks, and any Acts in amendment thereof, or any Acts in relation to the said banks now in force, shall respectively continue in force for the purposes of winding-up, and for such purposes only.

Bank of British Columbia.   2. The sections of this Act enumerated in the next following section shall continue to apply to the Bank of British Columbia, but only in so far as may be necessary to wind up the business of the bank. 63-64 V., c. 26, s. 5.

Banks in Liquidation.

The following banks, which are those named in Schedule A. to the Bank Act, 1890, and not named in Schedule A. to the present Bank Act, suspended payment or were absorbed by other banks and went into liquidation in the interval between 1890 and 1906:

1. Commercial Bank of Manitoba, suspended payment July 3, 1903.

2. Banque du Peuple, suspended payment July 16, 1895.

3. Banque Ville Marie, suspended payment July 25, 1899.

4. The Bank of Yarmouth, Nova Scotia, suspended payment March 6, 1905. Sec. 5.

5. The Halifax Banking Company, absorbed by the Canadian Bank of Commerce.

6. The Exchange Bank of Yarmouth, absorbed by the Bank of Montreal.

7. The Peoples Bank of Halifax, absorbed by the Bank of Montreal.

8. The Commercial Bank of Windsor, absorbed by the Union Bank of Halifax.

9. The Summerside Bank, absorbed by the Bank of New Brunswick.

10. The Merchants Bank of Prince Edward Island, absorbed by the Canadian Bank of Commerce.

The assets of the Bank of British Columbia were purchased by the Canadian Bank of Commerce, under the provisions now contained in secs. 99 to 111, the purchase taking effect the 2nd of January, 1901.

The Bank of British North America.

6. The sections of this Act which apply to the Bank of British North America are sections,— What provisions applicable.

one;

two;

six;

seven;

thirty-nine;

forty-five;

fifty-seven to sixty-one, both inclusive;

sixty-three to one hundred and twenty-four both inclusive;

one hundred and thirty;

one hundred and thirty-two to one hundred and fifty-two, both inclusive; and,

one hundred and fifty-four to one hundred and fifty-seven, both inclusive.

2. The other sections of this Act do not apply to the Bank of British North America. 53 V., c. 31, s. 6; 63-64 V., c. 26, s. 7.

Sec. 6.   Cf. next section.

Section not   The following sections of the Act do not apply to the Bank
applicable to of British North America.
Bank of
B. N. A.   3-5.   Application of the Act;
                 8-17.   Incorporation, and organization of banks;
                 18-32. Internal regulations;
                 33-35. Capital stock, increase or reduction;
                 36-38. Subscriptions and calls;
                 40-42. Recovery of calls;
                 43-44. Transfer of shares;
                 46. Sale of shares under execution.
                 47-51. Transmission of shares;
                 52-53. Shares subject to trusts;
                 54-56. Annual statement.
                 62. Note issue at agency in British possession outside of
                 Canada;
                 125-129. Double liability of shareholders, application of
                 limitations, forfeiture of charter by insolvency, calls in case of
                 insolvency;
                 131. Priority of charges in case of insolvency;
                 153. Penalties for making wilfully false statement, etc.;
                 158. Recovery of penalties by Crown.

Chief office
at Montreal.   7. For the purposes of the several sections of this Act made
                 applicable to the Bank of British North America the chief
                 office of the Bank of British North America shall be the office
                 of the bank at Montreal in the province of Quebec.   53 V., c.
                 31, s. 7.

                 The Bank of British North America was incorporated by
                 royal charter, and has a corporate existence independently of
                 the act (cf. Bank of B.N.A. v. Browne, 1850, 6 U.C.R. 490; Pat-
                 ton v. Foy, 1860, 9 C.P. 512).   Its head office is situated in Lon-
                 don, Eng.   The bank is subject to the Bank Act to the extent
                 specified in sec. 6.

CHAPTER V.

INCORPORATION AND ORGANIZATION OF BANKS.

The sections included in this chapter do not apply to the Bank of British North America (sec. 6).

8. The capital stock of every bank hereafter incorporated, the name of the bank, the place where its chief office is to be situated, and the name of the provisional directors, shall be declared in the Act of incorporation of every such bank respectively. 53 V., c. 31, s. 9.

Cf. sec. 4.

Particulars of Act of incorporation.

9. An Act of incorporation of a bank in the form set forth in schedule B to this Act shall be construed to confer upon the bank thereby incorporated all the powers, privileges and immunities, and to subject it to all the liabilities and provisions set forth in this Act. 53 V., c. 31, s. 9.

Form thereof.

The form of act of incorporation of new banks provides that the act shall remain in force until the 1st day of July, 1911, but subject to the provisions of sec. 16.

10. The capital stock of any bank hereafter incorporated shall be not less than five hundred thousand dollars, and shall be divided into shares of one hundred dollars each. 53 V., c. 31, s. 10.

Capital stock and shares.

This section dates from 1890, the provision as to the amount of the par value of shares being new in that year. The condition that the capital should be not less than $500,000 was implied in the provision of the Act of 1871, that no bank to be thereafter incorporated, unless otherwise provided by its charter, should issue notes or commence the business of banking until $500,000 should have been *bonâ fide* subscribed, etc., cf. sec. 13 of the present Act.

Sec. 11.

Provisional directors.

11. The number of provisional directors shall be not less than five.

Tenure.

2. The provisional directors shall hold office until directors are elected by the subscribers to the stock, as hereinafter provided. 53 V., c. 31, s. 11; 4-5 E. VII., c. 4, s. 1.

This section dates from 1890 except that prior to 1906 it was not divided into two sub-sections.

"As hereinafter provided," see sec. 13, which provides for the election of directors by the subscribers to the stock.

See notes to next section.

Opening of stock books.

12. For the purpose of organizing the bank, the provisional directors may, after giving public notice thereof, cause stock books to be opened, in which shall be recorded the subscriptions of such persons as desire to become shareholders in the bank.

Where.

2. Such books shall be opened at the place where the chief office of the bank is to be situate, and elsewhere, in the discretion of the provisional directors.

How long.

3. Such stock books may be kept open for such time as the provisional directors deem necessary. 53 V., c. 31, s. 12.

This section dates from 1890, except that in 1906 it was divided into its present sub-sections.

"Public Notice," see sec. 2, sub-sec. 2.

Quorum.

No provision is made as to what shall constitute a quorum or as to the filling of vacancies. A majority would be a quorum (see Interpretation Act); and casual vacancies in the board would not invalidate the acts of the board (York Tramways v. Willows, 1882, 8 Q.B.D. 685), unless the number of directors were thereby reduced below the legal minimum of five (In re Alma Spinning Co. Bottomly's case, 1880, 16 Ch.D. 681; Toronto Brewing, etc., Co. v. Blake, 1883, 2 O.R. 175; cf. notes to sec. 25).

Informality of proceedings.

It does not seem to be necessary that the provisional directors should actually meet together at one place if they are unanimous in coming to a decision (In re Great Northern, etc., Works, Ex parte Kennedy, 1890, 44 Ch. D. 472).

And the informality of their internal proceedings cannot affect a third person who deals with them (Allen v. Ontario & Rainy River, 1898, 29 O.R. 510); cf. Chapter VI. on Internal Regulations.

The powers of the provisional directors seem to be limited to the organization of the bank, and, for that purpose, to the opening of stock books and the obtaining of subscriptions and payments thereon sufficient to comply with sec. 13, and then under the last mentioned section the calling of a meeting of subscribers to supplant them by the election of directors from among the subscribers, which the provisional directors themselves may never be. (In re North Simcoe Railway Co. v. Toronto, 1874, 36 U.C.R. at p. 119.) They are merely trustees to start, as it were, the ordinary legal machinery into motion. Upon the meeting of the subscribers and the election of directors, the whole object of the appointment of provisional directors is satisfied, and their authority ceases. (Michie v. Erie & Huron, 1876, 26 C.P. at p. 574.)

The ordinary rules governing subscriptions for and allotments of stock would doubtless prevail. (See Chapter VIII., on Shares and Calls.)

The prohibition of section 14 against the bank's commencing the business of banking is not intended to prevent calls being made on stock subscribed for, or to prevent the board of provisional directors from doing any acts for and in the name of the bank within the power of directors, so long as such acts fall short of what might properly be termed "commencing operations." (North Sydney v. Greener, 1898, 31 N.S.R. 41.)

13. So soon as a sum not less than five hundred thousand dollars of the capital stock of the bank has been *bonâ fide* subscribed, and a sum not less than two hundred and fifty thousand dollars thereof has been paid to the Minister, the provisional directors may, by public notice, published for at least four weeks, call a meeting of the subscribers to the said stock, to be held in the place named in the Act of incorporation as the chief place of business of the bank, at such time and at such place therein as set forth in the said notice.

2. The subscribers shall at such meeting,—

(a) determine the day upon which the annual general meeting of the bank is to be held; and,

(b) elect such number of directors, duly qualified under this Act, not less than five, as they think necessary.

3. Such directors shall hold office until the annual general meeting in the year next succeeding their election.

4. Upon the election of directors as aforesaid the functions of the provisional directors shall cease. 53 V., c. 31, s. 13; 4-5 E. VII., c. 4, s. 2.

The *bonâ fide* subscription of $500,000 of capital and the payment of $250,000 thereof to the Minister of Finance are two of the conditions precedent to a new bank's commencing business. The amounts do not vary with the authorized capital of the bank because the object of the provision is to secure a safe minimum of subscribed capital and paid-up capital as evidence of good faith and stability. From this point of view there is no reason for requiring a larger minimum in the case of a bank with an authorized capital of $2,000,000 than in the case of a bank whose authorized capital is only $500,000 (the smallest amount allowed by the act). The provision operates of course as a discouragement of small local banks.

The section dates from 1890, except that in 1906 it was divided into its present sub-sections.   •

Prior to 1890 the amount of capital required to be *bonâ fide* subscribed before commencing business was the same as at present, but only $100,000 was required to be paid up. This last amount was required to be *bonâ fide* paid up, and the fact that the necessary amount had been subscribed and paid up had to be proved to the satisfaction of the Treasury Board, and its certificate obtained, before the bank commenced business. There was a further provision that at least $200,000 in all should be paid up within two years after the commencement of business. The provision of the present act that the minimum of paid-up capital shall be paid to the Minister of Finance was first enacted in 1890. It is designed to ensure the *bonâ fide* paying up of the necessary amount, and is aimed particularly against the practice of discounting paper of subscribers and crediting them with payment on stock subscribed.

The requirements to be satisfied before a new bank com- Sec. 13.
mences business as provided by this and the next following three Prerequisites
sections are, briefly, the following: to commencement of business.

1. *Bonâ fide* subscriptions of $500,000 and payment on account thereof to the Minister of Finance of $250,000 (Sec. 13).

2. Calling of meeting of subscribers by the provisional directors, and election of directors (Sec. 13).

3. Obtaining of certificate from the Treasury Board within one year from the passing of the act of incorporation (Secs. 14 and 16).

Upon the issue of the Treasury Board's certificate the Minister of Finance is required to pay to the bank without interest the amount deposited with him, after deducting therefrom $5,000 for the purposes of the Bank Circulation Redemption Fund under section 64. In the event of no certificate being issued within the year, the Minister is required to repay the amount deposited to the person depositing the same, and the charter of the bank lapses.

The "public notice" required is prescribed by sec. 2, subsec. 2. Inasmuch as the directors are authorized to call a meeting "by public notice," individual notices to subscribers are unnecessary. Cf. notes to secs. 21 and 31.

It is doubtful whether a minority of the subscribers can make a valid election of directors. (In re London & Southern, etc., Land Co., 1885, 31 Ch. D. 223; York Tramways v. Willows, 1882, 8 Q.B.D. 685 at p. 697).

All subscribers appear to be entitled to vote whether they have made any payments on account of stock subscribed or not. The form of subscription ought to be drawn so as to give the provisional directors power to enforce payment by suit or forfeiture.

14. The bank shall not issue notes or commence the business Permission of Treasury Board to of banking until it has obtained from the Treasury Board a mence business. certificate permitting it to do so.

2. No application for such certificate shall be made until No certificate until directors have been elected by the subscribers to the stock in directors the manner hereinbefore provided. 53 V., c. 31, s. 14. elected.

Sec 14.   See notes to section 13.

Sec 132 makes it an offence against this act to issue notes or
commence business before the obtaining of the certificate.

Sec. 15 prescribes the conditions to be performed before the
certificate of the Treasury Board may be given.

"Commence the business of banking," refers to the transaction of business with the public as distinguished from dealings
connected with subscriptions for stock. (Cf. North Sydney v.
Greener, referred to in the notes to sec. 12.)

This section was divided into its present sub-sections in 1906.

When cer-   **15.** No certificate shall be given by the Treasury Board
tificate may
be granted   until it has been shewn to the satisfaction of the Board, by
affidavit or otherwise, that all the requirements of this Act and
of the special Act of incorporation of the bank, as to the payment required to be made to the Minister, the election of directors, deposit for security for note issue, or other preliminaries,
have been complied with, and that the sum so paid is then held
by the Minister.

Within one   2. No such certificate shall be given except within one year
year.   from the passing of the Act of incorporation of the bank applying for the said certificate. 53 V., c. 31, s. 15.

This section was divided into its present sub-sections in 1906.

If certificate   **16.** If the bank does not obtain a certificate from the Treas-
not granted.
ury Board within one year from the time of the passing of
its Act of incorporation, all the rights, powers and privileges
conferred on the bank by its Act of incorporation shall there-
Powers to   upon cease and determine, and be of no force or effect what-
cease.   ever. 53 V., c. 31, s. 16.

See notes to sec. 13.

This and the two next preceding sections date from 1890.
Prior to that date there was no time limit for the commencement
of business other than the time set for the expiration in due
course of the charter of the bank.

Susan

275 20 Silverado

Crest PK SW

Calgary Alta

T2X 4L3

e in manner hereinbefore   Sec. 17.

h pay to the bank the Deposit, how
im as aforesaid, without disposed of
                                           if certificate
1e sum of five thousand granted.

er the provisions of this

d by the bank.

by the Treasury Board If certificate
thereof, the amount so not granted.

son depositing the same.

under any obligation to Minister not
way of the amount so re- bound.
turned.   53 V., c. 31, s. 17.

See notes to sec. 13.

Sec. 64 requires the Minister of Finance to retain the sum of $5,000 for the purposes of the Bank Circulation Redemption Fund.

This section was divided into its present sub-sections in 1906.

CHAPTER VI.

INTERNAL REGULATIONS.

Sec. 18.
(p. 52.)

The sections included in this chapter do not apply to the Bank of British North America (sec. 6).

Ultra vires acts.

A company is not bound by those acts of the directors, which as regards the company are *ultra vires,* and the subsequent approval of the whole body of shareholders cannot make such acts binding. Ashbury v. Riche, 1875, L.R. 7 H.L. 653; cf. Irvine v. Union Bank, 1877, 2 App. Cas. 366.)

Informality of internal proceedings.

But if the acts in question are *intra vires* of the company, the mere want of formality in the Company's proceedings will not affect a third party with whom it is dealing, even though such party is himself a director and has notice of all that is done. (Neelon v. Thorold, 1893, 22 S.C.R. 390, 396; Adams v. Bank of Montreal, 1899, 8 B.C. 314, and 1 Com. L.R. 248, and cases cited.)

There is no necessity on the part of persons dealing with companies to see that *de facto* directors are properly appointed. (Mahoney v. East Holyford, 1875, L.R. 7 H.L. 869.)

In any case where a person holds himself out as an agent or official of a company, and the circumstances are such that in law the company could repudiate such person or take proceedings to restrain him, but has not done so, then his acts within his apparent authority will bind the company as regards persons ignorant of his true position, even though his assumption of authority is entirely unwarranted. (Allen v. Ontario & Rainy River Railway, 1898, 29 O.R. 510, 513, and cases cited.)

In Ruben v. Great Fingall, [1906] A.C. 439, the appellants advanced in good faith a sum of money to the secretary of the respondent company for his own purposes on the security of a share certificate of the company issued to them by the secretary certifying that the appellants were registered in the company's register of shareholders as transferees of shares. This certificate was, in point of form, in accordance with the company's articles of association, inasmuch as it bore the seal of the company, and appeared to be signed by two of the directors and countersigned by the secretary. The seal of the company was,

however, affixed by the secretary fraudulently and without authority, and the signatures of the two directors were forged by him. In an action against the company for damages for refusing to register the appellants as owners of the shares, it was held that, in the absence of any evidence that the company ever held out the secretary as having authority in this behalf to do anything more than the ministerial act of delivering share certificates, when duly made, to the owners of shares, the company was not estopped by the forged certificate from disputing the claim of the appellants, or responsible to them for the wrongful act of the secretary. Sec. 18.
(p. 52.)

Further, persons dealing with companies are not obliged to see that directors exercise the powers they possess in the precise manner prescribed by the regulations of the company; and persons dealing with directors *bonâ fide,* and without notice of an irregular or improper exercise of the directors' powers are not affected by such irregularity or impropriety. (Royal British Bank v. Turquand, 1856, 5 E. & B. 248, 6 *ib.* 327; Ex parte Overend, Gurney & Co., 1869, L.R. 4 Ch. 460; County of Gloucester Bank v. Rudry, [1895] 1 Ch. 629; Duck v. Tower, [1901] 2 K.B. 314; Trusts & Guarantee v. Abbott Mitchell, 1902, 11 O. L.R. 403.)

The court will not interfere with the internal management of companies acting within their powers, and in fact, has no jurisdiction to do so. In order to redress a wrong done to the company or to recover moneys or damages alleged to be due to the company, the action should *primâ facie* be brought by the company itself. These cardinal principles are laid down in the well-known cases of Foss v. Harbottle, 1843, 2 Hare 461, and Mozley v. Alston, 1847, 1 Ph. 790 and in numerous later cases.' But an exception is made to the second rule, where the persons against whom the relief is sought themselves hold or control the majority of the shares of the company, and will not permit an action to be brought in the company's name. In such a case the courts allow the shareholders complaining to bring an action in their own names. This, however, is mere matter of procedure, in order to give a remedy for a wrong what would otherwise escape redress. It is obvious that in such an action the plaintiffs cannot have a larger right to relief than the company itself would have if it were plaintiff, and cannot complain of acts which would be valid if done with the approval of the Court, will not interfere with internal management.

majority of the shareholders, or which are capable of being confirmed by this majority. The cases in which the minority can maintain such an action are, therefore, confined to those in which the
acts complained of are of a fraudulent character or beyond the
powers of the company. A familiar example is the attempt of
a majority directly or indirectly to appropriate to themselves
money, property or advantages which belong to the company,
or in which the other shareholders are entitled to participate, as
was alleged in the case of Menier v. Hooper's Telegraph Works,
1874, L.R. 9 Ch. 350. It should be added that no mere informality or irregularity that can be remedied by the majority will
entitle the minority to sue, if the act when done regularly would
be within the powers of the company, and if the intention of
the majority of the shareholders is clear. This may be illustrated by the judgment of Mellish, L.J., in MacDougall v.
Gardiner, 1875, 1 Ch.D. 13 at p. 25; cf. Burland v. Earle, 1902,
A.C. 83, 94.

But a shareholder who has, with full knowledge of the facts,
himself received part of the proceeds of an *ultrâ vires* act committed by the directors—such as payment of a dividend out of
capital—and who still retains the money, cannot, either individually or as suing on behalf of the general body of shareholders,
maintain an action against those directors. (Towers v. African
Tug Co., [1904] 1 Ch. 558.)

Powers of Shareholders.

Under sub-section 1 of sec. 18 the shareholders may regulate
by by-law the following matters incident to the management and
administration of the affairs of the bank.

(1) The day upon which the annual general meeting of the
shareholders for the election of directors shall be held (cf. secs.
21, 22 and 23 as to the hour of the meeting, the public notice
thereof and the mode of electing directors).

2. The record to be kept of proxies.

(3) The time, not exceeding 30 days, within which proxies
must be produced and recorded prior to a meeting, in order to
entitle the holder to vote thereon. By sec. 32 only shareholders
entitled to vote may vote or act as proxies, and proxies must be
renewed within the two years preceding the time of the meeting.
In the absence of by-law proxies may be registered up to the

time of the meeting. A by-law must not provide that proxies Sec. 18. (p. 52.)
to be valid shall be registered more than 30 days before the meeting.

(4) The number of the directors, which shall not be less than
five. (Prior to 1905 the number of directors was limited to ten).

(5) The quorum of directors, which shall not be less than Powers of shareholders.
three.

(6) The qualification of directors subject to sec. 20.

(7) The method of filling vacancies in the board of directors whenever the same occur during any year. Cf. sec. 25.

(8) The time and proceedings for the election of directors
in case of a failure of any election on the day appointed for it.
(Cf. sec. 27 under which the old directors continue in office
until a new election is made).

(9) The remuneration of the president, vice-president and
other directors.

(10) The amount of discounts or loans which may be made
to directors, either jointly or severally, or to any one firm or
person, or to any shareholder, or to corporations. (The aggregate amount of loans to directors and firms of which they are
partners must be shewn in the monthly return, Schedule D.)

(11) The shareholders also have power to authorize the directors to establish guarantee and pension funds for the officers
and employees of the bank and their families, and to contribute
thereto out of the funds of the bank. (Sec. 18, sub-sec. 2.)

(12) To remove the president, vice-president or any director at a special general meeting called for the purpose. (Sec.
31, sub-sec. 4.)

(13) To increase or reduce the capital stock of the bank,
subject to the approval of the Treasury Board. (Secs. 33 and
35.)

(14) To approve of an agreement for the sale of the assets
of the bank to another bank, or for the purchase of the assets
of another bank, but in the latter case the shareholders need
consent only if it is necessary for the purpose of the purchase
to increase the capital stock of the bank. (Secs. 101 and 103.)

(15) To require the directors to submit further statements
of the affairs of the bank in addition to the regular annual statement. (Sec. 55.)

By-laws.   **18.** The shareholders of the bank may regulate, by by-law,
the following matters incident to the management and administration of the affairs of the bank, that is to say :—

    (a) The day upon which the annual general meeting of the
shareholders for the election of directors shall be held;

    (b) The record to be kept of proxies, and the time, not
exceeding thirty days, within which proxies must be produced and recorded prior to a meeting in order to entitle
the holder to vote thereon;

    (c) The number of the directors, which shall be not less than
five, and the quorum thereof, which shall be not less than
three;

    (d) Subject to the provisions hereinafter contained, the
qualifications of directors;

    (e) The method of filling vacancies in the board of direc-
tors, whenever the same occur during each year;

    (f) The time and proceedings for the election of directors,
in case of a failure of any election on the day appointed
for it;

    (g) The remuneration of the president, vice-president and
other directors; and,

    (h) The amount of discounts or loans which may be made to
directors, either jointly or severally, or to any one firm or
person, or to any shareholder, or to corporations.

Guarantee   **2.** The shareholders may authorize the directors to establish
and pension guarantee and pension funds for the officers and employees of
funds.
the bank and their families, and to contribute thereto out of the
funds of the bank.

Existing by-   **3.** Until it is otherwise prescribed by by-law under this
laws con-   section, the by-laws of the bank on any matter which may be
tinued.
regulated by by-law under this section shall remain in force,

Exception.   except as to any provision fixing the qualification of directors

at an amount less than that prescribed by this Act. 53 V.,
c. 31, s. 18; 4-5 E. VII., c. 4, s. 3.

See notes, *supra.*

The division of sub-section 1 into lettered clauses was made
in 1906. The corresponding provision of the Act of 1890, as
amended in 1900, contained also a clause prohibiting any person
from being elected or continuing a director unless he held stock
paid up to the amount required to qualify him. This clause is
now part of sec. 20.

19. The stock, property, affairs and concerns of the bank
shall be managed by a board of directors, who shall be elected
annually in manner hereinafter provided, and shall be eligible
for re-election. 53 V., c. 31, s. 19.

This section was sub-sec. 1 of sec. 19 of the Act of 1890.

The stock, property, affairs and concerns of a bank are to be
managed by a board of directors. (Sec. 19.)

The number of directors is to be not less than five and their
quorum not less than three, but otherwise their number and
quorum are subject to regulation by the shareholders. (Sec. 18.)
Cf. notes to sec. 12.

See also the following sections relating to directors.
20. Qualification.
21-27. Election.
28. Meetings.
29-30. General Powers.

Duties and Liabilities of directors.

At every annual meeting of the shareholders it is the duty
of the outgoing directors to submit a clear and full statement of
the affairs of the bank, containing the particulars required by
sec. 54 and any additional statements which may be lawfully
required by the shareholders under sec. 55.

The directors are responsible for knowingly and wilfully
concurring in declaring any dividend or bonus so as to impair
the paid-up capital. (Sec. 58).

A director is liable criminally if he pledges, assigns or hypothecates notes of the bank (sec. 139), if he refuses to make calls

Sec. 19.

Duties and
liabilities of
directors.
on the double liability of the shareholders after the expiration
of three months from the insolvency of the bank (sec. 154), if
he wilfully gives or concurs in giving any creditor of the bank
any fraudulent, undue or unfair preference over other creditors (sec. 155), or if he makes any wilfully false or deceptive
statement in any account, statement, return report or other
document respecting the affairs of the bank (sec. 153). In the
last case he is also responsible for all damages sustained by any
person in consequence of such statement.

The directors are bound to account to the company for all
profits made by them with the assets of the company, and for
all profits made by them at the expense of the company otherwise than with its knowledge and consent. (Imperial v. Coleman, 1873, L.R. 6 H.L. 189; Costa Rica v. Forwood, [1901] 1
Ch. 746.)

They are also responsible for the loss of the company's assets, if that loss is attributable to the employment by them of
the assets in a manner and for purposes not warranted by the
constitution of the company. (Cullerne v. London & Suburban,
1890, 25 Q.B.D. 485; In re Sharpe, [1892] 1 Ch. 154; Hirsche
v. Sims, [1894] A.C. 654.)

Directors of a bank are bound to exercise the care of a prudent administrator in the management of its business. Such
acts as allowing overdrafts by insolvent persons without proper
security, the impairment of the capital of the bank by the payment of unearned dividends, the furnishing of false and deceptive statements to the government, the expenditure of the funds
of the bank in illegal purchases of its own shares, are acts of
gross mismanagement which render the directors personally
liable, jointly and severally, for losses sustained by the shareholders by reason thereof.

Directors cannot divest themselves of their personal responsibility. While they are at liberty to employ such assistants as
may be required to carry on the business of the corporation,
they are nevertheless responsible for the misconduct of the employees appointed by them, unless such misconduct could not
have been guarded against by the exercise of reasonable diligence. (McDonald v. Rankin, 1890, M.L.R. 7 S.C. 44.)

If directors, in unwittingly assenting to what were in fact
payments of dividends out of capital and advances on improper
security, honestly relied on the judgment, information and ad-

vice of the chairman and general manager of the bank, by whose statements they were misled and whose integrity, skill and competence they had no reason to suspect, they are not negligent of their duties as directors and are not bound to look at the books for themselves. (Dovey v. Cory, [1901] A.C. 477, and cases cited; In re Denham & Co., 1883, 25 Ch. D. 752.) The trust reposed by directors in their manager must not be blind or unqualified, or to the exclusion of the exercise of their own judgment, nor may they disregard the directions contained in the by-laws and regulations of the bank. (Leeds Estate v. Shepherd, 1887, 36 Ch. D. 787.)

But directors who keep within the limits of their authority, and who, acting in good faith to the best of their judgment, exercise a reasonable amount of care, are not liable to make good to the company the losses which may result from their acts. (London Financial v. Kelk, 1883, 26 Ch.D. 107 and authorities there collected; Dovey v. Cory, *supra*.)

20. Each director shall,—   Qualifications.

   (a) when the paid-up capital stock of the bank is one million dollars or less, hold stock of the bank on which not less than three thousand dollars have been paid up;

   (b) when the paid-up capital stock of the bank is over one million dollars and does not exceed three million dollars, hold stock of the bank on which not less than four thousand dollars have been paid up; and,

   (c) when the paid-up capital stock of the bank exceeds three million dollars, hold stock of the bank on which not less than five thousand dollars have been paid up.

2. No person shall be elected or continue to be a director Idem. unless he holds stock paid up to the amount required by this Act, or such greater amount as is required by any by-law in that behalf.

3. A majority of the directors shall be natural born or natur- Majority to alized subjects of His Majesty. 53 V., c. 31, ss. 18 and 19.   be British subjects.

Qualification of Directors.

Prior to 1890 all the directors were required to be British subjects, but it was not necessary that their qualification shares should be paid up to any amount.

Sec. 20.　　　　The shareholders may under sec. 18 make by-laws requiring additional qualifications for a director.

In the Act of 1890 sub-sec. 2 was part of sec. 18, and sub-secs. 1 and 3, except for some verbal re-arrangement made in 1906, were part of sec. 19.

Qualification shares.　　　　Even if the by-laws require a director to hold qualification shares "in his own right," he need not be the beneficial owner of the shares, but he must be a person who holds shares in such a way that the company can safely deal with him in respect of his shares, whatever his interest in them may be. Holding in a representative character will not do. Holding as trustee without beneficial ownership will do, but the holder must so hold as that the company can safely deal with him as owner. (Sutton v. English, [1902] 2 Ch. 502, and cases cited at p. 506; Boschoek v. Fuke, [1906] 1 Ch. 148; cf. however, Ritchie v. Vermillion, 1902, 4 O.L.R. at p. 597, as to the meaning of "absolutely in his own right.")

If a by-law provides that no person shall be qualified to be a director who is not a holder of a certain number of shares, the holding of such shares is a condition precedent to the election of a director, and the election of an unqualified person is void. In re Percy, etc., Co., Jenner's case, 1877, 7 Ch. D. 132.) The necessity for holding shares does not oblige a director to take shares from the company. He may acquire them in any other legal mode, and therefore the mere acting as director does not amount to a contract by the person so acting to take the necessary number of unpaid shares from the company. In re Metropolitan, etc., Co., Brown's case. 1873, L.R. 9 Ch. 102, at p. 109; Jenner's case, *supra;* cf. Molineaux v. London, [1902] 2 K.B. 589).

Election of directors.　　　　**21.** The directors shall be elected by the shareholders on such day in each year as is appointed by the charter or by any by-law of the bank, and at such time of the day as the directors appoint.

At head office.　　　　2. The election shall take place at the head office of the bank.

Notice.　　　　3. Public notice of the election shall be given by the directors by publishing such notice, for at least four weeks previously to the time of holding the election, in a newspaper published

at the place where the head office of the bank is situate. 53 V.,
c. 31, s. 19.

The division into sub-sections was made in 1906.

Public notice.

The public notice required is defined by the section, whereas in other sections (*e.g.*, secs. 13 and 31), the words "public notice" are used without any limitation and therefore mean public notice as defined by sec. 2, sub-sec. 2.

Notice to shareholders.

Probably no notice other than the public notice mentioned in the section need be given to shareholders. It would be prudent perhaps to pass a by-law dispensing with any other notice. Cf. notes to sec. 31.

Election of directors.

The first directors are elected at the meeting of subscribers called by the provisional directors under sec. 13. Thereafter the directors are elected at the annual general meeting held each year on the day appointed by the charter or by by-law of the shareholders (secs. 18 and 21), or, if the election does not take place on such day, then on any other day according to the by-laws made by the shareholders in that behalf (secs. 18 and 27). The directors, as soon as may be after their own election, elect two of their number to be president and vice-president respectively, and they may also elect one of their number to be honorary president (sec. 24). A vacancy which occurs in the board is filled in the manner provided by the by-laws (secs. 18 and 25), and if such vacancy is in the office of president or vice-president the directors elect such officer from among themselves (sec. 26). The president, the vice-president or any director may be removed by the shareholders at a special general meeting called for the purpose (sec. 31).

22. The persons, to the number authorized to be elected, who Who shall
have the greatest number of votes at any election, shall be be directors.
directors. 53 V., c. 31, s. 19.

Sec. 23.   **23.** If it happens at any election that two or more persons
Provision in   have an equal number of votes, and the election or non-election
case of equal-
ity of votes.   of one or more of such persons as a director or directors depends
on such equality, then the directors who have a greater number
of votes, or the majority of them, shall in order to complete
the full number of directors, determine which of the said persons so having an equal number of votes shall be a director or
directors. 53 V., c. 31, s. 19.

Election of   **24.** The directors, as soon as may be after their election,
president
and vice-   shall proceed to elect, by ballot, two of their number to be pre-
president.   sident and vice-president respectively.

Honorary   2. The directors may also elect by ballot one of their number
president.   to be honorary president. 53 V., c. 31, s. 19; 4-5 E. VII., c. 4,
s. 4.

Sub-sec. 2 dates from 1905, sub-sec. 1 from 1890.

As to the duties of president and vice-president, see sec. 28.

Vacancies,   **25.** If a vacancy occurs in the board of directors the
how filled.
vacancy shall be filled in the manner provided by the by-laws:
Proviso.   Provided that, if the vacancy is not filled, the acts of a quorum
of the remaining directors shall not be thereby invalidated.
53 V., c. 31, s. 19.

Sec. 18, sub-sec. 1, clause (e), confers upon the shareholders
power to regulate by by-law the method of filling vacancies in
the board.

If the number of directors is reduced below the legal minimum of five (ibid, clause (c)) or below the number fixed by
by-law as a quorum of the board, the directors remaining in
office are incapable of doing any business of the bank, and in
order to fill the vacancies, it would be necessary to call a special
general meeting under sec. 31. (Sovereen Co. v. Whitside, 1906,
12 O.L.R. 638, and cases cited; cf. notes to sec 12; see, however,
In re Bank of Syria, [1901] 1 Ch. 115.)

26. If a vacancy occurs in the office of the president or vice-president, the directors shall, from among themselves, elect a president or vice-president, who shall continue in office for the remainder of the year. 53 V., c. 31, s. 19.

Sec. 26.
Vacancy of president or vice-president.

27. If an election of directors is not made on the day appointed for that purpose, such election may take place on any other day, according to the by-laws made by the shareholders in that behalf.

Failure of election.

2. The directors in office on the day appointed for the election of directors shall remain in office until a new election is made. 53 V., c. 31, s. 20.

Cf. sec. 18, sub-sec. 1 (*e*), and notes, *infra*, under "Shareholders' Meetings."

28. The president, or in his absence the vice-president, shall preside at all meetings of the directors.

Meetings of directors.

2. If at any meeting of the directors both president and vice-president are absent, one of the directors present, chosen to act *pro tempore*, shall preside.

Idem.

3. The president, vice-president or president *pro tempore*, so presiding, shall vote as a director, and shall, if there is an equal division on any question, also have a casting vote. 53 V., c. 31, s. 21.

Voting.

The division into sub-sections was made in 1906. This section contains the only provisions of the Act relating to directors' meetings, except the provision of sec. 18 giving power to the shareholders to regulate the quorum. Cf. notes to sec. 12.

Duties of President and Vice-President.

The only duties imposed specially upon the president (or in his absence the vice-president), by the Act are to preside at meetings of directors (sec. 28), to sign the bonds and other obligations of the bank (sec. 73), and to sign the monthly and other returns to the government (secs. 112, 113 and 114).

Sec. 28.   The signing of the returns may involve a greater liability than that of an ordinary director (see sec. 153), but except as above stated or as provided by by-law, the duties and liabilities of a president are the same as those of any other director.

By sec. 24 the directors shall elect a president and vice-president, and may also elect an honorary president. The honorary president has no duties assigned to him by the Act; cf. sec. 2 (*j*).

General powers of directors.   **29.** The directors may make by-laws and regulations, not repugnant to the provisions of this Act or to the laws of Canada, with respect to,—

> (*a*) the management and disposition of the stock, property, affairs and concerns of the bank;
>
> (*b*) the duties and conduct of the officers, clerks and servants employed therein; and,
>
> (*c*) all such other matters as appertain to the business of a bank.

Existing by-laws continued.   2. All by-laws of the bank heretofore lawfully made and now in force with regard to any matter respecting which the directors may make by-laws under this section, including any by-laws for the establishing of guarantee and pension funds for the employees of the bank, shall remain in force until they are repealed or altered by other by-laws made under this Act. 53 V., c. 31, s. 22.

The division into sub-sections was made in 1906.

The exercise by the directors of the powers given by this section is subject to any by-laws made by the shareholders under sec. 18.

By other sections powers in regard to the following specific matters are given to the directors.

(4) To appoint as many officers, clerks and servants for carrying on the business of the bank and with such salaries and allowances as they consider necessary, subject to the giving of a bond by an employee before he enters upon his duties (sec. 30).

(5). To call a special general meeting of the shareholders (sec. 31).

(6) To allot shares in the event of an increase of capital Sec. 29. stock (sec. 34).

(7) To make regulations as to the assignment and transfer of shares of capital stock (sec. 36).

(8) To make calls upon shares subscribed, cancel subscriptions for non-payment, or sue for calls, etc. (secs. 37, 38, 40-42).

(9) To inspect the books, correspondence and funds of the bank (sec. 56).

(10) To declare dividends out of profits (sec. 57).

(11) To depute an officer of the bank to sign notes intended for circulation (sec. 73).

Remuneration of directors.

The directors' remuneration is governed by by-law of the shareholders under sec. 18. Directors cannot pay themselves for their services or make presents to themselves out of the bank's assets unless authorized to do so by the shareholders at a properly convened meeting. In re George Newman & Co., [1895] 1 Ch. 674; cf. Boschoek v. Fuke, [1906] 1 Ch. 148.)

30. The directors may appoint as many officers, clerks and Appointservants as they consider necessary for the carrying on of the ment of officers. business of the bank.

2. The directors may also appoint a director or directors for Branches. any branch of the bank.

3. Such officers, clerks and servants may be paid such salaries Salaries. and allowances as the directors consider necessary.

4. The directors shall, before permitting any cashier, officer, Security. clerk or servant of the bank to enter upon the duties of his office, require him to give a bond, guarantee, or other security to the satisfaction of the directors, for the due and faithful performance of his duties. 53 V., c. 31, s. 23.

The present wording and division into sub-sections date from 1906.

Under this section the directors may appoint a general manager, and branch managers, and also subordinate officers and clerks. They may also assign to one or more members of the board of directors the special supervision of particular branches.

If a bond is taken for the due and faithful performance by a cashier, officer, etc. of his duties, the legal relation between the bank and the surety will be governed by the general provincial law relating to principal and surety. The shareholders may under sec. 18, sub-sec. 2, establish a guarantee fund.

Authority of general manager.

The general manager of a bank is its general agent in its banking business. (Barwick v. English Joint Stock Bank, 1867, L.R. 2 Ex. 259, 265). In the exercise of his authority he is sub-ject to the control of the directors, but whatever is done by him in the way of ordinary banking transactions may be presumed, until the contrary is shewn, to be within the scope of his authority; the bank would be liable for his mistakes, and under some circumstances for his frauds, in the management of the business of the bank. (Bank of N.S.W. v. Owston, 1879, 4 App. Cas. 270, at p. 289.)

In accordance with the general rule of the law of agency, a bank is answerable for every such wrong of its agent as is committed in the course of the employment and for the bank's benefit, although the directors have not authorized the particular wrong or given a general authority to commit wrongs. There is no distinction in this respect between frauds and other wrongs. (Mackay v. Commercial Bank, 1874, L.R. 5 P.C. 394; Wilson v. Hotchkiss, 1901, 2 O.L.R. at p. 271.)

But the arrest, and still less the prosecution, of offenders is not within the ordinary routine of banking business, and therefore not within the ordinary scope of a bank manager's authority. Evidence accordingly is required to shew that such arrest or prosecution is within the scope of the duties and class of acts such manager is in fact authorized to perform. The authority may be general, or it may be special and derived from the exigencies of the particular occasion on which it is exercised. In the former case it is usually enough to shew that the agent was acting in what he did on behalf of the principal; but in the latter case evidence must be given of a state of facts which shews that such exigency is present or might reasonably be supposed to be present. (Bank of N.S.W. v. Owston, *supra;* cf. Thompson v. Bank of Nova Scotia, 1893, 32 N.B.R. 335, a case of a branch manager instituting criminal proceedings.)

Where cheques were fraudulently initialed as accepted by the manager, and the drawer gave the bank certain securities which the bank retained, it was held that the cheques could not be repudiated as against a *bonâ fide* holder for value. (Banque Nationale v. City Bank, 1873, 17 L.C.J. 197.)

Authority of branch manager.

While the general manager of a bank is its general agent in its banking business, the authority of a branch manager ordinarily will be confined to the transaction of the local business of the bank. For instance, he will have implied power to call in money which has been advanced from his branch at call. (Robertson v. Sheward, 1843, 1 M. & G. 511, at p. 517; Collinson v. Lister, 1885, 7 De. G.M. & G. 634, at p. 637), or to accept the cheque of a customer to deliver to another customer on a particular day, or on the happening of a specified event. (Grieve v. Molsons Bank, 1885, 8 O.R. 162.) But, in the absence of actual authority, he has no apparent authority to exercise powers of a discretionary character (Morse on Banking), as for instance to compromise a claim of the bank. (Bank of Commerce v. Jenkins, 1888, 16 O.R. 215.)

Agent's knowledge imputed to principal.

The usual rules of the law of agency apply to a bank manager. If for instance he does an act outside of the apparent scope of his authority and makes a representation to advance his own private ends (or what is the same thing, the private ends of some one other than the bank), it can in no sense be called the representation of the bank—in other words, it is not a representation by him as agent, and the bank is not affected by reason of its agent's knowledge of the transaction. (Richards v. Bank of Nova Scotia, 1896, 26 S.C.R. 381.)

Liability of manager.

If a local manager does some act in breach of his instructions, he must make good the loss occasioned thereby, but in a case where he accepted a joint, instead of a joint and several, promissory note as security for an advance, he having been expressly instructed to require the latter, it was held that, as the form of the note which he did take was sufficient to secure the liability of the parties in Ontario as effectively to all intents and purposes as if the note had been in the exact form called for by his instructions, only nominal damages were recoverable against him for his breach of duty in this regard. After discovering the mistake as to the form of the note, the local manager inserted the words "jointly and severally," in the belief that this alteration was to be initialed by all the makers, which, however, was not done. After consulting the bank's solicitor, the defendant crossed out the inserted words. The note having thus been made void by reason of material alteration it was held that the manager was not liable for the result of the alteration, since he acted in good faith and in ignorance of the legal consequences, and exercised reasonable care and diligence under all the circumstances. The mere fact that his judgment was mistaken, and his acts prejudicial to the bank, was not enough to render him liable (Banque Provinciale v. Charbonneau, 1903, 6 O.L.R. 302, 2 Com. L.R. 478, where the degree of skill and knowledge which may reasonably be expected of a local manager is discussed).

Bank of Upper Canada v. Bradshaw, 1867, L.R. 1 P.C. 479, was an action brought by a bank against its late manager and cashier to recover moneys belonging to the bank, alleged to have been improperly applied in discounting bills, etc., for his own advantage, for the benefit of parties and companies with whom he was connected and in which he was interested. It appeared that the transactions in question were all in the ordinary course of the business of the bank, that the manager had not exceeded the authority with which he was entrusted and that no case of bad faith could be established, and an appeal from a judgment in favour of the defendant was dismissed.

Special general meeting. **31.** A special general meeting of the shareholders of the bank may be called at any time by,—

(a) the directors of the bank or any four of them; or,

(b) any number not less than twenty-five of the shareholders, acting by themselves or by their proxies, who are together proprietors of at least one-tenth of the paid-up capital stock of the bank.

Notice. 2. Such directors or shareholders shall give six weeks' previous public notice, specifying therein the object of such meeting.

3. Such meeting shall be held at the usual place of meeting of the shareholders.

Sec. 31.
Place.

4. If the object of the special general meeting is to consider the proposed removal, for maladministration or other specified and apparently just cause, of the president or vice-president, or of a director of the bank, and if a majority of the votes of the shareholders at the meeting is given for such removal, a director to replace him shall be elected or appointed in the manner provided by the by-laws of the bank, or, if there are no by-laws providing therefor, by the shareholders at the meeting.

Removal of president vice-president or director.

Another to replace.

5. If it is the president or vice-president who is removed, his office shall be filled by the directors in the manner provided in case of a vacancy occurring in the office of president or vice-president. 53 V., c. 31, s. 24.

Choosing another president or vice-president.

The shareholders meet and vote at the annual general meetings of the bank (the first of such meetings being held at a time appointed under sec. 13 and subsequent ones being regulated by by-law under sec. 18), and at special general meetings called by virtue of sec. 31. Sec. 32 regulates the voting at any shareholders' meetings. Although the shareholders may name the *day* of the annual meeting, the *hour* of the day is appointed by the directors, the place of meeting must be the head office of the bank and public notice must be given (sec. 21). It is advisable that the by-law appointing a day for the election of directors (sec. 18) should also provide for the possible failure of the election on that day, as by sec. 27 the election may take place on any other day appointed by by-law of the shareholders. A meeting held on the day first appointed could no doubt be legally adjourned to another named day, so as to allow of the election of directors. (Reg. v. Wimbledon, 1882, 8 Q.B.D. at p. 463). Failing an adjournment, a special general meeting of the shareholders would have to be called.

This section was divided into its present sub-sections in 1906. The first part of the section formerly read: "The directors of the bank, or any four of them—or any number not less than twenty-five of the shareholders of the bank, who are together

Notice of meeting

Sec. 3   proprietors of at least one-tenth of the paid-up capital stock of the bank, by themselves or by their proxies—may, at any time, call a special general meeting of the shareholders, to he held at their usual place of meeting, *upon giving six weeks' previous public notice,* specifying in such notice the object of such meeting.'' Under the old section it was clear that the only notice required was public notice, that is as defined in the Act (see sec. 2, sub-sec. 2). Presumably the present section is not intended to change the law. Cf. secs. 13 and 21.

The general rule is that in the absence of special provision in the by-laws, notice of a general meeting must be sent to every shareholder. A conditional notice is not sufficient. (Alexander v. Simpson, 1889, 43 Ch. D. 139.)

The business to be transacted at the meeting must be mentioned in the notice. In re London, etc., Bank, Wright's Case, 1871, L.R. 12 Eq. 335 n.; Boschoek v. Fuke, [1906] 1 Ch. 148.)

Irregularity in notifying directors (Browne v. La Trinidad, 1887, 27 Ch.D. at p. 11), as distinguished from irregularity in the constitution of the board (Harben v. Phillips, 1883, 23 Ch. D. 14), will not affect the validity of a meeting of shareholders called by the directors. Resolutions passed at a meeting called by *de facto* directors are valid. (Boschoek v. Fuke, *supra.*)

The conditions for the calling of a special general meeting prescribed by this section must be strictly complied with. Resolutions passed at a meeting which has not been properly summoned have no validity. (In re State of Wyoming Syndicate, [1901] 2 Ch. 431.)

Filling vacancies   If a vacancy is created by a proceeding under this section it may be filled in the manner provided by sec. 25.

Removing directors.   There is no inherent power in a corporation to remove directors before the expiration of the period for which they have been elected (Imperial Hydropathic Hotel v. Hampson, 1882, 23 Ch. D. 1) ; but, granted the power, the matter of the removal of directors is one entirely for the shareholders to decide, and the court will not interfere. (Harben v. Phillips, 1883, 23 Ch. D. 14.)

One vote for each share.   **32.** Every shareholder shall, on all occasions on which the votes of the shareholders are taken, have one vote for each

share held by him for at least thirty days before the time of Sec. 32.
meeting.

2. In all cases when the votes of the shareholders are taken, Ballot.
the voting shall be by ballot.

3. All questions proposed for the consideration of the share- Majority to determine.
holders shall be determined by a majority of the votes of the
shareholders present in person or represented by proxy.

4. The chairman elected to preside at any meeting of the Casting vote.
shareholders shall vote as a shareholder only, unless there is
a tie, in which case he shall, except as to the election of a
director, have a casting vote.

5. If two or more persons are joint holders of shares, any As to joint holders of shares.
one of the joint holders may be empowered, by letter of at-
torney from the other joint holder or holders, or a majority of
them, to represent the said shares, and to vote accordingly.

6. Shareholders may vote by proxy, but no person other than Proxies.
a shareholder eligible to vote shall be permitted to vote or act
as proxy.

7. No manager, cashier, clerk or other subordinate officer Officer not to vote.
of the bank shall vote either in person or by proxy, or hold a
proxy for the purpose of voting.

8. No appointment of a proxy to vote at any meeting of Renewal of proxies.
the shareholders of the bank shall be valid for that purpose,
unless it has been made or renewed in writing within the two
years last preceding the time of such meeting.

9. No shareholder shall vote, either in person or by proxy, Calls must be paid before voting.
on any question proposed for the consideration of the share-
holders of the bank at any meeting of the shareholders, or
in any case in which the votes of the shareholders of the bank
are taken, unless he has paid all calls made by the directors
which are then due and payable. 53 V., c. 31, s. 25.

Chairman.

The chairman of a general meeting is chosen by the shareholders, and is usually the president of the bank.

The chairman has *primâ facie* authority to decide all incidental questions which arise at such meeting and necessarily
require decision at the time.   The entry by him in the minute
book of the results of a poll or of his decision on all such questions, although not conclusive, is *primâ facie* evidence of that
result, or of the correctness of that decision, and the onus of
displacing that evidence is thrown on those who impeach the
entry.   In re Indian Zoedone Co., 1884, 26 Ch. D. 70.)

The chairman has a casting vote in case of a tie (except as
to a tie in the election of directors—this event being provided
for by sec. 23.)

Proxies.

A by-law requiring the signature to a proxy to be attested
is imperative.   The attestation is essential to the validity of
the proxy.   (Harben v. Phillips, 1883, 23 Ch. D. 14.)   *Quære,*
however, as to the powers to pass such a by-law under the Act;
cf. sec. 18 (*b*).

A proxy may be signed in blank, and the blank filled in by
the person to whom the proxy is entrusted or sent.   (Ex parte
Lancaster, 1877, 5 Ch. D. 911; Ernest v. Loma, [1897] 1 Ch. 1.)

A proxy must be not only a shareholder, but also eligible to
vote.

Eligible to Vote.

In order to be eligible to vote in respect of shares a shareholder must have held such shares for at least 30 days prior to
the meeting, he must be the sole holder or have a letter of attorney from the other joint holder or holders, or a majority of them,
to represent such shares, he must have paid all calls made by
the directors which are then due and payable thereon, and he
must not be a manager, cashier, clerk or other subordinate officer
of that bank.

The object of the condition excluding the vote of a manager, cashier, clerk or other subordinate officer of the bank is to
prevent subordinate officers of the bank from acquiring the
power to elect or control those whose duty it is to superintend
their conduct in the management of the affairs of the bank.
The president, the vice-president and probably the general manager, if he is also a director, are not excluded from voting by

this section. (Cf. Reg. v. Bank of Upper Canada, 1849, 5 U.C. R. 338.)

If a shareholder is in other respects entitled to vote, he is not disqualified from doing so because his stock is not paid up. Where there has been no default in paying a call, votes are to be computed upon the face value of the shares held and not upon the amount paid thereon. (Purdom v. Ontario Loan, 1892, 22 O.R. 597.)

A shareholder is not debarred from voting or from using his voting power to carry a resolution by the fact of his having a personal interest in the subject-matter of the vote. (North-West v. Beatty, 1887, 12 App. Cas. 589; Burland v. Earle, [1902] A.C. at p. 94.)

CHAPTER VII.

CAPITAL STOCK.

The sections included in this chapter do not apply to the Bank of British North America (sec. 6).

Increase.

By-law.

33. The capital stock of the bank may be increased, from time to time, by such percentage, or by such amount, as is determined upon by by-law passed by the shareholders, at the annual general meeting, or at any special general meeting called for the purpose.

Approval of Treasury Board.

2. No such by-law shall come into operation, or be of any force or effect, unless and until a certificate approving thereof has been issued by the Treasury Board.

Condition for approva

3. No such certificate shall be issued by the Treasury Board unless application therefor is made within three months from the time of the passing of the by-law, nor unless it appears to the satisfaction of the Treasury Board that a copy of the by-law, together with notice of intention to apply for the certificate has been published for at least four weeks in the *Canada Gazette,* and in one or more newspapers published in the place where the chief office or place of business of the bank is situate.

Treasury Board may refuse,

4. Nothing herein contained shall be construed to prevent the Treasury Board from refusing to issue such certificate if it thinks best so to do. 53 V., c. 31, s. 26.

The section dates in substance from 1890, when the provision requiring the certificate of the Treasury Board was added. The division into the present sub-sections was made in 1906.

Cf. sec. 35, which provides for the reduction of capital stock.

Prior to 1871 an increase of capital stock could be effected only by Act of Parliament.

It is not intended that the Treasury Board, before issuing a certificate, should make a thorough inspection of the condition

of the bank and estimate the value of its assets, or that the certi- Sec. 33.
ficate should be taken as a representation to the public that the
earnings and assets justify the increase of capital.

But in exercising the discretion given it by this section the
Board might take into consideration any special circumstances
brought to its attention by a dissenting minority or in any other
way. The granting of the certificate would not be merely a ministerial act. (Cf. In re Massey Manufacturing Co., 1886, 13 A.
R. 466.)

The benefit of a new issue of stock is an increment of the
old shares, so that a contract by which a person is entitled to
"the free annual dividends, interest and profits of 100 shares
of the Bank of Montreal" gives him the right to the income of
the new shares subscribed for under the privilege to subscribe
attaching to the old shares. (Hargrave v. Clouston, 1874, 18
L.C.J. 290, 26 R.J.R.Q. 70.)

The provisions of this and of the next section do not apply
to any increase of stock made or provided for under the authority of secs. 103 and 104 (sec. 105).

34. Any of the original unsubscribed capital stock, or of the Allotment.
increased stock of the bank, shall, when the directors so deter- To present
mine, be allotted to the then shareholders of the bank *pro rata,* shareholders
and at such rate as is fixed by the directors: Provided that,—

(a) no fraction of a share shall be so allotted; and,

(b) in no case shall a rate be fixed by the directors, which
will make the premium, if any, paid or payable on the
stock so allotted, exceed the percentage which the reserve
fund of the bank then bears to the paid-up capital stock
thereof.

2. Any of such allotted stock which is not taken up by the To the
shareholder to whom the allotment has been made, within six public.
months from the time when notice of the allotment was mailed
to his address, or which he declines to accept, may be offered
for subscription to the public, in such manner and on such terms
as the directors prescribe. 53 V., c. 31, s. 27.

The division into the present sub-sections was made in 1906.
When the capital of a bank has been increased the directors

Sec. 34.   may determine the time of the allotment of so much of the orig-
Allotment] in inal capital as had not been subscribed as well as the increased
case of   capital.   Before it is offered to the public, any of such stock
increase.   must be allotted to the shareholders *pro rata*, either at par, or
at a premium that shall not exceed the percentage which the
reserve fund of the bank then bears to the paid-up capital. Any
of the stock so allotted which is not taken up by a shareholder
within six months, or which he declines to accept, may then be
offered to the public at any rate the directors may determine.
But the directors must not allot stock at a discount either to
shareholders or to the public (Ooregum v. Roper, [1892] A.C.
125; North-West v. Walsh, 1898, 29 S.C.R. 33; Morris v. Union
Bank, 1899, 31 S.C.R. 594; Mosely v. Koffyfontein, [1904] 2
Ch. 108). If, however, a certificate that shares are fully paid
up is issued to an innocent holder, who changes his position upon
the faith thereof, the bank will be estopped as against such
holder from contending that there is an unpaid balance.
(Bloomenthal v. Ford, [1897] A.C. 156; Dixon v. Kennaway,
[1900] 1 Ch. 833.)

The act provides that no fraction of a share shall be allotted.
Any *pro rata* division of shares will usually result in there being a number of fractions of shares unallotted. The shares made
up of these fractions may be allotted in any way the directors
think fit, and need not be allotted to shareholders before being
offered for subscription to the public.

Reduction.   **35.** The capital stock of the bank may be reduced by by-law
passed by the shareholders at the annual general meeting, or at
a special general meeting called for the purpose.

Approval of   2. No such by-law shall come into operation or be of force or
Treasury   effect until a certificate approving thereof has been issued by
Board.   the Treasury Board.

Conditions   3. No such certificate shall be issued by the Treasury Board
for approval. unless application therefor is made within three months from
the time of the passing of the by-law, nor unless it appears to
the satisfaction of the Board that,—

> (*a*) the shareholders voting for the by-law represent a
> majority in value of all the shares then issued by the bank;
> and,

(b) a copy of the by-law, together with notice of intention to apply to the Treasury Board for the issue of a certificate approving thereof, has been published for at least four weeks in the *Canada Gazette,* and in one or more newspapers published in the place where the chief office or place of business of the bank is situate.

4. Nothing herein contained shall be construed to prevent Treasury the Treasury Board from refusing to issue the certificate if it Board may refuse. thinks best so to do.

5. In addition to evidence of the passing of the by-law, and Statments of the publication thereof in the manner in this section pro- to be submitted. vided, statements showing,—

(a) the amount of stock issued;

(b) the number of shareholders represented at the meeting at which the by-law passed;

(c) the amount of stock held by each such shareholder;

(d) the number of shareholders who voted for the by-law;

(e) the amount of stock held by each of such last mentioned shareholders;

(f) the assets and liabilities of the bank in full; and,

(g) the reasons and causes why the reduction is sought; To Treasury shall be laid before the Treasury Board at the time of the appli- Board. cation for the issue of a certificate approving the by-law.

6. The passing of the by-law, and any reduction of the Not to capital stock of the bank thereunder, shall not in any way affect liability of diminish or interfere with the liability of the shareholders of shareholders. the bank to the creditors thereof at the time of the issue of the certificate approving the by-law.

7. If in any case legislation is sought to sanction any reduc- If legislation tion of the capital stock of any bank, a copy of the by-law or is asked to sanction re- resolution passed by the shareholders in regard thereto, together duction. with statements similar to those by this section required to be laid before the Treasury Board, shall, at least one month prior to the introduction into Parliament of the Bill relating to such reduction, be filed with the Minister.

8. The capital shall not be reduced below the amount of two hundred and fifty thousand dollars of paid-up stock.   53 V., c. 31, s. 28.

This section dates in substance from 1890.   Before that year the capital of a bank could be reduced only by Act of Parliament.

Sub-sec. 7 prevents the paid-up capital of a bank after incorporation from being reduced below the amount which is declared by sec. 13 to be the minimum capital for a new bank. It is possible, however, subject to the approval of the Treasury Board, to reduce the capital not paid up to an amount less than the minimum of subscribed capital which the last mentioned section requires in the case of a new bank.

Cf. sec. 33, which provides for the increase of capital stock, and notes under that section as to the granting of the certificate of the Treasury Board.

It is a condition precedent to the granting of the certificate of the Treasury Board under this section that a majority in value of all the shareholders of the bank should vote in favour of the by-law.   There is no similar provision in sec. 33.

CHAPTER VIII.

The sections included in this chapter, with the exception of sec. 39, do not apply to the Bank of British North America (sec. 6).

36. The shares of the capital stock of the bank shall be personal property. Shares personalty.

2. Books of subscription may be opened at the chief place of business of the bank, or at such of its branches, or at such place or places in the United Kingdom or in any of the British colonies or possessions, as the directors prescribe. Books of subscription.

3. The shares shall be assignable and transferable at any of the places aforesaid, according to such forms and subject to such rules and regulations as the directors prescribe. Transfers.

4. The dividends accruing upon any shares of the capital stock of the bank may be made payable at any of the places aforesaid. Dividends.

5. The directors may appoint such agents in the United Kingdom, or in any of the British colonies or possessions, for the purposes of this section, as they deem necessary. 53 V., c. 31, s. 29. Agents.

The section in substance dates from 1890. The present arrangement and division into sub-sections are the result of the revision of 1906.

Nature of Shares.

Shares are declared to be personal property. They are not an interest in land within the meaning of the Mortmain Acts (Myers v. Perigal, 1851, 11 C.B. 90, 2 De G.M. & G. 599; Edwards v. Hall, 1855, 6 DeG.M. & G. 75; cf. Ashworth v. Munn, 1880, 15 Ch. D. 363 at pp. 368, 372, 375, 376), or of the 4th section of the Statute of Frauds (Humble v. Mitchell, 1839, 11 Shares are personal estate.

Sec. 36. A. & E. 205), nor are they goods and chattels within the meaning of the 17th section of the latter statute (Humble v. Mitchell,
supra). See also notes to sec. 43 where the provision of this
section as to the assignability of shares more properly belongs.

A share signifies a definite portion of the capital of the bank—
the interest of the shareholder in the bank, measured for the purposes of liability and dividend by a sum of money, but also consisting of a series of mutual contracts entered into by all the
shareholders *inter se* (Borland's Trustee v. Steel, [1901] 1 Ch.
279).

Locality of Shares.

Situs of
shares at
head office.
Shares have a situs or locality at the head office (Nickle v.
Douglas, 1875, 37 U.C.R. 51; In re Ewing, 1881, 6 P.D. at p.
23), notwithstanding that for the sake of convenience provision
may be made for their transfer at another place, as *e.g.*, if a
bank having its head office and stock register at Toronto has also
separate stock registers at Montreal and London, Eng. (Hughes
v. Rees, 1884, 5 O.R. at p. 666; In re Clarke, [1904] 1 Ch. at p.
297, in argument). In the last mentioned case, however, the head
office of the company was in South Africa, but the share certificates were in England, and it was held that the shares passed
under a bequest made by a testator domiciled in England, of all
his personal estate in the United Kingdom, on the ground that
the production of the certificate was by its terms essential to the
completion of a transfer. If shares are transferable only on a
local register at a place other than the head office, and in the
case of a transmission, the transmission must be registered before the shares can be removed from the local register to the
head-office register, it might be held on the same principle that
the shares are locally situate where the local register is.

Succession
duty under
provincial
Acts.
The question of the locality of shares may become one of importance in connection with the liability to succession duty under provincial Acts, and these Acts are likely to be a source
of embarrassment to banks in regard to the registration of transfers of shares which have been transmitted on the death of a
shareholder.

Powers of
provincial
legislature.
Under the British North America Act, 1867, sec. 92, clause 2,
a provincial legislature may make laws with regard to "Direct
taxation within the province in order to the raising of a revenue
for provincial purposes." By virtue of this authority a pro-

vince (1) may tax property within the province without regard to the place of residence or domicile of the owner, and (2) conversely, may tax a person "found within the province," in respect, or upon the basis, of property situate without the province or of income derived from extra-provincial sources. Clement's Canadian Constitution, 2nd ed. 1904, p. 256, citing Bank of Toronto v. Lambe, 1887, 12 App. Cas. 584; Nickle v. Douglas, 1875, 37 U.C.R. at p. 62; Colquhoun v. Brooks, 1887, 19 Q.B.D. 65; Lefroy, 760(*n*), 769(*n*), but see Leprohon v. Ottawa, 1878, 2 A. R. at p. 534.

Sec. 36.
Locality of shares.

A provincial legislature cannot, however, impose a lien or charge upon property beyond the province; a tax upon a person "found within the province," would be enforceable only by process against the person taxed or against his property within the province. (Clement, p. 256.)

If, for instance, shares in a bank with its head office in Province A. are registered in the local register of the bank in Province B., and belong to a person who at the time of his death is domiciled in Province C., what is the liability of the bank, and what is that of the estate to which the shares belong?

Either Province A. or Province B. may impose a duty on the transmission of shares by reason of their situs in the province. If they are locally situate in Province A., where the head office of the bank is (see notes above), then there is no property in Province B. subject to taxation. If they are locally situate within Province B., then there is no property in Province A. subject to taxation.

In the case suggested there would appear to be no property in Province C. subject to duty. This conclusion is in accordance with justice as well as law, for, *ex hypothesi*, the property is liable to duty where it is locally situate. Several of the provinces have, however, reached out "with both hands," as it has been expressed, and attempted to impose a tax on the transmission not only of property actually situate within the province, but also of property actually situate without the province belonging to a person who at the time of his death was domiciled within the province. The power of the provincial legislature to impose a personal tax upon the representative of the deceased person within the province is undoubted, but it seems equally clear that such legislature cannot alter the legal meaning of the

Sec. 36.   words '.property within the province" as used in the B.N.A.
Act, and thus extend its jurisdiction to property which is situate
within the province only by the application of the fiction that
"mobilia sequuntur personam," and cannot enforce such assumed jurisdiction against property actually situate in another province or country, either by lien or charge or interference with
its transfer or otherwise.

Lex loci not   The Privy Council has laid down the rule that "although
lex domicilii the law of the testator's domicile governs the foreign personal
governs.
assets of his estate for the purpose of succession and enjoyment,
yet those assets are, for the purpose of legal representation, of
collection and of administration, as distinguished from distribution among the successors, governed by the law of their own locality and not by that of the testator's domicile. (Blackwood
v. The Queen, 1882, 8 App. Cas. 82.) This rule would seem to
indicate that for the purpose of succession duty, the shares do
not by reason of the late owner's domicile have a fictitious locality at the place of such domicile. The fiction is confined in its
operation to pointing out the law which shall govern the succession and enjoyment of the property, but has not the effect
of rendering the property locally situate in a place where it is
not in fact situate.

In Lambe v. Manuel, [1903] A.C. 68, a Quebec Act provided
for a duty upon transmissions, owing to death, of property in
the province, and it was held that the Act applied only to property which the successor claimed under and by virtue of Quebec law, and therefore had no application to property belonging to a person domiciled in Ontario and consisting (*inter alia*)
of shares in the capital stock of a bank whose head office was in
Montreal, where its stock registers and transfer books were kept.
After this decision, however, the Quebec Act was amended so
as to render liable to duty all property actually situate within
the province, no matter where the deceased was domiciled or
where the transmission took place. Thus the Quebec Succession
Duty Act, like the Ontario Act, now contemplates a situs or
locality being given to all kinds of personal property without
regard to the maxim *mobilia sequuntur personam*. (Cf. Attorney-General v. Newman, 1901, 1 O.L.R. 511, a case in regard
to deposits in the province owing to a person domiciled without
the province; Rex v. Lovitt, 1906, 1 East. L.R. 513, a decision

on a similar statute in New Brunswick), without, however, re- Sec. 36.
linquishing the attempt to tax also property which is situate
without the province, but whose owner was domiciled within the
province.

Shares are declared by the Bank Act to be assignable (sec. Can province
36), and it has been held that the directors are bound to register impose limi-
a transfer except in the cases in which they are authorized to transfer or
refuse to do so (see Smith v. Bank of Nova Scotia, 1883, 8 S. transmis-
C.R. 558, and notes to sec. 43). Further, in the case of a trans- sion?
mission of shares, the proper officers are absolutely required,
upon certain proof being furnished, to register the name of the
person entitled under the transmission (sec. 50). *Quære*, as to
the power of a provincial legislature to impose any limitation
upon the registration of a transfer or transmission. It has been
held, however, that it is *intra vires* of such a legislature to enact
that ''no transfer of the properties of any estate or succession
shall be valid, nor shall any title vest in any person, if the
taxes payable under this section have not been paid,'' etc., and
that a bank is therefore justified in refusing to register a transfer of shares by executors under a will, until proof is given
that the duties have been paid. (Heneker v. Bank of Montreal, 1895, Q.R. 7 S.C. 257.) It is submitted that the principle
of this decision must not be extended to the transfer of shares
not actually situate within the jurisdiction of the legislature
which enacts a statute of this kind.

A bank is not directly liable, in the absence of an enactment Liability of
expressly creating such liability, for succession duty imposed bank.
upon transmission of its shares, but if a statute in effect renders
illegal a transfer by an executor without payment of the duty,
the bank might be liable if it knowingly became a party to an
illegal transfer.

In the application of English cases, it must be borne in mind English and
that succession duty under provincial acts resembles the English Succession
probate or estate duties, *i.e.*, duties on the collection or distribu- Duty Acts
tion of an estate passing on a person's death (cf. Attorney-Gen- distinguish-
eral v. Newman, 1901, 1 O.L.R. at p. 515), rather than what
are known in England as legacy or succession duties. The liability to legacy duty (Thompson v. Advocate-General, 1845, 12
Cl. & F. 1), and to some extent succession duty (Attorney-Gen-

eral v. Jewish Colonization Association, [1901] 1 Q.B. at p. 138), is dependent upon the British domicile of the deceased owner of property.

Shareholders.

Incorpora-
tors not
necessarily
shareholders. The act of incorporation of a bank (Schedule B), provides that the persons therein named together with such others as become shareholders in the corporation by the Act created are constituted a corporation, etc. The question of what constitutes a person a shareholder of a company is discussed at length in Lindley on Companies 6th ed. 1902, pp. 15 *et seq.*

Apparently in the case of a bank the original incorporators are members of the corporation, but are not shareholders unless they subscribe for stock after incorporation (unlike the incorporators of a company incorporated by letters patent based upon their previous subscription, see In re Haggert Bros. Mfg. Co., Peaker & Reunion's Case, 1892, 19 A.R. 582).

Subscription for Shares.

The applications for and allotments of shares must be treated upon the same principles as ordinary contracts between individuals. In re National Savings Bank Association, Hebb's Case, 1867, L.R. 4 Eq. 9, at p. 11.)

Offer and
Acceptance. There must be the consent of two parties to a contract, and when an individual applies for shares in a company, there being no obligation to let him have any, there must be, in order to bind the applicant, some communication either in writing or orally or by conduct to shew the applicant that his offer has been accepted. In re Universal Banking Corporation, Gunn's Case, 1867, L.R. 3 Ch. 40 at p. 45.)

The application must be accepted, and the enterprise of the company proceeded with, within a reasonable time. (Patterson v. Turner, 1902, 3 O.L.R. 373; Ramsgate v. Montefiore, 1866, L.R. 1 Ex. 109.)

An application for shares may be withdrawn even orally at any time before notice of allotment is given. In re Brewery Assets Corporation, Truman's Case, [1894] 3 Ch. 272; In re Publishers' Syndicate, Mallory's Case, 1902, 3 O.L.R. 552.)

But a subscription for and agreement to take shares made under seal is not revocable (Nelson v. Pellatt, 1902, 4 O.L.R.

481), and, if not repudiated by the company, becomes a complete contract whenever the company accepts it and gives notice of acceptance. (Re Provincial Grocers, Calderwood's Case, 1905, 10 O.L.R. 705.

If application is made for shares by post or under circumstances from which authority to send notice of acceptance by post may be implied, notice of allotment sent by post is sufficient even if the notice fail to reach the allottee, and the contract is complete when the notice is posted. (Household Fire v. Grant, 1879, 4 Ex. D. 216; In re Imperial Land Co., Harris' Case, 1872, L.R. 7 Ch. 587, and cases cited.) *Subscription for shares*

Moreover an applicant may dispense with notice of allotment, or preclude himself from objecting to its non-receipt, as by acting as director or shareholder (In re International Contract Co., Levita's Case, 1867, L.R. 3 Ch. 36; In re Peruvian Railway Co., Crawley's Case, 1869, L.R. 4 Ch. 322), or as manager (In re Richards v. Home Assurance, 1871, L. R. 6 C.P. 591.)

Allotment, however, is the ordinary evidence of acceptance; and where there has been no allotment, acceptance will not be inferred from the mere facts that the applicant paid a deposit on the shares at the time he applied for them, that he obtained a receipt and that the money had not been returned. In re Adelphi Co., Best's Case, 1865, 2 De G. J. & Sm. 650; Ramsgate v. Montefiore, *supra*.) As to what is necessary to constitute allotment, see Re Canadian Tin Plate Co., Morton's Case, 1906, 12 O.L.R. 594.

The acceptance must be unconditional and in strict conformity with the application, and must not depart from it in any material respect. (Harris' Case, *supra;* In re Aberaman Ironworks, Peek's Case, 1869, L.R. 4 Ch. 532; Jackson v. Turquand, 1869, L.R. 4 H.L. 305.)

A subscription for shares upon a certain condition is not enforceable unless the condition is performed (In re Richmond Hill Hotel Co., Pellatt's Case, 1867, L.R. 2 Ch. 527), and if the condition is one which it is *ultra vires* of the company to perform, there can be no binding contract (Bank of Hindustan v. Alison, 1871, L.R. 6 C.P. 222; Page v. Austin, 1882, 10 S.C.R. 132).

The directors, if authorized by the charter or articles of association of the company may delegate the allotment of shares

6—BANK ACT.

Sec. 36. to a committee (Harris' Case, *supra*), but the duty of allotment is a discretionary one which they cannot discharge by a resolution, "that its secretary be instructed to allot all stock as applications are passed in." (Re Pakenham Pork Packing Co., Calloway's Case, 1906, 12 O.L.R. 100.)

Shares must not be issued at a discount. See notes to sec. 34.

Payment of shares. 37. The shares of the capital stock shall be paid in by such instalments and at such times and places as the directors appoint.

Cancellation for non-payment. 2. The directors may cancel any subscription for any share, unless a sum equal to ten per centum at least on the amount subscribed for is actually paid at or within thirty days after the time of subscribing.

Not to relieve if bank insolvent. 3. Such cancellation shall not, in the event of insolvency, relieve the subscriber as hereinafter provided, from his liability to creditors. 53 V., c. 31, s. 30.

The section dates from 1890, except that in 1906 it was divided into its present sub-sections. Under it the subscriber, notwithstanding that he does not pay 10 per cent. of the amount subscribed for within 30 days after the time of subscribing, remains liable as a shareholder until his subscription is cancelled by the directors. The contention to the contrary could not be plausibly said, as it was (though unsuccessfully), under the prior act, which said, "Provided always that no share shall be held to be lawfully subscribed for unless a sum equal to at least 10 per cent." etc. Re Central Bank, Nasmith's and Baines' Cases, 1889, 16 O.R. 293, 16 A.R. 237, 18 A.R. 209.)

As the directors appoint.

See next section, which provides for calls on shares.

As hereinafter provided.

Sub-sec. 3 is awkwardly worded and probably unnecessary. It apparently refers to sec. 130, and means that even after the subscription is cancelled, the subscriber remains liable upon the shares if the bank suspends payment within 60 days after the cancellation.

38. The directors may make such calls of money from the Sec. 38.
several shareholders for the time being, upon the shares sub- Calls on
scribed for by them respectively, as they find necessary. shares.

2. Such calls shall be made at intervals of not less than thirty Intervals
days. for calls.

3. Notice of any such call shall be given at least thirty days Notice.
prior to the day on which the call is payable.

4. No such call shall exceed ten per centum of each share Limitation.
subscribed. 53 V., c. 31, s. 31.

Cf. secs. 125-130, as to calls to be made in the event of the
insolvency of the bank. There is no provision in sec. 38 such
as that contained in sec. 128, that any number of calls may be
made by one resolution.

Sub-sec. 2 of the corresponding section of the Act of 1890
reads as follows:—''2. Such calls shall be made at intervals of
not less than thirty days, and upon notice to be given at least
thirty days prior to the day on which such call shall be payable; and no such call shall exceed ten per cent. of each share
subscribed.'' In the revision of 1906, this sub-section has been
divided into three new sub-sections, and the clause providing
for notice has been altered in such a way as to strengthen the
probability that there must be an interval of at least thirty days
(*i.e.* thirty clear days excluding the first day and the last), between the passing of each by-law or resolution making a call,
and a similar interval between each call and the day fixed for
payment of such call. See notes to sec. 128.

The making of a call is the fixing of a time at which money
is payable in respect of shares subscribed for. It is essential
that the by-law or resolution of the directors making a call shall
fix a time for payment. (Re Cawley & Co., 1889, 42 Ch. D. 209;
Armstrong v. Merchants, 1900, 32 O.R. 387.)

If a meeting of directors is duly called, only a quorum and
not necessarily a majority of the directors need be present to
make a valid call. (Ontario Marine v. Ireland, 1855, 5 C.P.
139.)

39. If any part of the paid-up capital is lost the directors Capital lost
shall, if all the subscribed stock is not paid up, forthwith make to be called
for.

Sec. 39.   calls upon the shareholders to an amount equivalent to the
loss: Provided that all net profits shall be applied to make good
such loss.

Returns to   2. Any such loss of capital and the calls, if any made in re-
mention.   spect thereof, shall be mentioned in the next return made by
the bank to the Minister. 53 V., c. 31, s. 48.

In the Act of 1890 this section and section 58 constituted
one section. Sec. 58 provides that no dividend or bonus shall
ever be declared so as to impair the paid-up capital of the bank.
The separation of the two sections makes it quite clear that the
recoupment, as directed by sec. 39, of paid-up capital lost, is not
confined to the impairment of capital by reason of the declaration of dividends or bonuses.

Recovery   40. In case of the non-payment of any call, the directors
of calls.   may, in the corporate name of the bank, sue for, recover, collect and get in any such call, or may cause and declare the
Forfeiture. shares in respect of which any such call is made to be forfeited
to the bank. 53 V., c. 31, s. 32.

Shares declared forfeited under this section must under
sec. 41 be sold by the bank within six months. Sec. 41 also
provides for a money penalty for non-payment of calls, the
amount of such penalty to be deducted from the proceeds of the
sale of the shares. See sec. 42 as to what the declaration or
statement of claim in an action for calls shall contain.

See sec. 128 as to forfeiture resulting from non-payment of
a call when the bank is insolvent.

There must be properly appointed directors to declare a forfeiture. (Garden, Gully, etc. v. McLister, 1875, 1 App. Cas. 39,
but see notes to sec. 12.)

No forfeiture can be effected unless every condition precedent has been strictly and literally complied with. (Johnson
v. Lyttle, 1877, 5 Ch. D. at p. 694; In re New Chile Gold Mining Co., 1890, 45 Ch. D. 598.)

The power to sue or to declare a forfeiture is in the alternative. After threatening suit the directors cannot declare a
forfeiture without giving an express notice that they intend to
do so. (Robertson v. Banque d'Hochelaga, 1881, 4 L.N. 314.)

41. If any shareholder refuses or neglects to pay any in- Sec. 41.
stalment upon his shares of the capital stock at the time appoint- Fine for
ed therefor, such shareholder shall incur a penalty, to the use failure to pay call.
of the bank, of a sum of money equal to ten per centum of the
amount of such shares.

2. If the directors declare any shares to be forfeited to the Sale of for-
bank they shall, within six months thereafter, without any feited shares.
previous formality, other than thirty days' public notice of
their intention so to do, sell at public auction the said shares,
or so many of the said shares as shall, after deducting the
reasonable expenses of the sale, yield a sum of money sufficient
to pay the unpaid instalments due on the remainder of the said
shares, and the amount of penalties incurred upon the whole.

3. The president or vice-president, manager or cashier of Transfer,
the bank shall execute the transfer to the purchaser of the how execut-
shares so sold; and such transfer shall be as valid and effectual ed.
in law as if it had been executed by the original holder of the
shares thereby transferred.

4. The directors, or the shareholders at a general meeting, Remission of
may, notwithstanding anything in this section contained, forfeiture or penalty.
remit, either in whole or in part, and conditionally or unconditionally, any forfeiture or penalty incurred by the non-payment of instalments as aforesaid. 53 V., c. 31, s. 33.

This section makes a shareholder who fails to pay a call
liable to pay a money penalty to the use of the bank amounting
to 10 per cent. of the amount of his shares. The penalty is in
addition to the liability to forfeiture of the shares. The penalty or forfeiture may be remitted, or the bank instead of declaring the shares forfeited, may enforce payment of calls by
suit, the forfeiture and suit being alternative not cumulative
remedies.

The power to declare shares to be forfeited is given by sec.
40.

If the bank acquires shares by forfeiture it must within six
months sell them, or a sufficient part thereof to pay the amount
of penalties incurred for non-payment of the whole and the

Sec. 41.   unpaid instalments due on the part not sold. This is in accordance with the policy of sec. 76 of the Act, which forbids a bank
to deal in shares of its own capital stock.

Recovery by   **42.** In any action brought to recover any money due on any
action.   call, it shall not be necessary to set forth the special matter in
the declaration or statement of claim, but it shall be sufficient
Allegations. to allege that the defendant is the holder of one share or more,
as the case may be, in the capital stock of the bank, and that
he is indebted to the bank for a call or calls upon such share or
shares, in the sum to which the call or calls amount, as the case
may be, stating the amount and number of the calls.

Proof.   2. It shall not be necessary, in any such action, to prove the
appointment of the directors. 53 V., c. 31, s. 34.

This section dates from 1871, and is useful in practice. The
jurisdiction of the Dominion Parliament has been questioned
on the ground that procedure in an action for money due on
a call is not properly part of the law relating to banking, and
is not within the principle of Cushing v. Dupuy, 1880, 5 App.
Cas. 409. In that case it was laid down that procedure even
though it affected civil rights in the province necessarily forms
an essential part of any law dealing with insolvency. The section, however, makes for the convenient operation of the Bank
Act, and would seem to be *intra vires* of Parliament within the
principle of Tennant v. Union Bank, [1894] A.C. 31.

CHAPTER IX.

TRANSFER AND TRANSMISSION OF SHARES.

The sections included in this chapter, with the exception of sec. 45, do not apply to the Bank of British North America (sec. 6).

Shares have been held to be choses in action (Colonial Bank *Assignability* v. Whinney, 1886, 11 App. Cas. 426, at p. 439). They may be *of shares.* assigned in any legal manner. (Bank of Montreal v. Henderson, 1870, 14 L.C.J. 169, 20 R.J.R.Q. 98.) Sec. 36 expressly declares them to be personal estate and also assignable and transferable in the place and in the manner, and subject to the rules and regulations, prescribed by the directors. The following sections contain additional limitations and provisions as to the transfer and transmission of shares.

TRANSFER AND TRANSMISSION OF SHARES.

43. No assignment or transfer of the shares of the capital *Conditions* stock of the bank shall be valid unless,— *for transfer of shares.*

(*a*) made, registered and accepted by the person to whom the transfer is made in a book or books kept for that purpose; and,

(*b*) the person making the assignment or transfer has, if required by the bank, previously discharged all his debts or liabilities to the bank which exceed in amount the remaining stock, if any, belonging to such person, valued at the then current rate.

2. No fractional part of a share, or less than a whole share, *Fraction of* shall be assignable or transferable. 53 V., c. 31, s. 35. *share not transferable.*

This section was divided into its present sub-sections in 1906. In other respects it dates from 1890.

Its predecessor (R.S.C. 1886, c. 120, sec. 29), constituted one section with sub-sec. 1 and 3 of the present sec. 36.

Sec. 43.

Obligation of
bank to reg-
ister trans-
fer.

Sub-sec. 3 of sec. 36 is out of place where it now is, and belongs more properly to the subject of this chapter.

The shares being by the express provisions of the Act transferable (sec. 36), at the will of the holder, the directors are bound to register a transfer, unless some express provision of the act gives them the authority to refuse to do so, as in the two cases mentioned in section 43, namely, (1) if the transfer is not made, registered and accepted by the transferee in the books kept for that purpose, or (2) if the transferor, although required by the bank to do so, has not previously discharged all his debts or liabilities to the bank which exceed in amount the remaining stock, if any, belonging to him valued at the then current rate. (Smith v. Bank of Nova Scotia, 1883, 8 S.C.R. 558; cf. Barss v. Bank of Nova Scotia, 1885, 6 C.L.T. 443, 6 R. & G. (N.S.) 245.

Two cases are mentioned in which a transfer shall not be valid, and the rule *expressio unius exclusio alterius* applies (In re Smith, Knight & Co., Weston's Case, 1868, L.R. 4 Ch. 20, at p. 30.)

As illustrating the proposition that the directors have no discretionary power to refuse to register a transfer except in the cases in which they are expressly authorized to do so, see In re McKain and Canadian Birkbeck, 1904, 7 O.L.R. 241; In re Panton and the Cramp Steel Co., 1904, 9 O.L.R. 3.

As to the rights and obligations of the bank in regard to transfer of shares which are subject to trusts, see Chapter X., *infra*.

As to the obligation to register a transmission of shares upon proper proof of the fact of transmission, see sec. 50.

If registration of the transfer is wrongfully refused, the transferee has a right of action—the measure of damages being the value of the shares at the time of the refusal to register. In re Ottos Kopje Diamond Mines, [1893] 1 Ch. 618.)

Mode of
transfer.

The foregoing must be read subject to the power of the directors under sec. 36 to regulate the form and conditions of transfers in general.

In practice the transferor does not usually attend in person to execute the transfer in the books of the bank, but executes a power of attorney by virtue of which some officer of the bank executes the transfer and registers the same in the books of the bank. The transferee must accept the transfer, and this also is usually done in practice by means of a power of attorney. See In re Central Bank, Baines' Case, 1889, 16 O.R. 293, where it was held that the system of transferring shares by what is known as a "marginal transfer" is a sufficient compliance with, or at least is not in anyway a violation of, the statutory provisions of this section. (Cf. Boultbee v. Gzowski, 1896, 28 O.R. at p. 287; S.C. reversed 24 A.R. 502, restored 1898, 29 S.C.R. 54.)

If a broker or other agent although in good faith induces the Forged the bank to transfer shares upon a power purporting to be made power of in his favour by a shareholder, but which is in fact forged, the attorney. agent must be taken to have given an implied warranty that he had authority, upon the principle of Collen v. Wright, 1857, 8 E. & B. 647, 657, and is therefore liable to indemnify the bank against the claim of the stockholder for restitution. (Starkey v. Bank of England, [1903] A.C. 114.)

If the stock certificate states that in the event of sale or trans- Surrender of mission of the shares the certificate must be surrendered before certificate. the transfer is registered or new certificate issued, the performance of such a condition, if "prescribed by the directors" under sec. 36, may be insisted upon by the bank, but, no doubt, if the non-production of the certificate is accounted for, as by proof that it was lost or destroyed or that it was wrongfully withheld by someone who had no right to withhold it, the court would order registration upon proper indemnity being given. (Colonial Bank v. Whinney, 1886, 11 App. Cas. 426.)

But the bank is not bound to insist upon the production of the certificate before registering a transfer of the shares represented thereby, and a transfer to an innocent transferee, duly registered and accepted without production of the certificate, will have priority over an earlier but unregistered transfer, accompanied by delivery of the certificate. The bank is not estopped from denying the right to the shares of the holder of the certificate. The only effect of the certificate is to preclude the bank from denying that at the time the certificate was issued the person named therein as the owner was entitled to the shares. (Smith v. Walkerville, 1896, 23 A.R. 95; cf. Rainford v. Keith, [1905] 1 Ch. 296, [1905] 2 Ch. 147.)

This section gives the bank an implied lien upon shares of Lien. its own stock for debts of the holder; cf. sec. 77.

Sec. 43.

Acceptance
of transfer.

If a transferee does not accept the shares in the books of
the bank, but subsequently deals with the shares by selling and
transferring them, his transferee, being the holder at the time
of the suspension of the bank, is liable as a contributor. (Re
Central Bank, Nasmith's Case, 1889, 16 O.R. 293, 304; affirmed
on appeal 18 A.R. 209.)

After a winding up order has been made, it is then too late
for holders of shares entered as such in the books of the bank
to escape liability by shewing irregularities in transfers to more
or less remote predecessors in title. (In re Central Bank, Home
Savings & Loan Co.'s Case, 1891, 18 A.R. 489.)

If the transfer is not registered more than 60 days before
the bank suspends payment, the transferor is subject to the
double liability under secs. 125 and 130.

A transfer of shares cannot legally be accepted by a minor
or other person who by provincial law is incapable of contracting. (Dumont v. Aubert, 1879, 5 L.N. 295; Walsh v. Union
Bank, 1879, 5 Q.L.R. 289.)

Bank of Liverpool v. Bigelow, 1878, 3 R. & C. (N.S.) 236,
was an action for calls against the transferee of shares in the
plaintiff bank. There was no valid transfer under the act, but
the defendant had paid other calls, given a receipt for a dividend,
combined with other persons in appointing a proxy, and, being
present at the trial and hearing all the evidence, had not produced any evidence or offered his own evidence. *Held,* that he
must be treated as a shareholder.

List of trans-
fers.

44. A list of all transfers of shares registered each day in
the books of the bank, showing, in each case, the parties to such
transfers and the number of shares transferred, shall be made
up at the end of each day.

For inspec-
tion.

2. Such list shall be kept at the chief place of business
of the bank, for the inspection of its shareholders. 53 V., c. 31,
s. 36.

Cf. next section.

Require-
ments for
valid trans-
fer.

45. All sales or transfers of shares, and all contracts and
agreements in respect thereof, hereafter made or purporting to

be made, shall be null and void, unless the person making the sale or transfer, or the person in whose name or behalf the sale or transfer is made, at the time of the sale or transfer,—

(a) is the registered owner in the books of the bank of the share or shares so sold or transferred, or intended or purporting to be so sold or transferred; or,

(b) has the registered owner's assent to the sale.

2. The distinguishing number or numbers, if any, of such share or shares shall be designated in the contract of agreement of sale or transfer. [Contract to state number.]

3. Notwithstanding anything in this section contained, the rights and remedies under any contract of sale, which does not comply with the conditions and requirements in this section mentioned, of any purchaser who has no knowledge of such non-compliance, are hereby saved. 53 V.. c. 31, s. 37. [Purchasers without notice.]

This section dates from 1890. Similar provisions as to inserting numbers in transfers of shares of the English Joint Stock Banks "are regularly disregarded on the Stock Exchange, but the custom to do so is illegal and unreasonable" (Neilson v. James, 1882, 9 Q.B.D. 546); possibly it may be binding upon principals of a stockbroker who know of it when they employ him. (Perry v. Barnett, 1885, 15 Q.B.D. 388.) See further Loring v. Davis, 1886, 32 Ch. D. 625, and Mitchell v. Glasgow Bank, 1877, 4 App. Cas. 624.

Sec. 133 makes a contravention of this section "an offence against this act."

A bank is, however, under no obligation to distinguish its shares by numbers.

46. When any share of the capital stock has been sold under a writ of execution, the officer by whom the writ was executed shall, within thirty days after the sale, leave with the bank an attested copy of the writ, with the certificate of such officer endorsed thereon, certifying to whom the sale has been made. [Sale of shares under execution.]

Sec. 46.   2. The president, vice-president, manager or cashier of the
Transfer,   bank shall execute the transfer of the share so sold to the pur-
how
executed.   chaser, but not until after all debts and liabilities to the bank of
             the holder of the share, and all liens in favour of the bank ex-
             isting thereon, have been discharged as by this Act provided.

Validity.   3. Such transfer shall be to all intents and purposes as valid
             and effectual in law as if it had been executed by the holder of
             the said share.   53 V., c. 31, s. 38.

             The shares of a bank, the head office of which is in one pro-
             vince, may be sold under a writ of execution in another pro-
             vince where the bank has a branch office.   In re Bank of On-
             tario, 1879, 44 U.C.R. 247.)   The question of the locality of
             shares is discussed in the notes to sec. 36.

Transmission   **47.** If the interest in any share in the capital stock of any
of shares.   bank is transmitted by or in consequence of,—

             (a) the death, bankrupcy, or insolvency of any shareholder;
                 or,

             (b) the marriage of a female shareholder; or,

             (c) any lawful means, other than a transfer according to
                 the provisions of this Act;

How authen- the transmission shall be authenticated by a declaration in writ-
ticated.   ing, as hereinafter mentioned, or in such other manner as the
             directors of the bank require.

Declaration.   2. Every such declaration shall distinctly state the manner
             in which and the person to whom the share has been transmitted,
             and shall be made and signed by such person.

Acknowledg-   3. The person making and signing the declaration shall ack-
ment.   nowledge the same before a judge of a court of record, or before
             the mayor, provost or chief magistrate of a city, town, borough
             or other place, or before a notary public, where the same is made
             and signed.

To be left   4. Every declaration so signed and acknowledged shall be
with bank.   left with the cashier, manager, or other officer or agent of the

bank, who shall thereupon enter the name of the person entitled under the transmission in the register of shareholders.

Sec. 47.

5. Until the transmission has been so authenticated, no person claiming by virtue thereof shall be entitled to participate in the profits of the bank, or to vote in respect of any such share of the capital stock. 53 V., c. 31, s. 39.

Exercise of rights as shareholder.

"Transmission" in this and the next following sections is used in contradistinction to "transfer." The latter means a transfer by the act of the holder, the former a transmission by devolution of law. (In re Bentham Mills, 1879, 11 Ch. D. 900.)

If the Bank Act conflicts with provincial law, the latter is overruled. (Cf. notes to sec. 34.) These sections do not, however, purport to alter the transmission of shares as governed by the law of the domicile of the holder, but merely prescribe the method in which transmission shall be proved so as to authorize the bank to make the necessary alteration in its books. In order to establish his right to deal with the shares, the person to whom the shares have been transmitted must comply with the provisions of the act, and until he has done so he is not entitled to participate in the profits of the bank or to vote in respect of the shares.

Section merely provides for proof of transmission.

Two of the cases of transmission mentioned in this section, namely, the death of a shareholder and the marriage of a female shareholder, are further provided for by secs. 48, 50 and 51. In the Act of 1871 these sections were contained substantially in their present form. That act also contained a section providing that in case of transmission of shares, if the directors entertained reasonable doubts as to the legality of any claim to and upon such shares, they might apply to the court by way of petition for an order or judgment adjudicating and awarding the shares to the party or parties legally entitled to the same, etc. The division of the sections into their present sub-sections was made in 1906.

A bank cannot refuse to record a transmission of shares on the ground of any indebtedness or liability to the bank within sec. 43. (In re Bentham Mills, *supra;* cf. sec. 50.)

See sec. 49 as to the authentication of a declaration made under this section.

Sec. 47.   The bank is not obliged to see to the execution of trusts by
the person to whom the shares are transmitted. See notes to
sec. 52 where the obligation of the bank to register a transfer
which may be in breach of trust is discussed.

Transmis-   **48.** If the transmission of any share of the capital stock has
sion by
marriage of taken place by virtue of the marriage of a female shareholder,
female   the declaration shall be accompanied by a copy of the register
shareholder.
             of such marriage, or other particulars of the celebration thereof,
Declaration. and shall declare the identity of the wife with the holder of such
             share, and shall be made and signed by such female shareholder
             and her husband.

If separate   2. The declaration may include a statement to the effect
property
of wife.   that the share transmitted is the separate property and under
             the sole control of the wife, and that she may, without requir-
             ing the consent or authority of her husband, receive and grant
             receipts for the dividends and profits accruing in respect there-
             of, and dispose of and transfer the share itself.

Revocation.   3. The declaration shall be binding upon the bank and per-
             sons making the same, until the said persons see fit to revoke it
             by a written notice to the bank to that effect.

Omission   4. The omission of a statement in any such declaration that
not to
invalidate. the wife making the declaration is duly authorized by her
             husband to make the same shall not invalidate the declaration.
             53 V., c. 31, s. 40.

          The provisions of this section are supplementary to those of
sec. 47. It was proposed in 1890 to alter sec. 48, so as to permit
a married woman in Quebec to dispose of her shares without
·the consent of her husband, as she can do in Ontario. The
amendment, however, was withdrawn, and the section as it
stands does not permit a married woman in Quebec to dispose
of her shares unless both husband and wife file a declaration
which is in effect a power of attorney to enable the wife to
receive the dividends or dispose of the shares.
          See next section as to the authentication of a declaration
made under this section.

49. Every such declaration and instrument as are by the last two preceding sections required to perfect the transmission of a share in the bank shall, if made in any country other than Canada, the United Kingdom or a British colony,— Sec. 49.
Authentica-
tion of
declaration
etc., in cer-
tain cases.

   (*a*) be further authenticated by the clerk of a court of record under the seal of the court, or by the British consul or vice-consul, or other accredited representative of His Majesty's Government in the country where the declaration or instrument is made; or,

   (*b*) be made directly before such British consul, vice-consul or other accredited representative.

   2. The directors, cashier or other officer or agent of the bank may require corroborative evidence of any fact alleged in any such declaration. 53 V., c. 31, s. 39. Further
evidence.

Prior to 1906, this section constituted one section with sec. 47.

50. If the transmission has taken place by virtue of any testamentary instrument, or by intestacy, the probate of the will, or the letters of administration, or act of curatorship or tutorship, or an official extract therefrom, shall, together with the declaration, be produced and left with the cashier or other officer or agent of the bank. Transmis-
sion by will
or intestacy.

   2. The cashier or other officer or agent shall thereupon enter in the register of shareholders the name of the person entitled under the transmission. 53 V., c. 31, s. 41. Entry.

See next section.

The imperative nature of the phrase "shall thereupon enter in the register," deprives the directors or officers of any discretion in regard to the registration, provided proper proof of transmission has been furnished in accordance with the act. Cf. notes to sec. 47. As to the obligation to register a transfer, see notes to sec. 43.

51. If the transmission of any share of the capital stock has taken place by virtue of the decease of any shareholder, the production to the directors and the deposit with them of,— Transmis-
sion by
decease.

(a) any authenticated copy of the probate of the will of the deceased shareholder, or of letters of administration of his estate, or of letters of verification of heirship, or of the act of curatorship or tutorship, granted by any court in Canada having power to grant the same, or by any court or authority in England, Wales, Ireland, or any British colony, or of any testament, testamentary or testament dative expede in Scotland; or,

(b) an authentic notarial copy of the will of the deceased shareholder, if such will is in notarial form according to the law of the province of Quebec; or,

(c) if the deceased shareholder died out of His Majesty's dominions, any authenticated copy of the probate of his will or letters of administration of his property, or other document of like import, granted by any court or authority having the requisite power in such matters;

shall be sufficient justification and authority to the directors for paying any dividend, or for transferring or authorizing the transfer of any share, in pursuance of and in conformity to the probate, letters of administration, or other such document as aforesaid. 53 V., c. 31, s. 42.

The provisions of this section and of section 50, are supplementary to those of 47. See notes to the last mentioned section.

A will in notarial form according to the law of Quebec does not require to be admitted to probate. The section provides for production of an authentic notarial copy of such a will, or of an authenticated copy of the probate of any other will, as proof in each case of transmission of shares. Similarly the probate of a will, letters of administration, etc., granted by a competent court and valid according to the law of the particular province or country where the deceased shareholder was domiciled may be produced as evidence of the title to shares. An authenticated copy no doubt means a copy certified by a person or court properly having the custody of the original.

The words "in pursuance of and in conformity to such probate," etc., refer to the legal and not to the beneficial title conferred by such probate, etc. The probate would be "sufficient justification and authority" to the bank for paying dividends or transferring shares to the executor, *i.e.*, the person to whom by operation of law the transmission has taken place, and the bank would not be obliged to see that the executor did not divert the dividends or shares to his own use. (See notes to sec. 52.)

CHAPTER X.

Shares subject to Trusts.

The sections included in this chapter do not apply to the Bank of British North America (sec. 6).

Bank not bound to see to trusts. 52. The bank shall not be bound to see to the execution of any trust, whether expressed, implied or constructive, to which any share of its stock is subject.

Receipt. 2. The receipt of the person in whose name any such share stands in the books of the bank, or, if it stands in the names of more persons than one, the receipt of one of such persons, shall be a sufficient discharge to the bank for any dividend or any other sum of money payable in respect of such share, unless, previously to such payment, express notice to the contrary has been given to the bank.

Bank not bound. 3. The bank shall not be bound to see to the application of the money paid upon such receipt, whether given by one of such persons or all of them. 53 V., c. 31, s. 43.

This section refers only to trusts in regard to shares of the bank's own capital stock. It has no reference to trusts in respect of shares of other corporations taken by the bank as collateral security; see notes to sec. 76, *infra*.

By sec. 96, a bank is not bound to see to the execution of any trust to which any deposit is subject.

Sec. 53 deals with the question of the personal liability of a trustee-holder of shares.

Section refers to trusts of which bank has notice. The language of sub-sec. 1 is general and comprehensive. It cannot be construed as referring to trusts of which the bank has no notice, for it would require no legislative provision to save the bank from responsibility for not seeing to the execution of a trust, the existence of which has not in some way been brought to its knowledge. The provision seems to be directly applicable to trusts, of which the bank has knowledge or notice, and in regard to these the bank, it is declared, is not to be bound to see to their execution. (Simpson v. Molsons Bank, [1895] A.C. 270.) *Sec. 52.*

Where an executor filed with the bank a declaration under sec. 47, and a copy of the probate under sec. 50, and required the bank to transfer the testator's stock to him as executor, which the bank refused to do, on the ground that by the will the stock was specifically bequenthed to be divided among certain legatees, it was held that it was the bank's duty to make the transfer, and that the bank was under no obligation to see that the bequests of the will were carried out by the executor. (Boyd v. Bank of New Brunswick, 1891, N.B. Eq. Cas. 545; I Journal C.B.A. 80.) *Bank obliged to register. transfer.*

Apart from the statute it is not clear that notice to the bank of a trust affecting its shares would cast upon it the duty of ascertaining the terms of the trust. Section 30 of the English National Debt Act, 1870, provides that no notice of any trust in respect to any stock certificate or coupon shall be receivable by the Bank of England. But even before the last mentioned act, it had been held that the Bank of England could not prevent an executor from selling out or transferring stock into his own name. (Bank of England v. Parsons, 1800, 5 Ves. 665; cf. Hartga v. Bank of England, 1796, 3 Ves. 55.) In Lady Mayo's Case, 1772, Lofft, 65, a transfer of moneys in the bank in the name of a *feme covert* had been made by the husband. It was suspected that by virtue of a trust, the moneys were held to the wife's separate use, and the bank, on transferring the stock, made a memorandum of a defect of title suspected. It was held that to make such a memorandum was not permissible, and that no secret trust as against the party who had the open legal title, would affect the bank. Lord Mansfield added: "I won't say a word against the holder of the stock having his action against the bank for disparaging his title." Cf. Franklin v. Bank of England, 1829, 9 B. & C. 156; Humberstone v. Chase, 1836, 2 Y. & C. Ex. 209; Hart on Banking, 2nd ed., 1906, pp. 105-6. *Duty apart from the statute.*

By the clause now in question, however, the bank is relieved from the duty of making enquiry, and cannot be held responsible for registering a transfer, unless it can be shewn that the bank, at the time of the transfer, possessed actual knowledge sufficient to fix it with notice that the transfer is in breach of trust, or the circumstances connected with the transfer and breach of trust are such as to warrant a court in holding that the bank really and knowingly joined in committing the breach. *Effect of the section.*

Sec. 52.

Notice of trust a question of fact.

What amount of knowledge would be sufficient to imply that the bank must know that a transfer is in breach of trust depends on the circumstances of each case. In Simpson v. Molsons Bank, [1885] A.C. 270, a testator bequeathed stock in the Molsons Bank to his executors, of whom one was William Molson, president of the bank. Certain of the shares were to go to Alexander Molson, but with a substitution rendering it improper that the shares should be transferred absolutely to him, because he might, if that were done, defeat the substitution. A copy of the will was deposited with the bank (presumably to enable the bank to satisfy itself that the executors were entitled to be registered as owners), but there was apparently no evidence that the provisions relating to the substitution were brought specially to the bank's notice. The law agent of the bank was also law agent of the executors. Several transfers of shares from the same block as those in question in the action were transferred to trustees for the purpose of protecting similar substitutions. Subsequently the shares in question were conveyed outright to Alexander Molson, and he dealt with them as his own absolutely. Under a clause in the same words as those of the sub-section now under discussion, it was held that the bank was not liable, on the ground that it had not actual knowledge that a breach of trust was intended or was being committed by the transfer.

Law in Quebec.

It was argued in Simpson v. Molsons Bank that by virtue of the law of Quebec the executors were mere depositaries of the stock without power of disposition or sale, except with the consent of the succession or by authorization of the court, but the Privy Council held that whatever might be the position in the absence of a bequest to the executors, in this case the shares were specifically bequeathed to the executors by the will with a direction as to the disposition of them in certain ways by the executors, and that therefore the title to the shares was vested in the executors.

Nature of a trust.

In the province of Quebec a power of disposition is not a necessary incident to the execution of a trust. It has been suggested that notice to a bank that shares are held by a trustee in Quebec is in itself notice that the trustee is merely an administrator for the legal owner without power of sale unless such a power is expressly given by the instrument creating the trust, and that the bank is therefore bound to examine the whole of the document in order to ascertain whether or not the trustee has the power to sell. If, however, the statute is to receive the same interpretation in all the provinces, it would seem to follow that a trust must mean the same thing in all the provinces. The essentials of a trust are that the legal title should be in one person and the equitable or beneficial title in another. (Hardoon v. Belilios, [1901] A.C. at p. 123; Porteous v. Reynar, 1887, 13 App. Cas. at pp. 131-132.)

The legal title involves a power of sale. The trustee may pass the title, although in transferring the property, he commits a breach of trust.. (Shropshire v. The Queen, 1875, L.R. 7 H.L. 496, at p. 513.)

It is true that in Simpson v. Molsons Bank, *supra,* the members of the Judicial Committee did look at the trust document, but it does not appear that they did do so for any other purpose than to see whether the prerequisite to the application of the statute existed, namely, whether there was a trust, *i.e.,* a legal estate in one person and a beneficial interest in another; having found that there was a trust, they then applied the statute and held that the bank was not bound to see that the person who had the legal estate should transfer the shares in accordance with the trust.

The statute relieves the bank from entering upon their books under secs. 50 and 51, notice of trusts as between the legal owner and other persons. Testamentary and other instruments or ex- tracts therefrom may be produced to and left with the bank, and will constitute sufficient authority for the transfer of a share or the payment of a dividend. But in the case contemplated by those sections, the object of the legislature is not to make the bank responsible for the due administration of the fund according to the equitable right, but to enable it to ascertain, who, under such instrument, is the person legally entitled. (Cf. Lewin on Trusts, 11th ed. 1904, pp. 31-2.)

The provision that the bank shall not be obliged to see to the due execution of any trust is unqualified.. The ques- tion of notice under sub-sec. 2, only arises in regard to the sufficiency of the receipt of the person in whose name any share stands. The receipt of such person, or, if the share stands in the name of more than one, the receipt of one of such persons, is a sufficient discharge to the bank for any dividend or any other sum of money payable in respect of such share, *unless express notice to the contrary has been given to the bank.* If the receipt

Sec. 52. is sufficient, then the bank is not bound to see to the application of the money paid upon such receipt. Section 96 contains a somewhat similar provision in regard to deposits. See notes to that section, where the difference in the wording of the two sections is discussed.

Executor, etc., not personally liable as shareholders.

53. No person holding stock in the bank as executor, administrator, guardian, trustee, tutor or curator of or for any estate, trust or person named in the books of the bank as being so represented by him, shall be personally subject to any liability as a shareholder; but the estate and funds in his hands shall be liable in like manner and to the same extent as the testator, intestate, ward or person interested in such estate and funds would be, if living and competent to hold the stock in his own name.

Cestui que trust liable.

2. If the trust is for a living person, such person shall also himself be liable as a shareholder.

Executor, etc., liable if trust not named.

3. If the estate, trust or person so represented is not so named in the books of the bank, the executor, administrator, guardian, trustee, tutor or curator shall be personally liable in respect of the stock, as if he held it in his own name as owner thereof. 63-64 V., c. 26, s. 8.

The original of this section was passed in 1880. The division into sub-sections was made in 1906, but in other respects the section in its present form dates from 1900, when "tutor" and "curator" were added to the class of representatives, and the words "estate, trust or person so represented" were substituted for "testator, ward or person so represented."

Legal owner personally liable.

A loan company which advances money on the security of bank shares which are transferred to it and accepted by it, in the ordinary absolute form, cannot escape liability on the ground that it is merely a trustee for the borrower. In re Central Bank, Home Savings & Loan Co.'s Case, 1891, 18, A.R. 489.)

A person who is *sui juris* and beneficially entitled to shares which he cannot disclaim is personally bound to indemnify the registered holder thereof against calls upon them. (Hardoon v. Belilios, [1901] A.C. 118.) A trustee for infants or for

tenants for life (S.C. at p. 127), can, of course, be indemnified Sec. 53.
only to the extent of the trust funds, because there is no bene-
ficiary who can be required personally to indemnify the trustee
against the whole of the burdens incident to his legal ownership.
Cf. the case of an executor. In re Cheshire Banking Co., Duff's
Executors' Case, 1886, 32 Ch. D. 301.)

If a trustee, executor or other person belonging to one of Unless he
the classes of representative persons mentioned in sec. 53 does names
beneficial
not desire to rely upon the precarious security of a right of in- owner.
demnity, he may avoid all personal liability upon shares held
by him, by naming in the books of the bank as such the estate,
trust or person represented by him. If he does not adopt this
course he will himself be personally liable in respect of such
shares, as if he held them in his own name as absolute owner,
notwithstanding that he describes himself as trustee. (Muir v.
City of Glasgow Bank, 1879, 4 App. Cas. 337.)

In order to escape liability under this section, the person in
whose name the shares stand must be able to shew that there is
an existing and not a purely fictitious *cestui que* trust or trust
estate. But on the other hand the whole of the trust funds
might conceivably be invested in the shares of one bank, and in
such event, upon the failure of the bank, there would be no
assets of the estate available for the double liability.

CHAPTER XI.

ANNUAL STATEMENT AND INSPECTION.

The sub-heading of the Act which precedes sec. 54 is "Annual Statement and Inspection." The collocation of words is a misleading one, and would indicate that some provision was made for an inspection of the affairs of the bank. The inspection referred to is merely the right of inspection of the books, etc., which the directors have at all times. See sec. 56.

The sections included in this chapter do not apply to the Bank of British North America (sec. 6.)

Statement to be laid before annual meeting. **54.** At every annual meeting of the shareholders for the election of directors, the out-going directors shall submit a clear and full statement of the affairs of the bank, exhibiting, on the one hand, the liabilities of or the debts due by the bank, and, on the other hand, the assets and resources thereof.

Liabilities. 2. The statement shall show, on the one part,—

(a) the amount of the capital stock paid in;

(b) the amount of the notes of the bank in circulation;

(c) the net profits made;

(d) the balances due to other banks; and,

(e) the cash deposited in the bank, distinguishing deposits bearing interest from those not bearing interest.

Assets. 3. The statement shall show, on the other part,—

(a) the amount of the current coin, the gold and silver bullion and the Dominion notes held by the bank;

(b) the balances due to the bank from other banks;

(c) the value of the real and other property of the bank; and,

(d) the amount of debts owing to the bank, including and particularizing the amounts so owing upon bills of exchange, discounted notes, mortgages and other securities.

4. The statement shall also exhibit,— Sec. 54.

(a) the rate and amount of the last dividend declared by Other particulars.
the directors;

(b) the amount of reserved profits at the date of such statement; and,

(c) the amount of debts due to the bank, overdue and not paid, with an estimate of the loss which will probably accrue thereon. 53 V., c. 31, s. 45.

As to the annual and other meetings of the shareholders, see Chapter VI. on Internal Regulations.

See sec. 153 as to the liability for the making of a false statement.

55. The directors shall also submit to the shareholders such Further statements further statement of the affairs of the bank, other than state- as required ments with reference to the account of any person dealing with by by-law. the bank, as the shareholders require by by-law passed at the annual general meeting, or at any special general meeting of the shareholders called for the purpose.

2. The statements so required shall be submitted at the When to be annual general meeting, or at any special general meeting called submitted. for the purpose, or at such time and in such manner as is set forth in the by-law of the shareholders requiring such statements. 63-64 V., c. 26, s. 9.

This section was added to the act in 1900 as a sub-section of section 54. It provides in effect that whenever the shareholders by by-law require the directors to give any particular class of information at the annual or any special general meeting, the same is to be furnished in accordance with such by-law, provided, however, that the shareholders shall not be entitled to information with regard to the accounts of the customers of the bank, these accounts being guarded from inspection by sec. 56.

Cf. sec. 113, conferring power on the Minister of Finance to call for special returns in addition to the regular monthly returns required by sec. 112.

See sec. 153, as to the liability for the making of a false statement.

Sec. 56.

Inspection of books.

Customer's accounts.

56. The books, correspondence and funds of the bank shall, at all times, be subject to the inspection of the directors.

2. No person, who is not a director, shall be allowed to inspect the account of any person dealing with the bank. 53 V., c. 31, s. 46.

Bank cannot refuse to disclose transactions with customer in court proceedings.

At an early date it was held in Upper Canada that a shareholder of a bank, merely as such, has no right to inspect the stock books or other books of the bank. (In re The Bank of Upper Canada v. Baldwin, 1829, Draper 55.) Any right that he might possibly have asserted to inspect the account of any person dealing with the bank has been done away with by this section which dates from 1871. The section does not, however, create any privilege so as to enable a bank to refuse to disclose its transactions with one of its customers, when the propriety of those transactions is in question in a court of law between the bank and another customer who attacks them and shews good cause for requiring the information he seeks. (Re Chatham Banner Co., Bank of Montreal's Claim, 1901, 2 O.L.R. 672.)

No privilege at common law.

The evidence as to a customer's account is not privileged at common law, and this section amounts only to a prohibition against the bank's voluntarily permitting any examination of its customers' accounts save by a director. An officer of a bank, when served with a subpoena *duces tecum* to attend as a witness in an action, is bound, whether the bank is a party or not, to produce the bank books specified in the subpoena which are in his custody and control, and which contain any entry relevant to the matters in question in the action. He must also give evidence as to such entries. The books of a branch bank are *primâ facie* deemed to be in the custody and control of the local manager and their production within the scope of his authority. (Hannum v. McRae, 1898, 18 P.R. 185.) Inconvenience to the bank is no ground for refusing production. There is no statute in force in Canada corresponding to the English Bankers' Books Evidence Act, which was passed to remedy the inconvenience of producing the original books, and which allows examined copies of entries to be produced in their place. Even

in England, however, a banker remains bound at common law
to produce his books, except in so far as the inconvenience may
be modified by statute. (*Ibid.* pp. 187, 196.)

The question of the legal duty of a bank to keep its cus- Duty to keep cust-
tomers' affairs secret is not clear. The balance of judicial opin- omer's
ion seems to favour the view that there is an implied undertak- affairs secret.
ing in the contract between bank and customer that the bank
will not unreasonably disclose the state of its customer's account, the damages for breach being confined to actual damage
sustained by the customer. (Foster v. Bank of London, 1862,
3 F. & F. 214; Tassel v. Cooper, 1850, 9 C.B. 509; Hardy v.
Veasey, 1868, L.R. 3 Ex. 107; Hart on Banking, 2nd. ed., 1906,
p. 214.)

Probably if a cheque is presented for an amount greater than
the amount to the credit of the drawer's account, the bank
ought not to state the amount of the deficiency, or say more
than "not sufficient funds." (Foster v. Bank of London, *supra.*)

A director is not bound to examine entries in any of the Director's
company's books, nor is constructive notice to be so extended as liability.
to impute to him a knowledge of the contents of the books. In
re Denham & Co., 1883, 25 Ch. D. 752, and see Chapter VI.,
supra, as to Liability of Directors.)

CHAPTER XII.

DIVIDENDS.

Sec. 57 authorizes the payment of dividends out of profits, sec. 58 prohibits their payment so as to impair the paid-up capital, and sec. 59 forbids their being paid to an amount exceeding 8 per cent. per annum unless a certain rest or reserve fund is maintained. The provisions of secs. 58 and 59 expressly apply to bonuses as well as dividends. A bonus is merely an extra dividend or allowance to the shareholders, and the power to declare a bonus is covered by the power to declare a dividend given to the directors by sec. 57.

As to liability of directors see notes to sec. 39 and also Chapter VI., *supra.*

Sections 57 and 58 were divided into their present sub-sections in 1906.

Quarterly or half-yearly.

57. The directors of the bank shall, subject to the provisions of this Act, declare quarterly or half yearly dividends of so much of the profits of the bank as to the majority of them seems advisable.

Notice.

2. The directors shall give at least thirty days' public notice of the payment of such dividends previously to the date fixed for such payment.

Books closed.

3. The directors may close the transfer books during a certain time, not exceeding fifteen days, before the payment of each dividend. 53 V., c. 31, s. 47.

Public notice.—The nature of this is prescribed by sec. 2, sub-sec. 2.

Section 77 gives the bank a lien on unpaid dividends for any indebtedness or liability of the shareholder.

The practice of paying dividends quarterly instead of half-yearly is now becoming general.

Declaration of dividends discretionary.

Whether the whole or any part of the profits should be divided, or what portion should be divided and what portion retained, are entirely questions of internal management which the directors, subject to the control of the shareholders, must decide for themselves, and the court has no jurisdiction to control or review their decision. (Burland v. Earle, [1902] A.C. at pp. 95-97; and see notes to next section.) Sec. 57.

In the absence of any express or implied term in the bargain to the contrary, the purchaser of shares will be entitled to all benefits incidental to the ownership of the shares as from the time of sale. Purchaser's right to dividend.

In Black v. Homersham, 1878, 4 Ex. D. 24, shares of a company had been sold by auction on the 1st of August, and a deposit had been paid. By the conditions of sale, the purchase was to be completed on the 29th of August, which accordingly was done, and the transfers were signed. On the 24th, a dividend was declared in respect of a period antecedent to the sale by auction. The conditions of sale containing no provision as to dividends, it was held that the dividend belonged to the purchaser.

After a transfer of shares the seller becomes a trustee for the buyer, and is not entitled, except by arrangement with the buyer, to receive any advantage in respect of them by reason of his being the registered holder. (Hart on Banking, p. 966; Rooney v. Stanton, 1900, 17 T.L.R. 28.)

If under this section the transfer books are closed for a period after the declaration but before the payment of the dividend, the person in whose name a share stands at the time of the closing of the books is entitled to the dividend. The usage of the stock exchange is in accordance with this rule. If a sale is made after the closing of the books but before the payment of the dividend the vendor is nevertheless entitled to the dividend.

58. No dividend or bonus shall ever be declared so as to impair the paid-up capital of the bank. Dividend not to impair capital.

2. The directors who knowingly and wilfully concur in the declaration or making payable of any dividend or bonus, whereby the paid-up capital of the bank is impaired, shall be jointly and severally liable for the amount of such dividend or bonus, as a debt due by them to the bank. 53 V., c. 31, s. 48. Directors liable for such dividend.

Sec. 58.   The original of this section was passed in 1871. By it no
dividend or bonus is to be declared so as to impair the paid up
capital. If the capital is impaired then all the net profits are
to be applied to make up the loss, and in addition to this calls
are to be made upon unpaid subscribed stock to an amount equivalent to the loss (sec. 39). The directors knowingly and wilfully concurring in a declaration of dividends or bonus contrary
to this section are jointly liable for the amount thereof as a
debt due by them to the bank.

It was the frequent practice formerly for a bank, the capital of
which had been impaired, to apply to Parliament for a reduction of its capital so as to enable it to continue payment of dividends. Now the shareholders may by sec. 35, reduce the capital
under certain conditions and subject to the approval of the
Treasury Board.

What is
profit avail-
able for
dividend.

Where a banking company with a paid up capital of £500,-
000, sold part of its undertaking for £875,000, and after deducting the paid up capital and other incidental expenses, there remained a net balance of £205,000, and the directors proposed to
treat this balance as profit, it was held that the £205,000 was
profit on capital, and not part of the capital itself, and that the
directors would be justified in carrying this sum to the profit
and loss account, and after appropriating to the reserve fund
so much as they thought proper, might distribute the remainder
as dividends. (Lubbock v. British Bank, [1892] 2 Ch. 198.)

When it is said that dividends are not to be paid out of capital, the word "capital" means the money subscribed, or what
is represented by that money. Accretions to that capital may
be realized and turned into money, which may be divided
amongst the shareholders. (Verner v. General, etc., Trust,
[1894] 2 Ch. 239, 265; cf. Bond v. Barrow, [1902] 1 Ch. 353.)

The question of what is profit available for dividend depends
upon the result of the whole accounts fairly taken for the year
as well as profit and loss, and a realized accretion to the esti-
mated value of one item of the capital assets cannot be deemed
to be profit divisible amongst the shareholders without reference
to the result of the whole accounts fairly taken. (Foster v. New
Trinidad, [1901] 1 Ch. 208; the dictum in this case that dividends
may be paid out of earned profits in proper cases, notwithstanding that there has been a depreciation of capital, is inapplicable
to the case of a bank under the Act.)

59. No division of profits, either by way of dividends or bonus, or both combined, or in any other way, exceeding the rate of eight per centum per annum, shall be made by the bank, unless, after making the same, the bank has a rest or reserve fund, equal to at least thirty per centum of its paid-up capital after deducting all bad and doubtful debts. 53 V., c. 31, s. 49.

Sec. 59.
Dividend limited unless there is a certain reserve.

The original of this section was passed in 1871 and required a rest or reserve fund equal to 20 per cent. of the paid up capital. The object was to prevent a repetition of such extravagant distribution of assets under the guise of profits as had hastened the failure of some of the earlier banks, notably the Bank of Upper Canada. The percentage was increased to 30 per cent. in 1890.

Before any division of profits exceeding 8 per cent. is made, there must be a rest or reserve fund equal to 30 per cent. of the paid up capital after deducting all bad and doubtful debts. Directors are not liable for including in their accounts as good, debts which are in fact bad, when they are not fixed with knowledge of the fact or with negligence in regard thereto. (Dovey v. Cory, [1901] A.C. 477.)

CHAPTER XIII.

CASH RESERVES.

Forty per centum in Dominion notes.

60. The bank shall hold not less than forty per centum of its cash reserves in Dominion notes.

Supply of Dominion notes.

2. The Minister shall make such arrangements as are necessary for ensuring the delivery of Dominion notes to any bank, in exchange for an equivalent amount of specie, at the several offices at which Dominion notes are redeemable, in the cities of Toronto, Montreal, Halifax, St. John, Winnipeg, Victoria and Charlottetown, respectively.

Redemption.

3. Such notes shall be redeemable at the office for redemption of Dominion notes in the place where the specie is given in exchange. 53 V., c. 31, s. 50.

The Act of 1871 required the bank always to hold, as nearly as might be practicable, one-half of its cash reserves in Dominion notes, the proportion held in such notes never to be less than one-third. In 1880 one-third was changed to 40 per cent. The present provision dates from 1890.

The corresponding section of the Act of 1890 contained, as part of sub-sec. 1, a clause imposing upon the bank a penalty for contravention of the sub-section. This penalty clause is now sec. 134.

As to Dominion notes and specie, see Chapter XXIX. *infra.*

The question of requiring a bank to keep a fixed minimum cash reserve was fully discussed not only in 1871, but also in 1890, the proposal to that end being successfully opposed by the bankers.

Under the Act a bank is not obliged to keep any cash reserve, but if it does do so, it must hold 40 per cent. thereof in Dominion notes. This section is entirely in the interests of the Government, and seems to have no logical justification.

Discretionary power to retain profits undivided.

The court has no jurisdiction to say what is a fair or reasonable sum to retain undivided out of profits, or what reserve fund may properly be required, and it makes no difference whether the undividéd balance is retained to the credit of profit and loss account, or carried to the credit of a rest or reserve fund, or appropriated to any other use of the business. The power to form a reserve fund or retain a balance of undivided profits, involves the power to invest the moneys so retained. The investments may be on such securities as the directors may select (having regard to the business and powers of a bank under the Act), subject to the control of a general meeting, although different considerations might arise if it appeared that, under the guise of investing undivided profits or the reserve fund, the directors were in fact embarking the moneys of the company in speculative transactions, or otherwise abusing the powers vested in them for the management of its business. (Burland v. Earle, [1902] A.C. at pp. 95-97.)

No division of profits, either by way of dividends or bonus, or both combined, or in any other way, exceeding the rate of 8 per cent. per annum, may be made by a bank, unless, after making the same, the bank has a rest or reserve fund, equal to at least 30 per cent. of its paid-up capital after deducting all bad and doubtful debts (sec. 59).

CHAPTER XIV.

THE ISSUE AND CIRCULATION OF NOTES.

Sec. 61.

Character of Canadian bank note issue.

The distinctive feature of the note issue of Canadian banks has been already discussed in Chapter I., especially in connection with the legislation of 1890 and 1900. The notes are not secured by the pledge or special deposit with the government of bonds or other securities, but are simply credit instruments based upon the general assets of the bank issuing them. In order, however, that they may be not less secure than notes issued against bonds deposited with the government, they were made a first charge upon the assets (sec. 131). To avoid discount for geographical reasons each bank is obliged to arrange for the redemption of its notes in the commercial centres throughout the Dominion (sec. 70). Finally, to perfect the security for redemption and to avoid discount after the suspension of a bank, either because of delay in payment of note issues by the liquidator or of doubt as to ultimate payment, each bank is obliged to keep in the hands of the government a deposit equal to 5 per cent. of its average circulation (sec. 64). Should any liquidator fail to redeem the notes of an insolvent bank, recourse may be had to the entire fund if necessary. As a matter of fact, liquidators almost invariably are able to redeem notes as they are presented, but in order that the notes of an insolvent bank may be held or accepted without loss pending redemption, these notes bear 5 per cent. interest from the date of suspension to the date of the liquidator's announcement that he is ready to redeem (sec. 65).

Nature of bank note.

A bank note is the promissory note of a bank payable to bearer on demand. See notes to sec. 176 of the Bills of Exchange Act, Chapter LII., *infra*. In Canada the issue of notes intended for circulation is the exclusive privilege of the Dominion Government (see Chapter XXIX., *infra*), and the banks chartered under the Bank Act (see sec. 136).

Bank notes are not legal tender (see Chapter XXIX., *infra*), but must be received in payment or redeemed on demand by the issuing bank (see sec. 71).

A bank note contains a contract which is ambulatory by rea- Sec. 61.
son of the mere passing of it from hand to hand. It is also, a Nature of
thing which is in itself valued as money and currency. A mater- bank note.
ial alteration will invalidate it—such an alteration including
the alteration of the number which does not in fact affect the
contract or promise to pay. (Suffell v. Bank of England, 1882,
9 Q.B.D. 555, 567; 3 R.C. 640, 651.) But, by the effect of sec.
145 of the Bills of Exchange Act, the alteration of a bank note
if it is not apparent does not invalidate the note in the hands
of a holder in due course. (Leeds & County Bank v. Walker,
1883, 11 Q.B.D. 84.)

A stolen note or a note obtained by fraud, being like cash,
must on presentation be paid by the bank to any holder who is
not shewn to have come by it dishonestly. (Miller v. Race,
1758, 1 Burr. 452; 3 R.C. 626.)

But the bank is entitled to delay payment of a stopped note
for a reasonable time in order to make enquiries. (Solomons
v. Bank of England, 1791, 12 East 135 n., 3 R.C. 634, 12 R.R.
341.)

Negligence in taking a stolen note or forgetfulness of information regarding it is not sufficient to disentitle the holder to
payment (Raphael v. Bank of England, 1853, 17 C.B. 161),
but deliberate refusal to make enquiries when the circumstances
excite suspicion may be sufficient evidence of bad faith. (Solomons v. Bank of England, *supra;* Jones v. Gordon, 1877, 2 App.
Cas. 616.)

THE ISSUE AND CIRCULATION OF NOTES.

61. The bank may issue and re-issue notes payable to bearer Authority
on demand and intended for circulation: Provided that,— for.
Proviso.

   (*a*) the bank shall not, during any period of suspension of
      payment of its liabilities, issue or re-issue any such notes;
      and,

   (*b*) if, after any such suspension, the bank resumes business
      without the consent in writing of the curator, hereinafter
provided for, it shall not issue or re-issue any of such notes
until authorized by the Treasury Board so to do.

Sec. 61.

$5 or mul-
tiples there-
of.

Amount
limited.

Bank of
British
North
America.

2. No such note shall be for a sum less than five dollars, or for any sum which is not a multiple of five dollars.

3. The total amount of such notes, in circulation at any time, shall not exceed the amount of the unimpaired paid-up capital of the bank.

4. Notwithstanding anything in this section contained the total amount of such notes of the Bank of British North America in circulation at any time shall not exceed seventy-five per centum of the unimpaired paid-up capital of the Bank: Provided that,—

(a) the Bank may issue such notes in excess of the said seventy-five per centum upon depositing with the Minister, in respect of the excess, in cash or bonds of the Dominion of Canada, an amount equal to the excess; and the cash or bonds so deposited shall, in the event of the suspension of the Bank, be available by the Minister for the redemption of the notes issued in excess as aforesaid; and,

(b) the total amount of such notes of the Bank in circulation at any time shall in no case exceed its unimpaired paid-up capital.

Notes under
$5 or not in
multiples of
$5 to be
called in.

5. All notes heretofore issued or re-issued by any bank, and now in circulation, which are for a sum less than five dollars, or for a sum which is not a multiple of five dollars, shall be called in and cancelled as soon as practicable. 53 V., c. 31, s. 51; 63-64 V., c. 26, s. 10.

Under the Act of 1871 a bank was permitted to issue notes for $4 or more each, but in 1880 the present limitation to notes for $5 or a multiple thereof was introduced. Sec. 62 (the original of which was passed in 1899) permits the issue of notes for one pound sterling or a multiple thereof in British possessions other than Canada. By sec. 8 of the Currency Act (Chapter XXIX., *infra*), no bank note payable in any other currency than the currency of Canada shall be issued or re-issued by any bank.

The section was divided into its present sub-sections in 1906. The proviso of sub-section 1 was added to the Act in 1900, and is enforceable by penalty under section 138.

This proviso is designed to guard against the possible fraudulent action of the directors in issuing notes after the suspension of a bank, *e.g.*, to any depositors or any class of depositors,
and thus giving such depositors a prior lien upon the assets
of the bank. When a bank suspends payment its right to issue
notes ceases until (1) it resumes business with the consent in
writing of the curator, or (2) having resumed business without
such consent, it is authorized by the Treasury Board to issue
notes.

The authority from the Treasury Board is required as a
safeguard against a bank's only nominally resuming business,
and then issuing notes and thus defeating the purpose of the
other provisions of the section. The danger of course is that
notes once issued, even illegally, will be a charge on the Redemption Fund in case of the insolvency of the bank. The penalty
imposed for contravention of the section is therefore made very
heavy.

The limitation of the total amount of notes in circulation
at any time to the amount of the unimpaired paid up capital
has been in force since the passing of the General Banking Act of
1871. This limitation is enforceable by penalty under sec. 135.

As the creation of the Bank Circulation Redemption Fund
in 1890 (see sec. 64), gave added security to bank notes, and
facilitated their circulation in larger quantities, the penalties
upon excess of circulation were at the same time increased to
the amounts mentioned in sec. 135, (being nearly ten times as
large as the penalties provided by the previous Acts).

The form of monthly return (Schedule D.) provides for a
statement of the greatest amount of notes in circulation at any
time during the month to which the return relates, and by sec.
153 the making of any wilfully false or deceptive statement in
any return, etc., is made an offence.

See also secs. 63 and 139 forbidding under heavy penalties the
pledging assignment or hypothecation by a bank of its notes, and
sec. 140 imposing a penalty for issuing with intent to defraud,
or accepting with knowledge of such intent, bank notes intended
for circulation and not in circulation.

The Bank of British North America is not subject to the
double liability provision of sec. 125 (see sec. 6). That bank is
therefore, limited to a note circulation equal to 75 per cent. of
its unimpaired paid up capital, with power, however, to issue

Sec. 61. up to an amount not exceeding the whole of such capital upon depositing with the government, in cash or bonds of the Dominion, an amount equal to the excess of its circulation over 75 per cent.

Note issue at agency in British possession other than Canada. **62.** Notwithstanding the provisions of the last preceding section any bank may issue and re-issue at any office or agency of the bank in any British colony or possession other than Canada, notes of the bank payable to bearer on demand and intended for circulation in such colony or possession, for the sum of one pound sterling each, or for any multiple of such sum, or for the sum of five dollars each, or for any multiple of such sum, of the dollars in commercial use in such colony or possession, if the issue or re-issue of such notes is not forbidden by the laws of such colony or possession.

Governor in Council to fix rate for circulation. 2. No issue of notes of the denomination of five such dollars, or any multiple thereof, shall be made in any such British colony or possession unless nor until the Governor in Council, on the report of the Treasury Board, determines the rate, in Canadian currency, at which such notes shall be circulated as forming part of the total amount of the notes in circulation within the meaning of the last preceding section.

Redemption. 3. The notes so issued shall be redeemable at par at any office or agency of the bank in the colony or possession in which they are issued for circulation, and not elsewhere, except as in this section specially provided; and the place of redemption of such notes shall be legibly printed or stamped across the face of each note so issued.

Redemption if agency is abolished. 4. In the event of the bank ceasing to have an office or agency in any such British colony or possession, all notes issued in such colony or possession under the provisions of this section shall become payable and redeemable at the rate of four dollars and eighty-six and two-thirds cents per pound sterling, or, in the case of the issue of notes, of the denomination of five dollars, or any multiple thereof, of the dollars in commercial use in such colony or possession, at the rate established by the Governor in Council as required by this section, in the same manner as notes of the bank issued in Canada are payable and redeemable.

5. The amount of the notes at any time in circulation in any Total such colony or possession, issued under the provisions of this amount of circulation. section, shall, at the rate mentioned in the last preceding sub-section, form part of the total amount of the notes in circula-tion within the meaning of the last preceding section, and, ex-cept as herein otherwise specially provided, shall be subject to all the provisions of this Act.

6. No notes issued for circulation in a British colony or pos- No re-issue session other than Canada shall be re-issued in Canada. in Canada.

7. Nothing in this section contained shall be construed to Section authorize any bank,— limited.

(a) to increase the total amount of its notes in circulation in Canada and elsewhere beyond the limit fixed by the last preceding section; or,

(b) to issue or re-issue in Canada notes payable to bearer on demand, and intended for circulation, for a sum less than five dollars, or for a sum which is not a multiple of five dollars. 4 E. VII., c. 3, ss. 1, 2, 3 and 4.

This section dates from 1899. It does not apply to the Bank of British North America (sec. 6).

63. The bank shall not pledge, assign, or hypothecate its Pledge, etc., notes; and no advance or loan made on the security of the notes of notes prohibited. of a bank shall be recoverable from the bank or its assets. 53 V., c. 31, s. 52.

No advance or loan made on the security of the notes of a bank is recoverable from the bank or its assets, but if such notes came into the hands of some innocent holder he could enforce payment by the bank, and in the event of insolvency of the bank claim against its assets and against the Circulation Redemption Fund. The issue or pledge of notes within the prohibition of this section might possibly thus amount to giving a creditor a "fraudulent, undue or unfair preference over other creditors," an offence which is rendered criminal by sec. 155.

The prohibition of this section is made the subject of penalties under sec. 139; cf. also sec. 140. Both the last mentioned sections with sec. 63 constituted one section in the Act of 1890.

These sections are aimed, not so much against a bank's issuing a larger amount of its notes than it is authorized to do (see sec. 135), as against the fraudulent issue of notes otherwise than for circulation in the legitimate course of business, by the indirect method of pledging, assigning or hypothecation, or by the issue or delivery with intent to defraud or the taking or accepting with knowledge of such intent of notes intended for circulation, but not actually in circulation.

THE BANK CIRCULATION REDEMPTION FUND.

The provisions of the important group of sections relating to the Bank Circulation Redemption Fund may be summarized as follows:—

A fund is formed by a contribution from every bank of an amount equal to 5 per cent. of the average amount of its notes in circulation. When a new bank is authorized to commence business the sum of $5,000 is retained for the purposes of the fund out of the money in the government's hands under sec. 13. A re-adjustment of the fund is made as soon after the 30th of June of each year as is possible in such a way as to make the amount at the credit of each bank equal to 5 per cent. of the average note circulation of such bank during the twelve months next preceding the time of adjustment, or, in the case of a new bank, the average amount of its notes in circulation from the time it commenced business to the time of adjustment. The average is to be based upon the greatest amount of notes in circulation in each month as shewn by the monthly returns to the government. The fund bears interest at the rate of 3 per cent.

The purpose of the fund is to secure the payment of notes of any insolvent bank. When a bank suspends payment, its notes issued or re-issued and intended for circulation and then in circulation bear interest at 5 per cent. from the day of suspension. The liquidator may stop such interest from running by the publication of a notice and the payment in pursuance

thereof of notes as they are presented. In the event of failure Sec. 63.
on the part of the liquidator to arrange within two months of Circulation
the suspension for the payment with interest of all notes as they Redemption
are presented, the Minister of Finance may arrange for payment Fund.
out of the fund of all outstanding notes and interest, the notes
ceasing to bear interest from the day named by the Minister for
payment. Recourse may be had to the fund without regard to
the amount contributed thereto by the insolvent bank, but when
an amount has been paid out of the fund in excess of what had
been paid into the fund by the insolvent bank, including interest
thereon, the solvent banks are obliged on demand to make good
the excess in payments not exceeding in any one year 1 per
cent. of the average amount of the notes of each bank in circulation. Such payments are to be returned to the contributing
banks when the excess is repaid to the fund by the insolvent
bank. The impairment of the fund will be only temporary, except in the unlikely event that the assets of an insolvent bank,
including the double liability, are not sufficient ultimately to
meet all its notes. Any portion of an insolvent bank's contribution and interest thereon which is not used to pay the
notes of such bank, and the interest on such notes, may
be paid to the liquidator when proper arrangements have been
made to pay the notes still unpresented. Any amount paid out
of the fund in excess of the amount to the credit of the insolvent bank bears interest at 3 per cent. payable out of the assets
of such bank.

The sections date from 1890 except for the following three Amendments
amendments made in 1900. of 1900.

(1) The rate of interest which the notes of an insolvent bank
shall bear was changed from 6 to 5 per cent. (2) In sub-sec.
2 of sec. 66 the words "which each bank had or *should have* contributed to the fund at the time of the suspension of the bank
in respect of whose notes the payments are made," were substituted for the words "which each bank has at that time contributed to the fund." (3) Sub-sec. 9 of sec. 64 was added.

All the provisions of secs. 64 to 69, both inclusive, except
in so far as they are the result of the amendments of 1900, were
contained in sec. 54 of the Act of 1890. The division into separate sections, and the subdivision of such sections, are the result
of the revision of 1906.

Sec. 63.   It is in theory possible that a bank with relatively small capital may issue notes largely in excess of its authorized amount,
that the proceeds may be misappropriated, and that the other
banks may in effect have to redeem its notes. Practically, however such a contingency is effectually guarded against
by the system of frequent returns to the government, and
by the heavy penalties imposed for making false returns and
for excessive note issue, and also, by the action of the banks in
promptly presenting for redemption notes of other banks; cf.
also the supervisory powers of the Bankers' Association under
sec. 124.

Bank
circulation
redemption
fund
continued.

64. The moneys heretofore paid to and now deposited
with the Minister by the banks to which this Act applies, constituting the fund known as the Bank Circulation Redemption
Fund, shall continue to be held by the Minister for the purposes
and subject to the provisions in this section mentioned and contained.

$5,000 to be
retained
upon issue
certificate.

2. The Minister shall, upon the issue of a certificate under
this Act authorizing a bank to issue notes and commence the
business of banking, retain, out of any moneys of such bank
then in his possession, the sum of five thousand dollars, which
sum shall be held for the purposes of this section, until the
annual adjustment hereinafter provided for takes place in the
year then next following.

Adjustment

3. The amount at the credit of such bank shall, at such next
annual adjustment, be adjusted by payment to or by the bank
of such sum as is necessary to make the amount of money at
the credit of the bank equal to five per centum of the average

Five percent-
um of
average
circulation.

amount of its notes in circulation from the time it commenced
business to the time of such adjustment and such sum shall
thereafter be adjusted annually as hereinafter provided.

Circulation
Fund.

4. The amounts heretofore and from time to time hereafter
paid, to be retained and held by the Minister as by this section
provided, shall continue to form and shall form the Circulation
Fund.

5. The Circulation Fund shall continue to be held as here- Sec. 64.
tofore for the sole purpose of payment, in the event of the Its purposes.
suspension by a bank of payment in specie or Dominion notes
of any of its liabilities as they accrue, of the notes then issued
or re-issued by such bank, intended for circulation, and then
in circulation, and interest thereon.

6. The Circulation Fund shall bear interest at the rate of Fund to
three per centum per annum.   bear interest.

7. The Circulation Fund shall be adjusted, as soon as pos- Adjustment
sible after the thirtieth day of June in each year, in such a annually.
way as to make the amount at the credit of each bank contributing thereto, unless herein otherwise specially provided, equal
to five per centum of the average note circulation of such bank
during the then last preceding twelve months.

8. The average note circulation of a bank during any period Average
shall be determined from the average of the amount of its notes note circu-
in circulation, as shown by the monthly returns for such period determined.
made by the bank to the Minister; and where, in any return,
the greatest amount of notes in circulation at any time during
the month is given, such amount shall, for the purposes of this
section, be taken to be the amount of the notes of the bank in
circulation during the month to which such return relates.

9. The Minister shall with respect to all notes paid out Rights of
of the Circulation Fund have the same rights as any other Minister
holder of the notes of the bank: Provided that all such notes Proviso.
and all interest thereon, so paid by the Minister, after the
amount at the credit of such bank in the Circulation Fund, and
all interest due or accruing due thereon, has been exhausted,
shall bear interest, at the rate of three per centum per annum,
from the time such notes and interest are paid until such notes
and interest are repaid to the Minister by or out of the assets
of such bank.   53 V., c. 31, s. 54; 63-64 V., c. 26, s. 13.

See notes, *supra*.

Sec. 65.

Notes of
bank
suspending
payment to
bear
interest.

65. In the event of the suspension by a bank of payment in specie or Dominion notes of any of its liabilities as they accrue, the notes of the bank, issued or re-issued, intended for circulation, and then in circulation, shall bear interest at the rate of five per centum per annum, from the day of the suspension to such day as is named by the directors, or by the liquidator, receiver, assignee or other proper official, for the payment thereof.

Notice of
time for
payment.

2. Notice of such day shall be given by advertising for at least three days in a newspaper published in the place in which the head office of the bank is situate.

As to notes
not then
presented.

3. If any notes presented for payment on or after any day named for payment thereof are not paid, all notes then unpaid and in circulation shall continue to bear interest until such further day as is named for payment thereof, of which day notice shall be given in manner hereinbefore provided.

Notes not
redeemed to
be paid
out of
Circulation
Fund.

4. If the directors of the bank or the liquidator, receiver, assignee or other proper official fails to make arrangements, within two months from the day of the suspension of payment, by the bank, for the payment of all of its notes and interest thereon, the Minister may make arrangements for the payment, out of the Circulation Fund, of the notes remaining unpaid and all interest thereon, and the Minister shall give such notice of the payment as he thinks expedient.

Interest to
cease.

5. Notwithstanding anything herein contained all interest upon such notes shall cease upon and from the date named by the Minister for such payment.

Government
not liable.

6. Nothing herein contained shall be construed to impose any liability upon the Government of Canada, or upon the Minister, beyond the amount available from time to time out of the Circulation Fund. 53 V., c. 31, s. 54; 63-64 V., c. 26, s. 11.

See notes, *supra.*

By sec. 159 of the Winding-up Act (R.S.C. 1906, c. 144), publication in the *Canada Gazette* and in the official gazette of each province, and in two newspapers issued at or nearest to Sec. 65. the place where the head office of a bank is situate, of notice of any proceedings of which, under that act, creditors should be notified, is sufficient notice to holders of bank notes in circulation. If the head office is situated in the province of Quebec, one of the newspapers is to be a newspaper published in English and the other a newspaper published in French.

66. All payments made from the Circulation Fund shall be Payments without regard to the amount contributed thereto by the bank from Fund. in respect of whose notes the payments are made.

2. If the payments from the Circulation Fund exceed the If Fund amount contributed to the Circulation Fund by the bank so sus- exceeded. pending payment, and all interest due or accruing due to such bank thereon, the other banks to which this Act applies shall, on demand, make good to the Circulation Fund the amount of the excess, proportionately to the amount which each such other bank had or should have contributed to the Circulation Fund, at the time of the suspension of the bank in respect of whose notes the payments are made: Provided that,— Proviso.

(a) each of such other banks shall only be called upon to make good to the Circulation Fund its share of the excess in payments not exceeding, in any one year, one per centum of the average amount of its notes in circulation;

(b) such circulation shall be ascertained in such manner as the Minister decides; and,

(c) The Minister's decision shall be final.

3. All amounts recovered and received by the Minister from Amounts the bank on account of which such payments were made shall, recovered, how after the amount of such excess has been made good as afore- distributed. said, be distributed among the banks contributing to make good such excess, proportionately to the amount contributed by each. 53 V., c. 31, s. 54; 63-64 V., c. 26, s. 12.

See notes, *supra*.

Sec. 67.

Refund of
deposit if
bank is
wound up.

67. In the event of the winding-up of the business of a bank by reason of insolvency or otherwise, the Treasury Board may, on the application of the directors, or of the liquidator, receiver, assignee or other proper officials, and on being satisfied that proper arrangements have been made for the payment of the notes of the bank and any interest thereon, pay over to the directors, liquidator, receiver, assignee or other proper official, the amount of the Circulation Fund at the credit of the bank, or such portion thereof as it thinks expedient. 53 V., c. 31, s. 54.

See notes, *supra.*

Treasury
Board rules.

68. The Treasury Board may make all such rules and regulations as it thinks expedient with reference to,—

(*a*) the payment of any moneys out of the Circulation Fund, and the manner, place and time of such payments;

(*b*) the collection of all amounts due to the Circulation Fund;

(*c*) all accounts to be kept in connection therewith; and,

(*d*) generally the management of the Circulation Fund and all matters relating thereto. 53 V., c. 31, s. 54.

See notes, *supra.*

No rules and regulations have been made by the Treasury Board under this section.

Minister may
enforce
payments.

69. The Minister may, in his official name, by action in the Exchequer Court of Canada, enforce payment, with costs of action, of any sum due and payable by any bank which should form part of the Circulation Fund. 53 V., c. 31, s. 54.

See notes, *supra.*

Arrange-
ments to be
made for
circulation
at par.

70. The bank shall make such arrangements as are necessary to ensure the circulation at par, in any and every part of Canada, of all notes issued or re-issued by it and intended for circulation; and towards this purpose the bank shall establish agencies for the redemption and payment of its notes at the cities of Toronto, Montreal, Halifax, St. John, Winnipeg, Victoria and Charlottetown, and at such other places as are, from time to time, designated by the Treasury Board. 53 V., c. 31, s. 55.

This section was enacted in 1890 to meet the inconvenience resulting from the fact that bank notes circulating at a distance from the office where they were payable were frequently subject to a discount.

The arrangements made by the banks under this section and the establishment of the Bank Circulation Redemption Fund under secs. 64 *et seq.*, have resulted in maintaining the bank notes of all banks at par everywhere in Canada. Canadian bank notes now circulate as freely as if they were secured by a deposit of bonds.

See also the next section.

A bank must ensure the circulation of its notes at par, and, if necessary for this purpose, it must establish agencies for the redemption and payment of its notes at places other than those mentioned in the section or those which may be named by the Treasury Board. If, however, a bank neglected to establish an agency for redemption and payment of its notes at one of the places mentioned, the absence of such agency would probably not constitute dishonour of its notes at such place.

No places have been designated by the Treasury Board under this section.

71. The bank shall always receive in payment its own notes at par at any of its offices, and whether they are made payable there or not.

2. The chief place of business of the bank shall always be one of the places at which its notes are made payable. 53 V., c. 31, s. 56.

The obligation of this section is confined to *receiving in payment.* The section does not compel a bank to redeem its notes at any place except its head office or any other office at which

Sec. 71.
Bank must
take its own
notes.

such notes are payable, but see sec. 70, which requires arrangements to be made for redemption of bank notes at various principal cities in order to ensure their circulation at par throughout Canada.

As a matter of practice a bank always accepts at par the notes of other Canadian banks either in payment of a debt due to it or as a deposit by its customer. Any other practice would tend to disturb the confidence of the public in bank notes, a confidence which is largely a result of the arrangements made under sec. 70 and the establishment of the redemption fund under sec. 64. As a matter of legal right a bank is not obliged to accept in payment anything but legal tender (see Chapter XXIX, *infra*), or its own notes. There would be no legal objection to a bank's refusing to accept the notes of another bank in payment or to its charging a discount upon such notes as a condition of accepting them or upon notes of another bank deposited by a customer.

Quære, whether this section would apply to an office of a Canadian bank in a foreign country.

Payment in
Dominion
notes.

72. The bank, when making any payment, shall, on the request of the person to whom the payment is to be made, pay the same, or such part thereof, not exceeding one hundred dollars, as such person requests, in Dominion notes for one, two, or four dollars each, at the option of such person.

No torn
or defaced
notes.

2. No payment, whether in Dominion notes or bank notes, shall be made in bills that are torn or partially defaced by excessive handling. 53 V., c. 31, s. 57.

Formerly a person receiving payment might demand a sum not exceeding $50 to be paid in Dominion notes. The amount was increased to $100 in 1890, and sub-sec. 2 was added by the Senate in amendment to the House of Commons bill of that year. The latter amendment was characterized in the Commons as possibly a mischievous one, but was concurred in to avoid a postponement of the prorogation of Parliament.

The section would appear to authorize a person to whom a payment is to be made to require payment of the whole amount in Dominion notes of the denominations mentioned, notwithstanding that the amount payable exceeds $100, but the intention of the legislature probably was that the payee should be entitled to require payment in Dominion notes only up to $100 in any event. The payee is of course entitled to be paid in legal tender within the terms of the Currency Act (see Chapter XXIX., *infra*), and subject to this section the bank may pay in any form of legal tender it chooses.

73. The bonds, obligations and bills, obligatory or of credit, of the bank under its corporate seal, signed by the president or vice-president, and countersigned by a cashier or assistant cashier, which are made payable to any person, shall be assignable by endorsement thereon.

Bonds, obligations, etc.

Assignable by endorsement.

2. The bills or notes of the bank signed by the president, vice-president, cashier or other officer appointed by the directors of the bank to sign the same, promising the payment of money to any person, or to his order, or to the bearer, though not under the corporate seal of the bank, shall be binding and obligatory on the bank, in like manner and with the like force and effect as they would be upon any private person, if issued by him in his private or natural capacity, and shall be assignable in like manner as if they were so issued by a private person in his natural capacity.

Bills or notes binding.

Though not sealed.

3. The directors of the bank may, from time to time, authorize or depute any cashier, assistant cashier or officer of the bank, or any director other than the president or vice-president, or any cashier, manager or local director of any branch or office of discount and deposit of the bank, to sign the notes of the bank intended for circulation. 53 V., c. 31, s. 58.

Directors may depute officer to sign.

The section was divided into sub-sections in 1906, but in other respects it dates from 1871. It makes the bonds, obligations and bills, obligatory or of credit, of the bank under its corporate seal, etc., assignable by endorsement. The other documents mentioned in the section, not under the corporate seal, have no special assignability under the Act. Their assignment depends upon the general provincial law governing simi-

Sec. 73. lar documents issued by a private person in his natural capacity. Cf. notes to sec. 95, in regard to the negotiability or assignability of deposit receipts.

Bills may be signed oy machinery. **74.** All bank notes and bills whereon the name of any person entrusted or authorized to sign such notes or bills on behalf of the bank is impressed by machinery provided for that purpose, by or with the authority of the bank, shall be good and valid to all intents and purposes, as if such notes and bills had been subscribed in the proper handwriting of the person entrusted or authorized by the bank to sign the same respectively, and shall be bank notes and bills within the meaning of all laws and statutes whatever, and may be described as bank notes or bills in all indictments and civil or criminal proceedings whatever: Provided that at least one signature to each note or bill must be in the actual handwriting of a person authorized to sign such note or bill. 53 V., c. 31, s. 59.

One signature to be handwritten.

Counterfeit or fraudulent notes to be stamped. **75.** Every officer charged with the receipt or disbursement of public moneys, and every officer of any bank, and every person acting as or employed by any banker, shall stamp or write in plain letters, upon every counterfeit or fraudulent note issued in the form of a Dominion or bank note, and intended to circulate as money, which is presented to him at his place of business, the word *Counterfeit, Altered* or *Worthless.*

If wrongfully stamped. 2. If such officer or person wrongfully stamps any genuine note he shall, upon presentation, redeem it at the face value thereof. 53 V., c. 31, s. 62.

CHAPTER XV.

BUSINESS AND POWERS OF A BANK.

A bank chartered under the Bank Act, in addition to being Sec. 76. (P. 137.) a corporation with certain specified powers and subject to certain specified restrictions, is by sec. 76 of that act authorized to "engage in and carry on such business generally as appertains to the business of banking."

The nature of the business of banking is part of the law Business of Banking. merchant, and will be judicially noticed by the courts. (Per Lord Campbell in Bank of Australasia v. Breillat, 1847, 6 Moo. P.C. 152; see Chapter II., *supra*.) The specific provisions of the Bank Act must be considered as applied to a corporation which has general banking powers.

The heart of the law of banking is that a bank has such powers as are requisite for the safe and convenient attainment of the purposes of its incorporation, the chief of these being to provide a place of safety in which the public may keep money and other valuables, and to lend its own money, and that of others deposited with it (unless specially deposited), for a profit, and to act as agent in the remission and collection of money. If it is by its organic law, a bank of issue, it has one more fundamental purpose, namely, to provide the public with a convenient currency in the shape of promissory notes intended to circulate as money. (Morse on Banks & Banking, 4th ed., 1903, sec. 46 A.)

In regard to matters not clear upon statute or binding decisions, it is a proper method of ascertaining what is legitimately within the scope of the business of banking, and what are the powers of corporations formed for the purpose of carrying on that business, to refer to the history of banking and the definitions of lexicographers (*Ibid.*).

A "banker" is defined in Hart on Banking (2nd ed., 1906), Banker and customer defined. as "one who in the ordinary course of his business receives money, which he repays by honouring the cheques of the persons from or on whose account he receives it," and a "customer" as "one who has an account with a banker" (see Great Western v. London & County Bank, [1901] A.C. 414, where the term "customer" is discussed). See also Morse on Banks and Banking, Chapter I., where the definition of a bank is elaborately discussed. The following analysis of the business and powers of a bank is based in the main upon that of Hart.

1. *It follows from the definition of a banker given above that normally a bank is the debtor of its customer and bound to discharge its indebtedness by honouring its customer's cheques.*

Bank as drawee of cheques. A bank may be considered as primarily and naturally the depositary of money and the drawee of cheques. The balance standing to the credit of a customer represents money he has lent to the bank. The property in cash deposited, and in the proceeds of drafts and cheques collected for the customer, passes to the bank and forms part of its trading capital. Its liability to the customer is purely a personal obligation to honour cheques drawn upon it by him.

A bank under the Bank Act is a Bank of Deposit. Sec. 95 expressly recognizes the power of the bank to receive and repay deposits, and permits the bank to a certain extent to deal in this respect with persons incapable by law to enter into ordinary contracts. The rights and liabilities of the bank in regard to deposits made with it and cheques drawn upon it will be considered in the notes to that section and in Part III. of the Bills of Exchange Act entitled "Cheques on a Bank."

2. *A bank usually undertakes expressly or impliedly to honour bills of exchange accepted by its customer, and made payable at the bank, to the extent of its customer's balance, or to an agreed amount.*

Bank may pay customer's acceptance The bank is not bound to pay bills accepted by the customer and made payable at the bank (Robarts v. Tucker, 1851, 16 Q. B. 560), but may do so (Kymar v. Laurie, 1849, 18 L.J.Q.B. 218) ; except in the province of Quebec, where, it is said, special authority from the customer is required. A bank is not obliged to accept bills drawn upon it, in the absence of special agreement to do so, but such agreement may be inferred from the bank's having accepted previous bills and having funds to meet the bill in question (see Cumming v. Shand, 1860, 29 L.J. Ex. 129). If money is paid to the bank with its assent to meet a bill it may be sued by the holder (see De Bernales v. Fuller, as stated in 3 App. Cas. at p. 334).

3. *A bank invariably acts as the collecting agent of its customer.*   Sec. 76.
(P. 137.)

The current account involves the collection of cheques and The
orders delivered to the bank by its customer in order that their collecting
proceeds may be credited to him.   banker.

Incidentally the discounting of bills, etc., involves the collection thereof. Secs. 93 and 94 contain specific provisions for certain collection and agency charges in addition to the discount where such bills, etc., are payable at an office other than the office of discount.

A bank undertaking the duty of collecting mercantile paper is bound as agent to use due diligence in performing the duties of collection (Bank of Van Diemen's Land v. Bank of Victoria, 1871, L.R. 3 P.C. 526), and is liable to its principal for negligence in the performance of its duty, as for instance for failure to use due diligence in presenting a bill for acceptance, where acceptance is necessary (Bank of Van Diemen's Land v. Bank of Victoria, *supra;* Bills of Exchange Act, secs. 75, 76 and 77), and for payment (*Ibid.*, secs. 85 *et seq.;* Browne v. Commercial Bank, 1853, 10 U.C.R. 129; as to presentment of cheque for payment, see notes to sec. 166 of the Bills of Exchange Act).

A bank which engages to collect an unaccepted bill may leave it for two days with the drawee, in order that he may decide during that time whether he will accept. The duty of the bank is to obtain acceptance if possible, but not to press unduly for acceptance in such a way as to lead to refusal, provided the steps for obtaining acceptance or refusal are taken within that limit of time which will preserve the principal's right against the drawer. (Bank of Van Diemen's Land v. Bank of Victoria, *supra;* Bills of Exchange Act, sec. 80.)

A bank undertaking to collect an accepted bill must not part with the bill or permit it to be tampered with until it is paid, or if a conditional payment is made, until the condition has been accepted by the principal. (Bank of Scotland v. Dominion Bank, [1891] A.C. 592.)

As to notice of dishonour when a bill is dishonoured in the hands of an agent, see Bills of Exchange Act, sec. 100; cf. Steinhoff v. Merchants Bank, 1881, 46 U.C.R. 25.

When a bank receives a note for collection and in the regular course of business places the same in the hands of a responsible and solvent agent, it is not responsible for the loss of the note

in the mails. In any case the bank's offer to give security to
the maker and the endorser that they would never be troubled
if they pay the note, is sufficient. (Litman v. Montreal City &
District Savings Bank, 1897, Q.R. 13 S.C. 262.)

A bank to which a promissory note is endorsed "for collection" becomes for that purpose, the agent of the endorser, to
whom it is bound to account for the amount collected. (Perreault v. Merchants Bank, 1905, Q.R. 27 S.C. 149.) The bank
is the holder, but subject to any defence which might be set up
against the principal; see notes to sec. 56 of the Bills of Exchange Act.

If a cheque is deposited for collection and presented with
due diligence to the drawee bank and dishonoured, the mere
fact that the collecting bank has credited the payee with the
amount of the cheque is not evidence that the cheque was intended to be discounted, and the entry in the books of the collecting bank may be reversed and the payee of the cheque
charged with the amount (Reg. v. Bank of Montreal, 1886, 1
Can. Ex. C. R. 154). A bank accepting the deposit of
a certified cheque and crediting the depositor with the
amount accepts it for the purpose of cashing it as the depositor's
agent, and cannot, in the absence of express agreement to that
effect, be deemed to have acquired title to it in consideration of
the credit entry, and thus to have gratuitously guaranteed its
payment by the drawee bank. (Gaden v. Newfoundland Savings Bank, [1899] A.C. 281.) But it has been held in Capital
& Counties Bank v. Gordon, [1903] A.C. 240, that where a bank
credits a customer with the amount of a crossed cheque deposited by him, and allows him to draw against the amount so
credited before the cheque is cleared, the bank becomes a holder
for value, and therefore, when the cheque is paid, the bank does
not receive payment merely as agent for collection and "for
its customer" within the protection of sec. 175 of the Bills of
Exchange Act.

A collecting bank in accordance with the ordinary rule governing agents, can receive payment of a draft sent to it for
collection in money only, and cannot bind its principal by setting off an amount due to it by the acceptor against the amount
of the draft. (Donogh v. Gillespie, 1894, 21 A.R. 292.)

4. *Incidentally the business of a bank as a dealer in money,*   Sec. 76.
etc., involves the issue in exchange for money of instruments   (P. 137.)
whereby the bank in effect acknowledges its obligation to pay
money to or honour drafts of the holder or other person entitled
under the terms thereof, as the case may be.

A bank which sells a draft payable at another place is, in Issue of
one view of the transaction, an agent for the transmission of drafts and
money, but the transaction may rather be regarded as a deal- credit.
ing in money and instruments of credit. Similarly with letters of
credit issued by a bank. Sec. 76 authorizes the bank to carry
on business as a dealer in gold and silver coin and bullion, bills
of exchange, etc.

5. *A bank may serve the purpose of providing the public*
with a paper currency in the shape of its promissory notes.

A bank under the Bank Act is a Bank of Issue. By sec. 61 Bank of
of the Act it is authorized to issue and re-issue notes payable to issue.
bearer on demand and intended for circulation. See notes to
that section.

6. *A bank is also a lender of money.*

The profitable conduct of the business of banking necessar- Lending of
ily involves the lending of money by way of allowing money.
overdrafts on current accounts, making loans in the form of
advances on discounting bills and notes, etc. Lending is naturally accompanied by the acquisition of various kinds of security.

In so far as the bank lends to a customer the normal relation of the parties is inverted.

A bank chartered under the Bank Act is a Bank of Discount.
To ascertain its lending powers reference must be had particularly to sec. 76 which specifies various kinds of property upon
the security of which a bank may lend money, and other kinds
of property upon the security of which it may not do so, except
as expressly authorized in other parts of the Act. See notes to
that section where reference is made to all the sections relating
to the lending powers of a bank.

The funds in the hands of a bank available for lending, or Trading
its trading capital, are made up of capital.

1. The invested capital, that is the cash paid up on subscribed shares.

2. The borrowed capital, derived from

(a) Notes in circulation—the amount of which, except in the case of the Bank of British North America, may be equal to, but not greater than, the invested capital.

(b) Deposits of customers—the amount of which may be and usually is many times the invested capital.

(c) Money received for drafts, letters of credit, etc., which must be repaid in another place and at a future time.

The trading capital, borrowed from one group of persons in one way or another, is loaned to another group of persons in various ways. The difference between the amount the bank earns on its capital, its exchange and collection charges, charges for keeping accounts and for acting as depositary of valuables, etc., on the one hand, and on the other hand, the amount it pays to those from whom it borrows, expenses of the bank, deductions for bad debts, etc., form its profits. Out of these profits it may pay dividends and bonuses, and create a rest or reserve fund for contingencies.

7. *A bank is sometimes the bailee of title deeds and other valuables in small compass entrusted to it by its customer for safe custody.*

Safe custody of valuables.
The bank is a mere bailee of property deposited for safe keeping by the customer, and if it receives no special renumeration for allowing the deposit, it is not liable for loss by the theft of a bank servant, provided it took such care as a man would take of his own property. (Giblin v. McMullen, 1869, L.R. 2 P.C. 318; 16 E.R. 578, and cases noted at end of latter report; 3 R.C. 613.) The doctrine of Giblin v. McMullen is probably not applicable to cases of bailment arising under the Civil Code of Lower Canada; see an article by E. Fabre Surveyer in 11 Journal C.B.A. 346, 4 Can. L.R. 39, where the whole subject of the liability of a depositary or bailee is discussed with special reference to the law of Quebec.

But the law of Quebec, like that of the other provinces, recognizes the distinction between a bailment for reward and a gratuitous bailment, the latter being more properly called a deposit.

If a commission is paid for the safe-keeping, a higher degree of care is required than in the case of a gratuitous bailment. (In re United Service Co., Johnston's Claim, 1870, L.R. 6 Ch.

212.) The last mentioned case and Giblin v. McMullen are discussed, in connection with the recent case of Langtry v. Union Bank, in the Solicitors Journal for the 28th September, 1895, quoted at some length in 3 Journal C.B.A. 196. In Langtry v. Union Bank, a theft of jewels deposited with a bank was effected by means of a forged delivery order presented to the bank, and the bank was held liable to the owner. In this country the safe custody of valuables is usually undertaken by trust companies or safe deposit agencies which have special facilities for the purpose.

Property deposited for safe-keeping only is not subject to the bank's general lien; see notes to sec. 77.

THE BUSINESS AND POWERS OF A BANK.

76. The bank may,—

(a) open branches, agencies and offices;   Generally.

(b) engage in and carry on business as a dealer in gold and silver coin and bullion;

(c) deal in, discount and lend money and make advances upon the security of, and take as collateral security for any loan made by it, bills of exchange, promissory notes and other negotiable securities, or the stock, bonds, debentures and obligations of municipal and other corporations, whether secured by mortgage or otherwise, or Dominion, provincial, British, foreign and other public securities; and,

(d) engage in and carry on such business generally as appertains to the business of banking.

2. Except as authorized by this Act, the bank shall not, either Exceptions. directly or indirectly,—

(a) deal in the buying or selling, or bartering of goods, wares and merchandise, or engage or be engaged in any trade or business whatsoever;

(b) purchase, or deal in, or lend money, or make advances upon the security or pledge of any share of its own capital stock, or of the capital stock of any bank; or,

Sec. 76.   (c) lend money or make advances upon the security, mortgage or hypothecation of any lands, tenements or immovable property, or of any ships or other vessels, or upon the
security of any goods, wares and merchandise. 53 V., c. 31,
s. 64.

The negative portions of this section, except as to lending
money on the shares of other banks, are taken from the Act of
1871. The remainder of the section, granting certain powers to
the bank, was expressed in that act in the short clause: "The
bank may open branches or agencies and offices of discount and
deposit and transact business, at any place or places in the Dominion." These powers were amplified in subsequent acts. The
section was divided into its present sub-sections and clauses in
1906. In other respects the section in its present form dates
from 1890, and is a consolidation of secs. 45, 46, 59 and 60 of
R.S.C., 1886, c. 120.

This section expressly authorizes a bank to do certain specified classes of acts, and forbids it to do certain other specified
classes of acts—the prohibition, however, being subject to a very
important qualification.

Authorised   The authorized acts are as follows:—
business.
(a) To open branches, agencies and offices.
(b) To engage in and carry on business as a dealer in gold
and silver coin and bullion.

(c) To deal in To discount To lend money and make advances on the security of, and and to take as collateral security for any loan made by it	bills of exchange and promissory notes and other negotiable securities, or the stock, bonds, debentures and obligations of municipal and other corporations, whether secured by mortgage or otherwise, or Dominion, provincial, British, foreign and other public securities.

(d) To engage in and carry on such business as generally
appertains to the business of banking.

To open branches, agencies and offices.

Branches.   Branch banks are merely separate offices of the principal
bank (Prince v. Oriental Bank, 1878, 3 App. Cas. 325), so that

accounts kept at different branches may be consolidated by the   Sec. 76.
bank (Garrett v. McKewan, 1872, L.R. 8 Ex. 10), and a sum
payable at a branch may be paid by the bank at the head office
(Irwin v. Bank of Montreal, 1876, 38 U.C.R. 375; Bain v. Torrance, 1884, Man. R. 32).

Branches are, however, treated as distinct banks for purposes
of notice of dishonour and payment of cheques (Prince v. Oriental Bank, *supra;* London City, etc., Bank v. Gordon, [1903]
A.C. 240; Reg. v. Bank of Montreal, 1886, 1 Can. Ex. C.R. 154,
and cases cited; but see Steinhoff v. Merchants Bank, 1881, 46
U.C.R. 25; Fielding v. Corry, [1898] 1 Q.B. 268, and sec. 100
of the Bills of Exchange Act as to notice of dishonour).

An agency is a different thing from a branch. An agent or Agencies.
correspondent bank collects cheques, notes, etc., cashes drafts
drawn against it, retires bills according to instructions, and does
almost all that a branch bank may do. The main difference is
that an agency receives a commission as its remuneration while
a branch is merely an office of the bank in another place, and its
profits belong, and its expenses and losses are borne, by the
bank of which it is a branch.

A bank acting as agent may be liable for negligence according to the ordinary principles of the law of agency applicable
to the particular circumstances: see notes, *supra,* p. 133.

The agent bank is the agent of the bank which employs it,
and not the agent of the latter's customer, so that if the agent
collects money for the customer's account, the customer's bank
is liable to account for the money collected. (MacKersy v. Ramsay, 1843, 9 Cl. & F. 818.)

To deal in, discount, etc.

To deal in bills of exchange, etc., is to traffic or trade in
them, *i.e.,* to buy and sell them, or to lend on them. (Cf. Jones
v. Imperial Bank, 1876, 23 Gr. 268, at p. 275.)

A bill is *discounted* when in consideration of a sum paid by Discount
the bank, the transferor endorses it to the bank, or when, with- of bill.
out endorsement, he becomes liable to the bank by agreement or
custom in respect of the payment of the amount of the bill.
(Hart on Banking, 2nd. ed., 1906, p. 616.)

The discount is the deduction or drawback made from an
advance of money upon a bill; the difference between the price

Sec. 76.

Discounting not a form of loan.

paid and the face value of the bill. (In re Land Securities Co., Ex parte Farquhar, [1896] 2 Ch. 320; cf. London Financial Association v. Kelk, 1883, 26 Ch. D. 107, at pp. 134-5.)

Hart on Banking (p. 616) lays down the further propositions that discounting as carried on by banks is essentially a form of lending, and that the advance upon every bill or note discounted, without reference to its character as business or accommodation paper, is properly denominated a loan, for interest is predicable only of loans, being the price paid for the use of money (citing Fleckner v. Bank of the U.S., 1823, 21 U.S. (8 Wheaton) 338, at p. 350, and National Bank v. Johnson, 1881, 104 U.S. 271, at pp. 276-7). But, as pointed out by a reviewer in 22 L.Q.R. 453 (1906), an ordinary discounting is an absolute sale of a claim against a third party (embodied in a negotiable instrument of which the ownership passes to the purchaser), with an implied guarantee, on the vendor's part, of the payment of the claim at maturity. A bank which holds a bill, not as a mortgagee or pledgee, but as an out and out holder. (In re Hallett & Co., [1894], 2 Q.B. 256.) In every borrowing transaction the borrower has to repay the amount lent to him at a fixed date or at a fixed period after notice or on demand; if any property is transferred to the lender by way of security for the loan, the borrower is entitled to redeem such property on repayment of the loan with interest. On the other hand, a bank which discounts a bill for a customer does not become entitled to a claim for the repayment of the amount paid or credited to the customer; in the event of the bill being dishonoured, the bank, if it complies with the prescribed formalities, acquires a claim for damages under secs. 134 *et seq.*, of the Bills of Exchange Act, but this claim for damages is in the nature of a claim for breach of warranty, and cannot by any stretch of language be described as a claim for the repayment of a loan. The bank, while it holds the bill, is the absolute owner thereof; the customer would not under any circumstances have a right to redeem it.

If the customer is not the acceptor or maker of a bill or note discounted the bank must have recourse primarily against the acceptor or maker, and has recourse against the customer only after default and notice to him. (Rouquette v. Overmann, 1875, L.R. 10 Q.B. 525; cf. In re Gomersall, 1875, 1 Ch. D. 142.)

The discounted paper becomes the property of the bank, and if it is lost or destroyed the loss falls upon the bank. (Carstairs v. Bates, 1812, 3 Camp. 301.)

A bill is *pledged* when the holder in consideration of a loan, Sec. 76. deposits the bill with the lender merely as a security. In this Pledge of case the interest of the lender in the bill is limited to the bill. amount secured by the deposit. (Reid v. Furnival, 1833, 1 Cr. & M. 538.)

A bill is *bought* when, in consideration of a sum paid, it is Purchase of transferred without endorsement, or endorsed without recourse, bill. and the transferor does not become responsible for its payment to the person who takes it. This is a different transaction from one in which a person desiring to remit money to a distant place buys from a bank, and the bank sells to him, a bill drawn by it upon its correspondent in the place of payment. (See Misa v. Currie, 1876, 1 App. Cas. 554.)

All these forms of dealing in bills are covered by the comprehensive language of sec. 76. The powers given also include that of taking bills, etc., as collateral security for past loans.

Collateral security.

Collateral means literally situated at the side, hence parallel or additional, and not, if the nature of the transaction does not require it, secondary. (In re Athill, 1880, 16 Ch. D. 211.)

Collateral security is any property which is assigned or Collateral pledged to secure the performance of an obligation and as addi- security tional thereto, and which upon the performance of the obliga- defined. tion is to be surrendered or discharged. If the creditor upon payment of the debt fails to return the property taken as collateral security, he must account to the debtor for the face value of the property, in the absence of evidence to shew that such value could not be realized. (Union Bank v. Elliott, 1902, 14 Man. R. 187; Ryan v. McConnell, 1889, 18 O.R. 409.)

A bank can sue upon paper taken as collateral security when it becomes due, and before the maturity of the debt secured by such paper. (Shaw v. Crawford, 1857, 16 U.C.R. 101; Ross v. Tyson, 1869, 19 C.P. 294.) As to realization of security, after default in payment of the secured debt, see notes to sec. 78.

But, when a bank gives a customer "a line of credit, to be secured by collections deposited," it is bound to credit the customer with the payments made from time to time on collateral notes deposited with the bank by the customer in accordance with the memorandum. It cannot hold the payments in a suspense account until the maturity of the cus-

76. tomer's own paper given to the bank to cover the line of credit, and take judgment against the customer for the full amount of that paper. (Molsons Bank v. Cooper, 1898, 26 S.C.R. 611, affirmed by the Judicial Committee, reported 26 A.R. 571.)

DOCUMENTS WHICH MAY BE TAKEN AS COLLATERAL SECURITY.

Bills of exchange and promissory notes.

See Bills of Exchange Act, *infra.*

Other negotiable securities.

See Chapter XXX., where the subject of negotiable securities, other than bills, notes and cheques, is discussed.

Stocks, bonds, debentures and obligations of corporations.

The power to lend money upon shares, etc., involves the power to do any prudent or proper act with a view of obtaining the benefit of such security, as for instance to have the shares transferred absolutely to the bank and to register the bank as shareholder. (In re Asiatic Banking Corporation, Royal Bank of India's Case, 1869, L.R. 4 Ch. 252.) As to powers of realizing securities, see notes to sec. 78.

A bank is expressly authorized to take as collateral security bonds of corporations. By this means it may, in effect, lend money to the holder of such bonds on a mortgage of lands. The bank cannot take direct to itself a mortgage of lands except as additional security, but if a company issues bonds secured by mortgage and pledges the whole issue to the bank, the transaction will then be within the enabling clauses of this section. The company might be incorporated for the express purpose of acquiring lands and issuing bonds to be secured by mortgage of such lands, so as to enable the bank to lend money upon what would otherwise be unlawful security.

As to the validity and negotiability of bonds, etc., see Chapter XXX., *infra.*

Trusts and claims of the third parties relating to shares and negotiable securities taken by the bank as collateral security.

Under section 52 a bank is not bound to see to the execution of any trust to which any shares of its own stock is subject. If, however, it takes as security shares held in trust with actual Sec. 76. notice of the trust, as for instance, when the shares prior to their transfer to the bank stand in the transferor's name "in trust" (Bank of Montreal v. Sweeny, 1887, 12 App. Cas. 617; Birkbeck v. Johnston, 1902, 3 O.L.R. at p. 507, S.C. 6 O.L.R. 258), the bank must decline to accept the property until it has ascertained that the transfer is authorized by the trust, or it must take the chance of finding that there is somebody with a prior title to demand a transfer from the transferor. (Cf. Sheffield v. London Joint Stock Bank, 1888, 13 App. Cas. 333, distinguished in London Joint Stock Bank v. Simmons, [1892] A.C. 201; Raphael v. McFarlane, 1890, 18 S.C.R. 183; London & Canadian v. Duggan, [1893] A.C. 506; Petry v. Caisse d'Economie, 1891, 19 S.C.R. 713.)

Pledges of negotiable securities, or securities treated by the Pledge of market as negotiable (see Chapter XXX., *infra*), to a bank, negotiable which lends money upon them, in good faith and without notice securities. that they are the property of a third person, pledged without his authority, can be held as security by the bank against the owner. The bank can hold the securities notwithstanding that they are pledged in a block by a broker who in the common course is known to hold securities belonging to his principals. (London Joint Stock Bank v. Simmons, [1892] A.C. 201.) The same rule applies to the proceeds of a cheque carried to broker's account by a bank which did not know, and had made no enquiry, whether the money paid in was in the broker's hands as agent or otherwise. (Thompson v. Clydesdale Bank, [1893] A.C. 282.)

Share certificates and transfers are not negotiable instru- Share ments. In Rumball v. Metropolitian Bank, 1877, 1 Q.B.D. 194, certificate scrip certificates to bearer for shares in an English joint stock not company were held to be negotiable, but in London & County negotiable Bank v. London & River Plate Bank, 1887, 20 Q.B.D. 232, S. instruments. C. 21 Q.B.D. 535, share certificates of the Pennsylvania Railroad with blank transfer forms endorsed on the back were held not to be negotiable instruments notwithstanding evidence that these shares were treated as negotiable by delivery on the English market. See also Smith v. Walkerville, 1896, 23 A.R. 95, and an article by Z. A. Lash in 7 Journal C.B.A. 117.

A person taking share certificates for value without notice of any infirmity in the title would not have a right to hold them

as against a prior owner who had never intended to part with
the property in them. If there has been no intent on the part
of the owner to transfer them, a good title can be obtained
against him only if he has so acted as to preclude himself from
setting up a claim to them. (Colonial Bank v. Cady, 1890, 15
App. Cas. 267, 283, and see Société Générale v. Walker, 1885,
11 App. Cas. 20, and cases cited.) In Smith v. Rogers, 1899,
30 O.R. 256, (where many of the cases are collected), it was held
that the registered owner, by endorsing a certificate of shares
with a transfer and power of attorney in blank and delivering
it to a broker, had so acted as to estop himself from setting up
his title as against a bank with which the certificate was improperly deposited by the broker as security, in view of the evidence
given that according to the usages of the stock exchanges of
Ontario and Quebec such a share certificate so endorsed passes
from hand to hand and is recognized as entitling the holder to
deal with the shares as owner and pass the property in them by
delivery, or to fill in the blank with his own name and have the
shares so registered on the books of the company. It was held
in that case that the bank was entitled to hold the shares as
against the owner. There was no question of the rights of a subsequent transfer by the registered owner, and the case does not
decide that the bank was not obliged, as against another transferee, to complete its title by procuring itself to be registered
on the books of the company.

A note upon a share certificate that "without the production
of this certificate no transfer of the shares mentioned therein
can be registered" does not amount to a representation to or
contract with the holder of the certificate that the shares will
not be transferred without production of the certificate, but is
only a warning to the owner of the shares to take care of the
certificate because he cannot compel the company to register a
transfer without its production. (Rainford v. Keith, [1905]
1 Ch. 296; S.C, reversed on the ground that the company had
notice in fact of the claim of a third party, [1905] 2 Ch. 147.)

The effect of a certificate is to preclude the company issuing
it from denying that at the time it was issued the person named
therein as the owner was entitled to the shares. The certificate
will not give to a transferee from the person so named a good
title as against an innocent, though subsequent, transferee, whose
transfer is duly registered without production of the certificate.
(Smith v. Walkerville, 1896, 23 A.R. 95.)

See notes at the beginning of this chapter.

A bank may take as collateral security the assignment of a policy of fire insurance upon property in which the bank has no interest. The bank is entitled to payment of the proceeds of insurance maintained by the owner of the property and made payable in case of loss to the bank as its interest might appear under a verbal agreement between the bank and the owner that the property should be insured in the bank's favour as security for advances which the bank might make from time to time. This is within the general banking powers and not within the prohibition of sec. 76. (Re Shediac Boot & Shoe Co., 1905, 37 N.B.R. 98.)

A bond of the customer and other parties (Moffatt v. Merchants Bank, 1885, 11 S.C.R. 46), or an assignment of a debt (Rennie v. Quebec Bank, 1902, 3 O.L.R. 541; Merchants Bank v. Darveau, 1898, Q.R. 15 S.C. 325), may be taken as security.

A bank may also make advances upon the assignment of moneys payable under contracts existing or future, or upon the security of any chose in action, except in so far as the Bank Act expressly excludes such transactions. (Molsons Bank v. Carscaden, 1892, 8 Man. R. 451.)

PROHIBITIONS OF SECTION 76.

The second part of the section is in restriction of the powers of the bank, and provides that, *"except as authorized by this Act,"* the bank shall not, either directly or indirectly,

(*a*) Deal in the buying, or selling, or bartering of goods, wares and merchandise, or engage or be engaged in any trade or business whatsoever;

(*b*) Purchase, or deal in, or lend money, or make advances upon the security or pledge of any share of its own capital stock, or of the capital stock of any bank; or

(*c*) Lend money or make advances upon the security, mortgage, or hypothecation of any land, tenements or immovable property, or of any ships or other vessels, or upon the security of any goods, wares and merchandise.

10—BANK ACT.

Except as authorized by this Act.

The exceptions provided for by this clause are important, and are contained in the first sub-section of this section and in secs. 77-89; see especially secs. 80, 84, 86 and 88.

Effect of the Act upon transactions entered into in contravention of its provisions.

It has been said that the prohibition of the Act is a law of public policy in the public interest, and any transaction in violation thereof is necessarily null and void; that no court can be called upon to give effect to any such transaction or to enforce any contract or security on which money is lent or advances as thus prohibited are made. (Bank of Toronto v. Perkins, 1883, 8 S.C.R. at p. 610; cf. Bathgate v. Merchants Bank, 1888, 5 Man. R. at p. 215.)

Contract of loan valid although security invalid.

This dictum must, it would seem, be confined to the effect of the Act upon the validity of the security taken. If a bank takes as security for an advance an assignment of a kind forbidden by the Act, it cannot enforce the security. The bank incurs a penalty under sec. 146, but the contract of loan is valid and the property nevertheless passes to the bank (National Bank of Australasia v. Cherry, 1870, L.R. 3 P.C. 299, at p. 307; Ayers v. South Australian Banking Co., 1871, L.R. 3 P.C. 548, at p. 559). Upon repayment of the loan the bank is bound to restore the property or to pay its value (Exchange Bank v. Fletcher, 1890, 19 S.C.R. 278). The borrower who has received the money cannot, in his own defence, question the bank's power to lend, nor can his creditors, who have no other rights in this respect than the debtor himself. The fact that the taking of the security is *ultra vires* of the bank may perhaps affect the pledge as regards third parties interested in the property pledged but does not affect the borrower's contract to pay. (Rolland v. Caisse d'Economie, 1895, 24 S.C.R. 405; in this case there was in the charter of the bank no direct prohibition of the transaction in question.)

The invalidity of the security taken would not affect the existence of the debt; even if the contract should be deemed to be non-existent, the bank would be entitled to recover the money advanced. (In re Langlois, 1893, Q.R. 4 S.C. 65; Canadian Bank of Commerce v. McDonald, 1906, 3 West. L.R. 90.)

A prohibiting statute does not necessarily import nullity if the transaction is valid according to the general law, but if the

bank seeks to obtain a priority over other creditors by virtue of $\quad$ Sec. 76.
the Act, and the general law confers no priority, it is necessary
for the bank as against the creditors of the transferor to shew
that the transaction was in precise accordance with the provisions of the Act. (Royal Canadian Bank v. Ross, 1877, 40 U.
C.R. 466, and cases cited at p. 473.)

Dealing in the buying, selling or bartering.

The prohibition of the Act is against *dealing* in the buying Prohibited
or selling of goods, etc., that is against a transaction which is acts.
primarily a purchase or sale. The bank must not traffic in
goods; it cannot buy them with a view to selling them again at
a profit (Morse on Banks and Banking, sec. 77). Such traffic
would not fall within any department of banking, but would
be engaging in trade or business. If, however, a borrower who
has pledged goods to a bank as security for a debt, makes default and gives the bank a release of his interest in such goods,
the bank would not be prohibited from selling them, and to that
extent engaging in the buying and selling of goods.

The Act does not forbid the guaranteeing by the bank of
the purchase price of goods (Molsons Bank v. Kennedy, 1879,
10 Rev. Leg. 110), but a bank could not be bound by a warranty,
express or implied, on the sale of goods acquired by it in contravention of the Act. (Radford v. Merchants Bank, 1883, 3
O.R. 529.)

Trade or business.

This Act has already (in this same section and also, in sec.
14) referred to "the business of banking," and the word business in the sense of "the occupation of conducting trade or
monetary transactions of any kind" (Century Dictionary)
would include banking. Trade comprehends every species of
exchange or dealing, either in the produce of land, in manufactures, or in bills or money. It is chiefly used, however, to denote the barter or purchase and sale of goods, wares and merchandise, either by wholesale or retail.

Share of its own capital stock or of the capital stock of any bank.

The prohibition against a bank's lending on the security of
its own shares was contained in the general Banking Act of

1871. See, however, sec. 77 which gives the bank a privileged
lien upon its own shares for a debt due to it from a shareholder.

Bank not to lend on bank shares.   The privilege of taking as security the shares of another
bank was not abolished until 1879 (cf. Carnegie v. Federal
Bank. 1884, 5 O.R. 418). The prohibition to make advances on
the security of shares of another bank applies to the bank and
not to the borrower. (Exchange Bank v. Fletcher, 1890, 19 S.
C.R. 278 and see note, *supra*, under this section, as to the effect
of transactions entered into in contravention of the Act.)

The word ''bank'' is defined by sec. 2 as any bank to which
this Act applies, but *quære* whether dealing in the shares of a
foreign bank is not within the prohibition of this section.

The prohibition is subject to sec. 80. See also notes to sec.
77.

One of the obvious evils of permitting a bank to hold its own
stock absolutely is that the double liability imposed upon shareholders by sec. 125 would be rendered illusory as regards stock
held by the bank itself. The pledge to a bank of shares of its
own stock would be objectionable on the same ground because
there would always be the possibility of the borrower's making
default or becoming bankrupt and the bank's having to acquire
the shares absolutely.

If a bank acquires shares of its own stock by forfeiture under
sec. 40 for non-payment of calls, it is obliged under sec 41 to
sell them within six months.

Where a bank in contravention of the Act traffics in its own
shares, and in the course of such traffic certain shares are transferred to the cashier in trust for the bank, his transferees may
perhaps have a right to rescind before the failure of the bank,
but cannot do so afterwards. The transaction is not a nullity,
and becomes by the suspension of the bank, of unimpeachable
validity as between the transferee and the liquidator. (Re
Central Bank, Nasmith's Case, 1888, 16 O.R. 293, 18 A.R. 209;
cf. Henderson's Case, 1889, 17 O.R. 110.)

*Security mortgage or hypothecation of any lands, tenements
or immovable property.*

The prohibition as to mortgages of real estate is subject to
sec. 80.

The object of this prohibition and, to a less degree, that
against engaging in trade or business or dealing in the buying,
selling or bartering of goods, is to prevent a bank from locking
up its assets and to oblige it to keep them in the form that
renders them most available. Under the system governed by the
Act, the greater part of the assets of a bank including its paid-
up capital, its deposits, and the amount of its note issue, are
constantly in process of being collected or paid in and again
loaned out or circulated.

This enables the bank to meet the demands of the people and
to supply them with the money for the proper conduct of commercial transactions. It facilitates the bringing to the
markets of the world of the lumber, wheat and other products
of the Dominion.

Or of any ships or other vessels.

See McDonell v. Bank of Upper Canada, 1850, 7 U.C.R.
252.

This prohibition is now subject to the provisions of sec. 85.

Goods, wares and merchandise.

One clause of this section forbids dealing in the buying, selling, etc., of goods. Another clause prohibits lending money on
their security. The clauses are subject to the provisions of secs.
86 to 90, as well as of sec. 80.

The expression "goods, wares and merchandise," is defined
by sec. 2(*f*) to include, in addition to the things usually understood thereby, timber, deals, boards, staves, saw-logs and other
timber, petroleum, crude oil and all agricultural produce and
other articles of commerce.

Debts are not included in goods, wares and merchandise, and
therefore a bank may take an assignment of a debt due to the
borrower from his co-partners. (Rennie v. Quebec Bank, 1902,
3 O.L.R. 541, at p. 545; cf. cases cited, *supra*, under "General
Banking Powers.")

77. The bank shall have a privileged lien, for any debt
or liability for any debt to the bank, on the shares of its own
capital stock, and on any unpaid dividends of the debtor or person liable, and may decline to allow any transfer of the shares
of such debtor or person until the debt is paid.

Sale of
shares.
2. The bank shall, within twelve months after the debt has accrued and become payable, sell such shares: Provided that notice shall be given to the holder of the shares of the intention of the bank to sell the same, by mailing the notice,

Notice.
in the post office, post paid, to the last known address of the holder, at least thirty days prior to the sale.

Transfer.
3. Upon the sale being made the president, vice-president, manager or cashier shall execute a transfer of the shares to the purchaser thereof in the usual transfer book of the bank.

Effect of
transfer.
4. Such transfer shall vest in the purchaser all the rights in or to the said shares which were possessed by the holder thereof, with the same obligation of warranty on his part as if he were the vendor thereof, but without any warranty from the bank or by the officer of the bank executing the transfer. 53 V., c. 31, s. 65.

Lien upon
debtor's
shares.
Under the Act of 1871 the lien of the bank upon a debtor's shares or unpaid dividends secured only an "overdue debt" to the bank (see Cook v. Royal Canadian Bank, 1873, 20 Gr. 1; cf. In re Stockton Malleable Iron Co., 1875, 2 Ch. D. 101). In 1880 the lien was extended so as to cover "any debt or liability for a debt" to the bank.

Cf. secs. 43 and 44, which impliedly preserve the bank's lien in case of attempted transfer by the debtor, or of a sale under a writ of execution, of the shares to which the lien extends.

Such lien may be discharged by a new arrangement between the bank and the debtor, the terms of which are incompatible with the retention of the lien or which shew an intention to waive it. (Bank of Africa v. Salisbury, [1892] A.C. 281.)

Section 76 forbids a bank to make an advance upon the security or pledge of shares of its own capital stock. The only safeguard against the bank's making an advance, ostensibly upon other security, but really upon the security of its lien upon such shares, appears to be the necessity of selling the shares within 12 months after the debt has accrued and become payable. The bank is by sec. 145 liable to a penalty, if it neglects to sell such shares within 12 months or if it sells them without 30 days' previous notice in writing to the holder of the shares.

As to the effect of the bank's representation in regard to the amount of its claims against a shareholder made to a person who purposes making a loan to a third party upon the security of shares of the bank, see Cook v. Royal Canadian Bank, *supra*. It is incumbent upon the person seeking the information to notify the person of whom the enquiry is made of the purpose for which the information is sought, in order that the latter may have the opportunity of making such investigation as will enable him to reply correctly and with due caution. Otherwise the enquirer is not entitled to act upon the representation made or bind by such representation the person making it, or his principal (*ibid.*).

General lien.

The bank also has in the absence of any inconsistent special agreement (In re Bowes, 1886, 33 Ch. D. 586), a general lien for all that is due to it from the customer. (Re Williams, 1903, 7 O.L.R. 156.)

The lien extends to all the securities and moneys of the cus- tomer in its hands which have not been deposited for a particu- lar purpose (Davis v. Bowsher, 1794, 5 T.R. 488; 2 R.R. 650; Brandao v. Barnett, 1864, 12 Cl. & F. 787; 69 R.R. 204; Riddell v. Bank of Upper Canada, 1859, 18 U.C.R. 139), but not to property merely deposited for safekeeping (Brandao v. Barnett; Leese v. Martin, 1873, L.R. 17 Eq. 224). In re London and Globe Finance Corporation, [1902] 2 Ch. 416, it was held that securities deposited with brokers, as cover for specific advances, but left in the brokers' hands after repayment, became liable to the general lien. Neither the general lien (Jeffryes v. Agra Bank, 1866, L.R. 2 Eq. 674), nor an express charge, can extend to further advances made after notice that the property sought to be charged belongs, or is mortgaged to, a third person. (London & County Bank v. Ratcliff, 1881, 6 App. Cas. 722; Bradford Banking Co. v. Briggs, 1886, 12 App. Cas. 29.)

The general lien exists only for debts due to the bank, whereas the statutory lien upon its own shares covers not only any debt, but also any liability for a debt.

Enforcement of lien.

A mere lien carries with it no right of sale. (Donald v. Suckling, 1866, L.R. 1 Q.B. 585, at p. 604.)

Sec. 77.   But the court may treat a mere deposit, *e.g.*, of share certifi-
Enforcement cates, as a mortgage, and foreclosure may be obtained (Harrold
of lien.   v. Plenty, [1901] 2 Ch. 314). In Brandao v. Barnett, *supra*,
Lord Campbell says the right acquired by a general lien is an
implied pledge, and a banker's lien is usually so treated.

In the case of the statutory lien, the bank has a right to sell
the shares at any time within twelve months after the debt has
accrued and become payable, subject to the condition as to notice
mentioned in the section. If the bank allows the twelve months
to elapse without exercising the power of sale, it would not only
become liable to a penalty under sec. 145, but it would then be
confined to the appropriate remedy given by provincial law. The
lien would still exist, but the statutory right of sale would be
gone.

Collateral   **78.** The stocks, bonds, debentures or securities, acquired and
securities
may be sold. held by the bank as collateral security, may, in case of default
in the payment of the debt, for the securing of which they were
so acquired and held, be dealt with, sold and conveyed, either
in like manner and subject to the same restrictions as are herein provided in respect of stock of the bank on which it has
acquired a lien under this Act, or in like manner as and subject
to the restrictions under which a private individual might in
like circumstances deal with, sell and convey the same: Provided that the bank shall not be obliged to sell within twelve
months.

Right of sale   2. The right so to deal with and dispose of such stock, bonds,
may be
waived.   debentures or securities in manner aforesaid may be waived or
varied by any agreement between the bank and the owner of
the stock, bonds, debentures or securities, made at the time at
which such debt was incurred, or, if the time of payment of the
debt has been extended, then by an agreement made at the time
of the extension. 53 V., c. 31, s. 66.

The bank has a right to realize security which matures before
the maturity of the debt secured and apply the proceeds in payment of the debt (see *supra*, p. 141). This section has reference
to the realization of securities after the maturity of the debt.

In the event of default in repayment of an advance made
upon the security of stock of corporations other than the bank
or upon other security, the bank has a power of sale similar to
that which it has in regard to shares of its own stock upon which
it has acquired a privileged lien under sec. 77, but without obligation to sell the same within 12 months. This obligation is
designed only to prevent a bank's dealing in its own stock as
prohibited by sec. 76.

See also sec. 80, which confers the same rights upon the bank
in regard to personal or movable property as in regard to real or
immovable property mortgaged or hypothecated to it. These
rights include the power to purchase or sell given by sec. 81.

When the purchasers of goods give promissory notes for the
price, and also hire receipts by which the property remains in
the vendor until payment is made, and the vendor or other holder
of the notes discounts them with a bank, the bank is entitled also
to the hire receipts. The receipts are merely securities accessory
to the debts represented by the notes, the bank not being able
effectually to recover on the notes until the hire receipts are
forthcoming. (Central Bank v. Garland, 1890, 20 O.R. 142,
affirmed 1891, 18 A.R. 438.)

A bank selling under the first part of this section merely
transfers the rights of the pledgor and a warranty of title by
him, but gives no such warranty itself (see sec. 77). The case is
different, however, when the bank sells pursuant to sec 89; see
notes to that section.

Section 78 in its present form dates from 1890, the part of
subsection 1 after the words "this Act" having been inserted
in that year. The effect of the amendment is to confirm the
general right of realizing securities which the bank has in common with other pledgees of personalty. (Donald v. Suckling,
1866, L.R. 1 Q.B. 585, at p. 604.) A pledge as distinguished from
a lien (see notes to sec. 77), enables the pledgee to sell on default
in payment, after notice to the pledgor. (Deverges v. Sandeman,
[1902] 1 Ch. at p. 593, and authorities there cited.)

The method of realization is subject to the contract made at
the time of the pledge. If the contract of pledge of stock to
secure an advance authorizes the bank, in the event of default,
to sell or dispose of the security without notice, and to apply the
proceeds in liquidation of the advance, a sale or loan of the

security before default made is tortious, and the pledgor may elect, either to claim damages, or to affirm the sale and claim profits made by the bank. One element of the measure of damages is the highest point of the stock market between the conversion and the first default. (Carnegie v. Federal Bank, 1884, 5 O.R. 418.)

Where the authority was "from time to time to sell the said securities—by giving 15 days' notice in one daily paper published in the city of Ottawa—with power to the bank to buy in and resell without being liable for any loss occasioned thereby," it was held that the power given was to sell by auction, and that the bank had no power to sell by private contract. (Toronto General Trusts v. Central Ontario, 1905, 10 O.L.R. 347.)

In making a sale of property mortgaged to it, the bank must exercise proper care and discretion, and adopt such means as would be adopted by a prudent man to get the best price obtainable. Otherwise it is liable to the mortgagor if it sells the property at a grossly inadequate price (Prentice v. Consolidated Bank, 1886, 13 A.R. 69). In order that the best price may be obtained, it is usually advisable to sell collateral securities by public sale. (Toronto General Trusts v. Central Ontario, *supra*, and authorities cited at pp. 352-3.)

79. The bank may acquire and hold real and immovable property for its actual use and occupation and the management of its business, and may sell or dispose of the same, and acquire other property in its stead for the same purpose. 53 V., c. 31, s. 67.

A power of the kind conferred by this section will be construed liberally. (Morse on Banks & Banking, 4th ed., 1903, sec. 74.)

Where a company was empowered to acquire and hold for the purpose of its business, real or immovable estate, not exceeding a certain sum in yearly value, it was held that the company acting in good faith must be the sole judge of what is required for the purpose of its business. (Montreal v. Robert, [1906] A.C. 196.)

80. The bank may take, hold and dispose of mortgages and *hypothèques* upon real or personal, immovable or movable property, by way of additional security for debts contracted to the bank in the course of its business.

2. The rights, powers and privileges which the bank is by this Act declared to have, or to have had, in respect of real or immovable property mortgaged to it, shall be held and possessed by it in respect of any personal or movable property which is mortgaged or hypothecated to the bank. 53 V., c. 31, s. 68.

This section was divided into sub-sections in 1906. In other respects it is a transcript of the provision contained in the Acts of 1867 and of 1871, except that the words "movable" and "immovable" have been added wherever they occur in the present section.

The section is one of the important exceptions to the prohibition of sec. 76 against lending on the security or mortgage of lands, ships or goods. The investment of the money of a bank in property of this description would have the effect of locking up the assets of the bank and making them unavailable either for mercantile purposes, or for the purposes of meeting claims of depositors and of redeeming notes, etc. The same objection does not apply when additional security is taken on such property after an advance has once been made (cf. Rennie v. Quebec Bank, 1902, 3 O.L.R. 541, and cases cited at p. 551). If the security taken is really *additional*, it may at least save the bank from ultimate loss.

Primarily "contracted in the course of its business" means contracted in the past, and refers to advances made or indebtedness incurred prior to the giving of the mortgage.

Sometimes, however, it is sought to support a mortgage which is taken contemporaneously with the discounting of a bill or note. In such a case it has been said that it would be a question of fact for the judge or jury to determine whether the mortgage was in truth taken to secure the transaction on the bill or note, or whether the bill or note was created for the mere purpose of upholding and giving colour to the mortgage—a question of fact upon which the conclusion would be in general so uncertain as to make the mortgage very doubtful security (Commercial Bank v.

Sec. 80.

Mortgage as additional security.

Bank of Upper Canada, 1859, 7 Gr. 430). In Bank of Toronto v. Perkins, 1882, 8 S.C.R. 603, it was decided that a mortgage made as collateral security for a note discounted by the bank, the proceeds of which were placed to the mortgagor's credit on the same day as that on which the mortgage was made, was invalid.

In the case of Re The Essex Land & Timber Co., Trout's Case, 1891, 21 O.R. 367, the facts briefly stated were as follows: One Trout had before the 27th of January, 1890, become responsible to the Bank of Montreal for the sum of $14,500 for the accommodation of a company of which he was president. About that date he was requested to become further responsible by an endorsement of the company's notes, which he agreed to do, upon receiving from the company a mortgage upon certain lands. The mortgage was conditioned upon the payment by the company of the notes. It was assigned to the bank prior to the endorsement of the notes or the payment of the advances by the bank. Held no violation of this section.

The giving of a mortgage by way of security against which the customer may draw, is not authorized by this section, but in the event of a conflict of evidence as to whether a mortgage was taken to secure past advances only, or future advances as well, the court will lean to the construction which will make the transaction a lawful one. (Royal Canadian Bank v. Cummer, 1869, 15 Gr. 627.)

The bank may take a valid mortgage as additional security for an existing indebtedness, although the effect is to enable the customer to obtain further advances. In one case such a mortgage provided that it should continue a security for the existing indebtedness and all renewals or substitutions therefor and all indebtedness of the customer in respect thereof. After the mortgage was given the customer's line of credit was increased, but no separate account was kept of the liabilities secured by the mortgage and these further advances. The proceeds of the discounts and cash deposits were carried to the customer's credit in one open current account against which he drew cheques to retire the notes secured by the mortgage as they matured. It was held that this mode of book-keeping had not operated as a discharge of the mortgage debt. (Cameron v. Kerr, 1878, 3 A.R. 30; cf. Royal Canadian Bank v. Cummer, *supra*; Moffatt v. Merchants Bank, 1884, 11 S.C.R. 46.)

If a bank holding a mortgage as additional security for the
payment of certain notes, substitutes for these notes renewals
from time to time, without, however, receiving actual payment,
the whole series of notes and renewals form links in the same
chain of liability which is secured by the mortgage. Although
as a matter of book-keeping, the bank may have treated the first
notes, and the subsequent substituted notes, as paid by the application of the proceeds from time to time of the renewals, there is
no payment in fact of the notes for which the mortgage was
given. (Dominion Bank v. Oliver, 1889, 17 O.R. 402, and cf.
Commercial Bank v. Bank of Upper Canada, *supra.*)

- If a mortgage given to a bank is invalid on account of being
security for future or contemporaneous advances in contravention of the Act, another mortgage upon the same or different property may be executed as additional security after the debt has
been contracted in the course of business or the advances made.
Such mortgage is perfectly good (Commercial Bank v. Bank of
Upper Canada, *supra*; Grant v. Banque Nationale, 1885, 9 O.R.
411, 423; and cf. National Bank of Australasia v. Cherry, 1870,
L.R. 3 P.C. 299).

The taking of collateral security by way of mortgage does not
effect a merger, or relieve the parties to any bills or notes from
meeting them according to their terms before the mortgage itself
comes due. If the bills or notes secured are renewed beyond
the term of the mortgage, the security is not enforceable until
the maturity of the bills or notes. (Molsons Bank v. McDonald,
1877, 2 A.R. 102.)

The property which may be mortgaged to the bank under this
section is described in the widest possible language and would
include any of the kinds of property referred to in sec. 76. It
has been held, for instance, that a bank may under this section
take a bill of sale of horses by way of additional security from
the owner of the horses, and may recover on promissory notes
made in its favour by a person who purchases the horses from
the owner. (Bank of Hamilton v. Donaldson, 1901, 13 Man. R.
378.)

A bank may take a mortgage of timber limits (Grant v.
Banque Nationale, 1885, 9 O.R. 411). It may take as security
the interest of a railway company in a contract for the construction of certain cars and may lease them to the company (Bank

Sec. 80.

Mortgage as
additional
security.

of Upper Canada v. Killaly, 1861, 21 U.C.R. 9). It may also take a mortgage of stock in trade and all future stock in trade to be acquired during the currency of the mortgage, and an assignment of book debts and an agreement to assign all future book debts of the business. (Gillies v. Commercial Bank, 1895, 10 Man. R. 460, 464.)

No special priority is given by this section to mortgages authorized by it. It allows mortgages to be taken by the bank under certain circumstances, but their validity and priority must be determined by provincial law.

Rights, powers and privileges.

Sub-section 2 seems to be strangely misplaced in its present position. It makes applicable to personal or movable property mortgaged to the bank the rights, powers and privileges which the bank has in regard to real or immovable property, *i.e.*, those given by secs. 81, 82, and 83.

Purchases of
realty.

81. The bank may purchase any lands or real or immovable property offered for sale,—

(a) under execution, or in insolvency, or under the order or decree of a court, as belonging to any debtor to the bank; or,

(b) by a mortgagee or other encumbrancer, having priority over a mortgage or other encumbrance held by the bank; or,

(c) by the bank under a power of sale given to it for that purpose;

in cases in which, under similar circumstances, an individual could so purchase, without any restriction as to the value of the property which it may so purchase, and may acquire a title thereto as any individual, purchasing at sheriff's sale, or under a power of sale, in like circumstances could do, and may take, have, hold and dispose of the same at pleasure. 53 V., c. 31, s. 69.

The original of this section was enacted by the Act of 1867, from which it was transcribed into the Act of 1871.

According to these Acts the execution under which the lands ^{Sec. 81.} were offered for sale must have been issued "at the suit of the Purchases of bank." This limitation was struck out by the Act of 1880, which realty. also added the words "or in insolvency, or under the order or decree of a court of equity, as belonging to any debtor to the bank." The section was enacted substantially in its present form in 1890, when the words "or offered for sale by a mortgagee or other encumbrancer having priority over a mortgage or other encumbrance held by the bank" were added.

The powers given by this section also extend to personalty: see sec. 80, and notes to sec. 78.

Reference must be had to provincial law in each case in order to ascertain the rights of an individual to purchase under any of the circumstances mentioned.

82. The bank may acquire and hold an absolute title in or Bank may to real or immovable property mortgaged to it as security for a acquire absolute debt due or owing to it, either by the obtaining of a release of title to the equity of redemption in the mortgaged property, or by pro- mortgaged curing a foreclosure, or by other means whereby, as between individuals, an equity of redemption can, by law, be barred, and may purchase and acquire any prior mortgage or charge on such property.

2. Nothing in any charter, Act or law shall be construed as No Act or ever having been intended to prevent or as preventing the bank law to prevent. from acquiring and holding an absolute title to and in any such mortgaged real or immovable property, whatever the value thereof, or from exercising or acting upon any power of sale contained in any mortgage given to or held by the bank, author- izing or enabling it to sell or convey away any property so mort- gaged. 53 V., c. 31, s. 71; 63-64 V., c. 26, s. 14.

Sub-section 1 dates from the Acts of 1867 and 1871.

The section resolves any question that might have existed as to the bank's power to foreclose a mortgage which had been law- fully taken (cf. Bank of Upper Canada v. Scott, 1858, 6 Gr. 451). If such power is expressly given by the terms of the mortgage it could be validly exercised without any assistance from the Act. (Bank of N.S.W. v. Campbell, 1886, 11 App. Cas. 192.)

Sec. 82.
Acquiring
absolute
title.
The right of a bank to sell in pursuance of a power of sale contained in a mortgage is impliedly recognized by sec. 81.

The powers given by this section extend also to personalty—see sec. 80.

Where no express power of sale is contained in the mortgage, the right nevertheless is implied by law in the case of a mortgage of personalty. (Deverges v. Sandeman, [1902] 1 Ch. at p. 593, cited in notes to sec. 66.)

Sub-section 2 is a transcript of provisions contained in the Acts of 1867 and 1871. It confers no power to acquire or sell lands, but provides that nothing in any charter Act or law is to be construed as having prevented or as preventing the bank from acquiring, etc., or exercising any power of sale, etc.

Property to
be sold with-
in certain
time.
83. No bank shall hold any real or immovable property, howsoever acquired, except such as is required for its own use, for any period exceeding seven years from the date of the acquisition thereof, or any extension of such period as in this section provided, and such property shall be absolutely sold or disposed of, within such period or extended period, as the case may be, so that the bank shall no longer retain any interest therein unless by way of security.

Extension of
time.
2. The Treasury Board may direct that the time for the sale or disposal of any such real or immovable property shall be extended for a further period or periods, not to exceed five years.

Twelve
years.
3. The whole period during which the bank may so hold such property under the foregoing provisions of this section shall not exceed twelve years from the date of the acquisition thereof.

Property not
sold liable to
forfeiture.
4. Any real or immovable property, not required by the bank for its own use, held by the bank for a longer period than authorized by the foregoing provisions of this section shall be liable to be forfeited to His Majesty for the use of the Dominion of Canada: Provided that,—

Proviso.
(a) no such forfeiture shall take effect until the expiration of at least six calendar months after notice in writing to

the bank by the Minister of the intention of His Majesty   Sec. 83
to claim the forfeiture; and,

(*b*) the bank may, notwithstanding such notice, before the
forfeiture is effected sell or dispose of the property free
from liability to forfeiture.

5. The provisions of this section shall apply to any real or Provisions
immovable property heretofore acquired by the bank and held apply to
realty now
by it at the time of the coming into force of this Act. 63-64 V., held.
c. 26, s. 14.

Sub-section 1 down to and including "seven years from the
date of the acquisition thereof" dates from 1880. The remainder
of the section was added in 1900. The division into the present
sub-sections was made in 1906.

Prior to the last mentioned date, the section constituted one Property to
section with sub-sec. 1 of sec. 82. The words "howsoever acquired" be sold
refer to the acquiring of the absolute title in any of the ways within a
certain
mentioned in sec. 82. The seven years' limitation begins to run time after
from the getting in of the absolute title, not from the taking of acquiring
absolute
the security. title.

The limitation is a safeguard against investments of too
great permanence; cf. notes to sec. 76.

Previous to 1900 there was an absolute prohibition against
holding for a longer period than 7 years, but no provision as to
sale or forfeiture of the property. By the amended section the
bank must sell the property so as no longer to retain any interest
therein unless by way of security (*i.e.*, for the purchase price);
but the Treasury Board has power to extend the time for sale for
a further period or periods not exceeding in all five years, beyond the original seven. If a bank holds property beyond
the period authorized by the Act, the property does not become
ipso facto forfeited, but the Finance Minister by giving six
months' notice may cause a forfeiture unless the property is sold
before the expiration of such six months.

Probably under the Act as it existed prior to 1900 the title
to lands held beyond the authorized period would have remained
in the bank, subject to any right of entry or defeasance which the
Crown might possess. (McDiarmid v. Hughes, 1888, 16 O.R.
570.)

Sec. 84.
Loans on
standing
timber.

84. The bank may lend money upon the security of standing timber, and the rights or licenses held by persons to cut or remove such timber. 63-64 V., c. 26, s. 16.

This section was added to the Act in 1900.

A timber limit or the right or license to cut timber has been held to be personal property (Bennett v. O'Meara, 1868, 15 Gr. 396; but see Grant v. Banque Nationale, 1885, 9 O.R. 411, where a timber limit seems to be regarded as land). The standing timber itself would be real property as part of the land upon which it stands, and a mortgage thereof would, apart from this section, be within the prohibition of section 76. The effect of the amendment is that standing timber and the rights or licenses held by persons to cut or remove such timber may be the subject of mortgage or a pledge to the bank and such mortgage or pledge is not confined to the case mentioned in sec. 80, that is it need not be "by way of *additional* security for debts contracted to the bank in the course of its business." It may be to secure contemporaneous or future advances. The mortgage of standing timber must be registered in accordance with provincial law in order to preserve its priority, and it must contain a sufficient description of the lands for the purpose of registration. The assignment or pledge of a timber limit must conform to the regulations of the proper government department, and must be registered with, or notice thereof must be given to such department in accordance with such regulations (cf. Grant v. Banque Nationale, *supra*.)

As to
advances for
building
ships.

85. Every bank advancing money in aid of the building of any ship or vessel shall have the same right of acquiring and holding security upon such ship or vessel, while building and when completed, either by way of mortgage, *hypothèque*, hypothecation, privilege or lien thereon, or purchase or transfer thereof, as individuals have in the province wherein the ship or vessel is being built.

Rights and
obligations.

2. The bank may, for the purpose of obtaining and enforcing such security, avail itself of all such rights and means, and shall

be subject to all such obligations, limitations and conditions, as Sec. 85. are, by the law of such province, conferred or imposed upon individuals making such advances.   53 V., c. 31, s. 72.

This section forms an exception to sec. 76, which prohibits the Advances on security of ships. lending of money upon the security of any ships or other vessels.

Secs. 80 and 85, being read together, permit a bank to acquire and hold security upon a ship, (1) for the repayment of advances made in aid of the building of the ship, (2) by way of additional security for any debt contracted to the bank in the course of its business.

In the first case the power is limited to security for advances made for a specific purpose, in the second case the power is limited to additional security.   In both cases the rights of the bank are the same as those of individuals taking similar security uuder provincial law.

CHAPTER XVI

WAREHOUSE RECEIPTS, ETC., AS COLLATERAL SECURITY.

Review of earlier legislation.

Sec. 86.
(P. 167.)
Prior to 1859 the rights of banks in the late province of Canada to acquire bills of lading and warehouse receipts as securities for advances depended upon the general law affecting private individuals and upon the provisions of the charter of each bank.

Receipt by warehouse-man, etc.
An Act of 1859 entitled an Act Granting Additional Facilities in Commercial Transactions (consolidated as Chapter 54 of C.S.C., 1859), contemplated the giving of a bill of lading, specification of timber or receipt by a warehouseman, miller, wharfinger, master of a vessel, or carrier, for cereal grains, goods, wares or merchandise, stored or deposited, or to be stored or deposited, in any warehouse, mill-cove (sic), or other place in the province, or shipped in any vessel, or delivered to any carrier for carriage, and provided that such receipt, etc., when endorsed to a bank by the owner or person entitled to receive such cereal grains, etc., as collateral security for the due payment of any bill of exchange or note discounted by such bank in the regular course of its business, should vest in the bank all the right and title of the endorser, subject to the right of the endorser to have the receipt re-transferred to him if such bill, note or debt were paid when due.

Under this statute, it was held that the warehouseman, etc., giving the receipt must be a person occupying the position of bailee of the goods of which he was not himself the owner.

In 1861 the consolidated statute was amended so as to permit a warehouseman, etc., who was at the same time the owner of, (or entitled otherwise than as warehouseman, etc., to receive), cereal grains, etc., to give a receipt for the same and endorse the receipt, such receipt to be as valid and effectual for the purpose of the Act as if the person giving and endorsing the receipt were not one and the same person.

The effect of the amendment was to introduce, for the first time, the principle that the owner of goods might practically give the bank a mortgage upon his goods in the form of a ware- Sec. 86. house receipt. The persons entitled to do this, however, were (P. 167.) confined to the five classes mentioned in the Act of 1859 above Review of cited, and the receipt must have been given in the capacity of legislation. warehouseman, etc., otherwise it was of no value as a transfer of property. (Royal Canadian Bank v. Ross, 1877, 40 U.C.R. at p. 473.)

In 1865 the class of persons who might endorse a warehouse Receipt by receipt was extended so as to allow of its being given by the agent of attorney or agent of the owner. This provision was, however, owner. subsequently limited by the Act of 1871, which enacted that the receipt, etc., endorsed to the bank should vest in the bank "all the right and title of the last previous holder thereof, and if such holder be the agent of the owner within the meaning of the fifty-ninth chapter of the Consolidated Statutes of the late Province of Canada, then all the right and title of the owner thereof."

In 1880 the language of the previous Act was considerably changed. Warehouse receipt was defined to mean any receipt given by any person for any goods, wares and merchandise in his actual visible and continued possession, as bailee, in good faith, and not as of his own property, and also to include a receipt given by the keeper of any harbour, cove, pond, wharf, yard, warehouse, shed, storehouse, tannery, mill or other place in Canada, for goods, wares and merchandise, being in the place or in one or more of the places so kept by him, whether such person is engaged in other business or not, and to include specifications of timber. Bill of lading was declared to comprise all receipts for goods, wares and merchandise, accompanied by an obligation to transport the same from the place where they were received to some other place, whether by land or water, or partly by land or partly by water, and by any mode of carriage whatever.

The Act contained provisions similar to those of 1859, as amended in 1871, vesting in the bank upon endorsement of such warehouse receipt or bill of lading, all the right and title of the previous holder or owner (including the case where the previous holder is the owner's agent), and also, in amendment of the previous statutes, provided for the vesting in the bank of all the right and title of the person from whom the goods, etc., were received or acquired by the bank, if the receipt or bill of lading is made directly in favour of the bank, instead of to the previous holder or owner.

Review of earlier legislation.
The Act of 1880 likewise enumerated the privileged classes of occupations, in which, if a person were engaged, as his ostensible business, he might grant a receipt or a bill of lading directly to the bank upon his own goods, such receipt to have the same effect as if the owner or the person giving the receipt or bill of lading, were different persons.

We have seen that this privileged group of persons was first created in 1861. The list of such persons was gradually extended in 1865, 1871, 1872, 1880 and 1888, by the addition in each of the years mentioned of persons engaged in certain named occupations.

The power thus given to certain classes of persons in effect to give a mortgage upon their goods direct to the bank, was authorized by the legislature by means of a fiction: namely, by permitting such persons, as warehousemen, to issue receipts to themselves as owners, acknowledging that they had certain goods in their possession to their own order, and then, as owners, to endorse such receipts to a bank—a fiction that was only slightly disguised when the transaction took the form of a receipt from the owner direct to the bank.

Security in form of Schedule C.
In 1890 the law was greatly changed in form, though not in substance. The bank was still authorized to acquire and hold a warehouse receipt or bill of lading as collateral security, provided the goods mentioned in such receipt or bill of lading were in the possession of the person giving it as bailee in good faith and not as of his own property. But the right of the owners of goods to use the fiction of a warehouse receipt or bill of lading as a means of obtaining advances upon such goods was abolished, this right having been considerably abused (see Royal Canadian Bank v. Ross, *supra*).

Instead, a new form of security was authorized by sec. 74 of the Act of 1890 (now sec. 88). The privilege of pledging the pledger's own goods for advances was no longer limited to certain named classes, but any person engaged in business as a wholesale manufacturer of goods, wares and merchandise, and any wholesale purchaser or shipper of products of agriculture, the forest and mine, or the sea, lake and rivers, and any wholesale purchaser or shipper of live stock or dead stock and the products thereof, was authorized to give to the bank security as mentioned in the Act.

In regard to the purpose for which a bank might take a ware- *Purpose for which receipt may be taken.* house receipt or bill of lading, the Act of 1871 enabled the bank to acquire and hold such documents not only for the due payment of any bill or note discounted by the bank in the regular course of its banking business, (as provided in the Act of 1859), but also "for any debt which might become due to the bank under any credit opened or liability incurred by the bank for or on behalf of the holder or owner of such bill of lading, etc., or for any other debt to become due to the bank." In 1880, however, the right of the bank was confined to holding these documents as "collateral security for the payment of any debt incurred in its favour in the course of its banking business."

This provision was carried into the Bank Act of 1890 and remained unchanged until 1900, when the words "or as security for any liability incurred by it for any person" were added.

86. The bank may acquire and hold any warehouse receipt *Warehouse receipts and bills of lading.* or bill of lading as collateral security for the payment of any debt incurred in its favour, or as security for any liability incurred by it for any person, in the course of its banking business.

2. Any warehouse receipt or bill of lading so acquired shall *Effect of taking.* vest in the bank, from the date of the acquisition thereof,—

    (*a*) all the right and title to such warehouse receipt or bill of lading and to the goods covered thereby of the previous holder or owner thereof; or,

    (*b*) all the right and title to the goods, wares and merchandise mentioned therein of the person from whom the same were received or acquired by the bank, if the warehouse receipt or bill of lading is made directly in favour of the bank, instead of to the previous holder or owner of such goods, wares and merchandise. 53 V., c. 31, s. 73; 63-64 V., c. 26, s. 15.

This section prior to 1906 constituted one section with sec. 87. It was divided into its present sub-sections in that year.

This section and sec. 88 must be read subject to the provisions of sec. 90. They are both important exceptions to the provisions of sec. 76, which forbid a bank to lend money or make advances upon the security of any goods, wares and merchandise.

The bank may acquire.

The method of acquiring is not prescribed. A warehouse receipt or bill of lading may be transferred either by delivery, after endorsement in blank (Bank of Hamilton v. Noye, 1885, 9 O.R. 631), or by special endorsement to the bank. If the document at the time of delivery to the bank has not been endorsed by the person in whose favour it is, the omission could doubtless be supplied subsequently. Sec. 87 speaks of such a document being transferred either by endorsement or by delivery.

But the absence of the endorsement puts the bank upon enquiry, and the mere delivery of the document to the bank by the person who has possession of it will not by itself affect the outstanding interest of the person in whose favour the document is made out. (Gosselin v. Ontario Bank, 1905, 36 S.C.R. 407.)

Legislative power.

The question of legislative power in regard to warehouse receipts is discussed in the notes to sec. 88.

Warehouse receipt.

Warehouse receipt as used in this Act is defined by sec. 2(g).

A statement of the place where the goods are stored is not essential to the bank's security.

Inasmuch as the present Act, (unlike the Acts in force prior to 1890), does not provide for a warehouseman, etc., who is also the owner of goods giving a receipt to the bank upon such goods, it would seem to follow that if a person, though apparently a warehouseman, were really the owner of the goods mentioned in the receipt issued by him, such receipt would not afford to the bank any security as against execution creditors or others not claiming through the owner. A banker, before making an advance upon the security of a warehouse receipt, ought to satisfy himself that the receipt has been issued by a person whose possession is actual, visible and continuous, and who is himself a bailee in good faith.

The definition of warehouse receipt discriminates between Sec. 86. three classes of receipts, namely:

1. A receipt given by any person for goods in his actual vis- Warehouse ible and continued possession as bailee thereof in good faith and receipt. not as of his own property.

2. A receipt given by any person who is the owner or keeper of a warehouse, etc., or other place for the storage of goods, for goods delivered to him as bailee, and actually in the place or one of the places owned or kept by him, whether he is engaged in other business or not.

3. A receipt given by any person in charge of logs or timber in transit from timber limits or other lands to their place of destination.

It has been said that the same sort of proof is not required in the case of a warehouseman giving such receipts as in the case of a mere bailee of the goods. If a receipt is issued by a ware-houseman, the test of its validity does not necessarily depend upon proof that he was actually, visibly and continuously in possession. (Boyd, C., in Re Monteith, 1886, 10 O.R. at p. 540; but see judgment of Proudfoot, J., in the same case at p. 549, and note that the wording of the present Act is slightly differ-ent from that of the Act of 1880 under which that case arose.)

In giving effect to the transfer of vouchers of the class of warehouse receipts, the legislature has added a mode of trans-ferring personal property to those previously known to the law. The legislation which permits a change of property to be effected by the endorsement of the receipt of the custodian of the pro-perty, does not ignore the principle of the Bills of Sale Acts, because it deals only with property which is out of the actual possession of its owner. Similarly when the owner, under form-er Acts, now repealed, was in some cases enabled to give his own receipt as security, that power was extended only to an owner who was engaged in the calling of a warehouseman, etc., and who gave receipts in his capacity as such.

But the attempt to transfer the property by transfer of warehouse receipt while retaining the actual possession, is not authorized by this section. (Cf. Milloy v. Kerr, 1878, 3 A.R. at p. 368, S.C. affirmed, 8 S.C.R. 474.) See, however, sec. 88, which does authorize a transfer which conflicts directly with the principle of the Bills of Sales Acts.

It has been said that the words of the definition are aimed against the "casual creation of a warehouseman for a temporary purpose." (Moss, C.J.A., in Milloy v. Kerr, 1878, 3 A.R. at p. 360.)

While, however, the possession must not be fictitious and the premises in which the goods are stored must be kept by the bailee *bonâ fide* (Re Monteith, 1885, 10 O.R. 529), it is not strictly necessary that the premises must be kept by him for the purpose of warehousing goods in general, or the goods mentioned in the receipt in particular. A receipt granted by any person who has actual possession in the sense of the Act, and who is not the owner, is valid whether he keeps a warehouse or not, *e.g.*, if a person puts some furniture in his neighbour's house and takes a receipt in proper form, that is a warehouse receipt under the Act, though not, perhaps, a desirable banking security.

In Ontario Bank v. O'Reilly, 1906, 12 O.L.R. 420, a storage and warehouse firm consisted of A. and B., and a commission and produce firm consisted of A., B. and C. The commission firm purchased goods and warehoused them with the storage firm. A. issued receipts in the name of the storage firm to C., as representing the commission firm. The receipts were endorsed by C. to the plaintiff bank as security for notes discounted. It was held that A., in signing such receipts, was not in any sense giving receipts "as of his own property" within the meaning of sec. 2 of the Bank Act, the two firms being distinct entities, which, since the Judicature Act, were capable of maintaining an action at law one against the other.

A warehouse receipt within the Act could not formerly be given to a bank for logs or timber in transit from the woods where they were cut to the mill, because they were not actually in a place owned or kept by the warehouseman, etc. (Tennant v. Union Bank, 19 A.R. 4, 13, S.C., [1894] A.C. 31), but in 1900 the definition of warehouse receipt was enlarged so as to include receipts given by any person in charge of logs or timber in transit from timber limits or other lands to their place of destination.

On the other hand lumber stored in a millyard is in a place "kept by" the miller within the Act (*ibid.* 14).

Except as noted above, the section in its present form dates from 1890. Specifications of timber are included in the term warehouse receipt under the Act of 1880, but not under the present Act.

Bill of lading.

See notes to sec. 2(h). A bill of lading is defined as follows: "bill of lading" includes all receipts for goods, wares or merchandise, accompanied by an undertaking to transport the same from the place where they were received to some other place, by any mode of carriage whatever, whether by land or water, or partly by land and partly by water.

Collateral security.

As to the meaning of collateral security and the obligation of the lender, on payment of the debt secured, to return or account for the property taken as security, see notes to sec. 76.

On the re-endorsement and delivery of a receipt by the bank, the pledgor is in as of his former title, not as assignee of the bank with the rights given to the latter by the Bank Act. (Mason v. Great Western Ry., 1871, 31 U.C.R. 73).

For any debt . . . or liability incurred.

The debt or liability must be incurred either contemporaneously with the taking of the security or upon a written promise or agreement, etc. See sec. 90.

It is not essential that the borrower should be the owner or holder of the warehouse receipt. The bank may acquire it as collateral security for him from a third person, or the receipt may be issued to a third person for the purpose of being endorsed by him to the bank. (Tennant v. Union Bank, 19 A.R. at p. 6; S.C. [1894] A.C. 31.)

The bank may acquire the receipt from a previous private lender, in which case such lender might be regarded either as the "previous holder" or, the transfer being made at the request of and for the owner, as the agent of the owner.

or as security for any liability incurred by it for any person. .

These words, added in 1900, permit a bank to take security under this section for any liability incurred, that is, for that

Sec. 86.   which will or may result in a debt as, for instance, in the case of a letter of credit issued by the bank, where no money actually passes from the bank to the customer at the time the liability is incurred, but the credit of the bank is pledged to payment at a future time.

As security for liability.   The distinction between a debt and a liability is well known to the law; a liability of a guarantor, for instance, becomes a debt only when ·default is made by the principal debtor (cf. Cockburn v. Sylvester, 1877, 1 A.R. 471).

Shall vest in the bank.

Effect of taking of warehouse receipt.   The property in the goods passes to the bank with the risk of loss, so that if an insurance policy is subject to a condition that the insurance must be in the name of the owner, the bank must be named as the assured (McBride v. Gore Insurance Co., 1870, 30 U.C.R. 451), although the assignor also has an insurable interest in the goods (Parsons v. Queen Insurance Co., 1878, 29 C.P. 188).

The bank as owner is entitled to take possession of the goods whenever it deems it advisable. If the assignor refuses to give possession of the goods upon demand, the bank may take such appropriate proceedings under the law of the province where the goods are situated as any other owner of goods may take in the case of goods wrongfully detained by another person, and can follow the goods to the same extent as any such owner. The person withholding possession from the bank is also liable to a penalty (sec. 144).

The bank as pledgee of a bill of lading may return it to the pledgor for a limited purpose, (as for instance, to enable the pledgor to obtain delivery and sell on behalf of the pledgee, and account for the proceeds towards satisfaction of the debt), without thereby losing its rights under the contract of pledge. (North-Western Bank v. Poynter, [1895] A.C. 56; Inglis v. Robertson, [1898] A.C. 616, 626.) The fact that the bank endorses the bill of lading to the consignee in order to enable him to examine the goods does not transfer the right of property in them to the consignee, and if the latter deals with the goods as his own by re-shipping and selling them, he becomes liable to the bank, in an action for conversion for the goods or their value. (Imperial Bank v. Hull, 1901, 4 Terr. L.R. 498, varied 5 Terr. L.R. 313.)

From the date of its acquisition.

If the receipt is a security taken in conformity with the Priority of Act, the time of its acquisition is the test of its priority over security. an assignment or mortgage of the same goods to another party. If the provincial law requires a chattel mortgage or bill of sale to be registered in order to be valid as against creditors or a subsequent assignee or mortgagee for value without notice, then the taking of the receipt by the bank in good faith gives the bank priority over an unregistered assignment or mortgage of any date whatsoever. If by provincial law an assignment or mortgage is valid without registration as against creditors, etc., or has been registered in accordance with provincial law (Traders Bank v. Brown, 1889, 18 O.R. 430), priority of delivery is the sole test.

It is of course quite possible that innocent persons may suffer, but the doctrine of the Bills of Sale Acts is more infringed upon in theory than in practice by the Bank Act. The general practice which prevails on the part of the banks of making advances to wholesale manufacturers, dealers, etc., for the purpose of enabling them to carry forward their enterprises until the products are put on the market, is well known. Therefore, a private individual who proposes to make an advance to a wholesale manufacturer, dealer, etc., may be said to have notice that the raw products are probably pledged to the dealer's banker.

See sec. 89, sub-sec. 2.

Equitable title.

In Dominion Bank v. Davidson, 1885, 12 A.R. 90, a bank advanced money for the purchase of goods upon the security of the shipping receipt and then, in return for the purchaser's receipt and undertaking to sell the property and collect the proceeds and deposit same in the bank, (the purchaser thereby acknowledging himself to be bailee of the goods for the bank), returned the shipping receipt to the purchaser. The purchaser received the goods from the carriers and warehoused them, taking in his own name warehouse receipts, which he endorsed to the bank, the bank then giving up the bailee receipt. It was held that no property in the goods had passed to the purchaser when the bank made the advance, and the bank was therefore entitled at least as equitable owner, as against

Sec. 86. execution creditors of the purchaser. See also Cameron v. Perrin, 1887, 14 A.R. 565, 576.

Previous holder or owner.

A previous holder may be either a previous lender on the security of the same goods, or a person to whom the receipt or bill of lading is issued, to be by him endorsed to the bank (see *supra,* p. 171), or a person who comes within one of the classes mentioned in sec. 87.

The bank has no other or higher right than the consignor. (Imperial Bank v. Hull, 1901, 4 Terr. L.R. 498, S.C. 5 Terr. L. R. 313.)

If the warehouse receipt or bill of lading is made directly in favour of the bank.

This clause impliedly authorizes the receipt to be made direct to the bank, instead of its being made to the previous holder or owner and by him endorsed to the bank. It is preferable, however, to have the document in the form of a receipt to the bailor or shipper and that the bank should acquire it by endorsement in the usual way.

Under the original Act of 1859, which provided for a receipt, etc., being transferred to the bank by endorsement, it was held that a receipt could not be given direct to the bank within the Act. (Royal Canadian Bank v. Miller, 1870, 29 U.C.R. 266, and other cases.) The contrary was held under the Act of 1871, which authorized the bank to acquire such receipt without specifying the manner. (Merchants Bank v. Smith, 1884, 8 S.C.R. 512.)

Goods, wares and merchandise.

These words are defined by sec. 2(*f*), and see notes to sec. 76.

The transfer of the receipt, etc., vests in the bank only the particular goods mentioned in such receipt, and not goods substituted for such goods. (Llado v. Morgan, 1874, 23 C.P. 517.) Cf., however, sub-sec. 2 of sec. 88, as to goods substituted in cases within that sub-section, and see sub-sec. 1 of sec. 89, as to goods manufactured or produced from the goods covered by a receipt, etc.

If the person who gives the receipt fails to keep the goods *Sec. 86.* mentioned therein separate and distinguishable from other goods and sells some of them, so that he no longer has a sufficient quantity in all to answer the quantity mentioned in the receipt, the bank is, perhaps, entitled to hold all the goods in store of the kind mentioned in the receipt. (Smith v. Merchants Bank, 1881, 28 Gr. 629, and cases cited at p. 639; S.C. 8 S.C.R. 512.)

It has been said that if, after a wrongful commingling of *Goods, wares* goods, the receiptor indicates certain goods as equivalent to, and *and* partly the same as, those covered by the receipt, the bank is *merchandise.* entitled to such goods. (Bank of Hamilton v. Noye, 1885, 9 O. R. 631; cf. Banque d'Hochelaga v. Merchants Bank, 1895, 10 Man. R. 361.)

As to realization of security, see sec. 89, sub-sec. 3.

Sec. 143 renders it a criminal offence to make any false statement in any warehouse receipt, etc., given to a bank under this section.

87. If the previous holder of such warehouse receipt or bill *When* of lading is any person,— *previous holder is an*

(*a*) entrusted with the possession of the goods, wares and *agent.* merchandise mentioned therein, by or by the authority of the owner thereof; or,

(*b*) to whom such goods, wares and merchandise are, by or by the authority of the owner thereof, consigned; or,

(*c*) who, by or by the authority of the owner of such goods, wares and merchandise, is possessed of any bill of lading, receipt, order or other document covering the same, such as is used in the course of business as proof of the possession or control of goods, wares and merchandise, or as authorizing or purporting to authorize, either by endorsement or by delivery, the possessor of such a document to transfer or receive the goods, wares and merchandise thereby represented;

the bank shall be, upon the acquisition of such warehouse receipt or bill of lading, vested with all the right and title of the owner of such goods, wares and merchandise, subject to the right of

Sec. 87.   the owner to have the same transferred to him if the debt or
liability, as security for which such warehouse receipt or bill of
lading is held by the bank, is paid.

Presumption   2. Any person shall be deemed to be the possessor of such
of
possession.   goods, wares and merchandise, bill of lading, receipt, order or
other document as aforesaid,—

    (a) who is in actual possession thereof; or,

    (b) for whom, or subject to whose control, the same are held
by any person.   53 V., c. 31, s. 73; 63-64 V., c. 26, s. 15.

Agent of the   We have seen (see review of earlier legislation at the begin-
owner.   ning of this chapter) that the Act of 1871 included in the term
"previous holder" an agent of the owner within the meaning
of C.S.C. 1859, c. 59, (a statute founded on the English Factors
Acts and being the predecessor of Article 1740 of the Civil Code
of Lower Canada and of the Ontario Act entitled an Act respecting Contracts in relation to Goods entrusted to Agents, R.S.O.,
1897, c. 150).   In the Bank Act of 1880, also, the Consolidated
Statute was referred to in regard to the meaning of agent, but
in the Revised Statutes of 1886 the reference to C.S.C., c. 59 was
omitted and a definition of agent was substituted.   This definition was carried into the Act of 1890 with little modification.

Sub-secs. 2 and 3 of sec. 73 of the last mentioned Act are as
follows:

"2. If the previous holder of such warehouse receipt or bill
of lading is the agent of the owner of the goods, wares and merchandise mentioned therein, the bank shall be vested with all
the right and title of the owner thereof, subject to his right to
have the same re-transferred to him, if the debt, as security for
which they are held by the bank, is paid:

"3. In this section the expression agent means any person
intrusted with the possession of goods, wares and merchandise,
or to whom the same are consigned, or who is possessed of any
bill of lading, receipt, order or other document used in the course
of business as proof of the possession or control of goods, wares
and merchandise, or authorizing or purporting to authorize,
either by indorsement or by delivery, the possessor of such document to transfer or receive the goods, wares and merchandise
thereby represented; and such person shall be deemed the pos-

sessor of such goods, wares and merchandise, bill of lading, re- Sec. 87.
ceipt, order or other document as aforesaid, as well if the same
are held by any person for him or subject to his control as if
he is in actual possession thereof.''

In the revision of 1906 these two sub-sections were re-enacted
as a separate section (87), the clauses being re-arranged. The
new section contains all the elements of the former definition of
agent, but the word agent itself is omitted.

The terms of sec. 87, and of the definition of agent in the Goods
Act of 1890 are wider than those of the Consolidated Statute pledged by
and of the Factors Acts, and decisions must be read with due re- agent of
gard to the differences in wording. An agent under the Act of owner.
1890, or the person referred to in sec.87 of the present Act, means
(1) Any person entrusted with the possession of goods, wares
and merchandise; (2) or to whom the same are consigned; (3)
or who is possessed of (not ''entrusted with the possession of''
as in the Factors Acts), a bill of lading or other document of
title as mentioned in the Act, whether the goods are in his actual possession or only held by another person for him or subject to his control. The Act contains no provision similar to
that of the Factors Acts with regard to the effect of notice to the
pledgee of the fact of the pledgor's being only an agent or of
his want of authority to make a pledge.

The words of the Act seem wide and general, but, perhaps
all that was intended was to import the provisions of the Factors Acts into the Bank Act, and to give the same protection
(subject to the differences in wording above noted) to the bank
dealing with an agent as is given to other persons dealing in
good faith with him. (Cf. Tennant v. Union Bank, 1892, 19 A.
R. at p. 29; S.C., [1894] A.C. 31.)

If this is a correct view of the law, then it will be held that
an agent under the Bank Act must be an agent of that class,
which like factors, have a business, which, when carried to its
legitimate result, would properly end in selling or receiving payment for goods. (Cole v. North Western Bank, 1875, L.R.
10 C.P. 354; City Bank v. Barrow, 5 App. Cas. at 678; Bush v.
Fry, 1888, 15 O.R. 122, and cases cited.)

So far as the power of an agent under the Factors Acts to
pledge goods in his possession is concerned, the controlling word
is ''entrusted.'' It imports that confidence has been reposed in
the agent by the principal—the owner of the goods—and that

Sec. 87.   the possession of the goods, at the particular time and in the particular way they are in the hands of the agent, is intended and contemplated by the owner. If the possession has been obtained in violation of instructions or by means of a breach of faith, the goods are not "entrusted" within the Act. (Moshier v. Keenan, 1900, 31 O.R. at p. 660, and cases cited.)

Goods pledged by agent of owner.   But the' power of an agent who is consignee of goods or one who is possessed of the bill of lading or other document of title, to pledge such goods is not, so far as the bank is concerned, subject to any requirement that the goods must be entrusted to him by the owner. The mere fact that the agent is the consignee, or has possession of the bill of lading or other document of title is sufficient to give the bank a valid title by transfer from him.

Under the Factors Acts a document of title to goods may be safely taken by way of pledge from one known to be an agent without any enquiry as to his authority. (London Joint Stock Bank v. Simmons, [1892] A.C. at p. 217.) The same is doubtless true under the Bank Act, but it is possible that such a pledge would be valid only if it is taken in good faith, and without notice that the agent making the same has no authority to do so or that he is acting *mala fide* against the owner of the goods, notwithstanding the omission from the Bank Act of the words to this effect in the Factors Acts.

The general rule at common law was that a person in possession of goods could not confer on another, either by sale or pledge, any better title to the goods than he had himself. (Farquharson v. King, [1901] 2 K.B. at p. 715.)

If an agent within the Act pledges goods to one person for a debt which does not exhaust the whole value of the goods, they are still in his control, being held by the pledgee "for him and subject to his control," to the extent to which they are not exhausted by the pledge, and subject to such pledge they may be further pledged to a bank under this section. (Portalis v. Tetley, 1867, L.R. 5 Eq. 140.)

Loans to wholesale shippers or dealers.   **88.** The bank may lend money to any wholesale purchaser or shipper of or dealer in products of agriculture, the forest, quarry and mine, or the sea, lakes and rivers, or to any wholesale purchaser or shipper of or dealer in live stock or dead stock and the products thereof, upon the security of such products, or of such live stock or dead stock and the products thereof. _{Sec. 88. Upon security.}

2. The bank may allow the goods, wares and merchandise covered by such security to be removed and other goods, wares and merchandise, such as mentioned in the last preceding sub-section, to be substituted therefor, if the goods, wares and merchandise so substituted are of substantially the same character, and of substantially the same value as, or of less value than, those for which they have been so substituted; and the goods, wares and merchandise so substituted shall be covered by such security as if originally covered thereby. _{Removal of goods. Substitution.}

3. The bank may lend money to any person engaged in business as a wholesale manufacturer of any goods, wares and mechandise, upon the security of the goods, wares and merchandise manufactured by him, or procured for such manufacture. _{Loans to wholesale manufacturers. Security.}

4. Any such security, as mentioned in the foregoing provisions of this section, may be given by the owner of said goods, wares and merchandise, stock or products. _{Owner may give the security.}

5. The security may be taken in the form set forth in schedule C to this Act, or to the like effect. _{Form of security.}

6. The bank shall, by virtue of such security, acquire the same rights and powers in respect to the goods, wares and merchandise, stock or products covered thereby, as if it had acquired the same by virtue of a warehouse receipt. 53 V., c. 31, s. 74; 63-64 V., c. 26, s. 17. _{Same rights as upon warehouse receipts.}

This section reproduces the effect of sec. 74 of the Act of 1890, as amended by sec. 17 of the Act of 1900. The present subdivision, however, dates from 1906. It will be convenient, for the purpose of referring to the earlier statutes, to note that the sub-sections of the present Act are derived as follows: sub-sec. 1 from sub-sec. 2 (1890), as amended by sec. 17 (1900); sub-sec. 2 from sec. 17 (1900); sub-sec. 3 from sec. 1 (1890); and sub-secs. 4, 5 and 6 from sub-sec. 3 (1890).

The section must be read subject to sec. 90.

Sec. 88. *Previous legislation.*

At the beginning of this chapter reference is made to some of the earlier statutes which allowed the owner of goods to borrow money upon such goods by means of the fiction of issuing a receipt to himself and then endorsing it to the bank. Under the Act of 1859 it was held that this form of issue and endorsement must be strictly observed. (Bank of British North America v. Clarkson, 1869, 19 C.P. 182; cf. Royal Canadian Bank v. Miller, 1870, 29 U.C.R. 266.) But under the Act of 1871, it was held by the Supreme Court, reversing the Court of Appeal for Ontario, that in the case of a warehouse receipt given by the owner of goods who was engaged in the calling of warehouseman, etc., it was not necessary for such owner to go through the form of issuing a receipt to himself and then endorsing it to the bank. A simple acknowledgment that the goods had been received from the bank, (which was, in the case in question, the consignee of the goods), with a note that the document was to be regarded as a receipt under the provisions of the statute, was held to be sufficient. (Merchants Bank v. Smith, 1884, 8 S.C. R. 512.)

Security in form of Schedule C. The Act of 1890 abolished the use of the fiction of a warehouse receipt issued by the owner, and substituted a new security, being in form an assignment to the bank of goods, wares and merchandise, to secure the payment of advances made on bills or notes discounted or a debt contracted.

Although the form was the creation of the Act, its effect was to be the same as if the bank had acquired the same by virtue of a warehouse receipt. It is to be borne in mind that when in 1890 the law was thus re-framed respecting advances made upon the security of goods in the owner's possession, it was assumed that the form and not the essence was to be changed. The statute extended the classes to whom advances could be made to others than the particular classes of persons to whom it was previously limited. Except as above stated there is little difference between the law governing assignments under sec. 88 and that which formerly governed warehouse receipts given by parties for their own goods.

Legislative power.—Conflict with provincial legislation.

This section and sec. 86 raise an important question of legislative power as between the Dominion and the provincial legislatures.

Under the Banking Acts in force prior to the Act of 1890, Sec. 88.
as we have seen, a bank might acquire and hold, as security for
a loan, a warehouse receipt or bill of lading from any person
engaged in certain named occupations, (e.g., a saw miller), upon
such person's own goods, which warehouse receipt or bill of
lading should be as valid and effectual as if the owner and the
persons making such warehouse receipt or bill of lading were
different persons, and the warehouse receipt or bill of lading
was equally valid and effectual, although such person's business
might be confined to the manufacture of his own timber. (Tennant v. Union Bank, [1894] A.C. at p. 44.)

The Ontario Mercantile Amendment Act (now R.S.O., 1897, **Bank Act**
c. 145) also deals with warehouse receipts and other mercantile **overrides**
documents which are effectual to transmit the property of goods **provincial legislation.**
without actual delivery. It not only recognizes the negotiability
of warehouse receipts by custodiers who are not the owners of
goods; it extends the privilege to receipts by one who is both
owner and custodier, but only in cases where the grantor of
the receipts is, from the nature of his trade or calling, a custodier for others as well as for himself, and therefore in a position to give receipts to third parties. The enactments of the
Bank Act therefore go beyond the provisions of the Mercantile
Amendment Act. They omit the limitation of the provincial
statute, which requires, in order to validate a warehouse receipt
by a custodier who is also owner, that the trade or calling in
which he is ostensibly engaged must be one that admits of his
granting receipts on behalf of other owners.

The receipts in question in the case of Tennant v. Union
Bank did not comply with the Mercantile Amendment Act, because it was neither averred nor proved that the firm giving the
receipt had the custody of any goods except its own. It was
argued as against the bank's claim that the subject of warehouse receipts and of other negotiable documents which pass the
property in goods without delivery relates to ''Property and
Civil Rights in the Province,'' within clause 13 of sec. 92 of
the British North America Act, 1867, and is therefore within
the exclusive jurisdiction of the province. The trial judge and
the Court of Appeal felt bound by the decision of the Supreme
Court in Merchants Bank v. Smith, 1882, 8 S.C.R. 512, upholding the jurisdiction of Parliament. The Judicial Committee

held that warehouse receipts taken as security by a bank in the
course of the business of banking are matters coming within
the class of subjects described in clause 15 of sec. 91 as "Banking, incorporation of banks and the issue of paper money," and
that the provisions of the Bank Act with respect to such receipts are *intra vires*, even though the effect is to modify civil
rights in the province. Sec. 88 also is clearly within the ruling
in Tennant v. Union Bank, and *intra vires* of the Dominion Parliament, and may confer upon a bank privileges as a lender
which provincial legislation does not recognize.

This section also may conflict with, and for the protection of
a bank override the provincial Bills of Sales Acts in regard
to conveyances or mortgages of goods where possession is retained by the transferor. Provincial statutes providing that a
bill of sale or chattel mortgage, if not duly registered, shall be
void as against creditors of the grantor or mortgagor, must give
way in favour of a bank which takes security in accordance
with this section. (Tennant v. Union Bank, [1894] A.C. at p.
40.)

If, however, the security taken is not a valid security within
the Act, it must stand or fall in accordance with the general
law of the province applicable to it. (Halsted v. Bank of Hamilton, 1896, 27 O.R. at p. 440; S.C. 24 A.R. 152, 28 S.C.R. 235.)

It can now be taken as definitely settled that the exclusive
power to confer upon banks contractual and loaning rights, and
to provide the forms that all securities shall take in connection
therewith, is in the Dominion Parliament as incidental to banking, and that its enactments are *intra vires*, even if they are inconsistent with the provincial law relating to property and civil
rights. (Cf. Cushing v. Dupuy, 1880, 5 App. Cas. 409.) But
the provincial legislature has exclusive jurisdiction with regard
to warehouse receipts, bills of lading and other documents of
title, and with regard to chattel mortgages and other matters
of civil rights in the province, otherwise than in connection with
banking or some other subject over which exclusive jurisdiction
is given to Parliament.

May lend money.

The loan must be made direct to the manufacturer, etc., and
not to some other person, as for instance a private banker, on

the security of such manufacturer's note. The language of this section is not so wide as that of sec. 86 which permits the bank to acquire a warehouse receipt or bill of lading as collateral security for the payment of any debt incurred in its favour or as security for any liability incurred by it *for any person, etc.*

Wholesale.

The Act does not attempt to define this word. In the Century Dictionary wholesale is defined as "buying and selling by the price or in large quantity; as, a wholesale dealer." In the majority of cases the distinction between wholesale and retail is easily made. A wholesale manufacturer, for instance, is the person who manufactures for sale in bulk to those who sell in retail to others. Ordinarily he is the person whose goods reach the ultimate consumer, not directly but through an intermediary distributer. Yet a middleman might sometimes be properly classed as a wholesale purchaser, etc. The particular circumstances of each case would have to be considered. A banker ought of course to avoid transactions in which there is any ground for doubt.

Wholesale Purchaser or Shipper of or Dealer in.

In the Act of 1890 two classes of persons were mentioned to whom the bank might lend money under this section: (1) Wholesale manufacturers of any goods, wares and merchandise, and (2) wholesale purchasers or shippers of products of agriculture, the forest, etc., or of live stock or dead stock and the products thereof, the loan to be made upon the security of such goods, etc., products, stock and products thereof respectively.

The draft bill introduced into the House of Commons contained the words "manufacturer or producer," but it was pointed out that the interpretation clause defined goods, wares and merchandise as including "agricultural produce" and that a producer would therefore include a farmer. The words "or producer" were therefore struck out, as it was not intended that a farmer should be entitled to pledge his produce by virtue of this section.

The principle of the provisions of sec. 88 is not applicable to a farmer. These provisions are designed to enable wholesale manufacturers, purchasers or shippers to obtain advances upon

88. their goods, products, etc., in order to enable them to carry their goods to completion, and transport them from the place where they are manufactured or produced to the market (as the case may be). It would scarcely be a benefit to the farmer to bring him within the scope of this section and so render doubtful his credit with private lenders, who might otherwise be willing to make advances on the security of mortgage under the provincial law. When, however, he has his grain ready for the market, he may, like any other person, put his property in the hands of a bailee or warehouseman and obtain a loan under sec. 86, upon the security of the receipt.

Wholesale Dealer.

The words "or dealer in" were inserted in 1900.

Products of the Forest.

It was held by the Superior Court in Quebec, in Molsons Bank v. Beaudry, that lumber which has passed through the saw mill is no longer the product of the forest within this section. The judgment was affirmed by the Court of King's Bench upon other grounds, only one of the judges in appeal expressing himself in favour of, and another expressing himself against, such an interpretation of the words "products of the forest," 1901, Q.R. 11 K.B. 212, 1 Com. L.R. 201. Note, however, that a manufacturer of sawn lumber is included within the privileges of sub-sec. 3, by virtue of the definition of goods, wares and merchandise as including timber, deals, boards, etc., (sec. 2).

Quarry.

This word was added in 1900.

Substituted goods, wares and merchandise.

Sub-sec. 2, added in 1900, is a departure from previous policy in regard to the rights of a bank with respect to grain and other similar merchandise when the specific goods in existence at the time the security is taken have been removed and other like goods substituted by the owner. (Cf. Llado v. Morgan, 1874, 23 C.P. 517.) It is to be noted also that the provision applies only to security taken under sub-sec. 1, and not to security taken under sub-sec. 3. There is no similar provision ap-

plicable to goods covered by a warehouse receipt. Cf., however, Sec. 88.
notes to sec. 86 as to cases of commingling of goods covered by Substituted
warehouse receipt. These cases would doubtless be equally ap- goods.
plicable to securities under sec. 88.

The right of substitution does not apply, for instance, to sawn lumber, if Molsons Bank v. Beaudry, *supra,* decides that such lumber is not the product of the forest, because, in that event, it can be pledged only as manufactured goods under subsec. 3. The same principle applies to flour, etc.

The substitution clause says the "bank may allow the goods . . . . to be removed," etc. It is advisable to have the evidence of the bank's consent in writing, the most satisfactory way being to have the customer make a formal application for the bank's consent, and it would be advisable subsequently from time to time to obtain from the customer statements of the goods removed and substituted.

The goods substituted must be of substantially the same character and of substantially the same value as, or of less value than, those for which they have been substituted. If these conditions are not fulfilled the assignment would be entirely worthless as a security on the substituted goods, and the bank's consent to the removal of the original goods would estop it from claiming the original goods as against a third party acquiring title upon the faith of such consent. When there is any doubt as to the character or value of the substituted goods it is advisable, if there is a sufficiently comprehensive written promise, to take a new assignment of the substituted goods.

The bank's right to hold substituted goods under this section must be distinguished from the right under sec. 89 to retain its security on goods manufactured from the goods originally assigned to it. The latter right extends both to goods covered by a warehouse receipt and to goods assigned under sec. 88.

Manufacturer.

This word as defined by sec. 2(*i*) "includes manufacturers of logs, timber, or lumber, maltsters, distillers, brewers, refiners and producers of petroleum, tanners, curers, packers, canners of meat, pork, fish, fruit or vegetables, and any person who produces by hand, art, process or mechanical means any goods, wares or merchandise."

The word "manufacturer" in its widest sense of one who "makes" or "fabricates," or even in the narrower sense of one who "works materials into the form of" or "brings material into being as" (cf. McNichol v. Pinch, [1906] 2 K.B. 352), would doubtless include the various classes of persons mentioned in clause (i). The clause was framed, however, so as expressly to bring within the operation of the Act certain classes which might not be included in the popular meaning of manufacturer. It was thought that, as popularly understood, the term manufacturer is rather applied to products which are not so entirely changed in substance and appearance from the articles from which they are made as, for instance, distilled, or malt liquor. Distillers, maltsters and brewers were therefore expressly included. Similarly express mention is made of other classes of persons who are manufacturers in the strict legal sense, but not perhaps in the ordinary sense.

A manufacturer of "logs, timber and lumber," was, by the amendment of 1900, expressed to be included in the term manufacturer in order to permit of the pledge of logs, timber and lumber under sec. 88 as well as under sec. 86. (Cf. similar amendment of clause (g) in 1900.) The rest of clause (i) dates from 1890.

The goods of a manufacturer, upon the security of which the bank may, under this section, make advances, must be goods actually manufactured by him or procured for such manufacture. They must not be goods procured by him to be sold in substantially the same condition.

Schedule C. *May be given by the owner. . . . may be taken in the form set forth in Schedule C. to this Act or to the like effect.*

The security for loans authorized by this section may be taken in any form allowed by the law of the place where the transaction occurs and where the goods or products are, but, if the security is not taken in the form of Schedule C, the local law must be observed. If, for instance, the goods are in Ontario and a bank takes a chattel mortgage as security, it must protect itself by filing it in the proper office and otherwise complying with the Bills of Sale and Chattel Mortgage Act. (Halsted v. Bank of Hamilton, 1896, 27 O.R. at p. 440.)

Sub-sec. 5, however, permits the security to be taken in a special form and sub-sec. 6 declares the rights acquired by the

bank under such form. If this form is used it is valid notwithstanding that it does not comply with provincial law. (Tennant v. Union Bank, *supra*.)

The form is set out as Schedule C to the Act and, as amended in 1900 and with some slight verbal alterations introduced
in the revision of 1906, is as follows:

SCHEDULE C.

In consideration of an advance of   dollars made by
the   Bank to A.B., for which the said bank holds
the following bills or notes: (*describe the bills or notes, if any*),
[*or,* in consideration of the discounting of the following bills or
notes by the   Bank for A.B.: (*describe the bills or
notes*),] the goods, wares and merchandise mentioned below are
hereby assigned to the said bank as security for the payment
on or before the   day of   of the said advance,
together with interest thereon at the rate of   per centum
per annum from the   day of   (*or,* of the said bills
or notes, or renewals thereof, or substitutions therefor, and interest thereon, *or as the case may be*).

This security is given under the provisions of section 88 of
the Bank Act, and is subject to the provisions of the said Act.

The said goods, wares and merchandise are now owned by
          , are now in the possession of   , and are
free from any mortgage, lien or charge thereon (*or as the case
may be*), and are in (*place or places where the goods are*), and
are the following (*description of goods assigned*).

Dated, etc.

(N.B.—*The bills or notes and the goods, etc., may be set out
in schedules annexed.*)

Probably the intention of the Act is that under sub-sec. 3,
the same person shall own the goods as well as manufacture
them or procure them for manufacture, but this point is not
clear.

The form apparently contemplates that the person to whom
the advance is made and the person by whom the goods are
owned may be different persons.

The form contained in Schedule C to the original Bank Act
of 1890 contemplated only the net amount of the advance being

Sec. 88.   expressed as the consideration for the assignment. The present
form, substituted in 1900, contains an alternative consideration
clause which expressly sanctions the practice of mentioning, in
the case of a discount, only the gross amount of the bills or notes.
It might be highly inconvenient in some cases to have to calculate the charges and deduct them, so as to arrive at the net
amount of the advance, before the completion of the document.
The form of 1890 also required the bills or notes, if any, to be
fully described. The present form omits the word "fully."

Where a new assignment is taken under a written promise
in connection with a regular line of credit, the advance being
made by way of overdraft, it is advisable that such new assignment should be drawn to cover all the certain goods covered by
the promise as security for the whole overdraft at such time.

The name of the owner of the goods and also the name of
the person in whose possession they are (who may be a different
person, as, for instance, when the goods are at a railway sta-
tion where the agent cannot give a warehouse receipt, or in bond
under the charge of the Customs or the Excise Department),
and any mortgage lien or charge on such goods, should be mentioned.

Description
of the goods
pledged.

The form also provides for the mentioning of the "place or
places where the goods are" and the "description of the goods
assigned." The latter is an important essential of the form and
usually involves the former. The description in Schedule C
to the Act of 1890 required the description to be "particular,"
a word which is omitted in the present form. It cannot be assumed, however, that the change in the wording is intended to
do away with the necessity for identifying the goods by the
description, and in the absence of decisions under the Bank Act
it would be well to comply with the rule laid down in the Ontario Bills of Sales Act, namely, that all instruments under the
Act shall contain such sufficient and full description thereof
that the same may be thereby readily and easily known and distinguished.

The cases are exhaustively digested in Barron and O'Brien
on Chattel Mortgages and Bills of Sale (1897), at pp. 360 *et seq.*
The following are some of the cases which seem to be applicable
to a security under this section of the Bank Act.

The description need not be such a one as that, with the
deed in hand, without other enquiry, the property could be

identified, but there must be such material on the face of the
mortgage as would indicate how the property may be identified
if proper enquiries are instituted. (McCall v. Wolff, 1885, 13
S.C.R. at p. 133.)

It is not necessary that the property should be so described
as to enable a person to distinguish the article without having recourse to extrinsic evidence, and merely by casting his eye on them.
(Rose v. Scott, 1858, 17 U.C.R. 385, 387; Holt v. Carmichael,
1878, 2 A.R. 639, 641.)

Written descriptions are to be interpreted in the light of the
facts known to, and in the minds of, the parties at the time;
they are not prepared for strangers, but for those they are to
affect—the parties and their privies (Willey v. Snyder, 1876,
34 Mich. 60) ; yet they must be such as will enable the articles
to be identified as against third parties, creditors or others,
claiming an interest in the property. (McCall v. Wolff, *supra.*)

A mortgage of 100,000 feet of white pine saw logs now on
North Branch, so called ''Thunder Bay River,'' no data being
furnished for distinguishing the logs from the mass bearing the
same mark, is void for uncertainty (Richardson v. Alpena, 1879,
40 Mich. 203) ; but a description identifying the property by
its mark would be sufficient, if it provided a means of separat-
ing the mortgaged property from others of a like kind. (Merchants National Bank v. McLaughlin, 1880, 1 McCreary, 258.)
It is not sufficient to state merely the street in which the property mortgaged happens to be without saying that it is on the
premises of a named person situate in that street. Wilson v.
Kerr, 1858, 17 U.C.R. 168.)

The words ''also the stock of gold and silver watches, jewel-
lery and electro-silver plate, which at the date hereof is in the
possession of the mortgagor in his said store'' is a sufficient description, notwithstanding that the electro-plated goods and
watches were numbered, and might have been identified thereby.
(Segsworth v. Meriden, 1883, 3 O.R. 413.)

A description of goods as being ''now in and upon a certain locality,'' limits the goods to which the mortgage refers to
those goods only that were, at the time of the execution of the
mortgage, ''now in and upon'' the *locus in quo,* although goods
upon other premises were intended to be covered by the mortgage. (Donnelly v. Hall, 1885, 7 O.R. 581.)

Where the mortgage is of "all the staves I have in M. the same which I purchased from F.," and it appears that the mortgagor has no staves in M., but has some close thereto and purchased from F., the first part of the description may be rejected as false, the remainder being sufficient to pass the property, it being merely a matter of identification. (Pettis v. Kellogg, 1851, 7 Cush. (Mass.) 456.)

The best description often is a general one, such as "all the logs, lumber and products thereof, which are now in the following places, namely,   ." Such a description would be suitable even if it occurs in an assignment which is additional to one previously taken, and would, if it were valid in other respects, transfer the goods mentioned in the previous assignment subject to such previous assignment, and in addition, any goods added since such previous assignment or not covered thereby.

If a contest afterwards arises as to whether certain goods are covered by the mortgage, it will be necessary for the mortgagee to shew that such goods were the property of the mortgagor and in the specified place at the time of the execution of the mortgage.

If general words are employed it is necessary that the location of the property at the moment of the execution of the deed should be defined, and the statement should be added that the articles are all the goods answering the description on the premises (McCall v. Wolff, 1885, 13 S.C.R. 130; Harris v. Commercial Bank, 1857, 16 U.C.R. 437, 444; Howell v. McFarlane, 1857, 16 U.C.R. 469; Re Thirkell, 21 Gr. 492; Ross v. Conger, 1856, 14 U.C.R. 525; Fraser v. Bank of Toronto, 1860, 19 U.C.R. 381; Powell v. Bank of Upper Canada, 1871, 11 C.P. 303), or all the goods, etc., *of the mortgagor* on the premises described. (Whiting v. Hovey, 1887, 14 S.C.R. 515; Thompson v. Quirk, 1889, 18 S.C.R. (Appendix) 695, S.C. Cas. 436.)

The same rights and powers . . . . as if it had acquired the same by virtue of a warehouse receipt.

See sec. 86 and notes thereto as to the effect of the security taken, and see sec. 90 as to the conditions of its validity and priority.

89. If goods, wares and merchandise are manufactured or produced from the goods, wares and merchandise, or any of them, included in or covered by any warehouse receipt, or included in or covered by any security given under the last preceding section, while so covered, the bank holding such warehouse receipt or security shall hold or continue to hold such goods, wares and merchandise, during the process and after the completion of such manufacture or production, with the same right and title, and for the same purposes and upon the same conditions, as it held or could have held the original goods, wares and merchandise.

Sec. 89.

As to goods manufactured from articles pledged.

2. All advances made on the security of any bill of lading or warehouse receipt, or of any security given under the last preceding section, shall give to the bank making the advances a claim for the repayment of the advances on the goods, wares and merchandise therein mentioned, or into which they have been converted, prior to and by preference over the claim of any unpaid vendor: Provided that such preference shall not be given over the claim of any unpaid vendor who had a lien upon the goods, wares and merchandise at the time of the acquisition by the bank of such warehouse receipt, bill of lading, or security, unless the same was acquired without knowledge on the part of the bank of such lien.

Prior claim of bank over unpaid vendor.

Proviso.

3. In the event of the non-payment at maturity of any debt or liability secured by a warehouse receipt or bill of lading, or secured by any security given under the last preceding section, the bank may sell the goods, wares and merchandise mentioned therein, or so much thereof as will suffice to pay such debt or liability with interest and expenses, returning the surplus, if any, to the person from whom the warehouse receipt, bill of lading, or security, or the goods, wares, merchandise mentioned therein, as the case may be, were acquired: Provided that such power of sale shall be exercised subject to the following provisions, namely :—

Sale of goods on non-payment of debt.

Proviso.

Sec. 89.
Notice.

(*a*) No sale, without the consent in writing of the owner of any timber, boards, deals, staves, sawlogs or other lumber, shall be made under this Act until notice of the time and place of such sale has been given by a registered letter, mailed in the post office, post paid, to the last known address of the pledgor thereof, at least thirty days prior to the sale thereof;

Idem.

(*b*) No goods, wares and merchandise, other than timber, boards, deals, staves, saw-logs or other lumber, shall be sold by the bank under this Act without the consent of the owner, until notice of the time and place of sale has been given by a registered letter, mailed in the post office, post paid, to the last known address of the pledger thereof, at least ten days prior to the sale thereof;

Sale by
auction.

(*c*) Every sale, under such power of sale, without the consent of the owner, shall be made by public auction, after notice thereof by advertisement, in at least two newspapers published in or nearest to the place where the sale is to be made, stating the time and place thereof; and, if the sale is in the province of Quebec, then at least one of such newspapers shall be a newspaper published in the English language, and one other such newspaper shall be a newspaper published in the French language. 53 V., c. 31, ss. 76, 77 and 78; 63-64 V., c. 26, s. 19.

This section is a combination of secs. 76 and 77 of the Act of 1890, and of sec. 78 of the same Act, as amended by sec. 19 of the Act of 1900.

Goods manufactured or produced from goods pledged.

The Act of 1880 provided that a warehouse receipt given by a miller, maltster, or packer or cutter of pork for cereal grains or hogs, should also vest in the bank the title to flour or malt, pork, bacon or hams manufactured out of the grains or hogs •while held under such receipt. Sub-sec. 1 in its present form dates from 1890, and contains a similar provision of general application to any goods, wares or merchandise included in any warehouse receipt or any security given under sec. 88. A bill of lading is not mentioned because it covers goods in transit only.

Having regard to the usual course of business in such matters, flour which is set apart as being the product of wheat need not be that which has been made from the identical wheat mentioned in the receipt, it being physically impossible in many instances, as the mills are conducted, that the wheat delivered, and that only, should produce the flour given for it. (Mason v. Great Western, 1871, 31 U.C.R. 73, 93; cf. Llado v. Morgan, 1874, 23 C.P. 517, 525.)

An interesting question is raised by the possible case of two kinds of raw material entering into the manufacture of certain goods, and of the owner's having pledged one kind to one bank, and the other to another bank. *Quære,* as to the rights of the respective banks in the manufactured goods.

Doubt may also arise where other material than that covered by the security enters into the manufacture of goods.

Rights to proceeds in case of sale by the receiptor.

In Re Goodfallow, Traders Bank v. Goodfallow, 1890, 19 O. R. 299, a miller, as security for an advance, gave a warehouse receipt to a bank on some wheat "and its product" stored in his mill. He died shortly afterwards. In the interval, wheat was constantly going out of the mill, and fresh wheat coming in. Just before the receiptor's death, the bank took possession, and found a large shortage in the wheat, which had commenced shortly after the receipt had been given and had continued to a greater or less degree all the time. In the administration of the estate it appeared that during the period of shortage some of the wheat had been converted into flour which had been sold, and the proceeds, which were less than the value of the shortage, were paid to the administrator. It was held that the bank was entitled to the purchase money of the flour.

Re Goodfallow was a case between the bank and the pledgor's administrator (whose rights were no higher than those of the pledgor himself), and the case was distinguished on this ground by the Supreme Court of Nova Scotia in Union Bank v. Spinney, 1906, 1 East. L.R. 277. In this case one Churchill, who had pledged corn to a bank by assignment in the form of Sche-

13—BANK ACT.

dule C, ground the corn into meal, sold the product, and fraudulently sought to divert the purchase money to one of his creditors, the defendant Spinney, by making drafts upon the purchaser in Spinney's favour instead of the bank's. On appeal to the Supreme Court of Canada, however, it was held, reversing the Court below, that Spinney knew or, under the circumstances, ought to have known, that the meal was the property of the bank, and therefore, not being a purchaser in good faith for value and without notice of the bank's claim, he was liable to the bank for the purchase money in his hands: 38 S.C.R. 187.

Prior claim over unpaid vendor.

The Act of 1861 gave to a bank, which had made advances on the security of a bill of lading or receipt, a claim on the goods covered by the security, prior to and by way of preference over the claim of any unpaid vendor—an important provision, because, under the law of Lower Canada, and under certain circumstances under the law of Upper Canada, the claim of the unpaid vendor of the goods would prevail over that of a person making advances upon the security of the goods.

The Act of 1865 went further, and gave the bank priority in regard to advances on the security of timber, etc., over the claim of any unpaid vendor *or other creditor save and except claims for wages of labour performed in making and transporting such timber, etc.* In 1871, however, the italicized words were omitted.

Sub-sec. 2, in its present form, dates from 1890. It is to be noted that any unpaid vendor who had a lien on the goods at the time of the acquisition by the bank of the warehouse receipt or bill of lading is now protected unless the same was acquired without knowledge on the part of the bank of such lien.

The words "or into which they have been converted" refer to the extended effect given by sub-sec. 1 to a warehouse receipt taken as security by a bank.

Sale of goods on non-payment of debt.

Sub-sec. 3 dates from 1890, except that in 1900 it was amended by the insertion of the words "or liability" after the word debt, where it first occurs—an amendment rendered necessary by the insertion of these words in sec. 86.

The express power of sale given by this section is subject Sec. 89. to the following conditions:

1. There must be default in payment at maturity of the debt secured by the document under which the goods are held.

2. Except by the consent of the owner, 30 days' prior notice by registered letter to the last known address of the pledgor must be given of the time and place of sale of timber, boards, deals, staves, saw logs or other lumber, and ten days' notice in the case of other goods.

3. Except by the consent of the owner, the sale must be by public auction, of which a notice is to be duly published as required by the section.

In so far as a security is valid only by virtue of secs. 86 and 88, these conditions must be strictly observed in order to constitute a valid sale, and the bank is liable to a penalty (sec. 142) if it sells without complying with the conditions. If a security, however, is valid by the general law and in virtue of the general powers of the bank to take security, there is by the common law prevailing in the provinces other than Quebec, an implied power of sale on default in payment of the debt secured (see notes to sec. 81), and such a power would probably not be subject to the conditions of this section. The conditions ought to be read as referring only to a sale made by virtue of the Act.

The owner may not only waive the necessity of notice and Waiver of notice, and of public sale. public sale, but may also agree that the goods shall become the property of the bank, and authorize it to sell them by private sale and apply the proceeds upon the debt. Such a transaction would give the bank an absolute title notwithstanding that at its inception the pledge was invalid by reason of being for a past debt, the rights of creditors not having arisen at the time of the agreement releasing the title in the goods to the bank. (Armstrong v. Buchanan, 1903, 35 N.S.R. 559, 1 Com. L.R. 506.)

If goods are lawfully sold under this section, the money that Application of proceeds. remains after applying the proceeds of the sale to the debt secured by the warehouse receipt, bill of lading or security is simply money held to the use of the person from whom the document or the goods was or were acquired. Such money may be made the subject of a collateral agreement, oral or written, and it is competent for the bank and the borrower to agree that in

Sec. 89. the event of sale the surplus shall be applied by the bank in payment of other debts due by the borrower to the bank. (Thompson v. Molsons Bank, 1889, 16 S.C.R. 664.)

If the goods are of such a nature that they are capable of division a bank is not justified in selling a quantity greatly in excess of what will realize enough to pay its debt. (Gibbs v. Dominion Bank, 1879, 30 C.P. 36; cf. Prentice v. Consolidated Bank and Toronto General Trusts v. Central Ontario, cited in the notes to sec. 66.)

If a bank sells goods pledged under a bill of lading and endorses the bill to the purchaser but has not itself a good title, the purchaser may recover the price from the bank as upon an implied warranty of title and failure of consideration (Peuchen v. Imperial Bank, 1890, 20 O.R. 325), or may sue upon the implied warranty for the value of the goods. (Confederation Life v. Labatt, 1900, 27 A.R. 321.)

But a bank which has endorsed and delivered a bill of lading is not obliged by law to give notice of the arrival of the goods to the endorsee, even if the bank has itself received notice. (Masson v. Merchants Bank, 1898, Q.R. 14 S.C. 293.)

Conditions under which bank may take security.

90. The bank shall not acquire or hold any warehouse receipt or bill of lading, or any such security as aforesaid, to secure the payment of any bill, note, debt, or liability, unless such bill, note, debt or liability is negotiated or contracted,—

(a) at the time of the acquisition thereof by the bank; or,

(b) upon the written promise or agreement that such warehouse receipt or bill of lading or security would be given to the bank:

Proviso. Provided that such bill, note, debt, or liability may be renewed, or the time for the payment thereof extended, without affecting any such security.

2. The bank may,—

Exchanging of warehouse receipt for bill of lading and *vice versa.*

(a) on shipment of any goods, wares and merchandise for which it holds a warehouse receipt, or any such security as aforesaid, surrender such receipt or security and receive a bill of lading in exchange therefor; or,

(b) on the receipt of any goods, wares and merchandise for
which it holds a bill of lading, or any such security as
aforesaid, surrender such bill of lading or security, store
the goods, wares and merchandise, and take a warehouse
receipt therefor, or ship the goods, wares and merchandise,
or part of them, and take another bill of lading therefor.
53 V., c. 31, s. 75; 63-64 V., c. 26, s. 18.

The Statute of 1859, already referred to under sec. 86, pro- Earlier
vided that no transfer of a bill of lading or receipt should be legislation.
made to secure the payment of any bill, note or debt unless such
bill, note or debt was negotiated or contracted at the same time
with the endorsement of such bill of lading or receipt. Substantially this provision was preserved in all the subsequent banking statutes.

By the Bank Act of 1871 these words were added: "or upon
the understanding that such bill of lading, etc., would be transferred to the bank, but such bill, note or debt may be renewed
or the time for the payment thereof extended without affecting
such security."

A new section was substituted in 1890, which, as amended
in 1900, and with some immaterial verbal alterations made in
1906, is re-enacted in the present section.

Mortgages whether of real or personal property may be
taken by a bank only by way of additional security (see sec.
68). Security under secs. 86 and 88 cannot be taken for a
past advance, except upon a written promise or agreement contemporaneous with the advance. The reason of the special
powers given to banks to advance money to wholesale purchasers, shippers and dealers and to manufacturers is to enable such persons to bring their goods and products to completion and to the market, i.e., to tide over the time between the
purchase and the sale, between the raw product and the finished
article, to facilitate the "moving of the crops," etc. These objects can be accomplished by a transaction which results in an
advance being made at the time of the pledge, or thereafter from
time to time as it may be required, but would not be assisted by
allowing a bank to take security of this kind for an advance
which had been already made.

Debt or liability.

As to the meaning of debt or liability, see notes to sec. 86. The words "or liability" were added to this section and to sec. 89 in 1900, on account of the similar addition made in that year to sec. 86.

Negotiated or contracted.

Notes are not "negotiated or contracted at the time of the acquisition" of a warehouse receipt where there is simply a renewal of notes already in the hands of the bank, and a warehouse receipt is procured on the occasion of such renewal; no new advance is made and no valuable consideration is given or surrendered contemporaneously by the bank which might represent the inception of a new transaction or negotiation of securities. In the section "renewed" is put in contrast with "negotiated"; the latter term refers to the original transfer of the negotiable instrument from the maker or holder to the bank, but not to intermediate transfers or renewals taking place during the currency of the liability whereby no change is made in the condition of the parties except the mere giving of time. (Dominion Bank v. Oliver, 1889, 17 O.R. 402; Bank of Hamilton v. Halstead, 1897, 28 S.C.R. 235.)

Similarly a note substituted for an overdrawn account, (as, for instance, in produce accounts where the customer is permitted to overdraw to pay for grain, etc., and to cover by the discounting of a note as soon as he knows what his requirements are), would not constitute a debt contracted at the time of the discounting of the note so as to support a security taken at that time.

The fact that for the debt when originally contracted the bank held security, which it gave up when the renewals were made and new security taken, cannot assist it. A bill or note may be renewed without affecting the original security, but it is not contemplated by the Act that the original security may be given up and fresh security taken on the renewal. (The Bank of Hamilton v. Shepherd, 1894, 21 A.R. 156, overruling Bank of Hamilton v. Noye, 1885, 9 O.R. 631.)

A bill or note taken by a bank on acquiring a security under this section is not "negotiated at the time of the acquisition thereof" when the person giving the security and to whose account the

proceeds of the bill or note are credited, is not at liberty to draw
against them except on fulfilling certain other conditions. (Halsted v. Bank of Hamilton, 1896, 27 O.R. 435, affirmed, 24 A.R.
152, and by the Supreme Court, *sub nom*. Bank of Hamilton v.
Halstead, 1897, 28 S.C.R. 235.)

Sec. 90.
Negotiated
or
contracted.

Bank of Hamilton v. Halstead was distinguished by the
Court of Appeal for Ontario in Ontario Bank v. O'Reilly, 1906,
12 O.L.R. 420. Moss, C.J.O., at p. 432, says: "In regard to the
warehouse receipts now in question, each one was transferred
by indorsement and instrument of hypothecation contemporaneously with the discount of a promissory note made by the
holders or owners of the warehouse receipts. As a result of
each transaction the plaintiffs acquired and became the holders
of a promissory note on which the makers were liable, and the
latter received in their current account the proceeds of the
discount, and in consideration thereof made a transfer or hypothecation of a warehouse receipt. There was, therefore, a
negotiation of a note and an actual advance at the time of the
acquisition of the warehouse receipt. No doubt, it was the case
that on most occasions when a discount was effected the account
was overdrawn, but that was in the course of dealing, and the
circumstance did not deprive the transaction of its character of
a negotiation of the note, for the proceeds were placed freely at
the disposal of the customers, and the drawings on the account
continued as before. Therein lies the broad distinction between
this case and Halsted v. Bank of Hamilton, . . . , a distinction which renders this case analagous to the decision of the
Master of the Rolls in In re Carew's Estate Act, 1862, 31 Beav.
39, to which reference is made by the learned Chief Justice of
the Common Pleas in 27 O.R. at p. 439. On the same page the
learned Chief Justice states his reasons for thinking it impossible to treat any of the notes in respect of which the securities
in question were given as having been "negotiated" in the
sense in which the term is used in sec. 75, [now sec. 90], of the
Bank Act. He says: "It is true that the form was gone through
of taking the notes and passing the amount of them to the credit
of one of the accounts, but contemporaneously with this an
equal amount was placed to the debit of another of the accounts,
and not a farthing of the amounts which the notes represented
could be touched by Zoellner or made available by him for any

purpose, unless he should bring to the defendants and leave for collection or discount customers' paper, which would entitle him to credit in account No. 2, for an amount equal to that which he proposed to withdraw.'' In other words, the proceeds of the discounts were placed entirely out of the control of the customer, and he could make no use of them except upon further securing the amount of the withdrawals. No such state of facts exists in this case, and the decision does not assist the defendants.''

Upon the written promise or agreement.

If the bill, note, debt or liability is not negotiated or contracted at the time of the acquisition of the security by the bank, then the negotiation or contracting must be upon the written promise or agreement that such security shall be given. The writing must be given to the bank either at the time of the negotiation or contracting of the debt or anterior thereto, for a bill, etc., could not be said to be negotiated or contracted *upon* a written promise which is not then in existence.

It has been suggested that the ''agreement'' must contain the names of the parties and the consideration, but that the word ''promise'' is a wider term and might be sufficient although it does not contain the essentials of a legal agreement, *sed quære*.

In Re Central Bank, Canada Shipping Co.'s Case, 1891, 21 O.R. 515, a case arising under the corresponding section of R. S.C. 1886, c. 120, at the time of an advance of money to pay for cattle, the purchaser agreed that upon the shipment of the cattle the bill of lading should be issued to the bank as security for repayment of the advance. The cattle were delivered to the carriers who had notice and assented to the special property of the bank. It was held that the bank had priority over creditors who had attached the cattle on their delivery to the carriers, but before the bill of lading was made out, (following, but not altogether approving, Merchants Bank v. Suter, 1876, 24 Gr. 356). The effect of the case, if it is good law, is that a bank may acquire by anticipation a property in a nonexisting bill of lading, and this must be to acquire by anticipation some right or title of the previous owner to the goods, of which the document is but the symbol, before the date of the acquisition of the symbol.

That such warehouse receipt, etc., would be given.

It has been held that the goods need not be *in esse* or in the possession of the borrower at the time the promise or agreement to give the warehouse receipt is made. (Royal Canadian Bank v. Ross, 1877, 40 U.C.R. 466.)

There has been no decision, however, as to whether a general promise to give a warehouse receipt upon goods would be sufficient, or whether it is necessary to refer to the precise warehouse receipt which is afterwards actually acquired, *e.g.*, by mentioning the warehouse, the warehouseman, the quantity and the description of the goods. The latter would be sufficient, but in practice it would be well to avoid too much particularity, for if the receipt actually given did not correspond exactly to the description of it contained in the promise, awkward questions might arise.

The use of the word "such" would certainly indicate that more is required than a general promise to give a warehouse receipt. The goods need not be in existence at the time of the making of the promise, but their existence must be in contemplation, and it should be practicable to give sufficient particulars to identify them, as, *e.g.*, all the goods of a certain kind in a specified place. Such a description contained both in the promise and in the warehouse receipt afterwards given in pursuance of the promise would be sufficient.

Line of credit.

Where a regular line of credit is granted, it is essential that *before* or *at the time* that the first advance is made thereunder, a written promise should be taken to give security, and ordinarily no promise will meet the varying conditions of an active account except a general one by which the customer agrees to give security from time to time on all his goods, etc., for all advances made under the credit. The written promise must mention any class of product on which the bank afterwards lends, and any places where the goods, etc., are stored at the time of the taking of the security. In practice it would be advisable to include all classes of product on which it is likely the bank may be asked to lend and all places where the customer is likely to store goods. Such a promise will enable the bank to take security on such portions of his goods as may seem necessary from time to time.

If subsequently it is desired to make advances larger than
those mentioned in the written promise, but upon goods of the
same nature and stored in the same places as those mentioned
in the promise, a new written promise may be taken covering
the additional amount of advances to be made. If, however, it
is desired to make advances upon goods of a different nature,
or, whether of the same or of a different nature, stored in different places from those mentioned in the original promise, then
a new promise must be taken for the amount of advances to be
made upon such goods. In this case a separate account must
be kept of advances made under the second promise, and the
proceeds of advances made under one promise must not be used
to repay advances made under the other promise.

When new security is taken under a written promise it is
advisable usually that the bank should retain the old security
until the final repayment of all the advances.

May be renewed or the time for payment thereof extended.

The renewal or extension is only a continuation of the old
indebtedness. In the absence, however, of special agreement,
payments made by the debtor after the making of the advances
are in the ordinary course between debtor and creditor placed
against the earliest items of the indebtedness, when no special
direction has been given by the debtor and no special appropriation made by the creditor. (Gibbs v. Dominion Bank, 1879,
30 C.P. 36).

Exchange or substitution of securities.

A borrower had been in the habit of buying hops from time
to time and giving the bank pledges of the same for the purpose
of raising money to pay for them, and then at the request of
the bank, he constituted his bookkeeper his warehouseman, and
the latter issued warehouse receipts to the bank in substitution
for the pledges theretofore held, there being no further advance
made when the new securities were given. It was held that this
exchange of securities should be treated as authorized under
sub-sec. 2 of this section. (Conn. v. Smith, 1897, 28 O.R. 629.)

In the case of a casual or isolated loan it is necessary that
a security taken by a bank under section 86 or section
88 should not be given up, but should be held by
the bank until the debt or liability has been absolutely extin-

guished, unless such security is taken in pursuance of a written agreement drawn so as to admit of the substitution of a new security, or unless the substitution falls within the provisions of sub-sec. 2 of sec. 88. Otherwise the bank could not validly take any security other than the one taken at the time the loan is made. It is often advisable even when the loan is made at the time of the taking of the security that there should be a written promise to give further security, so that the bank would be in a position to take further security if it deemed it necessary without making any further advance.

Curing defects.

If an assignment taken is defective the security may be perfected by a new assignment in pursuance of a written promise made at the time of or before the making of the advances. If there is no written promise, but subsequent advances are made upon the security of new assignments, with or without a written promise to give further assignments, the liability account relating to the first advance should be closed so far as new advances are concerned. The old loan cannot of course be paid out of the proceeds of the new loan, but subsequent receipts on the customer's account can be . applied on the repayment of the old loan, which may thus be ultimately wiped out, and leave the outstanding advances all covered by the new assignment.

Penalties.

See secs. 143 and 144.

CHAPTER XVII.

INTEREST AND COLLECTION AND AGENCY FEES.

Interest at 7 per centum may be charged.   **91.** The bank may stipulate for, take, reserve or exact any rate of interest or discount, not exceeding seven per centum per annum, and may receive and take in advance, any such rate, but no higher rate of interest shall be recoverable by the bank. 53 V., c. 31, s. 80.

Any rate may be allowed.   **92.** The bank may allow any rate of interest whatever upon money deposited with it. 53 V., c. 31, s. 80.

Usury laws.   Prior to the statute 29 and 30 Vict., c. 10, (1866), a bank exacting a higher rate of interest and discount than seven per cent. was liable under the law of the late Province of Canada to the penalties and forfeitures of C.S.C. 1859, c. 58—these having been kept in force as regards banks after they were repealed against individuals. (Drake v. Bank of Toronto, 1862, 9 Gr. 116, 133.) The first mentioned statute enacted that no bank should be liable to any penalty or forfeiture for usury under the Consolidated Statute, but that the amount of interest or commission should remain as limited thereby. It was held that the amending statute relieved the bank not only from the penal consequences of contravening the former Act, but also from the loss or forfeiture of the money advanced and of the security received. (Commercial Bank v. Cotton, 1867, 17 C.P. 447.)

In 1867 the provision was enacted which was re-enacted by the General Banking Act of 1871, and from there transcribed into the Bank Act of 1890, as sec. 80, in the following words:

"80. The bank shall not be liable to incur any penalty or forfeiture for usury, and may stipulate for, take, reserve or exact any rate of interest or discount not exceeding seven per cent. per annum, and may receive and take in advance any such rate, but no higher rate of interest shall be recoverable by the bank; and the bank may allow any rate of interest whatever upon money deposited with it."

In the revision of 1906 the first clause of the section just quoted has been omitted, and the remainder of the section has been re-enacted as secs. 91 and 92.

In 1872 a further statute relating to interest was passed. It recited the provisions of the Act of 1871 (sec. 80 of the Act of 1890 above referred to), and recited further that in some of the provinces of Canada laws might be in force imposing penalties on parties other than banks for taking, or stipulating, or paying more than a certain rate of interest, and that doubts might arise as to the effect of such laws in certain cases as to parties, other than the bank, to negotiable securities discounted or otherwise acquired and held by any bank. The statute then enacted the provisions which were afterwards re-enacted in the Bank Act of 1890, as sec. 81, in the following words:

"81. No promissory note, bill of exchange or other negotiable security, discounted by or indorsed or otherwise assigned to the bank, shall be held to be void, usurious or tainted by usury, as regards such bank, or any maker, drawer, acceptor, indorser, or indorsee thereof, or other party thereto, or *bonâ fide* holder thereof, nor shall any party thereto be subject to any penalty or forfeiture by reason of any rate of interest taken, stipulated or received by such bank, on or with respect to such promissory note, bill of exchange, or other negotiable security, or paid or allowed by any party thereto to another in compensation for, or in consideration of the rate of interest taken or to be taken thereon by such bank; but no party thereto, other than the bank, shall be entitled to recover or liable to pay more than the lawful rate of interest in the province where the suit is brought, nor shall the bank be entitled to recover a higher rate than seven per cent. per annum; and no innocent holder of or party to any promissory note, bill of exchange or other negotiable security, shall, in any case be deprived of any remedy against any party thereto, or liable to any penalty or forfeiture, by reason of any usury or offence against the laws of any such province, respecting interest, committed in respect of such note, bill or negotiable security, without the complicity or consent of such innocent holder or party."

This section was omitted from the Bank Act in the revision of 1906. It became practically obsolete in 1890, when by 53 Vict., c. 34, the various provincial statutes relating to interest

Sec. 92.   and usury consolidated in R.S.C. 1886, c. 127, secs. 9 to 30,
Usury laws.   were repealed. It has been set out above, however, because
some of the recent decisions, presently to be noted, have referred
to its provisions. Cf. also sec. 59 of the Bills of Exchange Act,
infra.

Interest Act   The Interest Act (R.S.C., c. 120), provides (secs. 2 and 3):
"2. Except as otherwise provided by this or by any other Act
of the Parliament of Canada, any person may stipulate for, allow and exact, on any contract or agreement whatsoever, any
rate of interest or discount which is agreed upon. 3. Except
as to liabilities existing immediately before the seventh day of
July, one thousand nine hundred, whenever any interest is payable by the agreement of parties or by law, and no rate is fixed
by such agreement or by law, the rate of interest shall be five
per centum per annum." Prior to the 7th of July, 1900, the
rate in such cases was six per cent.

The Money-Lenders' Act (R.S.C., c. 122), which limits the
rate of interest in certain cases, applies only to "money-lenders"
as defined in the Act.

There is, then, no law now in force which renders a bank
"liable to incur any penalty or forfeiture for usury."

Any rate
may be
stipulated
for.   A bank may stipulate for any rate of interest or discount
whatever without thereby invalidating the contract of loan or
pledge. (Quinlan v. Gordon, 1861, 20 Gr. (Appendix) 1; Adams
v. Bank of Montreal, 1899, 8 B.C.R. at p. 316, 1 Com. L.R. at
p. 250; S.C. 31 S.C.R. 223.) But if compelled to sue for the
interest, the bank cannot recover more than seven per cent.
(Bank of Montreal v. Hartman, 1905, 2 West. L.R. 57); for all
beyond the legal rate, the court will hold the contract void.
(Quinlan v. Gordon, *supra.*)

After maturity the rate of interest is limited to seven per
cent. or other smaller rate stipulated for. If no particular rate
of interest after maturity has been stipulated for, the bank
can recover only the rate of interest allowed in such a case by
the general law. (Royal Canadian Bank v. Shaw, 1871, 21 C.
P. 455; Bank of B.N.A. v. Bossuyt, 15 Man. R. 266; cf. St.
John v. Rykert, 1884, 10 S.C.R. 278; People's Loan v. Grant,
1890, 18 S.C.R. 262.)

Debtor may
recover back
excess
charged.   If a bank retains or debits the debtor's account with interest
in excess of seven per cent., the debtor is entitled to recover

back the excess or is entitled to credit for the excess so charged in an action by the bank. (Canadian Bank of Commerce v. Mc-Donald, 1906, 3 West. L.R. 90, at pp. 101, *et seq.;* Banque de St. Hyacinthe v. Sarrazin, 1892, Q.R. 2 S.C. 96.) To allow recovery back of such interest is not in effect to enforce a penalty or forfeiture for usury; it is not a proceeding for usury, though the action is brought on account of usury. (Kierzkowski v. Dorion, 1868, L.R. 2 P.C. 291, at p. 314.)

If, however, the debtor voluntarily pays the excess of inter- But not if est over seven per cent. as, *e.g.,* by giving his cheque to the excess voluntarily bank for such excess as shewn by the bank's monthly statement, paid by him. he cannot recover back the excess and is not entitled in an action by the bank to have the amount of the excess so paid applied on account of the principal or of the interest calculated at seven per cent. only. (Canadian Bank of Commerce v. McDonald, *supra;* Bank of B.N.A. v. Bossuyt, *supra;* Quinlan v. Gordon, *supra;* Hutton v. Federal Bank, 1883, 9 P.R. at p. 581.) The dictum of Pagnuelo, J., in Banque de St. Hyacinthe, *supra,* to the effect that the prohibition of the Act is one "of public order," and that, therefore, a person who has paid to a bank interest in excess of the rate fixed by the Act, may recover back the excess, was not necessary to the decision of the case. In that case the excess of interest was retained by the bank, but was not in any other sense *paid* by the debtor.

It has been held that a third party, *e.g.,* an execution creditor of the debtor, is not entitled to compel the bank to account for interest charged by it in excess of seven per cent. (Benallack v. Bank of B.N.A., 1905, judgment of the Territorial Court of the Yukon Territory (cf. 36 S.C.R. 120), as explained in Ritchie v. Canadian Bank of Commerce, 1905, 2 West. L.R. 499, at p. 501.)

A bank may also receive and retain, in addition to the discount, the collection or agency charges authorized by secs. 93 and 94.

93. When any note, bill, or other negotiable security or Percentage paper, payable at any of the bank's places or seats of business, chargeable for branches, agencies or offices of discount and deposit in Canada, collection. is discounted at any other of the bank's places or seats of business, branches, agencies or offices of discount and deposit, the

Sec. 93.   bank may, in order to defray the expenses attending the collection thereof, receive or retain, in addition to the discount thereon, a percentage calculated upon the amount of such note, bill, or other negotiable security or paper, not exceeding, if the note, bill, or other negotiable security or paper is to run,—

(a) for less than thirty days, one-eighth of one per centum;

(b) for thirty days or over but less than sixty days, one-fourth of one per centum;

(c) for sixty days or over but less than ninety days, three-eighths of one per centum; and,

(d) for ninety days or over, one-half of one per centum. 53 V., c. 31, s. 82.

Except for some verbal re-arrangement made in the revision of 1906, this section dates from the Acts of 1867 and 1871. Cf. sec. 91 as to rate of interest allowed by law, and sec. 94 as to collection fees on negotiable paper payable at places other than the place of discount or a branch or agency of the same bank.

A bank is not entitled to charge any discount or commission for the cashing of any official cheque of the Government of Canada, or of any department thereof, whether drawn on the bank cashing the cheque or on any other bank (sec. 98).

Agency charges.   **94.** The bank may, in discounting any note, bill or other negotiable security or paper, *bonâ fide* payable at any place in Canada, other than that at which it is discounted, and other than one of its own places or seats of business, branches, agencies or offices of discount and deposit in Canada, receive and retain, in addition to the discount thereon, a sum not exceeding one-half of one per centum on the amount thereof, to defray the expenses of agency and charges in collecting the same. 53 V., c. 31, s. 83.

This section dates from the Acts of 1867 and 1871. Cf. sec. 93.

CHAPTER XVIII.

Deposits and the Current Account.

The receiving of deposits and the honouring of cheques upon them may be considered as the primary function of a bank, see Chapter XV., *supra,* on the "Business and Powers of a Bank." The discussion in this chapter will partially include the rights and liabilities of a bank in respect to cheques drawn upon it. See also secs. 165, *et seq.,* of the Bills of Exchange Act, Chapter LI., *infra.*

The subject of a bank's lien upon securities or money of the customer in its hands is discussed in the notes to sec. 77.

As to the duty of the bank in regard to its customer's acceptances made payable at the bank, see notes, *supra,* p. 132.

95. The bank may, subject to the provisions of this section, without the authority, aid, assistance or intervention of any other person or official being required,— *Deposits may be received from persons unable to contract.*

    (*a*) receive deposits from any person whomsoever, whatever his age, status or condition in life, and whether such person is qualified by law to enter into ordinary contracts or not; and,

    (*b*) from time to time repay any or all of the principal thereof, and pay the whole or any part of the interest thereon to such person, unless before such repayment the money so deposited in the bank is lawfully claimed as the property of some other person.

2. In the case of any such lawful claim the money so deposited may be paid to the depositor with the consent of the claimant, or to the claimant with the consent of the depositor. *Payments by consent.*

3. If the person making any such deposit could not, under the law of the province where the deposit is made, deposit and withdraw money in and from a bank without this section, the total amount to be received from such person on deposit shall *Deposit limited.*

not, at any time, exceed the sum of five hundred dollars. 53 V.,
c. 31, s. 84.

This section dates from 1890, except for some re-arrangement of the wording in 1906. The Acts of 1867 and 1871 authorized the bank merely to open offices of discount and deposit.

The section enables a bank in receiving deposits, to some extent, to deal with persons otherwise incompetent by provincial
law to contract (Re Central Bank, Morton and Block's
Claims, 1889, 17 O.R. at p. 584.) Up to an aggregate amount
of $500 the bank may receive deposits from any person without
regard to whether by provincial law such person could deposit
money in, and withdraw money from, a bank.

As to the jurisdiction of Parliament to override provincial
law in this respect, cf. Tennant v. Union Bank, discussed in
the notes to sec. 88.

Locality of deposits.

A bank with regard to deposits received and deposit receipts
issued is resident in the province where the transaction takes
place, and the deposit receipt has a locality in that province,
so that the estate to which it belongs may be liable to succession
duty in respect of it, although the deceased payee was domiciled
in a foreign country (Attorney-General v. Newman, 1901, 1 O.
L.R. 511; In re Succession Duty Act, 1902, 9 B.C.R. 174), and
the bank may be served and the deposit attached in that province as a debt due to the depositor. (County of Wentworth
v. Smith, 1893, 15 P.R. 372.) The bank is protected by payment into court in pursuance of order of court made in the province where the deposit is situate. (Harris v. Cordingly, 1899,
Q.R. 16 S.C. 501.)

Bank a debtor in respect of deposits.

The bank is a debtor to the customer (Foley v. Hill, 1848,
2 H.L.C. 28; Robarts v. Tucker, 1851, 16 Q.B. 560; Webb v.
Derbyshire, [1906] 1 Ch. 135), not a bailee or a trustee (Ex
parte Waring, 1866, 36 L.J. Ch. 151), in respect of money deposited with it, and not actually appropriated to a particular
purpose. (Farley v. Turner, 1857, 26 L.J. Ch. 710.)

And the relation is still that of debtor and creditor if the customer has overdrawn his account. (Cunliffe Brooks v. Blackburn, 1884, 9 App. Cas. 857.)

It follows that upon the insolvency of the bank the customer has merely a right of proof in respect of his current or deposit accounts. (Re Barned's Bank, 1870, 39 L.J. Ch. 635.)

It follows also that the bank can be discharged only by payments made to the customer, his agent or principal (Sims v. Bond, 1833, 5 B. & Ad. 389), or to some person who by mercantile law can give a good discharge.

Interest on deposits.

Interest is not payable on a deposit or loan except by statute or by express agreement (Edwards v. Vere, 1833, 5 B. & Ad. 282; in re Gosman, 1881, 17 Ch. D. 771), or where a contract to pay interest may be implied from the mode of dealing between the parties (In re Duncan & Co., [1905] 1 Ch. 307; In re East of England Banking Co., 1868, L.R. 4 Ch. 14), the usage of trade, or other circumstances.

By section 92 the bank may allow any rate of interest whatever upon money deposited with it. Interest-bearing deposits must be distinguished from other deposits in the annual statement (sec. 54).

Obligation to repay deposits and to honour cheques.

The bank must pay its customer's cheque on presentation if it has funds sufficient to meet the cheque. (Marzetti v. Williams, 1830, 1 B. & Ad. 415, 3 R.C. 746; Perreault v. Merchants Bank, 1905, Q.R. 27 S.C. 149.)

Substantial damages may be given for dishonouring a customer's cheque, even though proof of special damage be inadmissible (Fleming v. Bank of N.Z., [1900] A.C. 577). But if a non-trading depositor in the savings department of a bank has made his deposit subject to special terms, he may, on the wrongful refusal of the bank to pay to him personally the amount of the deposit, recover as damages only the interest and the money. The bank having received a deposit subject to certain notice of withdrawal, if required, cannot set up, as a defence to an action for the deposit, the absence of such notice, unless the refusal to pay was based on that ground. (Henderson v. Bank of Hamilton, 1894, 25 O.R. 641, 22 A.R. 414.)

If a customer's cheque is presented for payment, the bank must decide whether the state of the account between it and the customer will justify it in paying the cheque. If the cashier or teller counts out the amount of the cheque and places the money upon the counter or the ledge of the wicket in front of him, the payment is complete and cannot be revoked by the bank, even though the money has not been counted and accepted by the person presenting the cheque. (Chambers v. Miller, 1862, 13 C.B. N.S. 125; and cases cited in Hall v. Hatch, 1901, 3 O.L.R. 147.) The property in the money passes from the bank to the payee of the cheque so that it can be attached as his property even before he has touched it with his hand. (Hall v. Hatch, *supra.*)

The bank must pay cheques in the order of presentation (Kilsby v. Williams, 1822, 1 B. & Ald. 815), unless the bank has notice of the death of the customer or of a countermand of payment by him (Bills of Exchange Act, sec. 167). In Marzetti v. Williams, *supra,* and Robarts v. Tucker, 1851, 16 Q.B. 560, it is said that the banker is entitled to a reasonable time to satisfy himself of the genuineness of the signature to a cheque or bill of exchange. Cf. Todd v. Union Bank, 1887, 4 Man. R. 204. But in Bank of England v. Vagliano, [1891] A.C. at p. 157, Lord Macnaghten expressly lays it down that bankers who undertake the duty of paying their customers' acceptances must pay off-hand, and this reasoning would seem to apply equally to cheques.

A bank contracting for valuable consideration with a customer's agent or a third party to honour the customer's outstanding cheques is liable to be sued by the customer for breach of contract in the event of the specified cheques being subsequently dishonoured. (Fleming v. Bank of New Zealand, [1900] A.C. 577.)

Pass-book and vouchers.

The effect of receipt from a bank of a pass-book and vouchers, and their retention without comment by a customer, are considered in Rex v. Bank of Montreal, 10 O.L.R. 117, by Anglin, J., who decided that there is no contractual obligation on the part of the customer to examine his pass-book. This case was affirmed by the Court of Appeal, 1906, 11 O.L.R. 595. Maclaren, J.A., at p. 605, says: ''The trial judge has reviewed very

fully the leading English and American cases in which the
effect of the receipt from a bank of a pass-book and vouchers, and their retention by the customer have been considered
and discussed. He comes to the conclusion that under the principles laid down in Leather Manufacturers' Bank v. Morgan,
1866, 117 U.S. 96, and De Frees Critten v. Chemical National
Bank, 1902, 171 N.Y. 219, the customer might be held in the
United States to be estopped from objecting where he had failed
to check over his pass-book himself or had not exercised reasonable supervision over the clerk to whom he had entrusted it
under circumstances where he would not be estopped in England. In support of this conclusion he refers particularly to
the case of Chatterton v. London and County Bank, 1890-1,
a summarized report of which appears in Paget on Banking, at
pp. 120 *et seq.*, and also to the cases discussed in Hart on Banking at pp. 200-203. It is to be observed that in most of these
cases the question considered is whether the customer who receives his pass-book and vouchers owes a duty to the bank to
examine them, and whether he is estopped from objecting if he
does not do so, or does not object before the bank has altered
its position. In the present case there is more. The department regularly notified the bank each month that the cheques
and statement had been found correct. Such receipts are not
at all on the same footing as those that are frequently signed
by the messenger of the customer when he receives the cheques
and vouchers at the end of the month or at other periods. These
latter can have little binding effect unless there is an express
or implied contract that the customer will examine them and
report within a reasonable time as to their correctness. Ordinarily the retention of the pass-book and the vouchers without
objection could only operate against the customer where there
existed such a contract by way of estoppel, and where the facts
of the particular case were such as to justify the application of
this doctrine.'' Rex v. Bank of Montreal was affirmed by the
Supreme Court on the 19th of February, 1907.

A banker's pass-book, which is numbered and in which it is
stipulated that the deposits recorded in it will not be repaid
without its production, is a proper subject of *donatio mortis
causa*, and delivery of such a book in anticipation of death
operates as a transfer of the debt to take effect upon death.
(Brown v. Toronto General Trusts, 1900, 32 O.R. 319.)

Appropriation and set off in the current account.

Payments to and drawings upon current accounts are taken
to be set off against each other automatically the earliest drawing against the earliest payment and so on. (The "rule in Clayton's Case," Devaynes v. Noble, 1816, 1 Mer. 608, 3 R.C. 329,
15 R.R. 161, discussed in The Mecca, [1897] A.C. at pp. 293-
296.)

The rule does not apply to a case where there is no account
current between the parties, or where a contrary intention appears from the circumstances. (City Discount Co. v. McLean,
1874, L.R. 9 C.P. 692; Gillies v. Commercial Bank, 1895, 10
Man. R. 460, 479. It may appear from an account rendered
or other circumstances that the creditor intended not to make any
appropriation, but to reserve the right. The general rule is
that when a debtor is making a payment to his creditor, he
may appropriate the money as he pleases, and the creditor must
apply it accordingly. (McArthur v. McMillan, 1886, 3 Man. R.
377.) If the debtor does not make any appropriation at the
time when he makes the payment, the right of appropriation
devolves upon the creditor, and he has the right of election "up
to the very last moment" (The Mecca, *supra*) and he may make
an appropriation even when he is being examined as a witness
in an action by him against the debtor. (Seymour v. Pickett,
[1905] 1 K.B. 715.)

Where an account is continued after dissolution of partnership in the same mode as before, the rule in Clayton's Case will
apply (Laing v. Campbell, 1865, 36 Beav. 3), but it will be
otherwise where distinct accounts are kept and the new firm,
as creditors, have appropriated a payment to the new account.
(Simson v. Ingham, 1823, 2 B. & C. 65). As to what dealings
with a firm's account will discharge a retired partner from liability for an old overdraft, see Rouse v. Bradford, [1894] A.C.
586.

Where the members of a firm have separate private accounts
with the bankers of the firm, and a balance is due to the bankers
from the firm, the bankers have no lien for such balance on the
separate accounts. (Richards v. Bank of B.N.A., 1901, 8 B.C.
R. 143, 209; Watts v. Christie, 1849, 11 Beav. 546.)

On the death of a surety for a current account, it is common
practice for the bank to close the account and open a fresh one

with the customer. This prevents the surety's estate getting
the benefit of subsequent payments to current account by the
customer. (In re Sherry, 1884, 25 Ch. D. 692.)
Where an insolvent testator, having a deposit to his credit
in a bank at the time of his death, was indebted to the bank on
a note under discount, which had not then matured and the
executors did not withdraw or demand the deposit before the
maturity of the note, it was held that the bank might set off the
debt on the note against the deposit, and rank for the balance
of the debt against the estate. (Ontario Bank v. Routhier,
1900, 32 O.R. 67; cf. Thomas v. Smith, 1900, Q.R. 16 S.C. 354.)

The rule in Clayton's Case, *supra*, attributing the first
drawings out to the first payments in does not apply
where a person who holds money as a trustee or in
a fiduciary character pays it to his account at his bankers and mixes it with his own money, and afterwards
draws out sums by cheques in the ordinary manner. The
drawer must be taken to have drawn out his own money in preference to the trust money. (In re Hallett's Estate, Knatchbull
v. Hallett, 1879, 13 Ch. D. 696; In re Oatway, Hertslet v. Oatway, [1903] 2 Ch. 356.) But the rule does apply as between
two *cestui que trustent* whose money the trustee has paid into
his own account, so that the first sum paid in will be held to
have been first drawn out. (In re Hallett, *supra;* In re Stenning, Wood v. Stenning, [1895] 2 Ch. 433; Bailey v. Jellett,
1884, 9 A.R. 187.)

If money held by a person in a fiduciary character has been
paid by him to his account at his bankers, the person for whom
he held the money can follow it, and has a charge on the balance
in the banker's hands (In re Hallett's Estate, *supra*), but for
this purpose there must be a specific fund, capable of being
identified, into which the trust money has been converted. (In
re Hallett & Co., Ex parte Blane, [1894] 2 Q.B. 237.)

If a customer keeps several accounts at a bank they may be
treated as one by the bank for the purpose of setting off a debit
balance in one against a credit balance in another. (In re
European Bank, Agra Bank's Claim, 1872, L.R. 8 Ch. 41; cf.
Johnson v. Roberts, 1875, L.R. 10 Ch. 505; Mutton v. Peat,
[1900] 2 Ch. 79, and see also the subject of a bank's general
lien discussed in the notes to sec. 77.)

Deposit receipts.

A bank may under the Bank Act issue a certificate or receipt, commonly known as a "deposit receipt" acknowledging the deposit with the bank of a certain sum of money and the obligation of the bank to pay or account for the same with interest to the depositor or to the depositor "or order." The effect of the endorsement of such a receipt by the depositor depends largely on the wording of the receipt.

There is high authority in favour of the view that a document which is a receipt for a certain sum "payable to" the depositor or order, or "which the bank will repay" to the depositor or order, possesses all the qualities of a promissory note notwithstanding that it also contains clauses providing that the sum deposited, in order to bear interest, must remain in the bank for a certain period, and that it cannot be withdrawn except on a certain number of days' notice, and that the receipt must be given up to the bank when payment is required. (Richer v. Voyer, 1874, L.R. 5 P.C. at p. 477; Re Central Bank, Morton & Block's Claims, 1889, 17 O.R. 574.) It has been said (Re Central Bank, *supra*, at p. 585) that the term requiring the receipt to be given up merely expresses what the law would imply and may be regarded as surplusage, and that the other clauses referred to have not the effect of preventing the receipt from being a promissory note, as they do not make the time of payment uncertain. It is merely a matter of computation, having regard to the date of the receipt, to ascertain when the money may be withdrawn, and the requirements of previous notice merely make the receipt one payable so many days after the occurrence of a specified event, which the holder can determine, such as "after sight" or "after demand."

If a deposit receipt is a promissory note the effect of endorsement to a holder in due course would be to pass the legal right to the money payable thereunder to the endorsee, who might recover in his own name and free from all the equities that might exist between the original holder and the bank. If it is not a promissory note, but yet is expressed to be payable to the depositor or his order, it may nevertheless be so far negotiable as to pass a good title to a *bonâ fide* purchaser for value who takes without notice of any infirmity of title. This is on the ground of representation and estoppel. (Re Central Bank, *supra*, at p. 586 and cases there cited, *sed quære*.)

Where, however, the receipt is expressed to be payable to the depositor and not also to his order, it is said that negotiabil- Deposits ity is negatived (Re Central Bank, *supra,* at p. 583), and where receipt. the receipt is worded "for which the bank will account to" the depositor, it cannot be transferred merely by endorsement and delivery so as to entitle the holder to demand payment of the money represented by it. (Saderquist v. Ontario Bank, 1889, 15 A.R. 609; Lee v. Bank of British North America, 1879, 30 C.P. 255, and cases cited.) But if the depositor for valuable consideration endorses such a receipt, and delivers it to another person with the intention of passing all his right and title to the money represented by the receipt, which money the bank pays to such other person, this would be a good defence on equitable grounds to an action by the original depositor against the bank. (Mander v. Royal Canadian Bank, 1869, 20 C.P. 125; S.C. 21 C.P. 492.)

A deposit receipt which on its face states that it is not transferable and that cheques cannot be drawn against it is clearly not a negotiable instrument, but the endorsement upon it of an order to pay and the delivery of the document operate as an equitable assignment of the fund. It is not necessary to give notice to the bank in order to complete the assignment (In re Griffin, [1899] 1 Ch. 408; cf. In re Commercial Bank of Manitoba, Barkwell's Claim, 1897, 11 Man. R. 494), although notice may be necessary as against a subsequent assignee.

A deposit receipt is merely the evidence of a debt, and, notwithstanding a condition in the receipt requiring its production before payment, the bank cannot refuse to pay the assignee in insolvency of the depositor or the depositor himself, provided it is indemnified not only against double liability, but against double vexation. (Bank of Montreal v. Little, 1870, 17 Gr. 313, 316.)

96. The bank shall not be bound to see to the execution of Bank not to any trust, whether expressed, implied or constructive, to which see to trusts n deposits. any deposit made under the authority of this Act is subject.

2. Except only in the case of a lawful claim, by some other Receipt of one of two person before repayment, the receipt of the person in whose joint name any such deposit stands, or, if it stands in the names of depositors sufficient. two persons, the receipt of one, or, if it stands in the names of

Sec. 96.   more than two persons, the receipt of a majority of such persons, shall, notwithstanding any trust to which such deposit
is then subject, and whether or not the bank sought to be charged
Or of a   with such trust, and with which the deposit has been made, had
majority. notice thereof, be a sufficient discharge to all concerned for the
payment of any money payable in respect of such deposit.

Application.   3. The bank shall not be bound to see to the application of
the money paid upon such receipt. 53 V., c. 31, s. 84.

Section 52 provides that the bank shall not be bound to see
to the execution of any trust to which any share of its stock
is subject. This section contains a similar provision as to any
trust to which any deposit made under the authority of this
section is subject.

Sufficiency of   There are, however, differences in the wording of the two
receipt.   sections. Firstly, in the case of shareholders, the receipt of
one of two or more persons in whose name shares stand is a
sufficient receipt to the bank for any money payable in respect
of such shares. In the case of a deposit, the receipt of one of
two persons in whose name the deposit stands is sufficient, but
if it stands in the name of more than two, the receipt of a
majority is required.

Apart from this section the receipt of one of two joint depositors, not being partners in trade, would not have been sufficient. (Innes v. Stephenson, 1831, 1 M. & Rob. 145; Husband
v. Davis, 1851, 10 C.B. 645.)

Secondly, the foregoing provision as to the sufficiency of
shareholders' receipts is subject to the clause "unless express
notice to the contrary has been given to the bank." In the case
of depositors, "except only in the case of a lawful claim, by some
other person before repayment," the receipt is declared to be sufficient "notwithstanding any trust to which such deposit is then
subject, and whether or not the bank sought to be charged with
such trust, and with which the deposit has been made, had notice thereof."

The practical effect of the two sections, as regards the sufficiency of a receipt, is perhaps not very different. In the one
case an "express notice" that the receipt is insufficient, in the
other case a "lawful claim" by some person other than the person giving the receipt, before repayment, is required.

A "lawful claim" means one which is *primâ facie* substan- Sec. 96.
tial. (In re Bank of Toronto & Dickinson, 1906, 8 O.W.R. 323.) Lawful
In this case money had been deposited to the credit of "the claim.
executors of the estate of the late J.D." One of the executors
subsequently served formal written notice on the bank, forbidding it to pay out money except on cheques signed by all three
executors. It was held that the case came within the exception
to sub-sec. 2, and an order was made for payment of the money
into court, unless the parties would agree that it should be retained as if it were in court. Cf. Dominion Bank & Kennedy, 1906,
8 O.W.R. 755, 834.

So far as the obligation to see to the execution of any trust No obliga-
is concerned, this section is in the same terms as sec. 52, and tion to see to
the notes to that section may usefully be consulted in regard to trust.
this section. As there pointed out, the provision seems to be
directly applicable to trusts of which the bank has notice, for
it would require no legislative provision to free the bank from
responsibility for not seeing to the execution of a trust, the existence of which has not in some way been brought to its knowledge.

A bank is liable if it knowingly participates in a breach of
trust. (Cf. Gray v. Johnston, 1868, L.R. 3 H.L. 1.) Where
it is proposed by the customer of the bank to apply a balance
standing to the credit of the customer on a trust account or
other trust moneys in discharge or reduction of a debt due from
the customer upon his private account, the bank, *ex hypothesi,*
knows the intended application of the trust moneys, and therefore may readily be held to have known that the transaction
was a breach of trust. But, although the bank knows that the
money with which the customer repays an overdraft on his
private account is derived from the funds of a third party,
it does not necessarily follow that it knows of a misapplication.
The circumstances of the case may be consistent with a right
on the part of the customer to make the transfer or application
in question. Cf. Hart on Banking, 2nd ed., 1906, p. 161; and
see cases cited in next paragraph.

The bank may treat all a customer's personal accounts as
one (In re European Bank, 1872, L.R. 8 Ch. 41), but may not
use the balance of an account, as to which it has notice that it
is not a personal account, to meet a deficiency on a personal

Sec. 96.
No obliga-
tion to see to
execution of
trust.

account (Ex parte Kingston, 1871, L.R. 6 Ch. 632; cf. Union Bank of Australia v. Murray-Aynsley, [1898] A.C. 693; Shields v Bank of Ireland, [1901] 1 Ir. R. 222, and Bank of N.S.W. v. Goulburn, [1902] A.C. 543.)

If, however, the bank receives money in good faith as money belonging to an estate of which it is a creditor, without notice of any trust, it may retain the same as against an alleged *cestui que trust* of such money. (Giraldi v. Banque Jacques-Cartier, 1883, 9 S.C.R. 597.)

Where, however, a customer, who is a trustee, draws a cheque upon a trust account in favour of a third party, the bank will have its attention drawn to the object or purpose of the payment only under exceptional circumstances. It is under no obligation to enquire as to the purpose for which a cheque is drawn, and as it is not likely that the customer will voluntarily explain that he is about to misapply trust funds, it will obviously be very seldom that the bank will have notice of the breach intended. Hart, p. 163.

In order to hold a bank justified in refusing to pay a demand of a customer, the customer being a trustee and drawing a cheque as trustee, there must, in the first place, be some misapplication, some breach of trust, intended by the trustee, and there must be, in the second place, proof that the bank is privy to the intent to make this misapplication of the trust funds. (Gray v. Johnston, *supra;* Bailey v. Jephcott, 1884, 9 A.R. 187; Clench v. Consolidated Bank, 1880, 31 C.P. 169.) The fact that the bank is personally interested in the misapplication may be very good evidence of notice, but in point of law the personal interest is immaterial, and actual notice of, and participation in, the breach of trust is sufficient ground of liability. Hart, p. 165.

If depositor
dies, claim
not exceed-
ing $500, how
proved.

97. If a person dies, having a deposit with the bank not exceeding the sum of five hundred dollars, the production to the bank and deposit with it of,—

(a) any authenticated copy of the probate of the will of the deceased depositor, or of letters of administration of his estate, or of letters of verification of heirship, or of the act of curatorship or tutorship, granted by any court in Canada having power to grant the same, or by any court or authority in England, Wales, Ireland, or any British colony, or of any testament, testamentary or testament dative expede in Scotland; or,

(*b*) an authentic notarial copy of the will of the deceased depositor, if such will is in notarial form, according to the law of the province of Quebec; or,

(*c*) if the deceased depositor died out of His Majesty's dominions, any authenticated copy of the probate of his will, or letters of administration of his property, or other document of like import, granted by any court or authority having the requisite power in such matters;

shall be sufficient justification and authority to the directors for paying such deposit, in pursuance of and in conformity to such probate, letters of administration, or other document as aforesaid. 63-64 V., c. 26, s. 20.

This section dates from 1900 except for some re-arrangement of the wording in 1906.

Letters of administration are valid so long as they are un-revoked, even though their grant was based upon fraud or forgery, and a bank paying money in good faith to an administrator who, by the law of the province where the money is payable, is entitled to receive it, is protected from liability to pay a second time. (Irwin v. Bank of Montreal, 1876, 38 U.C.R. 375.)

By this section special provision is made authorizing the bank to pay the amount of a deposit, not exceeding $500, upon the production and deposit with it of an authentic notarial copy of the will, or an authenticated copy of the probate of the will or of letters of administration, etc., granted by a court of competent jurisdiction. This provision dispenses with the necessity of having letters of a foreign court resealed, or of obtaining grant of letters to a representative resident within the province where the debt is situate.

Even if the deposit exceeds $500, and a representative of the deceased depositor is appointed in another province where the bank has an office, the bank might pay such representative at the latter place (cf. notes to sec. 76, *supra*, pp. 138-9.

To be paid at par.

98. The bank shall not charge any discount or commission for the cashing of any official cheque of the Government of Canada or of any department thereof, whether drawn on the bank cashing the cheque or on any other bank.   53 V., c. 31, s. 103.

Cf. secs. 93 and 94 as to agency and collection charges in other cases.

CHAPTER XIX.

THE PURCHASE OF THE ASSETS OF A BANK.

The sections included in this chapter were first enacted by the Bank Act Amendment Act, 1900, and the Act amending the same (63 Vict., c. 27.) They are intended to provide a convenient method whereby a bank, which desires to dispose of its business, may be able to do so without applying to Parliament.

The first Order in Council passed under the provisions of the Act was that of the 31st of December, 1900, approving an agreement, dated the 15th day of December, 1900, between the Bank of British Columbia and the Canadian Bank of Commerce, and a proposed increase of the capital stock of the latter bank from $6,000,000 to $8,000,000 in order to provide for the payment to the former bank of $2,000,000 of fully paid-up shares of the latter bank as provided in the said agreement. See Dominion Statutes, 1902, p. LV.

THE PURCHASE OF THE ASSETS OF A BANK.

99. Any bank may sell the whole or any portion of its assets to any other bank which may purchase such assets; and the selling and purchasing banks may, for such purposes, enter into an agreement of sale and purchase, which agreement shall contain all the terms and conditions connected with the sale and purchase of such assets. 63-64 V., c. 26, s. 33. Bank may sell assets to another bank.

100. The consideration for any such sale and purchase may be as agreed upon between the selling and purchasing banks. Consideration.

2. If the consideration, or any portion thereof, is shares of the capital stock of the purchasing bank, the agreement shall provide for the amount of the shares of the purchasing bank to be paid to the selling bank. If in shares of capital stock.

3. Until such shares so paid to the selling bank have been sold by such bank, or have been distributed among and accepted Not considered issued until sold or distributed.

Sec. 100.   by the shareholders of such bank, they shall not be considered issued shares of the purchasing bank for the purposes of its note circulation. 63-64 V., c. 26, s. 34.

By section 61 the total amount of a bank's notes in circulation at any time shall not exceed the amount of the unimpaired paid-up capital of the bank.

Agreement of sale to be submitted to selling shareholders at meeting.   **101.** The agreement of sale and purchase shall be submitted to the shareholders of the selling bank, either at the annual general meeting of such bank or at a special general meeting thereof called for the purpose.

Copy to each shareholder by mail.   2. A copy of the agreement shall be mailed, postpaid, to each shareholder of such bank to his last known address, at least four weeks previously to the date of the meeting at which the agreement is to be submitted, together with a notice of the time and place of the holding of such meeting. 63-64 V., c. 26, s. 35.

A special general meeting of the shareholders may be called as provided by sec. 31. As to the annual meeting, see notes to that section.

Agreement may be executed if they approve.   **102.** If at such meeting the agreement is approved by resolution carried by the votes of shareholders, present in person or represented by proxy, representing not less than two-thirds of the amount of the subscribed capital stock of the bank, the agreement may be executed under the seals of the banks, parties thereto, and application may be made to the Governor in Council, through the Minister, for approval thereof.

Approval of Governor in Council.   2. Until the agreement is approved by the Governor in Council it shall not be of any force or effect. 63-64 V., c. 26, s. 36.

As to proxies and voting rights of shareholders, see sec. 32 and notes.

The Minister means the Minister of Finance and Receiver-General (sec. 2).

103. If the agreement provides for the payment of the con- Sec. 103.
sideration for such sale and purchase, in whole or in part, in Approval of
shares of the capital stock of the purchasing bank, and for such shareholders
purpose it is necessary to increase the capital stock of such bank, ing bank.
the agreement shall not be executed on behalf of the purchasing
bank, unless nor until it is approved by the shareholders thereof
at the annual general meeting, or at a special general meeting
of such shareholders. 63-64 V., c. 26, s. 37.

104. The Governor in Council may, on the application for Necessary
his approval of the agreement, approve of the increase of the increase of
capital stock of the purchasing bank, which is necessary to pro- approved.
vide for the payment of the shares of such bank to the selling
bank, as provided in the said agreement. 63-64 V., c. 26, s. 38.

105. The provisions of this Act with regard to,—   Ordinary
    (*a*) the increase of the capital stock of the bank by by-law provisions
        of the shareholders approved by the Treasury Board; and, not to
    (*b*) the allotment and sale of such increased stock; apply.
shall not apply to any increase of stock made or provided for
under the authority of the last two preceding sections.   63-64
V., c. 26, s. 38.

The provisions referred to are contained in secs. 33 and 34.

106. The approval of the Governor in Council shall not be Conditions
given to the agreement, unless,—   on which
    (*a*) the approval thereof is recommended by the Treasury Council may
        Board;   approve
    (*b*) the application for approval thereof is made, by or on
        behalf of the bank executing it, within three months from
        the date of execution of the agreement; and,
    (*c*) it appears to the satisfaction of the Governor in Council
        that all the requirements of this Act in connection with
        the approval of the agreement by the shareholders of the
15—BANK ACT.

Sec. 106.

selling and purchasing banks have been complied with, and that notice of the intention of the banks to apply to the Governor in Council for the approval of the agreement has been published for at least four weeks in the *Canada Gazette,* and in one or more newspapers published in places where the chief offices or places of business of the banks are situate.

Information.

2. Such banks shall afford all information that the Minister requires.

Approval may be refused.

3. Nothing herein contained shall be construed to prevent the Governor in Council or the Treasury Board from refusing to approve of the agreement or to recommend its approval. 63-64 V., c. 26, s. 39.

Further conditions.

107. The agreement shall not be approved of unless it appears that,—

(a) proper provisions have been made for the payment of the liabilities of the selling bank;

(b) the agreement provides for the assumption and payment by the purchasing bank of the notes of the selling bank issued and intended for circulation, outstanding and in circulation; and,

(c) the amounts of the notes of both the purchasing and selling banks, issued for circulation, outstanding and in circulation, as shown by the then last monthly returns of the banks, do not altogether exceed the then paid-up capital of the purchasing bank; or, if the amount of such notes does exceed such paid-up capital, an amount in cash, equal to the excess of such notes over such paid-up capital, has been deposited by the purchasing bank with the Minister.

Deposit.

2. The amount so deposited as aforesaid shall be held by the Minister as security for the redemption of the said excess of notes; and, when such excess, or any portion thereof, has been redeemed and cancelled, the amount so deposited, or an amount

equal to the amount of excess so redeemed and cancelled, shall Sec. 107.
from time to time, be repaid by the Minister to the purchasing
bank, but without interest, on the application of such bank, and
on the production of such evidence as the Minister may require
to show that the notes in regard to which such repayment is
asked have been redeemed and cancelled. 63-64 V., c. 27, s. 1.

108. The notes of the selling bank so assumed and to be Notes of
paid by the purchasing bank shall, on the approval of the agree- selling bank
ment, be deemed to be, for all intents and purposes, notes of the notes of
purchasing bank issued for circulation; and the purchasing bank.
bank shall be liable in the same manner and to the same extent
as if it had issued them for circulation.

2. The amount at the credit of the selling bank in the Circu- Circulation
lation Fund shall, on the approval of the agreement, be trans- Fund.
ferred to the credit of the purchasing bank.

3. The notes of the selling bank shall not be re-issued, but Notes to be
shall be called in, redeemed and cancelled as quickly as possible. called in.
63-64 V., c. 26, s. 41.

As to the issue and circulation of notes, see sec. 61. The
Circulation Fund is provided for by secs. 64 *et seq.*

109. The approval by the Governor in Council of the agree- Evidence of
ment shall be evidenced by a certified copy of the order in Governor in
council approving thereof. Council.

2. Such certified copy shall be conclusive evidence of the Order in
approval of the agreement therein referred to, and of the regu- clusive.
larity of all proceedings in connection therewith. 63-64 V., c.
26, s. 42.

110. On the agreement being approved of by the Governor On approval
in Council, the assets therein referred to as sold and purchased in Council
shall, in accordance with and subject to the terms thereof, and the assets
without any further conveyance, become vested in the purchas- pass.
ing bank.

Sec. 110.
Further
assurance.

2. The selling bank shall, from time to time, subject to the terms of the agreement, execute such formal and separate conveyances, assignments and assurances, for registration purposes or otherwise, as are reasonably required to confirm or evidence the vesting in the purchasing bank of the full title or ownership of the assets referred to in the agreement. 63-64 V., c. 26, s. 43.

Selling bank
to cease busi-
ness and be
wound up.

111. As soon as the agreement is approved of by the Governor in Council, the selling bank shall cease to issue or re-issue notes for circulation, and shall cease to transact any business, except such as is necessary to enable it to carry out the agreement, to realize upon any assets not included in the agreement, to pay and discharge its liabilities, and generally to wind up its business; and the charter or Act of incorporation of such bank, and any Acts in amendment thereof then in force, shall continue in force only for the purposes in this section specified. 63-64 V., c. 26, s. 44.

CHAPTER XX.

RETURNS BY A BANK.

The following returns to the government are required by the Bank Act.

Sec. 112, monthly returns in the form set forth in Schedule D.

Sec. 113, special returns called for by the Minister.

Sec. 114, a return of all dividends, etc., unpaid for more than five years.

Sec. 114, a return of all drafts or bills of exchange issued by the bank and unpaid for more than five years.

Sec. 114, a certified list of shareholders.

Secs. 147 to 151 impose penalties upon a bank which neglects to transmit any of the above mentioned returns.

Sec. 152 provides that when any return is transmitted by post, the date of deposit in the post office, as shown by the post office mark or stamp upon the envelope or wrapper enclosing the return, shall be taken *primâ facie* to be the day when the return was transmitted.

By sec. 153 provision is made for the criminal and civil liability of persons who make any wilfully false or deceptive statement in any account, statement, return, report or other document respecting the affairs of a bank, etc.

Minister in the Act means the Minister of Finance and Receiver-General (sec. 2).

RETURNS.

112. Monthly returns shall be made by the bank to the Minister in the form set forth in schedule D to this Act. Monthly.

2. Such returns shall be made up and sent in within the first fifteen days of each month, and shall exhibit the condition of the bank on the last juridical day of the month last preceding. Within first 15 days.

3. Such returns shall be signed by the chief accountant and by the president, or vice-president, or the director then acting How signed.

Sec. 112.

as president, and by the manager, cashier or other principal officer of the bank at its chief place of business. 53 V., c. 31, s. 85.

Monthly returns.

Cf. sec. 113 which empowers the Minister of Finance to call for special returns.

Monthly returns have been required since 1871. Sec 13 of 34 Vict., c. 5, provided as follows:

"Monthly returns shall be made by the bank to the government in the following form, and shall be made within the first ten days of each month, and shall exhibit the condition of the bank on the last juridical day of the month preceding; and such monthly returns shall be signed by the President or Vice-President, or the Director (or, if the bank be *en commandité*, the principal partner) then acting as President, and by the Manager, Cashier, or other principal officer of the bank at its chief seat of business."

The form prescribed in the Act of 1871 was itself an elaboration of the form of statement required to be published in certain cases under chapter 21 of the Consolidated Statutes of Canada, 1859.

By statutes subsequent to 1871 changes were made from time to time, the changes being designed to make the information given more detailed and trustworthy, without however disturbing that general continuity of form which is desirable for the purpose of comparison.

The present form was adopted in 1900. It is printed among the schedules in Chapter XXVI., *infra*.

The officers making the return should be careful to classify the items of assets and liabilities under the proper heads. Improper classification of items may constitute a false or deceptive statement within sec. 153.

The monthly returns of the various banks are published each month in a consolidated form by the government.

Special returns.

113. The Minister may also call for special returns from any bank, whenever, in his judgment, they are necessary to afford a full and complete knowledge of its condition.

How made.

2. Such special returns shall be made and signed in the manner and by the persons specified in the last preceding section.

3. Such special returns shall be made and sent in within Sec. 113.
thirty days from the date of the demand therefor by the Min- Within 30
ister: Provided that the Minister may extend the time for _{days from}
demand.
sending in such special returns for such further period, not
exceeding thirty days, as he thinks expedient. 53 V., c. 31, s.
86.

The special returns which may be called for under this section are in addition to the monthly returns required to be made
by sec. 112.

114. The bank shall, within twenty days after the close of Annual.
each calendar year, transmit or deliver to the Minister a return,—

(a) of all dividends which have remained unpaid for more
than five years; and,

(b) of all amounts or balances in respect of which no transactions have taken place, or upon which no interest has
been paid, during the five years prior to the date of such
return:

Provided that, in the case of moneys deposited for a fixed period,
the said term of five years shall be reckoned from the date of
the termination of such fixed period.

2. The return mentioned in the last preceding subsection What return
shall set forth,— shall show.

(a) the name of each shareholder or creditor to whom such
dividends, amounts or balances are, according to the books
of the bank, payable;

(b) the last known address of each such shareholder or creditor;

(c) the amount due to each such shareholder or creditor;

(d) the agency of the bank at which the last transaction took
place;

(e) the date of such last transaction; and,

(f) if such shareholder or creditor is known to the bank to
be dead, the names and addresses of his legal representatives, so far as known to the bank.

Sec. 114.

Further
annual
return.

3. The bank shall likewise, within twenty days after the close of each calendar year, transmit or deliver to the Minister a return of all drafts or bills of exchange, issued by the bank to any person, and remaining unpaid for more than five years prior to the date of such return, setting forth so far as known,—

Particulars.

(a) the names of the persons to whom, or at whose request such drafts or bills of exchange were issued;

(b) the addresses of such persons;

(c) the names of the payees of such drafts or bills of exchange;

(d) the amounts and dates of such drafts or bills of exchange;

(e) the names of the places where such drafts or bills of exchange were payable; and,

(f) the agencies of the bank respectively from which such drafts or bills of exchange were issued.

How annual
returns
signed.

4. The returns required by the foregoing provisions of this section shall be signed by the chief accountant, and by the president or vice-president or the director then acting as president, and by the manager, cashier or other principal officer of the bank, at its chief place of business.

Annual list.

5. The bank shall also, within twenty days after the close of each calendar year, transmit or deliver to the Minister a certified list showing,—

(a) the names of the shareholders of the bank on the last day of such calendar year, with their additions and residences;

(b) the number of shares then held by them respectively; and,

(c) the value at par of such shares.

To Parliament.

6. The Minister shall lay such returns and lists before Parliament at the next session thereof. 53 V., c. 31, ss. 87 and 88; 63-64 V., c. 26, s. 21.

Sec. 114.
Annual
returns of
unpaid
dividends,
etc.

This section dates from 1890, except sub-sec. 3. The present division into sub-sections is a result of the revision of 1906.

The effect of the first two sub-sections is to secure to a bank, so long as it is solvent, the benefit of unpaid dividends and other amounts and balances in respect of which transactions have ceased to take place or interest ceased to be paid. Until the dividends, etc., are claimed, the sole obligation of the bank is to make the required returns so as to give notice by means of the government publications to any persons who may be entitled and allow them an opportunity to claim payment.

Under sec. 126, the liability of a bank for moneys deposited with it or dividends declared and payable on its capital stock is never barred by any statute of limitations or enactment or law relating to prescription. It is therefore necessary, in the event of the winding-up of a bank, to provide a fund to meet claims which may be made from time to time to unpaid dividends and deposits, and interest, if any. This is done by sec. 115.

Sub-sec. 3 dates from 1900. Its purpose is to give notice to persons in whose favour any drafts or bills may have been issued, and to allow them an opportunity to claim the proceeds.

The lists of shareholders are published annually by the government.

CHAPTER XXI.

PAYMENTS TO THE MINISTER UPON WINDING-UP.

Unclaimed
moneys.

115. If, in the event of the winding-up of the business of the bank in insolvency, or under any general winding-up Act, or otherwise, any moneys payable by the liquidator, either to shareholders or depositors, remain unclaimed,—

(a) for the period of three years from the date of suspension of payment by the bank; or,

(b) for a like period from the commencement of the winding-up of such business; or,

(c) until the final winding-up of such business, if the business is finally wound up before the expiration of the said three years;

With
interest.

such moneys and all interest thereon shall, notwithstanding any statute of limitations or other Act relating to prescription, be paid to the Minister, to be held by him subject to all rightful claims on behalf of any person other than the bank.

Governor in
Council may
order pay-
ment to per-
son entitled.

2. If a claim to any moneys so paid is thereafter established to the satisfaction of the Treasury Board, the Governor in Council shall, on the report of the Treasury Board, direct payment thereof to be made to the person entitled thereto, together with interest on the principal sum thereof, at the rate of three per centum per annum, for a period not exceeding six years from the date of payment thereof to the Minister as aforesaid: Provided that no such interest shall be paid or payable on such principal sum, unless interest thereon was payable by the bank paying the same to the Minister.

Interest.

Bank dis-
charged.

3. Upon payment to the Minister as herein provided, the bank and its assets shall be held to be discharged from further liability for the amounts so paid. 53 V., c. 31, s. 88.

See notes to sec. 114.

By sec. 126 the liability of the bank, under any law, custom or agreement, to repay moneys deposited with it and interest, if any, and to pay dividends declared and payable on its capital stock, shall continue, notwithstanding any statute of limitations, or any enactment or law relating to prescription. Hence the necessity for this section.

The sections providing for the insolvency of a bank are sec. 125 *et seq.* As to the application to a bank of the provisions of the Dominion Winding-up Act, see Chapter XXIV., *infra.*

116. Upon the winding-up of a bank in insolvency or under any general winding-up Act, or otherwise, the assignees, liquidators, directors, or other officials in charge of such winding-up, shall, before the final distribution of the assets, or within three years from the commencement of the suspension of payment by the bank, whichever shall first happen, pay over to the Minister a sum, out of the assets of the bank, equal to the amount then outstanding of the notes intended for circulation issued by the bank. *Circulation outstanding at distribution of assets.*

2. Upon such payment being made, the bank and its assets shall be relieved from all further liability in respect of such outstanding notes. *Bank relieved.*

3. The sum so paid shall be held by the Minister and applied for the purpose of redeeming, whenever presented, such outstanding notes, without interest. 53 V., c. 31, s. 88. *Minister to redeem.*

This section is designed to guard against the charging of the Bank Circulation Redemption Fund with the payment of the notes of an insolvent bank which are presented after the liquidator has distributed the assets. This safeguard is necessary because by sec. 64 the principle is laid down that every bank note, once in circulation, shall be redeemable, no matter how long it may be outstanding. An incidental result of the section is that an insolvent bank is deprived of the profit, if any, derived from the loss or destruction of outstanding bank notes.

As to the payment of interest on the notes of a bank which has suspended payment and when such notes cease to bear interest, see sec. 65.

Sec. 116.   Cf. sec. 158 of the Winding-up Act which provides that the
Outstanding liquidators shall ascertain as nearly as possible the amount of
notes of   notes of the bank intended for circulation and actually outstand-
insolvent   ing, and shall reserve dividends on any part of the said amount
bank .   in respect of which claims are not filed, until the expiration of
at least two years after the date of the winding-up order, or
until the last dividend, if such last dividend is not made until
after the experation of the said time. And further (by sub-sec.
2) that if claims are not filed and dividends applied for in respect of any part of the said amount before the period by this
section limited, the dividends so reserved shall form the last or
part of the last dividend.

CHAPTER XXII.

The Curator.

Owing to the establishment in 1890 of the Bank Circulation Redemption Fund (secs. 64 *et seq.*) every chartered bank now has an interest in seeing that the affairs of a bank which has suspended payment shall be properly managed and that proper measures are taken for the redemption of the outstanding notes of such bank. The Canadian Bankers' Association, formerly existing as an unincorporated society, was incorporated in 1900 (see Chapter XXVII.), as a suitable medium for the necessary supervision. Power is given to the Association by the next following sections of the Act to appoint a curator in the event of the suspension of payment by a bank. The powers and duties of the curator are governed by these sections and also by "by-laws, rules and regulations" made by the Association in pursuance of the further authority conferred upon it by sec. 124 (see end of this chapter where the by-laws passed by the Association on this subject are set out).

117. The Association, shall, if a bank suspends payment in specie or Dominion notes of any of its liabilities as they accrue, forthwith appoint a curator to supervise the affairs of such bank. *Association to appoint.*

2. The Association may at any time remove the curator, and may appoint another person to act in his stead. 63-64 V., c. 26, s. 24. *Removal.*

The "Association" is defined by sec. 2 to mean the Canadian Bankers' Association.

118. The appointment of the curator shall be made in the manner provided for in the by-law of the Association made in that behalf as hereinafter provided. *Appointment to be made under by-law of Association.*

Sec. 118.
If no by-
law.

2. If there is no such by-law the appointment shall be made in writing by the president of the Association, or by the person acting as president. 63-64 V., c. 26, s. 25.

The by-law referred to is made in pursuance of sec. 124, and is set out below.

Powers and
duties of
curator.

119. The curator shall assume supervision of the affairs of the bank, and of all necessary arrangements for the payment of the notes of the bank issued for circulation, and, at the time of his appointment, outstanding and in circulation.

Idem.

2. The curator shall generally have all powers and shall take all steps and do all things necessary or expedient to protect the rights and interests of the creditors and shareholders of the bank, and to conserve and ensure the proper disposition, according to law, of the assets of the bank; and, for the purposes of this section, he shall have free and full access to all books, accounts, documents and papers of the bank.

Idem.

3. The curator shall continue to supervise the affairs of the bank until he is removed from office, or until the bank resumes business, or until a liquidator is duly appointed to wind up the business of the bank. 63-64 V., c. 26, s. 26.

A bank which has suspended payment is forbidden by sec. 61 to issue or re-issue its notes payable to bearer on demand and intended for circulation until it resumes business with the consent in writing of the curator or, having resumed business without such consent, until it is authorized by the Treasury Board to issue or re-issue such notes.

Officers and
clerks to as-
sist curator.

120. The president, vice-president, directors, general manager, managers, clerks and officers of the bank shall give and afford to the curator all such information and assistance as he requires in the discharge of his duties. 63-64 V., c. 26, s. 27.

No act of
directors
valid unless
approved by
curator.

121. No by-law, regulation, resolution or act, touching the affairs or management of the bank, passed, made or done by the directors during the time the curator is in charge of the bank,

shall be of any force or effect until approved in writing by the Sec. 121. curator. 63-64 V., c. 26, s. 27.

122. The curator shall make all returns and reports, and Curator to make re- shall give all information to the Minister, touching the affairs turns as of the bank, that the Minister requires of him. 63-64 V., c. 26, required by Minister. s. 28.

123. The remuneration of the curator for his services, and Remunera- tion of his expenses and disbursements in connection with the discharge curator. of his duties, shall be fixed and determined by the Association, and shall be paid out of the assets of the bank, and, in case of the winding-up of the bank, shall rank on the estate equally with the remuneration of the liquidator. 63-64 V., c. 26, s. 29.

By sec. 92 of the Winding-up Act all costs, charges and expenses properly incurred in the winding-up of a company, including the remuneration of the liquidator, shall be payable out of the assets of the company, in priority to all other claims.

BY-LAWS RESPECTING CURATOR.

In pursuance of the powers conferred by sec. 124 the following by-laws were passed at a general meeting of the Association held in Toronto on the 15th of November, 1900, and approved by the Treasury Board on the 10th of May, 1901.

CURATOR.

By-law No. 14.

Whenever any bank suspends payment, a curator, as men- By-laws res- tioned in sec. 24 of the Bank Act Amendment Act, 1900, [sec. pecting 117 of the present Act], shall be appointed to supervise the curator. affairs of such bank. Such appointment shall be made in writing by the president of the association or by the person who, during a vacancy in the office of, or in the absence of, the president, may be acting as president of the association.

If a curator so appointed dies, or resigns, another curator may be appointed in his stead in the manner aforesaid.

The executive council may by resolution at any time remove a curator from office and appoint another person curator in his stead.

By-laws respecting curator.

A curator so appointed shall have all the powers and subject to the provisions of By-law No. 15, shall perform all the duties imposed upon the curator by the said Bank Act Amendment Act; he shall also furnish all such returns and reports, and give all such information touching the affairs of the suspended bank as the president of the association or the executive council may require of him from time to time.

The remuneration of the curator for his service and his expenses and disbursements in connection with the discharge of his duties shall be fixed and determined from time to time by the executive council.

By-law No. 15.

Whenever a bank suspends payment and a curator is accordingly appointed, the president shall also appoint a local advisory board consisting of three members, selected generally as far as possible from among the general managers, assistant general managers, cashiers, inspectors or chief accountants, or branch managers of any bank at the place where the head office of such suspended bank is situated, and the curator shall advise from time to time with such advisory board, and it shall be his duty, before taking any important step in connection with his duties as curator, to obtain the approval of such advisory board thereto. With the sanction of such advisory board, he may employ such assistants as he may require for the full performance of his duties as curator.

CHAPTER XXIII.

BY-LAWS OF THE CANADIAN BANKERS' ASSOCIATION.

124. The Association may, at any meeting thereof, with the approval of two-thirds in number of the banks represented at such meeting, if the banks so approving have at least two-thirds in par value of the paid-up capital of the banks so represented, make by-laws, rules and regulations respecting,— ^{How made.}

- (*a*) all matters relating to the appointment or removal of the curator, and his powers and duties; ^{As to what subjects.}
- (*b*) the supervision of the making of the notes of the banks which are intended for circulation, and the delivery thereof to the banks;
- (*c*) the inspection of the disposition made by the banks of such notes;
- (*d*) the destruction of notes of the banks; and,
- (*e*) the imposition of penalties for the breach or non-observance of any by-law, rule or regulation made by virtue of this section.

2. No such by-law, rule or regulation, and no amendment or repeal thereof, shall be of any force or effect until approved by the Treasury Board. ^{Approval of Treasury Board.}

3. Before any such by-law, rule or regulation, or any amendment or repeal thereof is so approved, the Treasury Board shall submit it to every bank which is not a member of the Association, and give to each such bank an opportunity of being heard before the Treasury Board with respect thereto. ^{Notice to other banks.}

4. The Association shall have all powers necessary to carry out, or to enforce the carrying out, of any by-law, rule or regulation, or any amendment thereof, so approved by the Treasury Board. 63-64 V., c. 26, ss. 30 and 31. ^{Enforcement of by-laws.}

This section, like secs. 117 to 123, dates from 1900: See notes at the beginning of Chapter XXII., *supra*.

16—BANK ACT.

　　　　The Association is defined by sec. 2 to mean the Canadian Bankers' Association, and its Act of incorporation is set out in Chapter XXVII., *infra.*

The authority to appoint and remove a curator is conferred on the Association by sec. 117 of the Bank Act. Further provisions as to his appointment, removal, powers and duties are contained in secs. 118 to 123, and in by-laws 14 and 15 passed in pursuance of the power conferred by sec. 124, and printed in Chapter XXII.

Under sec. 119, in the case of a bank which has suspended payment, the Association may, through a curator appointed by it, exercise supervision of all necessary arrangements for the payment of the notes of the bank issued for circulation and, at the time of the appointment of the curator, outstanding and in circulation. The Association may also exercise supervision over the notes of all banks doing business under the Act in respect of the matters mentioned in sec. 124. In pursuance of the power conferred by this section, the following by-law (No. 13) was passed at a general meeting of the Association held in Toronto on the 15th of November, 1900, and amended at a general meeting held in Montreal on the 15th of April, 1901, and approved by the Treasury Board on the 10th of May, 1901.

CIRCULATION.

By-law of
Association
respecting
bank notes.

By-law No. 13.

(a) A monthly return shall be made to the President of the Canadian Bankers' Association by all banks doing business in Canada, whether members of the Canadian Bankers' Association or not, in the form hereinafter set forth; said return shall be made up and sent in within the first fifteen days of each month, and shall exhibit the condition of the bank's note circulation on the last juridical day of the month next preceding; and every such monthly return shall be signed by the chief accountant or acting chief accountant and by the president or vice-president, or by any director of the bank, and by the general manager, cashier, or other chief executive officer of the bank at its chief place of business. Every such monthly return which shews therein notes destroyed during such month shall be accompanied by a certificate or certificates in the form hereinafter set forth, covering all the notes mentioned as destroyed in such

return, signed by at least three of the directors of the bank, and Sec. 124.
by the chief executive officer or some officer of the bank acting By-law of
for him, stating that the notes mentioned in such certificate or Association
certificates have been destroyed in the presence of and under respecting
the supervision of the persons respectively signing such certificate or certificates respectively.

FORM OF MONTHLY RETURN OF CIRCULATION ABOVE MENTIONED.

CIRCULATION STATEMENT OF THE
                  (Here state name of bank)
for the month of ....190 .
Credit Balance of Bank Note Accounts on last day.........
        of preceding month (inclusive of unsigned
        notes)................................$
Add notes received from printers during month, viz:
From...............$
" ....$ $

Less notes destroyed during month (as per certifi-
        cate herewith).........................$

Balance of Bank Note Accounts on last day of
        month............................$
Less notes on hand, viz:
        Signed............$
        Undersigned.......$ $

Notes in circulation on last day of month........$

                  ....
                  Chief Accountant.
    We declare that the foregoing return, to the best of our
knowledge and belief, is correct, and shews truly and clearly
the state and position of the Note Circulation of said Bank dur-
and on the last day of the period covered by such returns
.... this .... day of ....19...
                  ....
                  President.
              ....
               General Manager.

Sec. 124.

By-law of Association respecting bank notes.

FORM OF CERTIFICATE OF DESTRUCTION OF NOTES ABOVE MENTIONED.

Certificate of Destruction of Notes of the (here mention name of bank) accompanying monthly Circulation Statement for month of .... A. D. 190..

We, the undersigned, hereby certify that we have examined bank notes of this Bank amounting to $............ consisting of the following, viz: (here set out the denominations) and have burned and destroyed the same, and that the said notes so burned and destroyed by us are not included in any other Certificate of Destruction of Notes signed by us or any of us, or to the best of our knowledge and belief, by any other person to accompany the present or any monthly circulation statement made or to be made to the President of the Canadian Bankers' Association.

.... this .... day of .... 19..

.... ⎫
.... ⎬ Directors of said bank.
.... ⎭

....
General Manager.

(b) For all purposes of this by-law, the chief place of business of the Bank of British North America shall be the chief office of the said bank of the City of Montreal, in the Province of Quebec.

And in the case of the said Bank of British North America the said monthly circulation return shall be signed by the general manager's clerk, or acting general manager's clerk, and by the general manager or the acting general manager of the said bank; and the said certificate of destruction of notes shall be signed by the general manager or acting general manager, the inspector or assistant inspector, and the local manager of the Montreal branch or the acting local manager of the Montreal branch of the said bank, instead of by the persons respectively hereinbefore directed to sign the said returns respectively.

(c) Every bank which neglects to make up and send in as aforesaid any monthly return required by this by-law within the time by this by-law limited, shall incur a penalty of fifty dollars for each and every day after the expiration of such time during which the bank neglects so to make up and send in such returns.

(*d*) The executive council of the Association shall have power, by resolution, at any time to direct that an inspection shall be made of the circulation accounts of any bank by an officer or officers to be named in such resolution, and such inspection shall be made accordingly.

(*e*) Some person or persons appointed from time to time by the executive council of the Association shall during the year 1901 (and during every year thereafter) make inspection of the circulation accounts of every bank doing business in Canada, whether members of the Association or not, and shall report thereon to the council; and upon every such inspection all and every the officers of the bank whose circulation account shall be so inspected, shall give and afford to the officer or officers making such inspection, all such information and assistance as he or they may require to enable him or them fully to inspect said circulation account, and to report to the council upon the same, and upon the means adopted for the destruction of the notes.

(*f*) The amount of all penalties imposed upon a bank for any violation of this by-law shall be recoverable and enforceable with costs, at the suit of the Canadian Bankers' Association, and such penalties shall belong to the Canadian Bankers' Association for the uses of the Association.

(*g*) The President of the Canadian Bankers' Association shall each month have printed and forwarded to the chief executive officer of every bank in Canada subject to the Bank Act, whether a member of the Association or not, a statement of the circulation returns of all the banks in Canada for the last preceding month, as received by him.

(*h*) In this by-law it is declared for greater certainty that the Canadian Bankers' Association herein mentioned and referred to is the Association incorporated by special Act of Parliament of Canada, 63 and 64 Vict., c. 93.

Sec. 124.
By-law of Association respecting bank notes.

CHAPTER XXIV.

INSOLVENCY OF A BANK.

Secs. 125 to 129 and 131 are not applicable to the Bank of British North America (sec. 6).

In the event of the insolvency of a bank, proceedings may be taken for its winding-up under the Dominion Winding-up Act (R.S.C., c. 144) enacted by Parliament by virtue of its jurisdiction over bankruptcy and insolvency. (Schoolbred v. Clarke, 1890, 17 S.C.R. 265.)

It would be competent for the Parliament of Canada to pass a special Winding-up Act applicable to banks alone (Quirt v. The Queen, 1891, 19 S.C.R. 510). Instead of doing so, it has made applicable to banks, with some variations, the general Act for the winding-up of incorporated companies.

Upon suspension of payment by a bank, and pending the resumption of business or the appointment of a liquidator, a curator (sec. 117) is to be appointed by the Canadian Bankers' Association, to supervise the affairs of the bank in order to protect the interests of shareholders and creditors, and ensure the proper disposition of the assets.

By sec. 128 the directors of an insolvent bank are required, after a certain time, and if no proceedings are taken under the Winding-up Act, to make calls on the shareholders under the double liability clause, without waiting for the collection of debts or sale of assets.

Application of Winding-up Act.

The Winding-up Act (sec. 6) applies "to incorporated banks, savings banks, incorporated insurance companies, loan companies having borrowing powers, building societies having a capital stock, and incorporated trading companies doing business in Canada wheresoever incorporated and, (a) which are insolvent; or, (b) which are in liquidation or in process of being wound up, and, on petition by any of their shareholders or creditors, assignees or liquidators ask to be brought under the provisions of this Act."

As to when a bank is deemed insolvent, see sec. 127 of the Bank Act, and notes.

It is outside the scope of this book to discuss all the provisions of the Winding-up Act which are of general application to insolvent companies. Certain sections of the Act apply only to banks (see secs. 8 and 149) and will be noted under the sections of the Bank Act included in this chapter. Certain other sections which relate to subjects dealt with in the Bank Act will also be noted.

In addition to the sections included in this chapter, the following earlier sections of the Act contemplate the insolvency of a bank: Sections of Bank Act relating to insolvency.

Sec. 61 forbids the issue by a bank of its notes during any period of suspension of payment, or, except under certain conditions, after the resumption of business.

Secs. 64 *et seq.* provide for payment out of the Bank Circulation Redemption Fund, under certain conditions, of outstanding notes of a bank which has suspended payment. The excess of any payments made for such purpose out of the fund over the amount in the fund to the credit of the bank in respect of whose notes the payments are made is recoverable out of the assets of such bank.

Sec. 115 provides for the payment to the Minister of Finance of the amount of any moneys payable to shareholders or depositors, which are unclaimed at the completion of the winding-up of a bank or at the expiration of three years from the suspension of payment or the commencement of winding-up proceedings. Sec. 116 contains a somewhat similar provision in regard to the amount of outstanding notes.

INSOLVENCY.

125. In the event of the property and assets of the bank being insufficient to pay its debts and liabilities, each shareholder of the bank shall be liable for the deficiency, to an amount equal to the par value of the shares held by him, in addition to any amount not paid up on such shares. 53 V., c. 31, s. 89. Double liability of shareholders

This section dates from 1871 and is commonly known as the double liability clause. Its effect is to render a shareholder liable (in addition to the extent to which his shares are not paid

Sec. 125. up) for an amount equal to the par value of the shares held by him, or so much of such amount as may be needed to pay the debts and liabilities of the bank.

As to what persons are shareholders, see secs. 37, 43 *et seq.*, 53 and 130, and notes to these sections.

The Winding-up Act (sec. 51) provides that "every shareholder or member of the company or his representative, shall be liable to contribute the amount unpaid on his shares at the capital, *or on his liability to the company, or its members or creditors, as the case may be, under the Act, charter or instrument of incorporation of the company,* or otherwise," and "the amount which he is liable to contribute shall be deemed an asset of the company, and a debt due to the company, payable as directed or appointed under this Act." Cf. also secs. 52 and 53 of the same Act.

Set-off. The Winding-up Act also provides that the law of set-off, as administered by the courts, whether of law or equity, shall apply to claims upon the estate of the company, and to all proceedings for the recovery of debts due or accruing due to the company at the commencement of the winding-up (sec. 71), except as to debts of the company transferred within 30 days next before the commencement of the winding-up of a company under the circumstances mentioned in sec. 100 of the Act.

A contributory under the double liability clause cannot, however, set off against such liability a debt due to him by the bank, there not being that mutuality between the cross-demands which is essential to set-off (Maritime Bank v. Troop, 1888, 16 S.C.R. 456). *Quære,* whether the liability of a shareholder for the amount of his shares not paid up is in the same position as regards set-off.

As to acquiring debts for the purpose of set-off, see In re Central Bank and the Winding-up Act, 1888, 15 O.R. 625; Maritime Bank v. Robinson, 1887, 26 N.B.R. 297.

See sec. 128 of the Bank Act and notes, as to the enforcement of the double liability. It was held in Brooke v. Bank of Upper Canada, 1869, 16 Gr. 249, in an action against the bank and certain creditors, that a bill would also lie in equity, at the suit of a creditor, to enforce the double liability, but that such bill must be on behalf of all the creditors.

An infant cannot be made liable upon shares standing in his name, he not having received the dividends and repudiating lia-

bility after coming of age. (Re Central Bank & Hogg, 1890, Sec. 125.
19 O.R. 7.)

126. The liability of the bank, under any law, custom or Liability
agreement to repay moneys deposited with it and interest, if of bank.
any, and to pay dividends declared and payable on its capital
stock, shall continue, notwithstanding any statute of limitations, or any enactment or law relating to prescription.   No prescrip-
                                                              tion.
2. This section applies to money heretofore or hereafter de- Retrospec-
dosited, and to dividends heretofore or hereafter declared. 53 V., tive.
c. 31, s. 90.

This section dates from 1890. It was proposed in that year
to oblige banks to pay to the government for the public use of
Canada any dividends and depositors' balances remaining unclaimed for a certain number of years, but the proposed amendment was modified so as to require only annual returns of such
dividends and balances (sec. 114).

This section expressly excludes the operation of any statute
of limitations or any contract or law relating to prescription in
such a case.

Unclaimed dividends and depositors' balances being simply
debts due by the bank, the provincial law of limitations would
otherwise apply, although no bank would perhaps venture to
plead the statute of limitations as a reason for non-payment.

As an incidental consequence of this section, a bank must
preserve for an indefinite time the vouchers for payments made
by it.

127. Any suspension by the bank of payment of any of Suspension
its liabilities as they accrue, in specie or Dominion notes, shall, for 90 days
                                                                     to constitute
if it continues for ninety days consecutively, or at intervals insolvency.
within twelve consecutive months, constitute the bank insolvent,
and work a forfeiture of its charter or Act of incorporation, so
far as regards all further banking operations.

2. The charter or Act of incorporation of the bank shall, in Charter to
                                                               remain in
such case, remain in force only for the purpose of enabling the force only for
directors, or other lawful authority, to make and enforce the winding up.

Sec. 127.   calls mentioned in the next following section of this Act, and
to wind up the business of the bank. 63 V., c. 31, s. 91.

The words "consecutively or at intervals within twelve consecutive months" were added in 1890. In other respects the
section dates, substantially in its present form, from 1871.

After a suspension of payment for a less period than would
constitute it insolvent under this section, a bank may resume
business, but if it does so without the consent of the curator, its
right to issue or re-issue notes is subject to the provisions of sec.
61. If the suspension continues for more than 90 days, either
consecutively, or at intervals within 12 consecutive months, such
suspension constitutes the bank insolvent and operates a forfeiture of its charter to the extent provided for by sec. 127.

When com-   This section is supplementary to the provisions of the Wind-
pany deemed ing-up Act by sec. 3 of which a company is deemed insolvent,—
insolvent.

(a) if it is unable to pay its debts as they become due;

(b) if it calls a meeting of its creditors for the purpose of
compounding with them;

(c) if.it exhibits a statement shewing its inability to meet
its liabilities;

(d) if it has otherwise acknowledged its insolvency;

(e) if it assigns, removes or disposes of, or attempts or is
about to assign, remove or dispose of, any of its property, with
intent to defraud, defeat or delay its creditors, or any of them;

(f) if, with such intent, it has procured its money, goods,
chattels, lands or property to be seized, levied on or taken, under or by any process or execution;

(g) if it has made any general conveyance or assignment of
its property for the benefit of its creditors, or if, being unable
to meet its liabilities in full, it makes any sale or conveyance of
the whole or the main part of its stock in trade or assets, without the consent of its creditors, or without satisfying their
claims; or,

(h) if it permits any execution issued against it, under which
any of its goods, chattels, land or property are seized, levied
upon or taken in execution, to remain unsatisfied till within four
days of the time fixed by the sheriff or proper officer for the sale
thereof, or for fifteen days after such seizure.

The same Act also provides that a company is deemed to be
unable to pay its debts as they become due, whenever a creditor,

to whom the company is indebted in a sum exceeding two hun- Sec. 127.
dred dollars then due has served on the company, in the manner When com-
in which process may legally be served on it in the place where pany deemed
service is made, a demand in writing, requiring the company to insolvent.
pay the sum so due, and the company has, for ninety days, in
the case of a bank, and for sixty days in all other cases, next
succeeding the service of the demand, neglected to pay such sum,
or to secure or compound for the same to the satisfaction of the
creditor. (Sec. 4.)

128. If any suspension of payment in full, in specie or If no pro-
Dominion notes, of all or any of the notes or other liabilities ceedings
of the bank, continues for three months after the expiration months
of the time which, under the last preceding section, would con- thereafter
stitute the bank insolvent, and if no proceedings are taken under make calls.
any Act for the winding-up of the bank, the directors shall make
calls on the shareholders thereof, to the amount they deem
necessary to pay all the debts and liabilities of the bank, without
waiting for the collection of any debts due to the bank or the
sale of any of its assets or property.

2. Such calls shall be made at intervals of thirty days.   Intervals.

3. Such calls shall be made upon notice to be given at least Notice.
thirty days prior to the day on which any such call shall be
payable.

4. Any number of such calls may be made by one resolution. Number.

5. No such call shall exceed twenty per centum on each share. Amount.

6. Payment of such calls may be enforced in like manner Payment.
as payment of calls on unpaid stock may be enforced.

7. The first of such calls may be made within ten days after First call.
the expiration of the said three months.

8. In the event of proceedings being taken, under any Act, Procedure.
for the winding-up of the bank in consequence of the insolvency of the bank, the said calls shall be made in the manner
prescribed for the making of such calls in such Act.

9. Any failure on the part of any shareholder liable to any Forfeiture
such call to pay the same when due, shall work a forfeiture by for non-payment.

such shareholder of all claim in or to any part of the assets of the bank: Provided that such call, and any further call thereafter, shall nevertheless be recoverable from him as if no such forfeiture had been incurred. 53 V., c. 31, ss. 92, 93 and 94.

This section is a consolidation of three separate sections of the Act of 1890, and was divided into its present sub-sections in 1906. In other respects the section dates from 1890. In the last mentioned year the law was amended in several particulars. Formerly the first calls on the double liability were to be made if the suspension of payment in full continued for six months, now they are to be made as above provided. The words "and any number of such calls may be made by one resolution" were added in 1890. Apart from these words it would be necessary to have separate meetings and resolutions at intervals of at least 30 days. (Robertson v. Banque d'Hochelaga, 1881, 4 L.N. 314.)

The principle that the double liability of shareholders should be enforced without waiting for the collection of debts or the sale of assets, was laid down by the Act of 1871. The provision giving effect to this principle is designed to ensure the prompt and effectual enforcement of such liability, and to guard against the recurrence of such cases as have been the cause of loss to creditors in the past. In the case of the Bank of Upper Canada, for instance, the entire assets of the bank were not realized for many years and, partly as a result of the delay, the double liability was in fact never enforced.

Proceedings after insolvency of bank.
After a bank has been constituted insolvent under sec. 127, proceedings may be taken under the Winding-up Act. If no such proceedings are taken, and the suspension of payment in full of all or any of the notes or other liabilities continues for three months after the bank has become insolvent under that section, the directors are obliged under sec. 128 to make calls on the shareholders to the amount the directors deem necessary to pay all the debts and liabilities of the bank, without waiting for the collection of any debts due to it or the sale of any of its assets or property.

If a winding-up order is made, the Winding-up Act provides that "the company from the time of the making of the winding-up order, shall cease to carry on its business, except in so far as is, in the opinion of the liquidator, required for the

beneficial winding-up thereof; but the corporate state and all Sec. 128.
the corporate powers of the company, notwithstanding it is
otherwise provided by the Act, charter or instrument of incorporation, shall continue until the affairs of the company are
wound up'' (sec. 20). Cf. secs. 21 to 23.

The settlement of the list of contributories, the making of calls
upon shareholders, etc., is provided for by secs. 48 *et seq.* of the
Winding-up Act.

By that Act the winding-up is deemed to commence at the
time of the service of the notice of presentation of the petition
for winding-up (sec. 5). When a bank becomes insolvent a
creditor for a sum not less than $1,000 may apply by petition
to the court in the province where the head office or other chief
place of business in Canada is situated. Before making the
order the court shall direct a meeting of the shareholders and a
meeting of the creditors of the bank to be summoned, held and
conducted as the court directs, for the purpose of ascertaining
their respective wishes as to the appointment of liquidators.
(Sec. 151; and cf. secs. 12 to 17 of general application to companies.)

The appointment of a chairman and the voting at each meeting is provided for (secs. 152 to 155).

The chairman of each meeting shall report the result thereof Appoint-
to the court, and, if a winding-up order is made, the court shall ment of
appoint one or more liquidators not exceeding three to be select- liquidator.
ed, in its discretion, after such hearing of the parties as it deems
expedient, from among the persons nominated by the majorities
and minorities of the shareholders and creditors at their respective meetings (sec. 156).

If no one is so nominated, the liquidator or liquidators shall
be chosen by the court (sec. 157).

In the case of the Bank of Liverpool, the judge appointed
liquidators from the nominees of the creditors, one of them being the defendant bank. Held, affirming the judgment of the
court below (22 N.S.R. 97), that there is nothing in the Winding-up Act that requires both creditors and shareholders to be
represented on the board of liquidators, that a bank may be
appointed liquidator, and that, if any appeal lies from the decision of the judge in exercising his judgment as to the appointment, his discretion was wisely exercised in this case. (Forsythe
v. Bank of Nova Scotia, 1890, 18 S.C.R. 707, S.C. Cas. 209.)

Sec. 128.

Appointment of liquidator.

If it appears that resort to the double liability of shareholders will be necessary to satisfy the claims of creditors, the creditors' choice of a liquidator should be adopted in preference to that of the shareholders. It is preferable that a liquidator should be appointed who is neither a creditor nor a shareholder. (Re Central Bank, 1888, 15 O.R. 309.)

While the court is confined to a selection between the persons nominated at the meetings of creditors and shareholders for the office of liquidator, it is not bound to adopt the choice of the majority, but must exercise its own discretion. If the bank is solvent, the court ought to have particular regard to the wishes of the shareholders, but if it is not absolutely clear that the bank is solvent, the interests of creditors in the liquidation are entitled to greater consideration than those of the shareholders. (In re Commercial Bank of Manitoba, 1893, 9 Man. R. 342.)

Under the Winding-up Act a company in liquidation retains its corporate powers, including the power to sue, although such powers must be exercised through the liquidator under the authority of the court. The liquidator must sue in his own name or in that of the company, according to the nature of the action: in his own name, when he acts as representative of creditors and contributories; in that of the company, to recover either its debts or its property. (Kent v. Communanté des Soeurs de Charité, [1903] A.C. 220.)

A shareholder has no right to set off against his double liability a debt due to him by the bank: see notes to sec. 125. Under this section if he fails to pay a call, any claim of his against the bank becomes forfeited. Non-payment alone under this section appears to operate a forfeiture, whereas under sec. 40 the non-payment of calls upon unpaid stock of a solvent bank results in a forfeiture only when the directors declare the shares forfeited.

A director who refuses to make or to enforce, or to concur in making or in enforcing, any call under sec. 128 is criminally liable under sec. 154.

Liability of directors not diminished.

129. Nothing contained in the four sections last preceding shall be construed to alter or diminish the additional liabilities of the directors as herein mentioned and declared. 53 V., c. 31, s. 95.

Additional liabilities of directors.

See sec. 58 (impairing capital) ; sec. 139 (pledging or improperly issuing or taking bank notes) ; sec. 153 (false or deceptive statement) ; sec. 155 (giving undue preference).

130. (*a*) Persons who, having been shareholders of the bank, have only transferred their shares, or any of them, to others, or registered the transfer thereof, within sixty days before the commencement of the suspension of payment by the bank; and, Liability of shareholders who have transferred their stock.

(*b*) Persons whose subscriptions to the stock of the bank have been cancelled, in manner hereinbefore provided, within the said period of sixty days before the commencement of the suspension of payment by the bank; Or whose subscriptions have been cancelled.

shall be liable to all calls on the shares held or subscribed for by them, as if they held such shares at the time of such suspension of payment, saving their recourse against those by whom such shares were then actually held. 53 V., c. 31, s. 96.

This section dates practically in its present form from 1890, when the corresponding section of the Act of 1871 was amended by the change of the time limit from one month to 60 days and by the addition of the words ''or persons whose subscriptions to the stock of the bank have been cancelled, etc.'' (referring to the power of cancellation for non-payment of calls given by sec. 37).

Cf. sec. 52 of the Winding-up Act, which provides generally that if a shareholder has transferred his shares under circumstances which do not, by law, free him from liability in respect thereof, he shall be liable to contribute independently of that Act.

Under section 125 every holder of a share of bank stock assumes a liability to contribute to the assets of the bank, in the event of its insolvency, a sum equal to the par value of the share. In the case of a person within sec. 37, this liability continues in force even after the registration upon the bank books of a transfer of the share to another person. It is extinguished only when the bank has continued for 60 days, after such registration, to carry on its business without any suspension of pay- Double liability of transferor of shares.

Sec. 130.
Double liability of transferor of shares.

ment. Every transaction in bank shares must be taken to be made subject to the possibility that this well-known statutory liability may be enforced in case the insolvency of the bank occurs within the statutory period. The transferee or actual holder of a share at the time of the suspension is liable himself, and he is bound, as between himself and the person from whom he purchased the share, to assume, and indemnify the latter against, the liability attached to the share. The obligation to indemnify arises not from the transfer but from the fact of purchase, and is based upon the principle that a person taking the advantage must take with it the burden. The liability of the purchaser of an equity of redemption to indemnify the mortgagor is based upon the same principle. (Boultbee v. Gzowski, 1896, 28 O.R. at pp. 302-3, and cases there cited; S.C. reversed 24 A.R. 502, restored 29 S.C.R. 54.)

The liquidator may, however, put upon the list of contributories both or all of the persons who have been holders of shares within 60 days prior to the suspension, until the full amount payable in respect of the shares has been paid. (In re Central Bank, Baines' Case, 1889, 16 O.R. at p. 305, 16 A.R. at p. 245; Henderson's Case, 1889, 17 O.R. 110.)

Where A. sells bank shares to B. within 60 days before the suspension of the bank, and B. sells to C., each of the three is liable upon the shares until the full amount payable in respect of them has been paid. C. is liable as the holder at the time. B. is liable notwithstanding that A. did not transfer the shares to him but executed a transfer in a form which was designed to enable B. to pass them to C. without B.'s taking the transfer in his own name. A. is entitled to indemnity from B., and B. from C. If A. has to pay, and recovers judgment against B., B. although he has not satisfied the judgment then has a cause of action against C. which he may assign to A. so as to enable A. to bring action directly against C. (Boultbee v. Gzowski, *supra.*)

Order of charges.
Notes.

131. In the case of the insolvency of any bank,—

(a) the payment of the notes issued or re-issued by such bank, intended for circulation, and then in circulation, together with any interest paid or payable thereon as hereinbefore provided, shall be the first charge upon the assets of the bank;

(*b*) the payment of any amount due to the Government of Canada, in trust or otherwise, shall be the second charge upon such assets; `Sec. 131.` `Dominion Government.`

(*c*) the payment of any amount due to the government of any of.the provinces, in trust or otherwise, shall be the third charge upon such assets; and, `Provincial governments.`

(*d*) the amount of any penalties for which the bank is liable shall not form a charge upon the assets of the bank, until all other liabilities are paid. 53 V., c. 31, s. 53. `Penalties.`

The provision made by this section that the payment of notes in circulation shall be the first charge upon the bank's assets in case of its insolvency was an important feature of the banking legislation of 1880 (see Chapter I.). The further security of the Bank Circulation Redemption Fund (see sec. 64) was created in 1890. See also secs. 71 and 72. `Priority of charges on assets of insolvent bank.`

The clauses making the payment of any amount due to the Government of Canada and to the government of any of the provinces the second and third charges respectively upon the assets, date from 1890. This is a re-enactment in modified form of the priority of the Crown as a simple contract creditor which existed at common law, and which was held to be applicable to the Crown as represented by the Dominion (Reg. v. Bank of Nova Scotia, 1885, 11 S.C.R. 1), or by a provincial government (Maritime Bank v. Receiver-General of N.B., [1892] A.C. 437). In the Province of Quebec the Crown has no general priority as a simple contract creditor (Exchange Bank v. Reg., 1886, 11 App. Cas. 157), so that in that province a material change in the law has been effected by the passing of this section.

Money deposited with the Government of Canada by a company under the Dominion Insurance Act is not the money of the Crown, but is held by the Finance Minister in trust for the company, and is not subject to the prerogative of payment in priority to other creditors. (Maritime Bank v. Reg., 1889, 17 S.C.R. 657.)

The claims of creditors are to be paid in priority to any penalties for which the bank is liable.

A depositor is simply an ordinary creditor and is entitled to be paid *pari passu* with other creditors.

17—BANK ACT.

A person who makes a deposit with a bank after its suspension, the deposit consisting of cheques of third parties drawn on and accepted by the bank in question, is not entitled to be paid by privilege the amount of such deposit. (Ontario Bank v. Chaplin, 1891, 20 S.C.R. 152.)

In Re Central Bank, Wells & McMurchy's Case, 1888, 15 O. R. 611, a deposit had been made in a bank, and it was shewn that, at a director's meeting held on the previous day, the necessity of seeking outside assistance or of suspending payment had been considered and a resolution passed to suspend payment if such assistance was refused. The bank closed on the day upon which the deposit was made and did not again open its doors, and notice of suspension of payment was given on the following morning. It was held that the depositor was entitled to be repaid the amount of his deposit as having been obtained from him by fraud, and the liquidators were ordered to pay the same with interest from the date of the deposit.

CHAPTER XXV.

OFFENCES AND PENALTIES.

The Commencement of Business.

132. Every director or provisional director of any bank and every other person, who, before the obtaining of the certificate from the Treasury Board, by this Act required, permitting the bank to issue notes or commence business, issues or authorizes the issue of any note of such bank, or transacts or authorizes the transaction of any business in connection with such bank, except such as is by this Act authorized to be transacted before the obtaining of such certificate, is guilty of an offence against this Act. 53 V., c. 31, s. 14.

Commencing business without certificate.

Offence.

See sec. 14 and notes thereto.
The penalty for an offence against this Act is provided for by sec. 157.

The Sale and Transfer of Shares.

133. Any person, whether principal, broker or agent, who wilfully sells or transfers or attempts to sell or transfer,—

If contrary to requirements.

(*a*) any share or shares of the capital stock of any bank by a false number; or,

(*b*) any share or shares of which the person making such sale or transfer, or in whose name or on whose behalf the same is made, is not at the time of such sale, or attempted sale, the registered owner; or,

(*c*) any share or shares, without the assent to such sale of the registered owner thereof;

is guilty of an offence against this Act. 53 V., c. 31, s. 37.

Offence.

See sec. 45.
The penalty for an offence against this Act is provided for by sec. 157.

The Cash Reserves.

Holding less   **134.** Every bank which at any time holds less than forty
than forty   per centum of its cash reserves in Dominion notes shall incur
p. c. in   a penalty of five hundred dollars for each such offence. 53 V.,
Dominion
notes.   c. 31, s. 50.

See sec. 60.
As to the procedure for enforcing the penalty, see sec. 158.

The Issue and Circulation of Notes.

Excess of   **135.** If the total amount of the notes of the bank in circula-
circulation.   tion at any time exceeds the amount authorized by this Act the
bank shall,—

Penalty.   (*a*) if the amount of such excess is not over one thousand
dollars, incur a penalty equal to the amount of such excess;
or,

Idem.   (*b*) if the amount of such excess is over one thousand dollars, and not over twenty thousand dollars, incur a penalty
of one thousand dollars; or,

Idem.   (*c*) if the amount of such excess is over twenty thousand
dollars, and not over one hundred thousand dollars, incur
a penalty of ten thousand dollars; or,

Idem.   (*d*) if the amount of such excess is over one hundred thousand dollars, and not over two hundred thousand dollars,
incur a penalty of fifty thousand dollars; or,

Idem.   (*e*) if the amount of such excess is over two hundred thousand dollars, incur a penalty of one hundred thousand
dollars. 53 V., c. 31, s. 51.

See sec. 61.
As to procedure, see sec. 158.

Unauthor-   **136.** Every person, except a bank to which this Act applies,
ised issue of   who issues or re-issues, makes, draws, or endorses any bill,
notes for
circulation.

bond, note, cheque or other instrument, intended to circulate Sec. 136.
as money, or to be used as a substitute for money, for any Penalty.
amount whatsoever, shall incur a penalty of four hundred dollars.

2. Such penalty shall be recoverable with costs, in any court How re-
of competent jurisdiction, by any person who sues for the same. coverable.

3. A moiety of such penalty shall belong to the person suing Appropria-
for the same, and the other moiety to His Majesty for the tion.
public uses of Canada.

4. If any such instrument is made for the payment of a less Intention
sum than twenty dollars, and is payable either in form or in presumed.
fact to the bearer thereof, or at sight, or on demand, or at less
than thirty days thereafter, or is overdue, or is in any way
calculated or designed for circulation, or as a substitute for
money, the intention to pass the same as money shall be presumed, unless such instrument is,—

    (a) a cheque on some chartered bank paid by the maker Exceptions.
        directly to his immediate creditor; or,

    (b) a promissory note, bill of exchange, bond or other under-
        taking for the payment of money made or delivered by the
        maker thereof to his immediate creditor; and,

    (c) not designed to circulate as money or as a substitute for
        money. 53 V., c. 31, s. 60.

The section was divided into its present sub-sections in 1906,
but in other respects it dates from 1890.

It is to be noted that under this section a moiety of any penalty recovered belongs to the person suing for the same. There
is no similar provision in other sections which impose penalties
upon individuals. Where the penalty is payable by the bank
the amount recovered belongs under sec. 158 to the Dominion,
but any portion thereof may be remitted to the bank or paid to
any person.

The joint effect of this section and of the Dominion Notes
Act is to reserve to the chartered banks and to the Government
of Canada the exclusive privilege of issuing notes intended to
circulate as money. See Chapter XXIX, *infra,* on Currency and
Dominion Notes.

Sec. 137.

Defacement of notes.

Penalty.

137. Every person who in any way defaces any Dominion or provincial note, or bank note, whether by writing, printing, drawing or stamping thereon, or by attaching or affixing thereto, anything in the nature or form of an advertisement, shall be liable to a penalty not exceeding twenty dollars. 53 V., c. 31, s. 61.

Cf. sec. 551 of the Criminal Code.

Issuing notes during period of suspension.

138. (a) Every person who, being president, vice-president, director, general manager, manager, clerk or other officer of the bank, issues or re-issues, during any period of suspension of payment by the bank of its liabilities, any notes of the bank payable to bearer on demand, and intended for circulation, or authorizes or is concerned in any such issue or re-issue; and,

Or without authority of Treasury Board.

(b) If, after any such suspension, the bank resumes business without the consent in writing of the curator, hereinbefore provided for, every person who being president, vice-president, director, general manager, manager, clerk or other officer of the bank issues or re-issues, or authorizes or is concerned in the issue or re-issue of any such notes before being thereunto authorized by the Treasury Board; and,

And accepting such notes.

(c) Every person who accepts, receives or takes, or authorizes or is concerned in, the acceptance, receipt or taking of any such notes, knowing the same to have been so issued or re-issued, from the bank, or from such president, vice-president, director, general manager, manager, clerk or other officer of the bank, in payment or part payment, or as security for the payment of any amount due or owing to such person by the bank;

Penalty

is guilty of an indictable offence, and liable to imprisonment for a term not exceeding seven years, or to a fine not exceeding two thousand dollars, or to both. 63-64 V., c. 26, s. 10.

This section was added to the Act in 1900. As first enacted it formed one section with the proviso to sec. 61. See notes to that section. Sec. 138.

139. (*a*) Every person who, being the president, vice-president, director, general manager, manager, cashier, or other officer of the bank, pledges, assigns, or hypothecates, or authorizes, or is concerned in the pledge, assignment or hypothecation of the notes of the bank; and, Pledging of notes

(*b*) Every person who accepts, receives or takes, or authorizes or is concerned in the acceptance or receipt or taking of such notes as a pledge, assignment or hypothecation; Accepting.

shall be liable to a fine of not less than four hundred dollars and not more than two thousand dollars, or to imprisonment for not more than two years, or to both. 53 V., c. 31, s. 52. Penalty.

See sec. 63.

140. (*a*) Every person who, being the president, vice-president, director, general manager, manager, cashier or other officer of a bank, with intent to defraud, issues or delivers, or authorizes or is concerned in the issue or delivery of notes of the bank intended for circulation and not then in circulation; and, Issuing notes fraudulently.

(*b*) Every person who, with knowledge of such intent, accepts, receives or takes, or authorizes or is concerned in the acceptance, receipt or taking of such notes; Knowingly accepting.

shall be guilty of an indictable offence, and liable to imprisonment for a term not exceeding seven years, or to a fine not exceeding two thousand dollars, or to both. 53 V., c. 31, s. 52. Penalty.

See sec. 63.

Warehouse Receipts, Bills of Lading and other Securities.

141. If any bank, to secure the payment of any bill, note, debt or liability, acquires or holds,— Bank acquiring warehouse receipt or bill of lading.

Sec. 141.   (*a*) any warehouse receipt or bill of lading; or,

(*b*) any instrument such as is by this Act authorized to be
taken by the bank to secure money lent,—

    (i) to any wholesale purchaser, or shipper of or dealer
in products of agriculture, the forest, quarry and
mine, or the sea, lakes and rivers, or to any wholesale
purchaser or shipper of or dealer in live or dead stock,
and the products thereof, upon the security of such
products, or of such live or dead stock, or the products
thereof; or,

    (ii) to any person engaged in business as a wholesale
manufacturer of any goods, wares and merchandise,
upon the security of the goods, wares and merchandise manufactured by such person, or procured for
such manufacture;

such bank shall, unless,—

Except in
certain cases   (*a*) such bill, note, debt or liability is negotiated or contracted at the time of the acquisition by the bank of such
warehouse receipt, bill of lading or security; or,

(*b*) such bill, note, debt or liability is negotiated or contracted upon the written promise or agreement that such
warehouse receipt, bill of lading or security would be given
to the bank; or,

(*c*) the acquisition or holding by the bank of such warehouse receipt, bill of lading or security is otherwise authorized by this Act;

Penalty.   incur a penalty not exceeding five hundred dollars. 53 V., c.
31, s. 79.

See secs. 86 to 90.

Secs. 141, 142, 145 and 146 in their present form date from
1906. They have replaced sec. 79 of the Act of 1890 which provides that "every bank which violates any provision contained
in any of the sections numbered sixty-four to seventy-eight
(both inclusive) shall incur for each violation thereof a penalty

not exceeding five hundred dollars.'' Secs. 64 to 78 of the Act Sec. 141. of 1890 are now secs. 76 to 90 (omitting sec. 84).

Sec. 76 forbids a bank to do certain things ''except as authorized by this Act,'' and secs. 141, 142, 145 and 146 set out the prohibited acts subject to the exceptions created by the other provisions of the Act.

Although the bank may be liable to a penalty in respect of a transaction entered into in contravention of the Bank Act, the transaction itself is not necessarily a nullity. See notes to sec. 76, *supra*, p. 146.

Clause (c) of sec. 141 protects a bank from liability to a penalty for doing an act which, although not authorized by secs. 86 to 90, is within the powers conferred by the enabling provisions of secs. 76 *et seq.*

142. If any debt or liability to the bank is secured by,— Non-compliance with

(a) any warehouse receipt, or bill of lading; or, requirements

(b) any other security such as is mentioned in the last pre- for sale. ceding section;

and is not paid at maturity, such bank shall, if it sells the goods, wares and merchandise or products, covered by such warehouse receipt, bill of lading or security, under the power of sale conferred upon it by this Act, without complying with the provisions to which the exercise of such power of sale is, by this Act, Penalty. made subject, incur a penalty not exceeding five hundred dollars. 53 V., c. 31, s. 79; 63-64 V., c. 26, s. 18.

See sec. 89, and cf. notes to sec. 141. As to procedure, see sec. 158.

143. Every person is guilty of an indictable offence and Making false liable to imprisonment for a term not exceeding two years who statements. wilfully makes any false statement,—

(a) in any warehouse receipt or bill of lading given under In warehouse receipt the authority of this Act to any bank; or, or bill of

(b) in any instrument given to any bank under the authority lading.
In security of this Act, as security for any loan of money made by upon
products.

Sec. 143.   the bank to any wholesale purchaser or shipper of or dealer in products of agriculture, the forest, quarry and mine, or the sea, lakes and rivers, or to any wholesale purchaser, or shipper of or dealer in live or dead stock and the products thereof, whereby any such products or stock is assigned or transferred to the bank as security for the payment of such loan; or,

In security upon manufactures.

(c) in any instrument given to any bank under the authority of this Act, as security for any loan of money made by the bank to any person engaged in business as a wholesale manufacturer of any goods, wares and merchandise, whereby any of the goods, wares and merchandise manufactured by him, or procured for such manufacture, are transferred or assigned to the bank as security for the payment of such loan. 53 V., c. 31, s. 75.

Prior to 1906, this section was part of the predecessor of the present sec. 90. The documents mentioned in clause (a) are those upon the security of which a bank may lend money under sec 86. Clauses (b) and (c) refer to documents which may be taken as security under sec. 88.

Cf. Criminal Code, secs. 425 and 427(a).

Wilfully disposing of or witholding goods covered by security.

144. Every person who, having possession or control of any goods, wares and merchandise covered by any warehouse receipt or bill of lading, or by any such security as in the last preceding section mentioned, and having knowledge of such receipt, bill of lading or security, without the consent of the bank in writing, and before the advance, bill, note, debt or liability thereby secured has been fully paid,—

(a) wilfully alienates or parts with any such goods, wares or merchandise; or,

(b) wilfully withholds from the bank possession of any such goods, wares and merchandise, upon demand, after default in payment of such advance, bill, note, debt or liability;

is guilty of an indictable offence, and liable to imprisonment Sec. 144.
for a term not exceeding two years. 53 V., c. 31, s. 75; 63-64 Penalty.
V., c. 26, s. 18.

Prior to 1906 this section was part of the predecessor of the
present sec. 90.

Cf. Crim. Code, secs. 426, 427(b).

145. (a) If any bank having, by virtue of the provisions Bank not
selling shares
of this Act, a privileged lien for any debt or liability for subject to
any debt to the bank, on the shares of its own capital privileged
lien.
stock of the debtor or person liable, neglects to sell such
shares within twelve months after such debt or liability
has accrued and become payable; or,

(b) If any such bank sells any such shares without giving Or selling
notice to the holder thereof of the intention of the bank without
notice.
to sell the same, by mailing such notice in the post office,
post paid, to the last known address of such holder, at
least thirty days prior to such sale;

such bank shall incur, for each such offence, a penalty not ex- Penalty.
ceeding five hundred dollars. 53 V., c. 31, s. 79.

See sec. 77, and cf. notes to sec 141.
As to procedure, see sec. 158.

Prohibited Business.

146. If any bank, except as authorized by this Act, either Bank doing.
directly or indirectly,—

(a) deals in the buying or selling or bartering of goods,
wares and merchandise, or engages or is engaged in any
trade or business whatsoever; or,

(b) purchases, deals in, or lends money or makes advances
upon the security or pledge of any share of its own capital
stock, or of the capital stock of any bank; or,

Sec. 146.   (c) lends money or makes advances upon the security, mortgage or hypothecation of any lands, tenements or immovable property, or of any ships or other vessels, or upon the security of any goods, wares and merchandise;

Penalty.   such bank shall incur a penalty not exceeding five hundred dollars. 53 V., c. 31, s. 79.

See sec. 76, and cf. notes to sec. 141.
As to procedure, see sec. 158.

Returns.

Bank not making monthly returns.   **147.** Every bank which neglects to make up and send to the Minister, within the first fifteen days of any month, any monthly return by this Act required to be made up and sent in within the said fifteen days, exhibiting the condition of the bank on the last juridical day of the month last preceding, and signed in the manner and by the persons by this Act required, shall incur a penalty of fifty dollars for each and every day,

Penalty.   after the expiration of such time, during which the bank neglects to make and send in such return. 53 V., c. 31, s. 85.

See secs. 112 and 152.
As to procedure, see sec. 158.

Not making returns required by Minister.   **148.** Every bank which neglects to make and send to the Minister, within thirty days from the date of the demand therefor by the Minister, or, if such time is extended by the Minister, within such extended time, not exceeding thirty days, as the Minister may allow, any special return, signed in the manner and by the persons by this Act required, which, under the provisions of this Act, the Minister may, for the purpose of affording a full and complete knowledge of the condition of the bank, call for, shall incur a penalty of five hundred dollars for each

Penalty.   and every day during which such neglect continues. 53 V., c. 31, s. 86.

See secs. 113 and 152.
As to procedure, see sec. 158.

149. Every bank which neglects to transmit or deliver to Bank not
the Minister, within twenty days after the close of any calendar making
year, a return, signed in the manner and by the persons and turns as to
setting forth the particulars by this Act required in that behalf, drafts, etc.
of all drafts or bills of exchange issued by the bank to any
person and remaining unpaid for more than five years prior to
the date of such return, shall incur a penalty of fifty dollars Penalty
for each and every day during which such neglect continues.
63-64 V., c. 26, s. 21.

See secs. 114 and 152.
As to procedure, see sec. 158.

150. Every bank which neglects to transmit or deliver to Not return-
the Minister, within twenty days after the close of any calendar ing annual
year, a certified list, as by this Act required, showing,— list.

(a) the names of the shareholders of the bank on the last
    day of such calendar year, with their additions and resi-
    dences;

(b) the number of shares then held by such shareholders
    respectively; and,

(c) the value at par of such shares;

shall incur a penalty of fifty dollars for each and every day Penalty.
during which such neglect continues.   53 V., c. 31, s. 87.

See secs. 114 and 152.
As to procedure, see sec. 158.

151. Every bank which neglects to transmit or deliver to Not making
the Minister, within twenty days after the close of any calendar annual re-
year, a return, signed in the manner and by the persons by this dends and
Act required, of all dividends which have remained unpaid for balances.
more than five years, and also of all amounts or balances in

respect of which no transactions have taken place, or upon which no interest has been paid, during the five years prior to the date of such return, and setting forth such further particulars as are by this Act required in that behalf, shall incur a penalty of fifty dollars for each and every day during which such neglect continues.

2. The said term of five years shall, in case of moneys deposited for a fixed period, be reckoned from the date of the termination of such fixed period. 53 V., c. 31, s. 88.

See secs. 114 and 152.
As to procedure, see sec. 158.

152. If any return or list, mentioned in either of the last five preceding sections, is transmitted by post, the date appearing, by the post office stamp or mark upon the envelope or wrapper enclosing the return or list received by the Minister, as the date of deposit in the post office of the place at which the chief office of the bank was situated, shall be taken *prima facie,* for the purpose of any of the said sections, to be the day upon which such return or list was transmitted to the Minister. 53 V., c. 31, ss. 85 and 86; 63-64 V., c. 26, s. 22.

153. The making of any wilfully false or deceptive statement in any account, statement, return, report or other document respecting the affairs of the bank is an indictable offence punishable, unless a greater punishment is in any case by law prescribed therefor, by imprisonment for a term not exceeding five years.

2. Every president, vice-president, director, auditor, manager, cashier or other officer of the bank, who,—

(a) prepares, signs, approves or concurs in any such account, statement, return, report or document containing such false or deceptive statement; or,

(b) uses the same with intent to deceive or mislead any person;

shall be held to have wilfully made such false or deceptive Sec. 153.
statement, and shall further be responsible for all damages sus- Offence.
tained by any person in consequence thereof. 53 V., c. 31, s. Damages.
99.

This section does not apply to the Bank of British North False state-
America (sec. 6). ment in
return, etc.
The section in its present form dates from 1906. It is a revision of sec. 99 of the Act of 1890, which is practically a transcript of the corresponding section of the Act of 1871, and reads
as follows: ''99. The making of any wilfully false or deceptive
statement in any account, statement, return, report or other
document respecting the affairs of the bank is, unless it amounts
to a higher offence, a misdemeanor punishable by imprisonment
for a term not exceeding five years; and every president, vice-
president, director, principal partner *en commandité*, auditor,
manager, cashier or other officer of the bank, who prepares,
signs, approves or concurs in such statement, return, report or
document, or uses the same with intent to deceive or mislead any
person, shall be held to have wilfully made such false statement,
and shall further be responsible for all damages sustained by
any person in consequence thereof.''

The revisers have been exceptionally free in their treatment
of the section. The change in the wording of the first part of
the section is consequential upon the abolition by the Criminal
Code, 1892, of the distinction between felony and misdemeanor
(R.S.C. 1906, c. 146, sec. 14). The changes in the wording of
the second part are presumably intended to be declaratory of
the meaning of the section (cf. Revised Statutes of Canada,
1906, Act, sec. 7).

It is to be noted that the word ''statement'' is used in two
senses in the section: (1) the false allegation contained in the
account, return, etc; (2) the document in which the false allegation is contained. It will simplify the consideration of the
section if the word ''statement'' is used exclusively in the first
sense, and the word ''account'' or ''return'' is used to express
the document in which the statement is contained.

The section appears to create but one offence, namely, ''the
making of any wilfully false or deceptive statement in any account, ... return, report or other document respecting

the affairs of the bank.'' This offence may be committed either by a bank officer or director, or by some other person. Any person, whether bank officer or director or not, who actually makes a false or deceptive statement, etc., and does it wilfully, is liable under sub-sec. 1.

Sub-sec. 2 seems to amplify the *primâ facie* meaning of "the *making* of any *wilfully* false or deceptive statement," and to declare that a bank officer or director shall be deemed to be guilty of the crime created by sub-sec. 1, *i.e.*, shall be deemed to have *made* a false or deceptive statement, and to have made it *wilfully*, (a) if he prepares, signs, approves or concurs in any account, return, report or other document respecting the affairs of the bank which in fact contains a wilfully false or deceptive statement, or (b) if he uses such account, etc., with intent to deceive or mislead any person.

It has been held, however, in some recent cases decided under sec. 99 of the Act of 1890, that knowledge of the falsity of the statement contained in the return is an essential element of the offence defined by the clause which is now lettered (a).

It is to be noted, also, that the form of certificate (Schedule D) to be signed by the president and general manager requires these officers to declare "that the foregoing return is made up from the books of the bank, and that *to the best of our knowledge and belief* it is correct, and shews truly and clearly the financial position of the bank.''

In a recent Quebec case it is laid down that it is not a duty cast on the president of a bank to watch the conduct of its cashier and inferior officers, nor to verify the exactness of the calculations of its auditors or of the entries in the books, nor to interfere with the employees who are put in a position of trust for the express purpose of attending to details of management. He is therefore not liable for loss arising from acts of gross mismanagement on their part of which he has no knowledge, and his signature of returns or statements required by the charter or the Bank Act, prepared and submitted by them, where he has no reason to suspect that they are inaccurate or false, does not amount to the making or approval of "wilfully false statements,'' etc., mentioned in sec. 99 of the Bank Act, 1890. (Préfontaine v. Grenier, 1906, Q.R. 15 K.B. 143.)

The judgment in favour of the defendant was affirmed by the Privy Council, [1907] A.C. 110. The first branch of the plaintiff's case as based upon alleged misrepresentations contained in an annual report. On this branch the members of the Judicial Committee found that there was no misrepresentation in fact by which the plaintiff was induced to act to his prejudice, and that it was therefore unnecessary to consider any of the questions of law which might otherwise have arisen. The second branch of the plaintiff's case was based upon alleged negligence on the part of the defendant in the discharge of his functions as president of the bank, the main ground of negligence charged being that he had not exercised such a control over the details of the bank's business as to enable him to detect and put a stop to the irregular practices of the cashier in regard to allowing overdrafts. On this branch of the case the committee found that the charge of negligence had not been established in fact and referred especially to the principles expressed in Dovey v. Cory, [1901] A.C. 477; cf. p. 55, *supra*.

Rex v. Lovitt, 1907, 2 East. L.R. 384, was a case reserved after the conviction of the president of the Yarmouth Bank for making a false and deceptive statement under sec. 99 of the Act of 1890. The false statement alleged was that certain items which were classed in a monthly return to the government as "current loans" ought to have been included under the head of "overdue debts." The Supreme Court of Nova Scotia set aside the verdict. Weatherbe, C.J., reviewed the evidence and came to the conclusion that there was no evidence that the persons who actually prepared the return in question did so with a fraudulent design or that the classification was wilfully false, and that in any case the president, who had no knowledge of the fraud or falsity, was not liable. Another member of the court came to the same conclusion as the Chief Justice, and two other members concurred in setting aside the verdict for reasons which are not relevant to the subject under discussion.

In Rex v. Cockburn, a case tried before the Police Magistrate for the City of Toronto, judgment was delivered at the close of the case on the 4th of February, 1907. The magistrate found as a fact that the defendant, the president of the Ontario Bank, had no knowledge of the falsity of the returns he signed, and held, as a matter of law, that such knowledge was an essential element of the crime. The only authority cited by the magistrate was the charge to the jury made by Longley, J., in Rex v. Lovitt.

18—BANK ACT.

Sec. 153. False statement in return, etc.

Wilfully.

In Préfontaine v. Grenier, the Court of King's Bench adopts
the dictum of Erle, J., in Reg. v. Badger, 1856, 6 E. & B. 136,
at p. 158, that the word wilfully means knowingly and fraudulently.

The word "wilful" generally implies nothing blameable, but
merely that the person of whose action or default the expression
is used is a free agent, and that what has been done arises from
the spontaneous action of his will.   It means that the act is
deliberate and intentional, not accidental or inadvertent.   (In
re Young, 1885, 31 Ch. D. 168; Reg. v. Senior, [1899] 1 Q.B.
283, 291; Wilson v. Manes, 1899, 26 A.R. 398.)

But as applied to a misstatement, the word wilful means that
the misstatement as distinguished from the statement is wilful.
An unintentional error in a statement does not make the misstatement wilful, although the statement is made deliberately and
therefore wilfully.   A wilfully false or deceptive statement
necessarily implies that the person making it does so deliberately with knowledge of its false or deceptive character.   Cf. In
re London & Tubbs' Contract, [1894] 2 Ch. 524, 536-538.

Mens rea.

Although *primâ facie* and as a general rule there must be a
mind at fault before there can be a crime, it is not an inflexible
rule, and a statute may relate to such a subject matter and may
be so framed as to make an act criminal whether there has been
any intention to break the law or otherwise to do wrong or not.
In such a case the statute is properly construed as imposing the
penalty when the act is done, no matter how innocently, and the
substance of the enactment is that a man shall take care that
the statutory direction is obeyed and that if he fails to do so
he does it at his peril.   Whether an enactment is to be construed
in this sense or with the qualification ordinarily imported into
the construction of criminal statutes, that there must be a guilty
mind, must depend upon the subject matter of the enactment,
and the various circumstances that make the one construction
or the other reasonable or unreasonable.   (Reg. v. Tolson, 1889,
23 Q.B.D. 168 at p. 172, and cases cited.)

False statements and fraudulent intent.

Reports made and accounts rendered by the directors in the course of their duty, though made and issued to the share-holders only, as to the state of affairs of the company, are considered the representations of the company not only to the share-holders but also to the public, if they are published and circu-lated by the authority of the directors or a general meeting. Directors of a company are personally liable for injury caused to third parties by false representations contained in a report of the directors to the shareholders, but the injury must be the immediate and not the remote consequence of the representation, and it must appear that the false representation was made with the intent that it should be acted upon by such third persons. A shareholder cannot claim damages against directors for hav-ing been induced to purchase shares by misrepresentation, if he has continued to hold them long after he had knowledge, or full means of knowledge, of the untruth of the representations on which he bought them. (Rhodes v. Starnes, 1878, 22 L.C.J. 113.)

The nature of the fraud required to sustain a charge of false statements knowingly made with a fraudulent intent is consid-ered and many authorities are reviewed in Parker v. McQuesten, 1872, 32 U.C.R. 273.

In Reg. v. Hincks, 1879, 24 L.C.J. 116, 2 L.N. 422, it was held that the instruction to the jury ''that wilful intent to make a false return may be inferred by the jury from all the circum-stances of the case proved to their satisfaction'' is correct, and that such wilful intent may be inferred from an improper clas-sification of items in a return. The conviction of the defendant (the president of the bank) was, however, quashed on the ground that the question whether certain items had been improperly classed was a question of fact for the jury and not one of law for the judge, namely, (1) whether sums borrowed by the bank from other banks, for which deposit receipts were given, were improperly classed as ''other deposits payable after notice or at a fixed day,'' and (2) whether demand notes were improperly classed as ''bills and notes discounted and current.''

In an indictment charging the cashier of a bank with having un-lawfully and wilfully made a wilful, false and deceptive statement in a return respecting the affairs of the bank, it is not necessary

Sec. 153.   to allege that the return referred to was one required by law to
False state- be made by the accused, or that any use was made by him of
ment and   such return, nor is it necessary to specify in what particulars
fraudulent
intent.   the return was false or to allege that the false statement was
             made with intent to deceive or mislead. (Reg. v. Cotté, 1877,
             22 L.C.J. 141.)

In an indictment under sec. 99 of the Act of 1890 the allegation that the defendant unlawfully made and sent to the Minister of Finance and Receiver-General a monthly report of and
concerning the affairs of the bank, adding, by way of para-
phrase, to characterize the term "monthly report," the words
"a wilful, false and deceptive statement of and concerning the
affairs of the said bank," and that such monthly report was
made with intent to deceive and mislead, sufficiently sets forth
the ingredients of the offence. (Reg. v. Weir (No. 1), 1899,
Q.R. 8 Q.B. 521, 3 Can. Crim. Cas. 102.)

An information under this section may be sworn by a non-
shareholder and even by a debtor of the bank. (Molleur v. Loupret, 1885, 8 L.N. 305.)

A *de facto* director or officer cannot protect himself by shewing that he is not a director or officer *de jure*. (Gibson v. Barton, 1875, L.R. 10 Q.B. 329.)

Calls in the Case of Suspension of Payment.

Director   **154.** (a) If any suspension of payment in full, in specie or
refusing to
make.   Dominion notes, of all or any of the notes or other liabili-
                  ties of the bank continues for three months after the ex-
                  piration of the time which, under the provisions of this
                  Act, would constitute the bank insolvent; and,

(b) if no proceedings are taken under any Act for the wind-
    ing-up of the bank; and,

(c) if any director of the bank refuses to make or enforce,
    or to concur in the making or enforcing of any call on the
    shareholders of the bank, to any amount which the direc-
    tors deem necessary to pay all the debts and liabilities of
    the bank;

such director shall be guilty of an indictable offence, and liable,—

(*a*) to imprisonment for any term not exceeding two years; Sec. 154.
and,   Penalty.

(*b*) personally for any damages suffered by any such default.
53 V., c. 21, s. 92.

See sec. 128.

Undue Preference to the Bank's Creditors.

155. Every person who, being the president, vice-presi- President,
dent, director, manager, cashier or other officer of the bank, undue pre-
wilfully gives or concurs in giving to any creditor of the bank ference to
any fraudulent, undue or unfair preference over other creditors, any creditor.
by giving security to such creditor, or by changing the nature
of his claim, or otherwise howsoever, is guilty of an indictable
offence, and liable,—

(*a*) to imprisonment for a term not exceeding two years; Penalty.
and,

(*b*) for all damages sustained by any person in consequence Damages.
of such preference. 53 V., c. 31, s. 97.

A fraudulent issue of bank notes under sec. 140, if made to
a creditor in order to give him a prior claim upon the assets of
the bank in the event of insolvency, might also amount to an
offence under this section.

Where a director of a bank, who was also a creditor for about
$13,000, after a resolution to suspend payment had been passed,
withdrew $10,000 from the bank with the concurrence of the
president, it was held that he had conspired with the president
to obtain, and had thereby obtained, an undue preference over
the other creditors. (Reg. v. Buntin, 1884, 7 L.N. 228, 395.)

The Using of the Title 'Bank,' etc.

156. Every person assuming or using the title of 'bank,' Unauthor-
'banking company,' 'banking house,' 'banking association' or ised use of
title.

Sec. 156.
Penalty.

'banking institution,' without being authorized so to do by this Act, or by some other Act in force in that behalf, is guilty of an offence against this Act. 53 V., c. 31, s. 100.

The unauthorized use of the word "bank" was first forbidden in 1880. The prohibition of the other terms contained in this section dates from 1883, although until 1890 the use of these terms was permitted if the words "not incorporated" were added to the title.

The section is designed to prevent persons doing business under any name which might mislead the public into the belief that it is doing business with a chartered bank.

Sec. 157 provides a penalty for "an offence against this Act."

Sec. 156 does not prevent a foreign bank from suing in Canada (cf. Larocque v. Franklin Co. Bank, 1858, 8 L.C.R. 328, 15 R.J.R.Q. 164).

As to the meaning of "bank" in the Act, see sec. 2.

Penalty for Offence against this Act.

Offence against this Act.

157. Every person committing an offence, declared to be an offence against this Act, shall be liable to a fine not exceeding one thousand dollars ,or to imprisonment for a term not exceeding five years, or to both, in the discretion of the court before which the conviction is had. 53 V., c. 31, s. 101.

Penalty.

See secs. 132, 133 and 156, each of which creates "an offence against this Act."

PROCEDURE.

Penalties enforceable at suit of Attorney General of Canada.

158. The amount of all penalties imposed upon a bank for any violation of this Act shall be recoverable and enforceable, with costs, at the suit of His Majesty instituted by the Attorney General of Canada, or by the Minister.

Appropriation.
Proviso.

2. Such penalties shall belong to the Crown for the public uses of Canada: Provided that the Governor in Council, on the

report of the Treasury Board, may direct that any portion of any penalty be remitted, or paid to any person, or applied in any manner deemed best adapted to attain the objects of this Act, and to secure the due administration thereof. 53 V., c. 31, s. 98.

This section dates from 1890. It does not apply to the Bank of British North America (sec. 6).

Secs. 134, 135, 141, 142, 145 to 151, impose penalties on the bank for violations of the Act.

A bank compelled to pay a penalty under this section would have its recourse against the officer whose act or neglect caused the violation. (Cf. Drake v. Bank of Toronto, 1862, 9 Gr. 116.)

The section provides that suits for penalties imposed upon a bank may be brought by and for the benefit of the Crown. It grants to the Governor in Council, on the report of the Treasury Board, discretionary powers to remit to the bank, or to pay to any person, any portion of a penalty. The power may be properly exercised so as to relieve a bank from the liability incurred by a technical, but not wilful, breach of the Act, as for instance where a bank with a large number of branches temporarily and unintentionally issues notes in excess of the authorized amount. The power may also be exercised for the purpose of rewarding an informer.

An important provision of the Act is that of sec. 131, which enacts that the amount of penalties for which the bank is liable shall not form a charge upon the assets, in case of insolvency, until all other liabilities are paid.

CHAPTER XXVI.

SCHEDULES TO THE BANK ACT.

SCHEDULE A.

1. The Bank of Montreal.
2. The Bank of New Brunswick.
3. The Quebec Bank.
4. The Bank of Nova Scotia.
5. The St. Stephen's Bank.
6. The Bank of Toronto.
7. The Molsons Bank.
8. The Eastern Townships Bank.
9. The Union Bank of Halifax.
10. The Ontario Bank.
11. La Banque Nationale.
12. The Merchants Bank of Canada.
13. La Banque Provinciale du Canada.
14. The People's Bank of New Brunswick.
15. The Union Bank of Canada.
16. The Canadian Bank of Commerce.
17. The Royal Bank of Canada.
18. The Dominion Bank.
19. The Bank of Hamilton.
20. The Standard Bank of Canada.
21. La Banque de St. Jean.
22. La Banque d'Hochelaga.
23. La Banque de St. Hyacinthe.
24. The Bank of Ottawa.
25. The Imperial Bank of Canada.
26. The Western Bank of Canada.

27. The Traders' Bank of Canada.
28. The Sovereign Bank of Canada.
29. The Metropolitan Bank.
30. The Crown Bank of Canada.
31. The Home Bank of Canada.
32. The Northern Bank.
33. The Sterling Bank of Canada.
34. The United Empire Bank of Canada.

63-64 V., c. 26, s. 4, and sch. A.

See notes to secs. 3, 4, and 5.

SCHEDULE B.

An Act to incorporate the   Bank.

Whereas the persons hereinafter named have, by their petition, prayed that an Act be passed for the purpose of establishing a bank in   , and it is expedient to grant the
prayer of the said petition:

Therefore His Majesty, by and with the advice and consent
of the Senate and House of Commons of Canada, enacts as
follows:—

1. The persons hereinafter named, together with such others
as become shareholders in the corporation by this Act created,
are hereby constituted a corporation by the name of   ,
hereinafter called the Bank.

2. The capital stock of the Bank shall be   dollars.

3. The chief office of the Bank shall be at   .

4.

shall be the provisional
directors of the Bank.

5. This Act shall, subject to the provisions of section six-
teen of the Bank Act, remain in force until the first day of
July, in the year one thousand nine hundred and eleven.

53 V., c. 31, sch. B.; 63-64 V., c. 26, s. 45.

See notes to sec. 9.

SCHEDULE C.

In consideration of an advance of...................dollars made by the...................Bank to A. B., for which the said Bank holds the following bills or notes: (*describe the bills or notes, if any*), [*or*, in consideration of the discounting of the following bills or notes by the..................Bank for A. B.: (*describe the bills or notes*),] the goods, wares and merchandise mentioned below are hereby assigned to the said Bank as security for the payment on or before the................. day of.....................of the said advance, together with interest thereon at the rate of....per centum per annum from the...........day of..........(*or*, of the said bills or notes, or renewals thereof, or substitutions therefor, and interest thereon, *or as the case may be*).

This security is given under the provisions of section eighty-eight of the Bank Act, and is subject to the provisions of the said Act.

The said goods, wares and merchandise, are now owned by .... , and are now in the possession of .... , and are free from any mortgage, lien or charge thereon (*or as the case may be*), and are in (*place or places where the goods are*), and are the following (*description of goods assigned*).

Dated, etc.

(*N.B.—The bills or notes and the goods, etc., may be set out in schedules annexed.*)

63-64 V., c. 26, s. 46 and sch. C.

See notes to sec. 88.

SCHEDULE D.

Return of the liabilities and assets of the   bank on
the   day of   , A.D.
   Capital authorized. . . . .$
   Capital subscribed. . . . .
   Capital paid up. . . . .
   Amount of rest or reserve fund. . . . .
   Rate per cent. of last dividend declared. . . . . .   per cent.

LIABILITIES.

1. Notes in circulation. . . . .$
2. Balance due to Dominion Government, after
       deducting advances for credits, pay-lists,
       etc. . . . .
3. Balances due to provincial governments. . . . .
4. Deposits by the public, payable on demand,
       in Canada. . . . .$
5. Deposits by the public, payable after notice
       or on a fixed day, in Canada. . . . .
6. Deposits elsewhere than in Canada. . . . .
7. Loans from other banks in Canada, secured,
       including bills rediscounted. . . . .
8. Deposits made by and balances due to other
       banks in Canada. . . . .
9. Balances due to agencies of the bank, or to
       other banks or agencies, in the United
       Kingdom. . . . .
10. Balances due to agencies of the bank, or to
       other banks or agencies, elsewhere than in
       Canada and the United Kingdom. . . . . . .
11. Liabilities not included under foregoing heads

                                            $

ASSETS.

1. Specie. . . . .$

2. Dominion notes. . . . .$

3. Deposits with Dominion Government for
    security of note circulation. . . . .

4. Notes of and cheques on other banks. . . . .

5. Loans to other banks in Canada, secured, in-
    cluding bills rediscounted. . . . .

6. Deposits made with and balances due from
    other banks in Canada. . . . .

7. Balances due from agencies of the bank, or
    from other banks or agencies, in the
    United Kingdom. . . . .

8. Balances due from agencies of the bank, or
    from other banks or agencies, elsewhere
    than in Canada and the United Kingdom.

9. Dominion Government and provincial govern-
    ments securities. . . . .

10. Canadian municipal securities, and British,
    or foreign, or colonial public securities,
    other than Canadian. . . . .

11. Railway and other bonds, debentures and
    stocks. . . . .

12. Call and short loans on stocks and bonds in
    Canada. . . . .

13. Call and short loans elsewhere than in
    Canada. . . . .

14. Current loans in Canada. . . . .

15. Current loans elsewhere than in Canada. . . .

16. Loans to the Government of Canada. . . . .

17. Loans to provincial governments. . . . .

18. Overdue debts. . . . .

19. Real estate other than bank premises. . . . . . .

Schedule D. 20. Mortgages on real estate sold by the bank....
    21. Bank premises.........................
    22. Other assets not included under the foregoing
      heads.............................

                        $

  Aggregate amount of loans to directors, and firms of which they are partners, $.

  Average amount of specie held during the month, $.

  Average amount of Dominion notes held during the month, $.

  Greatest amount of notes in circulation at any time during the month, $.

  I declare that the above return has been prepared under my directions and is correct according to the books of the bank.

            E. F.,
             Chief Accountant.

  We declare that the foregoing return is made up from the books of the bank, and that to the best of our knowledge and belief it is correct, and shows truly and clearly the financial position of the bank; and we further declare that the bank has never, at any time during the period to which the said return relates, held less than forty per centum of its cash reserves in Dominion notes.

(*Place*)   this   day of   .

            A. B., *President.*

            C. D., *General Manager.*

63-64 V., c. 26, s. 47 and sch. D.

  See notes to sec. 112.

CHAPTER XXVII.

THE CANADIAN BANKERS' ASSOCIATION.

Prior to its incorporation, the Canadian Bankers' Association existed as a voluntary association of banks and bankers. At its second annual meeting held in Toronto in June, 1893, the Association decided upon the publication of a quarterly journal, the first number of which appeared in September of the same year. The journal is now in the fourteenth year of its existence and contains much valuable matter relating to banking practice and law. The ''questions on points of practical interest'' and the answers of the editing committee given, in cases of difficulty, under advice of Counsel, published in the various numbers of the Journal, have been republished in book form by the secretary of the association. (Knight's Canadian Banking Practice, 2nd ed., 1906.)

In 1900 the Association was incorporated by Act of Parliament and important powers were conferred upon it under the Bank Act Amendment Act, 1900. See secs. 5, 6, and 7 of the Act of incorporation, which, for convenience of reference, is here printed in full.

AN ACT TO INCORPORATE THE CANADIAN BANKERS' ASSOCIATION.

(63-64 Vict. c. 93, assented to 7th July, 1900.)

WHEREAS the voluntary association now existing under the Preamble. name of the Canadian Bankers' Association has, by its petition, prayed that it may be enacted as hereinafter set forth, and it is expedient to grant the prayer of the said petition: Therefore Her Majesty, by and with the advoce and consent of the Senate and House of Commons of Canada, enacts as follows:—

1. There is hereby created and constituted a corporation Incorporation. under the name of ''The Canadian Bankers' Association,'' hereinafter called ''the Association.''

Sec. 2.

2. The Association shall consist of members and associates;

Association, how composed.

(*a*) The members, hereinafter referred to as members, shall be the banks named in the schedule to this Act, and such new banks hereafter incorporated by or under the authority of the Parliament of Canada as become entitled to carry on the business of banking in Canada, and to which *The Bank Act* in force at the time of its incorporation applies. Any

Members.

bank to which *The Bank Act* applies, carrying on business in Canada, and not named in the schedule to this Act, shall on its own application at the time be admitted as a member of the Association by resolution of the Executive Council hereinafter named;

Associates.

(*b*) The associates, hereinafter referred to as associates, shall be the bank officers who are associates of the voluntary association mentioned in the preamble at the time this Act is passed, and such other officers of the banks which are members of the Association as may be elected at a meeting of the executive council hereinafter named or at any annual meeting of the Association. An associate may at any time by written notice to the president of the Association withdraw from the Association.

The schedule to the Act is not printed. All the banks carrying on business under the Bank Act are members of the Association. Banks incorporated since the 7th of July, 1900, become members as soon as they become entitled to carry on the business of banking in Canada, *i.e.*, when they have obtained the certificate of the Treasury Board under sec. 14 of the Bank Act.

Effects of bank suspending.

3. Upon the suspension of payment of a bank being a member of the Association, such bank shall cease to be a member. Provided, however, that if and when such bank resumes the carrying on of its business in Canada it may again become a member of the Association.

4. Upon an associate ceasing to be an officer of a bank carrying on business in Canada, he shall, at the end of the then current calendar year, cease to be an associate. Sec. 4.
When associate ceases to be such.

5. The objects and powers of the Association shall be, to promote generally the interests and efficiency of banks and bank officers and the education and training of those contemplating employment in banks, and for such purposes, among other means, to arrange for lectures, discussions, competitive papers and examinations on commercial law and banking, and to acquire, publish and carry on the "Journal of The Canadian Bankers' Association." Objects of Association.

In addition to the powers conferred upon the Association by its Act of incorporation, the Association enjoys important powers under secs. 117 to 124 of the Bank Act: see Chapters XXII. and XXIII., *supra*.

The objects and powers of the Association are to be carried out by the executive council: see sec. 16, *infra*.

6. The Association may from time to time establish in any place in Canada a sub-section of the Association under such constitution and with such powers (not exceeding the powers of the Association) as may be thought best. Sub-sections of Association.

7. The Association may from time to time establish in any place in Canada a clearing house for banks, and make rules and regulations for the operations of such clearing house: Provided always, that no bank shall be or become a member of such clearing house except with its own consent, and a bank may after becoming such member at any time withdraw therefrom. Clearing houses.

2. All banks, whether members of the Association or not, shall have an equal voice in making from time to time the rules and regulations for the clearing house; but no such rule or regulation shall have any force or effect until approved of by the Treasury Board. Regulations.

Sec. 7.   The rules and regulations made by virtue of this Act in respect to clearing houses are set out in Chapter XXVIII., *infra*. See also sec. 16 of the Act.

Voting powers.

8. Members of the Association shall vote and act in all matters relating to the Association through their chief executive officers. For the purpose of this Act the chief executive officer of a member shall be its general manager or cashier, or in his absence the officer designated for the purpose by him, or in default of such designation the officer next in authority. Where the president or vice-president of a member performs the duties of a general manager or cashier he shall be the chief executive officer, and in his absence the officer designated for the purpose by him, and in default of such designation the officer next in authority to him. At all meetings of the Association each member shall have one vote upon each matter submitted for vote. The chairman shall, in addition to any vote he may have as chief executive officer or proxy, have a casting vote in case of a tie. Associates shall have only such powers of voting and otherwise taking part at meetings as may be provided by by-law.

Officers.

9. There shall be a president and one or more vice-presidents and an executive council of the Association, of which council five shall form a quorum unless the by-laws otherwise provide.

Officers of existing association continued.

10. The persons who are the president, vice-presidents and executive council of the voluntary association mentioned in the preamble at the time this Act is passed shall be the president, vice-presidents and executive council respectively of the Association until the first general meeting of the Association or until their successors are appointed.

General meetings.

11. The first general meeting of the Association shall be held during the present calendar year at such time and place and upon such notice as the executive council may decide.   Subsequent general meetings shall be held as the by-laws of the Association Sec. 11. may provide at least once in each calendar year.

12. At the first general meeting and at such annual meeting Election of thereafter the members of the Association shall elect a president, officers. one or more vice-presidents, and an executive council, all of whom shall hold office until the next general meeting or until their successors are appointed.

13. The president, vice-president and executive council shall Executive be chosen from among the chief executive officers of members of officers. the Association.

14. Unless the by-laws otherwise provide, the executive coun- Executive cil shall consist of the president and vice-president of the Associ- council. ation and fourteen chief executive officers, and five shall form a quorum for the transaction of business.

15. Each member and associate shall from time to time pay Dues. to the Association for the purpose thereof such dues and assessments as shall from time to time be fixed in that behalf by the Association at any annual meeting, or at any special meeting called for the purpose, by a vote of not less than two-thirds of those present or represented by proxy.

16. The objects and powers of the Association shall be carried By-laws out and exercised by the executive council, or under by-laws, governing Association. resolutions, rules and regulations passed by it, but every such by-law, rule and regulation, unless in the meantime confirmed at a general meeting of the Association called for the purpose of considering the same, shall only have force until the next annual meeting, and in default of confirmation thereat shall cease to have force. Provided always, that any by-law, rule or regulation passed by the executive council may be repealed, amended,

Sec. 16.

varied or otherwise dealt with by the Association at any annual general meeting or at a special general meeting called for the purpose.

Power of executive to pass by-laws.

2. For greater certainty, but not so as to restrict the generality of the foregoing, it is declared that the executive council shall have power to pass by-laws, resolutions, rules and regulations, not contrary to law or to the provisions of this Act, respecting,—

(a) lectures, discussions, competitive papers, examinations;

(b) the journal of the Association;

(c) the sub-sections of the Association;

(d) clearing houses for banks;

(e) general meetings, special and annual, of the Association and of the executive council, and the procedure and quorum thereat, including the part to be taken by associates and their powers of voting;

(f) voting by proxy at meetings of the Association and of the executive council;

(g) the appointment, functions, duties, remuneration and removal of officers, agents and servants of the Association.

Approva o Treasury Board.

3. No by-law, resolution, rule or regulation respecting clearing houses, and no repeal, amendment or variation of or other dealing with any such by-law, resolution, rule or regulation shall have any force or effect until approved of by the Treasury Board.

As to the objects and powers of the Association, cf. secs. 5, 6 and 7 of the Act.

R.S.C. c. 118

17. The provisions of *The Companies Clauses Act*, being chapter 118 of the Revised Statutes [1886], shall not apply to the Association.

The Companies Clauses Act is now Part II. of the Companies Act, R.S.C., 1906, c. 79.

CHAPTER XXVIII.

THE CLEARING HOUSE.

The following authorities may be usefully consulted as to the history and operation of clearing houses: Jevons, Money and the Mechanism of Exchange, Cannon's History of Clearing Houses (reviewed by J. T. P. Knight in an article in 10 Journal C.B.A. 40 on the history and operation of the Montreal Clearing House), Watson's Law of the Clearing House (where the American cases are exhaustively collected). See also Boddington v. Schlencker, 1833, 4 B. & Ad. 752, and the special verdict in Warwick v. Rogers, 1843, 5 M. & G. at p. 348, as to the early practice in the London clearing house, and cf. Hart, pp. 324, 327, where the rules of the London clearing house are set out. In Banque Nationale v. Merchants Bank, 1891, M.L.R. 7 S.C. 336, the beginning of the Montreal Clearing House is described.

In Canada clearing houses for banks are governed by the Act of incorporation of the Canadian Bankers' Association (see Chapter XXVII., *supra*). By that Act the Association may from time to time establish in any place in Canada a clearing house for banks, and make rules and regulations for its operations: provided always, that no bank shall be or become a member of such clearing house except with its own consent, and a bank may after becoming such member at any time withdraw therefrom, (sec. 7). It is further provided that all banks whether members of the Association or not, shall have an equal voice in making from time to time the rules and regulations for the clearing house, but no such rule or regulation shall have any force or effect until approved by the Treasury Board (sec. 7). The powers of the Association are to be exercised by its executive council, which is specifically authorized to pass by-laws, resolutions, rules and regulations not contrary to law, or to the provisions of the Act, respecting clearing houses for banks, but no such by-law, etc., and no repeal, amendment, or variation of or other dealing with, any such by-law, etc., is to have any force or effect until approved of by the Treasury Board (sec. 16).

Power to establish clearing houses.

In pursuance of the powers contained in the Act the Association has adopted the rules and regulations contained in By-law No. 16, set out below, being part of the by-laws passed at a general meeting of the Association held in Toronto on the 15th of November, 1900, and amended at a general meeting held in Montreal on the 15th of April, 1901, and approved by the Treasury Board on the 10th of May, 1901.

Clearing house a voluntary association. A clearing house is a voluntary association. The Bankers' Association has not exercised its power to "establish in any place in Canada a clearing house for banks" except by authorizing the chartered banks doing business in any city or town or such of them as may desire to do so to form themselves into a clearing house (Rule 1). Other banks may be admitted subsequently (Rule 1), and any member may withdraw upon giving the proper notice (sec. 7 and Rule 9).

Any clearing house may enact by-laws, rules and regulations for the government of its members, not inconsistent with the rules contained in By-law No. 16 (Rule 17).

To facilitate daily exchanges. A clearing house is established for the purpose of facilitating daily exchanges and settlements between banks (Rule 2).

It may be defined as a place or institution where the settlement of mutual claims of banks is effected by the payment of differences, called "balances."

Operation of clearing house. Its operation in a simple case may be illustrated as follows:

A clerk from each bank attends the clearing house at a stated hour with bank notes, cheques, drafts, bills and other items, usually called "exchanges," on the other banks belonging to the clearing house. These exchanges are distributed at the clearing house by messengers among the clerks of the banks that must pay them. The exchanges which a bank sends to the clearing house are called creditor exchanges; those which it receives from the other banks are called debtor exchanges. If the creditor exchanges of a bank exceed its debtor exchanges, it is a "creditor bank." If the reverse is the case, it is a "debtor bank."

By arrangement with the board of management of the clearing house, one bank acts as clearing bank for the receipt and disbursement of balances due by and to the various banks, and some bank officer acts as manager of the clearing house (Rule 10).

On completion of the exchanges, the balances due to or by each bank are settled and declared by the clearing house manager, and the balances due by debtor banks must be paid into the clearing bank at or during stated hours. Subsequently the credit balances are paid by the clearing bank to the creditor banks (Rule 11).

Operation of clearing house.

The hours for making the exchanges at the clearing house, for payment of the debit balances to the clearing bank, and for payment out of the balances due to the creditor banks, are fixed by by-law of the clearing house passed under Rule 17, provided that no credit balance, or portion thereof, shall be paid until all debit balances have been received by the clearing bank (Rule 11).

In the case of a large clearing house two or more representatives may be sent from each bank. Where two are sent the procedure may be as follows. A messenger delivers his parcels of credit exchanges and receives in return parcels of debit exchanges, and then returns to his own bank with his delivery statement initialed by the clerks who have received the parcels he has delivered. A clerk from each bank remains to transcribe the amounts received, as shewn by tickets removed from the parcels delivered to his messenger, to a settling sheet, and proceeds to calculate the difference between the amounts delivered and the amounts received—the difference constituting the credit or debit balance for which the manager of the clearing house signs vouchers to be used later at the clearing bank. If the calculations of all the clerks are accurately made, the amount due to the clearing bank will of course be the same as the amount due by it.

A clearing house substitutes a settlement made at a fixed time and place each day by representatives of all the members, for a separate settlement over the counter by each bank with every other bank. No other object is contemplated or provided for. The clearing house does not provide for any united action for any business purpose. It does not contemplate the employment of capital or credit in any enterprise. It contemplates and provides for co-operation to expedite and simplify the transaction by each member of its own proper business in one particular, namely, the settlement of daily balances with the other banks doing business in the same city or town. Incidentally, co-operation in this particular will tend to bring the banks belonging

Purpose of clearing house.

Purpose of clearing house.

to the clearing house into closer relations, enable them to become more familiar with the volume of business and the actual conditions of each other, and open the way to make them mutually helpful in times of financial stringency; but these results are incidental only.

The importance of these so-called incidental results of the clearing house, however, should not be overlooked. For instance, in times of extreme stringency, bankers in the United States have sometimes resorted to clearing house certificates as a method of giving each other assistance. The object is accomplished by the deposit by banks with the clearing house of bills receivable and other securities, and the issue to such banks of loan certificates which may be used in settling balances at the clearing house. The result is simply to give to the depositing banks the benefit of re-discount, and to shift the burden of the lender from day to day to the banks best able to carry it. This expedient was first resorted to by the New York bankers in 1873, and has since been used at several different periods. 2 Journal C.B.A. 208; and cf. Watson, p. 6.

The necessity for the issue of clearing house certificates in the United States has been due, in the main, to the lack of elasticity in the American currency. Since the Canadian system of bank note issue obviates this defect to some extent, there has hitherto been no occasion for the issue of such certificates. Although efforts have sometimes been made to widen the scope and extend the functions of the clearing house, it remains in Canada simply a time and labour-saving device, and is not, what it has been claimed to be in the United States, "a medium for united action upon all questions affecting the mutual welfare and prosperity of its members." 10 Journal C.B.A. at pp. 41, 49.

The exchanges sent to the clearing house by a bank are usually enclosed in sealed envelopes, which are not opened in the clearing house room. Only the aggregate amount of the exchanges contained in each package is noted upon the cover.

Objections to items.

Each bank upon receipt of the packages containing its debtor exchanges verifies the cash and bank notes, examines the cheques and other items with regard to the genuineness of its customers' signatures, the state of their accounts, regularity of endorsements, etc. If the bank objects to any item delivered to it or charge made against it in the exchanges of the day, it should first make application direct to the bank interested for repayment of the amount or charge objected to, but in default of obtaining payment from such bank, the objecting bank may, under Rule 12, notify the clearing house manager of the objection and non-payment.

Although the last mentioned rule provides that the objecting bank shall make such application for repayment and give notice of such objection within certain limited times, the omission to comply with the rule does not deprive the objecting bank of any rights it would have had if the exchanges had been made directly between the banks concerned instead of through the clearing house. Rule 12 is expressly made subject to the important Rule 2, which guards against the use of the clearing house as a means of obtaining payment of any item, charge or claim disputed or objected to.

By virtue of the last mentioned rule, payment through the clearing house is provisional only. If an item or charge is, for good cause, objected to on the day of its receipt from the clearing house and within the hours allowed by the rules, the objecting bank is entitled to repayment or to a reversal of the charge against it in respect of such item. Payment provisional only.

In Warwick v. Rogers, 1843, 5 M. & G. 340, a banker received through the clearing house a bill payable at his banking house accepted by a customer, and after examination of the bill and having funds in his hands, cancelled the acceptance by drawing lines across the customer's name, without rendering the acceptance illegible. In the course of the day, the customer, finding himself to be insolvent, ordered the banker not to pay the bill, whereupon the latter wrote thereon "cancelled by mistake—orders not to pay." The banker then returned the bill in this state to the clearing house before the settling hour in accordance with the custom of the trade in London (a custom which appears to have continued in its essential particulars down to the present time: Hart, p. 326). Held, that the banker was not under any legal liability. Cf. Prince v. Oriental Bank, 1878, 3 App. Cas. 325.

If the objection is not made within the time allowed by the clearing house rules, the fact of the payment through the clearing house does not affect the bank's rights. Its rights will be subject to the ordinary rules of law governing recovery by the payer of money paid by mistake to a person who is not entitled Bank not prejudiced by payment through clearing house.

298
28. THE CLEARING HOUSE.

Bank not prejudiced by payment through clearing house.

to receive payment and who cannot give a discharge (see Chapter XXXVIII., *infra*, notes to sec. 50 of the Bills of Exchange Act). Recent examples are to be found in the cases of Imperial Bank v. Bank of Hamilton, [1903] A.C. 49, and Rex v. Bank of Montreal, 1906, 11 O.L.R. 595, affirmed by the Supreme Court of Canada, 19th of February, 1907. In the former case the paying bank was held entitled to recover, notwithstanding payment through the clearing house and the fact that in accordance with a custom of the clearing house applicable to certified cheques, the cheque there in question was not objected to until the day following its receipt, the receiving bank not having been prejudiced by the delay (see clearing house rules referred to in 31 O.R. at p. 102). In the latter case it was held that the paying bank was estopped from claiming repayment of the cheque by its delay in objecting to it.

A custom of trade or banking in derogation of the common law must be strictly proved. In Banque Nationale v. Merchants Bank, 1891, M.L.R. 7 S.C. 336, a cheque was returned on the afternoon of the day of its receipt, and therefore with sufficient diligence according to the common law standard, but too late according to a temporary rule adopted by the then newly-formed Montreal Clearing House. It appeared in evidence that this rule was not generally observed by the banks belonging to the clearing house, and it was held that the objecting bank had the right to return the cheque.

In the United States the decisions are conflicting. In some cases absolute effect has been given to a clearing house rule requiring items to which objection is taken to be returned by a certain hour, irrespective of whether the presenting bank has altered its position prior to the return of the item. In other cases it has been considered necessary, in order to make such a rule effective, to shew that the presenting bank has been induced by the delay in returning the item to alter its position, as, for instance, by abandoning securities in its hands in the belief that the conditional acceptance of the item in the morning clearing had been meanwhile verified and made absolute. Banque Nationale v. Merchants Bank, *supra;* Watson, pp. 35 *et seq.*

Presentment through clearing house.

If a bill is accepted payable at a particular bank, presentment for payment through the clearing house is sufficient presentment to such bank. (Reynolds v. Chettle, 1811, 2 Camp. 595; Harris v. Parker, 1833, 3 Tyr. 370.)

The delivery of items to a bank through the clearing house is provisional and such items are held by the receiving bank as trustee until such bank pays to the clearing bank at the proper time the balance, if any, found against it as a result of the clearings of the day. See Rules 13, 14 and 15 which provide for the case of a bank's making default in payment of its debit balance.

The following is the text of

By-law No. 16.

The rules and regulations contained in this by-law are made Rules in pursuance of the powers contained in the Act to incorporate respecting the Canadian Bankers' Association, 63 and 64 Vict., c. 93 (1900), houses. and shall be adopted by, and shall be the rules and regulations governing all clearing houses now existing and established, or that may be hereafter established.

See notes, *supra*, at the beginning of this chapter.

Rule 1. The chartered banks doing business in any city or town, or such of them as may desire to do so, may form themselves into a Clearing House. Chartered banks thereafter establishing offices in such city or town may be admitted to the Clearing House by a vote of the members.

Rule 2. The Clearing House is established for the purpose of facilitating daily exchanges and settlements between banks. It shall not either directly or indirectly be used as a means of obtaining payment of any item, charge or claim disputed, or objected to. It is expressly agreed that any bank receiving exchanges through the Clearing House shall have the same rights to return any item, and to refuse to credit any sum which it would have had were the changes made directly between the banks concerned, instead of through the Clearing House; and nothing in these or any future rules, and nothing done, or omitted to be done thereunder, and no failure to comply therewith shall deprive a bank of any rights it might have possessed had such rules not been made, to return any item or refuse to credit any sum; and payment through the Clearing House of any item, charge or claim shall not deprive a bank of any right to recover back the amount so paid.

See notes, *supra*, p. 297.

Rule 3. The Annual Meeting of the members shall be held on such day in each year, and at such time and place as the members may fix by by-law. Special meetings may be called by the Chairman or Vice-Chairman whenever it may be deemed necessary, and the Chairman shall call a special meeting whenever requested to do so in writing by three or more members.

Rule 4. At any meeting each member may be represented by one or more of its officers, but each bank shall have one vote only.

Rule 5. At every Annual Meeting there shall be elected by Ballot a Board of Management who shall hold office until the next Annual Meeting, and thereafter until their successors are appointed. They shall have the general oversight and management of the Clearing House. They shall also deal with the expenses of the Clearing House, and the assessments made therefor. In the absence of any member of the Board of Management he may be represented by another officer of the bank of which he is an officer.

Rule 6. The Board of Management shall at their first meeting after their appointment elect out of their own number a Chairman, a Vice-Chairman, and a Secretary-Treasurer, who shall perform the duties customarily appertaining to these offices.

The officers so selected shall be respectively the Chairman, Vice-Chairman and Secretary-Treasurer of the Clearing House.

Should the bank of which the Chairman is an officer be interested in any matter, his powers and duties shall, with respect to such matter, be exercised by the Vice-Chairman, who shall also exercise the Chairman's duties and powers in his absence.

Rule 7. Meetings of the Board may be held at such times as the members of the same may determine. A special meeting shall be called by the Secretary-Treasurer on the written requisition of any member of the Clearing House for the consideration of any matter submitted by it, of which meeting 24 hours' notice shall be given, but if such meeting is for action under Rules 15 or 16, it shall be called immediately.

Rule 8. The expenses of the Clearing House shall be met by an equal assessment upon the members, to be made by the Board of Management.

Rule 9. Any bank may withdraw from the Clearing House by giving notice in writing to the Chairman or Secretary-Treasurer, between the hours of 1 and 3 o'clock p.m., and paying its due proportion of expenses and obligations then due. Said retirement to take effect from the close of business of the day on which such notice is given. The other banks shall be promptly notified of such withdrawal.

Rule 10. The Board of Management shall arrange with a bank to act as clearing bank for the receipt and disbursement of balances due by and to the various banks, but such bank shall be responsible only for the moneys actually received by it from the debtor banks, and for the distribution of such moneys amongst the creditor banks, on the presentation of the Clearing House certificates properly discharged. The clearing bank shall give receipts for balances received from the debtor banks. The Board of Management shall also arrange for an officer to act as Manager of the Clearing House from time to time, but not necessarily the same officer each day.

Rule 11. The hours for making the exchanges at the Clearing House, for payment of the debit balances to the clearing bank, and for payment out of the balances due the creditor banks, shall be fixed by by-law under clause 17. On completion of the exchanges, the balance due to or by each bank shall be settled and declared by the Clearing House Manager, and if the clearing statements are readjusted under the provisions of these rules, the balances must then be similarly declared settled, and the balances due by debtor banks must be paid into the clearing bank, at or during the hours fixed by by-law as aforesaid, provided that no credit balance, or portion thereof, shall be paid until all debit balances have been received by the clearing bank. At Clearing Houses where balances are payable in money they shall be paid in legal tender notes of large denominations.

At Clearing Houses where balances are payable by draft, should any settlement draft given to the clearing bank not be paid on presentation, the clearing bank shall at once notify in writing all the other banks of such default; and the amount of the unpaid draft shall be repaid to the clearing bank by the banks whose clearances were against the defaulting bank on the day the unpaid draft was drawn, in proportion to such balances.

The clearing bank shall collect the unpaid draft, and pay the same to the other banks in the above proportion. It is understood that the clearing bank is to be the agent of the associated banks, and to be liable only for moneys actually received by it.

Should any bank make default in paying to the clearing bank its debit balance, within the time fixed by this rule, such debit balance and interest thereon shall then be paid by the bank so in default to the Chairman of the Clearing House for the time being. and such Chairman and his successor in office from time to time shall be a creditor of and entitled to recover the said debit balance, and interest thereon from the defaulting bank. Such balances, when received by the said Chairman or his successor in office, shall be paid by him to the clearing bank for the benefit of the banks entitled thereto.

Rule 12. In order that the clearing statements may not be unnecessarily interfered with, it is agreed that a bank objecting to any item delivered to it through the Clearing House, or to any charge against it in the exchanges of the day, shall, before notifying the Clearing House Manager of the objection, apply to the bank interested for payment of the amount of the item or charge objected to, and such amount shall thereupon be immediately paid to the objecting bank. Should such payment not be made, the objecting bank may notify the Clearing House Manager of such objection and non-payment, and he shall thereupon deduct the said amount from the settling sheets of the banks concerned and readjust the clearing statements and declare the correct balances in conformity with the changes so made, provided that such notice shall be given at least half an hour before the earliest hour fixed by by-law, as provided in clause 11, for payment of the balances due to the creditor banks. But notwithstanding that the objecting bank may not have so notified the Clearing House Manager, it shall be the duty under these rules of the bank interested to make such payment on demand therefor being made at any time up to 3 o'clock; provided, however, that if the objection is based on the absence from the deposit of any parcel or of any cheque or other item entered on the deposit slip, notice of such absence shall have been given to the bank interested before 12 o'clock noon, the whole, however, subject to the provisions of Rule No. 2.

Rule 13. All bank notes, cheques, drafts, bills and other items (hereafter referred to as "items") delivered through the Clearing House to a bank in the exchanges of the day, shall be received by such bank as a trustee only, and not as its own property, to be held upon the following trust, namely, upon payment by such bank at the proper hour to the clearing bank of the balance (if any) against it, to retain such items freed from said trust; and in default of payment of such balance to return immediately and before 12.30 o'clock p.m., the said items unmarked and unmutilated through the Clearing House to the respective banks, and the fact that any item cannot be so returned shall not relieve the bank from the obligation to return the remaining items, including the amount of the bank's own notes so delivered in trust.

Upon such default and return of said items, each of the other banks shall immediately return all items which may have been received from the bank so in default, or pay the amount thereof to the defaulting bank through the Clearing House. The items returned by the bank in default shall remain the property of the respective banks from which they were received, and the Clearing House Manager shall adjust the settlement of balances anew.

A bank receiving through the Clearing House such items as aforesaid, shall be responsible for the proper carrying out of the trust upon which the same are received as aforesaid, and shall make good to the other banks respectively all loss and damage which may be suffered by the default in carrying out such trust.

Rule 14. In the event of any bank receiving exchanges through the Clearing House making default in payment of its debit balance (if any), then in lieu of its returning the items received by it as provided by Rule 13, the Board of Management may require the banks to which the defaulting bank, on an account being taken of the exchanges of the day between it and the other banks, would be a debtor, in proportion to the amounts which, on such accounting, would be respectively due to them, to furnish the Chairman of the Clearing House for the time being with the amount of the balance due by the defaulting bank, and such amount shall be furnished accordingly and shall be paid by the Chairman to the clearing bank, which shall then pay

over to the creditor banks the balances due to them in accordance with Rule 11. The said funds for the Chairman shall be
furnished by being deposited in the clearing bank for the purpose aforesaid. The defaulting bank shall repay to the Chairman
for the time being, or to his successor in office, the amount of
such debit balance and interest thereon, and the said Chairman,
and his successor in office, shall be entitled to recover the same
from the defaulting bank. Any moneys so recovered shall be
held in trust for and deposited in the clearing bank for the
benefit of the banks entitled thereto.

[This rule is intended to cover a case where for any reason
the banks which have balances against a defaulting bank pre-
fer, instead of having their items returned, to obtain the benefit
of the balances due to the defaulting bank by other banks, a benefit which under some circumstances might be very important. The
wording of the rule is rendered complicated by the fact that the
defaulting bank is not the debtor of the several banks in the
clearing house, but owes its debtor balance to the chairman of
the clearing house (Rule 11).]

Rule 15. If a bank neglects or refuses to pay its debit balance to the clearing bank, and if such default be made not because of inability to pay, the Board of Management may direct
that the exchanges for the day between the defaulting bank and
each of the other banks be eliminated from the Clearing House
Statements, and that the settlements upon such exchanges be
made directly between the banks interested and not through the
Clearing House. Upon such direction being given the Clearing
House Manager shall comply therewith and adjust the settlement of balances anew, and the settlements of the exchanges so
eliminated shall thereupon be made directly between the banks
interested.

Rule 16. Should any case arise to which, in the opinion of
the Board of Management, the foregoing rules are inapplicable,
or in which their operation would be inequitable, the Board shall
have power at any time to suspend the clearings and settlements
of the day; but immediately upon such suspension the Board
shall call a meeting of the members of the Clearing House to
take such measures as may be necessary.

Rule 17. Every Clearing House now existing, or that may
hereafter be established, may enact by-laws, rules and regula-

tions for the government of its members, not inconsistent with these rules, and may fix therein among other things :— Rules respecting clearing houses.

1. The name of the Clearing House;
2. The number of members of the Board of Management and the quorum thereof;
3. The date, time and place for the Annual Meeting;
4. The mode of providing for the expenses of the Clearing House;
5. The hours for making exchanges, and for payment of the balances to or by the clearing bank;
6. The mode or medium in which balances are to be paid.

Any by-law, rule, or regulation passed or adopted under this clause may be amended at any meeting of the members, provided that not less than two weeks' notice of such meeting and of the proposed amendments, has been given.

CHAPTER XXIX.

CURRENCY AND DOMINION NOTES.

Uniform currency established.

The Dominion statute 34 Vict., c. 4, passed in 1871, after reciting that "it is expedient to establish one uniform currency for the whole Dominion of Canada," enacted that on and after the first day of July, 1871, the currency of the province of Nova Scotia should be the same as that of the provinces of Quebec, Ontario, and New Brunswick, in all of which one currency, of the uniform value thereinafter mentioned, had been and was then used. The Act repealed a tentative Dominion Act of 1868, passed in anticipation of the adoption by the United States of an international standard of currency by which it was proposed that a five dollar gold coin should be of the same value as a French gold coin of twenty-five francs. It also repealed certain statutes of the provinces of Canada, Nova Scotia and New Brunswick, and enacted substantially the provisions contained in secs. 2, 3, 4, 6, 8, 9, 10, 11, 12 and 13 of the present statute.

These sections continue throughout the Dominion the decimal currency which was in use in the provinces other than Nova Scotia prior to Confederation, the pound sterling being the equivalent of $4.86 2-3.

Sec. 6 makes provision for the conversion of Nova Scotia currency into Canadian currency at the ratio of 73 to 75.

Legal tender is regulated by secs. 9 to 12, gold coins of the United States of the values, dates and weights specified being legal tender to any amount, Canadian silver coins to the amount of ten dollars, and Canadian copper or bronze coins to the amount of twenty-five cents, in any one payment. Dominion notes are also legal tender in every part of Canada except at the offices at which they are redeemable (R.S.C. c. 27, sec. 3, infra).

The repealing clause of the Act of 1871 excepted from its operation sec. 2 of the Act of 1868, part of which is now contained in sec. 5.

The provisions of secs. 14 and 16 also date from a time prior to the Act of 1871, they having been enacted by 32-33 Vict., c. 18, secs. 17 and 24.

The statute 44 Vict., c. 4, sec. 4, passed in 1881, enacted the Currency provisions now contained in sec. 7 relating to the conversion into legislation the currency of Canada of any debt or obligation contracted before the 1st of July, 1881, in the currency of British Columbia or Prince Edward Island, but payable thereafter.

The provisions of sec. 15 were enacted in 1906.

R.S.C., 1906, CHAPTER 25.

AN ACT RESPECTING THE CURRENCY.

SHORT TITLE.

1. This Act may be cited as the Currency Act.　　　Short title.

STANDARD OF VALUE.

2. The currency of Canada shall be such, that the British sovereign of the weight and fineness now prescribed by the laws of the United Kingdom, shall be equal to and shall pass current for four dollars eighty-six cents and two-thirds of a cent of the currency of Canada, and the half sovereign of proportionate weight and like fineness, for one-half the said sum. R.S., c. 30, s. 2. *Standard of value of currency.*

Gold is unlimited legal tender in Canada (secs. 9 to 12). It is also the standard of value. Any individual is entitled to take gold bullion to the English mint and have it coined into sovereigns at the rate of £3 17s. 10½d. an ounce, free of charge for coining, although the common practice is to sell bullion to the Bank of England at 1½d. less than the mint price. English sovereigns are made of standard gold, which is an alloy or mixture of eleven parts pure gold and one part composed chiefly of copper. Standard gold is therefore said to be "eleven-twelfths" fine or twenty-two carats fine, a carat being a goldsmith's term for a twenty-fourth part of an ounce.

At the mint price a sovereign should weigh 123.27447 grains troy, or 7.98805 grams, and should contain 113.00160 grains, or

Sec. 2.   7.32238 grams, of pure gold, but since absolute accuracy is a matter of difficulty (and was especially so in former times when the machinery for coining was somewhat primitive), the Mint is allowed a slight deviation called a "remedy," amounting to two-tenths of a grain in each sovereign. There is also a remedy in the fineness of the gold of two parts in a thousand.

Denomina-   3. The denominations of money in the currency of Canada,
tions in   shall be dollars, cents and mills,—the cent being one-hundredth
currency.   part of a dollar, and the mill one-tenth part of a cent. R.S.,
             c. 30, s. 1.

PUBLIC ACCOUNTS, DEBTS AND OBLIGATIONS.

Public   4. All public accounts throughout Canada shall be kept in
accounts,   the currency of Canada; and in any statement as to money or
etc.   money value, in any indictment or legal proceeding, the same
             shall be stated in such currency.

Private   2. In all private accounts and agreements rendered or en-
accounts,   tered into, on or subsequent to the first day of July, one thou-
etc., from   sand eight hundred and seventy-one, all sums mentioned shall be
July 1st,   understood to be in the currency of Canada, unless some other
1871.   is clearly expressed, or must, from the circumstances of the
             case, have been intended by the parties. R.S., c. 30, s. 2.

Sums   5. All sums mentioned in dollars and cents in *The British
mentioned   North America Act*, 1867, and in all Acts of the Parliament of
in certain   Canada shall, unless it is otherwise expressed, be understood to
Acts to be in
currency.   be sums in the currency of Canada as by this Act established.
             R.S., c. 30, s. 12.

Payments in 6. All sums of money payable on and after the first day of
Nova Scotia, July, one thousand eight hundred and seventy-one, to Her late
July, 1st,   Majesty Queen Victoria, or to any person, under any Act or
1871, to be
in Canada   law in force in Nova Scotia, passed before the said day, or under
currency.   any bill, note, contract, agreement or other document or instru-

ment made before the said day in and with reference to that
province, or made after the said day out of Nova Scotia and
with reference thereto, and which were intended to be, and but
for such alteration would have been payable in the currency of
Nova Scotia, as fixed by law previous to the fourteenth day of
April, one thousand eight hundred and seventy-one, shall hereafter be represented and payable, respectively, by equivalent
sums in the currency of Canada, that is to say, for every seventy-
five cents of Nova Scotia currency, by seventy-three cents of
Canada currency, and so in proportion for any greater or less
sum; and if in any such sum there is a fraction of a cent in the
equivalent in Canada currency, the nearest whole cent shall be
taken.   R.S., c. 30, s. 10.

The ratio of 73 to 75 represents the relation between the
currency of Nova Scotia prior to Confederation, of which it
requires $5 to make a pound sterling, and the currency of the
other provinces, in which a pound sterling was the equivalent of
$4.86⅔. By sec. 2, the latter currency is established as the
currency of Canada.

An interesting discussion of the old currencies of Nova Scotia is contained in an article by J. W. H. Rowley in 2 Journal
C.B.A. 413.

7. Any debt or obligation contracted before the first day of As to debts
July, in the year one thousand eight hundred and eighty-one, P.E.I. C. and
in the currency then lawfully used in the province of British contracted
Columbia, or in the province of Prince Edward Island, shall, 1st, 1881.
if payable thereafter, be payable by an equivalent sum in the
currency of Canada as hereby established.   R.S., c. 30, s. 11.

DOMINION AND BANK NOTES.

8. No Dominion note or bank note payable in any other No bank
currency than the currency of Canada, shall be issued or re- notes, etc.,
issued by the Government of Canada, or by any bank, and all in other
such notes issued before the first day of July, one thousand eight currency.

Sec. 8. hundred and seventy-one, shall be redeemed, or notes payable in the currency of Canada shall be substituted or exchanged for them. R.S., c. 30, s. 3.

Dominion notes are governed by the Dominion Notes Act, printed in this chapter, *infra.* Bank notes are governed by secs. 61 *et seq.*, of the Bank Act, *supra.* Section 62 of the Bank Act permits in certain cases the issue and reissue, at any office of a bank in any British colony or possession other than Canada, notes of the bank payable in the currency in use in such colony or possession.

COINS, LEGAL TENDER, ETC.

Gold coins may be struck for Canada.

9. Any gold coins struck for circulation in Canada by authority of the Crown, of the standard of fineness prescribed by law for the gold coins of the United Kingdom, and bearing the same proportion in weight to that of the British sovereign, which five dollars bear to four dollars eighty-six cents and two-thirds of a cent, shall pass current and be a legal tender in Canada for five dollars; and any multiples or division of such coin, struck by the same authority for like purposes, shall pass current and be a legal tender in Canada at rates proportionate to their intrinsic value respectively; and any such coins shall pass by such names as are assigned to them by Royal Proclamation declaring them a legal tender, and shall be subject to the like allowance for remedy as British coin. R.S., c. 30, s. 4.

No gold coins have ever been struck for circulation in Canada under this section. As to the standard of fineness and weight and allowance for remedy of the British sovereign, see notes to sec. 2. Gold coins of the United States of America of the dates, weight and standard of fineness mentioned in sec. 12 are legal tender in Canada.

Dominion notes are also legal tender (see sec. 3 of the Dominion Notes Act, *infra,* in this chapter).

10. The silver, copper or bronze coins heretofore struck by Sec. 10.
authority of the Crown for circulation in the provinces of Silver,
Ontario, Quebec and New Brunswick under the Acts at the copper or bronze coins
time in force in the said provinces respectively, shall be current struck before
Confedera-
and a legal tender throughout Canada, at the rates in the said tion.
currency of Canada assigned to them respectively by the said Legal tender
Acts, and under the like conditions and provisions.

2. Such other silver, copper or bronze coins as are by the Likewise
same authority struck for circulation in Canada, shall pass cur- those struck for circula-
rent and be a legal tender in Canada, at the rates assigned to tion in
them respectively by Royal Proclamation, such silver coins being Canada.
of the fineness now fixed by the laws of the United Kingdom,
and of weights bearing respectively the same proportion to the
value to be assigned to them which the weights of the silver
coins of the United Kingdom bear to their nominal value.

3. All such silver coins aforesaid, shall be a legal tender to To what
the amount of ten dollars, and such copper or bronze coins to amount.
the amount of twenty-five cents, in any one payment.

4. The holder of the notes of any person to the amount of As to holders
more than ten dollars, shall not be bound to receive more than of notes.
that amount in such silver coins in payment of such notes, if
presented for payment at one time, although any of such notes
is for a less sum. R.S., c. 30, s. 5.

Canadian silver and copper or bronze coins are tokens, *i.e.*,
coins the exchange value of which is greater than the value of
the metal contained in them. They are, however, coined only
in sufficient quantities to provide the country with coin for small
payments, and are legal tender only to limited amounts. No
other silver, copper or bronze coins than those which the Crown
has heretofore caused to be struck or may hereafter cause to be
struck for circulation in Canada, or in some province thereof,
shall be legal tender in Canada (sec. 11). As to gold coins, see
secs. 9 to 12.

11. No other silver, copper or bronze coins than those which No other
coins of
the Crown has heretofore caused to be struck or may hereafter silver or

Sec. 11.
copper to be
legal tender.
cause to be struck for circulation in Canada, or in some province thereof, shall be a legal tender in Canada. R.S., c. 30, s. 6.

As to foreign
gold coins.

Proviso as
to U. S.
eagle.
12. His Majesty may, by proclamation, from time to time, fix the rates at which any foreign gold coins of the description, date, weight and fineness mentioned in such proclamation, shall pass current, and be a legal tender in Canada: Provided that until it is otherwise ordered by any such proclamation, the gold eagle of the United States of America, coined after the first day of July, one thousand eight hundred and thirty-four, and before the first day of January, one thousand eight hundred and fifty-two, or after the said last-mentioned day, but while the standard of fineness for gold coins then fixed by the laws of the said United States remains unchanged, and weighing ten pennyweights, eighteen grain, troy weight, shall pass current and be a legal tender in Canada for ten dollars.

U. S. gold
coins.
2. The gold coins of the said United States being multiples and halves of the said eagle, and of like date and proportionate weights, shall pass current and be a legal tender in Canada for proportionate sums. R.S., c. 30, s. 7.

The gold eagle as coined since the 1st of July, 1834, weighs 258 grains troy, nine-tenths fine.

As to the weight and fineness of a British sovereign, see notes to sec. 2.

Proof of
date, etc., of
coins.
13. The stamp of the year on any foreign coin made current by this Act, or any proclamation issued under it, shall establish *prima facie* the fact of its having been coined in that year; and the stamp of the country on any foreign coin shall establish *prima facie* the fact of its being of the coinage of such country. R.S., c. 30, s. 8.

Defaced coin
not a legal
tender.
14. No tender of payment in money in any gold, silver or copper coin which has been defaced by stamping thereon any

name or word, whether such coin is or is not thereby diminished or lightened, shall be a legal tender. R.S., c. 30, s. 9. Sec. 14.

REDEMPTION OF COINS.

15. The Minister of Finance may, under regulations of the Governor in Council, redeem any silver, copper or bronze coins issued for circulation in Canada which by reason of abrasion through legitimate usage are no longer deemed fit for circulation. 6 E. VII., c. 8, s. 1. Redemption of light coin.

COUNTERFEIT OR DIMINISHED COIN TO BE BROKEN.

16. If any coin is tendered as current gold or silver coin to any person who suspects the same to be diminished otherwise than by reasonable wearing, or to be counterfeit, such person may cut, break, bend or deface such coin, and if any coin so cut, broken, bent or defaced appears to be diminished otherwise than by reasonable wearing, or to be counterfeit, the person tendering the same shall bear the loss thereof; but if the coin is of due weight, and appears to be lawful coin, the person cutting, breaking, bending or defacing it, shall be bound to receive the coin at the rate for which it was coined. By person to whom tendered. Who shall bear the loss.

2. If any dispute arises whether the coin so cut, broken, bent or defaced, is diminished in manner aforesaid, or counterfeit, it shall be heard and finally determined in a summary manner by any justice of the peace, who may examine, upon oath, the parties as well as any other person, for the purpose of deciding such dispute, and if he entertains any doubt in that behalf, he may summon three persons, the decision of a majority of whom shall be final. Disputes how decided.

3. Every officer employed in the collection of the revenue in Canada shall cut, break or deface, or cause to be cut, broken or defaced, every piece of counterfeit or unlawfully diminished gold or silver coin which is tendered to him in payment of any part of the revenue in Canada. Revenue officers to destroy such coin

Sig. 16.   4. For the purposes of this section 'current gold or silver
Definition.   coin' includes any coin which it is by Part IX. of the Criminal
              Code defined to include. R.S., c. 167, s. 26.

         This section was formerly part of an "Act respecting Offen-
    ces relating to the Coin," the other provisions of which are now
    incorporated in the Criminal Code (R.S.C. c. 146, Part IX.).
    By sec. 546 of the Code, "current gold or silver coin" includes
    any gold or silver coin of any of His Majesty's mints, or gold
    or silver coin of any foreign prince or state or country, or other
    gold or silver coin lawfully current, by virtue of any proclama-
    tion or otherwise, in any part of His Majesty's dominions.

                            DOMINION NOTES.

Dominion   As pointed out in Chapter I., *supra*, p. 4, the statute 31
Note   Vict., c. 46, passed in 1868, in effect extended to the whole Do-
legislation. minion the operation of the Provincial Notes Act, 1866. The
    $8,000,000 of provincial notes prepared in 1866, and the $5,000,-
    000 thereof in circulation in 1868 were declared to be Dominion
    notes, redeemable in specie on presentation at offices established
    or to be established at Montreal, Toronto, Halifax and St. John,
    N.B., and at that one of the said places at which they might be
    respectively made payable, the notes payable at Halifax to be
    redeemable in Nova Scotia currency, *i.e.*, at the rate of $5 per
    pound sterling. The Governor was authorized to establish
    branches of the Receiver-General's department in Montreal, To-
    ronto, Halifax and St. John, respectively, for the issue and re-
    demption of provincial or Dominion notes, or to make arrange-
    ments with any chartered bank or banks for this purpose. The
    government was also authorized either to re-issue any of such
    provincial notes or to issue Dominion notes to an amount not
    exceeding that of the provincial notes redeemed.
         From an early date bank charters granted in Upper and
    Lower Canada had permitted banks to issue notes as small as
    one dollar or five shillings. Notwithstanding the criticism and
    remonstrance of the Colonial Office, the officials of which urged
    that "a currency founded in a sound and metallic basis" be sub-
    stituted for this small note circulation, the privilege was en-
    joyed by the banks until 1870. In that year the right to issue

notes under $4 was voluntarily surrendered by the banks in Dominion return for valuable concessions, namely the abolition of the tax legislation. of one per cent. per annum upon their note circulation and the repeal of the statute requiring them to hold one-tenth of their capital in Dominion securities. At the same time the banks were required to hold, as nearly as might be, one-half of their cash reserves in Dominion notes, the proportion of such reserves held in Dominion notes never to be less than one-third thereof.

These provisions were subsequently modified so as to require a bank to hold not less than forty per centum of its cash reserves in Dominion notes (Bank Act, sec. 60), and to prohibit a bank's issuing any note for a sum less than $5 or for any sum which is not a multiple of $5 (*ibid.*, sec. 61).

In 1876 the laws respecting Dominion notes were extended to the provinces of Prince Edward Island, British Columbia and Manitoba, and the government was authorized to establish branch offices of the Receiver-General's department at Charlottetown, Victoria, and Winnipeg.

By statutes passed in 1870, 1872, 1875 and 1880 the Dominion note circulation was enlarged from time to time, and changes were made in the proportions of Dominion securities and specie respectively required to be held against outstanding notes. These Acts and that of 1868, were all consolidated by R.S.C., 1886, c. 31. An Act of 1895 (59 Vict., c. 16), repealing an Act of 1894, removed the limitation of $20,000,000 which had existed immediately prior to 1894, and provided that the Minister of Finance, in addition to any amount required to be held by him in gold under the revised statute, should hold an amount in gold equal to the amount of Dominion notes issued and outstanding in excess of $20,000,000.

In 1903, R.S.C. 1886, c. 31 and amending Acts were repealed and a new Act substituted, the provisions of which are reproduced in the present statute.

R.S.C., 1906, CHAPTER 27.

· AN ACT RESPECTING DOMINION NOTES.

SHORT TITLE.

1. This Act may be cited as the Dominion Notes Act.   Short title.

DOMINION NOTES ACT.

INTERPRETATION.

2. In this Act, unless the context otherwise requires,—

(*a*) 'specie' means coin current by law in Canada, at the rates and subject to the provisions of the law in that behalf, or bullion of equal value according to its weight and fineness.

(*b*) 'Dominion notes' means notes of the Dominion of Canada issued and outstanding under the authority of this Act. 3 E. VII., c. 43, ss. 1 and 2.

As to "coin current by law in Canada," see the Currency Act, *supra*.

ISSUE AND REDEMPTION.

3. Dominion notes may be issued and outstanding at any time to any amount, and such notes shall be a legal tender in every part of Canada except at the offices at which they are redeemable. 3 E. VII., c. 43, s. 2.

Legal tender is also provided for by secs. 9 to 12 of the Currency Act, *supra*.

As to the offices at which Dominion notes are redeemable, see secs. 5 and 9, *infra*.

4. Dominion notes shall be of such denominational values as the Governor in Council determines, and shall be in such form, and signed by such persons and in such manner, by lithograph, printing or otherwise, as the Minister of Finance from time to time directs.

n · 2. Such notes shall be redeemable in specie on presentation at branch offices established or at banks with which arrangements are made for the redemption thereof as hereinafter provided. 3 E. VII., c. 43, s. 3.

As to agencies for redemption of notes, see sec. 9.

5. The Minister of Finance shall always hold as security for the redemption of Dominion notes up to and including thirty million dollars, issued and outstanding at any one time an amount equal to not less than twenty-five per centum of the amount of such notes in gold, or in gold and securities of Canada, the principal and interest of which are guaranteed by the Government of the United Kingdom. *Amount held as security for redemption.*

2. The amount so held in gold shall be not less than fifteen per centum of the amount of such notes so issued and outstanding. *Amount held in gold.*

3. As security for the redemption of Dominion notes issued in excess of thirty million dollars the Minister shall hold an amount in gold equal to such excess. 3 E. VII., c. 43, s. 4. *Notes in excess of $30,000,000.*

By sec. 3, Dominion notes may be issued and outstanding at any time to any amount.

6. In case the amount held in accordance with the provisions of this Act as security for the redemption of Dominion notes is not sufficient to pay the Dominion notes presented for redemption, or in case the amount so held is reduced below the amount required by this Act to be held, the Governor in Council may raise, by way of loan, temporary or otherwise, such sums of money as are necessary to pay such notes or to provide the amount required to be held as security for the redemption of Dominion notes issued and outstanding. 3 E. VII., c. 43, s. 5. *Loan may be raised if amount of security is insufficient.*

PROCEEDS AND EXPENSES.

7. The proceeds of Dominion notes so issued shall form part of the Consolidated Revenue Fund of Canada, and all expenses incurred or required to be paid in connection with the engraving, printing or preparation of such notes, or the signing, issue *Proceeds of notes; expenses incurred.*

Sec. 7.   or redemption thereof, shall be paid out of the said fund. 3 E.
VII., c. 43, s. 5.

MONTHLY STATEMENT.

Monthly   8. The Minister of Finance shall publish monthly in the
statement
by Minister   *Canada Gazette* a statement of the amount of Dominion notes
in *Canada*   outstanding on the last day of the preceding month, and of the
Gazette.
gold and guaranteed debentures then held by him for securing
the redemption thereof. 3 E. VII., c. 43, s. 6.

AGENCIES FOR REDEMPTION.

Officers of   9. The Governor in Council may establish branch offices of
agencies for
redemption.   the Department of Finance at Toronto, Montreal, Halifax, St.
John, Winnipeg, Victoria and Charlottetown, for the redemption
of Dominion notes, or may make arrangements with a chartered
bank at any of the said places for the redemption thereof.

Assistant   2. Every assistant receiver general appointed at any of the
receiver
general.   said places under Part II. of the Savings Banks Act shall be an
agent for the issue and redemption of such notes. 3 E. VII., c.
43, s. 7.

The Minister of Finance is required to make such arrangements as are necessary for ensuring the delivery of Dominion
notes to any bank, in exchange for an equivalent amount of
specie, at the several offices at which Dominion notes are redeemable, in the cities mentioned in this section, respectively; such
notes are redeemable at the office for redemption of Dominion
notes in the place where the specie is given in exchange (Bank
Act, *supra*, sec. 60).

NOTES OF LATE PROVINCE OF CANADA.

Redemption   10. Provincial notes under the Act of the late province of
of notes of
old province Canada, passed in the session held in the twenty-ninth and
of Canada.   thirtieth years of Her late Majesty Queen Victoria's reign,

chapter ten, intituled *An Act to provide for the issue of Pro-* Sec. 10.
vincial Notes, shall be held to be notes of the Dominion of Canada, and shall be redeemable in specie on presentation at Toronto,
Montreal, Halifax, or St. John, according as the same are
respectively made payable, and shall be legal tender except at
the offices at which they so are respectively made payable. 3
E. VII., c. 43, s. 8.

BOOK II.

NEGOTIABLE INSTRUMENTS AND THE BILLS OF EXCHANGE ACT.

CHAPTER XXX.

Negotiable Instruments.

In Crouch v. Credit Foncier, 1873, L.R. 8 Q.B. at p. 381, Blackburn, J., quoting the editors of Smith's Leading Cases, states the tests of negotiability thus:

"It may be laid down as a safe rule that where an instrument is by the custom of trade transferable, like cash, by delivery, and is also capable of being sued upon by the person holding it pro tempore, then it is entitled to the name of a *negotiable instrument,* and the property in it passes to a *bonâ fide* transferee for value, though the transfer may not have taken place in market overt. But that if either of the above requisites be wanting, *i.e.,* if it be either not accustomably transferable, or, though it be accustomably transferable, yet, if its nature be such as to render it incapable of being put in suit by the party holding it pro tempore, it is not a *negotiable instrument,* nor will delivery of it pass the property of it to a vendee, however *bonâ fide,* if the transferor himself have not a good title to it, and the transfer be made out of market overt."

According to Chalmers (p. 317), Blackburn, J.'s statement requires modification in two respects. Firstly, an instrument, not otherwise negotiable, may be made negotiable by statute. Secondly, foreign government bonds to bearer may undoubtedly be negotiable, yet the holder cannot sue the foreign government upon them in the courts of this country; the explanation may, however, be that the exemption of a foreign government from suit in this country is a personal exemption, and does not arise out of any defect of title on the part of the holder.

Blackburn, J., in the same case at p. 382, continues:

"Bills of exchange and promissory notes, whether payable
to order or to bearer, are by the law merchant negotiable in both
senses of the word. The person who, by a genuine endorsement,
or, where it is payable to bearer, by a delivery, becomes holder,
may sue in his own name on the contract, and if he is a *bonâ
fide* holder for value, he has a good title notwithstanding any
defect of title in the party (whether indorser or deliverer)
from whom he took it.''

Yet, when the two characteristics just mentioned as belonging to bills and notes are considered, it is evident that they do
not afford satisfactory tests to distinguish so-called negotiable
instruments from other choses in action.

(1) All choses in action might formerly be sued on in equity,
and by the effect of statute may now be sued on in law, in the
name of the transferee. The characteristic which has been
spoken of as one peculiar to bills and notes is really but a matter of practice upon which different courts took different views.
This characteristic, as a peciliar one, either never existed or,
if it did, has been abolished.

(2) As to the second characteristic, a bill or note does not
cease to be a "negotiable instrument" when it becomes overdue, yet in that case "it can be negotiated only subject to any
defect of title affecting it at its maturity" (Bills of Exchange
Act, sec. 70). Even before maturity, honest acquisition of a
bill or note does not always confer title (*e.g.*, if the signature
has been obtained by fraud, or if a simple signature not delivered
in order that it may be converted into a bill has been fraudulently filled up as a complete bill, or if a completed but unissued
bill is stolen: cf. effect of material alteration before the passing of the Bills of Exchange Act).

Nor on the other hand is the characteristic in question one
which attaches only to bills and notes or other so-called negotiable instruments. "Generally speaking a chose in action assignable only in equity must be assigned subject to the equities
existing between the original parties to the contract; but this
is a rule which must yield when it appears from the nature or
terms of the contract that it must have been intended to be assignable free from, and unaffected by, such equities." (Re Agra
and Masterman's Bank, 1867, L.R. 2 Ch. at p. 397.)

Thus when bills and notes are distinguished from other Tests of
negotiability choses in action by being described as negotiable, they are so distinguished by a peculiarity of which they not only have no exclusive possession but which frequently they have not themselves.

Some of the difficulties of defining the word negotiable disappear when it is noted that it has an original and an acquired meaning. Originally it meant (1) transferable; but afterwards it was used to indicate the effects of transfer, namely, that the transferee (2) could sue in his own name, and (3) took free from the equities.

The primary meaning truly indicated at one time a real distinction among choses in action. Now any chose in action arising out of contract may be transferred, and it is not essential to the validity of a bill that it shall be transferable from one person to another, except under the ordinary rules governing the assignment of choses in action, as for instance a ''non-negotiable'' bill.

Nevertheless there does exist a real distinction among choses Real
distinction. in action, namely between those intended to be assignable free from equities, and those not so intended. All contracts are now transferable by the obligee, but some are made with the intention that they shall be payable to persons other than the immediate promisee, that is, are intended to be ambulatory.

Ambulatory intent is perhaps more truly the distinguishing Ambulatory
intent. characteristic of ''negotiable'' instruments than the characteristics usually assigned. This characteristic is not confined to bills and notes, although the non-recognition of the true distinguishing characteristic made the admission of other instruments to the class called negotiable unnecessarily difficult. Other instruments are equally negotiable instruments ''when it appears from the nature or terms of the contract that it must have been intended to be assignable free from, and unaffected by, such equities.'' (Re Agra & Masterman's Bank, *supra*.)

As to the foregoing, cf. Ewart in 16 L.Q.R. 135, especially at pp. 140-142, and his book on Estoppel by Misrepresentation, Chapter XXIV, where the confusion surrounding the meaning of ''negotiable'' is discussed.

''Negotiability'' may affect the rights of holders of instru- Negotia-
bility. ments (1) in regard to the equities of the person liable as against

the transferee in good faith, and (2) in regard to the equities
of the real owner as against some holder who claims through a
finder, a thief, or a fraudulent trustee.

1. *As to the equities of persons liable.* The reason
why the person liable may not set up his equities may
be either (*a*) that the contract is an original promise by
the person liable to pay the transferee, that is, not a promise to
the original payee but an original and direct promise moving
from the person liable to the transferee, by virtue of the ambulatory nature of the contract (cf. Bullard v. Bell, 1817, Mason
243), or more probably, (*b*) that the person liable is estopped, by
making a contract that he will pay to the order of the original
payee, from setting up his equities as against third parties who
have acted upon the faith of his promise. (Cf. Re General Es-
tates Co. 1868, L.R. 3 Ch. 758; McKenzie v. Montreal, 1878, 29
C.P. at pp. 338-339.)

2. *As to the title of a transferee from a finder, a thief, or a
fraudulent trustee.* Such transferee of a bill or note is said to
obtain a good title by reason of the "negotiability" of the instrument. "The law merchant validates in the interest of commerce a transaction which the common law would declare void
for want of title or authority." (Swan v. North British, 1862,
7 H. & N. 634.)

Negotia-
bility by
estoppel.

The negotiable character of bonds and scrip payable to bearer
was not readily admitted by the courts but it was nevertheless
held that the persons dealing with such documents were estopped from denying it. This doctrine of "negotiability by estoppel," (so named by Bowen, L.J., in Easton v. London, etc.,
Bank, 1886, 34 Ch. D. at p. 113), was formulated by Lord
Cairns in Goodwin v. Robarts, 1876, 1 App. Cas. at p. 490, 5 R.
C. at p. 212, where he says: "Let it be assumed, for the moment,
that the instrument was not negotiable, that no right of action
was transferred by the delivery, and that no legal claim could
be made by the taker in his own name against the foreign government; still the appellant is in the position of a person who
has made a representation, on the face of his scrip, that it would
pass with a good title to anyone on his taking it in good faith
and for value, and who has put it in the power of his agent to
hand over the scrip with this representation to those who are
induced to alter their position on the faith of the representation
so made."

Ewart suggests that the true foundation for the decision of cases where a man apparently may give a better title than he has is to be found, not in negotiability real or by estoppel, but in estoppel by ostensible ownership or ostensible agency. The maxim *nemo dat quod non habet* is, he says, universally true; but its truth in no way prevents an owner of property from being estopped by his conduct from setting up his good title as against a transferee who has none. In the case of an ambulatory instrument, mere possession constitutes apparent ownership. Therefore if the true owner of such an instrument gives possession of it to another he gives such other person the apparent ownership, and is estopped as against a transferee in good faith from such person from denying that the apparent is the real ownership. Sometimes the validity of a transferee's title must be attributed to ostensible agency rather than to ostensible ownership. Bills are entrusted to a bill-broker. As against a transferee in good faith, the owner is estopped from setting up that the agent by private instructions had no authority to sell. An owner of ambulatory instruments is aware that possession is apparent ownership. He may protect himself against loss by restricting their transferability by appropriate endorsement. If he leaves them payable to bearer, and they are lost or stolen, he ought to bear the loss rather than an innocent transferee from the finder or thief. Cf. Young v. MacNider, 1895, 25 S.C.R. at p. 279.

Definition of negotiable instrument.

The following definition by a recent writer of high authority expresses clearly the distinction between the original and the acquired meaning of the word negotiable.

A negotiable instrument is one which, when transferred by delivery or by endorsement and delivery, as the case may be, passes to the transferee a good title to payment according to its tenor, and irrespective of the title of the transferor, provided, in the case of a bill of exchange, note, or cheque, that the transferee is a holder in due course (Bills of Exchange Act, sec. 56), and in the case of other instruments, that he is a holder for value in good faith without notice of any defect attaching to the instrument or the title of the transferor. Negotiability in the above sense must be carefully distinguished from the mere

Negotiabil-
ity defined.
quality of being subject to negotiation. Negotiation is the appropriate transfer of a bill, note, or cheque, by delivery or by endorsement and delivery (Bills of Exchange Act, sec. 60), and may take place where the instrument, by reason of being overdue or otherwise, has lost the quality of negotiability in the first-mentioned sense. Hart on Banking, p. 816. Cf. Chapter XL., *infra*.

What instruments are negotiable.

The negotiability of bills, notes and cheques, in both senses of the term negotiability, will be discussed in connection with the Bills of Exchange Act which is the subject of commentary in the following chapters of the book. The remainder of this chapter will consist of a statement of the principal classes of documents other than bills, notes and cheques which are entitled to a place in the conventional category of negotiable instruments, *i.e.*, negotiable in the sense firstly mentioned in Hart's definition.

The meaning of "a holder for value in good faith without notice of any defect attaching to the instrument or to the title of the transferor" need not be further discussed here, as all the elements of the expression are discussed in connection with the appropriate sections of the Bills of Exchange Act: see notes to sec. 56.

The title of a bank which takes negotiable instruments from a broker or other agent is discussed in Chapter XV., *supra*, p. 143.

A bank when taking the bonds or other obligations of a corporation as security must assure itself either that the issue of such obligations is within the ordinary scope of the power of the corporation or that the issue has been duly authorized in pursuance of special powers in that behalf contained in the charter of the corporation or in any statutes applicable to it.

In Webb v. Herne Bay Commissioners, 1870, L.R. 5 Q.B. 642, the commissioners had power under a local Act to levy certain rates and to. mortgage such rates to secure money borrowed from time to time. In payment of goods supplied to them by one of their own members, they issued to the vendor, in alleged contravention of the Act, mortgages in the form prescribed by the Act, which purported upon the face of them to be mortgages given for money advanced to them. The mortgages were duly transferred to the plaintiff in the form prescribed by the Act. It was held that inasmuch as there was power to issue What instruments are negotiable. mortgages for the purposes stated on their face, the commissioners were estopped from saying that the mortgages were not good and valid in the hands of an innocent holder.

The principle of Webb v. Herne Bay Commissioners is not applicable, however, to instruments which on their face do not purport to be duly executed and issued in pursuance of the power given to the corporation and for an authorized purpose. If a municipal debenture purports to be issued in pursuance of a by-law, and the by-law on its face purports to be passed for a purpose for which the corporation has no power to pass such a by-law, the debenture is void even in the hands of an innocent holder for value. (Confederation Life v. Howard, 1894, 25 O. R. 197.)

The quality of negotiability is an incident annexed by the Usage the test of negotiability usage of the money market where the instruments are transferred, and is not determined by the law of the place of issue. (Picker v. London & County Bank, 1887, 18 Q.B.D. 515.)

The law, as thus governed by usage, is of a progressive character (cf. Chapter II., *supra*, p. 22). Instruments which at one time are not negotiable, may, by the usage of the money market, afterwards become so. (Goodwin v. Robarts, 1875, L. R. 10 Ex. 337, 1 App. Cas. 476: see judgment of the Exchequer Chamber, where the history of the doctrine of negotiability to that date is traced.)

Bonds payable to bearer or order.

"In my opinion," says Bigham, J., in Edelstein v. Schuler, Proof of usage unnecessary. [1902] 2 K.B. at p. 155, "the time has passed when the negotiability of bearer bonds, whether government bonds or trading bonds, foreign or English, can be called in question in our courts. The existence of the usage has been so often proved and its convenience is so obvious that it must be taken now to be part of the law; the very expression "bearer bond" connotes the idea of negotiability, so that the moment such bonds are issued to the public they rank themselves among the class of negotiable securities."

The bonds in question in Edelstein v. Schuler were debenture Company bonds to bearer. bonds, some issued by an English company in England, others by foreign corporations abroad, in the ordinary form of such securities. Both classes of bonds were held to be negotiable so as to give a holder in good faith and for value a perfect title; following Bechuanaland v. London, [1898] 2 Q.B. 658.

The case of Crouch v. Crédit Foncier, 1873, L.R. 8 Q.B. 374, so far as it is inconsistent with the doctrine just laid down, can no longer be considered law in view of the doubt expressed in Goodwin v. Robarts, and the disapproval expressed in Bechuanaland v. London. Cf. the explanation of Crouch v. Crédit Foncier in London & County Bank v. River Plate Bank, 1887, 20 Q.B.D. at p. 240, where, however, a different kind of document was in question, namely share certificates.

Bonds to order. In the case of In re General Estate Co., 1868, L.R. 3 Ch. 758, the doctrine of negotiability was held to extend to bonds payable to the order of a named person and by him endorsed, distinguishing In re Natal Company's Case, 1868, L.R. 3 Ch. 355 on the ground of the peculiar wording of the bond in the latter case, which was payable to a named person "his executors, administrators, or transferees or to the holder for the time being of this debenture bond." See also Bank of Toronto v. Cobourg Ry. Co., 1884, 7 O.R. 1, where the nature of debentures is discussed, and the particular debentures in question (payable to order and expressed to be made in pursuance of a statute which made them a charge on the property of the company, with a right of foreclosure and sale) are characterized as "strictly, on the face of them, negotiable instruments."

In Venables v. Baring, [1892] 3 Ch. 527, the bonds of an American railroad company were in question. On the face of each bond it was stated that it and the other bonds of the series were secured by a mortgage of even date made by the company to trustees upon the company's property. It was held that the bonds were negotiable, without deciding whether or not any of the limitations or provisions expressed in the mortgage passed with the bond.

Foreign government bonds. The negotiability of foreign government bonds payable to bearer has been established since the case of Gorgier v. Mievell, 1824, 3 B. & C. 45, 5 R.C. 198. Cf. Goodwin v. Robarts, 1875, L.R. 10 Ex. 337, 1 App. Cas. 476, 5 R.C. 199.

Scrip. In Goodwin v. Robarts the principle of negotiability was held to extend to the scrip issued by a foreign government, on negotiating a loan. The scrip contained a promise to give to the bearer, after all instalments of the loan were made, a bond for the amount paid.

The question of the negotiability of such bonds and scrip is independent of the fact that the holder cannot sue the foreign government or its agents within the jurisdiction. (Goodwin v. Robarts; Twycross v. Dreyfus, 1877, 5 Ch. D. 206.)

It has been said that the mere fact that bonds are overdue will not prevent a transferee in good faith and for value from acquiring a good title by estoppel. (Young v. Macnider, 1895, 25 S.C.R. 272, 278.)

Interest coupons are independent negotiable instruments (McKenzie v. Montreal, etc., 1878, 29 C.P. 333; DesRosiers v. Montreal, etc., 1883, 6 L.N. 388).

Other negotiable instruments.

Circular notes issued by a bank are negotiable instruments. The law and practice respecting them is discussed in Conflans v. Parker, 1867, L.R. 3 C.P. 1, 11-12.

Dividend warrants payable to a named person and not to his order, or to bearer, are not negotiable (Partridge v. Bank of England, 1846, 9 Q.B. 396, but see Goodwin v. Robarts, 1875, L.R. 10 Ex. at p. 354) unless they come within the definition of a bill of exchange or cheque (see Bills of Exchange Act, sec. 22). The provisions of the Act as to crossed cheques are applicable to a warrant for payment of dividend (*ibid.* sec. 7).

Exchequer bills are negotiable instruments. (Brandao v. Barnett, 1846, 12 Cl. & F. 787, at p. 805.)

Instruments not negotiable.

Post office orders have been held in England not to be negotiable although the Post Office regulations provide in effect that a banker's stamp will be accepted in place of the payee's receipt. (Fine Art v. Union Bank, 1886, 17 Q.B.D. 705; cf. McEntire v. Potter, 1889, 22 Q.B.D. at pp. 441-2.)

Share certificates and transfers are not negotiable instruments: see Chapter XV., *supra,* p. 143.

Bills of lading are not negotiable instruments: see Chapter III., *supra,* notes to sec. 2, of the Bank Act, p. 35. They are, however, by the custom of merchants, transferable by endorsement.

A letter of credit signed by the provincial secretary with the assent of his colleagues, but not being authorized by order in council, constitutes no contract with the government and is not a negotiable instrument within the Bills of Exchange Act or the Bank Act so as to enable a bank to lend money upon it. (Banque Jacques-Cartier v. The Queen, 1895, 25 S.C.R. 84.)

CHAPTER XXXI.

INTRODUCTION TO THE BILLS OF EXCHANGE ACT.

The Bills of Exchange Act, 1890, being 53 Vict., c. 33, intituled "An Act relating to Bills of Exchange, Cheques and Promissory Notes," was a re-enactment with little modification of the English Bills of Exchange Act, 1882. The draftsman of the English Act was M. D. Chalmers, C.S.I., author of "A Digest of the Law of Bills of Exchange, Promissory Notes, Cheques and Negotiable Securities."

In the introduction to the third edition of that work the author said:—

"Soon after the publication of the second edition of this Digest the law relating to bills, notes, and cheques was codified by the Bills of Exchange Act, 1882. For the most part the propositions of the Act were taken word for word from the propositions of the Digest. In the introduction to the second edition it was pointed out that the general propositions of the Digest could only be considered as law in so far as they were correct and logical inductions from the decided cases which were cited as illustrations. Now the position is reversed. The cases decided before the Act are only law in so far as they can be shewn to be correct and logical deductions from the general propositions of the Act. The illustrations, therefore, must always be tested by the language of the Act itself." *Illustrations must be tested by language of Act.*

The Bills of Exchange Act, 1882, was the first enactment codifying any branch of the Common Law. The conditions under which the experiment was successfully carried out is described by Chalmers in the following language:—

"The success of the Bills of Exchange Bill depended on the wise lines laid down by Lord Herschell. He insisted that the bill should be introduced in a form which did nothing more than codify the existing law, and that all amendments should be left to Parliament. A bill which merely improves the form, without altering the substance, of the law creates no opposition, and gives very little room for controversy. Of course codification pure and simple is an impossibility. The draftsman comes across doubtful points of law which he must decide one way or *Codification of law relating to bills.*

Codification of law relating to bills.

the other. Again, voluminous though our case law is, there are occasional gaps which a codifying bill must bridge over if it aims at anything like completeness. Still, in drafting the Bills of Exchange bill, my aim was to reproduce as exactly as possible the existing law, whether it seemed good, bad, or indifferent in its effects. The idea of codifying the law of negotiable instruments was first suggested to me by Sir Fitz-James Stephen's Digest of the Law of Evidence, and Sir F. Pollock's Digest of the Law of Partnership. Bills, notes, and cheques seemed to form a well isolated subject, and I therefore set to work to prepare a digest of the law relating to them. I found that the law was contained in some 2,500 cases, and 17 statutory enactments. I read through the whole of the decisions, beginning with the first reported case in 1603. But the cases on the subject were comparatively few and unimportant until the time of Lord Mansfield. The general principles of the law were then settled, and subsequent decisions, though very numerous, have been for the most part illustrations of, or deductions from, the general propositions then laid down. On some points there was a curious dearth of authority. As regards such points I had recourse to American decisions, and to inquiry as to the usages among bankers and merchants. As the result, a good many propositions in the Digest, even on points of frequent occurrence, had to be stated with a (probably) or a (perhaps). Some two years after the publication of my Digest, I read a paper on the question of codifying the law of negotiable instruments before the Institute of Bankers. Mr. John Hollams, the well-known commercial lawyer, who was present, pointed out the advantages of a code to the mercantile community; and mainly I think on his advice, I received instructions from the Institute of Bankers and the Associated Chambers of Commerce to prepare a bill on the subject. The draft of the bill was first submitted to a sub-committee of the Council of the Institute of Bankers, who carefully tested such portions of it as dealt with matters of usage uncovered by authority. The bill was then introduced by Sir John Lubbock, the president of the Institute. After it had been read a second time in the Commons, it was referred to a strong select committee of merchants, bankers, and lawyers, with Sir Farrer Herschell as chairman.

"As the Scotch law of negotiable instruments differed in certain particulars from English law, the bill was originally drafted to apply to England and Ireland only. The first work of the select committee was to take the evidence of Sheriff Dove-Wilson of Aberdeen, a well-known authority on Scotch commercial law. He pointed out the particulars in which the bill, if applied to Scotland, would alter the law there. With three exceptions the points of difference were insignificant. The committee thereupon resolved to apply the bill to Scotland, and Sheriff Dove-Wilson undertook the drafting of the necessary amendments. Eventually the Scotch rules were in three cases preserved as to Scotland, while on other points the Scotch rule was either adopted for England, or the English rule applied to Scotland. A few amendments in the law were made when the committee was unanimous in their favour, but very wisely no amendments were pressed on which there was a difference of opinion. Sir Farrer Herschell reported the bill to the House, and it was read a third time and sent up to the Lords without alteration. In the House of Lords it was again referred to a select committee with Lord Bramwell for chairman. A few amendments were there inserted, mainly at Lord Bramwell's suggestion. These were agreed to by the Commons, and the bill passed without opposition. *[margin: Codification of law relating to bills.]*

"The Act has now been in operation for more than eight years, so that some estimate can be formed as to its results. Merchants and bankers say that it is a great convenience to them to have the whole of the general principles of the laws of bills, notes, and cheques contained in a single Act of 100 sections. As regards particular cases which arise, it is seldom necessary to go beyond the Act itself. It must also be an advantage to foreigners who have English bill transactions to have an authoritative statement of the English law on the subject in an accessible form. If I could do the work over again, I certainly could do it better and should profit by past experience. But as it is, the Act, as yet, has given rise to very little litigation."

In Canada, early in the Parliamentary Session of 1889, a bill to enact the English Bills of Exchange Act with the necessary modifications was introduced into the House of Commons by Sir John Thompson, the Minister of Justice, and considered to some extent in committee. Before its introduction the bill had been distributed throughout the Dominion among the banks, chambers of commerce and boards of trade, and to other persons who manifested interest in the subject. This distribution re- *[margin: Codification in Canada.]*

sulted in a number of suggestions being made, some of which were incorporated in the bill in committee. Subsequently, in view of the importance of the subject, and the desire of the House to have an opportunity to consider the bill more carefully, the bill was withdrawn, upon the understanding that it should be introduced again at the next session. In the interval it was again widely distributed, and copies were furnished to members of both Houses of Parliament.

On the 20th of January, 1890, the Minister of Justice reintroduced the bill. It was discussed in committee and some amendments were made both in the Commons and in the Senate. The bill received the royal assent on the 16th of May, 1890, and came into force on the 1st of September, 1890.

In the following chapters of this book attention will be drawn to the respects in which the English Act changed the existing law of England, and no good purpose would be served by ennumerating them here.

Differences between English and Canadian Act. In the course of its passage through Parliament, the Canadian bill underwent a number of changes, chiefly in the direction of sanctioning some usage or law already in force in some one or more of the provinces of Canada. In its ultimate form the Act presented the following chief points of difference from the English Act.

1. Whenever the last day of grace falls on a legal holiday or non-juridical day in the province where any such bill is payable, then the day next following, not being a legal holiday or non-juridical day in such province, shall be the last day of grace (sec. 42). For the English law, see notes to that section.

2. The legal holidays or non-juridical days in Canada are not in every case the days which are non-business days in England (notes to sec. 43). Some days are legal holidays in Quebec which are not holidays in the other provinces.

3. A sight draft in England is a demand bill and is not entitled to days of grace. In Canada a sight draft is a bill payable at a determinable future time and is entitled to days of grace (secs. 24 and 42).

4. The propriety of the practice of protesting inland bills upon dishonour is recognized by the Canadian Act (sec. 113). In Quebec protest of such bills is necessary to preserve the liability of drawer or endorsers (sec. 114).

5. The section of the English Act which protects a banker who, in good faith and in the ordinary course of business, pays a cheque upon a forged or unauthorized endorsement has not been re-enacted in Canada. See secs. 49 and 50, and notes.

Since 1882 only one amendment has been made to the Eng- Amend-
lish Act (see notes to sec. 175). The Canadian Act has been ments.
amended in various particulars. When the Canadian bill was altered by taking sight drafts out of the class of demand bills, the incidental effect of this change upon other parts of the Act was overlooked, and several of the subsequent amendments were intended merely to render the various parts of the Act consistent with each other.

The Canadian Act, as originally passed in 1890, also differed Rules of
from the English Act in omitting the important section 97, sub- common law
sec. 2, of the latter Act which provides that "the rules of the applicable.
common law, including the law merchant, save in so far as they are inconsistent with the express provisions of this Act, shall continue to apply to bills of exchange, promissory notes, and cheques."

In the following session, (1891), this omission was rectified by the addition of the provision contained in sec. 10 of the present Act.

The Act has had the effect of creating one uniform law re- Effect of
lating to bills, notes and cheques for all the provinces, except the Act.
that (1) it preserved the necessity of protesting inland bills in the Province of Quebec, (2) it left untouched the tariffs of fees for notarial services existing in the several provinces, and (3) it retained in the Province of Quebec certain holidays not observed in the other provinces. See, however, notes to sec. 10 of the Act, as to the extent to which reference must still be had to provincial law in transactions connected with bills, notes and cheques.

Inasmuch as recourse in unprovided cases must be had to the common law of England relating to bills, notes and cheques, and not to the provincial law on these subjects, there does not seem to be any practical advantage in discussing in detail the matters in respect of which the law of the different provinces may have differed from the law of England prior to the Act. In the English-speaking provinces the differences were few, and, excepting in so far as they have been incorporated into the Act, unimportant. The statutes which were repealed by the Act were not numerous and did not purport to deal comprehensively with the general subject of bills of exchange.

Quebec.

The only province in which any comprehensive enactment existed was Quebec. Articles 2279 to 2354 of the Civil Code of Lower Canada, 1866, related to the subject of bills, notes and cheques. Article 2340, which was also applicable to notes and cheques, provided that "in all matters relating to bills of exchange not provided for in this code recourse must be had to the laws of England in force on the thirtieth day of May, one thousand eight hundred and forty-nine." These articles were all repealed by the Bills of Exchange Act, 1890, "except in so far as such articles, or any of them, relate to evidence in regard to bills of exchange, cheques and promissory notes." The law in Quebec prior to the enactment of the Code of 1866 will be presently referred to.

Origin and history of bills of exchange.

The origin and history of bills of exchange and other negotiable instruments are traced by Cockburn, C.J., in his judgment in the case of Goodwin v. Robarts, 1875, L.R. 10 Ex. 347, in language which need not be quoted at length. The introduction and use of bills of exchange in England, as indeed everywhere else, seems to have been founded on the mere practice of merchants and gradually to have acquired the force of a custom. The old form of declaration of a bill used always to state that it was drawn "*secundum usum et consuetudinem mercatorum.*" The practice of making bills negotiable by endorsement was at first unknown, but from its obvious convenience it speedily came into general use, and, as part of the general custom of merchants, received the sanction of the courts. In the beginning the use of bills of exchange seems to have been confined to foreign bills between English and foreign merchants. It was afterwards extended to domestic bills between traders, and finally to bills of all persons, whether traders or not. In the time of Chief Justice Holt, a controversy arose between the courts and the merchants, as to whether the customary incidents of negotiability were to be recognized in the case of promissory notes. The dispute was settled by the stat. 3 & 4 Anne, c. 9, which vindicated the custom and confirmed the negotiability of notes.

Growth of the law merchant.

In Chapter II., *supra*, reference has been made to the growth of the law merchant and its incorporation into the common law. The results of this formation of the law by custom, as pointed out by Chalmers, are instructive:

"A reference to Marius' treatise on Bills of Exchange, written about 1670, or Beawes' Lex Mercatoria, written about 1720, will shew that the law, or perhaps rather the practice, as to bills of exchange, was even then pretty well defined. Comparing the usage of that time with the law as it now stands, it will be seen that it has been modified in some important respects. Comparing English law with French, it will be seen that, for the most part, where they differ, French law is in strict accordance with the rules laid down by Beawes. The fact is that when Beawes wrote, the law or practice of both nations on this subject was uniform. The French law, however, was embodied in a code by the "Ordonnance de 1673," which is amplified but substantially adopted by the Code de Commerce of 1818. Its development was thus arrested, and it remains in substance what it was 200 years ago. English law has been developed piecemeal by judi- English and cial decisions founded on custom. The result has been to work French law out a theory of bills widely different from the original. The of exchange English theory may be called the Banking or Currency theory, contrasted. as opposed to the French or Mercantile theory. A bill of exchange in its origin was an instrument by which a trade debt, due in one place, was transferred in another. It merely avoided the necessity of transmitting cash from place to place. This theory the French law steadily keeps in view. In England bills have developed into a perfectly flexible paper currency. In France a bill represents a trade transaction; in England it is merely an instrument of credit. English law gives full play to the system of accommodation paper; French law endeavours to stamp it out. A comparison of some of the main points of divergence between English and French law will shew how the two theories are worked out. In England it is no longer necessary to express on a bill that value has been given, for the law raises a presumption to that effect. In France the nature of the' value must be expressed, and a false statement of value avoids the bill in the hands of all parties with notice. In England a bill may now be drawn and payable in the same place (formerly it was otherwise, see the definition of bill in Comyns' Digest). In France the place where a bill is drawn must be so far distant from the place where it is payable, that there may be a possible rate of exchange between the two. A false statement of places, so as to evade this rule, avoids the bill in the hands of a holder with notice. As French lawyers put it, a bill of exchange neces-

English and
French law
of exchange
contrasted.

sarily presupposes a contract of exchange. In England, since 1765, a bill may be drawn payable to bearer, though formerly it was otherwise. In France it must be payable to order; if it were not so, it is clear that the rule acquiring the consideration to be expressed would be an absurdity. In England a bill originally payable to order becomes payable to bearer when endorsed in blank. In France an indorsement in blank merely operates as a procuration. An endorsement to operate as a negotiation must be an endorsement to order, and must state the consideration; in short, it must conform to the conditions of an original draft. In England, if a bill be refused acceptance, a right of action at once accrues to the holder. This is a logical consequence of the currency theory. In France no cause of action arises unless the bill is again dishonoured at maturity; the holder, in the meantime, is only entitled to demand security from the drawer and indorsers. In England a sharp distinction is drawn between current and overdue bills. In France no such distinction is drawn. In England no protest is required in the case of an inland bill, notice of dishonour alone being sufficient. In France every dishonoured bill must be protested. Grave doubts may exist as to whether the English or the French system is the soundest and most beneficial to the mercantile community, but this is a problem which it is beyond the province of a lawyer to attempt to solve.''

Sources of
law of ex-
change in
Quebec.

As noted in Chapter II., *supra*, p. 25, it is still a matter of controversy whether the celebrated ordinance of 1673 above mentioned, which codified the law relating to bills of exchange, was ever in force in what is now the province of Quebec. Whatever may be the correct view, the courts of Quebec were frequently uncertain and divided as to the sources of law to which they should have recourse. Their guide in some instances was the old French law, as it existed at the time of the Treaty of 1763, and as modified by competent authority in the province. Owing to the doubts which existed in regard to the ordinance of 1673, old text books had to be consulted to ascertain to what extent it had altered the law, and modern commentators consulted in so far as they were deemed to be the exponents of the old law.

In 1849 the legislature of the province of Canada passed the Statute 12 Vict., c. 22, which, although not expressly confined in its operation to Lower Canada, was afterwards held not to

apply to Upper Canada (Ridout v. Manning, 1850, 7 U.C.R. Sources of
35). This statute was the most comprehensive enactment relat-_{law of ex-} _{change in}
ing to bills and notes which was passed in any part of Canada _{Quebec.}
prior to the Civil Code. In effect it introduced into Lower Canada many of the rules of English law and some of the statutes of
Upper Canada, and provided that in all matters relating to bills
and notes, in regard to which no provision was made in the
Act, recourse should be had to the laws then in force in Lower
Canada, and, in cases not provided for by such laws, then to
the laws of England as at the time of the passing of the Act,
i.e., the 30th day of May, 1849.

The statute just mentioned did not remedy the uncertainty
of the law in Lower Canada, inasmuch as resort was to be had
to the laws of England only when the existing laws of Lower
Canada were silent. See the whole subject learnedly discussed
in Girouard's Essai sur les Lettres de change et les Billets prom-
issoires, Montreal, 1860.

The seventh report of the commissioners appointed to codify
the laws of Lower Canada in civil matters contains the following remarks in regard to bills, notes and cheques:—

"The works of Savary, a writer of great experience and
industry, are based chiefly upon the Ordinance of 1673, which,
according to the prevailing opinion, is not received as law with
us. The same observation is true of the *Traité du Change* of
Pothier, and thus the guidance of that admirable jurist, which
in almost all instances is so complete and unerring, cannot be
implicitly followed in this.

"Looking from these authors, to the usages among our merchants, and to the adjudged cases in the courts, more or less
sanctioned by special statutory provisions, it would seem that
our law in relation to bills of exchange has gradually been
formed, less from the ancient French law, which is its legitimate source, than from the commercial usages and jurisprudence of England, aided by the legislation and learning of
modern France. It can scarcely, however, for that reason, be
regarded as new law; for the observation of Heineccius, as cited
by Story, shews the breadth of the basis of all municipal laws
on the subject of bills of exchange. The laws of all nations on
this subject, he justly says, entirely agree in most things; there
are certain principles common to all nations which constitute
the proper foundations upon which the whole law of exchange

Sources of
law of ex-
change in
Quebec.

rests as a part of the municipal jurisprudence of each country. These principles, having their origin in the customs and practice of exchange, are considered so proper in themselves that all the just conclusions deducible from them are deemed of universal obligation.''

As already noted above, the Civil Code of 1866 resolved the doubts previously existing as to the law of Lower Canada by providing that in all cases not provided for by the code resort should be had to the laws of England as of the 30th of May, 1849.

CHAPTER XXXII.

THE BILLS OF EXCHANGE ACT: SHORT TITLE AND INTERPRETA-
TION.

THE REVISED STATUTES OF CANADA, 1906,

CHAPTER 119.

AN ACT RELATING TO BILLS OF EXCHANGE, CHEQUES AND
PROMISSORY NOTES.

SHORT TITLE.

1. This Act may be cited as the Bills of Exchange Act. 53 Short title.
V., c. 33, s. 1. Eng. s. 1.

The original of this Act was passed in 1890 (see last chapter)
by virtue of the exclusive jurisdiction conferred upon the Dominion Parliament by the 91st section of the British North America Act, 1867, to make laws with regard to Bills of Exchange
and Promissory Notes. Its short title was "The Bills of Exchange Act, 1890."

The Act of 1890 both in arrangement and wording, was a
copy of the English Bills of Exchange Act, 1882, except in a
few particulars. In the revision of the Dominion Statutes in
1906, however, many material alterations were made in the arrangement and constitution of the sections. Many of the sections of the new Act consist of sub-sections and parts of different sections of the old Act, and even more frequently sections
of the old Act have been divided into parts and sub-sections
and now appear in separate sections of the new Act.

At the end of each section of the Act, a note is made of the Correspond-
corresponding section or parts of sections of the English Act ing sections
of 1882. The number of the section of the English Act is pre- Act.
ceded by the abbreviation "Eng." in order to distinguish this
reference from the official reference at the end of each section

Sec. 1. to the Canadian Act of 1890 and amending Acts. It is in no case to be taken for granted that the corresponding English section is in exactly the same words as the Canadian Statute. Owing to the re-arrangement of sections effected by the revision of 1906, there is very often some verbal difference between the English and Canadian statutes. Whenever the difference is significant, a special note will be made of the fact.

The Act is a codifying Act, and the rule for its construction was stated by Lord Herschell in Bank of England v. Vagliano, [1891] A.C. at pp. 144-5, as follows:—

Rule of construction of code. "I think the proper course is in the first instance to examine the language of the statute and to ask what is its natural meaning, uninfluenced by any consideration derived from the previous state of the law, and not to start with inquiring how the law previously stood, and then, assuming that it was probably intended to leave it unaltered, to see if the words of the enactment will bear an interpretation in conformity with this view.

"If a statute, intended to embody in a code a particular branch of law, is to be treated in this fashion, it appears to me its utility will be almost entirely destroyed, and the very object with which it was enacted will be frustrated. The purpose of such a statute surely was that on any point specifically dealt with by it, the law should be ascertained by interpreting the language used instead of, as before, by roaming over a vast number of authorities in order to discover what the law was, extracting it by a minute, critical examination of the prior decisions, dependent upon a knowledge of the exact effect even of an obsolete proceeding such as a demurrer to evidence. I am of course far from asserting that resort may never be had to the previous state of the law for the purpose of aiding in the construction of the provisions of the code. If, for example, a provision be of doubtful import, such resort would be perfectly legitimate. Or, again, if in a code of the law of negotiable instruments words be found which have previously acquired a technical meaning or been used in a sense other than their ordinary one, in relation to such instruments, the same interpretation might well be put upon them in the code. I give these as examples merely; they, of course, do not exhaust the category. What, however, I am venturing to insist upon is, that the first step taken should be to interpret the language of the statute, and that an appeal to early decisions can only be justified on some special ground."

This rule of construction was approved by Lord Watson in Robinson v. C.P.R., [1892] A.C. at p. 487. See also Abbott v. Fraser, 1874, L.R. 6 P.C. at pp. 116-117, where the Judicial Committee says of the Civil Code of Lower Canada, "When this code contains rules on any given subject complete in themselves, they alone are binding, and cannot be controlled by the pre-existing laws on the subject, which can then be properly referred to only to elucidate, in cases of doubtful construction, the language of the code," and compare Bank of Toronto v. St. Lawrence, [1903] A.C. at p. 66, and Hinton v. Bank of Montreal, 1903, 9 B.C.R. 545, 548-550.

INTERPRETATION.

2. In this Act, unless the context otherwise requires,—

(a) 'acceptance' means an acceptance completed by delivery or notification;

(b) 'action' includes counter-claim and set off;

(c) 'bank' means an incorporated bank or savings bank carrying on business in Canada;

(d) 'bearer' means the person in possession of a bill or note which is payable to bearer;

(e) 'bill' means bill of exchange, and 'note' means promissory note;

(f) 'delivery' means transfer of possession, actual or constructive, from one person to another;

(g) 'holder' means the payee or endorsee of a bill or note who is in possession of it, or the bearer thereof;

(h) 'endorsement' means an endorsement completed by delivery;

(i) 'issue' means the first delivery of a bill or note, complete in form, to a person who takes it as a holder;

(j) 'value' means valuable consideration;

(k) 'defence' includes counter-claim;

(l) 'non-business days' means days directed by this Act to be observed as legal holidays or non-juridical days.

2. Any day other than as aforesaid is a business day. 53 V., c. 33, ss. 2 and 91. Eng. ss. 2 and 92.

Definitions.

'Acceptance.'

'Action.'

'Bank.'

'Bearer.'

'Bill,' 'note.'

'Delivery.'

'Holder.'

'Endorsement.'

'Issue.'

'Value.'

'Defence.'

'Non-business days.'

Business days.

An interpretation clause should be used for the purpose of interpreting words which are ambiguous or equivocal, and not so as to disturb the meaning of such as are plain (Reg. v. Pearce, 1880, 5 Q.B.D. 389). Such a clause is not intended to exclude the rule, alike of good sense and of grammar and law, that general words are to be restrained to the subject matter dealt with. (Chorlton v. Lings, 1868, L.R. 4 C.P. 387.)

The definitions in sec. 2 are verbal, that is, they define the sense in which the particular terms are used in the Act. The substantial or operative definitions are referred to below, and appear in their appropriate places in the Act.

(a) *Acceptance.*

As to the operative definition and requisites of an acceptance, see secs. 35 *et seq.*

As to delivery or notification to complete a contract on a bill, see secs. 39, 40 and 41. Delivery is defined by clause (f).

(b) *Action.*

The word "action" is used in secs. 11, 49, 58, 93, 157 and 183. By clause (k) defence includes counterclaim.

Set off is of a different nature from counter-claim. A set off consists of a defence to the original claim of the plaintiff. A counter-claim is an assertion of a separate and independent demand which does not answer or destroy the original claim of the plaintiff (Stoke v. Taylor, 1880, 5 Q.B.D. at p. 577). The right to set up a counter-claim was first given by the Judicature Acts. The right to rely on a set off has long existed. Set off corresponds approximately to compensation under the Civil Code, counterclaim is analogous to a cross-demand under the Quebec Code of Civil Procedure: Maclaren, p. 22.

(c) *Bank.*

Cf. the Bank Act, sec. 2(a).

The corresponding clause of the English Act is as follows:— "Banker" includes a body of persons, whether incorporated or not, who carry on the business of banking. Banking in Canada is carried on by the chartered banks, certain savings banks, and private bankers. A bank under the Act does not include a private banker: see notes to sec. 165. Savings banks are governed by R.S.C. cc. 30 and 32.

(d) Bearer.

As to when a bill or note is payable to bearer, see sec. 21. A bill payable to bearer is negotiated by delivery (sec. 60). The possessor of a bill or note payable to order is not technically the "bearer" of it, but "bearer" is included in "holder" as defined by clause (g).

(e) Bill and note.

The operative definitions of these words are contained in secs. 17 and 176. A cheque is defined by sec. 165.

(f) Delivery.

Delivery is necessary to make any contract on a bill complete and irrevocable (sec. 39). A person is said to have constructive possession of a thing when it is in the actual possession of his servant or agent on his behalf; therefore delivery may be effected without change of actual possession in three cases, namely: (1) A bill is held by C. on his own account; he subsequently holds it as agent for D: (2) A bill is held by C.'s agent, who subsequently attorns to D. and holds it as his agent: (3) A bill is held by D. as agent for C; he subsequently holds it on his own account. Chalmers, p. 4.

(g) Holder.

Holder as here defined includes classes of persons who are holders in different senses:—

(1) The lawful holder or holder in due course (sec. 56). In this sense holder includes a person to whom a bill is by its terms payable and whose title is good against all the world; and also a person to whom a bill is by its terms payable, and who, as against third parties, is entitled to enforce payment thereof, though, as between himself and his transferor, he is a mere agent or bailee with a defeasible title, e.g., an endorsee for collection.

(2) An unlawful holder, that is, a person to whom a bill is by its terms payable, whose possession is unlawful (e.g., the finder of a bill endorsed in blank), but who nevertheless can give a valid discharge to a person paying it in good faith, and also a good title to a person who takes it before maturity in good faith and for value (sec. 74). An unlawful holder must be dis-

tinguished from a mere wrongful possessor, *e.g.*, a person holding under a forged endorsement, or a person who has stolen a
bill payable to the order of another (sec. 49). A wrongful possessor has no title and gives none. Chalmers, p. 5.

Possession is an essential part of the definition. As to holder
for value, see sec. 54. Bearer is defined by clause (*d*).

(*h*) *Endorsement.*
As to delivery, see clause (*f*).
As to the other requisites of an endorsement to operate as
a negotiation, see secs. 62, *et seq.*

The word endorser primarily denotes the holder of a bill who
endorses it, but it is also used to denote any person who signs a
bill otherwise than as drawer or acceptor and thereby incurs
the liabilities of an endorser to a holder in due course (sec. 131).
A person who signs a bill although not the holder of it is called
under the foreign codes the giver of an "aval."

The term endorsee is used to denote not only the person to
whom a bill is specially endorsed, but also any person who makes
title through an endorsement, *e.g.*, the bearer of a bill endorsed
in blank. Chalmers, p. 6. Cf. also notes to clause (*g*) *supra*,
as to a holder for collection.

(*i*) *Issue.*
The term issue is used in secs. 28, 30 and 160. The "re-
issue" of a bill is provided for by sec. 73. As to a "complete"
bill; cf. secs. 31 and 56.

(*j*) *Value.*
The operative definition of valuable consideration is contained in sec. 53. See also secs. 54 to 58.

(*k*) *Defence.*
The word is used in secs 15 and 74. Cf. clause (*b*), *supra*.
There is no corresponding clause in the English Act.

(*l*) *Non-business days.*
Sec. 43 provides that in all matters relating to bills, certain
days and no others shall be observed as legal holidays or non-
juridical days.
See secs. 6, 42, and notes to sec. 43.

Person—written—writing.

The English Act also contains definitions of the words bankrupt, person, written and writing. By the Interpretation Act (R.S.C. c. 1, sec. 34), "person" includes any body corporate and politic, and the heirs, executors, administrators or other legal representatives of such person, according to the law of that part of Canada to which the context extends, and "writing," "written," or any term of like import, includes words printed, painted, engraved, lithographed or otherwise traced or copied.

As to "bankrupt" see notes to sec. 78.

CHAPTER XXXIII.

Bills of Exchange Act; General Provisions.

In the present statute, "Part I." includes secs. 3 to 16, under the heading "General," these being, for the most part, the sections which, in the Act of 1890, are contained in "Part V." entitled "Supplementary." The short title and the interpretation clauses (secs. 1 and 2) compose "Part I." in the Act of 1890. In both statutes the second, third and fourth "Parts" contain substantially the same provisions and are entitled respectively:

II. Bills of Exchange;

III. Cheques on a Bank;

IV. Promissory Notes.

PART I.

GENERAL.

Thing done in good faith. 3. A thing is deemed to be done in good faith, within the meaning of this Act, where it is in fact done honestly whether it is done negligently or not. 53 V.,.c. 33, s. 89. Eng. s. 90.

The expression "in good faith" is used in secs. 56, 139, 172 and 175.

This clause is obviously founded upon the distinction pointed out by Lord Blackburn, in Jones v. Gordon, 1877, 2 App. Cas. 616 at p. 629 (4 R.C. 415 at p. 427), between honest blundering or carelessness and a dishonest refraining from enquiry. (Tatam v. Haslar, 1889, 23 Q.B.D. at p. 348.)

Negligence and good faith. Negligence on the part of the holder of a bill is not of itself sufficient to deprive him of his remedies for procuring its payment. But negligence, when considered in connection with the surrounding circumstances, may be evidence of *mala fides*. Good faith or bad faith is a question of fact depending on the circumstances of the individual case. It is for the tribunal, whether judge or jury, that has to decide questions of fact, to determine

whether a particular holder took a bill in good faith or not. Sec. 3.
The tribunal must make use of its general knowledge of business and of the moving motives of mankind in order to appre-
ciate the evidence which is before it (In re Gomersall, 1875, 1
Ch. D. 137, 146, S.C. *sub nom.* Jones v. Gordon, *supra.* In
this case the whole subject of good faith is fully discussed.) See
also Chalmers, p. 276.

4. Where by this Act, any instrument or writing is required Signature.
to be signed by any person, it is not necessary that he should
sign it with his own hand, but it is sufficient if his signature
is written thereon by some other person by or under his authority. 53 V., c. 33, s. 90. Eng. s. 91.

Sec. 131 provides that no person is liable as drawer, endorser, or acceptor of a bill who has not signed it as such. Cf. secs.
17, 36, 62, 63, 132, 151 and 176.

A signature may be defined as the writing of a person's name What is
on a bill in order to authenticate and give effect to some con- sufficient
tract thereon. A pencil signature (Geary v. Physic, 1826, 5 B. signature.
& C. 234), and also a lithographed or stamped signature (Ex
parte Birmingham Bank, 1868, L.R. 3 Ch. at pp. 653-4) is
sufficient: see definition of "writing" in the Interpretation Act,
noted under sec. 2, *supra.* A signature made by another person
but attested by mark is sufficient. (George v. Surrey, 1830, M.
& M. 516). A note which runs "I, William Smith, promise to
pay, etc." is sufficiently signed. (Taylor v. Dobbins, 1719, 1
Stra. 399; cf. Ruff v. Webb, 1794, 1 Esp. 129.)

As to the signature of a corporation, see sec. 5 and notes.

As to the liability of an agent who signs without authority,
see notes to sec. 51.

If a person is induced by fraud to sign a bill under the belief
that he is signing a wholly different document and if in so signing he has acted without negligence, his signature is null and
void. Thus:—

D., an old man with enfeebled sight, is induced to sign his
name on the back of a bill by being told that it is a railway
guarantee which he had promised to sign. The bill is negotiated
to a holder in due course. D. is not liable as an endorser. (Foster

Sec. 4.   v. McKinnon, 1869, L.R. 4 C.P. 704; cf. Banque Jacques Cartier v. Lescard, 1886, 13 Q.L.R. 39; Banque Jacques Cartier v.
Lalonde, 1901, Q.R. 20 S.C. 43.)

By or under his authority.

Signature   Subject to the provisions of the Act, a forged or unauthor-
by agent.   ized signature is wholly inoperative, unless the party against
whom it is sought to retain or enforce payment is precluded
from setting up the forgery or want of authority (sec. 49). An
unauthorized signature may become binding by ratification (see
notes to sec. 49).

A signature by procuration operates as notice that the agent
has but a limited authority to sign, and the principal is bound
by such signatures only if the agent in so signing was acting
within the actual limits of his authority (sec. 51, and see cases
there cited).

A signature by an agent must be the principal's signature,
or the agent's signature for or on his behalf; if the agent merely
adds words to his own signature describing himself as agent, he
will be liable and not the principal: cf. sec. 52.

Where a bill is payable to order, the delivery of the bill by
the payee to another person with the intention of transferring
the property, does not itself constitute an authority to the latter
person to endorse the bill in the name of the former. (Harrop
v. Fisher, 1861, 4 R.C. 338, 30 L.J.C.P. 283, 10 C.B.N.S. 196.)
There is nothing in the Act explicitly to point out this rule, but
the rule is consistent with the general principle stated in sec.
4. By sec. 61 where the holder of a bill payable to his order
transfers it for value without endorsing it, the transferee acquires the right to have the endorsement of the transferor.

A general power to sign bills, notes, etc., and to superintend,
manage, and direct all the affairs of the principal, gives the
agent power to endorse notes (Auldjo v. McDougall, 1833, 3
O.S. 199), but a power of attorney to administer the affairs of
the principal does not authorize the endorsement of a note.
(Banque Molson v. Cooke, 1905, Q.R. 27 S.C. 130.)

Bill payable to C.'s order and endorsed in his name. It is
proved that C.'s wife had authority to endorse bills for him and
that in this case C.'s endorsement was written by his daughter
in the presence and by the direction of his wife. Held, sufficient. (Lord v. Hall, 1849, 8 C.B. 627; cf. Lindus v. Bradwell,
1848, 5 C.B. at p. 591.)

Bill addressed to B and accepted in his name. It is shewn
that C. who wrote the acceptance, is in the habit of accepting
bills in B.'s name, and that B. is aware of it and duly honours
such bills. This is evidence from which an authority to C. to
accept bills for B. may be implied. (Cf. Morris v. Bethell, 1869,
L.R. 5 C.P. at p. 51.)

It is shewn that C. has express authority to draw bills in A.'s
name. This of itself is not sufficient to shew that he has authority to endorse bills for A. (Cf. Prescott v. Flinn, 1832, 9 Bing.
at p. 22.)

An express authority to an agent to receive payment from
B., by drawing on him, does not authorize an agent to draw a
bill payable to his own order. (Hogarth v. Wherley, 1875, L.R.
10 C.P. 630.)

An authority to a partner in a non-trading firm to draw
cheques does not authorize drawing post-dated cheques, which
for most purposes are equivalent to bills payable after date.
(Forster v. Mackreth, 1867, L.R. 2 Ex. 163.)

5. In the case of a corporation, where, by this Act, any instrument or writing is required to be signed, it is sufficient if
the instrument or writing is duly sealed with the corporate seal;
but nothing in this section shall be construed as requiring the
bill or note of a corporation to be under seal. 53 V., c. 33, s.
90. Eng. s. 91.

The word "duly" in this section does not occur in the corresponding section of the English Act. It was inserted by the
Senate in amendment to the House of Commons bill.

By the law merchant an instrument under seal is not negotiable, but this section makes an exception in the case of bills
and notes sealed with the corporate seal of a company.

The section deals only with the form of signature. It does
not touch the question of capacity to contract; see secs. 47 and
48.

A corporation, otherwise competent to contract, could always be bound by a bill or note duly signed on its behalf. This
was one of the recognized exceptions to the rule that corporations
can contract only under seal. (Crouch v. Crédit Foncier, 1873,
L.R. 8 Q.B. at pp. 382, 383.)

In order to determine whether a company is liable on a bill, three questions must be asked:

(1) Has the company the requisite capacity to bind itself by a bill?

(2) Is the signature on the bill sufficient in form to bind the company?

(3) Was the signature placed there by a person who had authority to sign bills for the company? If, however, the person signing is acting within the apparent scope of his authority, it is immaterial that he exceeds or contravenes private instructions. (In re Land Credit Co., Ex parte Overend, 1869, L.R. 4 Ch. 460.)

Sec. 47 of the English Companies Act, 1862 (which is applicable to the bills or notes of all companies under the Companies Acts, 1862 to 1900, including limited banks under the Companies Act, 1879; Chalmers, p. 345) provides as follows: "A promissory note or bill of exchange shall be deemed to have been made, accepted, or indorsed on behalf of any company under this Act, if made, accepted, or indorsed in the name of the company by any person acting under the authority of the company, or if made, accepted, or indorsed by or on behalf or on account of the company, by any person acting under the authority of the company."

The section does not confer on all companies under the Companies Acts capacity to issue bills and notes. It merely prescribes the mode in which such companies as have the requisite capacity may exercise it. (Peruvian Railways Co. v. Thames, &c., Co., 1867, L.R. 2 Ch. 617.)

As to the liability of an agent who signs without authority, see notes to sec. 51.

The section expressly provides that nothing therein shall be construed as requiring the bill or note of a corporation to be under seal.

The Dominion Companies Act (R.S.C. c. 79, sec. 32) provides that every bill of exchange drawn, accepted or endorsed, and every promissory note and cheque made, drawn or endorsed on behalf of the company, by any agent, officer or servant of the company, in general accordance with his powers as such under the by-laws of the company, shall be binding upon the company, and that in no case shall it be necessary to have the seal of the company affixed to any such bill, note or cheque, or

to prove that the same was made, drawn, accepted or endorsed, Sec. 5.
as the case may be, in pursuance of any by-law or special note Liability of
or order. The same section also provides that no person so act- corporation
ing as such agent, officer or servant of the company shall be on a bill.
thereby subjected individually to any liability whatever to
any person. But by sec. 115 of the same Act every director,
manager or officer of the company, and every person on its behalf, who signs or authorizes to be signed on behalf of the company, any bill of exchange, promissory note, endorsement, cheque,
etc., wherein the name of the company, with the word "limited"
after it, is not mentioned in legible characters, as required by
sec. 33 of the Act, shall incur a penalty of two hundred dollars,
and shall also be personally liable to the holder of any such
bill, note, cheque, etc., for the amount thereof, unless the same
is duly paid by the company.

The provisions just recited apply to companies incorporated
under Part I. of the Act by letters patent and to companies incorporated under R.S.C., 1886, c. 119, or to which that Act applied before its repeal by 2 Edw. VII., c. 15, excepting loan
companies. Sec. 160 contains provisions similar to those of sec.
32 applicable to companies incorporated by special Acts of
Parliament. Similar provisions are also contained in several of
the provincial Companies Acts. In every case of a bill or note
signed by or on behalf of a company, it is necessary to consult
the statute which is applicable in the particular instance.

In the case of a bank, see secs. 73 and 74 of the Bank Act,
supra.

See also notes to sec. 35, as to acceptance by or on behalf
of a company.

6. Where, by this Act, the time limited for doing any act Computa-
or thing is less than three days, in reckoning time, non-business tion of time.
days are excluded. 53 V., c. 33, s. 91. Eng. s. 92.

Non-business days, as defined by sec. 2(*l*) are the days directed by the Act to be observed as legal holidays or non-juridical days. What days are to be so observed is defined by sec.
43.

This section will be applicable to sec 80 (acceptance), and When non-
sec. 94 (presentment to acceptor for honour). Cf. also secs. 97 business
and 103 (notice of dishonour). days ex-
cluded.

Sec. 6.

In the English Act a distinction is made between bank holidays and other non-business days; see notes in Chapter XXXVII., *infra.*

Crossing
dividend
warrants.

7. The provisions of this Act as to crossed cheques shall apply to a warrant for payment of dividend. 53 V., c. 33, s. 94. Eng. s. 95.

In Partridge v. Bank of England, 1846, 9 Q.B. 396, it appeared that the bank was in the habit of paying dividends to those entitled to them by warrants. It was pleaded and proved that by a usage of sixty years' standing of the bankers and merchants of London, these warrants, which are not made to bearer, were nevertheless negotiable so soon as the party to whom they were made payable had annexed to them the receipt which the bank required before payment would be made. The Court of Exchequer held that the custom relied on was "rather a *practice of trade* than a *custom* properly so called, and that such a practice could not alter the law according to which such an instrument conferred no right of action on an assignee." (Cf. Goodwin v. Robarts, 1875, L.R. 10 Ex. at p. 354.)

The provisions as to crossed cheques are contained in secs. 168 *et seq.*

The English Act (sec. 97) further provides that nothing in the Act shall affect the validity of any usage relating to dividend warrants, or the endorsement thereof. This provision, which is not in the Canadian Act, was probably intended to protect the usage of paying dividend warrants on the endorsement of one of several payees, but otherwise it seems to contemplate them as falling within the Act. Chalmers, p. 327.

The Bank
Act not
affected.

8. Nothing in this Act shall affect the provisions of the Bank Act. 53 V., c. 33, s. 95. Eng. s. 97.

See Bank Act especially secs. 61 to 75 in Chapter XIV. (The Issue and Circulation of Notes), *supra.*

The corresponding section of the English Act is differently worded, and applies to a number of statutes besides those directly relating to banks.

9. The Act of the Parliament of Great Britain passed in the fifteenth year of the reign of His late Majesty George III., intituled *An Act to restrain the negotiation of Promissory Notes and Inland Bills of Exchange under a limited sum within that part of Great Britain called England*, and the Act of the said Parliament passed in the seventeenth year of His said Majesty's reign, intituled *An Act for further restraining the negotiation of Promissory Notes and Inland Bills of Exchange under a limited sum within that part of Great Britain called England*, shall not extend to or be in force in any province of Canada, nor shall the said Acts make void any bills, notes, drafts or orders made or uttered therein. 53 V., c. 33, s. 95.

Sec. 9. Imperial Acts 15 Geo. III. c. 51 and 17 Geo. III. c. 30.

The Act of 1890 repealed certain Dominion and provincial statutes then in force, but contained no provision, other than this section, expressly affecting any Imperial Statute. The statutes mentioned in this section are no longer in force in England. Chalmers, p. 267, says: "A promissory note for less than £5 payable to bearer on demand is, it seems, void in England. The legislation on the subject is confused, but this seems to be the effect of it."

10. The rules of the common law of England, including the law merchant, save in so far as they are inconsistent with the express provisions of this Act, shall apply to bills of exchange, promissory notes and cheques. 54-55 V., c. 17, s. 8. Eng. s. 97.

Common law of England.

This section was added to the Act by the amending Act of 1891, which provided that the section should be taken and held to have applied to bills of exchange, promissory notes and cheques from the date when the original Act of 1890 came into force. The importance of the amendment in the unification of the law for the whole Dominion has been already pointed out in Chapter XXXI., *supra.* As to the meaning of the "law merchant," see Chapter II., *supra.*

Sec. 10 has been added to meet cases not exhaustively dealt with by other sections. (In re Gillespie, Ex parte Robarts, 1886, 18 Q.B.D. at p. 292; and see notes to sec. 134.)

Sec. 10.

Common
law how
determined.

The rules of the common law of England, save in so far as they are inconsistent with the provisions of the Act, must be applied, and, in order to determine what is the common law of England, resort must be had primarily to English decisions. Canadian cases decided prior to the passing of the Act are authority only in so far as they correctly declare the common law of England. This conclusion received some support from the judgment of the Privy Council in Macdonald v. Whitefield, 1883, 8 App. Cas. at p. 749, 4 R.C. at p. 545, where the somewhat similar provision of the Civil Code of Lower Canada (now repealed in this respect) was in question.

In that case, Lord Watson, delivering the judgment of the Judicial Committee, refers to the fact that the case of Ianson v. Paxton, 1873, 28 C.P. 439, decided by the Court of Error and Appeal in Upper Canada, and three other decisions of Canadian Courts, as well as a New York decision, were relied on by the respondent's counsel, as supporting the doctrine for which they were contending. Without entering into "a minute criticism of these cases," Lord Watson disposes of them in the following language: "If they are to be regarded as authorities to that effect, their Lordships cannot accept these cases as conclusive of the law of England, or as precedents which ought to govern the decision of this appeal. The Civil Code of Lower Canada (article 2340) enacts that in all matters relating to bills of exchange not provided for in the Code, recourse must be had to the laws of England in force on the 30th day of May, 1849," and seeing that the Code makes no provision regarding the question raised between the appellant and the respondent, that question must, in the opinion of their Lordships, be decided according to the law of England, as laid down by the Court of Common Pleas in Reynolds v. Wheeler, 10 C.B.N.S. 561; 30 L.J.C.P. 350.''

As to the general rule of construction of the provisions of the Act itself as a statute intended to embody in a code a particular branch of the law, see Chapter XXXII., *supra*, p. 342.

Any case decided before the Act in regard to a matter for which provision is made by the Act, is law only in so far as it can be shewn to be a correct and logical deduction from the general propositions of the Act. See Chapter XXXI., *supra*, p. 331.

Reference must still be had, however, in many instances, to provincial law in matters connected with bills of exchange, etc.

The Act governs the form, issue, negotiation and discharge of bills, the manner in which persons become liable, as parties thereto, etc., but neither the Act itself, nor the common law of England made applicable by sec. 10, regulates all matters of civil obligation resulting from the substance of the contracts entered into by parties to bills or determines all the consequences of such contracts. These, as a general rule, are governed by provincial law, and, where the places of drawing, accepting and payment are in different provinces, recourse must be had to the provisions of secs. 160 to 164, or to the general rules applicable to cases of conflict of laws, in order to determine what particular local law is applicable.

For instance, the Act declares what persons are liable as endorsers, but the appropriate provincial law decides whether an endorser, as being in the nature of a surety, is discharged by dealings between the creditor and the principal debtor. (Guy v. Paré, 1892, Q.R. 1 S.C. 443, a case decided under Article 2340 of the Civil Code, referred to above.)

Again, the Act and the common law declare whether a note in a particular form is a joint note or a joint and several note (Noble v. Forgrave, 1899, Q.R. 17 S.C. 234), but the provincial law regulates the consequences of joint or joint and several liability. Thus, where the common law rule as to joint contracts has been altered by provincial statute, the statute governs (Cook v. Dodds, 1903, 6 O.L.R. 608).

Likewise, the Act contains provisions as to the discharge of a bill by payment, or the avoiding of a bill by reason of fraud, duress, illegality of consideration, etc. What is payment, fraud, duress or illegality must be determined by provincial law. The Act provides only as to the extent to which fraud, etc., will affect parties other than the immediate parties to the frauds, etc.

The question of capacity is expressly referred by the Act to the general law governing capacity.

No less certainly questions of limitations or prescription, set-off or compensation, and evidence are to be governed by provincial law.

11. A protest of any bill or note within Canada, and any copy thereof as copied by the notary or justice of the peace, shall, in any action be *prima facie* evidence of presentation and dishonour, and also of service of notice of such presentation and dishonour as stated in such protest or copy. 53 V., c. 33, s. 93.

There is no corresponding section in the English Act.

Independently of this section it would be necessary to prove, by *viva voce* evidence in court, the facts of presentment of an inland bill or note, and of giving of notice of dishonour. (Codd v. Lewis, 1851, 8 U.C.R. 242.)

Protest as
evidence.

The *primâ facie* evidence afforded by the production of the protest or copy may be rebutted. But, inasmuch as by sec. 104, if a notice of dishonour is duly addressed and posted, the sender is deemed to have given due notice notwithstanding any miscarriage by the post office, it would seem that the mere denial of the receipt of the notice alleged to have been given by post is not a sufficient answer. (Cf. Merchants Bank v. Macdougall, 1879, 30 C.P. 236; Southam v. Ranton, 1883, 9 A.R. 530; but see Ontario Bank v. Burke, 1885, 10 P.R. 561.)

As to foreign protest, see next section.

Copy of protest, *prima facie* evidence.

12. If a bill or note, presented for acceptance, or payable out of Canada, is protested for non-acceptance or non-payment, a notarial copy of the protest and of the notice of dishonour, and a notarial certificate of the service of such notice, shall be received in all courts, as *prima facie* evidence of such protest, notice and service. 53 V., c. 33, s. 71.

This section was added by the Senate in amendment of the House of Commons bill, 1890. There is no corresponding section in the English Act.

Foreign
protest.

Prior to this Act it was held in Upper Canada that the production of a protest of a notary in a foreign country was no evidence of the facts therein stated (Griffin v. Judson, 1862, 12 C.P. 430; cf., however, Ross v. McKindsay, 1845, 1 U.C.R. 507). The giving of notice of dishonour is not usually part of a notary's duties, and the protest could be evidence only of the non-acceptance or non-payment. (Ewing v. Cameron, 1843, 6 O.S. 541.)

Under this section a notarial copy of the protest alone is not made *primâ facie* evidence of the giving of notice. A notarial copy of the notice and a notarial certificate of the service must be produced.

As to the protest of an inland bill, see sec. 11.

13. No clerk, teller or agent of any bank shall act as a notary in the protesting of any bill or note payable at the bank or at any of the branches of the bank in which he is employed. 53 V., c. 33, s. 61.

Officer of bank not to act as notary.

This section is a re-enactment of R.S.C. 1886, c. 123, sec. 11, and has been law in Ontario and Quebec since 1850. There is no corresponding section in the English Act.

Especially in view of sec. 11, which makes a protest *primâ facie* evidence of dishonour and notice, it is considered important that a bill or note should be protested by an independent person—not by a clerk, teller or agent of the bank whose interest it is to establish the facts of dishonour and notice.

14. Every bill or note the consideration of which consists, in whole or in part, of the purchase money of a patent right, or of a partial interest, limited geographically or otherwise, in a patent right, shall have written or printed prominently and legibly across the face thereof, before the same is issued, the words *Given for a patent right.*

Consideration, purchase money of patent.

2. Without such words thereon, such instrument and any renewal thereof shall be void, except in the hands of a holder in due course without notice of such consideration. 53 V., c. 33, s. 30.

Absence of necessary words.

Sub-sec. 2 was added to the Act by the Senate in amendment to the House of Commons bill in 1890. Sub-sec. 1 of this section, and also secs. 15 and 16 are a re-enactment of R.S.C. 1886, c. 123, secs. 12, 13 and 14. The original Act, passed in 1884, was entitled "An Act for the better prevention of fraud in connection with the sale of patent rights."

Sec. 14.

Bill void in hands of endorsee with notice.

Even under the Act as it stood before the enactment of sub-sec. 2, it was held that a note, the consideration of which consisted of the purchase money of a patent right, was void in the hands of an endorsee for value with notice of the consideration, by reason of the absence of the words "given for a patent right." (Johnson v. Martin, 1892, 19 A.R. 592, overruling Girvin v. Burke, 1890, 19 O.R. 204.)

A joint and several note made by two persons in partnership is invalid under this section, although one of the makers was already indebted to the payee on a personal account to more than the amount of the note, and the consideration for the note was the purchase of a patent right only as regards the other maker. C. & F. were partners in the manufacture of certain articles under a patent owned by F. F. assigned to C. a part interest in the patent in consideration of C.'s authorizing F. to sign the firm name to a note in favour of F.'s creditor. It was held that the note was void because it had not "given for a patent right" written or printed across its face. (Craig v. Benjamin, 1894, 24 S.C.R. 278.) "The endeavour in this case was to render legal by indirect means that which it was the aim and very object of the statute to prevent. The cases demonstrating the futility of such attempts are collected in Johnson v. Martin, 19 A.R. at pp. 595, 597." (Samuel v. Fairgrieve, 1893, 24 O.R. at p. 490.)

Without notice.

See notes to sec. 56, as to what constitutes notice of illegality.

Transferee to take with equities.

15. The endorsee or other transferee of any such instrument having the words aforesaid so printed or written thereon, shall take the same subject to any defence or set-off in respect of the whole or any part thereof which would have existed between the original parties. 53 V., c. 33, s. 30.

It is evident from these sections, that the object of this legislation is to protect persons who give bills or notes for patent rights, and to enable them to defend themselves against transferees to the same extent as they could against the original payee. In order to secure this object more effectually, the legislature by the next following section, makes it an indictable offence knowingly to issue, sell or transfer such notes, without having Sec. 15. the prescribed words written or printed thereon. (Johnson v. Martin, 1892, 19 A.R. at p. 600.)

By sec. 2, clause (*b*) set off is included in action, and by clause (*k*) defence includes counter-claim.

16. Every one who issues, sells or transfers, by endorsement Transferring or delivery, any such instrument not having the words *Given* defective *for a patent right* printed or written in manner aforesaid across the face thereof, knowing the consideration of such instrument to have consisted, in whole or in part, of the purchase money Indictable of a patent right, or of a partial interest, limited geographically offence. or otherwise, in a patent right, is guilty of an indictable offence and liable to imprisonment for any term not exceeding one Penalty. year, or to such fine, not exceeding two hundred dollars, as the court thinks fit. 53 V., c. 33, s. 30.

See notes to secs. 14 and 15.

CHAPTER XXXIV.

BILLS OF EXCHANGE: FORM OF BILL AND INTERPRETATION.

Part II. of the Act, entitled "Bills of Exchange," extends from sec. 17 to sec. 164. These sections are contained in Chapters XXXIV. to L. of this book. The subsequent "Parts" of the Act are:

III. Cheques on a Bank: secs. 165 to 175.

IV. Promissory Notes: secs. 176 to 187.

Cheques. By sec. 165, except as otherwise provided in Part III., the provisions of this Act applicable to a bill of exchange payable on demand apply to a cheque. Part III. contains special provisions with regard to a cheque which is not presented for payment within a reasonable time, and the termination of a bank's duty and authority to pay a cheque, and also with regard to crossed cheques.

Promissory notes. By sec. 186, subject to the provisions of Part IV. and except as provided by sec. 186, the provisions of the Act relating to bills of exchange apply, with the necessary modifications, to promissory notes. In the application of such provisions the maker of a note shall be deemed to correspond with the acceptor of a bill, and the first endorser of a note shall be deemed to correspond with the drawer of an accepted bill payable to drawer's order. The following provisions as to bills do not apply to notes, namely; those relating to (a) presentment for acceptance; (b) acceptance; (c) acceptance *supra* protest; (d) bills in a set.

PART II.

BILLS OF EXCHANGE.

Form of Bill and Interpretation.

Bill of exchange defined. 17. A bill of exchange is an unconditional order in writing, addressed by one person to another, signed by the person giving it, requiring the person to whom it is addressed to pay, on de-

mand or at a fixed or determinable future time, a sum certain Sec. 17.
in money to or the order of a specific person, or to bearer.

2. An instrument which does not comply with the requisites Non-compli-
aforesaid, or which orders any act to be done in addition to the ance with requisites.
payment of money, is not, except as hereinafter provided, a bill
of exchange.

3. An order to pay out of a particular fund is not uncondi- Unconditional within the meaning of this section: Provided that an tional order.
unqualified order to pay, coupled with,—

    (a) an indication of a particular fund out of which the
       drawee is to reimburse himself, or a particular account to
       be debited with the amount; or,

    (b) a statement of the transaction which gives rise to the
       bill;

is unconditional. 53 V., c. 33, s. 3. Eng. s. 3.

Bill of exchange.

A bill is sometimes called a draft and an accepted bill an
acceptance. The person who gives the order is called the drawer.
The person to whom it is addressed is called the drawee, and
if he signifies his assent to the order (sec. 35), he is then called
the acceptor. The person to whom the money is payable is called
the payee or bearer (sec. 2), as the case may be. If he transfers
the bill by indorsement (sec. 2) he is called the endorser (sec.
131); if by delivery only, he is called the transferor by delivery
(sec. 137). The holder is defined by sec. 2.

No special form of words is essential to the validity of a bill.
Thus an order, sufficient in other respects, running "Credit C.
or order in cash" instead of "Pay" is a valid bill (Ellison v.
Collingridge, 1850, 9 C.B. 570; Lovell v. Hill, 1838, 6 C. & P.
238).

A bill may be drawn in any language. (See, e.g., Re Marseilles Co., 1885, 30 Ch. D. 598.)

Where an instrument is so ambiguously worded that it is
doubtful whether it was intended for a bill or for a note, the
holder may treat it as either at his option. (Chalmers, p. 9;
Golding v. Waterhouse, 1876, 3 Pugs. (N.B.) 313.) See also
sec. 26, by which certain instruments may be treated either as
bills or notes at the holder's option.

Sec. 17.   *Unconditional.*

See sub-sec. 3.

As to an instrument payable on a contingency, see sec. 18.

Neither a bill nor a note may be drawn conditionally, but a bill may be accepted conditionally (sec. 38). The condition in an endorsement may be disregarded (sec. 66). As between the immediate parties, and as regards a remote party other than a holder in due course, the delivery of a bill may be shewn to have been conditional (sec. 40).

The following words written on an instrument do not make it conditional:

Uncondi-tional.   1. as per memorandum of agreement (Jury v. Barker, 1858, E.B. & E. 459) or as per advice. (Chalmers, p. 11.)

2. no time given to or security taken from or composition or arrangement entered into with either party hereto shall prejudice the rights of the holder to proceed against any other party. (Kirkwood v. Carroll [1903] 1 K.B. 531; overruling Kirkwood v. Smith, [1896] 1 Q.B. 582, and approving Yates v. Evans, 1892, 61 L.J.Q.B. 446.)

3. on policy No. 33,386. (Taylor v. Currie, 1871, 109, Mass. 36.)

4. which when paid is to be endorsed on the mortgage bearing even date with this note. (Chesney v. St. John, 1879, 4 A.R. 150.)

The following words written upon an instrument make it conditional:

Conditional.   1. cheque conditional. (Hately v. Elliott, 1905, 9 O.L.R. 185, 189.)

2. the title and right to the possession of the property for which this note is given shall remain in the vendors until this note is paid. Dominion Bank v. Wiggins, 1894, 21 A.R. 275).

3. provided the receipt form at foot hereof is duly signed, stamped and dated. (Bavins v. London & S.W. Bank, [1900] 1 Q.B. 270.)

4. it is agreed that this note is to be paid by a lawful mortgage. (Newhorn v. Lawrence, 1848, 5 U.C.R. 359; cf. Drury v. Macauley, 1846, 16 M. & W. 146.)

5. out of my salary during such time as I am indebted to the said A. for money or otherwise. Amount due him now is $292. (Angers v. Dillon, 1898, Q.R. 15 S.C. 435.)

Order.

A bill is an "order"; therefore it must in its terms be imperative and not precatory, but the insertion of mere terms of courtesy will not make it precatory (Chalmers, p. 11).

An instrument running "Mr. B. will much oblige Mr. A. by paying to the order of C., etc.," was held good as a bill. (Ruff v. Webb, 1794, 1 Esp. 129; cf. Reg. v. Tuke, 1858, 17 U.C.R. 296. The common form of a French bill runs "il vous plaira payer").

An instrument running "Please let bearer have £100 and you will much oblige me," was held not to be a bill. (Little v. Slackford, 1828, 1 M. & M. 171.)

A document running "we authorize you to pay" is not a bill. (Hamilton v. Spottiswoode, 1849, 4 Ex. 200.)

In writing.

See notes to sec. 2, *supra*, p. 347.

Addressed by one person to another.

An instrument not addressed to anyone is not a bill: see notes to sec. 20.

A warrant issued by a police committee to the city treasurer is not a bill, the drawer and drawee being really the same person. (Charlebois v. Montreal, 1898, Q.R. 15 S.C. 96); cf. sec. 26.

As to the meaning of "person," see notes to sec. 2, *supra*, p. 347.

Signed by the person giving it.

See sec. 4 and notes, as to the signature.

A bill may be accepted before it is signed (sec. 37), but until a bill is signed it is inchoate and of no effect. (Reg. v. Harper, 1881, 7 Q.B.D. 78; Reg. v. Bowerman, [1891] 1 Q.B. 112.)

See sec. 31 as to the effect of delivery of a simple signature on a blank paper.

The person to whom it is addressed.

The drawee must be named or otherwise indicated in a bill with reasonable certainty (sec. 20). A bill may be addressed to two or more drawees but not to two drawees in the alternative or to two or more drawees in succession (sec. 18).

On demand or at a fixed or determinable future time.

As to when a bill is payable on demand, see sec. 23.

As to when a bill is payable at a determinable future time, see sec. 24. A bill must not be expressed to be payable on a contingency (sec. 18).

A sum certain.

As to the meaning of a sum certain, see also sec. 28 (sum required to be paid with interest, by instalments, or according to an indicated or ascertainable rate of exchange).

The following are invalid as not being for a sum certain:

1. An order for "the amount of my account furnished" which the drawee wrote "correct for, say, $75" and signed his initials. (Kennedy v. Adams, 1874, 2 Pugs (N.B.) 162.)

2. An order to pay C. "£100 and all other sums which may be due to him." (Smith v. Nightingale, 1818, 2 Stark 375.)

3. An order to pay "the proceeds of a shipment of goods value £2,000 consigned by me to you." (Jones v. Simpson, 1823, 2 B. & C. 318.)

4. An order to pay "the balance due to me for building the Baptist College Chapel." (Crowfoot v. Gurney, 1832, 9 Bing. 372.)

5. A promise to pay "£100 and the demands of the Sick Club." (Bolton v. Dugdale, 1833, 4 B. & Ad. 619.)

6. A promise to pay "£100 and all fines according to rule." (Ayrey v. Fearnsides, 1838, 4 M. & W. 168.)

In money.

A bill must be payable in money, *i.e.*, legal tender.

The money may be foreign money. A note made in Canada payable at Chicago in "American currency" is good (Third National Bank v. Cosby, 1877, 41 U.C.R. 402, 43 U.C.R. 58; cf. St. Stephen Ry. Co. v. Black, 1870, 2 Han. (N.B.) 139). If a note is payable in the United States "in currency," currency means American currency. (Wallace v. Souther, 1888, 16 S.C.R. 717.)

A note payable in "legal tender money" (North-Western v. Jarvis, 1883, 2 Man. R. 53) or in "bankable currency" (Dunn v. Allen, 1884, 24 N.B.R. 1) is good.

The following are invalid bills or notes, namely orders or promises to pay a sum,

1. "in Canada bills" (Gray v. Worden, 1870, 29 U.C. R. 535), or in bonds or bank notes (Chalmers, p. 10).

2. "in cash or mortgage upon real estate," although the maker elects to pay in cash (Going v. Barwick, 1858, 16 U.C.R. 45), "half in cash and half in goods." (Gillin v. Cutler, 1857, 1 L.C.J. 277; Burnham v. Watts, 1844, 2 Kerr (N.B.) 377; Melville v. Bedell, 1832, Chipman (N.B.) 349; Turner v. Crane, 1833, *ibid.* 370.

3. a note running "I will pay A. $90 for B. or otherwise settle the sum of $90 for him on a note that he says he gave A. for $100. (Cochrane v. Caie, 1875, 3 Pugs. N.B.) 224.)

4. "in merchantable timber, etc. If not so paid within the time, then the same is to be paid in cash. (Boulton v. Jones, 1860, 19 U.C.R. 517.)

Specified person or bearer.

Where a bill is not payable to bearer, the payee must be named or otherwise indicated therein with reasonable certainty: see sec. 21 and notes. See also sec. 19.

As to bearer, see sec. 2(d) and sec. 21.

Except as hereinafter provided.

These words are not in the English Act. They were added to the Canadian bill of 1889 in committee in view of the provisions of sec. 28, sub-sec. 1, clause (d), but seem to be unnecessary for this purpose inasmuch as a sum payable as therein provided is still a "sum certain" within sec. 17.

The definition of a bill contemplates three parties to the instrument. Any two of them may, however, be the same person (secs. 19 and 26). The drawee or payee may be fictitious (secs. 21 and 26). Words may be added prohibiting transfer (sec. 21). No time for payment need be expressed (sec. 23). Blanks in material particulars may be filled up (sec. 31) including the date (sec. 31).

Particular fund.

An order to pay out of a particular fund is not a bill of exchange but may be an equitable assignment: see notes to sec. 127.

The following are not bills or notes, being orders or promises to pay out of a particular fund, namely orders or promises to pay money:

1. out of the money in your hands belonging to the company. (Jenney v. Herle, 1723, 2 Ld. Raym. 1361.)

2. out of the money due from A as soon as you receive it. (Dawkes v. Lord Deloraine, 1771, 3 Wils. 287; 2 W. Bl. 782.)

3. out of the money arising from my reversion when sold. (Carlos v. Fancourt, 1794, 5 T.R. 482; 4 R.C. 180.)

4. on the sale or produce when sold of the A. Hotel. (Hill v. Halford, 1801, 2 B. & P. 413.)

5. out of the moneys now due, or hereafter to become due, to me under the will of my late father, and before making any payment to me thereout. (Fisher v. Calvert, 1879, 27 W.R. 301.)

6. out of S.'s money. (Ockerman v. Blacklock, 1862, 12 C.P. 362.)

7. out of the first moneys received by you on my account. (Fullerton v. Chapman, 1871, 2 N.S.D. 470.)

8. and deduct the same from my share of the profits of the partnership. (Munger v. Shannon, 1874, 61 N.Y. 251, where the English and American cases are reviewed.)

9. out of certificate of money due me on 1st June for materials furnished to above church. (Bank of B.N.A. v. Gibson, 1892, 21 O.R. 613.)

The following are valid bills or notes, namely orders or promises to pay money,

1. as my quarterly half-pay due 1st February by advance. (Macleod v. Snee, 1728, 2 Stra. 762.)

2. being a portion of a value as under, deposited in security for the payment hereof. (Haussoulier v. Hartsinck, 1798, 7 T.R. 733.)

3. against cotton, per "Swallow." (Cf. Truman v. Clare, 1858, Johns. 769.)

4. on account of moneys advanced by me for the A company. (Griffin v. Weatherby, 1868, L.R. 3 Q.B. 753.)

5. against credit No. 20, and place it to account, as advised per A. & Co. (Cf. Banner v. Johnston, 1871, L.R. 5 H.L. 157.)

6. which you will please charge to my account, and credit according to a registered letter I have addressed to you. (Re Boyse, 1886, 33 Ch. D. 612.)

7. for flooring supplied to your buildings on D road, and Sec. 17
charge to my account. (Hall v. Prittie, 1890, 17 A.R. 306; see Particular
also notes to sec. 127.) Fund.

18. An instrument expressed to be payable on a contingency Instrument
is not a bill, and the happening of the event does not cure the payable on
defect. contingency.

2. A bill may be addressed to two or more drawees, whether Addressed to
they are partners or not; but an order addressed to two drawees drawees.
in the alternative, or to two or more drawees in succession, is
not a bill of exchange. 53 V., c. 33, ss. 6 and 11. Eng. ss. 6
and 11.

Payable on a contingency.

A bill may be payable on or at a fixed period after the occurrence of a specified event which is certain to happen, though
the time of happening is uncertain: see sec. 24 which prior to
1906 constituted one section with sub-sec. 1 of this section.

An instrument creating a liability to payment upon a contingency *e.g.*, one payable 90 days after sight, or when realized,
cannot be a negotiable bill or note. (Carlos v. Fancourt, 1794,
4 R.C. 180, 5 T.R. 482, 2 R.R. 647, affirmed on a writ of error
2 Str. 1217; Alexander v. Thomas, 1851, 16 Q.B. 333.)

The following are invalid bills or notes namely instruments
payable,

1. "three days after the sailing" of a vessel. (Dooley v.
Ryarson, 1873, 1 Q.L.R. 219, 28 R. J. R. Q. 243; cf. Palmer v.
Pratt, 1824, 2 Bing. 185; Duchaine v. Maguire, 1882, 8 Q.L.R.
295.)

2. at the sale, or delivery, of the timber marked "P.A." in
Quebec or elsewhere. (Russell v. Wells, 1848, 5 O. S. 725.)

3. on account of the plaintiff's claim in this suit. (Perth v.
McGregor, 1862, 21 U.C.R. 459.)

4. so long as the drawer shall be indebted to the payee. (Angers v. Dillon, 1899, Q.R. 15 S.C. 435.)

5. when I marry B. (Pearson v. Garret, 1689, 4 Mod. 242.)

6. when I am in good circumstances. (Ex parte Tootell,
1798, 4 Ves. 372.)

24—BANK ACT.

Sec. 18.

Payable on a contingency.

7. on completion of building now in course of erection. (Thomson v. Huggins, 1896, 23 A.R. 191; Garner v. Hayes, 1884, 10 A.R. 24.)

Two or more drawees.

Prior to 1906, sub-sec. 2 and sec. 20 formed one section.

The acceptance of some one or more of the drawees but not of all is a qualified acceptance (sec. 38.)

A bill may not be addressed to two drawees in succession, or in the alternative, but it may name a drawee in case of need (sec. 33). A bill may be made payable in the alternative (sec. 19).

The acceptors of a bill can be liable only jointly, whereas the makers of a note may be liable jointly or jointly and severally according to its tenor (sec. 179).

Payee, drawer or drawee.

19. A bill may be drawn payable to, or to the order of, the drawer; or it may be drawn payable to, or to the order of, the drawee.

Two or more payees.

2. A bill may be made payable to two or more payees jointly, or it may be made payable in the alternative to one of two, or one or some of several payees.

Holder of office payee.

3. A bill may be made payable to the holder of an office for the time being. 53 V., c. 33, ss. 5 and 7. Eng. ss. 5 and 7.

Payable to or to the order of.

Cf. secs. 21 and 22.

Prior to 1906, sub-sec. 1 and sec. 26 formed one section. The latter section provides for the case in which the drawer and drawee are the same person or where the drawee is a fictitious person or a person not having capacity to contract.

A bill may be drawn payable to the drawer's order. (Golding v. Waterhouse, 1876, 3 Pugs. (N.B.) 313; cf. Butler v. Crips, 1704, 1 Salk. 130). A bill payable to "——— order," which is endorsed by the drawer, is deemed to be payable to drawer's order. (Chamberlain v. Young, [1893] 2 Q.B. 206.)

A bill is sometimes drawn in the form "pay to your own order" when the drawee acts in two different capacities, *e.g.*, if he be in business on his own account, and also agent for some

other person interested in the bill (Chalmers, p. 17; see Holdsworth v. Hunter, 1830, 10 B. & C. 449). In such a case the instrument is not a bill which can be enforced until the drawee has
endorsed it away. (Cf. R. v. Bartlett, 1841, 2 M. & R. 362.)

The payee.

The provisions of the Act relating to a payee apply, with the necessary modifications, to an endorsee under a special endorsement (sec. 67.)

Payable to two or more payees, etc.

Prior to 1906, sub-secs. 2 and 3 of this section and sub-secs. 4 and 5 of sec. 21 formed one section.

The Act makes a material alteration in the law in allowing a bill to be made payable to persons in the alternative, unless there is apparent community of interest. Blanckenhagen v. Blundell, 1819, 2 B. & Ald. 417; cf. Holmes v. Jacques, 1866, L.R. 1 Q.B. 376, and Watson v. Evans, 1863, 32 L.J. Ex. 137; Chalmers, p. 21.)

An instrument payable to the "order of J.B.G. for W.M." is a note, and negotiable, but the endorser must see that the proceeds are applied for M. (Munro v. Cox, 1870, 30 U.C.R. 363.)

A note payable to A. "or to his wife and to no other person" is the same as if payable to A. alone. (Moodie v. Rowatt, 1856, 14 U.C.R. 273.)

A note in the alternative is payable to, and may be sued on by, either one of the payees. (Spaulding v. Evans, 1840, 2 McLean (Am.) 139.)

Payable to the holder of an office.

Prior to the Act a bill drawn payable to the "treasurer for the time being" of a society was void for uncertainty. (Cowie v. Sterling, 1856, 6 E. & B. 333; Yates v. Nash, 1860, 29 L.J. C.P. 306), but an instrument payable to A.B., treasurer of, etc., or to his successor in office, or order was held to be a note, the words "or to his successors in office" being void. (McGregor v. Daly, 1855, 5 C.P. 126; cf. Patton v. Melville, 1861, 21 U.C. R. 263, where the words following the payee's name were held to be descriptive only.)

20. The drawee must be named or otherwise indicated in a bill with reasonable certainty. 53 V., c. 33, s. 6.   Eng. s. 6.

As to a fictitious drawee, see sec. 26.

As to filling up blanks, see sec. 31.

The indication of the drawee seems indispensable to the rights, duties and obligations of all the parties, for the payee cannot otherwise know upon whom he is to call to accept and pay the bill; nor can any other person know whether it is addressed to him or not, and whether he would be justified in accepting and paying the bill on account of the drawer (Story, sec. 58).

An order not directed to any person is not a bill. (Forward v. Thompson, 1854, 12 U.C.R. 103; McPherson v. Johnston, 1894, 3 B.C.R. 465.)

B. writes an acceptance upon an instrument in the form of a bill, but addressed to no one. He is not liable as an acceptor (Peto v. Reynolds, 1854, 9 Ex. 410, 11 Ex. 418), but may be liable as the maker of a note. (Fielder v. Marshall, 1861, 30 L.J. C.P. 158.)

Instrument in the form of a bill payable to drawer's order, not containing the name of a drawee, but expressed to be payable "at No. 1 Union Street, London." B., who lives there, accepts it. He is liable as acceptor. (Gray v. Milner, 1819, 9 Taunt. 739.)

An instrument in the form of a bill containing, where the address to the drawee should be, the words "at Messrs. B. & Co. is a bill addressed to B. & Co. (Shuttleworth v. Stephens, 1808, 1 Camp. 407.)

21. When a bill contains words prohibiting transfer, or indicating an intention that it should not be transferable, it is valid as between the parties thereto, but it is not negotiable.

2. A negotiable bill may be payable either to order or to bearer.

3. A bill is payable to bearer which is expressed to be so payable, or on which the only or last endorsement is an endorsement in blank.

4. Where a bill is not payable to bearer, the payee must be Sec. 21.
named or otherwise indicated therein with reasonable certainty. Certainty of
payee.

5. Where the payee is a fictitious or non-existing person, the Fictitious
bill may be treated as payable to bearer. 53 V., c. 33, ss. 7 payee.
and 8. Eng. ss. 7 and 8.

Prior to 1906 the first three sub-sections of this section and
sec. 22 formed one section, and sub-secs. 4 and 5 formed one section with sec. 19.

Prohibiting transfer.

A bill expressed to be payable to a particular person is payable to order, if it does not contain words prohibiting transfer
or indicating an intention that it shall not be transferable (sec.
22). The acceptor of a bill payable to drawer or order, when
accepting it, strikes out to the words "or order" and writes over
his acceptance the words "in favour of drawer only." The
negotiability of the bill is not affected. (Decroix v. Meyer, 1890,
25 Q.B.D. 343, affirmed *sub nom.* Meyer v. Decroix, [1891] A.
C. 520, 4 R.C. 249.) A bill negotiable in its origin continues to
be negotiable until it has been (*a*) restrictively endorsed or (*b*)
discharged by payment or otherwise (sec. 69).

Where a cheque payable to C.'s order was crossed "account
of C., National Bank, Dublin," it was held that these words
did not prohibit further transfer, and that the bank, having
credited C. with the amount, could sue the drawer. (National
Bank v. Silke, [1891] 1 Q.B. 435.)

A person who puts his name on the back of a non-negotiable
note payable to another cannot be sued as endorser (West v.
Bown, 1847, 3 U.C.R. 290; a case of a note payable to a particular person, but not expressed to be payable to his order.
Such a note is now payable to order if it does not contain words
prohibiting transfer or indicating an intention that it shall not
be transferable (sec. 22). As to the other objection to the liability of the defendant in the case cited, namely, that when he
put his name on the back the note had not been endorsed by the
payee, see now notes to sec. 131.)

As to the assignment of a non-negotiable bill as a chose in
action, see notes at the beginning of Chapter XL., *infra*.

Payable either to order or bearer.

As to when a bill is payable to order, see sec. 22.

Where a bill is negotiable in its origin, it continues to be negotiable until it has been, (*a*) restrictively endorsed; or, (*b*) discharged by payment or otherwise (sec. 69.)

The only or last endorsement.

Sub-sec. 3 alters the law. It was intended to bring the law into accordance with the mercantile understanding by making a special endorsement control a previous endorsement in blank (Chalmers p. 25). Before the Act it was held that where a bill was endorsed in blank, its negotiability to bearer was not affected by a subsequent special endorsement (Walker v. Macdonald. 1848, 2 Ex. 527), though the special endorser was liable on his endorsement only to such parties as made title through it (Smith v. Clarke, 1794, Peake, 225), cf. Sovereign Bank v. Gordon, 1905, 9 O.L.R. at p. 150.

A blank endorsement may be converted by any holder of the bill into a special endorsement (sec. 67).

Payee must be named or otherwise indicated with reasonable certainty.

A bill may be made payable to the holder of an office for the time being (sec. 19).

Extrinsic evidence is admissible to identify the payee when misnamed, or when designated by description only, but not to explain away an uncertainty patent on the bill. (Soares v. Glyn, 1845, 8 Q.B. 24.)

Thus, an instrument payable "to the order of the Treasurer of Portugal" (Soares v. Glyn, *supra;* cf. Holmes v. Jaques, 1866, L.R. 1 Q.B. 376) or to the trustees of an insolvent firm, without naming them (Auldo v. McDougall, 1833, 3 O.S. 199) is sufficiently certain, and extrinsic evidence may be given to identify the payee or payees described.

Similarly if a bill is payable to John Souther & Son, evidence may be given that John Souther & Co. were intended to be named. (Wallace v. Souther, 1889, 16 S.C.R. 717; cf. Willis v. Barrett, 1816, 2 Stark, 29.)

But if a bill be drawn in the form "pay —— or order" evidence is not admissible to shew that C. was intended to be

the payee (R. v. Randall, 1811, R. & R. 195) and the bill cannot be recovered on by the person to whom it was given, either
as payee or bearer, unless he inserts his name in the blank.
(Mutual Safety v. Porter, 1851, 2 Allen (N.B.) 230.) The person in possession of a bill has *primâ facie* authority to fill up
the blank in any way he thinks fit (secs. 31 and 32).

A bill payable to "—— order" and endorsed by the drawer,
is payable to the drawer's order. (Chamberlain v. Young,
[1893] 2 Q.B. 206.)

If the payee is wrongly designated or his name is misspelt,
he may endorse the bill as therein described, adding his proper
signature (sec. 64).

Payee a fictitious or non-existing person.

For the sake of convenience of comparison a summary of the
facts of some of the leading cases precedes the discussion of sub-
sec. 5.

1. A bill purporting to be drawn by A. to the order of C.
& Co., and to be endorsed by them, is accepted by the drawee
payable at his bankers'. The bankers pay it at maturity. A.
is a correspondent of the acceptor's, who often draws bills in
favour of C. & Co. It turns out afterwards that the names and
signatures of the drawer and payees were forged by the acceptor's clerk, who obtained the money. Under these circumstances
C. & Co., are fictitious payees and the bankers can debit the
acceptor's account with the sum so paid (Bank of England v.
Vagliano, [1891] A.C. 107; discussed, 7 L.Q.R. 216, 10 L.Q.R.
40). As to the result if the bill had really been drawn in favour
of C. & Co., and their signature had been forged, see sec. 49.

2. A clerk, by false pretences, induces the plaintiff, his employer, to draw cheques in favour of B., a fictitious, non-existing
person. He then forges an endorsement in B.'s name, and negotiates the cheques to the defendant for value. The bankers pay
the defendant. The plaintiff cannot recover from the defendant
the money so paid. (Clutton v. Attenborough, [1897] A.C. 90;
cf. Vinden v. Hughes, [1905] 1 K.B. at p. 800.)

3. N. was the assistant superintendent of the plaintiff, a life
insurance company, and the local agent at one of its branches.
N. sent in a number of fictitious applications for insurance in
the names of existing persons. Subsequently he represented to
the company that the insured persons were dead and that the

Sec. 21.

Payee a fictitious or non-existing person.

claims were payable, and sent in to the head office claim papers with forged signatures. Thereupon the company sent to N. cheques made by the company in favour of the alleged claimants and payable at a branch of the defendant bank. N. forged the payees' names, and the cheques were presented to and paid by the bank in good faith (to whom or how did not appear) and the amounts charged to the company's account. Held, that under the circumstances the cheques must be regarded as payable to fictitious or non-existent persons, and therefore payable to bearer, and the bank was justified in paying and charging the company with the amounts. (London Life Ins. Co. v. Molsons Bank, 1904, 8 O.L.R. 238.)

4. The plaintiffs' confidential clerk made out a number of cheques to the order of various customers of the plaintiffs' for sums not actually owing to the respective customers at the time the cheques were signed, obtained the plaintiffs' signature thereto, misappropriated the cheques, forged the payees' endorsements and negotiated the cheques with the defendant, who gave full value for them in good faith and obtained payment of them from the plaintiffs' bankers. Held, that the payees were not "fictitious" persons, and the plaintiffs were entitled to judgment for the amounts of the cheques. (Vinden v. Hughes, [1905] 1 K.B. 795.)

5. W. by falsely representing to the plaintiff that he had agreed to purchase from K. certain shares then held by K. in a company, and that he had arranged to resell the shares at a profit, induced the plaintiff to agree to assist ·him in financing the transaction. For this purpose the plaintiff drew a cheque on the C. Bank payable to K. or order for the amount of the purchase-money, which cheque was delivered to W. in order that he might hand it to K. in payment for the shares. W. forged K.'s endorsement to the cheque and paid it into his own account with the defendant bank, who credited him with the amount, and collected the money from the C. Bank. W. had not agreed to buy any shares from K., and K. had at the time no shares in the company. Held, that the payee was not a "fictitious person" and that the defendant bank was liable to pay to the plaintiff the amount of the cheque as damages for conversion of the cheque. (Macbeth v. North and South Wales Bank, [1906] 2 K.B. 718.)

6. A bill purporting to be drawn by A. and endorsed in blank **Sec. 21.** by C, the payee, is accepted *supra* protest for the honour of the **Payee a** drawer. It turns out that A.'s signature was forged, and that **fictitious or** C. was a fictitious person. The acceptor for honour is estopped **non-existing** from setting up these facts if the bill is in the hands of a holder **person.** in due course. (Phillips v. im Thurn, 1865, 18 C.B.N.S. 694, L. R. 1 C.P. 463.)

7. By arrangement between the endorsee and acceptor a bill is drawn and endorsed in the name of a deceased person. The endorsee can recover from the acceptor. (Ashpitel v. Bryan, 1863, 33 L.J. Q.B. 328; cf. Vagliano v. Bank of England, 1889, 23 Q.B.D. at p. 260.)

Payee a fictitious or non-existing person.

Sub-sec. 5 was inserted in committee in place of a clause working out in detail the effect of the cases. The words "or non-existing" seem superfluous; but they were probably intended to cover the case given in Illustration 7 (see summary of the facts of the leading cases, *supra*). Chalmers, p. 22.

The acceptor of a bill by accepting it is precluded from denying to a holder in due course the existence of the drawer, the genuineness of his signature, and his capacity and authority to draw the bill, or the existence of the payee and his capacity to endorse (sec. 129). This was the law before the Act, the law in this respect being based on the principle of estoppel. The genuineness of the endorsement of the payee was, however, a matter as to which, except in one special instance, no estoppel prevailed. This exception was that a bill drawn to the order of a fictitious or non-existing payee might be treated as payable to bearer but the estoppel applied only against the parties who at the time they became liable on the bill were cognizant of the fictitious character or of the non-existence of the supposed payee. After the passing of the Act, the Court of Appeal in England, in its celebrated case of Vagliano v. Bank of England, held that the Act did not extend the exception, and that "fictitious" meant fictitious to the knowledge of the party sought to be charged upon a bill (23 Q.B.D. 243; see the judgment of Bowen, L.J., especially at pp. 257, *et seq.*, where the cases are reviewed). It was held, however, by the House of Lords (Bank of England v. Vagliano, [1891] A.C. 107) that such a qualification of the express words of the statute could not be properly implied from

Sec. 21.

Payee a fictitious or non-existing person.

the earlier cases. If the payee is fictitious or non-existing, the bill may, as regards all persons, be treated as payable to bearer. It was held further that the word "fictitious" is applicable not only to a creature of the imagination having no real existence, but also to a real person named as payee who has not, and never was intended by the drawer to have, any right upon or arising out of the bill. The section applies, although the bill (so called) is not in reality a bill, but is in fact a document in the form of a bill manufactured by a person who forges the signature of the named drawer, obtains by fraud the signature of the acceptor, forges the signature of the named payee, and presents the documents for payment, both the named drawer and the named payee being entirely ignorant of the circumstances (*ibid.*).

The Vagliano Case was applied by the Court of Appeal for Ontario in London Life v. Molsons Bank, 1904, 8 O.L.R. 238. In the London Life Case there was a real drawer. In the Vagliano Case the name of the pretended drawer was forged, but the acceptor was estopped from denying the genuineness of the drawer's signature. In neither case was there any genuine transaction on which the bills could be based. A real difference between the two cases is that in the London Life Case the drawer really intended its cheques to be paid to the named payees while in the Vagliano Case the drawer had no intention to pay any one, his name having been forged.

In Clutton v. Attenborough, [1897] A.C. 90 the drawers believed and intended the cheque to be payable to the order of a real person, but in fact there was no such person as the named payee, and it was held that the case came within the section, and the cheque might be treated as payable to bearer.

Both the Vagliano Case and Clutton v. Attenborough were distinguished in Vinden v. Hughes, [1905] 1 K.B. 795. In that case the drawers signed cheques at the instance of their clerk and cashier in favour of various customers to whom the drawers did not owe anything or did not owe an amount equal to that mentioned in the cheques payable to them respectively. The clerk forged the payees' endorsements, and negotiated the cheques to a holder for value in good faith who in turn obtained payment from the drawers' bankers. Warrington, J., who tried the case distinguished Clutton v. Attenborough because there the payee was a non-existing rather than a fictitious person. He

also distinguished the Vagliano Case because in that case there
was no drawer in fact and the use of a name as payee was a
mere fiction, whereas in the case before him the drawer intended
to issue the document and intended to issue it with the name of
the particular payee upon it, that payee being a real person.
Warrington, J., refers especially to the judgment of Lord Herschell, [1891] A.C. at p. 152, as summing up the meaning of
"fictitious" as applied to a real person, namely that the payee
is named "by way of pretence only, without the intention that
he shall be the person to receive payment."

Vinden v. Hughes was approved and followed in the case of
Macbeth v. North & South Wales Bank, [1906] 2 K.B. 718,
decided by Bray, J. At p. 725, he says:—

"The plaintiff was told that Kerr was an engineer formerly
living at Bootle, but then near Manchester. That was true. He
was told that Kerr had agreed to sell the 5,000 shares to White.
That was untrue, and he in fact held no shares. There had
been no such transaction, but the plaintiff believed the statements made to him, and made the cheque payable to Kerr in
order that he and no one else should get the money. Can Kerr,
under such circumstances, be said to be a fictitious payee? I
will first examine the authorities. In Vinden v. Hughes, [1905]
1 K.B. 795, the facts were, in my opinion, indistinguishable
from the present case. Vinden had a real person in his mind
when he drew the cheque, although in fact the payee was not
his creditor as he supposed, and had had no transaction with
him giving rise to such a debt. He had been deceived by his
clerk, but he intended the payee and no one else to receive the
money. Warrington, J., held that the payee was not fictitious.
He says (at p. 802) : "It was not a mere pretence at the time he
drew it. He had every reason to believe, and he did believe,
that the cheques were being drawn in the ordinary course of
business for the purpose of the money being paid to the persons
whose names appeared on the face of those cheques." That
seems to me to fit exactly the present case. . . . . . . Kerr
was a real person intended by the plaintiff, the drawer, as I
have found, to be the person who should receive payment. It
is a fallacy to say that Kerr was fictitious because he had no
shares and had never agreed to sell any to White. The plaintiff
believed he had, and intended him, and no one else, to receive
the money. It seems to me that when there is a real drawer who

Sec. 21.

Payee a
fictitious or
non-existing
person.

has designated an existing person as the payee and intended that that person should be the payee, it is impossible that that payee can be fictitious. I think that the word "fictitious" implies that the name has been inserted by the person who has put it in for some dishonest purpose, without any intention that the cheque should be paid to that person only, and therefore it is that such a drawer is not permitted to say what he did not intend, viz., that the cheque shall be paid to that person only, and the only way of effecting this is to say that it shall be payable to bearer. It matters not in my opinion how much the drawer of the cheque may have been deceived, if he honestly intends that the cheque shall be paid to the person designated by him. I think Warrington, J., has not in any way misread the judgments in Bank of England v. Vagliano. I think his decision and mine are really founded on the principles laid down in that case."

It is difficult to reconcile Vinden v. Hughes and Macbeth v. North & South Wales Bank with London Life v. Molsons Bank. If Warrington and Bray, JJ., have not "misread the judgments in Bank of England v. Vagliano," the last mentioned case decides that a named payee, being a real person intended by the drawer to be the payee, is not "fictitious or non-existing" within the section, notwithstanding that there is no real transaction between the drawer and the payee upon which the bill might be based and which would justify the payee in endorsing the bill. If, however, this proposition is applied to the facts in the London Life Case, one seems to be driven to a conclusion contrary to that at which the Court of Appeal for Ontario arrived. If the local insurance agent in that case had invented names instead of using the names of actual persons who lived in his district, cheques made out in favour of such invented names would have been payable to "non-existing" persons within the principle of Clutton v. Attenborough. The agent, for his own purposes and doubtless in order to lessen the risk of the company's discovering that the insurances had no real existence, used the names of real persons. Such persons were intended by the drawer to receive payment. "It matters not in my opinion," says Bray, J., *supra*, "how much the drawer of the cheque may have been deceived if he honestly intends that the cheque shall be paid to the person designated by him." According to Bray, J., the principle of the statutory provision is that the drawer, who for some dishonest purpose has inserted

the name of a fictitious or non-existing person, necessarily could
not have intended that the cheque should be payable to such
person only, and therefore he must be deemed to have made it
payable to bearer.

In the Australian case of City Bank v. Rowan, 1893, 14 N.S.
W.R. (Law) 127, the facts were very similar to those in Vinden v.
Hughes. It was falsely represented to the defendants that certain goods had been sold to them by James Shackell & Co. and
were ready to be delivered, and the defendants were induced to
become makers of a note in favour of the alleged vendors for
the purchase price of the goods. In fact the firm of James
Shackell & Co., had ceased to exist, although James Shackell a
former member of the firm resided in Melbourne, where the firm
formerly carried on business. The payees' name was forged and
the note negotiated to the plaintiff who took in good faith. It
would seem that the case might have been disposed of in the
plaintiff's favour on the ground that the note was payable to a
non-existing person. The court reached the same conclusion,
but based its decision upon the ground that the case fell ''precisely within the law laid down in Bank of England v. Vagliano,
which is to the effect that wherever the name inserted as that
of payee in a bill or note is inserted without any intention that
payment shall only be made in conformity therewith, the payee
becomes a fictitious person within the meaning of the Bills of
Exchange Act and that such bill or note may be treated by a
legal holder as payable to bearer.'' It is not easy to see the
application of this doctrine to the facts before the court as the
makers of the note did in fact intend that the named payees
should receive payment in conformity with the terms of the
note. The judgment then proceeds, as follows, laying down a
similar doctrine to that upon which the Court of Appeal relied
in the London Life Case: ''Here James Shackell & Co. the supposed payees, even if an existing firm, had no interest in the
note, no right to endorse it or be paid upon it, and as they had
not, then no person as payee had any such right. The payees
were accordingly fictitious persons, and the plaintiffs are therefore holders of this note as if it were payable to bearer, and may
as such holders sue the defendants as makers.''

When a bill is payable to the order of a fictitious person,
it is obvious that a genuine endorsement can never be obtained.
The Act makes such a bill payable to bearer. But inasmuch

Sec. 21.

Payee a
fictitious or
non-existing
person.

as a bill payable to one person, in the hands of another, is patently irregular, it is clear that the bill should be endorsed, and perhaps a *bonâ fide* holder would be justified in endorsing it in the payee's name. Though the bill may be payable to bearer, it is clear that a holder who is party or privy to any fraud acquires no title. What the Act has done is to declare that the mere fact that a bill is payable to a fictitious person shall not affect the rights of a person who has received or paid it in good faith. Chalmers, p. 23.

The signature of a fictitious person must be distinguished from (a) the forged signature of a real person, and (b) the signature of a real person using a fictitious name—for instance, John Smith may trade as "The Birmingham Hardware Company," and sign accordingly. (Chalmers, p. 24; see, too, Schultz v. Astley, 1836, 2 Bing, N.C. 544, where Thomas Wilson Richardson drew a bill as Thomas Wilson; see sec. 132.)

The estoppels which bind an acceptor as such have been referred to above; those which bind a drawer or endorser as such are defined by sec. 130. As to estoppel by negligence, see notes to sec. 49.

Where a bill is drawn payable to a deceased person in ignorance of his death, his personal representatives may enforce the bill. (Murray v. East India, 1821, 5 B. & Ald. 204.)

Bill payable
to order
when.

22. A bill is payable to order which is expressed to be so payable, or which is expressed to be payable to a particular person, and does not contain words prohibiting transfer or indicating an intention that it should not be transferable.

When payable to person or order.

2. Where a bill, either originally or by endorsement, is expressed to be payable to the order of a specified person, and not to him or his order, it is nevertheless payable to him or his order, at his option. 53 V., c. 33, s. 8. Eng. s. 8.

Prior to 1906, this section and the first three sub-sections of sec. 21 formed one section.

Sub-sec. 1 alters the law and adopts the Scotch rule. Before the Act it was held that a bill or note drawn payable to a particular person, without the addition of "or order" or other words authorizing transfer, was not negotiable, Plimley v. Westley, 1835, 2 Bing, N.C. at p. 251; Harvey v. Bank of Hamilton,

1888, 16 S.C.R. 714, S.C. Cas. 129; otherwise as to an endorsement, Edie v. East India Co., 1761, 2 Burr, 1216; cf. Goodwin v. Robarts, 1875, L.R. 10 Ex. at p. 357; see notes to sec. 67.)

If the acceptor of a bill payable to drawer or order, when accepting it, strikes out the words "or order," and writes over his acceptance the words "in favour of drawer only," the alteration is immaterial and the negotiability of the bill is not affected. (Decroix v. Meyer, [1891] A.C. 520, 4 R.C. 249.)

If a person writes across a bill that which unqualified would, in ordinary course, import a clean acceptance of a bill, and intends to qualify its operation, he must do so by plain and intelligible language, and make that qualification sufficiently part of the acceptance itself to be intelligible in the ordinary course of business. (Decroix v. Meyer, *supra*.)

Words qualifying negotiability must be unambiguous.

If a bill contains words prohibiting transfer or indicating an intention that it should not be transferable, it is valid as between the parties, but it is not negotiable (sec. 21).

Cf. secs. 68 and 69.

Sub-sec. 2 is declaratory (Smith v. McClure, 1804, 5 East, 476). It provides that a bill payable "to the order of C." is in legal effect the same as "to C. or order." C. can demand payment without giving an endorsement except by way of receipt. He need not endorse so as to make himself liable on the bill (cf. Carlon v. Kenealy, 1843, 12 M. & W. 139). Like any other person who receives money, he is bound to give a receipt (cf. Lockridge v. Lacey, 1870, 30 U.C.R. 494.)

Cf. notes to sec. 95 of the Bank Act, *supra*, p. 216 as to deposit receipts.

23. A bill is payable on demand,—

Payable on demand when.

(a) which is expressed to be payable on demand, or on presentation; or,

(b) in which no time for payment is expressed.

2. Where a bill is accepted or endorsed when it is overdue, it shall, as regards the acceptor who so accepts, or any endorser who so endorses it, be deemed a bill payable on demand. 53 V., c. 33, s. 10. Eng. s. 10.

Endorsed when overdue.

The corresponding section of the English Act has in sub-sec. 1, clause (a), the words "or at sight" after the words "on

Sec. 23.   demand.'' These words were in the Canadian bill as introduced
into the House of Commons in 1890, but were struck out in committee.

If a bill is not payable on demand, three days of grace are,
in every case, where the bill itself does not otherwise provide,
added to the time of payment (sec. 42). The effect of the Act
is that bills payable on presentation are demand drafts and are
not entitled to days of grace, but that sight drafts, in accordance with the custom prevailing in this country prior to the
Act, are entitled to days of grace. In England bills payable at
sight as well as those payable on presentation are demand drafts
and not entitled to days of grace.

The English Act in this respect reproduced the effect of the
statute, 34 & 35 Vict., c. 74. Prior to that statute it was doubtful whether or no days of grace attached to such bills. Chalmers, p. 30.

Clause (b) of sub-sec. 1 is declaratory. Before the Act a
bill payable generally was payable on demand. (Whitlock v.
Underwood, 1823, 2 B. & C. 157.)

When bill
overdue.
A bill payable on demand is deemed to be overdue for the
purposes of negotiation, when it appears on the face of it to
have been in circulation for an unreasonable length of time
(sec. 70). A demand bill must be presented for payment within
a reasonable time after its issue, in order to render the drawer
liable, and within a reasonable time after its endorsement, in
order to render the endorser liable (sec. 86). The provisions of
the Act applicable to a bill payable on demand apply to a cheque
except as otherwise provided in Part III. (sec. 165). As to
presentment for payment of a note payable on demand, see
secs. 180 & 181. As to presentment for acceptance, see sec. 75.

A bill payable otherwise than on demand is overdue after
the expiration of the last day of grace (cf. Leftley v. Mills,
1791, 4 T.R. 170). As to the negotiation of an overdue bill, see
sec. 70.

Acceptance
or endorse-
ment after
maturity.
A bill may be accepted when it is overdue (sec. 37).

Before the enactment of sub-sec. 2 the English law on the
subject dealt with was very obscure; but it had been held in the
United States that where a bill was endorsed after maturity,
the endorser was entitled to have it presented for payment, and
to receive notice of dishonour in the event of non-payment,
within a reasonable time. Otherwise, if an endorser took up a

dishonoured bill, and re-issued it on his original endorsement, Sig. 23. for his liability was then fixed. The present sub-section gives effect to the American rule. Chalmers, p. 31. The rule here before the Act was probably the same as it was in the United States. (Davis v. Dunn, 1850, 6 U.C.R. 327.)

24. A bill is payable at a determinable future time, within Determinable future time. the meaning of this Act, which is expressed to be payable,—

    (*a*) at sight or at a fixed period after date or sight; Sight.

    (*b*) on or at a fixed period after the occurrence of a specified Specified event. event which is certain to happen, though the time of happening is uncertain. 53 V., c. 33, s. 11; 54-55 V., c. 17, s. 1. Eng. s. 11.

The corresponding section of the English Act omits the words "at sight or" at the beginning of clause (*a*). These words were added to the Canadian Act by amendment in 1891.

When similar words were struck out of the section in the bill of 1890 which corresponds to the present sec. 23 (see notes to that section) the effect was to declare that a sight draft was not payable on demand. Hence the necessity to insert the words in sec. 24, so as to include sight drafts in the category of bills payable at a determinable future time.

Subject to the provisions of the Act, when a bill payable at sight or after sight is negotiated, the holder must either present it for acceptance or negotiate it within a reasonable time (sec. 77). Presentment of such a bill for acceptance is necessary in order to fix the maturity of the instrument (sec. 75).

As to the due date of bills payable as described in this section, see secs. 44, 45 and 46. See also sec. 150 (acceptance for honour).

When a bill is not payable on demand, it is duly presented for payment if presented on the day it falls due (sec. 86). Three days of grace, where the bill itself does not otherwise provide, are added to the time of payment as fixed by the bill, and the bill is due and payable on the last day of grace (sec. 42).

Event which is certain to ·happen.

An instrument payable on a contingency is not a bill and the happening of the event does not cure the defect (sec. 18).

25—BANK ACT.

Sec. 24.

Event which
is certain
to happen.

The following are valid, namely orders or promises to pay:—
1. ten days after the death of A. (Colehan v. Cooke, 1742,
Willes, 393, 399, 4 R.C. 184, 190.)

2. two months after H. M. Ship Swallow is paid off. (Colehan v. Cooke, *supra.*)

3. on the 1st of January, when A. comes of age. (Goss v.
Nelson, 1757, 1 Burr. 226.)

4. one year after notice. (Clayton v. Gosling, 1826, 5 B. &
C. 360.)

5. one year after my death. (Roffey v. Greenwell, 1839, 10
A. & E. 222.)

6. two months after demand in writing. (Price v. Taylor,
1860, 5 H. & N. 540, 29 L.J. Ex. 331.)

7. five years after the opening of the S. Railway. (Ex parte,
Gibson, 1869, L.R. 4 Ch. 662, *sed quære;* see *contra,* Blackman
v. Lehman, 1879, 35 Amer. R. 57.)

8. at a specified date, with a proviso that "if the defendant
should sooner dispose of or sell certain lands, etc., then the note
shall be payable on demand at said bank." (Elliott v. Beech.
1886, 3 Man. R. 213; cf. Massey v. Perrin, 1892, 8 Man. R. 457.)

9. seventeen months after date I promise to pay to A. or
order £50 without interest, or three years and five months after
date with two years' interest. (Hogg v. Marsh, 1849, 5 U.C.R.
319.)

Inland bill
defined.

25. An inland bill is a bill which is, or on the face of it purports to be,—

(*a*) both drawn and payable within Canada; or,

(*b*) drawn within Canada upon some person resident therein.

Other bills.

2. Any other bill is a foreign bill.

Presump-
tion.

3. Unless the contrary appears on the face of the bill, the
holder may treat it as an inland bill. 53 V., c. 33, s. 4. Eng.
s. 4.

A foreign bill if dishonoured must be duly protested (sec.
112) whereas, except in the Province of Quebec, it is not necessary to note or protest an inland bill (sec. 113), notice of dishonour alone being sufficient.

Where a foreign note is dishonoured, protest thereof is unnecessary, except for the preservation of the liabilities of endor-

sers (sec. 187). See sec. 177 as to when a note is a foreign or Sec. 25.
an inland note.

Inland or foreign bill.

Sub-sec. 2 is new. The result appears to be that though a
bill purports to be a foreign bill, the holder may nevertheless
shew that it is in fact an inland bill for the purpose of excusing
protest; while if it purports to be an inland bill though really
a foreign bill, he may treat it, at his option, as either. Chalmers,
p. 17.

"Unless the contrary appears on the face of the bill," *i.e.*,
unless something on the face of the bill indicates that it is a foreign bill, the holder may treat it as an inland bill, although it
does not purport to be (a) both drawn and payable within
Canada, or (b) drawn within Canada upon some person resident
therein.

As to place of payment for purposes of presentment, if no
place of payment is specified in the bill, see sec. 88. As to measure of damages when a bill is dishonoured abroad, see sec. 136.
As to conflict of laws, see secs. 160 *et seq.*

In order to determine whether a bill is inland or foreign,
Canada is treated as one country, but for the purposes of private international law or conflict of laws, the various provinces
are to be treated as separate countries, and the consequence of
the contracts entered into by the various parties to a bill may be
governed by provincial law. (See Chapter L., secs. 160, *et seq.*,
infra, and notes to sec. 10, *supra*.)

The following are inland bills:—

1. A bill is drawn in Toronto on a merchant in Montreal.
It is accepted payable in Montreal, but is endorsed in New York.
(Chalmers p. 16; cf. sec. 161 and Lebel v. Tucker, 1867, L.R.
3 Q.B. 77.)

2. A bill is drawn in Toronto on B. who resides in Montreal, B. accepts it payable in New York. (Chalmers, p. 16.)

3. A bill is drawn in Toronto upon a merchant in New York,
payable in Toronto, and is accepted. (Cf. Amner v. Clark,
1835, 2 C.M. & R. 468, and sec. 162; if the bill were not drawn
payable in Toronto, it would in its origin be a foreign bill, and
would, presumably, continue so, though subsequently accepted
payable in Toronto: Chalmers, p. 16.)

26. Where in a bill drawer and drawee are the same person, Bill or note.
or where the drawee is a fictitious person or a person not hav-

ing capacity to contract, the holder may treat the instrument, at his option, either as a bill of exchange or as a promissory note. 53 V., c. 33, s. 5. Eng. s. 5.

Cf. sec. 21 as to fictitious payee.

As to incapacity to contract, see sec. 47, which provides that capacity to incur liability as a party to a bill is co-extensive with capacity to contract.

Presentment for acceptance is excused where the drawee is a fictitious person or a person not having capacity to contract by bill (sec. 79). Presentment for payment is dispensed with where the drawee is a fictitious person (sec. 92).

Notice of dishonour is dispensed with as regards the drawer where (a) the drawer and drawee are the same person; (b) the drawee is a fictitious person or a person not having capacity to contract (sec. 107). Notice of dishonour is dispensed with as regards the endorser, where the drawee is a fictitious person or a person not having capacity to contract, and the endorser was aware of the fact at the time he endorsed the bill (sec. 108).

Bill or note. If both drawer and drawee are fictitious persons, the bill might perhaps be treated as a note made by the first endorser. (Chalmers, p. 18.)

A firm carries on business in London and Liverpool. The London house drew a bill on the Liverpool house. The holder may treat it as a note made by the London house payable in Liverpool; and if it be not paid, the omission to give notice of dishonour to the London house is immaterial. (Miller v. Thomson, 1841, 3 M. & G. 576; Willans v. Ayers, 1877, 3 App. Cas. 133.)

A. draws a bill on B. and negotiates it away; B. is a fictitious person. The holder may treat the bill as a note made by A. He need not prove presentment or give notice of dishonour. (Smith v. Bellamy, 1817, 2 Stark. 223.)

The directors of a joint stock company draw a bill in the name of the company, addressed "To the Cashier." The holder may treat it as a note by the company. (Allen v. Sea, 1850, 9 C.B. 574.)

A document in the form of a banker's draft drawn by a branch bank upon its head office cannot be treated by the bank as a bill of exchange, although a holder may sue the bank upon it and treat it as either a bill or a note. (London City, etc., Bank v. Gordon, [1903] A.C. at p. 250.)

Sec. 26.
Bill or note.

27. A bill is not invalid by reason only,— — Valid bill.

(a) that it is not dated; — Not dated.

(b) that it does not specify the value given, or that any value has been given therefor; — Statement of value.

(c) that it does not specify the place where it is drawn or the place where it is payable; — Statement of place.

(d) that it is antedated or postdated, or that it bears date on a Sunday or other non-juridical day. 53 V., c. 33, ss. 3 and 13. Eng. ss. 3 and 13. — Irregular date.

Prior to 1906, clauses (a), (b) and (c) were part of sec. 17, and clause (d) was part of sec. 29.

Although an undated bill may be valid, the issue of an undated bill is irregular and may be attended with some practical inconvenience.

As to inserting the date of issue or acceptance, see sec. 30; cf. sec. 31.

If a date is given, it is presumed to be the true date (sec. 29.)

Any alteration of the date is a material alteration (sec. 146). As to conflict of law, see secs. 160 and 164.

If the date is omitted, the bill is considered as dated on the day on which it was drawn (Giles v. Bourne, 1817, 6 M. & S. 73), and such date may be shewn by parol evidence. (Davis v. Jones, 1856, 17 C.B. 625.)

A note dated 7 Nov. 1905, payable "21st November next" is payable 21st November, 1906. (Drapeau v. Pominville, 1897, Q.R. 11 S.C. 326.)

Value.

The law raises a *primâ facie* presumption of consideration, and therefore it is not necessary to express on the face of the bill that value has been given (Hatch v. Trayes, 1840, 3 P. & D. 402, 11 A. & E. 702). The words "value received" in the case of an accepted bill payable to drawer's order, mean value received by the acceptor (Highmore v. Primrose, 1816, 5 M. &

S. 65), but in a bill payable to a third party, they mean *primâ facie* value received by the drawer. (Grant v. DaCosta, 1815, 3 M. & S. 352.)

Every party whose signature appears upon a bill is *primâ facie* deemed to have become a party thereto for value (sec. 58). But the value may be impeached; see notes to that section.

See also notes to secs. 40 and 41 for the rule as to the admissibility of oral evidence in regard to the contracts upon a bill.

Place.

A bill may state an alternative place of payment. (Beeching v. Gower, 1816, Holt, N.P.C. 313; cf. Pollard v. Herries, 1803, 3 B. & P. 335.)

A bill which is made payable elsewhere than at the residence or place of business of the drawee, is said to be "domiciled" where payable. (Chalmers, p. 15.)

As to presentment for payment of a bill in which no place of payment is specified, see sec. 88.

Under some of the foreign codes, it is necessary that a bill should be payable in a place different from that in which it was made. This rule prevailed under the old French law and, for a long time, in the Province of Quebec. Long ago, however, the merchants of Quebec had adopted the English custom, which was sanctioned by the Civil Code of 1866, "la remise de place en place" not being mentioned in that code as an essential of a bill of exchange. (Girouard, p. 16.)

A bank which discounts a bill or note payable at a place in Canada different from the place of discount may charge collection or agency fees as authorized by secs. 93 and 94 of the Bank Act.

An acceptance to pay at a particular specified place is not on that account conditional or qualified (sec. 38).

Any alteration of the place of payment, or the alteration of a bill by the addition of a place of payment without the acceptor's assent where the bill has been accepted generally, is a material alteration (sec. 146).

Ante-dating and post-dating.

For many purposes a post-dated cheque is equivalent to a bill payable after date (Forster v. Mackreth, 1867, 36 L.J. Ex. 94, L.R. 2 Ex. 163, 4 R.C. 210). For instance, if the cheque is

presented to the bank on or after the date, the bank paying it Sec. 27.
is entitled to charge the customer in the same way as any other Ante-dating
drawee of a bill payable on demand, and any other person tak- and post-
ing the cheque for value (within a reasonable time after the dating.
date) would doubtless be entitled to treat it as a bill of exchange
payable on demand. In any case, the person liable upon the
instrument would be bound to make his arrangements to meet
it as if it were a bill payable on demand on or after the day of
its date. (4 R.C. at p. 214.)

A bill bearing date the 1st May, is endorsed by the payee to
D. It appears that the payee died in the previous April. D.
may shew that the bill was post-dated, and he can then recover
on the bill. (Pasmore v. North, 1811, 13 East 517; Usher v.
Dauncey, 1814, 4 Camp. 97.)

A post-dated cheque given and received with the intention
that it should be held over and not presented for payment until
the day of its date, is a bill of exchange, and therefore, in the
absence of express authority, one partner of a firm of solicitors
cannot bind his co-partners by drawing a post-dated cheque in
the name of the firm. (Forster v. Mackreth, *supra*.)

The fact that a cheque is post-dated does not make it irregular within the meaning of sec. 56, so as to charge the holder with
equities of which he had no notice. (Hitchcock v. Edwards,
1889, 60 L.T.N.S. 636; Royal Bank v. Tottenham, [1894] 2 Q.
B. 715; Chalmers, p. 34; but see 4 R.C. 214, where the editor
says "it could hardly be maintained that a person taking a
cheque before the apparent date would not be put upon enquiry,
or would have a better title than the person from whom he received it.)

To ante-date a deed in order to defraud a third party is a
forgery. (Reg. v. Ritson, 1869, L.R. 1 C.C.R. 200. As to bills
which were ante-dated to defraud creditors, see Re Gomersall,
1875, 1 Ch. D. 137; Jones v. Gordon, 1877, 2 App. Cas. 625.)

Sunday or other non-juridical day.

The words "or other non-juridical day" are not in the English Act. They were added by the Senate. Their utility is not
obvious, as no days except Sundays are *dies nefasti* in Canada.

Legislation having for its object the compulsory observance
of Sunday, or the fixing of rules of conduct (with the usual
sanctions) to be followed on that day, is within the jurisdiction

of the Dominion Parliament (In re Legislation respecting Abstention from Labour on Sunday, 1905, 35 S.C.R. 581, 592, following Attorney-General for Ontario v. Hamilton Street Railway, [1903] A.C. 524). In the latter case the Judicial Committee held that the Ontario Act "to prevent the Profanation
of the Lord's Day" is *ultra vires* of the Ontario Legislature, as
being within the exclusive power given to Parliament to legislate with regard to criminal law.

It is possible that the decisions just referred to would not
affect a provincial Act declaring a contract made on Sunday to
be invalid.

R.S.C. c. 153, sec. 5, provides that it shall not be lawful for
any person on the Lord's Day, except as provided in the Act,
or in any provincial Act or law now or hereafter in force, to
sell or offer for sale or purchase any goods, chattels, or other
personal property, or any real estate, or to carry on or transact
any business of his ordinary calling, or in connection with such
calling, or for gain to do, or employ any other person to do, on
that day, any work, business, or labour. Sec. 16 of the same
Act provides that nothing in the Act shall be construed to repeal
or in any way affect any provisions of any Act or law relating
in any way to the observance of the Lord's Day in force in any
province of Canada when the Act comes into force.

So far as bills are concerned, sec. 27 declares that a bill is
not invalid by reason only that it bears date on a Sunday. The
Act does not say that a bill made on Sunday shall be valid.
Such a bill would seem to be affected with illegality, except as
against a holder in due course (sec. 58), if the consideration is
a contract forbidden by statute to be made on Sunday.

In Quebec, before the Act it was held that a note made or
dated on Sunday for a trade transaction closed the same day
was void between the immediate parties (Coté v. Lemieux, 1859,
9 L.C.R. 221; cf. Kearney v. Kerich, 1863, 7 L.C.J. 31, where
the plaintiff, apparently a holder in due course, was held entitled
to recover on a note made on Sunday. The decision was based
on the ground that the Quebec Statute merely imposed a penalty, but was silent as to the effect upon contracts. It was there
said "The court does not know of any law, either in Canada or
in England, which declares that a note made on a Sunday, is
a nullity or void."

Under the Ontario Lord's Day Act a note made on Sunday Sec. 27. in payment of goods sold on that day, is void, as between the Bill made or original parties, but not as against an endorsee for value and dated on without notice (Houliston v. Parsons, 1852, 9 U.C.R. 681; Crom- Sunday. bie v. Overholtzer, 1853, 11 U.C.R. 55). In the latter case it was said ''The statute makes void all contracts of sale made on a Sunday; but that affects merely the consideration. The plea relies on the bare fact that the transaction out of which this note arose was illegal as between the parties, without averring anything that might make such a defence available against this plaintiff, an innocent holder, for all that appears, for value.''

In Begbie v. Levi, 1830, 1 Cr. & J. 180, the court seemed to think that a bill issued on a Sunday would be void in the hands of a holder with notice, but they suggested qualifications. (Chalmers, p. 35.)

28. The sum payable by a bill is a sum certain within the Sum certain. meaning of this Act, although it is required to be paid,—

   (a) with interest;   Interest.

   (b) by stated instalments;   Instalments.

   (c) by stated instalments, with a provision that upon default Default.
      in payment of any instalment the whole shall become due;

   (d) according to an indicated rate of exchange or according Exchange.
      to a rate of exchange to be ascertained as directed by the
      bill.

2. Where the sum payable is expressed in words and also Figures and in figures, and there is a discrepancy between the two, the sum words. denoted by the words is the amount payable.

3. Where a bill is expressed to be payable with interest, un- With less the instrument otherwise provides, interest runs from the interest. date of the bill, and if the bill is undated, from the issue thereof. 53 V., c. 33, s. 9. Eng. s. 9.

A bill or a note must be for the payment of a ''sum certain'' (secs. 17 and 176). See notes to sec. 17.

An alteration of the sum payable is a material alteration (sec. 146).

Sec. 28. *With interest.*

A bill for £100 payable "with lawful interest" is valid. (Warrington v. Early, 1853, 2 E. & B. 763.)

The rate of interest in Canada, whenever any interest is payable by the agreement of parties or by law, and no rate is fixed by such agreement or by law, is five per centum per annum (R.S.C. c. 120, sec. 3). See also notes to secs. 91 and 92 of the Bank Act.

Where a bill is dishonoured, the measure of damages, which are deemed to be liquidated damages, include interest on the amount of the bill from the time of presentment for payment, if the bill is payable on demand, and from the maturity of the bill in any other case (sec. 134).

In case of conflict of laws, see notes to sec. 161, *infra.*

Interest from date or issue.

A bill does not bear interest until maturity, unless it is expressed to be payable with interest. Interest expressly made payable by a bill is part of the debt, and not merely damages for detaining the debt. (Crouse v. Park, 1847, 3 U.C.R. 458.)

As to date, see notes to sec. 27. Issue is defined by sec. 2.

By stated instalments.

A bill payable by two instalments due 1st January and 1st July is valid (Carlon v. Kenealy, 1843, 12 M. & W. 139; Gaskin v. Davis, 1860, 2 F. & F. 294), but a bill payable "by instalments," not specifying dates or amounts (Moffatt v. Edwards, 1841, Car. & M. 16), or "by ten equal instalments, payable, etc., all instalments to cease on the death of A." (Worley v. Harrison, 1835, 3 A. & E. 669) is invalid.

Days of grace must be added to the instalment due-dates (Oridge v. Sherborne, 1843, 11 M. & W. 374.)

A promise to pay $100 "to be paid in yearly proportions" is a note payable in two years, and parol evidence to shew that it was intended to give four years for payment is not admissible. (McQueen v. McQueen, 1852, 9 U.C.R. 536.)

An illustration of clause (c) is afforded by Carlon v. Kenealy, *supra.* In the absence of an acceleration clause, only the overdue instalment can be sued for. (Clearahue v. Morris, 1820, 2 Rev. de Leg. 30.)

Each instalment is to be treated as a separate bill for purposes of presentment and notice of dishonour.

Rate of exchange.

A bill payable "at exchange as per last endorsement" (Chalmers, p. 27), or "payable in Paris or London, at the choice of the holder, according to the course of exchange upon Paris (Pollard v. Herries, 1803, 3 B. & P. 335) is valid.

Where a bill drawn in a foreign country is made payable in Canada but not in the currency of Canada, the amount, in the absence of express stipulation, is to be calculated according to the rate of exchange for sight drafts at the place of payment on the day the bill is payable (sec. 163).

The general rule is that a sum payable in a currency other than that of the place of payment is to be calculated upon the value of such currency at the time of payment. (Cf. Hirschfield v. Smith, 1866, L.R. 1 C.P. 340, 353, and Chalmers, p. 28, disapproving of Da Costa v. Cole, 1688, Skinner, 272; cf. sec. 164.)

Prior to the Act it had been held in a number of cases in this country that a bill payable according to an indicated rate of exchange was invalid as not being for a sum certain.

Discrepancy between words and figures.

A bill is drawn "Pay to the order of C. two hundred pounds." In the margin is superscribed £250. This is a bill for £200 only and evidence to the contrary is inadmissible. Saunderson v. Piper, 1839, 5 Bing. N.C. 425, 2 R.C. 707, 712.)

A bill is drawn "Pay to the order of C. one hundred," with £100 in the margin. This is a bill for £100. (Rex. v. Elliott, 1777, 1 Leach, C.C. 175.)

A bill in the form "Pay to my order, twenty-five, ten shillings" is sufficient as a bill for £25 10s. (Phipps v. Tanner, 1833, 5 C. & P. 488.)

Parol evidence is inadmissible to explain a patent ambiguity (Saunderson v. Piper, *supra*). If the sum payable is omitted, evidence could not be given to shew the sum for which the bill was intended to be drawn, but the holder would have *primâ facie* authority to fill up the omission (sec. 31).

A bill in which the sum payable is expressed in figures only is valid, although there are grave practical objections to drawing a bill in that form.

B. signs as acceptor a bill with the amount left blank. In the
margin is £14 (in figures). This is fraudulently altered to £164
and the bill is filled up for one hundred and sixty-four pounds.
A holder in due course can recover £40 from B., the giving of
the acceptance in blank constituting authority to fill up the bill
for any amount the stamp will cover. (Garrard v. Lewis, 1882,
10 Q.B.D. 30: see secs. 31 and 32.)

29. Where a bill or an acceptance, or any endorsement on
a bill, is dated, the date shall, unless the contrary is proved, be
deemed to be the true date of the drawing, acceptance or endorsement, as the case may be. 53 V., c. 33, s. 13. Eng. s. 13.

This section is declaratory of the common law. (Roberts v.
Bethel, 1852, 12 C.B. at p. 778; Hays v. David, 1852, 3 L.C.R.
112, 115.)

The *primâ facie* presumption arising from the date may be
rebutted and the true date shewn, *e.g.*, for the purpose of oust-
ing the Statute of Limitations (Montague v. Perkins, 1853, 22
L.J.C.P. 187; cf. Inkiel v. Laforest, 1897, Q.R. 7 Q.B. 456.)

B. gives a blank acceptance in 1857. The drawer, by inad-
vertence, fills it up as a bill dated 1856. The holder can recover
from the acceptor. (Armfield v. Allport, 1857, 27 L.J. Ex. 42;
cf. Pasmore v. North, cited, *supra,* in the notes to sec. 27 (post-
dated bill.)

30. Where a bill expressed to be payable at a fixed period
after date is issued undated, or where the acceptance of a bill
payable at sight or at a fixed period after sight is undated, any
holder may insert therein the true date of issue or acceptance,
and the bill shall be payable accordingly: Provided that,—

(*a*) where the holder in good faith and by mistake inserts
a wrong date; and,

(*b*) in every other case where a wrong date is inserted;
if the bill subsequently comes into the hands of a holder in due
course the bill shall not be voided thereby, but shall operate
and be payable as if the date so inserted had been the true date.
53 V., c. 33, s. 12; 54-55 V., c. 17, s. 2. Eng. s. 12.

This section is supplementary to sec. 31.

The English Act omits the words "at sight or." These words were added to the Canadian Act in 1891; cf. notes to sec. 24. The section was added to the English bill in committee. Before its enactment the English law on the subject was very obscure. When a bill comes from a foreign country undated, the holder frequently cannot know the exact date intended. He knows when the mail left, but does not know on what previous day the bill was issued. The present section throws any possible inconvenience that may arise upon the negligent party who omitted to date the bill or acceptance. Chalmers, p. 33.

As to "issue" and "holder," see sec. 2. "Good faith" is defined by sec. 3, and "holder in due course" by sec. 56.

A bill is not invalid by reason only that it is not dated (sec. 27), but the omission, being a material one (cf. sec. 146). may be filled up by the person in possession of the bill (sec. 31).

31. Where a simple signature on a blank paper is delivered *Perfecting bill.* by the signer in order that it may be converted into a bill, it operates as a *prima facie* authority to fill it up as a complete bill for any amount, using the signature for that of the drawer or acceptor, or an endorser; and, in like manner, when a bill *Authority* is wanting in any material particular, the person in possession of it has a *prima facie* authority to fill up the omission in any way he thinks fit. 53 V., c. 33, s. 20. Eng. s. 20.

Prior to 1906 this section and sec. 32 constituted one section. The two sections must be read together, for the completed instrument cannot be enforced against any person who became a party to it prior to its completion, unless it was filled up within a reasonable time and strictly in accordance with the authority given or unless, after completion, it is negotiated to a holder in due course (sec. 32).

The English Act provides that where a simple signature on a blank *stamped* paper is delivered, etc., it operates as a *primâ facie* authority to fill it up as a complete bill for any amount *the stamp will cover*, etc.

Sec. 30 provides for the special case where a bill payable after date is issued undated or an acceptance payable at sight or after sight is undated.

Sec. 31.

Filling up
incomplete
bill.

Every contract on a bill, whether it is the drawer's, the acceptor's, or an endorser's, is incomplete and revocable, until delivery of the instrument in order to give effect thereto (sec. 39; cf. secs. 40 and 41).

Delivery means transfer of possession, actual or constructive, from one person to another (sec. 2).

The simple signature on a blank paper must be delivered by the signer in order that it may be converted into a bill, and a bill wanting in a material particular must be delivered within the meaning of the Act, before any authority is implied to complete the bill.

B. puts a blank acceptance in his desk. It is *stolen*, and then filled up as a bill. Even a holder in due course cannot recover from B., for the inchoate instrument was never delivered for the purpose of being converted into a bill. (Baxendale v. Bennett, 1878, 3 Q.B.D. 525.)

Likewise a note written over a signature given merely for the purpose of indicating the signer's address (Ford v. Auger, 1874, 18 L.C.J. 296), or for the purpose of a receipt (Banque Jacques Cartier v. Lescard, 1886, 13 Q.L.R. 39) cannot be recovered on: cf. notes to sec. 4.

The expression "*primâ facie* authority" in the section perhaps hardly expresses the extent of the power of the holder of a blank instrument. The power to complete the bill is not merely that of an agent, but arises from a contract that the person to whom the bill is given or anyone authorized by him should be at liberty to fill it up. (Notes to Baxendale v. Bennett, 4 R.C. at p. 645). The nature and effect of the contract made by a person who signs and delivers an instrument other than a bill or note is further considered in 5 R.C. 140, under the title "Blank" and in the ruling cases of Swan v. North British, 1863, 2 H. & C. 175 and Société Générale v. Walker, 1885, 11 App. Cas. 20.)

Where a note is signed and endorsed with a blank space for the rate of interest in an existing clause providing for interest any person in possession of the note has *primâ facie* authority to fill in any rate of interest, but if the note when signed and endorsed had no clause providing for interest, the addition of such a clause is an alteration not contemplated when the note was made and endorsed and avoids the note. (British Columbia

v. Ellis, 1897, 6 B.C.R. 82; cf. Burton v. Goffin, 1897, 5 B.C.R. Sec. 31.
454.)

Filling up

A bill is drawn payable to —— or order. Any holder for incomplete
value may write his own name in the blank and sue on the bill. bill.
(Crutchly v. Mann, 1814, 5 Taunt. 529; Mutual Safety v. Porter, 1851, 2 Allen (N.B.) 230; cf. Chamberlain v. Young, [1893]
2 Q.B. 206 where it was held that a bill made payable to "——
order," and issued by the drawer endorsed by him without filling up the blank, was perfect, "—— order" being construed
to mean "my order," *i.e.*, to the order of the drawer.)

32. In order that any such instrument when completed may When to be
be enforceable against any person who became a party thereto complete.
prior to its completion, it must be filled up within a reasonable
time, and strictly in accordance with the authority given: Provided that if any such instrument, after completion, is negotiated to a holder in due course, it shall be valid and effectual
for all purposes in his hands, and he may enforce it as if it had
been filled up within a reasonable time and strictly in accordance with the authority given.

2. Reasonable time within the meaning of this section is a Reasonable
question of fact. 53 V., c. 33, s. 20. Eng. s. 20. time.

This section is supplementary to sec. 31. "Such instrument"
in sec. 32 refers to an instrument which has been delivered in
an incomplete state, *i.e.*, a simple signature on a blank paper
delivered by the signer in order that it may be converted into
a bill, or a bill delivered as a bill but wanting in a material particular (sec. 31.)

Although a person who issues a bill leaving a blank in a
material part of it, is estopped, as between himself and a *bonâ
fide* holder for value to whom it has passed with the blank filled
up, from disputing the authority so to fill it up, there is no'
estoppel or presumption of authority in the case of a bill which
has not been issued—that is to say delivered with the intention
that it should operate as a bill—by the person charged upon it.
(Baxendale v. Bennett, 1878, 3 Q.B.D. 525, 4 R.C. 637.)

When com-

There seem to be cases which would arise fairly often in pleted in-
practice which would not be within the proviso, and where the strument
may be en-
forced.

Sec. 32.

When completed instrument may be enforced.

first part of the section would take effect. The proviso can never operate in favour of a person who knows the acceptance of the bill to have been in blank. So in all cases where the plaintiff has been allowed to recover on a bill in which he had inserted his own name as payee he would probably now have to shew that this was done within the authority given by the defendant. (Herdman v. Wheeler, [1902] 1 K.B. at p. 370, and cases cited.)

B. and A. sign as makers a joint and several note, with blanks for date and payee's name. B. signs on condition that the note shall be issued only if C. also will join as maker. C. refuses to join. A. who is in possession of the note, represents to plaintiff that he has authority to issue it. He fills in plaintiff's name as payee, and transfers the note to him for value. Plaintiff cannot recover from B. Awde v. Dixon, 1851, 6 Ex. 869; cf. Hogarth v. Latham, 1878, 3 Q.B.D. 643.)

If, however, the signature or incomplete instrument has been delivered within the meaning of sec. 31, and, after completion, is negotiated to a holder in due course, it is valid and effectual for all purposes in his hands although it had not been filled up within a reasonable time or in accordance with the authority given.

A "holder in due course" is a holder (sec. 2) who has taken a bill, complete and regular on the face of it, under the conditions mentioned in sec. 56. If the bill is not complete and regular on its face, the holder has notice of the imperfection and can be in no better position than the person who took the bill in blank (Hatch v. Searles, 1854, 2 Sm. & G. 147; France v. Clark, 1884, 26 Ch. D. 257, at p. 262.)

As to "reasonable time," cf. secs. 77, 86, 166, 181 and 182, where this expression is used.

"Negotiated" in the proviso to the section means transferred by one holder to another (cf. sec. 60). A delivery of a bill to a payee for value is the issue of the bill (cf. sec. 2) and not its negotiating. B., intending to borrow £15 from A., signs a blank stamped paper, and authorizes A. to fill it up as a note for £15 payable to A. A., instead of so doing, fills up the document as a note for £30 payable to C., and then hands it to C., who takes it in good faith and for value. Held, that, even if C. is a holder in due course (which is doubtful), the delivery of the note to him is not a negotiation of the instrument, and therefore he cannot recover, the note not having been filled up by A. in accordance with B.'s authority. (Herdman v. Wheeler, [1902] 1 K.B. 361.

"Completion" in the section refers to completing the form of the bill or supplying the wanting "material particular." It does not include delivery, as in secs. 39 and 178, where a bill or note is said to be inchoate and incomplete until delivery (*ibid.*, p. 371).

Sec. 32.
When completed instrument may be enforced.

Defendant signed, as maker, a printed form of promissory note, and handed it to A. by whom it was filled up for $55. The plaintiffs became endorsees for value without notice. Defendant held liable, though the note may have been fraudulently or improperly filled up or endorsed (McInnes v. Milton, 1870, 30 U. C.R. 489; cf. Garrard v. Lewis, 1882, 10 Q.B.D. 30, cited in notes to sec. 28.)

Where the payee of a note endorsed it in November for the accommodation of the maker, leaving the date and sum blank, and the blanks were filled up in February by the maker, the date inserted being a day in January, it was held that the endorsee could recover against the payee. (Sanford v. Ross, 1841, 6 O.S. 104.)

An endorser placed his name upon a note without maker's name or sum or payee's name, and the maker's name was afterwards signed by another person without authority, and the note negotiated. The endorsee must shew that he is a *bonâ fide* holder for value. (Harscombe v. Cotton, 1857, 15 U.C.R. 42; cf. Rossin v. McCarty, 1850, 7 U.C.R. 100.)

In 1840 B. gives a blank acceptance on a 5s. stamp to A. to accommodate him. In 1852 A. fills up the document as a bill for £200, and signs as drawer. He then negotiates it to a holder in due course. The holder can recover from the acceptor. (Montague v. Perkins, 1853, 22 L.J.C.P. 187.)

An instrument which is wanting in some one or more of the requisites of a complete bill is in effect a transferable authority to create a bill, and while incomplete is subject to the ordinary rules of law relating to authorities, *e.g.*, an authority coupled with an interest is not revoked by the death of donor or donee, while an authority not coupled with an interest is revoked by the donor's death. Chalmers, p. 53, citing the four following cases as illustrations:

Death of acceptor of incomplete bill.

1. B., who is indebted to C., gives him a blank acceptance for £100. C. dies. If C.'s administrator fills up the paper as a bill

Sec. 32.   payable to drawer's order, and inserts his own name as drawer, he can enforce payment thereof against the acceptor. (Scard v. Jackson, 1875, 34 L.T.N.S. 65.)

2. B., who is indebted to C., gives him a blank acceptance for £100, and then dies. C. may fill in his own name as drawer and payee after B.'s death, and recover the amount from B.'s estate. (Carter v. White, 1882, 20 Ch. D. 225, affirmed, 1883, 25 Ch. D. 666, C.A., where it was held that a surety for the acceptor, not party to the bill, was not discharged.)

3. B., having authority to do so, gives a blank acceptance for £100 in the name of the firm. It is filled up after B.'s death. The surviving partners are liable. (Usher v. Dauncey, 1814, 4 Camp. 97.)

4. B. gives C. a blank acceptance to accommodate him, and without receiving value. After B.'s death it is filled up and discounted with D., who sees it filled up. D. cannot recover the amount from B.'s estate. (Hatch v. Searles, 1854, 2 Sm. & G. 147, approved in France v. Clark, 1884, 26 Ch. D. at p. 262.)

Referee in   **33.** The drawer of a bill and any endorser may insert there-
case of need. in the name of a person, who shall be called the referee in case of need, to whom the holder may resort in case of need, that is to say, in case the bill is dishonoured by non-acceptance or non-payment.

Option.   2. It is in the option of the holder to resort to the referee in case of need or not, as he thinks fit. 53 V., c. 33, s. 15. Eng. s. 15.

In the province of Quebec presentment to the referee in case of need (besoin or recommandataire) was, prior to the Act, obligatory, as it is under some of the foreign codes.

In England the question was a doubtful one prior to the Act.

It may possibly be necessary in some cases to present to the case of need in Canada, in order to charge a foreign drawer or endorser in his own country, for a Canadian Statute is only binding in Canadian Courts. However in most countries the duties of the holder would be held to be regulated by the *lex loci solutionis*. Cf. Chalmers, p. 39.

The referee in case of need is sometimes called the drawee in case of need (cf. the French version, "tiré au besoin"), or simply the "case of need."

A bill must be protested or noted for protest before it can be ╎Sec. 33.
presented to the case of need (secs. 117 and 147, *et seq.*).

34. The drawer of a bill, and any endorser, may insert there-╎Stipulations.
in an express stipulation,—

    (*a*) negativing or limiting his own liability to the holder;   Limiting.

    (*b*) waiving, as regards himself, some or all of the holder's ╎Waiving
       duties. 53 V., c. 33, s. 16. Eng. s. 16.   ╎rights.

Negativing or limiting, etc.

An endorsement negativing or limiting the endorser's liability is sometimes called a qualified endorsement.

Such an endorsement must be distinguished from a conditional endorsement (sec. 66) or a restrictive endorsement (sec.
68).

The holder of a bill endorses it to D. thus: "Pay D. or order
without recourse to me," or "Pay D. sans recours" (Goupy v.
Harden, 1816, 7 Taunt. at p. 163), or Pay D. or order at his own
risk (Rice v. Stearns, 1807, 3 Mass. 224) or "Pay D. or order
without recourse, unless presented within 30 days" (Chalmers,
p. 40). The endorser thereby passes his interest to D., but negatives or limits his liability as an endorser. (Cf. Castrique v.
Buttigieg, 1855, 10 Moo. P.C. pp. 110-2, 117.

In order to escape personal liability the person signing must
do more than merely add words to his signature describing himself as an agent or as filling a representative character (sec.
52).

As to the ordinary liabilities of parties to a bill, see secs. 127,
et seq.

An acceptance may be qualified (sec. 38).

Waiving as regards himself, etc.

The drawer or any endorser may under clause (*b*) waive his
right to presentment, notice or dishonour, etc. Such an endorsement is sometimes spoken of as a facultative endorsement.

It does not affect the negotiation of the bill. C. adds the
words "notice of dishonour waived" to his endorsement. This
relieves any subsequent party from the necessity of giving notice
of dishonour to C. The addition of the words "protest waived"

"return without protest" "retour sans frais" or "retour sans protêt" would have the same effect. But it is doubtful whether any of these forms of endorsement could have the effect of dispensing with notice of dishonour to parties subsequent to C. The express authority of the section extends only to the waiver by a party "as regards himself" of some or all of the holder's duties.

CHAPTER XXXV.

The sections of this Act which relate to acceptance do not apply to promissory notes: see sec. 186.

Acceptance is defined by secs. 35 and 36.

It may be general or qualified (sec. 38).

The time of acceptance is provided for by sec. 37.

As to acceptance *supra* protest, see sec. 147, and as to acceptance of bills in a set, see secs. 158 and 159.

Acceptance and Interpretation.

35. The acceptance of a bill is the signification by the drawee of his assent to the order of the drawer. Acceptance defined.

2. Where in a bill the drawee is wrongly designated or his name is misspelt, he may accept the bill as therein described, adding, if he thinks fit, his proper signature, or he may accept by his proper signature. 53 V., c. 33, s. 17. Eng. s. 17. Drawee's name wrong.

Prior to 1906 this section and sec. 36 constituted one section.

Unless the context otherwise requires, "acceptance" means an acceptance completed by delivery or notification, (sec. 2), for until delivery or notification the contract of acceptance is incomplete and revocable (sec. 39). After the drawee has accepted a bill he is termed the "acceptor."

The liability of an acceptor is defined by secs. 128 and 129.

Acceptance must be by drawee.

There cannot be an acceptor of a bill other than the drawee or one who accepts as his agent (see notes to sec. 51) or for his honour (sec. 147, *et seq.*). Steele v. McKinley, 1880, 5 App. Cas. 754, at p. 782, 4 R.C. 218, at p. 235.

The same principle is not applicable to a note. Any number of persons may become bound as promisors along with the original maker (see *ibid.*).

In Steele v. McKinley, *supra*, W., addressed a bill to W. M. and T. M. The drawees accepted. Their father, J. M., then wrote his own signature across the back of the bill, and handed it to W. who remitted its amount, less discount, to the drawees. In an action by the representative of the drawer against the representative of J. M., it was held that what was done could not be effectual as a guarantee for want of a writing sufficient to satisfy the Statute of Frauds, or as an acceptance because the bill was not addressed to J. M.

It was urged that J. M.'s signature was operative as an endorsement to W., but the court held that W., being the drawer, was by virtue of that fact liable to an endorser, and could not at the same time be entitled to sue on the endorsement.

It is true that there may be an endorsement by a person who puts his name on the bill to facilitate its negotiation to a holder. Such an endorsement is known as the giving of an aval. But an aval for the honour of the acceptor is not effectual in English law. The endorsement by a stranger to a bill to one who is about to take it has the effect of making the endorser responsible to subsequent holders, but creates no obligation to those who were parties previously. See notes to sec. 131.

In Steele v. McKinley the liability of the defendant was discussed with reference to some Scotch authorities which seemed to indicate the contrary. The English authorities were already clear upon the point.

A bill is addressed to B. C. writes an acceptance upon it. C. is not liable as acceptor. (Davis v. Clarke, 1844, 6 Q.B. 16.)

A bill is addressed to B. B. accepts it. C. also writes an acceptance upon it. C. is not liable as acceptor (Jackson v. Hudson, 1810, 2 Camp. 447), but might be liable as endorser.

A bill is addressed to the "Directors of the B. Co., Ltd." The acceptance is signed by two directors and the manager. The manager is not liable as acceptor. (Bult v. Morrell, 1840, 12 A. & E. 745.)

A bill is addressed to William B. His wife accepts it, signing the acceptance "Mary B." If he authorizes her so to accept, or afterwards promises to pay the bill, he is liable as acceptor. (Lindus v. Bradwell, 1849, 5 C.B. 583, on the ground that the drawee may accept in any name he chooses to adopt, and that in this case William B., chose to adopt *pro hac vice* the name of his wife to accept in: Chalmers, p. 43.)

Firm and partners.

When a bill is addressed to two or more persons, whether partners or not, any one of them may accept so as to bind himself (Owen v. Von Uster, 1850, 10 C.B. 318). If all do not accept, the acceptance is a qualified acceptance (sec. 38).

The signature of the name of a firm is equivalent to the signature by the person so signing of the names of all persons liable as partners in that firm (sec. 132). If a bill is addressed to B. & Co., and D., a partner in the firm, accepts it in his own name, he is liable as acceptor (Owen v. Von Uster, *supra*), but the firm is not liable. (Mason v. Ramsay, 1808, 1 Camp. 384, to the contrary, is not good law since the Act requiring the acceptance to be signed by the drawee: Chalmers, p. 44, see sec. 36.)

A bill is addressed to B. & Co. B., a partner in the firm, accepts it in the firm name, adding also his own name. This is the acceptance of the firm, and not of B. personally. (Re Barnard, Edwards v. Barnard, 1886, 32 Ch. D. 447.)

A bill is addressed to D., who is a partner in the firm of B. & Co. D., accepts in the firm name. He is liable personally as acceptor. (Nicholls v. Diamond, 1853, 9 Ex. 154.)

A firm of "Cormack Bros," dissolved partnership, and Carter, an agent, was appointed to wind it up. M. Cormack had been a partner in the firm. Carter accepted, for his own purposes, a bill drawn on Cormack Bros., signing the acceptance "M. Cormack and R. Carter." M. Cormack is not liable on this acceptance. (Odell v. Cormack, 1887, 19 Q.B.D. 223.)

Incorporated company.

The acceptance of a company is sufficiently signed if it is duly sealed with the corporate seal (sec. 5). A company may however be bound by an acceptance duly signed on its behalf by an agent: see notes to sec. 5.

A bill is addressed to the B. Co., Ltd. Two of the directors accept it, signing thus: "J. S. and H. T., directors of the B. Co., Ltd." This is an acceptance by the company. (Okell v. Charles, 1876, 34 L.T.N.S. 822.)

A bill is addressed to the S. S. P. Co., the proper name of the company being the S. S. P. Co., *Limited*. It is accepted by "J. M., secretary to the company." This is not the acceptance of the company. (Penrose v. Martyr, 1858, E.B. & E. 499;

Sec. 35.
Acceptance
by a
company.

Atkins v. Wardle, 1889, 58 L.J.Q.B. 377; Brown v. Howland, 1885, 9 O.R. 48, affirmed, 15 A.R. 750.)

If a bill is addressed to an officer of a company either by name or by the title of his office, the company cannot be liable as acceptor because it is not the drawee; the officer will be liable personally if he accepts either as officer of the company or "for the company," but not if he accepts in the company's name, per himself. (Madden v. Cox, 1880, 5 A.R. 473, where the previous cases in Upper Canada are discussed.)

Drawee wrongly designated or his name misspelt.

There is no provision in the English Act corresponding to sub-sec. 2. Sec. 64 contains a similar provision in regard to the payee or endorsee of a bill payable to order, except that the words "if he thinks fit" are omitted.

A bill is addressed to D. & Co. The proper style of the firm is C. D. & Co., and the bill is accepted in that name. This is a valid acceptance. (Lloyd v. Ashby, 1831, 2 B. & Ad. 23.)

A bill is addressed to M. & McQ., for goods supplied M. McQ. & Co. Acceptance in the name of M. McQ. & Co. Held not a valid acceptance. (Quebec Bank v. Miller, 1885, 3 Man. R. 17; under the Act the acceptance would be valid.)

Acceptance.

36. An acceptance is invalid unless it complies with the following conditions, namely:—

On the bill.

(a) It must be written on the bill and be signed by the drawee;

For money.

(b) It must not express that the drawee will perform his promise by any other means than the payment of money.

Mere
signature.

2. The mere signature of the drawee written on the bill without additional words is a sufficient acceptance. 53 V., c. 33, s. 17. Eng. s. 17.

Cf. notes to sec. 35.

At common law not only might an acceptance be by a separate letter, but it might be oral. The requirement that the acceptance be in writing on the bill itself and signed, was introduced into the law of England bv the Mercantile Amendment Act of 1856. In Hindhaugh v. Blakey, 1878, 3 C.P.D. 136, it was

held that the signature of the acceptor without words of accep- Sec. 36.
tance did not satisfy the statute. This decision was a surprise Requisites
to the mercantile community. An Act of 1878 provided that of accept-
the signature of the drawee without additional words should be ance.
sufficient, the Act being "equivalent to a declaration that the
case of Hindhaugh v. Blakey was wrongly decided." (Steele
v. McKinley, 1880, 5 App. Cas. at p. 782, 4 R.C. at p. 235.)
The effect of these enactments is reproduced by the Bills of
Exchange Act.

As to the signature see sec. 4; as to what the word "written"
includes, see note, *supra*, p. 347.

An acceptance written on the back of a bill is (probably)
sufficient. (Young v. Glover, 1857, 3 Jur. N.S. 637; Chalmers,
p. 44.)

A bill is left with B. for acceptance. He does not accept it
but retains it for a long time and ultimately destroys it. B. is
not liable as acceptor. The holder's remedy is by action for the
conversion of the bill. (Jeune v. Ward, 1818, 1 B. & Ald. 653,
at p. 660.)

An acceptance may be cancelled by the drawee as long as
he retains possession of the bill *qua* drawee. Chalmers, p. 45.

The usual mode of accepting is for the drawee to write
"accepted" across the face of the bill, and then to sign his name
underneath: but any words which stipulate that the drawee
means to pay is a sufficient acceptance. The simple meaning
of an acceptance is, "I will pay." (Smith v. Vertue, 1860, 30
L.J.C.P. at p. 60, 4 R.C. at p. 248.)

Other means than the payment of money.

An acceptance "payable in bills" or "payable in goods" is
invalid (Russell v. Phillips, 1850, 14 Q.B. 891; cf. Boehm v.
Garcias, 1807, 1 Camp, 425*n*.). When the time of payment comes,
the holder may of course accept goods or bills in satisfaction
of the debt due to him. An acceptance may be an acceptance
to pay part only of the amount for which the bill is drawn
(sec. 38).

37. A bill may be accepted,— Acceptance.

(a) before it has been signed by the drawer, or while other- Before
   wise incomplete; completion.

(b) when it is overdue, or after it has been dishonoured by a previous refusal to accept, or by non-payment.

2. When a bill payable at sight or after sight is dishonoured by non-acceptance, and the drawee subsequently accepts it, the holder, in the absence of any different agreement, is entitled to have the bill accepted as of the date of first presentment to the drawee for acceptance. 53 V., c. 33, s. 18; 54-55 V., c. 17, s. 3. Eng. s. 18.

The words "at sight or" in sub-sec. 2 are not in the English Act. They were added to the Canadian Act in 1891. See notes to sec. 24.

Incomplete instruments.

See sec. 31, as to filling up signed blank paper as a bill, or filling up any material omission.

The drawer's signature may be added at any time, but until the drawer has signed, the instrument is inchoate and without effect. A. addresses a bill to B. but does not sign it. B. accepts and the instrument is transferred for value to C. The instrument is neither a bill not a note. (McCall v. Taylor, 1865, 34 L.J.C.P. 356; cf. Goldsmid v. Hampton, 1858, 5 C.B.N.S. 94; Ex parte Hayward, 1871, L.R. 6 Ch. 546.)

Overdue.

A. draws a bill on B., dated 1 January, payable one month after date. The holder presents it for acceptance in March. B., accepts. As regards B., this is a valid acceptance of a bill payable on demand. Mutford v. Walcott, 1698, 1 L. Raym. 574, 4 R.C. 216.)

See sec. 23 which provides that where a bill is accepted when it is overdue, it shall, as regards the acceptor who so accepts, be deemed a bill payable on demand, and also contains a similar provision in regard to endorsement of an overdue bill. See notes to the same section as to when a bill is overdue.

After dishonour.

The holder of a bill payable one month after date presents it to the drawee for acceptance. Acceptance is refused. A week later it is again presented and accepted. The acceptance is valid. (Wynne v. Raikes, 1804, 5 East, 514.

In case a bill is dishonoured by non-acceptance, it may be presented to the referee in case of need, if there be one named in the bill (sec. 33). As to acceptance for honour, see sec. 147.

Sec. 37.

As of the date of first presentment.

Sub-sec. 3 was added to the English Act in committee. It accords with mercantile practice, and was intended to put the holder as far as possible in the same position as if the bill had not been dishonoured. Chalmers, p. 46.

The ordinary rule is that the holder is entitled to have the acceptance of a bill which is payable at or after sight dated as of the day of presentment or of either of the two next following days, but in any case not later than the day of the drawee's actual acceptance (sec. 80).

Presumption as to time.

Unless the contrary appears by its terms, a bill is *primâ facie* deemed to have been accepted before maturity and within a reasonable time after its issue, but there is no presumption as to the exact time of acceptance. For example, B. accepts, without dating, a bill drawn payable three months after date. He attains his majority the day before the bill matures. This is *primâ facie* evidence that B. accepted it while an infant. (Roberts v. Bethell, 1852, 12 C.B. 778.)

38. An acceptance is either,— Kinds.

(a) general; or,

(b) qualified.

2. A general acceptance assents without qualification to the order of the drawer. General.

3. A qualified acceptance in express terms varies the effect of the bill as drawn and in particular, an acceptance is qualified which is,— Qualified.

    (a) conditional, that is to say, which makes payment by the acceptor dependent on the fulfilment of a condition therein stated; Conditional.

    (b) partial, that is to say, an acceptance to pay part only of the amount for which the bill is drawn; Partial.

    (c) qualified as to time; Time.

(d) the acceptance of some one or more of the drawees, but
not of all.

4. An acceptance to pay at a particular specified place is not
on that account conditional or qualified. 53 V., c. 33, s. 19. Eng.
s. 19.

Qualified acceptance.

The holder may refuse to take a qualified acceptance (sec.
83). If a qualified acceptance is taken, the drawer or the endorser will be discharged from his liability upon the bill unless he
has authorized the taking of such an acceptance, or subsequently
assented thereto, or unless after he has received notice of a qualified acceptance, he does not within a reasonable time express
his dissent (secs. 83 and 84).

Conditional.

Although a bill may not be drawn in terms importing a
condition, it may be accepted conditionally. Cf. notes to sec.
17.

Words importing a conditional or qualified acceptance will
be construed most strongly against the restriction of the acceptor's liability, and, to have effect, must shew in clear and inequi-
vocal terms on the face of the bill that the acceptance is so qualified. Thus it was held that an acceptance worded "accepted payable, on giving up bill of lading for 76 bags clover-seed, at the
London and Westminister Bank" merely postponed the liability
to pay until the delivery up of the bill of lading, but that the
acceptor was not discharged by the failure to present the bill for
payment and deliver up the bill of lading on the very day of
maturity (Smith v. Vertue, 1860, 30 L.J.C.P. 59, 4 R.C. 246);
cf. Decroix v. Meyer, cited in notes to sec. 22; see also sec. 93.)

An acceptance worded "acceptable—payable when in funds"
is conditional. (Julian v. Shobrooke, 1753, 2 Wils. 9; as to the
meaning of such a condition, see Smith v. Vertue, *supra*.)

Examples of conditional acceptances are "When in funds
as a first preference out of the estate (Potters v. Taylor, 1888,
20 N.S.R. (8 R. & G.) 362) or "Provided they have done sufficient to earn that sum." (McLean v. Shields, 1884, 1 Man. R.
278. Upon the performance of the condition before action
brought, the acceptance becomes absolute. (Ontario Bank v.
McArthur, 1889, 5 Man. R. 381; Potters v. Taylor, *supra*.)

Partial.

Examples are:

1. Bill drawn on B. for $100. B. accepts it as to $50. (Cf. Wegersloffe v. Keene, 1709, 1 Stra. 214.)

2. Bill drawn on B. for $100. B., accepts it, payable half in money, half in goods. This is valid as a qualified acceptance for $50. (Petit v. Benson, 1697, Comberb, 452; cf. Rowe v. Young, 1820, 2 Bligh, H.L. at p. 409; 2 B. & B. 165.)

The drawer or endorser is not discharged by the taking of a partial acceptance, whereof due notice has been given (sec. 84).

Qualified as to time.

A bill drawn 28 Nov., 1836, payable 42 months after date was accepted "on condition of its being renewed until the 28th Nov., 1844." The endorsee is at liberty to treat the acceptance as an extension of the time of payment specified in the bill, and to declare on it accordingly. (Russell v. Phillips, 1850, 14 Q.B. 891.)

Words introduced into the memorandum of acceptance which are contrary to the tenor of the bill, will, unless the intention is clear, be rejected as not forming·part of the acceptance. Thus a bill dated 8th Sept., 1856, drawn payable four months after date was accepted. Between the words of acceptance and the signature of the acceptor was the memorandum "due 11th December, 1856." The memorandum of the due date was rejected. (Fanshawe v. Peat, 1857, 2 H. & N. 1, 4 R.C. 243.)

At a particular specified place.

The English Act provides that a qualified acceptance may be "(c) local, that is to say, an acceptance to pay only at a particular specified place: an acceptance to pay at a particular place is a general acceptance, unless it expressly states that the bill is to be paid there only, and not elsewhere."

Acceptance payable at a particular specified place.

The House of Lords had held that an acceptance "payable at the house of P. & Co.," bankers, was a qualified acceptance (Rowe v. Young, 1820, 2 B. & B. 165, 2 Bligh 391). The Statute 1 and 2 Geo. IV., c. 78, altered the law as thus declared, and enacted the provisions which have been re-enacted in the clauses of the English Act above quoted."

The bill as originally introduced into the House of Commons in 1889, followed the English Act. This was in accordance with

Sec. 38.

Acceptance payable at a particular specified place.

the law already prevailing in Ontario and Prince Edward Island. (R.S.C. 1886, c. 123, secs. 9 and 16.)

In 1890 the clause referring to an acceptance payable at a particular specified place was omitted from the bill, owing to the strong opinion expressed at the previous session against making the Ontario provisions applicable to the whole Dominion. Under the Ontario Statute, a convenient practice had grown up of persons accepting their bills at particular banks, not with the intention of restricting their liability upon the bills, but with the intention that the banks at which they kept their accounts should pay the bills when they matured without cheque and without further instructions. In other provinces the same practice had been followed to some extent, but except in Prince Edward Island without the sanction of statute. The practice was especially convenient in cases where an acceptance had to be procured by a bank at a considerable distance away. By stamping upon the bill "accepted payable at the A. Bank," and procuring the drawee's signature to the acceptance in that form, a bank avoided the necessity of having to present it to the drawee, as presentment at the place specified in the acceptance, i.e., at the bank itself, was sufficient (sec. 88).

The omission of the clause would have had the effect of making an acceptance to pay at a particular specified place a qualified acceptance, which a bank would take at the risk of discharging the other parties to the bill (secs. 83 and 84). Under the English and Ontario statutes, the bank might take an acceptance payable at a particular specified place, provided the acceptor did not expressly provide that the bill should be paid there only and not elsewhere.

The English clauses were restored in committee. In the Senate, however, the clause relating to a local acceptance was struck out and the present clause inserted, providing generally that the acceptance to pay at a particular specified place is not conditional or qualified.

The difference between the English and the Canadian law may be illustrated as follows:—

1. The drawee of a bill accepts "payable at Smith & Co." his bankers. This is a general acceptance in England (cf. Halstead v. Skelton, 1843, 5 Q.B. 86) and in Canada.

2. The drawee of a bill accepts it "payable at the Union Bank and not elsewhere," or "pay only at the Union Bank."

This is a qualified acceptance in England (*ibid.*), but a general acceptance in Canada.

A bill is presented at the proper place if a place of payment is specified in the bill and the bill is there presented (sec. 88).

As to presentment as regards drawer and endorsers, see sec. 85, and as regards acceptor, see sec. 93.

Sec. 38.
Acceptance
payable at a
particular
specified
place.

39. Every contract on a bill, whether it is the drawer's, the acceptor's or an endorser's, is incomplete and revocable, until delivery of the instrument in order to give effect thereto: Provided, that where an acceptance is written on a bill, and the drawee gives notice to, or according to the directions of, the person entitled to the bill that he has accepted it, the acceptance then becomes complete and irrevocable. 53 V., c. 33, s. 21, Eng. s. 21.

When
acceptance
complete.

Proviso.

Prior to 1906 this section and secs. 40 and 41 constituted one section. The sections must be read together.

The following sections contain provisions relating to the different "contracts on a bill":—

Secs. 130 to 133: drawer or endorser;

Secs. 35, 38 and 128: acceptor.

Delivery means transfer of possession, actual or constructive, from one person to another: see notes to sec. 2, sub-sec. 1(*f*).

"To constitute a contract there must be a delivery over of the instrument by the drawer or endorser for a good consideration, and as soon as such delivery takes place the contract is complete and it becomes a contract in writing." (Abrey v. Crux, 1869, L.R. 5 C.P. 37, at p. 42, 4 R.C. 195, at p. 199; cf. Denton v. Peters, 1870, L.R. 5 Q.B. 475; Ex parte Cote, 1873, L.R. 9 Ch. 27.)

As to the admission of oral evidence to contradict or vary the contract in writing, see notes to sec. 40.

"It is not the mere act of writing on the bill, but the making a communication of what is so written, that binds the acceptor; for the making the communication is a pledge by him to the party, and enables the holder to act upon it." (Cox v. Troy, 1822, 5 B. & Ald. at p. 478.)

The drawee, unlike the drawer or endorser, has no property in the bill; therefore less is required to make him attorn to the holder. Chalmers, p. 53.

Sec. 30.

Bill incom-
plete and
revocable
until
delivery.

The following illustrations of this section are given by Chalmers, pp. 53-55 :—

1. B., who owes C. £100, makes a note for the amount payable to C. B. dies, and the note is afterwards found among his papers. C. has no right to this note, and if it be given to him he cannot enforce it. (Cf. Bromage v. Lloyd, 1847, 1 Ex. 32.)

2. B. makes a note in favour of his servant and hands it to his solicitor, telling the solicitor to retain the note till his death, and then hand it to the servant, if still in his service. B. dies, and the solicitor hands the note to the servant. The servant can (perhaps) prove for the amount in the administration of B.'s estate. (Re Richards, 1887, 36 Ch. D. 541, criticized, Re Whitaker, 1889, 42 Ch. D. 119, at p. 125.)

3. B. makes a note in favour of C. and delivers it to a stakeholder (e.g., trustee under composition deed). C. thereby acquires no property in the note. (Cf. Latter v. White, 1872, L.R. 5 H.L. 578.)

4. C., the holder of a bill, specially endorses it to D., and encloses it in a letter addressed to D. The letter, which is put in the office letter box, is stolen by a clerk of C.'s, who forges D.'s endorsement and negotiates the bill. The property in the bill remains in C. (Cf. Arnold v. Cheque Bank, 1876, 1 C.P.D. at p. 684.)

5. By the regulations of the English Post Office, a letter once posted cannot be reclaimed. If, then, the endorsee of a bill authorize the endorser to transmit it to him by post, the property in the bill passes to the endorsee, and the endorsement becomes complete as soon as the letter is posted. (Ex parte Cote, 1873, L.R. 9 Ch. 27; Sichel v. Borch, 1864, 2 H. & C. 954; but if there be no authority to send by post, the instrument is so sent at sender's risk, Pennington v. Crossley, 1897, 13 Times L.R. 513.)

6. The holder of a note payable to bearer wishes to remit money to D. For safety of transmission he cuts the note in two and posts one-half to D. Before he posts the second half he changes his mind, and writes to D. demanding back the half he has sent. He is entitled to do so, for a partial delivery is ineffectual. (Smith v. Mundy, 1860, 29 L.J. Q.B. 172; cf. Redmayne v. Burton, 1860, 2 L.T.N.S. 324.)

7. A bill is left with the drawee for acceptance. The drawee writes an acceptance on it. The next day the holder calls for the

bill; he is merely informed that it is mislaid, and is requested to call the next day. In the meantime the drawee hears that the drawer has failed. He accordingly cancels his acceptance, and the next day delivers the dishonoured bill back to the holder. This is no acceptance; the drawee is entitled to cancel it. (Bank of Van Diemen's Land v. Bank of Victoria, 1871, L.R. 3 P.C. 526.)

8. A firm is indebted to D. B., who is a member of the firm, and also agent for D., writes the firm's endorsement on a bill held by the firm, and puts the bill with some other papers of D.'s of which he has the custody. This is a valid endorsement by the firm, and the property in the bill passes to D. (Lysaght v. Bryant, 1850, 9 C.B. 46.)

Sec. 39.
Bill incomplete and revocable until delivery.

CHAPTER XXXVI.

DELIVERY AND ORAL EVIDENCE.

Sec. 39, subject to a proviso specially applicable to acceptance, provides that "Every contract on a bill, whether it is the drawer's, the acceptor's or an endorser's, is incomplete and revocable, until delivery of the instrument in order to give effect thereto."

The other sections relating to delivery of a bill are secs. 40 and 41. Prior to 1906 all three sections formed one section. Section 39 is now placed in the Act under the heading "Acceptance and interpretation," and has therefore been included in the chapter so entitled. The section and the illustrations cited in connection with it must, however, be read along with the sections, which are included in this chapter.

If a bill is in the hands of a holder in due course a valid delivery by all parties prior to him is conclusively presumed. (sec. 40). In other cases where a bill is no longer in the hands of a party who has signed it, a valid and unconditional delivery by him is presumed until the contrary is proved (sec. 41). See sec. 40 and notes as to when the contrary may be proved.

Delivery.

Requisites. 40. As between immediate parties, and as regards a remote party, other than a holder in due course, the delivery,—

Authority. (*a*) in order to be effectual must be made either by or under the authority of the party drawing, accepting or endorsing, as the case may be;

Conditional. (*b*) may be shown to have been conditional or for a special purpose only, and not for the purpose of transferring the property in the bill.

Presumption. 2. If the bill is in the hands of a holder in due course, a valid delivery of the bill by all parties prior to him, so as to make them liable to him, is conclusively presumed. 53 V., c. 33, s. 21. Eng. s. 21.

41. Where a bill is no longer in the possession of a party who has signed it as drawer, acceptor or endorser, a valid and unconditional delivery by him is presumed until the contrary is proved. 53 V., c. 33, s. 21. Eng. s. 21.

In the hands of a holder in due course.

"Holder in due course" is defined by sec. 56.

A. makes a note and leaves it with B. to be used by him in procuring an advance from the payee. In an action by the payee, the maker alleges that he made and delivered the note to B. for a purpose other than that for which B. deposited it with the plaintiff, but does not state that the plaintiff had notice. Held no defence. (Ontario Bank v. Young, 1901, 2 O.L.R. 761.)

B., by means of a false pretence, or a promise on a condition which he does not fulfil, induces A. to draw a cheque in favour of C. B. delivers it to C., who receives it in good faith and for value. C. acquires a good title, and can sue the drawer, for B. is ostensibly the drawer's agent. (Watson v. Russell, 1862, 3 B. & S. 34, 5 B. & S. 968; cf. Clutton v. Attenborough, [1897] A.C. 90; but see Herdman v. Wheeler, [1902] 1 K.B. 361, as to the original payee of a note.)

A. draws a cheque payable to bearer, intending to pay it to B. It is stolen from his desk before he issues it, and is subsequently negotiated to C., who takes it for value and without notice. C. (perhaps) acquires a good title and can sue A. (Ingham v. Primrose, 1859, 7 C.B.N.S., at p. 85; but see Baxendale v. Bennett, 1878, 3 Q.B.D. 531.)

C., the holder of a bill, endorses it specially to D. in order that he may get it discounted for him. D., in breach of trust, negotiates the bill to E. If E. takes the bill in good faith and for value, he acquires a good title, and can sue all the parties thereto. If he do not so take it, he cannot sue C.; and if he sue the acceptor, the latter can set up that the bill is C.'s; further C. can bring an action against E. to recover the bill or the proceeds. (Goggerley v. Cuthbert, 1806, 2 B. & P. N.R. 170; cf. Alsager v. Close, 1842, 10 M. & W. 576; Muttyloll v. Dent, 1853, 8 Moo. P.C. 319.)

By or under the authority of the party drawing, etc.

The holder of a bill specially endorses it to D. and dies before delivering it, but his executor subsequently hands the bill to D.

Sec. 41.   The endorsement to D. is invalid, for an executor is not the
agent of his testator. D. cannot sue on the bill. (Bromage v.
Lloyd, 1847, 1 Ex. 32; cf. Re Richards, cited in notes to sec. 39.)

Conditional delivery, etc.

It has long been settled law that the delivery of a bill may
be conditional, and that effect will be given to the condition.
The same principle applies to such a bill as to the delivery of a
deed in escrow, with this difference, that a deed cannot be delivered conditionally to the obligee, the delivery must be to a
third party (Bell v. Lord Ingestre, 1848, 12 Q.B. 317, at p. 319,
4 R.C. 203, at p. 205). If a bill is delivered conditionally or
for a special purpose, the relation between the person who so
delivers it and the person to whom it is delivered is substantially
that of principal and agent. (Maguire v. Dodd, 1859, 9 Ir. Ch.
452.)

B. makes a note payable to C., who sues him on it. B. can
defend by shewing that the note was delivered to C. on condition that it was to operate only if he should procure B. to be
restored to a certain office, and that B. was not so restored.
(Jeffries v. Austin, 1725, 1 Stra. 674.)

C., the holder of a bill, endorses it in blank and hands it to
D. on the express condition that he shall forthwith retire certain
other bills therewith. D. does not do so. He cannot sue C., and
if he sues the acceptor, the latter can set up the *jus tertii*
(Bell v. Lord Ingestre, *supra;* cf. Wismer v. Wismer, 1863, 22
U.C.R. 446.)

C., the payee of a bill, endorses it to D. D. sues C. as endorser. C. may shew that he and D. were jointly interested in the
bill, and that he endorsed to the latter to collect on joint account. (Denton v. Peters, 1870, L.R. 5 Q.B. 475.)

B. makes a note for £100 payable to C. or order. C. sues B.
Evidence is admissible to shew that the note was given as collateral security for a running account, and what the state of
that account is. (Cf. Ex parte Twogood, 1812, 19 Ves. 227; Re
Boys, 1870, L.R. 10 Eq. 467.)

A note was signed by defendant and delivered to his joint
maker S., upon condition that S., before delivering it to the
agent of the plaintiff, should obtain the additional signature of
H. This condition was known to the plaintiff's agent and was
never fulfilled. Held, that the plaintiff could not succeed.
(Commercial Bank v. Morrison, 1902, 32 S.C.R. 98.)

Oral evidence.

A bill or note must be in writing, and so must the supervening contracts therein, such as acceptance or endorsement. The contracts of the various parties, as interpreted by this Act and by the law merchant, are subject to the ordinary rule as to written contracts. Oral evidence is inadmissible in any way to contradict or vary their effect.

Oral evidence is not admissible to shew an agreement that the liability of a party as it appears on the face of the bill is contingent on the happening of some event (Foster v. Jolly, 1835, 1 C. M. & R. 703; Abrey v. Crux, 1869, L.R. 5 C.P. 37, 4 R.C. 194; McNeil v. Cullen, 1904, 37 N.S.R. 13); or that such party shall not be liable on the bill in any event (Emerson v. Erwin, 1903, 10 B.C.R. 101); or unless he choose (Adams v. Thomas, 1850, 7 U.C.R. 249); or that interest shall be payable, although the bill is not expressed to be payable with interest (Dombroski v. Laliberté, 1905, Q.R. 27 S.C. 57); or that the bill shall be renewed at maturity (Letellier v. Cantin, 1897, Q.R. 11 S.C. 64; New London v. Neale, [1898] 2 Q.B. 487; Vidal v. Ford, 1859, 19 U.C.R. 88); or that it shall be payable in instalments, or that part only shall be paid (Besant v. Cross, 1851, 10 C.B. 895; Hill v. Wilson, 1873, L.R. 8 Ch. 888, at p. 898); or that it shall be payable out of a particular fund which is no longer available (Campbell v. Hodgson, 1819, Gow 74; cf. Richards v. Richards, 1831, 2 B. & Ad., at pp. 454, 455; Vidal v. Ford, *supra*); or that it shall be payable at a different time from that mentioned on the face. (Cf. Drain v. Harvey, 1855, 17 C.B. 257.)

(marginal note: When oral evidence admissible.)

But oral evidence is admissible, as between the immediate parties,

(*a*) to shew that what purports to be a complete contract has never come into operative existence. (Brown v. Howland, 1885, 9 O.R. 48, affirmed 15 A.R. 750; and see secs. 40 and 41 and cases cited.)

(*b*) To impeach the consideration for the contract. See Chapter XXXIX., *infra.*

(*c*) To shew that the contract has been discharged by payment, release or otherwise. See Chapter XLVI., *infra*, but note that under sec. 142 a renunciation must be in writing.

Action by payee against maker of a note. Held, a good defence that at the time of the making of the note an oral agreement (which was afterwards fully performed before action

brought) was entered into that if the maker would pay interest
on the note and support for life a relative of the payee's, the
note should be considered paid. (McQuarrie v. Brand, 1896, 28
O.R. 69.)

Oral evidence is also admissible to shew that the party apparently primarily liable on the bill is really a surety for another
party to the knowledge of the holder, and that the holder has
discharged the surety by agreeing for a consideration to give
time to the principal. (Ewin v. Lancaster, 1865, 6 B. & S. 571;
Overend v. Oriental, 1874, L.R. 7 H.L. 348.)

Although *primâ facie* the liabilities *inter se* of successive endorsers of a bill are that every prior endorser must indemnify
a subsequent one, the presumption may be rebutted by oral evidence of circumstances shewing the real intention and agreement
of the parties. (Macdonald v. Whitfield, 1883, 8 App. Cas. 733,
4 R.C. 530.)

As between immediate parties, a contemporaneous writing
(cf. Brown v. Langley, 1842, 4 M. & Gr. 466; Salmon v. Webb,
1852, 3 H.L. Cas. 510; Maillard v. Page, 1870, L.R. 5 Ex. 312,
at p. 319), or a subsequent written agreement (McManus v.
Bark, 1870, L.R. 5 Ex. 65), may control the effect of a bill,
subject to the same conditions that would be requisite in the case
of an ordinary contract, but the mere fact that a bill refers to
a collateral writing or agreement which is conditional in its
terms, will not vitiate the bill in the hands of a person who had
no notice of its contents. (Jury v. Barker, 1858, E. B. & E. 459;
see English and American cases reviewed in Taylor v. Curry,
1871, 109 Mass. 36.)

Though the terms of a bill may not be contradicted by oral
evidence, yet effect may be given to a collateral or prior oral
agreement by cross-action or counterclaim. (Lindley v. Lacey,
1864, 34 L.J.C.P. 7, at p. 9.)

As to evidence of the true date of the drawing, acceptance or
endorsement of a bill, see notes to sec. 27.

As to evidence to identify the payee of a bill, see notes to sec.
21.

CHAPTER XXXVII.

Under both the English Act and the Canadian Act days are either business days or non-business days. The latter are excluded in reckoning time where by this Act the time limited for doing any act or thing is less than three days (sec. 6).

Under the Canadian Act non-business days are the same as legal holidays or non-juridical days (sec. 2) and are the days mentioned in sec. 43. If the last day of grace falls on a legal holiday or non-juridical day in the province where a bill entitled to days of grace is payable, then the day next following, not being a legal holiday or non-juridical day in such province, shall be the last day of grace (sec. 42). *Non-business days.*

Under the English Act, however, non-business days are divided into two classes. (1) If the last day of grace falls on Sunday, Christmas Day, Good Friday, or a day appointed by royal proclamation as a public fast or thanksgiving day, the bill is, except in the case hereinafter provided for, due and payable on the preceding business day; (2) if the last day of grace is a bank holiday (other than Christmas Day or Good Friday) under the Bank Holiday Act, 1871, and Acts amending or extending it, or if the last day of grace is a Sunday and the second day of grace is a bank holiday, the bill is due and payable on the succeeding business day.

Where a bill is drawn in one country and is payable in another, the due date thereof is determined according to the law of the place where it is payable (sec. 164).

Computation of Time, non-juridical days and days of grace.

42. Where a bill is not payable on demand, three days, called days of grace, are, in every case, where the bill itself does not otherwise provide, added to the time of payment as fixed by the bill, and the bill is due and payable on the last day of grace: Provided that whenever the last day of grace falls *Computation of time.*

Sec. 42.
Last day of
grace.

on a legal holiday or non-juridical day in the province where any such bill is payable, then the day next following, not being a legal holiday or non-juridical day in such province, shall be the last day of grace. 53 V., c. 33, s. 14. Eng. s. 14.

Payable on demand.

As to when a bill is payable on demand, see sec. 23. In Canada sight bills are not payable on demand and are entitled to days of grace.

Days of grace.

A suggestion to abolish days of grace, in accordance with recent legislation in many continental countries, was made in committee, when the English bill was under consideration, but was withdrawn. Chalmers, p. 36.

A note is made payable by two equal instalments on January 1st and February 1st. The instalments fall due on January 4th and February 4th. (Oridge v. Sherborne, 1843, 11 M. & W. 374.)

A bill dated January 1st payable 30 days after date is due on February 3rd.

The proviso to this section is a re-enactment of the similar provision originally contained in the Bank Act of 1872 (35 Vict., c. 8).

A non-negotiable note, not payable on demand, is entitled to days of grace (Smith v. Kendall, 1794, 6 T.R. 123).

Notice of dishonour and action.

Notice of dishonour may be given at any time on the third day of grace immediately upon payment being refused by the acceptor (sec. 98), but action cannot be brought on a bill until the following day. See notes to sec. 95.

Non-juri-
dical days.

43. In all matters relating to bills of exchange, the following and no other days shall be observed as legal holidays or non-juridical days:—

General.

(*a*) In all the provinces of Canada,

Sundays,

New Year's Day,

Good Friday,   Sec. 43.
Easter Monday,
Victoria Day,
Dominion Day,
Labour Day,
Christmas Day,
The birthday (or the day fixed by proclamation for the celebration of the birthday) of the reigning sovereign;

Any day appointed by proclamation for a public holiday, or for a general fast, or a general thanksgiving throughout Canada,

The day next following New Year's Day, Christmas Day, Victoria Day, Dominion Day, and the birthday of the reigning sovereign when such days respectively fall on Sunday;

(b) In the province of Quebec in addition to the said days, Quebec.
The Epiphany,
The Ascension,
All Saint's Day,
Conception Day;

(c) In any one of the provinces of Canada, any day ap-Provincial pointed by proclamation of the Lieutenant Governor of proclama-tion. such province for a public holiday, or for a fast or thanksgiving within the same, and any non-juridical day by virtue of a statute of such province. 53 V., c. 23, s. 14; 56 V., c. 30, s. 1; 57-58 V., c. 55, s. 2; 1 Ed. VII., c. 12, sec. 2 and 4. Cf. Eng. ss. 14 and 92.

The provisions relating to legal holidays or non-juridical days were originally contained in the Bank Act of 1872. Dominion Day was added in 1879, and Easter Monday in 1883. Under the Bills of Exchange Act, 1890, the Annunciation, Corpus Christi, and the Festival of St. Peter and St. Paul were legal holidays in Quebec, but they were struck out in 1893. In 1894 Labour Day and in 1901 Victoria Day were added to the

Sec. 43.   list of Dominion legal holidays.   The present Bank Act contains no provision as to legal holidays.
As to non-business days, see notes, *supra*.

Time of payment.

44. Where a bill is payable at sight, or at a fixed period after date, after sight, or after the happening of a specified event, the time of payment is determined by excluding the day from which the time is to begin to run and by including the day of payment. 53 V., c. 33, s. 14. Cf. Eng. s. 14.

The words "at sight or" are not in the English Act. See notes to sec. 23.

Sight bill.

45. Where a bill is payable at sight or at a fixed period after sight, the time begins to run from the date of the acceptance if the bill is accepted, and from the date of noting or protest if the bill is noted or protested for non-acceptance, or for non-delivery. 53 V., c. 33, s. 14. Cf. Eng. s. 14.

The words "at sight or" are not in the English Act. See notes to sec. 23.

A bill is payable at sight. The acceptance bears date March 1st. The bill is due March 4th.

The date is presumed to be the true date unless the contrary be proved (sec. 29). As to omission of date see sec. 30. The proper date of an acceptance after a previous refusal to accept is the date of the first presentment (sec. 37). As to date of acceptance of a bill payable at sight or after sight, see sec. 80.

A bill payable after sight is noted for non-acceptance on January 1st. It is accepted *supra* protest on January 5th. The time of payment must be calculated from January 1st (sec. 150).

The holder of a foreign bill, payable 60 days after sight, makes an agreement that if it is dishonoured by non-acceptance, he will re-present it for payment at maturity. Acceptance is refused. The time of payment must be calculated from the day the bill was protested, and not from the day of presentment to the drawee for acceptance. (Campbell v. French, 1795, 6 T. R. 200.)

There is no acceptance of a note (sec. 186); "after sight" in a note therefore means after mere exhibition to the maker. (Sturdy v. Henderson, 1821, 4 B. & Ald. 592.)

As to protest for non-delivery, see sec. 120.

46. Every bill which is made payable at a month or months Due date. after date becomes due on the same numbered day of the month in which it is made payable as the day on which it is dated, unless there is no such day in the month in which it is made payable, in which case it becomes due on the last day of that month, with the addition, in all cases, of the days of grace.

2. The term 'month' in a bill means the calendar month. 'Month.' 53 V., c. 33, s. 14. Cf. Eng. s. 14.

The only provision in the English Act corresponding to this section is that "The term month in a bill means calendar month." Sub-sec. 1 is a re-enactment of a provision which was originally contained in the statute 35 Vict., c. 10 (1872). It is declaratory of the usage of merchants.

A bill dated 31st January payable "without grace" one month after date is due February 28th. A similar note dated January 1st is due February 1st.

Bills dated 28th, 29th and 30th November, respectively, payable three months after date, all fall due on March 3rd, except in a leap year, when the first note would fall due on March 2nd.

CHAPTER XXXVIII.

CAPACITY AND AUTHORITY OF PARTIES.

Capacity distinguished from authority.

Capacity must be distinguished from authority. Capacity means power to contract so as to bind oneself. Authority means power to contract on behalf of another so as to bind him. Capacity to contract is the creation of law. Authority is derived from the act of the parties themselves. Want of capacity is incurable. Want of authority may be cured by ratification. Capacity or no capacity is a question of law. Authority or no authority is usually a question of fact. Again, capacity to incur liability must be distinguished from capacity to transfer. An executed contract is often valid where an executory contract cannot be enforced. An endorsement usually consists of two distinct contracts, one executed, the other executory. It transfers the property in the bill, and it also involves a contingent assumption of liability on the part of the endorser. Chalmers, p. 61.

Capacity and Authority of Parties.

Capacity of parties.

Corporations.

47. Capacity to incur liability as a party to a bill is co-extensive with capacity to contract: Provided that nothing in this section shall enable a corporation to make itself liable as drawer, acceptor or endorser, of a bill, unless it is competent to it so to do under the law for the time being in force relating to such corporation. 53 V., c. 33, s. 22. Eng. s. 22.

This section is declaratory.

The last words of the provision of the English Act corresponding to this section are "relating to corporations" instead of "relating to *such* corporation." The change was intended to make it clear that the proviso referred to a special Act relating to any particular corporation in question as well as to the law respecting companies in general.

There is no special law of capacity applicable to parties to bills and notes. The rule laid down by this section refers the question of capacity to the general law of contracts in the province in which the transactions upon the bill take place.

As to conflict of laws, see Chapter L., *infra.*

If by the local law applicable to the case, the incapacity of a party renders the contract void, the bill is a nullity as regards such person, even in the hands of a holder in due course. For instance, by English law an infant incurs no liability by drawing, endorsing or accepting a bill, even though the bill is given for the price of necessaries supplied to him during infancy. (In re Soltykoff, Ex parte Margrett, [1891] 1 Q.B. 413; cf. Ricard v. Banque Nationale, 1893, Q.R. 3 Q.B. 161, a case of a married woman in the Province of Quebec.)

But if the law renders such contract voidable and not void, the incapacity can be set up only against a party with notice. For instance, by English law, the contracts of a lunatic or drunken man, known to be such, are voidable only. Neither lunacy nor drunkenness can be set up against a holder in due course. (Imperial Loan v. Stone, [1892] 1 Q.B. 599.)

Bills of corporations.

The bills of corporations, so far as the form is concerned are discussed in the notes to secs. 5 and 35. Sec. 47 relates only to capacity. As to the liability of a person who signs on behalf of a corporation without authority, see notes to sec. 52.

A corporation incurs no liability by drawing, endorsing or accepting a bill, unless expressly or impliedly empowered by its Act of incorporation or charter so to do. In the case of a trading corporation the fact of incorporation for the purposes of trade confers capacity. In the case of non-trading corporations, the power must be expressly given or there must be terms in its charter wide enough to include such power. (Re Peruvian Railway Co., 1867, L.R. 2 Ch. 617; Bateman v. Mid Wales Railway Co., 1866, L.R. 1 C.P. 499, at p. 505; cf., however, the statutory provisions applicable to companies referred to in the notes to sec. 5.)

48. Where a bill is drawn or endorsed by an infant, minor, or corporation having no capacity or power to incur liability on a bill, the drawing or endorsement entitles the holder to receive payment of the bill, and to enforce it against any other party thereto. 53 V., c. 33, s. 22. Eng. s. 22. *Effect of disability on holder.*

Sec. 48.

The world "minor" was added to the English bill in committee as the Scotch equivalent of the English term "infant." Chalmers, p. 61.

Under this section, the endorsement passes the property in the bill, though from want of capacity the infant, minor or corporation may not be liable as endorser. (Cf. Smith v. Johnson, 1858, 3 H. & N. 222.)

A bank may be justified in paying cheques out of the funds of a company although, on account of the form of the cheques, the company would not be liable as drawer if they had not been paid. (Mahony v. East Holyford, 1875, L.R. 7 H.L. 869, 884.)

Incapacity of one party.

The incapacity of one or more of the parties to a bill in no way diminishes the liability of the other parties. Thus the acceptor cannot set up the incapacity of the drawer or payee (sec. 129), nor the drawee that of the acceptor or payee (sec. 130), nor the endorser that of the drawer or any previous endorser (sec. 133).

Forgery.

49. Subject to the provisions of this Act, where a signature on a bill is forged, or placed thereon without the authority of the person whose signature it purports to be, the forged or unauthorized signature is wholly inoperative, and no right to retain the bill or to give a discharge therefor or to enforce payment thereof against any party thereto can be acquired through or under that signature, unless the party against whom it is

Estoppel.

sought to retain or enforce payment of the bill is precluded from setting up the forgery or want of authority: Provided that,—

Ratification.

(*a*) nothing in this section shall affect the ratification of an unauthorized signature not amounting to a forgery;

Recovery of amount paid on forged cheque.

(*b*) if a cheque payable to order is paid by the drawee upon a forged endorsement out of the funds of the drawer, or is so paid and charged to his account, the drawer shall have no right of action against the drawee for the recovery back of the amount so paid, nor any defence to any claim made by the drawee for the amount so paid, as the case may be, unless he gives notice in writing of such forgery to the drawee within one year after he has acquired notice of such forgery.

Sec. 49.

2. In case of failure by the drawer to give such notice within the said period, such cheque shall be held to have been paid in due course as respects every other party thereto or named therein, who has not previously instituted proceedings for the protection of his rights. 53 V., c. 33, s. 24. Cf. Eng. ss. 24 and 60.

Default of notice.

This section down to and including clause (a) of the proviso is a transcript of sec. 24 of the English Act. The Canadian bill of 1890 also contained a section corresponding to sec. 60 of the English Act (see notes to next section), but the section was withdrawn in committee. In the Senate clause (b) of the proviso and sub-sec. 2 were added. At a subsequent date the provisions of the present sec. 50 were added.

A bill held under a forged signature must be distinguished from a bill with genuine signatures which has been fraudulently altered (sec. 145), though such alteration may amount to the crime of forgery, and must also be distinguished from a bill, with genuine signatures, in which material omissions have been filled up (sec. 31).

Subject to the provisions of this Act.

See sec. 50 as to recovery of amount paid on forged endorsement in good faith and in the ordinary course of business, sec. 173 as to protection of bank and drawer, and sec. 175 as to protection of collecting bank, where cheque is crossed. See also sec. 21 and notes as to fictitious or non-existing payee, and sec. 26 as to fictitious drawee.

The general rule is that even a holder in due course cannot make title through a forgery (Roberts v. Tucker, 1851, 16 Q. B. 560, 3 R.C. 680), or an unauthorized signature. (Jenks v. Doran, 1880, 5 A.R. 538, 562.)

Forged or unauthorized signature is wholly inoperative.

As to forgery, cf. Criminal Code, secs. 466, *et seq.*

A bill is payable to the order of J. S. Another person of the same name gets hold of it, and endorses it to D., who takes it as

Sec. 49.

Forged or
unauthor-
ized signa-
ture is
wholly in-
operative.

a holder in due course. D., acquires no title to the bill, he cannot enforce payment against any party thereto (Mead v. Young,
1790, 4 T.R. 28), and should any party pay him, the payment
is invalid. (Graves v. American Bank, 1858, 17 N.Y. 205; cf.
Ogden v. Benas, 1874, L.R. 9 C.P. 513.)

A note payable to order is stolen from the payee. The thief
forges the payee's endorsement, and collects the note from the
maker's banker who returns the note to the maker. The payee
can recover the amount of the note from the maker in an action
for conversion of the note. (Johnston v. Windle, 1836, 3 Bing.
N.C. 225.)

　A bill is payable to C.'s order. His endorsement is forged.
D., a subsequent holder, presents the bill for acceptance. The
drawee accepts it payable at his bankers. The bankers pay D.
They cannot debit the acceptor with this payment. (Roberts v.
Tucker, *supra*.)

C. specially endorses a bill to D. It is stolen before delivery
to D., and D.'s endorsement in blank is forged on it. It comes
into B.'s hands, and he gets his bankers to present it for payment. They receive payment and credit B. with the amount,
B. subsequently draws out the whole sum. C. can recover the
amount of the bill from the bankers. (Arnold v. Cheque Bank,
1876, 1 C.P.D. 578; cf. Charles v. Blackwell, 1877, 2 C.P.D. at
p. 157.)

A letter of credit on a bank is granted in favour of C., whose
clerk gets possession of it, forges C.'s name to a draft, and
obtains the money. The bank is not discharged by this payment.
(Orr v. Union Bank, 1854, 1 Macq. H.L. 513.)

The payee of a note made and payable in Ontario, who had
absconded to Michigan, while there and after a writ of attach-
ment in insolvency had issued against him in Ontario, endorsed
the note for good consideration to the plaintiffs, who took it in
good faith. By the law of Ontario the title to the note had
vested in the assignee in bankruptcy before the endorsement.
Held, that the plaintiffs could not recover, the payee having no
authority to endorse. (Jenks v. Doran, 1880, 5 A.R. 558.)

Ratification of unauthorized or forged signature.

A. forges B.'s signature to a note as maker. Before the
note matures the holder finds out that B.'s signature is a forgery, and threatens to prosecute A. In order to prevent this,

B. gives the holder a memorandum which says: "I hold myself responsible for the note for £100 bearing my signature." The ratification is invalid. B. is not liable on the note. (Brook v. Hook, 1871, L.R. 6 Ex. 89; Ex parte Edwards, 1841, 2 Mon. D. & D. 241; and cf. Williams v. Bayley, 1866, L.R. 1 H.L. 200, at p. 221.)

Sec. 49. Ratification of unauthorized or forged signature.

An unauthorized signature not amounting to a forgery may be ratified by the principal, but, as a general rule, a forgery cannot be ratified. This general rule (see Brook v. Hook, *supra*) is, however, subject to modification. An act professing to have been done for or under the authority of the person sought to be charged is capable of ratification, so as to make such person civilly responsible as if he had originally authorized it, but not so as to make a defence for the forger against a criminal charge. (Cf. McKenzie v. British Linen Co., 1881, 6 App. Cas, at p. 99; Dominion Bank v. Ewing, 1904, 7 O.L.R. at p. 95, S.C. 35 S.C.R. 133.)

Precluded from setting up the forgery or want of authority.

By the fact of becoming a party to a bill, a person may be estopped from setting up that the signatures of other parties thereto are forged or unauthorized. As to drawer, see sec. 130; endorser, sec. 133; acceptor, sec. 129; acceptor for honour, notes to sec. 152; maker of note, sec. 185.

The word "precluded" was inserted in committee in lieu of the word "estopped," an English technical term, unknown to Scotch law. Chalmers, p. 75.

A party to a bill may be estopped by his conduct from denying to an innocent holder, the genuineness of his signature, or from setting up that the signatures of other parties to the bill are forged or unauthorized.

The acceptor of a bill forges A.'s name thereon as drawer, and discounts the bill with a bank. The bill is dishonoured, and notice sent to A. The acceptor gets the bill renewed for a smaller sum, paying the difference in cash to the bank, and on renewal again forges A.'s name as drawer. The renewed bill is dishonoured and notice is sent to A. A. does not repudiate the transaction for fourteen days. He is not estopped from setting up that his signature is forged. (McKenzie v. British Linen Co., 1881, 6 App. Cas. 82; *Secus*, if the bank had been prejudiced by the delay: see Ewing v. Dominion Bank, *infra*.)

Sec. 49.

Precluded from setting up the forgery or want of authority.

A. forges B.'s acceptance. B. pays the holder. Afterwards A. again forges B.'s acceptance, which, unknown to B., gets into the hands of the same holder. B. may set up that his signature was forged. (Morris v. Bethell, 1869, L.R. 5 C.P. 47.)

A cheque payable to the order of a company is endorsed by the secretary, who has no authority under the by-laws to give a valid endorsement. The company is estopped from denying the want of authority by the fact that on previous occasions the secretary has drawn money on cheques on his sole endorsement, and no notice was ever given to the bank that he was exceeding his authority. (Thorold v. Imperial Bank, 1887, 13 O.R. 330; cf. Imperial Bank v. Farmers' Trading Co., 1901, 13 Man. R. 412.)

A local manager of a company is authorized to endorse cheques for deposit with the Bank of B.C. He endorses and cashes at the Bank of M., a cheque drawn on the latter bank. The Bank of M., is liable to the company if there have been no other dealings sufficient to estop the company. (Hinton v. Bank of Montreal, 1903, 9 B.C.R. 545.)

The case of Ewing v. Dominion Bank, 1904, 35 S.C.R. 133, perhaps, goes further than any English decision in the direction of holding a person liable, on the ground of estoppel, upon a note to which his signature has been forged. In that case E. & Co., merchants at Montreal, received from the Dominion Bank, Toronto, on the morning of the 16th of August, a letter notifying them that their note for $2,000 to the T. P. Co., would fall due at the bank on a date named and requesting them to provide for the same. The name of E. & Co., had been forged to the note. E. & Co. communicated at once with the forger, but did not communicate with the bank till the following December, a few days before the note fell due. On the 15th and 16th of August the T. P. Co., issued cheques on the bank, payment of which left a balance to their credit at the close of business on the 15th of $1,611, on the 16th of $1,355, and on the 17th of $84. It was held by the Supreme Court, by a majority judgment, that, on receipt of the notice, E. & Co. were under a legal obligation to inform the bank, by telegraph or telephone, that they had not made the note, and that as they had not done so they were estopped from denying their signature.

The members of the Judicial Committee, upon application to them for special leave to appeal, treated the matter as absolutely a question of fact and dismissed the application upon the ground that they could not say that there was not evidence upon which the courts below might fairly find as they did: 1904, A.C. 806. The judgments of the members of the Supreme Court lay down the following propositions of law, which are of importance in connection with the question of estoppel.

Sec. 49. Precluded from setting up the forgery or want of authority.

1. If a person becomes aware that by the unauthorized use of his name, a fraud is being practised upon a bank, there may be a duty to notify the bank of the fraud, although no business relation previously existed between him and the bank; sufficient relation is created by the fact that express notice is given by the bank to such person that his name is being used (referring especially to Freeman v. Cooke, 2 Ex. 654, 663, and McKenzie v. British Linen Co., 1881, 6 App. Cas. 82, 109; but cf. Merchants Bank v. Lucas, 1889, 15 A.R. 573, 18 S.C.R. 704.)

2. Assuming the duty to notify the bank, modern business methods may require the use of the telegraph or the telephone. *Quære,* however, whether the business custom is not merely to write in due course: cf. 18 Harv. L.R. 141 (1904).

3. If a person is under such a duty, and, by reason of his neglect to notify the bank, the bank is prejudiced, the liability of the person whose name has been used is not limited to the actual amount of the loss sustained by the bank; he is estopped from denying the genuineness of his signature and is liable to the full amount of the document. The loss need not be the direct and necessary consequence of the neglect. (Cf. Ogilvie v. West Australian, [1896] A.C. 257, 270.)

Unless he gives notice in writing.

The effect of clause (b) of the proviso is that if a cheque payable to order is paid by the drawee upon a forged endorsement, there is a special period of limitation applicable to the claim or defence of the drawer against the drawee in respect of the payment made, namely one year after the drawer has acquired notice of the forgery. Until the year expires, the payment as between the drawer and drawee is invalid in accordance with the general rule that a forged endorsement is wholly inoperative. After the year, the drawer is concluded as against the drawee.

By sub-sec. 2 the same period of limitation is made applicable as respects every other party to the cheque or named therein who has not previously instituted proceedings for the protection of his rights.

Sec. 49.
Unless he
gives notice
in writing.

For example, A. draws a cheque in favour of B., and hands it to B., in payment of a debt. It is stolen from or lost by B., and the thief or finder forges B.'s name and obtains payment from the drawee bank. B. has no claim against A., because the delivery of the cheque operates as payment subject only to the condition that, if upon due presentment the cheque is not paid, the original debt revives. (Cf. Charles v. Blackwell, 1887, 2 C.P.D. at p. 158). A. cannot be charged by the bank with the amount of the payment unless a year passes after A. acquires notice of the forgery without A.'s having given notice in writing to the bank. If A. fails to give such notice and B. neglects to institute proceedings for the protection of his rights within the year after A. acquires notice of the forged or unauthorized signature, the cheque shall be deemed to have been paid in due course as respects B.

Recovery of
amount paid
on forged
endorsement.

50. If a bill bearing a forged or unauthorized endorsement is paid in good faith and in the ordinary course of business, by or on behalf of the drawee or acceptor, the person by whom or on whose behalf such payment is made shall have the right to recover the amount so paid from the person to whom it was so paid or from any endorser who has endorsed the bill subsequently to the forged or unauthorized endorsement if notice of the endorsement being a forged or unauthorized endorsement is given to each such subsequent endorser within the time and in the manner in this section mentioned.

Rights over.

2. Any such person or endorser from whom said amount has been recovered shall have the like right of recovery against any prior endorser subsequent to the forged or unauthorized endorsement.

Notice of
forgery.

3. Such notice of the endorsement being a forged or unauthorized endorsement shall be given within a reasonable time after the person seeking to recover the amount has acquired notice that the endorsement is forged or unauthorized, and may be given in the same manner, and if sent by post may be addressed in the same way, as notice of protest or dishonour of

a bill may be given or addressed under this Act. 60-61 V., c. Sec. 50.
10, s. 1. Cf. Eng. s. 60.

This section is not in the English Act. The history of the
section and its predecessor is discussed, and their contents an-
alyzed by Z. A. Lash, K.C., in 4 Journal C.B.A. at pp. 22 *et seq.*

In England prior to 1853 a banker paying a cheque to a English Act
holder, whose title depended upon a forged or unauthorized en- as to banker
paying on
dorsement, could not under ordinary circumstances debit the forged or
customer with the payment. In that year an Act was passed unauthor-
which was afterwards re-enacted in substance by sec. 60 of the endorse-
English Bills of Exchange Act, 1882. That section is as follows: ment.

''60. When a bill payable to order on demand is drawn on
a banker, and the banker on whom it is drawn pays the bill in
good faith and in the ordinary course of business, it is not incumbent on the banker to shew that the indorsement of the
payee or any subsequent indorsement was made by or under
the authority of the person whose indorsement it purports to
be, and the banker is deemed to have paid the bill in due course,
although such indorsement has been forged or made without
authority.''

The leading case on the English section is Charles v. Blackwell, 1887, 2 C.P.D. 151, in which it was held the banker who
pays a cheque in good faith and in the ordinary course of business is protected, notwithstanding that the endorsement of the
payee has been forged or made without authority, that the customer who draws the cheque is protected, the cheque having
been paid, and that the loss must fall upon the payee, who alone
of the three innocent parties could have contributed to the circumstances occasioning the loss.

A section in the same words as sec. 60 of the English Act English Act
was contained in the Canadian bill in 1890, but was struck out not adopted
in Canada.
in committee, probably as a result of a misunderstanding of
the effect of the section. In its place clause (*b*) and sub-sec. 2
of the present section 49 were added to the bill in the Senate. Amendment
It was doubtful under the Act of 1890 whether an acceptor of 1891.
or endorser would, after payment of the bill, have any remedy
against endorsers subsequent to the forged endorsement, and in
1891 the following sub-section was added to what is now sec 49:

''If the drawee of a cheque bearing a forged endorsement
pays the amount thereof to a subsequent endorser, or to the

Sec. 50.

Recovery of
money paid
on forged or
unauthorized
endorsement.

bearer thereof, he shall have all the rights of a holder in due
course for the recovery back of the amount so paid from any
endorser who has endorsed the same subsequent to the forged
endorsement, as well as his legal recourse against the bearer
thereof as a transferrer by delivery; and any endorser who has
made such payment shall have the like rights and recourse
against any antecedent endorser subsequent to the forged indorsement,—the whole, however, subject to the provisions and
limitations contained in the last preceding sub-section."

Finally in 1897 the amendment of 1891 was repealed and the
present sec. 50 enacted in its place.

Act of 1897
compared
with Act of
1891.

The meaning of the present section may be illustrated by
comparing its terms with those of the former section.

1. The former section applied only to a cheque. The present section applies to a bill of exchange whether drawn on a
bank or not and whether payable on demand or otherwise. By
virtue of sec. 186, it applies also to promissory notes.

2. The former section was confined to the case of a forged
endorsement. The present section applies also to an unauthorized endorsement.

3. A payment to be recovered back under the present section
must have been made in good faith, (i.e., honestly whether negligently or not: sec. 3), and in the ordinary course of business.

4. The former section in terms conferred the right of recovery back only upon the bank which had paid the cheque.
The present section gives the right to claim repayment to the
bank which has made the payment and to the customer on whose
behalf the payment has been made.

5. The former section gave the "rights of a holder in due
course" for the recovery back of the amount paid from any
endorser who had endorsed the same subsequent to the forged
endorsement. If the "rights of a holder in due course" meant
merely the ordinary rights of a holder of a bill, the bank was
confined to a remedy upon the bill itself against the prior endorsers. In that event the section meant one of three things, either
(1) that notice of dishonour must have been given within the
time limited by the Act in ordinary cases—a meaning which
gave no practical relief to the bank and made the section illusory; or, (2) that the bank had the rights of a holder without
the necessity of giving notice and might claim repayment at

any time before the Statute of Limitations had run its course; Sec. 50.
or (3) that by virtue of the concluding words—"the whole, Act of 1897
however, subject to the provisions and limitations contained in compared
the last preceding sub-section"—the bank had one year after with Act of
acquiring notice of the forgery to notify the endorser. The 1891.
third is the most probable meaning, but if the Act meant either
(2) or (3), it was unjust to the endorser in not requiring notice
to be given promptly after the discovery of the forgery.

The present section gives the right to recover back the
amount paid from the person to whom it was paid or from any
endorser subsequent to the forged or unauthorized endorsement,
but, like the former section in this respect, it confers no right
of recovery against an intermediate holder who may have transferred the bill, but who did not endorse it. The present section requires notice of the forgery or want of authority to be
given to each endorser subsequent to the endorsement in question, and not merely to the endorser sought to be charged. The
notice must be given within a reasonable time after the person
seeking to recover the amount has acquired notice that the
endorsement is forged or unauthorized, and may be given in the
same manner as notice of protest or dishonour under the Act.

As to "reasonable time," cf. secs. 77, 86 and 166, where the
same expression is used.

The present section does not affect the rights or position of
the drawer or endorsers prior to the forged or unauthorized endorsement, they being in no way responsible for the forgery
or want of authority. As a loss must be suffered by some innocent party, it is only right that it should fall upon him who by
his negligence or failure to enquire, was imposed upon, and who
had it entirely within his power to protect himself at the time
of acquiring the bill. This principle is applicable to the first
endorser after the forged or unauthorized endorsement and to
each subsequent endorsement. But an acceptor is in a different position. When a bill is presented for payment, he has no
time to verify the endorsement, and usually has no means of
doing so. He must pay at once or let the bill go to protest,—
and he is therefore required only to act in good faith and in the
ordinary course of business.

Recovery by payer of money paid by mistake.

Where payment of a bill or note is made by mistake to a person who is not entitled to receive payment, and who cannot give

a discharge, the payer can recover the money so paid from the
person who received it when such person did not act in good
faith in demanding payment of the bill. (Martin v. Morgan,
1819, 3 Moore, 635; Kendal v. Wood, 1871, L.R. 6 Ex. 243).
Subject to the provisions of the Act as to a collecting bank in the
case of a crossed cheque (sec. 175), the payer can recover the
money paid from the person who received it when such person
acted in good faith in demanding payment of the bill, provided
(a) that the payer was not guilty of negligence in making the
payment, and (probably) (b) that the position of the party receiving payment has not been altered before the discovery of
the mistake and notification thereof. Chalmers, p. 210.

A banker is bound to know the handwriting of his customer.
(Smith v. Mercer, 1815, 6 Taunt. 76; cf. Chalmers, p. 211.) If
in the ordinary course of dealing there comes through one bank
to another a cheque purporting to bear the signature of a customer of the latter, which accepts it, pays it and charges it to
the customer, the implication from the transaction is that the
drawee bank dealt with the cheque in reliance upon its knowledge of the customer's signature, and not upon any supposed
representation or warranty of its genuineness by the bank presenting it. (Rex v. Bank of Montreal, 1906, 11 O.L.R. 595, 601;
S.C. affirmed by the Supreme Court the 19th February, 1907.)
Cf. Bank of Ottawa v. Harty, 1906, 12 O.L.R. 218, in which
a person who had presented to the plaintiff bank a cheque on a
New York bank purporting to be endorsed by the payee, but not
in fact endorsed by the payee, was held liable as on a warranty
that he, as agent for the rightful owner, was entitled to payment.

There may be a duty on the part of the drawer of a cheque
towards his banker which does not exist on the part of the acceptor of a bill towards the holder. If the customer by any
act of his has induced the banker to act upon the document by
his act, or neglect of some act usual in the course of dealings
between them, it is quite intelligible that he should not be permitted to set up his own act or neglect to the prejudice of the
banker whom he has thus misled, or by neglect permitted to
be misled (Scholfield v. Londesborough, [1896] A.C. at p. 523).
But whatever the duty of a customer towards his banker may
be with reference to his drawing of cheques, the mere fact that
the cheque is drawn with spaces such that a forger can utilize

them for the purpose of forgery is not itself any violation of
that obligation. (Colonial Bank v. Marshall, [1906] A.C. 559,
568; cf. Imperial Bank v. Bank of Hamilton, [1903] A.C. at
p. 54.)

In Cocks v. Masterman, 1829, 9 B. & C. 902, it is said "that
the holder of a bill is entitled to know on the day when it becomes due whether it is an honoured or dishonoured bill, and
that if he receives the money and is suffered to retain it during
the whole of that day the parties who paid it cannot recover it
back. This stringent rule, recently asserted in even wider language in London & River Plate Bank v. Bank of Liverpool,
[1896] 1 Q.B. 7, has reference only to negotiable instruments,
on the dishonour of which notice has to be given to some one,
namely, to some drawer or endorser, who would be discharged
from liability unless such notice were given in proper time, and
is not to be applied to other cases. (Imperial Bank v. Bank of
Hamilton, [1903] A.C. at p. 58.)

In Bank of Toronto v. Hamilton, 1896, 28 O.R. 51, the plaintiff bank under telegraphic instructions from one of its branches,
telephoned to one of its sub-agencies to credit the defendant
with $2,000. The sub-agency by error credited him with $3,000,
which he drew out. The $2,000 had been paid into the branch
bank in the first instance by a third person as an advance on
the shipping bills of certain cattle bought from the defendant
for about $2,800, but of this fact the bank had no notice. The
defendant refused to repay the difference between the $2,000
and the price of the cattle, on the ground that on the faith of
the payment to him he had allowed them to be shipped abroad,
and that by his agreement for sale this was not to be done till
payment of the price in full. Held, that the bank was entitled
to recover the excess over $1,000.

51. A signature by procuration operates as notice that the
agent has but a limited authority to sign, and the principal is
bound by such signature only if the agent in so signing was
acting within the actual limits of his authority. 53 V., c. 33,
s. 25. Eng. s. 25.

This section is declaratory.

A person taking a bill signed by procuration ought to exercise due caution, and it would be only reasonable prudence to

Sec. 50. Recovery by payer of money paid by mistake.

Procuration signatures.

require the production of the authority in pursuance of which the bill is signed. (Attwood v. Munnings, 1827, 7 B. & C. 278, 4 R.C. 364.)

The section provides for the case of an instrument which shews on its face that it is signed by the hand of an agent. Cf. sec. 4, which provides that an instrument is sufficiently signed by a person if his signature is written thereon by some other person by or under his authority.

As to the signature of a corporation and notes signed on behalf of a corporation, see sec. 5.

As to the form of signature by an agent which is sufficient to shew that the agent is not to be personally liable, providing the authority is sufficient, see sec. 52.

If C. signs a bill by power of attorney from D., the form of signature should indicate the fact, as "D. per C.," "D. by C., atty.," "C. p. p. D." or "per proc. D., C." "D. p. p. C. means that D. is the agent and C. the principal.

An agent draws a cheque "per proc." in excess of his authority. The person in whose name it is drawn is not liable on the cheque to a person who has cashed it in good faith, but he must account for any money which has come into his possession. (Reid v. Rigby, [1894] 2 Q.B. 40.)

In Bridgewater v. Murphy, 1896, 23 A.R. 66, affirmed, 26 S.C.R. 443, the president of a company made a note in the company's name without authority, and discounted it with the company's bankers. The proceeds were credited to the company's account, and paid out by cheque in the company's name to its creditors whose claims should have been paid by the president out of moneys which he had previously misappropriated. It was held that the bankers, who took in good faith, were entitled to charge the amount of the note, when it fell due, against the company's account.

Notwithstanding the existence of a written power of attorney, the real scope of the agency may be ascertained from any admissible evidence. (Cooper v. Blacklock, 1880, 5 A.R. 535.)

If the agent has authority, his abuse of it does not affect a holder in due course; the agent's apparent authority is the real authority. (Bryant v. Quebec Bank, [1903] A.C. 170.)

By a resolution of the directors, the chairman of a company is authorized to accept bills drawn by A., against the deposit of securities. He accepts a bill drawn by A., signing per proc. the

company, without requiring the deposit of security. The bill
is negotiated to a *bonâ fide* holder. The company is liable. (Re
Land Credit Co., 1869, L.R. 4 Ch. 460.)

Detinue for a note. The note was payable to the plaintiff's
order, and was endorsed in the form "D., by his attorney, B."
in pledge for a private debt of the agent's, though this was not
known to the endorsee. The right of the endorsee to retain the
note depends on the proper construction of the power of attorney held by B., and in construing the power, it will be held
that a power to sell does not include a power to pledge. (Jonmenjoy v. Watson, 1884, 9 App. Cas. 561; cf. Jacobs v. Morris,
[1902] 1 Ch. 816, an action to restrain the negotiation of a bill
accepted by an agent in excess of his authority.)

B., who carries on business for himself, and is also in partnership with S., goes abroad; he gives S. an authority to accept
bills in his name in respect of his private business. S. accepts
a bill in B.'s name per proc., in respect to the partnership business. The bill is negotiated. B., is not liable on the acceptance.
(Attwood v. Munnings, 1827, 7 B. & C. 278; Stagg v. Elliott,
1862, 12 C.B.N.S. 373.)

Liability of agent who signs a bill on behalf of a principal.

By the Dominion Companies Act (R.S.C. c. 79, sec 115), any
director, manager or officer of a company, and every person on
its behalf who signs or authorizes to be signed on behalf of the
company any bill, note, endorsement, cheque, etc., wherein the
company's name, with the word "limited" after it, is not mentioned in legible characters, incurs a penalty and is personally
liable to the holder for the amount of such bill, etc., unless the
same is duly paid by the company.

By virtue of this Act or some similar provincial Act applicable to the company on behalf of which a person signs, the person signing may be liable on the instrument. (See Howell v.
Brethour, 1899, 30 O.R. 204.)

He is also liable on the instrument if the alleged principal
is fictitious or non-existing. (Cf. Kelner v. Baxter, 1866, L.R.
2 C.P. 174.)

In other cases a person who, without authority, signs the
name of another person to a bill, either simply or by a procuration signature, is not liable on the bill itself. (Polhill v. Walter,
1832, 3 B. & A. 114.)

Sec. 51.

Liability of agent who signs a bill on behalf of a principal.

A person signing without authority may, however be liable in an action for misrepresentation or fraud. (Polhill v. Walter, *supra;* West London v. Kitson, 1884, 13 Q.B.D. 360.) In such an action the holder must prove damage. (Eastwood v. Bain, 1858, 3 H. & N. 738.) The fraud which is sufficient to be a ground for an action of deceit is discussed in Derry v. Peek, 1889, 14 App. Cas. 337. (Cf. Low v. Bouverie, [1891] 3 Ch. at 100; Le Lievre v. Gould, [1893] 1 Q.B. at 501; negligent misrepresentation is sufficient where there is a contract between the parties and therefore a duty not to be negligent.)

Although a person who signs a bill in the name of another without authority is not liable on the bill itself, because he is not a party to it, and although he is not liable to an action of deceit because he acted innocently, he may, nevertheless, be liable on the ground of an implied warranty of authority (Collen v. Wright, 1857, 8 E. & B. 647; Firbanks v. Humphreys, 18 Q.B.D. 54, better report 56 L.J.Q.B. 57; Starkey v. Bank of England, [1903] A.C. 114). The person signing is liable on an implied warranty of authority only if the other contracting party relied on the existence of authority in fact. (Halbot v. Lens, [1901] 1 Ch. 344.)

Signing in representative capacity.

52. Where a person signs a bill as drawer, endorser or acceptor, and adds words to his signature indicating that he signs for or on behalf of a principal, or in a representative character, he is not personally liable thereon; but the mere addition to his signature of words describing him as an agent, or as filling a representative character, does not exempt him from personal liability.

Rule for determining capacity.

2. In determining whether a signature on a bill is that of the principal or that of the agent by whose hand it is written, the construction most favourable to the validity of the instrument shall be adopted. 53 V., c. 33, s. 26. Eng. s. 26.

The question of the sufficiency of the authority of an agent to sign a bill on behalf of a principal is discussed in the notes to secs. 4, 5 and 51. Sec. 52 deals only with the question whether the form of the signature is such as to render the principal and not the agent liable.

See sec. 132 as to signing a bill in a trade or assumed name or in the name of a firm.

Where a person is under obligation to endorse a bill in a representative capacity, he may endorse the bill in such terms as to negative personal liability (sec. 61).

This section was re-drafted in committee, and perhaps somewhat modifies the rigour of the common law rule. At any rate the older cases must be examined carefully with regard to the words of the section. The principle is this: the terms agent, manager, etc., attached to a signature are regarded as mere *designatio personæ*. The rule is applied with peculiar strictness to bills, because of the non-liability of the principal (cf. sec. 131). Chalmers, p. 80.

A man who puts his name to a bill makes himself personally liable, unless he states upon the face of the bill that he subscribes for another or by procuration of another, which are words of exclusion. Unless he says plainly, "I am the mere scribe," he is liable. (Leadbitter v. Farrow, 1816, 5 M. & S. at p. 349.)

In considering the question raised by this section, one must not overlook the distinction between bills of exchange and promissory notes. As pointed out in Alexander v. Sizer, 1869, L. R. 4 Ex. at p. 105, a bill of exchange is drawn on the intended acceptor in a personal character and if he accepts, he must do so in that character or not at all. The acceptance of a bill is the signification by the *drawee* of his assent to the order of the drawer (sec. 35; cf. notes to that section). This distinction explains many of the cases in which the principal has been held not liable on a bill, as not being the drawee, although otherwise the bill has been sufficiently signed for him or on his behalf by an agent.

Principal liable; agent not liable.

A leading case is that of Fairchild v. Ferguson, 1892, 21 S.C.R. 484. The manager of a company, in payment for goods purchased by him as such, gave a promissory note beginning "sixty days after date *we* promise to pay" and signed "R., manager O. L. Co." Evidence was given that both R. and the payees intended to make the company liable and that R. had authority to bind the contract by note. Held, the company's

note and not R.'s. Many of the cases are discussed in the judgments. Cf. Canada Paper Co. v. Gazette, 1893, 32 N.B.R. 689;
City Bank v. Cheney, 1857, 15 U.C.R. 400.

Money is lent to the S. Ry. Co. A note for the amount is given
in the form "I promise to pay," etc., and signed "for the S.
Ry. Co., J. B., secretary. J. B. is not personally liable. (Alexander v. Sizer, 1869, L.R. 4 Ex. 102; but see Gray v. Raper,
1866, L.R. 1 C.P. 694.)

Agent personally liable.

Many of the cases are collected in Boyd v. Mortimer, 1899,
30 O.R. 290. In that case an assignee for the benefit of the
creditors of a partnership signed notes in the firm name, followed by his own with the word assignee added, and was held
personally liable.

A bill is drawn upon "P. C. D., president N. D. & H. Co.,"
and accepted by him in the same terms. He is personally liable
(Bank of Montreal v. De Latre, 1848, 5 U.C.R. 362); he would
not have been liable if he had accepted in the company's name,
per himself. (Cf. Madden v. Cox, 1880, 5 A.R. 473, cited in
notes to sec. 35.)   ·

A bill addressed to A. M., is accepted "A. M., executor of
J. P." A. M. is personally liable. (Campbell v. McKay, 1892,
24 N.S.R. 404.)

A note is signed by an agent or officer in his own name, with
the addition after his name of, his agency or office, or of the
word "attorney," "executor." etc. He is personally liable.
(McDonald v. Smaill, 1893, 25 N.S.R. 440; Armour v. Gates,
1859, 8 C.P. 548; Hamilton v. Jones, 1896, Q.R. 10 S.C. 496;
Peele v. Robinson, 1860, 4 Allen (N.B.) 561; Hagarty v. Squier,
1877, 42 U.C.R. 165, and cases cited.)

A note made in the form "We, the directors of the K. Co.,
Ltd.," is signed "J. F., J. S." In the corner of the note is
the seal of the company and the signature of an attesting witness. J. F., and J. S., are personally liable. (Dutton v. Marsh.
1871, L.R. 6 Q.B. 361.)

CHAPTER XXXIX.

CONSIDERATION.

53. Valuable consideration for a bill may be constituted Valuable.
by,—

(a) any consideration sufficient to support a simple contract; Sufficiency.

(b) an antecedent debt or liability; Antecedent debt.

2. Such a debt or liability is deemed valuable consideration, Form of bill.
whether the bill is payable on demand or at a future time. 53
V., c. 33, s. 27. Eng. s. 27.

"Value" in the Act means valuable consideration (sec. 2).

Consideration has been thus defined in the case of Currie v.
Misa, 1875, L.R. 10 Ex. 153, 4 R.C. 316: "A valuable consideration in the sense of the law may consist either in some right,
interest, profit or benefit, accruing to one party, or some forbearance, detriment, loss or responsibility given, suffered, or
undertaken by the other." Consideration is therefore something done, forborne, or suffered, or promised to be done, forborne, or suffered by the promisee in respect of the promise.
It must necessarily be *in respect of the promise*, since consideration gives the promise a binding force. Anson on Contracts,
8th ed. 74.

As to an accommodation party and an accommodation bill,
see sec. 55.

As to a bill or note the consideration of which consists, in
whole or in part, of the purchase money of a patent right, or
of a partial interest in such right, see secs. 14, 15 and 16.

The question whether the consideration for a bill is sufficient to support a simple contract must be determined by provincial law.

It has been held that each of the following constitutes valu- Valuable
able consideration: considera-
tion.
—a cross acceptance (Rose v. Sims, 1830, 1 B. & Ad. at p.
526);

Sec. 53.   —the compromise of a disputed liability (Cook v. Wright, 1861, 30 L.J.Q.B. 321);

—a promise to give up a bill thought to be invalid (Smith v. Smith, 1863, 13 C.B.N.S. 418);

—a debt barred by the Statute of Limitations (Latouche v. Latouche, 1865, 3 H. & C. at p. 576; Wright v. Wright, 1876, 6 P.R. 295);

—the obligation on the part of a thief to restore stolen property (London, etc., Bank v. River Plate Bank, 1888, 21 Q.B. D. 535);

—the forbearance to sue a third party for a debt (Crears v. Hunter, 1887, 19 Q.B.D. 341; Creelman v. Stewart, 1896, 28 N.S.R. 185; Dickenson v. Clemow, 1850, 7 U.C.R. 421).

Not valuable consideration.   It has been held that the following do not constitute valuable consideration:

—a mere moral obligation (Eastwood v. Kenyon, 1840, 11 A. & E. 438; cf. In re Whittaker, 1889, 42 Ch. D. 119);

—a debt represented to be due though not really due (Southall v. Rigg, 1851, 11 C.B. 481);

—the giving up of a void note (Coward v. Hughes, 1855, 1 K. & J. 443);

—a voluntary gift of money (Hill v. Wilson, 1873, L.R. 8 Ch. at p. 894);

—a debt from a third person to the payee of a note upon no consideration for forbearance to sue and upon no privity between the debtor and the maker (McGillivray v. Keefer, 1847, 4 U.C.R. 456; Ryan v. McKerrall, 1888, 15 O.R. 460);

—where A. is indebted to B., and B. to C., and A makes a note in favour of C., unless there is evidence of novation (Cossitt v. Cook, 1884, 17 N.S.R. 84).

Antecedent debt or liability.

The words "or liability" were added to the English bill in committee. They perhaps extend the law. Chalmers, p. 82.

Otherwise, sub-sec. 2 embodies the rule laid down by the majority of the Court of Exchequer Chamber in Currie v. Misa, 1875, L.R. 10 Ex. 153, 4 R.C. 316 (S.C. *sub nom.* Misa v. Currie, 1876, 1 App. Cas. 554). Prior to that case it was uncertain how far an antecedent debt constituted a sufficient consideration for an instrument payable on demand. In the case of a bill or note

payable in futuro it was said that the suspension of the credi- Sec. 53.
tor's remedies during the currency of the bill or note constituted Antecedent
valuable consideration, but that when the instrument was pay- debt or
able on demand there was no such giving of time. The Court liability.
decided that this was not a valid distinction, and that the title
of a creditor to a bill given on account of a pre-existing debt,
whether payable on demand or at a future day, does not rest
upon an implied agreement to suspend his remedies, but upon
the fact that the giving of the bill is a conditional payment of
the debt, the condition being that the debt revives if the bill is
not realized. The instrument is taken by the creditor as money's
worth and becomes his property as truly as the money which
it represents would have been his had the payment been made
in gold. The judgment of the Court of Exchequer in this case
was approved in McLean v. Clydesdale Banking Co., 1883, 9
App. Cas. 95. In the latter case, a customer, being indebted to
his bankers, got a cheque on another bank from a friend, for the
purpose of reducing his overdraft. The cheque was paid in
and credited to the customer's account. It was held that the
bankers held the cheque for value, and could recover from the
drawer, who had stopped payment at the drawee bank. (Cf.
Gordon v. London, etc., Bank, [1903] A.C. 240; Ryan v. Mc-
Kerrall, 1888, 15 O.R. 460,)

Adequacy of consideration.

The courts do not enquire into the adequacy of a *bonâ fide*
consideration, but inadequacy may be evidence of bad faith or
fraud. (Jones v. Gordon, 1877, 2 App. Cas. 616.)

As to impeachment of consideration, see notes to sec. 58.

54. Where value has, at any time, been given for a bill, the Holder for
holder is deemed to be a holder for value as regards the accep- value.
tor and all parties to the bill who became parties prior to such
time.

2. Where the holder of a bill has a lien on it, arising either In case of
from contract or by implication of law, he is deemed to be a lien.
holder for value to the extent of the sum for which he has a lien.
53 V., c. 33, s. 27. Eng. s. 27.

Holder for value.

"Holder" is defined by sec. 2, and "holder in due course" by sec. 56. The latter must take the bill for value, but a holder for value may or may not be a holder in due course. (Raphael v. Bank of England, 1855, 17 C.B. at p. 174.)

The holder of a bill who receives it from a holder for value but does not himself give value for it, has all the rights of a holder for value against all parties to the bill except the person from whom he received it. The payee of a bill who holds it for value, endorses it to D. without value, *e.g.*, by way of gift or for collection. D., as regards the drawer and acceptor, is a holder for value.

Every party whose signature appears on a bill is *primâ facie* deemed to have become a party thereto for value (sec. 58).

A holder, whether for value or not, who derives his title to a bill through a holder in due course, and who is not himself a party to any fraud or illegality affecting it, has all the rights of a holder in due course as regards the acceptor and all parties to the bill prior to that holder (sec. 57).

Chalmers (p. 84) gives the following illustrations:

1. B. owes C. $50. In order to pay C., A. at B.'s request draws a bill on B. for $50 in favour of C. C. is a holder for value and can sue A., though A has received no value. (Scott v. Lifford, 1808, 1 Camp. 246.)

2. A. draws a bill on B., payable to his own order. B., to accommodate A., accepts it. Subsequently A. gives value to B. A. is a holder for value. (Burdon v. Benton, 1847, 9 Q.B. 843.)

3. B. makes a note in favour of C. C. is the treasurer of a loan society, and the consideration for the note is money advanced by the society to B. C. is a holder for value. (Lomas v. Bradshaw, 1850, 19 L.J.C.P. 273.)

4. C., the holder of a bill, endorses it in blank to D., receiving no value. D., for value transfers it by delivery to E. E. is a holder for value. (Barber v. Richards, 1851, 6 Ex. 63.)

5. A., at the request of B., draws a bill payable to C. for B.'s account with C. B. remits the bill to C. C. is a holder for value. It is immaterial that there is no consideration between A. and B., or that the consideration fails. (Munroe v. Bordier, 1849, 8 C.B. 862; Watson v. Russell, 1862, 3 B. & S. 34; 1864, 5 B. & S. 968.)

Holder having a lien.

The person who discounts a bill is a holder for full value. The pledgee of a bill is a holder for value to the extent of the debt secured, and if he sues a third party, he sues as trustee for the pledgor, as regards the difference between the amount of the debt secured and the amount of the bill.

As to the discount of bills and the rights and liabilities of pledgees of bills, see Chapter XV., *supra.*

As to bank's lien, see notes to Bank Act, sec. 77.

C., the holder of a bill for $100, deposits it with D. as security for a running account. At the time the bill matures the balance is in C.'s favour, but subsequently the balance turns against him to the extent of $50. D. is a holder for value as to $50. (Atwood v. Crowdie, 1816, 1 Stark. 483; cf. Pease v. Hirst, 1829, 10 B. & C. 122; Gray v. Seckham, 1872, L.R. 7 Ch. at p. 683.)

C., the holder of a bill for $100 endorses it to D. as a pledge for $50. D. is a holder for value to the extent of $50, and this is the sum he can recover if he sues C. (Attenborough v. Clarke, 1858, 27 L.J. Ex. 138.)

C. keeps with his bank a loan account and a general account. C., endorses to the bank, as collateral security for his loan account, a bill for $1,000, and draws against it to the extent of $500. C. becomes bankrupt, and his general account is overdrawn more than $500. The bank is holder of the bill for full value. (In re European Bank, 1872, L.R. 8 Ch. 41.)

The drawer of a bill for $100, which has been accepted for his accommodation, endorses it to C. as security for $50. If the acceptor becomes bankrupt, C. can tender a proof for $100, but is entitled to dividends only to the extent of $50. (Ex parte Newton, 1880, 16 Ch. D. 330.)

55. An accommodation party to a bill is a person who has Accommosigned a bill as drawer, acceptor or endorser, without receiving dation bil. value therefor, and for the purpose of lending his name to some other person.

2. An accommodation party is liable on the bill to a holder Liability of for value; and it is immaterial whether, when such holder took party. the bill, he knew such party to be an accommodation party or not. 53 V., c. 33, s. 28. Eng. s. 28.

Sec. 55.

Accommo-
dation bill
and accom-
modation
parties.

An accommodation bill is a bill whereof the acceptor (*i.e.*, the principal debtor according to the terms of the instrument) is in substance a mere surety for some other person who may or may not be a party to the bill. Any other bill is not correctly spoken of as an accommodation bill, although it may be signed by one or more accommodation parties. The distinction is important in regard to the discharge of the bill. An accommodation bill is discharged when it is paid in due course by the party accommodated (sec. 139), although in form he may not be the principal debtor (cf. sec. 140). It may be discharged by the giving of time to such party. (Oriental v. Overend, 1871, L.R. 7 Ch. 142; 1874, L.R. 7 H.L. 348.)

If two or more persons endorse a bill to accommodate the acceptor, their relations inter se are those of co-sureties, and not of sureties in succession according to the order of their names on the bill (see notes to sec. 133). Cf. Bowes v. Holland, 1856, 14 U.C.R. 316.

As a general rule the drawer or endorser for whose accommodation a bill is accepted, cannot avail himself of want of due presentment for payment (sec. 92), or of notice of dishonour (secs. 108 and 109), or of protest (sec. 110), because it is his own duty to provide the funds to meet the bill at maturity. As to negotiation of an overdue accommodation bill, see notes to sec. 70.

Not only is an accommodation party liable to a holder for value, although such holder knew, when he took the bill, that such party was an accommodation party (sec. 55), but, conversely, an accommodation party, known to be such, may avail himself of any defence, arising out of the bill transaction, which the person accommodated could have set up. (Bechervaise v. Lewis, 1872, L.R. 7 C.P. 372, 377.)

"Holder for value" is defined by sec. 54.

Every party whose signature appears on a bill is *primâ facie* deemed to have become a party thereto for value (sec. 58). See notes to that section as to the cases in which evidence may be given to impeach the value.

G., agrees to lend M. $100, provided M. will make a note for the amount in G.'s favour and procure W. to endorse the note as surety for the payment thereof to G. In pursuance of the agreement M. made a note in G.'s favour, G. endorsed to W., and W. endorsed to G. for M.'s accommodation. The fact

Sec. 55.

Accommo-
dation bill
and accom-
modation
parties.

that W. is surety for the payment of the note to G., negatives G.'s liability upon his previous endorsement to W., and W. may be sued on his endorsement by G. (Gunn v. McPherson, 1859, 18 U.C.R. 244; cf. Wilders v. Stevens, 1846, 15 M. & W. 208, and notes to sec. 73.)

As to G.'s right to sue W., if W. had endorsed before the endorsement by G. (the payee), see notes to sec. 131.

Action by holder of a note payable to bearer against the maker. Plea that the defendant made the note for the accommodation of C.D. and that there never was any consideration or value for the payment by the defendant of the note, and that the plaintiff holds the same without any value or consideration. Held bad, on demurrer, for the plea does not shew that there was not valid consideration as between C. D. and the plaintiff or shew facts which would disable the plaintiff from suing. (Muir v. Cameron, 1853, 10 U.C.R. 356.)

Accommodation bill and accommodation parties.

Bill drawn, endorsed and accepted for the accommodation of D., who is not a party thereto. The drawer and acceptor receive a commission for becoming parties. This is an accommodation bill. (Oriental v. Overend, 1871, L.R. 7 Ch. 142.)

Bill accepted for the accommodation of the drawer. This is an accommodation bill, and the acceptor is an accommodation acceptor. (Collott v. Haigh, 1812, 3 Camp. 281.)

Bill drawn payable to the order of C. and accepted. The acceptor was indebted to C., but the drawer signed to accommodate the acceptor. This is not an accommodation bill, though the drawer is an accommodation drawer. (Scott v. Lifford, 1808, 1 Camp. 246; cf. Sleigh v. Sleigh, 1850, 5 Ex. 514.)

Bill drawn against a running account, and accepted. This, it seems, is not an accommodation bill, though the account may have been against the drawer when the bill was drawn, or accepted, or payable. (In re Overend, Ex parte Swan, 1868, L. R. 6 Eq. at p. 356; cf. Wilks v. Hornby, 1862, 10 W.R. 742; Chalmers, p. 88.)

56. A holder in due course is a holder who has taken a bill, Holder in complete and regular on the face of it, under the following con- due course. ditions, namely:—

Sec. 56.   (a) That he became the holder of it before it was overdue
Notice.   and without notice that it had been previously dishonoured,
                   if such was the fact;

Good faith.   (b) That he took the bill in good faith and for value, and
                   that at the time the bill was negotiated to him he had no
                   notice of any defect in the title of the person who nego-
                   tiated it.

Title defec-   2. In particular the title of a person who negotiates a bill is
tive.
defective within the meaning of this Act when he obtained the
bill, or the acceptance thereof, by fraud, duress or force and
fear, or other unlawful means, or for an illegal consideration,
ɩr when he negotiates it in breach of faith, or under such circumstances as amount to a fraud. 53 V., c. 33, s. 29. Eng. s. 29.

"Holder" means the payee or endorsee of a bill or note
who is in possession of it (sec. 2). "Bearer" is defined by sec.
2. The rights and powers of a holder are defined by sec. 74. As
to negotiation, see secs. 60, *et seq.*, and as to overdue or dishonoured bills, see secs. 70, *et seq.*

Holder in   The Act has substituted "holder in due course" for "*bonâ
due course.
fide* holder for value without notice." The French version substitutes "*détenteur régulier*" for the old expression "*tiers por-
teur de bonne foi.*"

Good faith and value.

A thing is deemed to be done in good faith within the meaning of the Act, where it is in fact done honestly whether it is
done negligently or not (sec. 3).

Value means valuable consideration (sec. 2). The latter is
defined by sec. 53. As to "holder for value," see sec. 54.

There is a *primâ facie* presumption that value has been
given by a party to a bill (sec. 58).

Every holder of a bill is *primâ facie* deemed to be a holder
in due course, but if in an action on a bill it is admitted or proved
that the acceptance, issue or subsequent negotiation of the bill
is affected with fraud, duress or force and fear, or illegality,
the burden of proof that he is a holder in due course is on him,
unless and until he proves that subsequent to the alleged fraud

or illegality, value has in good faith been given for the bill by some other holder in due course (sec. 58).

Notice.

Notice means actual, though not formal notice, that is to say, either knowledge of the facts, or a suspicion of something wrong, combined with a wilful disregard of the means of knowledge (Raphael v. Bank of England, 1855, 17 C.B. at p. 174; cf. Ex parte Snowball, 1872, L.R. 7 Ch. at p. 549). As to notice of suspicious circumstances, cf. Swaisland v. Davidson, 1883, 3 O.R. 320; Reinhardt v. Shirley, 1894, Q.R. 6 S.C. 11.

As regards the parties affected with notice, the ordinary rules of law apply to bills and notes. Notice to the principal is notice to the agent; and notice to the agent is notice to the principal (cf. Collinson v. Lister, 1855, 7 De G. M. & G. at p. 637, branch bank), subject to the proviso (1) that when the agent is himself a party to the fraud he is not to be taken to have disclosed it to his principal (Ex parte Oriental Bank, 1870, L. R. 5 Ch. 358; Commercial Bank v. Morrison, 1902, 32 S.C.R. 98); and (2) where a bill is negotiated to an agent, and notice is given to the principal, or *vice versa*, there must be a reasonable time for communication. (Cf. Willis v. Bank of England, 1835, 4 A. & E. at p. 39.)

Complete and regular on the face of it.

If the bill itself contains a warning, *caveat emptor*. The holder, however honest, can acquire no better title than the person from whom he took it had. Thus, if the holder takes a blank acceptance, or a bill wanting in any material particular, he takes it at his peril (Awde v. Dixon, 1851, 6 Ex. 869; cf. notes to sec. 32, *supra*); so also if the holder takes a bill which has been torn and the pieces of which have been pasted together, if the tears appear to shew an intention to cancel it. (Ingham v. Primrose, 1859, 7 C.B.N.S. 82; Chalmers, p. 92.)

Holder in due course.

Quære, whether the payee of a bill, being one of the immediate parties and not a person to whom the bill is "negotiated," can ever be a holder in due course; but see sec. 2 which defines "holder" as including "payee." (Herdman v. Wheeler, [1902] 1 K.B. at pp. 367, 371-2.)

Sec. 56.

Holder in
due course.

A holder, whether for value or not, who derives his title to a bill through a holder in due course, and who is not himself a party to any fraud or illegality affecting it, has all the rights of that holder in due course as regards the acceptor and all parties to the bill prior to that holder (sec. 57).

C., the holder of a bill payable to his order, transfers it to D. for value but without endorsing it. C. has obtained this bill by fraud, but D. has no notice of this. D. is not a holder in due course. (Whistler v. Forster, 1863, 14 C.B.N.S. at p. 258; D. is not the holder as defined by sec. 2, until he obtains C.'s endorsement; cf. Jenkins v. Coomber, [1898] 2 Q.B. 168, cited in notes to sec. 131.)

C., who resides abroad, transmits a bill for collection to his agent in England. C. has obtained this bill by fraud, but his agent does not know it. At the time the agent receives the bill, C. is indebted to him on the balance of account. The agent is not a holder in due course and cannot recover on the bill. *Aliter*, if the bill had been transmitted to the agent in payment of his debt. (De la Chaumette v. Bank of England, 1829, 9 B. & C. 208, as explained by Currie v. Misa, 1875, L.R. 10 Ex. at p. 164; and McLean v. Clydesdale Bank, 1883, 9 App. Cas. at p. 114.)

C. endorses a bill to D. for value. D. suspects that C. stole the bill. As a fact he obtained it by false pretences. D. is not a holder in due course. (Cf. Jones v. Gordon, 1877, 2 App. Cas. at p. 628.)

The manager of a bank steals negotiable securities from the bank, and pledges them with C. He afterwards obtains them back from C. by a fraud, and replaces them in the bank. The bank knows nothing of the transactions. The bank is the holder in due course of these securities, and is entitled to retain them against C. (London & County Bank v. River Plate Bank, 1888, 21 Q.B.D. 535; cf. London Bank v. Simmons, [1892] A.C. 201.)

D., by false pretences, induces A. to draw a cheque in favour of C., who takes it in good faith and for value. C. is a holder in due course. (Watson v. Russell, 1862, 3 B. & S. 34.)

Defective title.

The list of defects in sub-sec. 2 may not be exhaustive.

The words "force and fear" were inserted in the English bill in committee as the equivalent of the English technical term duress, which is unknown to Scotch law. Chalmers, p. 93.

A person whose title is defective must be distinguished from a person who has no title at all, and can give none, as, for in- stance, a person making title through a forged or unauthorized endorsement (sec. 49).

The ordinary rules of the law of contract in the province where the transaction takes place determine what constitutes fraud, duress, etc: cf. notes to sec. 10 as to the application of provincial law to cases relating to bills and notes. As to conflict of laws, see Chapter L., *infra*.

The Act (secs. 56 and 57) provides only as to the extent to which fraud or illegality, which may be a defence as between the immediate parties, shall affect other parties.

57. A holder, whether for value or not, who derives his title to a bill through a holder in due course, and who is not himself a party to any fraud or illegality affecting it, has all the rights of that holder in due course as regards the acceptor and all parties to the bill prior to that holder. 53 V., c. 33, s. 29. Eng. s. 29.

See sec. 54 as to a holder for value.

As to a holder in due course, see secs. 56 and 58.

A partner in a firm fraudulently endorses a firm bill to D. in payment of a private debt. F. is cognizant of the fraud, but is not a party to it. D. endorses the bill to E., who takes it for value and without notice. E. endorses it to F. F. acquires E.'s rights. If he gave value to E., he can sue all the parties to the bill; if he did not give value, he can sue all parties except E. (May v. Chapman, 1847, 16 M. & W. 355; cf. Wallbridge v. Becket, 1855, 13 U.C.R. 395; Clarkson v. Lawson, 1856, 14 U. C.R. 67; Gauthier v. Reinhardt, 1904, Q.R. 26 S.C. 134.)

C., by fraud, induces B. to make a note in his favour. C. endorses the note to D., who takes it for value and without notice. Subsequently D. endorses the note for value back to C. C. cannot sue B. (Cf. Sawyer v. Wisewell, 1864, 91 Mass. at p. 42.)

58. Every party whose signature appears on a bill is *prima* *facie* deemed to have become a party thereto for value.

2. Every holder of a bill is *prima facie* deemed to be a holder in due course; but if, in an action on a bill it is admitted or proved that the acceptance, issue or subsequent negotiation of the bill is affected with fraud, duress or force and fear, or illegality, the burden of proof that he is such holder in due course shall be on him, unless and until he proves that, subsequent to the alleged fraud or illegality, value has in good faith been given for the bill by some other holder in due course. 53 V., c. 33, s. 30. Eng. s. 30.

As to a holder for value, see notes to sec. 54.

As to a holder in due course, see sec. 56.

As to fraud, etc., as between the immediate parties, see sec. 56, sub-sec. 2.

The rule expressed in secs. 57 and 58 embodies the effect of the case of Jones v. Gordon, 1877, 2 App. Cas. 616, 627, 4 R. C. 415, 452, and particularly Lord Blackburn's judgment.

Before the passing of the Act, it was uncertain how much the plaintiff had to prove when evidence of fraud had been given, *i.e.*, whether the onus was shifted only to the extent of making it necessary for the plaintiff to prove that value was in fact given, or whether he also had to prove that it was given in good faith. Lord Blackburn in Jones v. Gordon, *supra*, says: "The language of the quotation from Mr. Baron Parke would seem to shew that the onus as to both is shifted, but I do not think that has ever been decided, nor do I think it is necessary to decide it in the present case."

The Act has settled the law in accordance with the opinion expressed by Parke, B. A holder in due course must have taken the bill in good faith and for value and without notice of any defect in the title of the person who negotiated it (sec. 56). A holder is presumed to be a holder in due course until fraud, etc., is proved, but when that is proved, then the onus is shifted to the holder to prove that he is a holder in due course. He must prove not only that value has been given but that it has been given in good faith without notice of the fraud, etc. (Tatam v. Haslar, 1889, 23 Q.B.D. 345; cf. Gibson v. Coates, 1905, 1 West. L.R. 556.)

As to value, see sec. 53, and as to good faith, see sec. 3.

As to the rights of a holder, whether for value or not, who derives his title through a holder in due course, see sec. 57.

The words "if it is admitted or proved" mean no more than that some evidence in the nature of fraud must be given sufficient to be left to the jury (Tatam v. Haslar, *supra*). An affidavit by a defendant on a motion for summary judgment shewing facts affecting the note sued on with fraud is a sufficient answer to the motion, notwithstanding the plaintiff's affidavit that he is a holder in due course. (Farmer v. Ellis, 1901, 2 O.L.R. 544; cf. Flour City Bank v. Connery, 1898, 12 Man. R. 305.)

A. draws a bill on B., and endorses it to C. C. sues B. It is shewn that B. accepted it for A.'s accommodation. C. is not called on to prove that he gave value; he can recover without doing so. (Mills v. Barber, 1836, 1 M. & W. 425; cf. Mair v. McLean, 1841, 1 U.C.R. 455; Farmers' Bank v. Dominion Coal Co., 1893, 9 Man. R. 542.)

B. makes a note payable to C. C. endorses it to D., who sues B. If it appears that B. made the note for an illegal consideration, D., must prove that he gave value in good faith. (Bailey v. Bidwell, 1844, 13 M. & W. 73.) But if the consideration was merely void and not illegal, D. is not called upon to prove that he gave value. (Fitch v. Jones, 1855, 5 E. & B. 238; Belfast v. Doherty, 1879, 4 Ir. L.R. 124.)

The holder of a bill endorses it to D. to get it discounted. D. fraudulently negotiates it to E., who negotiates it to F. F. sues the acceptor. Evidence is given of D.'s fraud. F. must prove that he is an honest holder for value. (Cf. Smith v. Braine, 1851, 16 Q.B. 244; Berry v. Alderman, 1853, 14 C.B. 95; Tatam v. Haslar, 1889, 23 Q.B.D. 535.)

Action against the maker of a note payable to bearer. It is shewn to have been stolen from the true owner. It lies on the holder to prove that he gave value in good faith. (Raphael v. Bank of England, 1855, 17 C.B. 161.)

An acceptance is given in renewal of a bill which turns out to be a forgery. The genuine bill is negotiated, and the holder sues the acceptor. Evidence is given of these facts. It lies on the holder to prove that he is an honest holder for value. (Mather v. Maidstone, 1856, 18 C.B. 273.)

A partner accepts a bill in the firm's name for a private debt and in fraud of his co-partners. The bill is negotiated. The

Sec. 58.
Onus of proving value and good faith.

holder sues the firm as acceptors. As soon as it appears that
the bill was given for a private debt, the holder is called upon
to prove that he is an honest holder for value. (Hogg v. Skeen,
1865, 18 C.B.N.S. 426.)

Impeachment of value.

Every party whose signature appears on a bill is *primâ facie*
deemed to have become a party thereto for value (sec. 58), but
oral evidence may be given of absence of consideration, or its
failure, total or partial, or of fraud or illegality of consideration. Cf. Chalmers, pp. 96, *et seq.,* where the rules as to impeachment of consideration are stated (in part) as follows:

Mere absence of consideration, total or partial, is matter of
defence against an immediate party, or a remote party who is
not a holder for value, but it is not a defence against a remote
party who is a holder for value. (Cf. Forman v. Wright, 1851,
11 C.B. at p. 492.) See also secs 54, 55 and 57.

Total failure of consideration is a defence against an immediate party (Bullion v. Cartwright, 1905, 10 O.L.R. 438), but
it is not a defence against a remote party who is a holder in
due course. (Robinson v. Reynolds, 1841, 2 Q.B. at p. 211; as
to what amounts to total failure, see Wells v. Hopkins, 1839, 5
M. & W. 7; Hooper v. Treffry, 1847, 1 Ex. 17; Goldie v. Harper,
1899, 31 O.R. 284.)

Partial failure of consideration is a defence *pro tanto* against
an immediate party when the failure is an ascertained and liquidated amount, but not otherwise. (Day v. Nix, 1824, 9 Moore
159; Warwick v. Nairn, 1855, 10 Ex. 762; Goldie v. Harper,
supra; O'Donohue v. Swain, 1887, 4 Man. R. 476; Home Life v.
Walsh, 1903, 36 N.S.R. 73; Agra Bank v. Leighton, 1866, L.R.
2 Ex. at pp. 64-5; cf. McGregor v. Bishop, 1887, 14 O.R. 7.) It
is not a defence against a remote party who is a holder for value.
(Archer v. Bamford, 1822, 3 Stark. 175.) The rule as to partial failure of consideration is, however, largely a matter of
pleading, and, as against an immediate party, if such failure
is not a defence, it can under modern rules of practice usually
be set up by way of counterclaim. Cf. Maclaren on Bills, etc.,
3rd ed. 168-9.

Fraud is a defence against an immediate party and against
a remote party who is not a holder in due course. (Whistler v.
Forster, 1863, 14 C.B.N.S. at p. 258; cf. sec. 58.)

Illegality of consideration, total or partial, is a defence against an immediate party, but not against a holder in due course. (Hay v. Ayling 1851, 16 Q.B. at p. 431; Leggatt v. Brown, 1899, 30 O.R. 225; cf. Laprès v. Massé, 1901, Q.R. 19 S.C. 275, where a note, part of the consideration for which was illegal, was held good in part; Bellemare v. Gray, 1899, Q.R. 16 S.C. 581.)

When a bill is given for a consideration which a statute expressly declares shall make the bill void, the bill is, as against the party who gave it, void in the hands of all parties whether immediate or remote. (Edwards v. Dick, 1821, 4 B. & Ald, 212; Shillito v. Theed, 1831, 7 Bing. 405.)

Cf. next section, as to a bill given for a usurious consideration or upon a usurious contract.

59. No bill, although given for a usurious consideration or upon a usurious contract, is void in the hands of a holder, unless such holder had at the time of its transfer to him actual knowledge that it was originally given for a usurious consideration, or upon a usurious contract. 53 V., c. 33, s. 30.

There is no corresponding section in the English Act. The section is practically obsolete, as there is no usury law in force in Canada. See notes to the Bank Act, secs. 91 and 92.

The protection of the section is not limited to a holder in due course or a holder for value, the sole condition being that the holder shall not have actual knowledge, etc.

CHAPTER XL.

NEGOTIATION.

Two points must be carefully noted in regard to the negotiation of bills.

Two meanings of negotiable.
1. Every bill which does not contain words prohibiting transfer or indicating an intention that it should not be transferable (sec. 21) is negotiable in the sense that it is subject to negotiation, negotiation being the appropriate transfer by delivery or by endorsement and delivery (sec. 60). A bill negotiable in its origin continues to be negotiable until it has been (*a*) restrictively endorsed, or (*b*) discharged by payment or otherwise (sec. 69). But negotiability in this sense must be distinguished from the quality of negotiability which confers upon a holder in due course (sec. 56) a good title to payment according to the tenor of the bill and irrespective of defects in the title of the transferor. Negotiation in the one sense may take place under the Act even where the bill is overdue (sec. 70) or otherwise under circumstances which deprive the bill of the quality of negotiability in the other sense. See Chapter XXX., *supra,* where the meaning of negotiability is discussed.

Negotiation distinguished from transmission or transfer by assignment.
2. The Act deals only with transfer by negotiation, that is, transfer according to the law merchant. It leaves untouched (1) the rules of general law which regulate the transmission of bills by act of law, and (2) their transfer as *choses in action,* or chattels according to the general law.

The transmission and transfer of bills, otherwise than by negotiation under the Act, are regulated by the appropriate provincial law. See, *e.g.,* McCorkill v. Barrabe, 1885, M.L.R. 1 S.C. 319, in which it was held that a non-negotiable note specially endorsed by the payee and transferred to a third party might be sued on by the latter in his own name, after signification of the transfer is duly served upon the maker in accordance with Quebec law.

Willes, J., in Whistler v. Forster, 1863, 14 C.B.N.S. at p. 164, 4 R.C. at p. 334, says: "The general rule of law is undoubted that no one can transfer a better title than he himself possesses,—*nemo dat quod non habet.* To this there are some

exceptions, one of which arises out of the rule of the law mer- Sec. 60.
chant as to negotiable instruments. If such an instrument be Negotiation
transferred in good faith for value before it is overdue, it be- by the law
comes available in the hands of the holder, notwithstanding merchant.
fraud, which would have rendered it unavailable in the hands
of a previous holder. This rule, however, is only intended to
favour transfers in the ordinary and usual manner whereby a
title is acquired according to the law merchant, and not a
transfer which is valid in equity according to the doctrine respecting the assignment of *choses in action,* now, indeed, recognized and in many instances enforced by courts of law; and it
is therefore clear that in order to acquire the benefit of this rule
the holder of the bill must, if it be payable to order, obtain an
indorsement, and that he is affected by notice of a fraud received before he does so. Until he does so, he is merely in the
position of the assignee of an ordinary *chose in action,* and has
no better right than his assignor; when he does so he is affected
by fraud which he heard of before the indorsement.''

Negotiation.

60. A bill is negotiated when it is transferred from one By transfer.
person to another in such a manner as to constitute the transferee the holder of the bill.

2. A bill payable to bearer is negotiated by delivery. By delivery.

3. A bill payable to order is negotiated by the endorsement By endorse-
of the holder completed by delivery. 53 V., c. 33, s. 31. Eng. ment.
s. 31.

As to ''holder,'' see sec. 2.
As to ''bearer,'' see sec. 2. A bill is payable to bearer which
is expressed to be so payable, or on which the only or last endorsement is an endorsement in blank (sec. 21).
As to ''delivery,'' see secs. 2, 40, and 41.
As to ''endorsement,'' see secs. 62, *et seq.*
A bill is payable to order which is expressed to be so payable,
or which is expressed to be payable to a particular person, and
does not contain words prohibiting transfer or indicating an
intention that it should not be transferable (sec. 22).

Sec. 60.   This section deals only with negotiation by the law merchant, see notes, *supra*.

The delivery of a bill to the payee is the issue (cf. sec. 2), not the negotiation, of the bill. See Herdman v. Wheeler, [1902] 1 K.B. 361, and notes to sec. 32, *supra*, pp. 400, 401.

Without endorsement.   **61.** Where the holder of a bill payable to his order transfers it for value without endorsing it, the transfer gives the transferee such title as the transferrer had in the bill, and the transferee in addition acquires the right to have the endorsement of the transferrer.

Representative capacity.   2. Where any person is under obligation to endorse a bill in a representative capacity, he may endorse the bill in such terms as to negative personal liability. 53 V., c. 33, s. 31. Eng. s. 31.

The holder without endorsement of a bill payable to order, though taken by him in good faith and for value, has no better title than the person from whom he took it; and such holder is affected by fraud, of which he has notice before he obtains the formal endorsement. (Whistler v. Forster, 1863, 14 C.B.N.S. 248, 4 R.C. 332; such a bill is not negotiated (sec. 60) until the endorsement is made.)

A., the payee of a bill payable to order, transfers it to B. for value without endorsing. B. can compel A. to endorse, but he has no authority to endorse in A.'s name, and until he gets A.'s endorsement he cannot sue the acceptor in his own name or negotiate the bill to another person. (Harrop v. Fisher, 1861, 10 C.B.N.S. 196, 203; 4 R.C. 338, 342.)

If A., in the last case, dies before endorsing, the court will compel his executor or administrator to endorse, but the representative may endorse in such terms as to negative personal liability. (Cf. Watkins v. Maule, 1820, 2 Jac. & W. 243.) If B. returns the bill to A., for his endorsement, and A. destroys it, B. cannot sue the acceptor. (Edge v. Bumford, 1862, 31 L. J. Ch. 805.)

Negative personal liability.

The drawer of a bill and any endorser may insert therein an express stipulation negativing or limiting his own liability to

the holder (sec. 34). It is not sufficient, in order to avoid per- Sec. 61.
sonal liability, merely to add words to the signature describing the person who signs as filling a representative character
(sec. 52).

62. An endorsement in order to operate as a negotiation,— Endorsing.
(a) must be written on the bill itself and be signed by the Writing.
    endorser;
(b) must be an endorsement of the entire bill.   Entire bill.

2. An endorsement written on an allonge, or on a *copy* of Allonge.
a bill issued or negotiated in a country where *copies* are recognized, is deemed to be written on the bill itself.

3. A partial endorsement, that is to say, an endorsement Partial en-
which purports to transfer to the endorsee a part only of the dorsement.
amount payable, or which purports to transfer the bill to two
or more endorsees severally, does not operate as a negotiation
of the bill. 53 V., c. 33, s. 32. Eng. s. 32.

See also sec. 63. The provisions of secs. 62 and 63 were contained in one section prior to 1906. In the revision of that
year their internal arrangement was considerably altered.

As to the meaning of "written," cf. notes to secs. 2 and 17.

An endorsement means an endorsement completed by delivery (sec. 2). As to delivery, see secs. 40 and 41.

It is sufficient if the signature of the endorser is written by
some other person by or under his authority (sec. 4).

As to endorsement of bills in a set, see sec. 159.

An endorsement is usually made on the back of a bill, but
it may be validly made on the face of it (Young v. Glover, 1857,
3 Jur. N.S.Q.B. 637; Ex parte Yates, 1858, 2 DeG. & J. 191.)

But the assignment of a bill by a separate writing (Re Barrington, 1804, 2 Scho. & Lef. 112, 9 R.R. 61) or an express promise in writing to endorse a bill (cf. Harrop v. Fisher, 1861,
10 C.B.N.S. at p. 204, 4 R.C. at p. 342) is not an endorsement.

A signed memorandum on a bill "I hereby assign this draft
and all benefit of the money secured thereby to D." is a valid
endorsement. (Richards v. Frankum, 1840, 9 C. & P. at p. 225.)

Where there is no room on a bill for further endorsements,
a slip of paper, called an allonge, may be attached thereto. It

30—BANK ACT.

Sec. 62.

Requisites of endorsement.

becomes part of the bill, and endorsements may be written thereon. Some of the foreign codes contain minute provisions to prevent frauds, *e.g.*, that the first endorsement on the allonge must begin on the bill and end on the allonge; otherwise an allonge might be taken from one bill and stuck on to another. Chalmers, pp. 108-109.

"Copies" of bills are not used in England, Canada or the United States; but on the continent of Europe, where the practice of drawing bills in sets is not followed, copies are sometimes used for convenience of transfer while the original is being forwarded for acceptance. Maclaren on Bills, etc., 3rd ed. 203.

Partial endorsement.

C., the holder of a bill for $100, signs a memorandum on the back "Pay $50 to D. or order, and $50 to E. or order." This is not a valid endorsement, and neither D. nor E. can sue on the bill or further endorse it, but the memorandum although invalid as a negotiation may operate as an authority to receive payment of the amounts thereby specified. (Cf. Heilbut v. Nevill, 1869, L.R. 4 C.P. at p. 358; Conova v. Earl, 1868, 26 Iowa 169; Chalmers, p. 109.)

C., the holder of a bill for $100, endorses it "Pay D. or order, $30." This is invalid, unless C. also acknowledges the receipt of $70. (Hawkins v. Cardy, 1699, 1 Ld. Raym. 360.)

Signature sufficient.

63. The simple signature of the endorser on the bill, without additional words, is a sufficient endorsement.

Two or more payees.

2. Where a bill is payable to the order of two or more payees or endorsees who are not partners, all must endorse, unless the one endorsing has authority to endorse for the others. 53 V., c. 33, s. 32. Eng. s. 32.

See notes to sec. 62.

A bill payable to the order of C. and D. is endorsed by D. alone to E. E. cannot sue the acceptor. (Carvick v. Vickery, 1781, 2 Dougl. 652; cf. Heilbut v. Nevill, 1869, L.R. 4 C.P. at pp. 356, 358.)

A bill payable to the order of C. and D. is endorsed by C., with D.'s authority, " for self and D." This is a good endorsement by C., but, *quære*, as to D.'s liability. Chalmers, p. 110.

A bill payable to "C. and D., or the order of either of them" is endorsed by C. alone. C. is liable (Watson v. Evans, 1863, 32 L.J. Ex. 137). D. is not liable even though he has authorized C. to endorse, if C. has not in fact endorsed D.'s name.

Sec. 63.

If two or more payees or endorsees are partners, the signature of the name of the firm is equivalent to the signature by the person signing of the names of all persons liable as partners in that firm (sec. 132).

As to dividend warrants, see notes to sec. 7.

64. Where, in a bill payable to order, the payee or endorsee is wrongly designated, or his name is misspelt, he may endorse the bill as therein described, adding his proper signature; or he may endorse by his own proper signature. 53 V., c. 33, s. 32. Eng. s. 32.

Misspelling payee's name.

Where a bill is not payable to bearer, the payee must be named or otherwise indicated therein with reasonable certainty (sec. 21).

The English Act has the words "if he thinks fit" after the word "adding": cf. sec. 35.

A bill is endorsed to J. Smythe. The endorsee's real name is T. Smith. He can, under the English Act, validly negotiate the bill by endorsing it as J. Smythe. (Cf. Willis v. Barrett, 1816, 2 Stark. 29; *sed quære* under the Canadian Act.)

The usual and proper course is for the payee to sign first the name as described or spelt in the bill, and then to put underneath his proper signature.

A bill payable to Mrs. John Jones, should be endorsed "Ellen Jones, wife of John Jones." Chalmers, p. 111. The more usual, and a perfectly valid form, in such a case is for the payee to sign "Mrs. John Jones," adding underneath "Ellen Jones." The signature "Mrs. John Jones" alone is clearly irregular, and probably invalid.

A bill payable to Brown & Co. is endorsed in his individual name by John Smith who carries on business as Brown & Co. The endorsement is irregular, but probably valid. (Cf. Bryant v. Eastman, 1851, 61 Mass. 111; Walker v. Macdonald, 1848, 2 527; Chalmers, p. 110.)

Sec. 64.
Payee
wrongly
designated
or name
misspelt.

See also the Conventions and Rules respecting Endorsements (printed in the notes to sec. 68, *infra*), which may be usefully consulted, as indicating correct and convenient commercial practice.

Presumption as to order of endorsement.

65. Where there are two or more endorsements on a bill, each endorsement is deemed to have been made in the order in which it appears on the bill, until the contrary is proved. 53 V., c. 33, s. 32. Eng. s. 32.

The endorser of a bill by endorsing it engages that if it be dishonoured he will compensate the holder or a subsequent endorser who is compelled to pay it, provided that the requisite proceedings on dishonour be duly taken (sec. 133).

The order in which the endorsements appear on the bill may be shewn to be different from the order in which they were in fact made. The *primâ facie* presumption of the liability of prior endorser to subsequent endorser may be rebutted by circumstances shewing the real intention and agreement of the parties. (Macdonald v. Whitfield, 1883, 8 App. Cas. 530; and see notes to sec. 133.)

Disregarding condition.

66. Where a bill purports to be endorsed conditionally, the condition may be disregarded by the payer, and payment to the endorsee is valid, whether the condition has been fulfilled or not. 53 V., c. 33, s. 33. Eng. s. 33.

Cf. notes to sec. 17 ("unconditional" order). An acceptance may be conditional (sec. 38), although a bill must be drawn unconditionally.

This section alters the common law rule. Formerly the acceptor of a bill which had been endorsed conditionally paid the endorsee at his peril if the condition was not fulfilled (Robertson v. Kensington, 1811, 4 Taunt. 30). As between the endorser and endorsee the condition is binding (Commercial Bank v. Morrison, 1902, 32 S.C.R. 98), and in the event of payment to the endorsee, the endorser is entitled to recover the proceeds paid to the endorsee, if the condition is not fulfilled.

Cf. sec. 68 as to restrictive endorsements.

67. An endorsement may be made in blank or special. Sec. 67.

2. An endorsement in blank specifies no endorsee, and a bill Endorse-ment in blank.
so endorsed becomes payable to bearer.

3. A special endorsement specifies the person to whom, or Special en-dorsement.
to whose order, the bill is to be payable.

4. The provisions of this Act relating to a payee apply, with Application of Act to.
the necessary modifications, to an endorsee under a special endorsement.

5. Where a bill has been endorsed in blank, any holder may Conversion of blank en-dorsement.
convert the blank endorsement into a special endorsement by
writing above the endorser's signature a direction to pay the
bill to or to the order of himself or some other person. 53 V., c.
33, ss. 32 and 34. Eng. ss. 32 and 34.

Prior to 1906 sub-sec. 1 of this section, sub-sec. 1 of sec. 68,
and secs. 62, 63, 64, and 65 all formed one section.

Endorsement in blank.

Bill payable to the order of John Smith. He signs "John
Smith" on the back. This Act is interpreted by the law merchant as an endorsement in blank by John Smith, and operates
as if he had written: (1) I hereby assign this bill to bearer.
(2) I hereby undertake that if this bill be dishonoured, I, on
receiving due notice thereof, will indemnity the bearer. Chalmers, p. 112.

A bill payable to bearer is negotiated by delivery (sec. 60).

Special endorsement.

An endorsement "Pay to D." or "Pay to the order of D."
is equivalent to "Pay to D. or order" (sec. 22). A bill endorsed
in any of these ways is specially endorsed, and is negotiated by
the endorsement of the payee completed by delivery (sec. 60).

Before the Act an endorsement "Pay to D." meant "Pay
to D. or order" (Edie v. East India Co., 1761, 2 Burr. 1216, 4
R.C. 344), but a bill originally payable to D. could not be further negotiated by D. (see notes to sec. 22).

A special endorsement following an endorsement in blank
controls the effect of the endorsement in blank (sec. 21).

Sec. 67.   *Provisions relating to a payee.*
See secs. 19, 21 and 22.

Conversion of blank into special endorsement.

The holder of a bill endorsed by C. in blank, writes over C.'s signature the words "Pay to the order of D." The holder who does this is not liable as an endorser, but the transaction operates as a special endorsement from C. to D. (Vincent v. Horlock, 1808, 1 Camp. 442, 10 R.R. 724.)

If the holder has already converted the blank endorsement into a special one by writing a direction to pay to his own order over C.'s signature, and he desires to transfer the bill to D., without being liable as an endorser, the ordinary and proper method of doing so is for him to endorse the bill himself "without recourse." It has been held, however, that such holder may with D.'s consent, strike out his own as payee and substitute D.'s name as payee, and by this act and delivery to D., constitute E. a holder in due course (Sovereign Bank v. Gordon, 1905, 9 O.L.R. 146). This was a judgment of a divisional court on appeal from a county court, and under the Ontario practice no further appeal could be taken. The court was not unanimous, and the cases cited are conflicting. This rough and ready method of transferring a bill should therefore never be adopted. It need hardly be stated that the case is no authority for the proposition that if C., who transferred the bill to the holder in question, had endorsed the bill specially to such holder, the holder would have had any right to strike out his own name and substitute D.'s name as payee. The majority of the court held merely that the holder having converted the blank endorsement into a special one might subsequently, while he was still the holder, restore the endorsement to its original condition, and then convert it into a special endorsement by making the bill payable to D.

Striking out endorsements.

The holder may at any time (Mayer v. Jadis, 1833, 1 M. & Rob. 247) strike out any endorsement which is not necessary to his title, *e.g.,* intermediate endorsements in blank. (Cf. Barthe v. Armstrong, 1869, 5 R.L. 213, 25 R.J.R.Q. 130; Fairclough v. Pavia, 1854, 9 Ex. at p. 695; Bartlett v. Benson, 1845, 14 M. &

W. 733.) The endorser, whose endorsement is intentionally struck out, and all endorsers subsequent to him, are discharged from their liabilities. (Wilkinson v. Johnson, 1824, 3 B. & C. 428.)

The owner of a bill may strike out endorsements for collection. If the endorser of a bill takes it up or pays it when dishonoured, he may strike out his own and all subsequent endorsements, whether blank or special, and he is remitted to his original rights against the acceptor and antecedent parties, and may re-issue the bill though overdue. The fact that he is in possession of the bill is *primâ facie* evidence that he is the owner. (Callow v. Lawrence, 1814, 3 M. & S. 95; Black v. Strickland, 1883, 3 O.R. 217; cf. sec. 140.)

68. An endorsement may also contain terms making it restrictive.

2. An endorsement is restrictive which prohibits the further negotiation of the bill, or which expresses that it is a mere authority to deal with the bill as thereby directed, and not a transfer of the ownership thereof, as, for example, if a bill is endorsed 'Pay D only,' or 'Pay D for the account of X,' or 'Pay D, or order, for collection.'

3. A restrictive endorsement gives the endorsee the right to receive payment of the bill and to sue any party thereto that his endorser could have sued, but gives him no power to transfer his rights as endorsee unless it expressly authorizes him to do so.

4. Where a restrictive endorsement authorizes further transfer, all subsequent endorsees take the bill with the same rights and subject to the same liabilities as the first endorsee under the restrictive endorsement. 53 V., c. 33, ss. 32 and 35. Eng. ss. 32 and 35.

Prior to 1906, sub-sec. 1 was not part of this section: see notes to sec. 67.

Restrictive endorsement.

The following endorsements are restrictive:

1. Pay D. or order for the use of E. (Evans v. Cramlington, 1687, 1 Show. 4; 2 Show. 509.)

2. The within must be credited to D., value in account (Archer v. Bank of England, 1781, 2 Dougl. 637.)

3. Pay the contents to my use, or Pay the contents to the use of C., or Carry this bill to the credit of C. (Cf. Rice v. Stearns, 1807, 3 Mass. at p. 226.)

The object of a restrictive endorsement is to prevent the money received in respect of the bill from being applied to the use of any person other than the person specified: to whomsoever the money may be paid, it will be paid in trust for such person, and into whose hands soever the bill travels, it carries that trust on the face of it. (Cf. Lloyd v. Sigourney, 1828, 5 Bing. at p. 531, 4 R.C. at p. 361.)

Although a restrictive endorsement may be notice that no valuable consideration has been given by the endorsee (4 R.C. at p. 343), the statement in an endorsement that the value for it has been furnished by some person other than the endorsee does not make it restrictive (Potts v. Reed, 1806, 6 Esp. 57; Murrow v. Stuart, 1853, 8 Moo. P.C. 267) ; e.g., a bill endorsed "Pay D. or order value in account with E.," is in effect a simple endorsement to D. or order. (Buckley v. Jackson, 1868, L.R. 3 Ex. 135.)

The mere omission to add words of negotiability to a special endorsement does not make it restrictive (see secs. 21 and 22). A cheque payable to bearer cannot be restrictively endorsed for deposit so as to render the bank liable for paying the amount to the bearer without notice of the endorsement. (Exchange Bank v. Quebec Bank, 1890, M.L.R. 6 S.C. 10.)

Right to receive payment.

A bill endorsed "Pay D. for my account" or "for collection" must be paid to D. personally. The only effect of adding "or order" after D.'s name is to obviate the inconvenience of D.'s having to attend in person to obtain payment, and to enable D. by endorsing the bill to authorize another person to receive payment. The amount is nevertheless received to the use of A. (Lloyd v. Sigourney, 1828, 5 Bing. at p. 532, 4 R. C. at p. 362.) It has never been attempted to make the payer responsible in such a case for the due application of the proceeds by the endorsee, and it is clear that he is not responsible. Chalmers p. 116. Cf. Munro v. Cox, 1870, 30 U.C.R. 363.

A bill is endorsed "Pay D. or order for collection per account of C. Bank." If the C. Bank receives payment before maturity, D. cannot recover from the acceptor, although he has credited the C. Bank with the amount of the bill (Williams v. Shadbolt, 1885, 1 C. & E. 529). The relation of endorser and endorsee is substantially that of principal and agent.

Subsequent endorsees.

C. endorses a bill "Pay D. or order for my use." D. endorses it to, and discounts it with, E. on his own account. E. collects it at maturity. C. can recover the amount of the bill from E. (Lloyd v. Sigourney, 1829, 5 Bing. 525.)

C. endorses a bill "Pay D. or order for the use of F." D. collects the bill at maturity. If he misappropriates the money, F. cannot sue him (Wedlake v. Hurley, 1830, Lloyd v. Welsley, 330; 1 C. & J. 83). The action must be brought by C. (*Ibid.*, at pp. 332, 88.)

C. endorses a bill "Pay D. or order for account of F." D. is F.'s agent. D. endorses the bill to E., who collects it. F. can sue E. for the amount so received. (Trentell v. Barandon, 1817, 8 Taunt. 100; if D. had not been F.'s agent, C. must have brought the action.)

A. draws a bill on B., and endorses it to C. C. endorses it "Pay D or order for my use." The bill is dishonoured, and D. sues A. If A. has any defence against C., he may set it up against D. (Wilson v. Holmes, 1809, 5 Mass. 543.)

CONVENTIONS AND RULES RESPECTING ENDORSEMENTS.

Adopted by the Council of the Canadian Bankers' Association on the 26th February, 1898, under authority of a resolution passed at the annual meeting of the Association, 6th October, 1897.

(See 5 Journal C.B.A. 323, and discussion of "Endorsements of various kinds, restrictive, stamped and otherwise," by Z. A. Lash at p. 182 of the same volume. These conventions and rules are not of binding force except as between persons who agree to be bound by them. They have been adopted by the Association in order to encourage the general use of regular and well-understood endorsements and to attain a maximum of convenience in the exchange of items.)

Mode of endorsement.

1. An endorsement may be either written or stamped, in whole or in part.

Regular endorsements.

2. A regular endorsement within the meaning of these Conventions and Rules must be neither restrictive nor conditional, and must be so placed and worded as to shew clearly that an endorsement is intended.

If purporting to be the endorsement of the person or firm to whom the item is payable (whether originally or by endorsement), the names must correspond, subject, however, to section 32, sub-sec. 2, of the Bills of Exchange Act, which is as follows: —[now sec. 64, *supra*].

If purporting to be the endorsement of a corporation, the name of the corporation and the official position of the person or persons signing for it must be stated.

If purporting to be made by some one on behalf of the endorser, it must indicate by words that the person signing has been authorized to sign; *ex. gr.*, "John Smith, by his attorney, Thomas Robinson," or "Brown, Jones & Co., by Thomas Robinson, their attorney," or Per Pro. or P. P. the Smith Brown Company limited, Thomas Robinson."

Irregular endorsements.

3. An endorsement, other than a restrictive endorsement, which is not in accordance with the foregoing definition of a regular endorsement, or which is so placed or worded as to raise doubts whether it is intended as an endorsement, is an irregular endorsement within the meaning of these Conventions and Rules.

Restrictive endorsements.

4. Section 35 of the Bills of Exchange Act defines a restrictive endorsement as follows:—[now sec. 68, sub-sec. 2, *supra*].

The following further examples shall be treated as restrictive endorsements within the meaning of these Conventions and Rules, without prejudice, however, to their true character, should the question arise in court, viz:—

"For deposit only to credit of.............."

"For deposit in...........bank to credit of..........."

"Deposited in...........bank for account of.........."

"Credit..............bank."

Form and effect of guarantee.

⸴ 5. A guarantee of endorsements shall be in the following form or to the like effect:—

"Prior endorsements guaranteed by.........(name of bank)."

It may be written or stamped, but shall be signed in writing by an authorized officer of the bank giving it.

By virtue of such guarantee and of these Conventions and Rules, the bank giving same shall return to the paying bank the amount of the item bearing the guarantee, if, owing to the nature of any endorsement, or to its being forged, or unauthorized, it should appear that such payment was improperly made.

Endorsement by depositing bank.

6. When one bank deposits with or presents for payment to another bank (whether through the Clearing House or otherwise) a bill, note or cheque, the item so deposited or presented shall bear the stamped open endorsement of the depositing or presenting bank. Such stamp shall contain the name of the bank, its branch or agency, and the date, and shall for all purposes be the endorsement of the depositing or presenting bank, and, except as hereinafter specified, no further or other endorsement shall be required, whether the item be specially payable to the bank or otherwise, or be payable at the chief office or elsewhere.

Restrictively endorsed items.

7. If a bill, note or cheque bearing a restrictive endorsement be so deposited or presented, the depositing or presenting bank shall *ipso facto*, and by virtue of these Conventions and Rules, be deemed to have guaranteed such endorsement in accordance with sec. 5 hereof, and shall be liable to the paying bank to the same extent as if such guarantee had been actually placed upon the item, but payment may, notwithstanding, be refused until the restriction be removed.

Irregularly endorsed items.

8. If a bill, note or cheque, bearing an irregular endorsement as above defined, be so deposited or presented, the depositing or presenting bank shall endorse thereon the guarantee re-

Sec. 68.
Conventions
and rules
respecting
endorse-
ments.

ferred to in section 5 hereof, but payment may, notwithstanding, be refused, until the irregularity be removed.

Letters of credit, deposit receipts, etc.

9. When a letter of credit, deposit receipt, or other item not negotiable, and to which the provisions of the Bills of Exchange Act do not apply, is so deposited or presented, a receipt and indemnity in the following form, or to the like effect shall be written or stamped thereon, signed in writing by an authorized officer of the presenting or depositing bank, viz:—

"Received amount of within from the within named bank, which is hereby indemnified against all claims hereunder by any person."

Agreement as to practice.

10. While it is understood that in general, for convenience of the depositing or presenting bank, no objection will be made to a restrictive endorsement, or to an irregular endorsement if the guarantee above provided for be given, yet in view of the responsibility which a depositing or presenting bank incurs in connection therewith, each bank undertakes to make all reasonable efforts to have all endorsements on items deposited or presented by it made regular in order that its customers and the public generally may ultimately be led to adopt a regular and uniform system.

It is also understood that endorsements regularly made within the meaning of these Conventions and Rules shall not be objected to except for special reasons to be assigned with the objection.

Amendment.

Adopted by the Canadian Bankers' Association, February 22nd, 1906.

In case of all items, whether restrictively endorsed or otherwise, sent through the exchanges by members of the Association, the member sending the items shall be deemed and held as guaranteeing the authenticity of all endorsements thereon, and if such guaranty do not expressly appear it shall be implied.

When nego-
tiability
ceases.

69. Where a bill is negotiable in its origin, it continues to be negotiable until it has been,—

(*a*) restrictively endorsed; or,

(*b*) discharged by payment or otherwise. 53 V., c. 33, s. 36.
Eng. s. 36.

As to the meaning of "negotiable" see notes at the beginning
of this chapter. As to restrictive endorsements, see sec. 68, and
as to discharge, see secs. 139 to 146.

As to' delivery of an incomplete bill, and' its negotiation
after completion, see secs. 31 and 32.

70. Where an overdue bill is negotiated, it can be negotiated Overdue bill.
only subject to any defect of title affecting it at its maturity,
and thenceforward no person who takes it can acquire or give a
better title than that which had the person from whom he took Equities.
it.

2. A bill payable on demand is deemed to be overdue within Demand bill
the meaning and for the purposes of this section, when it ap- when.
pears on the face of it to have been in circulation for an unreasonable length of time.

3. What is an unreasonable length of time for such purpose Time.
is a question of fact. 53 V., c. 33, s. 36. Eng. s. 36.

Defect in title.

The term "defect of title" (cf. sec. 56), was substituted in Equity at-
the English bill for the equivalent expression "equity attach- bill.
ing to the bill," as that expression was unknown in Scotch law.
(Alcock v. Smith, [1892] 1 Ch. at p. 263.)

In the case of In re Overend, Gurney & Co., Ex parte Swan,
1868, L.R. 6 Eq. 344, 4 R.C. 375, the cases previous to that date
in regard to what is an equity attaching to a bill are reviewed
in the elaborate judgment of Malins, V.C. (approved in Ex
parte Oriental Commercial Bank, 1870, L.R. 5 Ch. 358). The
endorsee of a bill which is overdue takes it subject to all its
equities, that is the equities of the bill, not the equities of the
parties. He does not take it subject to a mere right of set off
or other right not inherent in the contractual relation represented by the bill. (*Ibid.*; cf. Amazon v. Quebec, 1876, 2 Q.L.
R. 310; Oulds v. Harrison, 1854, 10 Ex. 572; Whitehead v.

Walker, 1842, 10 M. & W. 696.) It is no defence to an action
by the endorsee that the bill was accepted for the accommodation
of the drawer without consideration and was endorsed after it
became due. (Ex parte Swan, *supra*.)

But if there be an agreement express or implied not to negotiate an accommodation bill after maturity, the agreement constitutes an equity attaching to the bill (Parr v. Jewell, 1855, 16
C.B. 684), and if it is agreed between the acceptor and drawer
that the drawer is to be at liberty to sell certain goods, deposited
with him by the acceptor, to provide for the bill, his agreement
constitutes an equity attaching to the bill. (Holmes v. Kidd,
1858, 3 H. & N. 891; cf. Ching v. Jeffery, 1885, 12 A.R. 432, and
cases there cited as to what equities attach to a bill.)

Illegality of consideration is an equity attaching to the bill
(Amory v. Meryweather, 1824, 2 B. & C. 573), but a holder in
due course may negotiate an overdue bill to a holder who is
not himself a party to any fraud or illegality affecting it (sec.
57; cf. Chalmers v. Lanion, 1808, 1 Camp. 383; Fairclough v.
Pavia, 1854, 9 Ex. 690).

Part payment is an equity attaching to the bill (Graves v.
Key, 1832, 3 B. & Ad. at p. 319.) If a bill has been actually
paid or otherwise discharged, the endorsee after maturity cannot recover, but payment or other discharge is rather a ground
of nullity than a defect of title. Cf. Chalmers, p. 120.

An agreement between the maker and payee of a promissory
note that it shall only be used for a particular purpose constitutes an equity attaching to the bill. (MacArthur v. MacDowall,
1892, 23 S.C.R. 571; cf. Lloyd v. Howard, 1850, 15 Q.B. 995;
Redfern v. Rosenthal, 1902, 86 L.T. 855, 18 T.L.R. 718.)

Action by third endorsee of a bill against the first endorser.
Although the plaintiff took the bill when overdue, the defendant
cannot set off a debt due to him from an intermediate holder and
endorser. (Whitehead v. Walker, 1842, 10 M. & W. 696.)

A *bonâ fide* holder acquiring a bill after dishonour takes
subject not merely to the equities of prior parties to the bill,
but also to those of all parties having an interest therein.
(Young v. MacNider, 1895, 25 S.C.R. 272, a case of an agent
disposing of commercial paper in fraud of his principal; cf. In
re European Bank, Ex parte Oriental Bank, 1870, L.R. 5 Ch.
358; Warren v. Haigh, 1875, 65 N.Y. 171.)

The provisions of the section perhaps do not apply to a bill Sec. 70.
which is negotiated in a foreign country, where no distinction Equity at-
is recognized between overdue and current bills. (Alcock v. taching to
Smith, [1892] 1 Ch. 238, affirmed on the ground that the evi- bill:
dence disclosed no defect of title; Chalmers, p. 120.)

When overdue.

Where a bill is not payable on demand, it is overdue after When de-
the expiration of the last day of grace (cf. sec. 42). mand bill is
overdue.

See sec. 23 defining what bills are payable on demand. Sub-
sec. 2 does not apply to notes (sec. 182), but, by virtue of sec.
165, does apply to cheques. A promissory note payable on demand is intended to be a continuing security. It is quite unlike
the case of a cheque which is intended to be presented speedily.
(Brooks v. Mitchell, 1841, 9 M. & W. at p. 18, 4 R.C. at p. 401.)

As to bills, the enactment is probably declaratory. Chalmers,
p. 121.

The cases as to cheques are elaborately reviewed in the
judgment of Field, J., in London & County Banking Co. v.
Groome, 1881, 8 Q.B.D. 288. In this case a cheque 8 days old
was held not to be overdue for the purposes of this section. The
cases chiefly commented on were Down v. Halling, 1825, 4 B.
& C. 330, and Rothschild v. Corney, 1829, 9 B. & C. 388. In
the former it is held that a cheque 5 days' old is to be regarded
as overdue; in the latter it is said that the fact that a cheque
is 6 days old is merely a circumstance to be taken into consideration by the jury.

The editor of the Ruling Cases (4 R.C. at p. 407), says:
"Although the law laid down in the judgment of the court in
the former case is flatly contradicted in the latter, and although
the direction to the jury in neither case is beyond the reach of
criticism, the two cases together support these propositions:
(*a*) That where a cheque is tendered for negotiation, the time
which has elapsed from its date (if long enough) may be sufficient alone to put the person to whom it is tendered upon enquiry as to the title of a person tendering it;

(*b*) That no fixed time can be assigned for this purpose;

(*c*) That a lapse of time so short as even 5 or 6 days may
combine with other circumstances to form such reasonable
ground of suspicion of want of title that the person acting in

Sec. 70.
When de-
mand bill is
overdue.

defiance of the suspicious facts will be chargeable with notice of the want of title if there is want of title in fact. The decision in London & County Banking Co. v. Groome is quite in accord-, ance with this view of the two previous decisions. Where (as in this case) a person pays a cheque on another bank to his account with his own bankers, the elements of suspicion, other than the lapse of time itself, appear to be minimized.''

Sub-secs. 2 and 3 are no doubt intended to be declaratory. The phrases ''unreasonable time'' (cf. sec. 77) and ''question of fact'' give abundant latitude for interpretation by judge and jury. As to reasonable time, cf. notes to sec. 166.

Presump-
tion as to.

71. Except where an endorsement bears date after the maturity of the bill, every negotiation is *primâ facie* deemed to have' been effected before the bill was overdue. 53 V., c. 33, s. 36. Eng. s. 36.

Cf. sec. 70.

This is declaratory (Lewis v. Parker, 1836, 4 A. & E. 838; cf. sec. 58); but apart from the general rule there is no presumption as to the exact time of negotiation (Anderson v. Weston, 1840, 6 Bing. N.C. 296), and it seems that circumstances of strong suspicion, short of direct evidence, may rebut the *primâ facie* presumption, and make it a case for the jury whether the bill was negotiated before or after maturity (Bounsall v. Harrison, 1836, 1 M. & W. 611). Chalmers, p. 122.

Taking bill
with notice
of dishonour.

72. Where a bill which is not overdue has been dishonoured, any person who takes it with notice of the dishonour takes it subject to any defect of title attaching thereto at the time of dishonour; but nothing in this section shall affect the rights of a holder in due course. 53 V., c. 33, s. 36. Eng. s. 36.

This section settles a disputed point, by putting a bill known to be dishonoured on the same footing as an overdue bill (see sec. 70). It affirms Crossley v. Ham, 1811, 13 East 498, and *quoad hoc* overrides Goodman v. Harvey, 1836, 6 Nev. & Man. 372. Chalmers, p. 122.

As to dishonour by non-acceptance, see sec. 81. ''Holder in due course'' is defined by sec. 56; see notes to that section as to the meaning of notice.

73. Where a bill is negotiated back to the drawer, or to a   Sec. 73.
prior endorser, or to the acceptor, such party may, subject to Re-issue of
the provisions of this Act, re-issue and further negotiate the bill.
bill, but he is not entitled to enforce the payment of the bill
against any intervening party to whom he was previously liable.
53 V., c. 33, s. 37. Eng. s. 37.

Subject to the provisions of this Act.

Where a bill is negotiable in its origin it continues to be
negotiable until it has been restrictively endorsed or discharged
(sec. 69). As to discharge, see secs. 139 to 146, and especially
140 and 141.

Bill payable three months after date is endorsed by the
holder to the acceptor. At any time before maturity the acceptor may re-issue the bill and endorse it away. (Attenborough
v. Mackenzie, 1856, 25 L.J. Ex. 244.)

The drawer of a bill payable to drawer's order endorses it
to C., who endorses it to D., who endorses it back to the drawer.
Subject to secs. 140 and 141, the drawer, either before or after
its maturity, may re-issue the bill and endorse it to E. (Cf.
Hubbard v. Jackson, 1827, 4 Bing. 390; Jones v. Broadhurst,
1850, 9 C.B. 173.)

To whom he was previously liable.

The rule of the latter part of the section is a rule against Rule against
circuity of action.   circuity of
action.
The drawer of a bill payable to drawer's order endorses it
for value to C., who endorses it back to D., who endorses it back
to the drawer. The drawer cannot recover from C. or D.,
for each of them in turn could recover from him as drawer.
(Cf. Wilders v. Stevens, 1846, 15 M. & W. at p. 212.)

The payee of a bill endorses it "without recourse" to D.,
who endorses it to E. who endorses it back to the payee. The
payee, in his character of third endorsee, can sue D. and E., for
they have no claim against him as prior endorser. (Cf. Morris
v. Walker, 1850, 15 Q.B. at p. 594; there is here no circuity
of action.)

The drawer of a bill endorses it to C., who has previously
undertaken to be responsible for the price of goods supplied to

31—BANK ACT.

the acceptor. C. endorses the bill back to the drawer. The drawer, in his character of endorsee can sue C., for C. has no remedy over against him. (Wilkinson v. Unwin, 1881, 7 Q. B.D. 636); cf. Pegg v. Howlett, 1897, 28 O.R. 473.

When it was desired to obtain the benefit of the endorsement of a person for the accommodation of the acceptor and for the purpose of facilitating the negotiation of the bill, the end was formerly accomplished by the payee's first endorsing to such person "without recourse," and then again endorsing after such person in case of negotiation to a subsequent holder. (Duthie v. Essery, 1895, 22 A.R. at p. 192.) Even if the payee did not add words to his endorsement negativing his liability, evidence could be given to shew that the other person endorsed for the acceptor's accommodation and with the intention of becoming liable as surety for the payment of the bill to the payee. (Wilkinson v. Unwin, *supra;* Foster v. Farewell, 1856, 13 U.C.R. 451; Gunn v. McPherson, 1859, 18 U.C.R. 244; Smith v. Richardson, 1865, 16 C.P. 210.)

The prior endorsement of the payee is not, however, necessary. An endorsement on a bill to one who is about to take it is valid, without the payee's prior endorsement, but the endorsement creates no obligations to those who were previously parties to the bill; it is solely for the benefit of those who take subsequently. (Duthie v. Essery, *supra;* cf. cases cited in the notes to sec. 131.)

74. The rights and powers of the holder of a bill are as follows:—

(*a*) He may sue on the bill in his own name;

(*b*) Where he is a holder in due course, he holds the bill free from any defect of title of prior parties, as well as from mere personal defences available to prior parties among themselves, and may enforce payment against all parties liable on the bill;

(*c*) Where his title is defective, if he negotiates the bill to a holder in due course, that holder obtains a good and complete title to the bill; and,

(*d*) Where his title is defective if he obtains payment of the
bill the person who pays him in due course gets a valid
discharge for the bill. 53 V., c. 33, s. 38. Eng. s. 37.

Clauses (*a*) and (*b*) express the two essentials which constitute the quality of negotiability as laid down by Blackburn, J., in Crouch v. Credit Foncier, 1873, L.R. 8 Q.B. at pp. 381-2, quoted and discussed in Chapter XXX., *supra.* See also note at the beginning of this chapter. This section deals only with the rights acquired by negotiation (sec. 60), that is, by transfer according to the form required by the law merchant.

See sec. 2, as to holder;

Sec. 56, as to holder in due course;

Secs. 56 and 70, as to defect of title;

Sec. 139, as to payment in due course.

By sec. 2, clause (*k*) defence includes counter-claim.

The power to negotiate a bill must be distinguished from the
right to negotiate it. The right is an incident of ownership;
the power is an incident of apparent ownership. Again the
right to sue must be, distinguished from the right to recover,
which depends on the further question whether the holder is
a holder for value, and in some cases whether he is a holder for value without notice. See Chalmers, pp. 124, *et seq.*, where the law as to the holder's rights of action and proof is stated in a series of rules.

CHAPTER XLI.

PRESENTMENT FOR ACCEPTANCE.

General
duties of
holder.

Prior to 1906 secs. 75 and 126 (with a few exceptions) were grouped under the heading "General Duties of the Holder." These duties comprise presentment for acceptance, presentment for payment, notice of dishonour and protest in the cases provided for by the sections contained in this and the next following three chapters. The duties in question are not absolute duties, but the holder is required to use reasonable diligence in order to fulfil them (cf. sec. 79).

If a party to a bill is discharged from his liability thereon by reason of the holder's omission to perform his duties, such party is also discharged from liability on the debt or other consideration for which the bill was given (cf. notes to sec. 96).

The sections relating to presentment for acceptance do not apply to promissory notes: see sec. 186.

Presentment for
acceptance
compared
with presentment for
payment.

Comparing presentment for acceptance with presentment for payment, it is clear that the two cases are governed by somewhat different considerations. Speaking generally, presentment for acceptance should be personal, while presentment for payment should be local. A bill should be presented for payment where the money is. Any one can then hand over the money. A bill should be presented for acceptance to the drawee himself, for he has to write the acceptance; but the place where it is presented to him is comparatively immaterial, for all he has to do is to take the bill. Again, (except in the case of demand drafts), the day for payment is a fixed day; but the drawee cannot tell on what day it may suit the holder to present a bill for acceptance. These considerations are material as bearing on the question whether the holder has used reasonable diligence to effect presentment. Chalmers, p. 141.

Presentment for acceptance.

When
necessary.

75. Where a bill is payable at sight or after sight, presentment for acceptance is necessary in order to fix the maturity of the instrument.

2. Where a bill expressly stipulates that it shall be presented for acceptance, or where a bill is drawn payable elsewhere than at the residence or place of business of the drawee, it must be presented for acceptance before it can be presented for payment. *Sec. 75.*
Express stipulation.

3. In no other case is presentment for acceptance necessary in order to render liable any party to the bill. 53 V., c. 33, s. 39. Eng. s. 39. *Other cases.*

The words "at sight or" are omitted from sub-sec. 1 of the corresponding section of the English Act, sight drafts in England being payable on demand (see notes to sec. 23). Sub-sec. 1 as it reads in the Canadian Act is declaratory of the common law.

Sub-sec. 2 settles a doubtful point. Chalmers, p. 134. Except in the cases mentioned in that sub-section, it has long been settled law that the holder need not present for acceptance a bill payable after date. (Ramchurn Mullick v. Luchmeechund Radikissen, 1854, 9 Moo. P.C. at p. 66, 4 R.C. at p. 463.) The same rule applies to a bill payable on demand or payable on or at a fixed period after the occurrence of a specified event which is certain to happen, though the time of happening is uncertain. But in the case of a bill payable at or after sight, presentment is necessary because otherwise the due date cannot be known. An acceptance of such a bill should be dated so that it may be known from what date the time runs.

Subject to the provisions of the Act, if a bill payable at or after sight is negotiated, the holder must either present it for acceptance or negotiate it within a reasonable time (sec. 77).

Sub-sec. 2 must be read subject to sec. 76.

Except in the case of bills payable at or after sight (secs. 75 and 77) and in the cases mentioned in sub-sec. 2 of sec. 75, presentment for acceptance is not necessary in order to render liable any party to the bill. Presentment may nevertheless be made with the object (1) of obtaining the acceptance of the drawee and thereby securing his liability as a party to the bill, or (2) of obtaining an immediate right of recourse against antecedent parties in case the bill is dishonoured by non-acceptance (sec. 82). *When presentment for acceptance necessary.*

Sec. 75.   As to the duties of agent, see Chapter XV., *supra*, p. 133.

The rules for due presentment for acceptance are contained in sec. 78.

As to the cases in which presentment is excused, see sec. 79.

Present-
ment ex-
cused.
76. Where the holder of a bill, drawn payable elsewhere than at the place of business or residence of the drawee, has not time, with the exercise of reasonable diligence, to present the bill for acceptance before presenting it for payment on the day that it falls due, the delay caused by presenting the bill for acceptance before presenting it for payment is excused, and does not discharge the drawer and endorsers. 53 V., c. 33, s. 39. Eng. s. 39.

This section was added to the English bill in committee. It settles a moot point and perhaps alters the law.

Where a bill is drawn payable elsewhere than at the residence or place of business of the drawee, it must be presented for acceptance before it can be presented for payment (sec. 75). It may be impossible in fact to present such a bill for acceptance before presenting it for payment on the due date, as, *e.g.*, where the holder or his agent at the place where the bill is payable receives it on the due date, or so shortly before such date that he has not sufficient time to send it for presentment to the drawee and get it back again on or before the due date. In such a case the holder or his agent must nevertheless present the bill for acceptance, but the delay in presenting it for payment thus caused is excused (sec. 76).

Sight bill.
77. Subject to the provisions of this Act, when a bill payable at sight or after sight is negotiated, the holder must either present it for acceptance or negotiate it within a reasonable time.

If not pre-
sented.
2. If he does not do so, the drawer and all endorsers prior to that holder are discharged.

Reasonable
time.
3. In determining what is a reasonable time within the meaning of this section, regard shall be had to the nature of the bill, the usage of trade with respect to similar bills, and the facts of the particular case. 53 V., c. 33, s. 40; 54-55 V., c. 17, s. 5. Eng. s. 40.

The words "at sight or" were added to the Canadian Act by amendment in 1891. They are not in the corresponding section of the English Act, sight bills in England being payable on demand (see notes to sec. 23), and therefore requiring no presentment for acceptance (see notes to sec. 75).

In determining the question of "reasonable time," (which is a mixed question of law and fact), regard must be had not only to the interest of the drawer to put the bill into circulation and to the interest of the drawee to have the bill speedily presented, but also to the interest of the holder who is entitled to a reasonable time to put the bill into circulation. The continued solvency of the drawer and the want of proof of actual loss by the laches of the holder constitute no answer to the objection that the holder has not presented or negotiated the bill within a reasonable time. Ramchurn Mullick v. Luchmeechund Radakissen, 1854, 9 Moo. P.C. at pp. 67-69, 4 R.C. at pp. 464-5.

As to reasonable time, cf. secs. 70 and 165.

In the case just cited, A. in Calcutta drew a bill on B. in Hong Kong, payable 60 days after sight. The holder retained it for more than five months during which time China bills were at a discount. He then negotiated it. The court held on the facts that the delay was unreasonable. The holder might, in the opinion of the court, have held the bill for some time if there was a reasonable prospect of the state of the market improving, but had no right to keep it as long as he did when there was no hope of the amendment of market conditions.

A. in London draws a bill on B. in Rio, payable 60 days after sight. The payee holds it back for four months, during which time Rio bills are at a discount. He then negotiates it. This may not be an unreasonable delay. (Mellish v. Rawdon, 1832, 9 Bing. 416.)

A. in Newfoundland draws a bill (in a set) on B. in London, payable 90 days after sight. The payee holds it back for two months, although there are tri-weekly mails, and then forwards it for presentment. No reason for holding back is shewn. This may be an unreasonable delay. (Straker v. Graham, 1839, 4 M. & W. 721; if the bill is accepted when presented, but the acceptor fails before the due date, A. is probably discharged; otherwise, if there was no unreasonable delay: Wylde v. Wetmore, 1869, 1 G. & O. (N.S.) 504, a case in which it was held that it was not an unreasonable delay to hold a bill drawn on

Sec. 77.
What is
reasonable
time.

Liverpool over two mails, and then to negotiate it about a month after its endorsement.)

The effect of allowing negotiation as an alternative to presentment is not very clear. Chalmers asks the question: "Does not negotiation within a reasonable time *toties quoties*, excuse presentment?

Rules.

78. A bill is duly presented for acceptance which is presented in accordance with the following rules, namely:—

By holder to drawee.

(*a*) The presentment must be made by or on behalf of the holder to the drawee or to some person authorized to accept or refuse acceptance on his behalf, at a reasonable hour on a business day and before the bill is overdue;

To all drawees.

(*b*) Where a bill is addressed to two or more drawees, who are not partners, presentment must be made to them all, unless one has authority to accept for all, when presentment may be made to him only;

To personal representative.

(*c*) Where the drawee is dead, presentment may be made to his personal representative;

Post office.

(*d*) Where authorized by agreement or usage, a presentment through the post office is sufficient. 53 V., c. 33, s. 41. Eng. s. 41.

As to the cases in which presentment for acceptance is necessary, see secs. 75 to 77.

The question of due presentment is material only where the holder of a bill payable at or after sight fails to present it for acceptance or to negotiate it within a reasonable time (sec. 77), or when acceptance cannot be obtained. Acceptance cures the informality of the presentment.

Bankrupt.

The corresponding section of the English Act contains also the following words: "Where the drawee is bankrupt, presentment may be made to him or to his trustee." Presentment is excused in the cases mentioned in sec. 79. The English Act excuses presentment also where the drawee is bankrupt, and defines "bankrupt" as including "any person whose estate is vested in a trustee or assignee under the law for the time being in force relating to bankruptcy." These provisions regarding bankrupts are all omitted from the Canadian Act, as there is no bankruptcy or insolvency law in force in Canada (see Atty - Gen. for Ontario v. Atty.-Gen. for Canada, [1894] A.C. 189). Cf. notes to secs. 97 and 116.

By or on behalf of the holder.

Holder means the payee or endorsee of a bill or note who is in possession of it, or the bearer thereof (sec. 2). For the purpose of presentment the holder need not be the lawful holder. (Cf. Morrison v. Buchanan, 1833, 6 C. & P. 18.)

The holder may, without endorsing the bill, present it through an agent.

To the drawee or to some person authorized, etc.

Speaking generally, presentment for acceptance should be personal, while presentment for payment should be local: see note preceding sec. 75, *supra.*

Presentment to a servant who opened the door would not be sufficient; and if a bill is domiciled for payment at a bank, presentment at the bank would not suffice. Chalmers, p. 138.

As to "business day" see sec. 2.

As to reasonable hour, see notes to sec. 87.

A bill must be presented before it is overdue. It may be accepted when it is overdue (sec. 37), but an acceptance in such a case does not preserve or revive the liability of the drawer and endorsers, except in the case provided for by sec. 76.

The acceptance of some one or more of the drawees, but not of all, is a qualified acceptance (sec. 38).

Where the drawee is dead, presentment is excused (sec. 79), but the holder has the option of presenting the bill to the drawee's personal representative.

The provision as to presentment through the post office gives effect to the recognized practice among English merchants: cf. notes to sec. 90 (presentment for payment).

79. Presentment in accordance with the aforesaid rules is excused, and a bill may be treated as dishonoured by non-acceptance,—

(a) where the drawee is dead, or is a fictitious person or a person not having capacity to contract by bill;

Sec. 79.
Impracti-
cability.
Waiver.

(b) where, after the exercise of reasonable diligence, such presentment cannot be effected;

(c) where although the presentment has been irregular, acceptance has been refused on some other ground.

Excuse.

2. The fact that the holder has reason to believe that the bill, on presentment, will be dishonoured does not excuse presentment. 53 V., c. 33, s. 41; 54-55 V., c. 17, s. 6. Eng. s. 41.

Where presentment would otherwise be obligatory, it is excused in the cases mentioned in this section.

As to the cases in which presentment for acceptance is necessary, see secs. 75 to 77.

As to what is due presentment, see sec. 78.

Where the drawee is dead, presentment to his personal representative is optional (sec. 78).

As to capacity to contract by bill, see sec. 47.

Clause (c) is perhaps new law. Chalmers, p. 140.

Time for
acceptance.

80. The drawee may accept a bill on the day of its due presentment to him for acceptance, or at any time within two days thereafter.

Dishonour.

2. When a bill is so duly presented for acceptance and is not accepted within the time aforesaid, the person presenting it must treat it as dishonoured by non-acceptance.

Loss of
rights.

3. If he does not so treat the bill as dishonoured, the holder shall lose his right of recourse against the drawer and endorsers.

Date of
acceptance.

4. In the case of a bill payable at sight or after sight, the acceptor may date his acceptance thereon as of any of the days aforesaid but not later than the day of his actual acceptance of the bill.

Refusing
acceptance.

5. If the acceptance is not so dated, the holder may refuse to take the acceptance and may treat the bill as dishonoured by non-acceptance. 2 E. VII., c. 2, s. 1. Eng. s. 42.

The corresponding section of the English Act reads as follows:

"When a bill is duly presented for acceptance, and is not Sec. 80.
accepted within the customary time, the person presenting it
must treat it as dishonoured by non-acceptance. If he do not,
the holder shall lose his right of recourse against the drawer and
indorsers."

The English section was much discussed in committee and
was eventually reduced to its present vague form, as the bankers and merchants took different views as to the exact rights of
the parties. Chalmers, p. 141.

When the Canadian bill was under discussion in 1890, the Time for
expression "within the customary time" was considered too acceptance.
vague, especially in view of the fact that the time might vary
in the different provinces, and therefore the words "on the day
of presentment or within two days thereafter" were substituted.
In 1902 the section then in force was repealed, and the present
section substituted. The division into the present sub-sections
is a result of the revision of 1906.

The effect of the section probably is to allow a longer time
for acceptance than is given by the English Act. See Bank of
Van Dieman's Land v. Victoria Bank, 1871, L.R. 3 P.C. at pp.
542-3, 546-7, and notes in Chapter XV., *supra*, p. 133, as to the
duties of an agent to whom a bill is sent for presentment.

In reckoning the time non-business days are to be excluded
(sec. 6).

The destruction or wrongful retention of the bill by the
drawee does not amount to an acceptance. Protest may be made
on a copy or written particulars (sec. 120), and the holder's
remedy against the drawee is an action for damages.

As to the date of acceptance, cf. sec. 37, *supra*, in regard to
acceptance after dishonour.

81. A bill is dishonoured by non-acceptance,—   Dishonour.

(a) when it is duly presented for acceptance, and such an Present-
acceptance as is prescribed by this Act is refused or cannot ment.
be obtained; or,

(b) when presentment for acceptance is excused and the bill Excuse.
is not accepted. 53 V., c. 33, s. 43. Eng. s. 43.

As to due presentment, see sec. 78.

As to the cases in which presentment is excused, see sec. 79.

Sec. 81.   As to acceptance, see secs. 35, *et seq.*, Chapter XXXV., *supra.*

If the holder does not obtain an unqualified acceptance, he may treat the bill as dishonoured by non-acceptance (sec. 83).

As to the holder's right of recourse in the event of the dishonour of a bill by non-acceptance, see sec. 82.

Secs. 81 and 82 would be more logically situated if placed with sec. 95 under the heading ''Dishonour.''

Recourse in such case.   **82.** Subject to the provisions of this Act, when a bill is dishonoured by non-acceptance an immediate right of recourse against the drawer and endorsers accrues to the holder, and no presentment for payment is necessary. 53 V., 33, s. 43. Eng. s. 43.

Subject to the provisions of the Act (see sec. 147, *infra,* as to acceptance for honour), the holder has an immediate right of recourse against drawer and endorsers. This right is suspended in the event of acceptance for honour with the holder's consent. Even if a bill has been dishonoured by refusal to accept, it is open to the holder to allow the bill to be accepted subsequently (sec. 37).

Right of recourse and right of action.   Although, except as above noted, the holder has an immediate right of recourse upon non-acceptance, his right of action is not complete until the defendant has received, or ought to have received, notice of dishonour, and, in the cases where protest is necessary, the bill has been protested. (Whitehead v. Walker, 1842, 9 M. & W. at p. 516; Castrique v. Bernabo, 1844, 6 Q.B. 498; cf. notes to sec. 95.)

Subject to the provisions of the Act, when a bill has been dishonoured by non-acceptance, notice of dishonour must be given to the drawer and each endorser, and any drawer or endorser to whom such notice is not given is discharged, provided that the rights of a holder in due course subsequent to the omission shall not be prejudiced by the omission (sec. 96).

As to the necessity for protest, see secs. 112 and 113.

As to right of recourse and right of action, and the time from which the Statute of Limitations begins to run, see notes to sec. 95.

83. The holder of a bill may refuse to take a qualified acceptance, and if he does not obtain an unqualified acceptance
may treat the bill as dishonoured by non-acceptance.

2. When the drawer or endorser of a bill receives notice of a
qualified acceptance, and does not within a reasonable time
express his dissent to the holder, he shall be deemed tó have
assented thereto. 53 V., c. 33, s. 44. Eng. s. 44.

As to what acceptances are qualified, see sec. 38.

As to the holder's rights in the event of the dishonour of a
bill by non-acceptance, see sec. 82 and notes.

The holder is entitled to treat a qualified acceptance as no
acceptance, and if he elects to take such an acceptance without
having been expressly or impliedly authorized by the drawer
or any endorser, the effect, except in the case of a partial acceptance, is to discharge any such drawer or endorser, who does
not subsequently assent to the taking of the qualified acceptance
(see sec. 84). The holder who takes a qualified acceptance
should at once give notice of the qualification to prior parties
who have not expressly or impliedly authorized the taking of
such acceptance. The notice is sufficient to bind a prior party
by a partial acceptance (sec. 84), but in the case of any other
qualified acceptance, the prior party may discharge himself
from liability on the bill by expressing his dissent to the holder
within a reasonable time after the receipt of the notice.

Sub-sec. 2 of sec. 83 settles a doubtful point in favour of the
holder. Chalmers, p. 144; Rowe v. Young, 1820, 2 Bligh, 391.

In some trades the practice of accepting against delivery of
bills of lading is so common that an authority to take such an
acceptance might perhaps be implied. Sometimes, too, the
terms of a documentary bill are such as impliedly to authorize
it. Chalmers, p. 144.

84. Where a qualified acceptance is taken, and the drawer
or an endorser has not expressedly or impliedly authorized the
holder to take a qualified acceptance, or does not subsequently
assent thereto, such drawer or endorser is discharged from his
liability on the bill: Provided that this section shall not apply
to a partial acceptance, whereof due notice has been given. 53
V., c. 33, s. 44. Eng. s. 44.

Sec. 84.   See notes to sec. 83.

Assent to a qualified acceptance will be implied as against a drawer or any endorser who receives notice of such an acceptance and does not within a reasonable time express his dissent to the holder (sec. 83).

Prior to the revision of 1906, this section and sub-sec. 3 of sec. 112 (protest of unaccepted part of a foreign bill) were placed, as they are in the English Act, between sub-secs. 1 and 2 of sec. 83.

CHAPTER XLII.

Presentment for payment as provided for in the sections contained in this chapter, is one of the general duties of the holder of a bill. See note at the beginning of Chapter XLI., *supra*. See also notes to sec. 96, as to the consequence of the holder's omission to perform such duties, and p. 484 where presentment for acceptance and presentment for payment are compared.

The provisions as to presentment of a bill for payment apply in part to a promissory note: see sec. 186, and secs. 180 to 184.

As to dishonour by non-payment, see sec. 95.

Presentment for Payment.

85. Subject to the provisions of this Act, a bill must be duly Necessity. presented for payment.

2. If it is not so presented, the drawer and endorsers shall be Result of discharged. none.

3. Where the holder of a bill presents it for payment, he Manner of. shall exhibit the bill to the person from whom he demands payment. 53 V., c. 33, ss. 45 and 52. Eng. ss. 45 and 52.

Prior to 1906 sub-sec. 3 was included in one section with sec. 93.

As to when presentment for payment is dispensed with, see sec. 92. Delay in making presentment is excused when the delay is caused by circumstances beyond the control of the holder, and not imputable to his default, misconduct or negligence (sec. 91). Sec. 76 provides for the special case of a domiciled bill coming forward late.

As to due presentment, see sec. 86 (time of presentment), sec. 87 (by and to whom presentment must be made), secs. 88 to 90 (place of presentment).

Except where delay is excused or presentment is dispensed with, the failure duly to present a bill for payment discharges

Sec. 85.

Who is entitled to presentment for payment.

the drawer and endorsers. But the acceptor in the absence of express stipulation, is not discharged by failure to present a bill for payment (sec. 93).

As to presentment to an acceptor for honour, see sec. 94.

Presentment for payment is necessary in order to render the endorser of a note liable (sec. 184). The endorser of a note in this respect is in the same position as the drawer or endorser of a bill. (Gibb v. Mather, 1832, 2 Cr. & J. at pp. 262, 263, 4 R.C. at p. 474; cf. sec. 186.)

But the maker (or, as he is sometimes called, the drawer) of a note is in a different position, being, like the acceptor of a bill, the party primarily liable (sec. 183).

As to presentment of a cheque for payment, see notes to next section.

As presentment for payment is not necessary to charge the acceptor or maker, so presentment is not generally a condition precedent to the liability of a person who has given a guarantee for the payment by the acceptor or maker. (Walton v. Mascall, 1844, 13 M. & W. 452, 4 R.C. 483; Carter v. White, 1883, 25 Ch. D. 666.)

Time for.

Due date.

Demand bill.

Reasonable time.

86. A bill is duly presented for payment which is presented,—

(a) when the bill is not payable on demand, on the day it falls due;

(b) when the bill is payable on demand, within a reasonable time after its issue, in order to render the drawer liable, and within a reasonable time after its endorsement, in order to render the endorser liable.

2. In determining what is a reasonable time within the meaning of this section regard shall be had to the nature of the bill, the usage of trade with regard to similar bills and the facts of the particular case. 53 V., c. 33, s. 45. Eng. s. 45.

As to when a bill is payable on demand, see sec. 23. When a bill is not payable on demand, it is due and payable on the third day of grace (sec. 42).

So far as an endorser is concerned this section applies to a cheque. A cheque is a bill drawn on a bank payable on demand (sec. 165). But the effect, so far as the drawer of a cheque is concerned, of the failure to present a cheque for payment within a reasonable time of its issue is the subject of special provisions (sec. 166; cf. exception to sub-sec. 2, sec. 165).

As to the presentment for payment of a note payable on demand, see sec. 180.

As to what is reasonable time, cf. notes to sec. 77.

Due presentment as regards time is required as regards the drawer and endorsers (sec. 85), but not as regards the acceptor (sec. 93).

Sec. 86. Presentment as regards drawer of a cheque.

87. Presentment must be made by the holder or by some person authorized to receive payment on his behalf, at the proper place as hereinafter defined, and either to the person designated by the bill as payer or to his representative or some person authorized to pay or to refuse payment on his behalf, if, with the exercise of reasonable diligence such person can there be found.

By and to whom.

2. When a bill is drawn upon, or accepted by two or more persons who are not partners, and no place of payment is specified, presentment must be made to them all.

Two acceptors.

3. When the drawee or acceptor of a bill is dead, and no place of payment is specified, presentment must be made to a personal representative if such there is, and with the exercise of reasonable diligence, he can be found. 53 V., c. 33, s. 45. Eng. s. 45.

Personal representation.

By whom.

A bill is discharged by payment made by or on behalf of the drawee or acceptor at or after the maturity of the bill to the holder thereof in good faith and without notice that his title to the bill is defective (sec. 139). Presentment for payment must be made by the holder or by some person authorized to receive payment on his behalf, i.e., by the person who can give a good discharge. The person who presents the bill must exhibit it to the person from whom he demands payment (sec. 85), and upon payment must deliver it up to the party who pays it (sec. 93), As to bills in a set, see sec. 159.

Sec. 87. *At the proper place.*
See secs. 88 to 90.

To whom.

In an action against drawer or endorsers (sec. 85) the holder must prove due presentment (sec. 86) to the drawee or acceptor, but need not prove any demand of the drawer. (Heylyn v. Adamson, 1758, 2 Burr. 669 at p. 678, 4 R.C. at p. 454.) In the case of a promissory note, presentment must be made to the maker (*ibid.*).

Presentment is sufficient if made to the representative of the person designated by the bill as payer or some person authorized to pay or to refuse payment on the payer's behalf. The words "or his representative" in sub-sec. 1 are not in the corresponding section of the English Act.

Sub-sec. 2 is probably declaratory, but the point was not clear. Of course if one of two or more acceptors pays or, in refusing payment, acts as the agent of the others, that is enough. Chalmers, p. 149.

Sub-sec. 3 is declaratory. Where the drawee of a bill is dead, presentment for *acceptance* is excused (sec. 79), but in the case of presentment for payment different considerations apply, and if no place of payment is specified reasonable diligence must be exercised to present the bill to the personal representative of the drawee. If a place of payment is specified, presentment at such place is sufficient without any effort being made to present to the personal representative. (Philpot v. Briant, 1827, 3 C. & P. 244; cf. sec. 88, and Wilkins v. Jadis, 1831, 2 B. & Ad. 188.)

Where authorized by agreement or usage, a presentment through the post office is sufficient (sec. 90).

Time for presentment.

Sub-sec. 1 also differs from the English Act in that the latter requires the presentment to be made "at a reasonable hour on a business day." These words are omitted from this section of the Canadian Act, but have been retained in sec. 78, which deals with presentment for acceptance.

The English rule is stated by Chalmers, p. 147, as follows:—

The reasonableness of the hour must depend on whether the bill is payable at a place of business or at a private house. The payer is not bound to stay at his place of business after a reasonable hour. If a bill be payable at a bank it must be presented within banking hours (Elford v. Teed, 1813, 1 M. & S. 28; Parker v. Gordon, 1806, 7 East 385); if at a trader's place of business, then within ordinary business hours (cf. Allen v. Edmundson, 1848, 2 Ex. at p. 723); if at a private house, probably a presentment up to bed-time would be sufficient. Triggs v. Newnham, 1825, 10 Moore 249; Wilkins v. Jadis, 1831, 2 B. & Ad. 188.) Cf. also, Maclaren on Bills, etc., 3rd ed., 1904, p. 245.

The Canadian Act provides that protest for non-payment may be made at any time after three o'clock in the afternoon (sec. 121). There is no similar provision in the English Act.

Where by the Act the time limited for doing any act or thing is less than three days, in reckoning time, non-business days are excluded (sec. 6).

88. A bill is presented at the proper place,— Place of.

(*a*) where a place of payment is specified in the bill or acceptance, and the bill is there presented; When specified.

(*b*) where no place of payment is specified, but the address of the drawee or acceptor is given in the bill, and the bill is there presented; When not specified.

(*c*) where no place of payment is specified and no address given, and the bill is presented at the drawee's or acceptor's place of business, if known, and if not at his ordinary residence, if known; When no address is given.

(*d*) in any other case, if presented to the drawee or acceptor wherever he can be found, or if presented at his last known place of business or residence. 53 V., c. 33, s. 45. Eng. s. 45. Other cases.

This section and secs. 89 and 90 deal with the place of presentment. As to the necessity for presentment, see sec. 85, as to time, see sec. 86, and as to the persons by and to whom presentment must be made, see sec. 87.

The words "or acceptance" in clause (*a*) of sec. 88 are not in the English Act.

The place of payment may be specified either by the drawer (Gibb v. Mather, 1832, 2 Cr. & J. 254, 4 R.C. 467), or by the acceptor (Saul v. Jones, 1858, 28 L.J.Q.B. 37). If a place of payment is specified by the acceptor, the acceptance is not thereby rendered conditional or qualified (sec. 38). It is still a general acceptance and therefore does not require the authority or consent of the drawer or endorsers (sec. 84). The change made in the law in this respect (see notes to sec. 38) does not, however, affect the question of presentment for payment as regards the drawer or endorsers. If a place of payment is specified either originally by the drawer, or in the acceptance, it is necessary to present the bill at such place in order to preserve the liability of the drawer or endorsers. (Gibb v. Mather, *supra.*)

As to the acceptor see sec. 93.

Place of payment specified.

Where a note is in the body of it made payable at a particular place, it must be presented for payment at that place (sec. 183).

If alternative places of payment are mentioned or specified, presentment at either is sufficient. (Beeching v. Gower, 1816, Holt N.P.C. 313; cf. Pollard v. Herries, 1803, 3 B. & P. 335.)

A bill is drawn payable at one place and accepted payable at another. Presentment for payment at the latter place would be sufficient.

The drawee of a bill accepts it payable at his banker's. The bill must be presented at the bank. A presentment to the acceptor personally is insufficient (Gibb v. Mather, *supra;* Saul v. Jones, *supra*). Presentment through the clearing house of which the bank is a member is deemed to be presentment at the bank. (Reynolds v. Chettle, 1811, 2 Camp. 595; Harris v. Parker, 1833, 3 Tyr. 370.)

A bill is accepted payable at a bank. When the bill matures, the bank is the holder of the bill, but the acceptor has no assets there. This is sufficient presentment. No personal demand on the acceptor is necessary. (Bailey v. Porter, 1845, 14 M. & W. 44; Union Bank v. McKilligan, 1887, 4 Man. R. 29; Rice v. Bowker, 1853, 3 L.C.R. 305, 4 R.J.R.Q. 23.)

Address given in the bill.

See Hine v. Alleby, and Buxton v. Jones, cited under sec. 89.

Place of business.

See Fitch v. Kelly, 1879, 44 U.C.R. 578, where it was held that a certain place, although not the ordinary place of business of the maker of the note, was, under the circumstances shewn in evidence, his office for the day, or that the person to whom the note was actually presented was there representing the maker authorized by him to receive and answer the presentment. As to proof that a place was the maker's last place of residence, see Kinnear v. Goddard, 1860, 4 Allen (N.B.) 559.

89. Where a bill is presented at the proper place as afore- Sufficient said and after the exercise of reasonable diligence, no person present- authorized to pay or refuse payment can there be found no ment. further presentment to the drawee or acceptor is required. 53 V., c. 33, s. 45. Eng. s. 45.

Cf. secs. 88 and 90.

A bill is addressed to "Mr. B., 1 Duke Street, London." B. accepts it generally. The bill is presented at the address mentioned and the house is found shut up. This is sufficient. (Hine v. Allely, 1833, 4 B. & Ad. 624; cf. Crosse v. Smith, 1813, 1 M. & S. at p. 554.) If the holder takes the bill to the address mentioned and a person living in the house informs him that B. has left, no further presentment is required. (Buxton v. Jones, 1840, 1 M. & Gr. 83.)

90. Where the place of payment specified in the bill or Present- acceptance is any city, town or village, and no place therein is ment at post specified, and the bill is presented at the drawee's or acceptor's office. known place of business or known ordinary residence therein, and if there is no such place of business or residence, the bill is presented at the post office, or principal post office in such city, town or village, such presentment is sufficient.

2. Where authorized by agreement or usage, a presentment Through through the post office is sufficient. 53 V., c. 33, s. 45. Cf. Eng. post office. s. 45.

Sec. 90.   Cf. secs. 88 and 89.

Sub-sec. 1 is not in the English Act. It was added to the Canadian bill in committee in 1890.

Sub-sec. 2 recognizes a customary practice. (Cf. Heywood v. Pickering, 1874, L.R. 9 Q.B. 428, at p. 432; Prideaux v. Criddle, 1869, L.R. 4 Q.B. 455, at p. 461; Reg. v. Bank of Montreal, 1886, 1 Can. Ex. C.R. 154, at p .167.)

Delay in presentment.

91. Delay in making presentment for payment is excused when the delay is caused by circumstances beyond the control of the holder, and not imputable to his default, misconduct or negligence.

Diligence.

2. When the cause of delay ceases to operate, presentment must be made with reasonable diligence.   53 V., c. 33, s. 46. Eng. s. 46.

As to causes excusing delay, cf. sec 105 (notice of dishonour) and sec. 111 (protest).

As to the cases in which presentment for payment is dispensed with, see sec. 92.

If presentment is delayed at the request of the drawer or endorser sought to be charged, the delay is presumably excused. (Lord Ward v. Oxford Ry. Co., 1852, 2 De G., M. & G. 750.)

The holder of a bill dies suddenly just before it matures. The circumstances may be such as to excuse delay. Chalmers, p. 151; cf. Rothschild v. Currie, 1841, 1 Q.B. at p. 47.)

A bill is presented through the post office (sec. 90). It is sent off in time to reach the drawee on the day of maturity, but by mistake of the post office is delayed some days. The delay is probably excused. (Windham Bank v. Morton, 1852, 22 Conn. 214; Pier v. Heinrichschoffer, 1877, 29 Am. R. 501; cf. sec. 104.)

Bill drawn in England, payable in Leghorn. At the time the bill matures Leghorn is besieged. The holder is not in Leghorn. Delay is excused. (Patience v. Townley, 1805, 2 Smith, 223.)

Bill drawn in England payable in Paris. By a French moratory law, passed in consequence of war, the maturity of bills payable in Paris is postponed three months. The delay in making presentment is excused. (Rouquette v. Overmann, 1875, L.R. 10 Q.B. 525; cf. notes to sec. 162.)

Sec. 91. Causes excusing delay.

92. Presentment for payment is dispensed with,—

(a) where, after the exercise of reasonable diligence, presentment, as required by this Act, cannot be effected;

(b) where the drawee is a fictitious person;

(c) as regards the drawer, where the drawee or acceptor is not bound, as between himself and the drawer, to accept or pay the bill, and the drawer has no reason to believe that the bill would be paid if presented;

(d) as regards an endorser, where the bill was accepted or made for the accommodation of that endorser, and he has no reason to expect that the bill would be paid if presented;

(e) by waiver of presentment, express or implied.

Dispense with.
Impracticable.
Fictitious drawee.
Useless.
Accommodation bill.
Waiver.

2. The fact that the holder has reason to believe that the bill will, on presentment, be dishonoured, does not dispense with the necessity for presentment. 53 V., c. 33, s. 46. Eng. s. 46.

Not dispense with.

Causes which dispense with presentment must be distinguished from causes which merely excuse delay.

Clause (a).

The drawee of a bill goes abroad, leaving an agent at home with power to accept bills, and who does in fact accept the bill. The bill must be presented for payment to the agent, if the drawee at the time of maturity continues absent. (Phillips v. Astling, 1809, 2 Taunt, 206, 4 R.C. 477.) The neglect to present the bill to the agent would be a want of the "reasonable diligence" required in order to dispense with presentment to the drawee.

Presentment for payment dispensed with.

The fact that the maker of a note is dangerously ill does not excuse presentment at his residence or place of business, and presentment to his brother in the street near the residence is not sufficient. (Nowton v. Roach, 1843, 2 Kerr (N.B.) 337.)

Clause (b).

This is declaratory. (Smith v. Bellamy, 1817, 2 Stark, 223.)

Sec. 92.

Present-
ment for
payment
dispensed
with.

Presentment for acceptance is excused not only where the drawee is a fictitious person, but also where he is a person not having capacity to contract by bill. Incapacity of acceptor in itself does not excuse presentment for payment.

Clauses (c) and (d).

Cf. secs. 107 and 108, *infra,* and notes, as to dispensing with notice of dishonour.

Bill payable to drawer's order is accepted and endorsed to accommodate the drawer. The drawer discounts it, but does not provide the acceptor with funds to meet it at maturity. Presentment is not necessary to charge the drawer (Terry v. Parker, 1837, 6 A. & E. 502), but is necessary to charge the accommodation endorser. (Saul v. Jones, 1858, 28 L.J.Q.B. 37; cf. Turner v. Samson, 1876, 2 Q.B.D. 23.)

A cheque is drawn on the A. Bank, the drawer not having sufficient funds there to meet it, and having no reason to expect that it will be honoured. Presentment is not necessary to charge the drawer. (Wirth v. Austin, 1875, L.R. 10 C.P. 689.)

Clause (e).

This is declaratory. (Hopley v. Dufresne, 1812, 15 East, 275; cf. Bank of Upper Canada v. Turcotte, 1865, 15 L.C.R. 203, 13 R.J.R.Q. 197, 199.)

Cf. sec. 106, as to waiver of notice of dishonour.

The waiver may be either before or after the time for presentment. A promise to pay after the bill is due is waiver of notice. (McCarthy v. Phelps, 1870, 30 U.C.R. 57; Deering v. Hayden, 1886, 3 Man. R. 219), if made with knowledge of the want of presentment. (Nowton v. Roach, 1843, 2 Kerr (N.B.) 337; Mc-Fatridge v. Williston, 1892, 25 N.S.R. 11.)

As to express stipulation in the bill waiving some or all of the holder's duties, see sec. 34.

Waiver of notice of dishonour does not of itself include a waiver of presentment for payment. (Hill v. Heap, 1823, D. & R. N.P.C. 57; Nowton v. Roach, *supra.*)

Waiver of demand of payment is waiver of presentment. (Burton v. Goffin, 1897, 5 B.C.R. 454.)

A memorandum running "my note coming due the 10th inst. good for 10 days after date," given by the endorser of a note

to the holder in reference to a note coming due the 11th, held Sec. 92.
sufficient waiver. (Burnett v. Monaghan, 1871, 3 R.L. 448, 24 Present-
R.J.R.Q. 29.) ment for
Part payment is a waiver of presentment. (Rice v. Bowker, payment dispensed
1853, 3 L.C.R. 305-6, 4 R.J.R.Q. 23.) with.

Sub-sec. 2.

The drawer of a bill orders the acceptor not to pay it. The
holder hears of this. Presentment is not dispensed with. (Hill
v. Heap, *supra.*)

The acceptor of a bill informs the holder that he cannot, or
will not, pay it when due. Presentment is not dispensed with.
(Baker v. Birch, 1811, 3 Camp. 107; Ex parte Bignold, 1836,
1 Deac. 712.)

The acceptor of a bill becomes bankrupt before it matures.
Presentment is not excused. (Esdaile v. Sowerby, 1809, 11 East,
at p. 117; Bowes v. Howe, 1813, 5 Taunt. 30.)

B. makes a note payable at "1 B. Street, London." Before
it becomes due he becomes insolvent and absconds. Presentment at the address mentioned is not dispensed with. (Sands
v. Clarke, 1849, 19 L.J.C.P. 84; Pierce v. Cate, 1853, 66 Mass.
190.)

93. When no place of payment is specified in the bill or When no
place
acceptance, presentment for payment is not necessary in order specified.
to render the acceptor liable.

2. When a place of payment is specified in the bill or accept- If place
specified.
ance, the acceptor, in the absence of an express stipulation to Neglect.
that effect, is not discharged by the omission to present the bill
for payment on the day that it matures, but if any suit or action
be instituted thereon before presentation the costs thereof shall
.be in the discretion of the court.

3. When a bill is paid the holder shall forthwith deliver it Delivery on
payment.
up to the party paying it. 53 V., c. 33, s. 52. Eng. s. 52.

The sub-sections of sec. 52 of the English Act corresponding
to sub-secs. 1 and 2 of this section are as follows:—

(1) When a bill is accepted generally presentment for payment is not necessary in order to render the acceptor liable.

Sec. 93.

Present-
ment for
payment,
when ne-
cessary in
order to
render
acceptor
liable.

(2) When by the terms of a qualified acceptance presentment for payment is required, the acceptor, in the absence of an
express stipulation to that effect, is not discharged by the omission to present the bill for payment on the day that it matures.

In regard to the difference in the wording of the two acts the
difference explained in the notes to sec. 38 must also be carefully noted. An acceptance payable at a particular place is a
general acceptance in England as in Canada, but an acceptance
payable only at a particular place is a qualified acceptance in
England but a general acceptance in Canada.

In England, when a bill is accepted payable at a particular
place, but not there only, presentment is not necessary in order
to render the acceptor liable. But if the acceptance is to pay
at a particular place and not elsewhere, as, *e.g.*, "payable at the
A. Bank only" the effect is to require presentment at the specified place before the acceptor can be sued (Halstead v. Skelton,
1843, 5 Q.B. at pp. 93, 94), but the presentment need not be
made on the day the bill matures, in the absence of an express
stipulation to that effect.

In Canada, when a bill is accepted payable at a particular
place, whether there only or not, presentment is not dispensed
with by the Act, but the omission to present the bill on the day
it matures does not discharge the acceptor, in the absence of an
express stipulation to that effect. If, however, a suit or action
is instituted on the bill before presentation the costs shall be in
the discretion of the court. As to sub-sec. 2, see the notes to sec.
183, which contains a similar provision in regard to presentment as regards the maker, but which also provides that, where
a note is in the body of it made payable at a particular place,
it must be presented for payment at that place. (Cf. sec. 88.)

Chalmers, p. 180, says: "When a bill is accepted payable at
a particular place and there only, the acceptor's position is for
many purposes analogous to that of the drawer of a cheque
(Bishop v. Chitty, 1742, 2 Stra. 1195; Ramchurn Mullick v.
Luckmeechund Radakissen, 1854, 9 Moo. P.C. at p. 70, 4 R.C. at
p. 466). If, then, he could shew that he was damnified by the
holder's omission to present it on the proper day, he would
probably be discharged. (Cf. Alexander v. Burchfield, 1842, 7
M. & G. 1061, case of a cheque where bank failed.)"

This conclusion does not seem to be consistent with the provisions of the Act that the acceptor, in the absence of an express

stipulation to that effect, is not discharged by the omission. The cases cited by Chalmers were decided before the passing of the Act. The "express stipulation" required by the English Act seems to be something different from the terms of the qualified acceptance which require presentment. An acceptance to pay at a particular place and there only requires presentment (Halstead v. Skelton, *supra*), but such qualified acceptance cannot reasonably be regarded as also amounting to an express stipulation that presentment shall be made on the day of maturity, especially in view of the rule laid down in Smith v. Vertue, 1860, 9 C.B.N.S. 214, 4 R.C. 246, that qualifications in acceptances should not be extended beyond the terms in which they are expressed. In that case an acceptance "payable, on delivering bill of lading, at the London and Westminister Bank" was held not to require presentment on the day of maturity, as regards the acceptor's liability.

Unlike the acceptor, the drawer and endorsers are entitled, subject to the provisions of the Act (sec. 85), to have the bill presented for payment. As to the proper place for presentment, see secs. 88 to 90.

The reason why presentment is not necessary as regards the maker or acceptor if no place of payment is specified is that at common law the debtor is bound to seek out his creditor to pay him. (Cranley v. Hillary, 1813, 2 M. & S. 120; Walton v. Mascall, 1844, 13 M. & W. at p. 458, 4 R.C. at p. 458.)

Delivery up of bill.

Prior to the revision of 1906, sub-sec. 3 formed one section with sub-sec. 3 of sec. 85, as in sec. 52 of the English Act.

The acceptor paying the bill has a right to the possession of the instrument for his own security, and as his voucher and discharge *pro tanto* in his account with the drawer. (Hansard v. Robinson, 1827, 7 B. & C. at p. 94; Crowe v. Clay, 1854, 9 Ex. 604; cf. Jones v. Broadhurst, 1850, 9 C.B. at p. 182, and Duncan v. North and South Wales Bank, 1880, 6 App. Cas. at p. 18, as to payment by drawer or endorser; and Cornes v. Taylor, 1854, 10 Ex. 441; Woodward v. Pell, 1868, L.R. 4 Q.B. 55, lien for costs.)

94. Where the address of the acceptor for honour of a bill is in the same place where the bill is protested for non-payment,

Margin notes: Sec. 93. Presentment for payment, when necessary in order to render acceptor liable.

Margin notes: Time for presentment.

Sec. 94. the bill must be presented to him not later than the day following its maturity.

Parties in
different
places.
 2. Where the address of the acceptor for honour is in some place other than the place where it is protested for non-payment, the bill must be forwarded not later than the day following its maturity for presentment to him.

Excuses for
delay.
 3. Delay in presentment or non-presentment is excused by any circumstance which would in case of acceptance by a drawee excuse delay in presentment for payment or non-presentment for payment. 53 V., c. 33, s. 66. Eng. s. 67.

As to acceptance for honour, see secs. 147 to 152.

Where a dishonoured bill has been accepted for honour *supra* protest, or contains a reference in case of need, it must be protested for non-payment before it is presented for payment to the acceptor for honour or referee in case of need, and if the bill is dishonoured by the acceptor for honour it must be protested for non-payment by him (sec. 117).

Sub-secs. 1 and 2 reproduce the effect of the English statute 6 and 7 Will. 4, c. 58. Non-business days are excluded in reckoning the time (sec. 6).

If the bill be not presented in due time to the acceptor for honour, it is conceived that he, and any party who would have been discharged if he had paid the bill, are discharged by the holder's laches; but there is no decision in point. Chalmers, p. 233.

As to circumstances which would excuse delay in presentment for payment or non-presentment for payment to the drawee, see secs. 91 and 92.

CHAPTER XLIII.

Subject to the provisions of the Act, when a bill has been dishonoured by non-acceptance (sec. 81) or non-payment (sec. 95) notice of honour must be given to the drawer and to each endorser (sec. 96). The giving of notice is one of the duties of the holder. As to these duties generally, see notes at the beginning of Chapter XLI., *supra*, p. 484.

Dishonour.

95. A bill is dishonoured by non-payment,— Non-payment on presentment.

(*a*) when it is duly presented for payment and payment is refused or cannot be obtained; or,

(*b*) when presentment is excused and the bill is overdue and unpaid. Excuse.

2. Subject to the provisions of this Act, when a bill is dishonoured by non-payment, an immediate right of recourse against the drawer, acceptor and endorsers accrues to the holder. 53 V., c. 33, s. 47. Eng. s. 47. Recourse.

As to due presentment, see sec. 86.

As to the cases in which presentment is excused, see sec. 92.

Sections 81 and 82 dealing with dishonour by non-acceptance are as follows:— Dishonour by non-acceptance.

81. A bill is dishonoured by non-acceptance,—

(*a*) When it is duly presented for acceptance, and such acceptance as is prescribed by this Act is refused or cannot be obtained; or,

(*b*) When presentment for acceptance is excused and the bill is not accepted.

82. Subject to the provisions of this Act, when a bill is dishonoured by non-acceptance an immediate right of recourse against the drawer and endorsers accrues to the holder, and no presentment for payment is necessary.

Sec. 95.
Dishonour.

These two sections are strictly parallel with sec. 95, and the revisers might more logically have placed all three sections under the heading "Dishonour." If secs. 81 and 82 are properly relegated to "Presentment for Acceptance" (Chapter XLI.), then sec. 95 belongs to "Presentment for Payment" (Chapter XLII.).

Subject to the provisions of this Act.

See secs. 147 to 155 as to acceptance and payment for honour.

Dishonour by non-payment.

If a note is payable with interest and an instalment of interest comes due before the maturity of the note, non-payment of such instalment probably constitutes dishonour of the note. (Moore v. Scott, 1906, 5 West. L.R. 8, 11, following Jennings v. Napanee, 1885, 4 C.L.T. 595.)

Right of recourse and right of action.

Right of recourse must be distinguished from right of action.

As against the acceptor, no notice of dishonour is necessary (sec. 96), and the holder's right of action accrues as soon as the bill is overdue. The word "acceptor" in sub-sec. 2 is not in the English Act, but no change in the law appears to have been made by the insertion of the word in the Canadian Act. The similar provision in regard to dishonour by non-acceptance (sec. 82) omits the word "acceptor."

As against the drawer and each endorser, subject to the provisions of the Act, notice of dishonour must be given (sec. 96). The bill may be, and in certain cases must be, noted or protested (secs. 112 and 113). The holder's right of action dates from the time when notice of dishonour is or ought to be received and not from the time when it is sent. (Castrique v. Bernabo, 1844, 6 Q.B. 498.)

At any time on the day when a bill is payable the holder of a bill may, immediately upon payment being refused by the acceptor, give notice of dishonour to the drawer and the endorsers (sec. 98). But the drawer and endorsers, as well as the acceptor, still have the whole of such day in which to pay the bill, and if payment is made subsequently on the same day, the payment is good and the notice of dishonour becomes of no avail. (Kennedy v. Thomas, [1894] 2 Q.B. at pp. 764, 765.)

In Kennedy v. Thomas, the English Court of Appeal decided that an action brought by the holder against the acceptor on the last day of grace must be dismissed as premature. In Upper Canada, however, the Court of Queen's Bench had previously held the contrary. (Sinclair v. Robson, 1858, 16 U.C.R. 211.) Sinclair v. Robson was a case of a promissory note payable at a bank. The note was dishonoured, and by virtue of a statute similar to the provision of sec. 121 (authorizing protest for non-payment on the day of dishonour at any time after three o'clock) was protested for non-payment on the same day. The plaintiff, an endorsee, paid the note at four o'clock, and sued out a writ at five o'clock. Held, that the action was not premature.

A similar question in regard to a bill of exchange came before the Ontario Queen's Bench Division in Edgar v. Magee, 1882, 1 O.R. 287. The case of Sinclair v. Robson was remarked upon but not overruled. One member of the court approved of it, one disapproved, and the third distinguished it on the ground that a cause of action would accrue upon a bill or note on the last day of grace provided it was presented at the place of payment on that day and payment refused. In the result it was held, that by reason of the Statute of Limitations a writ issued on the 1st December, 1881, upon a note falling due on 1st December, 1875, was not too late.

The rule was laid down by the Judicial Committee in Trimble v. Hill, 1879, 5 App. Cas. 342, that where a colonial legislature has passed an Act in the same terms as an Imperial Statute, and the latter has been authoritatively construed by the Court of Appeal in England, such construction should be adopted by the courts of the colony. This rule has not been always observed in Ontario (see McDonald v. Elliott, 1886, 12 O.R. 98, under the authority of which in Bank of Toronto v. McBean, 1900, 21 C.L.T. 44, Sinclair v. Robson was followed in preference to Kennedy v. Thomas). The rule has, however, since been applied in various cases. (See Hollender v. Ffoulkes, 1894, 26 O.R. 1; McVity v. Trenmouth, 1905, 9 O.L.R. at p. 109; but see Toronto v. Toronto Ry. Co., 1905, 9 O.L.R. at p. 339, where it is suggested that owing to a provision in the Ontario Judicature Act, the courts of Ontario must follow a decision of the Court of Appeal for Ontario notwithstanding any later expres-

Sec. 95.

No right of
action on
the last day
of grace.

sion of opinion in any English court, except the Judicial Committee itself.)

It would appear therefore that Kennedy v. Thomas must be followed in preference to Sinclair v. Robson, unless the absence from the English Act of any provision similar to that of sec. 121 referred to above constitutes a sufficient difference between the two statutes to take the case out of the rule laid down in Trimble v. Hill. Demers v. Rousseau, 1892, Q.R. 1 S.C. 440, is a decision to the same effect as Kennedy v. Thomas.

Accrues to the holder.

A. draws a bill upon B., payable at a bank. The bank is A.'s agent to procure acceptance and payment. A. may bring an action in his own name against B. (Richards v. Bowes, 1892, 31 N.B.R. 144.)

Limitations and prescription.

Limitation of action is usually governed by the law of the place where the action is brought: see Chapter L., *infra*.

Chalmers (p. 293) lays down the following rules as to the Statute of Limitations:

1. Subject to the case provided for by sec. 96(a) ["where a bill is dishonoured by non-acceptance, and notice of non-acceptance is not given, the rights of a holder in due course subsequent to the omission shall not be prejudiced by the omission"], and subject to rule 5, no action on a bill can be maintained against any party thereto after the expiration of six years from the time when a cause of action first accrued to the *then* holder against such party. (Whitehead v. Walker, 1842, 9 M. & W. 506; Woodruff v. Moore, 1850, 8 Barb. (N.Y.) 171.)

2. As against the acceptor, time begins to run from the maturity of the bill, unless,—

(1) Presentment for payment is necessary in order to charge the acceptor, in which case time (probably) runs from the date of such presentment (cf. sec. 93); or,

(2) The bill is accepted after its maturity, in which case time (probably) runs from the date of acceptance (cf. sec. 23).

3. As regards the drawer or an endorser, time (generally) begins to run from the date when notice of dishonour is received. (Cf. Castrique v. Bernabo, 1844, 6 Q.B. 498; and notes to sec. 82.)

Sec. 95.

4. When an action is brought against a party to a bill, to enforce an obligation collateral to the bill, though arising out of the bill transaction, the nature of the particular transaction determines the period from which time begins to run.

5. Any circumstance which postpones or defeats the operation of the Statute of Limitations in the case of an ordinary contract postpones or defeats it in like manner in the case of a bill.

No endorsement or memorandum of any payment written or made upon a bill by or on behalf of the party to whom such payment is made is sufficient to defeat the operation of the statute. (9 Geo. IV., c. 14, sec. 3.)

96. Subject to the provisions of this Act, when a bill has been dishonoured by non-acceptance or by non-payment, notice of dishonour must be given to the drawer, and each endorser, and any drawer or endorser to whom such notice is not given is discharged: Provided that,— *(Notice of dishonour.)*

(a) where a bill is dishonoured by non-acceptance, and due notice of dishonour is not given, the rights of a holder in due course subsequent to the omission shall not be prejudiced by the omission; *(Subsequent holder.)*

(b) where a bill is dishonoured by non-acceptance, and due notice of dishonour is given, it shall not be necessary to give notice of a subsequent dishonour by non-payment, unless the bill shall in the meantime have been accepted. *(Notice of non-payment.)*

2. In order to render the acceptor of a bill liable it is not necessary that notice of dishonour should be given to him. 53 V., c. 33, ss. 48 and 52. Eng. ss. 48 and 52. *(Notice to acceptor.)*

Prior to 1906 sub-sec. 2 and sec. 109 formed one sub-section of a section which included the provisions of sec. 93 and sub-sec. 3 of sec. 85.

As to dishonour by non-acceptance, see sec. 81, and by non-payment, see sec. 95.

As to holder in due course, see sec. 56.

Secs. 97, *et seq.*, contain the rules regarding the time and manner of giving notice of dishonour, the persons by whom and

Sec. 95.   to whom it should be given and the persons for whose benefit
it enures.

Delay in giving notice may be excused (sec. 105), and notice
may be dispensed with (secs. 106 to 108) under certain circumstances. Otherwise, notice of dishonour is essential to the
holder's cause of action against the drawer or an endorser. Berridge v. Fitzgerald, 1869, L.R. 4 Q.B. 639, 4 R.C. 494.)

"Notice of dishonour" means notification of dishonour, *i.e.*,
formal notice. Chalmers, p. 157. The fact that the drawer or
endorser knows that it has been dishonoured does not dispense
with the necessity for giving him notice. (Miers v. Brown,
1843, 11 M. & W. 372; East v. Smith, 1847, 16 L.J.Q.B. 292; cf.
In re Fenwick, Deep Sea Fishery Co.'s Claim, [1902] 1 Ch.
507.)

Discharge of
party by
omission to
give notice
of dishonour.

The discharge of a party to a bill must be distinguished
from the discharge of the bill (cf. secs. 139, *et seq.*).

An endorser of a bill who has not received due notice of
dishonour is discharged; and if he then pays the bill, he does
so in his own wrong, and cannot recover upon it against a prior
endorser, although the latter receives notice of dishonour on
the same day on which he would have received it if all the
notices had been given in due course. (Turner v. Leach, 1821,
4 B. & Ald. 451, 4 R.C. 523; cf. Savaria v. Paquette, 1899, Q.
R. 20 S.C. 314.)

Where a bill is endorsed when it is overdue, as regards such
endorser, it is a bill payable on demand (sec. 23). Therefore the
endorser is entitled to have it presented within a reasonable
time and is entitled to notice of dishonour.

No notice of dishonour need be given to the acceptor of a bill
or the maker of a note (cf. sec. 186).

A person who has given a guarantee for the payment of a
bill by the acceptor is not entitled to notice of dishonour (Walton v. Mascall, 1844, 13 M. & W. 72, 452, 4 R.C. 483). Secus,
in the case of a person who signs a bill otherwise than as drawer
or acceptor (sec. 131).

A person who is not a party to a bill, but who is liable on the
consideration for which it was given, is (probably) entitled to
notice of dishonour, though the same strict and technical notice
of dishonour would not apparently be required to charge such
party as is requisite to charge a party liable on the bill. Chalmers, p. 173.

Party discharged from liability on the consideration as well as from that on the bill.

A bill taken for and on account of a debt suspends the remedy by action to recover the amount of the debt (Walton v. Mascall, 1844, 13 M. & W. 452, 4 R.C. 483), but if the bill is taken as collateral security only, the right of action on the debt is not suspended. Even in the latter case the creditor by taking the bill becomes bound to perform the duties of holder, and if by his omission, as, for instance, to give due notice of dishonour, the bill is rendered worthless or deteriorated in value, then as between the creditor and the debtor the bill must be treated as payment, to the extent of its full amount, of the debt. (Peacock v. Purssell, 1863, 14 C.B.N.S. 728, 4 R.C. 526.)

A creditor who takes a bill for a pre-existing debt presumably takes it as conditional payment of the debt (Currie v. Misa, 1875, L.R. 10 Ex. at p. 163, 4 R.C. at pp. 320-1). So taken, the bill is subject to the law incident to bills, and if the debtor is discharged from liability on the bill by non-presentment for payment (Soward v. Palmer, 1818, 8 Taunt. 277; Hart v. McDougall, 1892, 25 N.S.R. 38), or by omission to give notice of dishonour (Bridges v. Berry, 1810, 3 Taunt. 130), he is also discharged from his liability on the debt which entered into the consideration of the bill. *Payment by bill.*

But where the bill has been dishonoured by non-payment on the part of the acceptor, notice of dishonour being duly given or waived, the condition of the payment of the debt is unfulfilled, and the right to sue on the original consideration revives. (Yglesias v. River Plate Bank, 1877, 3 C.P.D. 60.)

The bill and the consideration do not, however, constitute two separate causes of action, and a judgment (although unsatisfied) on a bill given for the price of goods sold operates as a bar to an action on the original contract. (Cambefort v. Chapman, 1887, 19 Q.B.D. 229.)

97. Notice of dishonour in order to be valid and effectual must be given,— *Notice.*

    (*a*) not later than the juridical or business day next following the dishonour of the bill; *Time for.*

Sec. 97.
By holder or
endorser.

(b) by or on behalf of the holder, or by or on behalf of an endorser, who at the time of giving it, is himself liable on the bill;

Personal
representa-
tive.

(c) in the case of the death, if known to the party giving notice, of the drawer or endorser, to a personal representative, if such there is and with the exercise of reasonable diligence he can be found;

Two
drawees.

(d) in case of two or more drawers or endorsers who are not partners, to each of them, unless one of them has authority to receive notice for the others. 53 V., c. 33, s. 49. Cf. Eng. s. 49 (1), (9), (11), (12).

Sec. 49 of the English Act, re-enacted with some important modifications by sec. 49 of the Canadian Act of 1890, contains fifteen rules in accordance with which notice of dishonour must be given in order to be valid and effectual. The revision of 1906 has effected a complete re-arrangement of the provisions of the old section and these provisions are now contained in secs. 97 to 104.

Clause (10) of the English section which provides that "where the drawer or endorser is bankrupt, notice may be given either to the party himself or to the trustee," is omitted from the Canadian Act. Cf. notes to sec. 78.

The English and Canadian Acts are different in respect to two other matters relating to notice of dishonour. One is noted under sec. 103; the other concerns the time when notice must be given.

Time for
giving notice
of dishonour

Both Acts provide that the notice may be given as soon as the bill is dishonoured (sec. 98). In Canada, however, the notice must be given not later than the juridical or business day next following the dishonour of the bill, while in England it must be given "within a reasonable time thereafter." The English Act further provides that "In the absence of special circumstances notice is not deemed to have been given within a reasonable time, unless,—

(a) where the person giving and the person to receive notice reside in the same place, the notice is given or sent off in time to reach the latter on the day after the dishonour of the bill;

(b) where the person giving and the person to receive notice reside in different places, the notice is sent off on the day after the dishonour of the bill, if there be a post at a convenient hour on that day, and if there be no such post on that day then by the next post thereafter.''

These provisions of the English Act simply express the law as clearly laid down in the old cases (see e.g., Smith v. Mullett, 1809, 2 Camp. 208, 11 R.R. 605, and Bray v. Hadwen, 1816, 5 M. & S. 68, 17 R.R. 277). See the matter fully discussed in Studdy v. Beesty, 1889, 60 L.T. 647, at p. 648, 4 R.C. at p. 500. See also notes to secs. 105 (excuse for delay in giving notice of dishonour) and 106 (notice dispensed with).

Any hardship which might result from the application of the absolute requirement of the Canadian Act that notice of dishonour must be given not later than the juridical or business day next following the dishonour of the bill is avoided by the provisions of sec. 103. That section permits notice of dishonour of any bill payable in Canada to be given by post, and provides that the notice is sufficient if addressed to any party at the place at which the bill is dated unless any such party has, under his signature, designated another place, in which case such notice is sufficiently given if addressed to him at such other place. By sec. 104, the sender is deemed to have given due notice of dishonour, notwithstanding any miscarriage by the post office.

If a bill is payable out of Canada, the necessity for and sufficiency of notice of dishonour is determined by the law of the place where the bill is dishonoured (sec. 162), and therefore sec. 97 would not apply.

As to what are juridical or business days, see secs. 2 and 43.

Although notice of dishonour need not be given until the following day, protest where necessary (secs. 112 and 113) must be made or noted on the day the bill is dishonoured (sec. 119).

A person who gives notice to a remote party must give notice within the same time as is limited for giving notice to an immediate party (Rowe v. Tipper, 1853, 22 L.J. C.P. 135), but if he gives due notice to his immediate endorser, but not to remote parties, his right as against the remote parties may yet be saved by due notice given by his immediate endorsers (cf. secs. 101 and 102).

Sec. 97.   *By whom notice must be given.*

Where the attorney duly authorized by the holder has given notice, but by mistake states it as given by the authority of an endorser who is also liable on the bill, the notice was held good, as there was in fact notice authorized by a competent person, and the mistake could not mislead—the notice being good on its face (Harrison v. Ruscoe, 1846, 15 M. & W. 231). It is observed in this case, at p. 235, that an acceptor, as he himself could not sue upon the bill after taking it up, is excluded from the category of persons who can give notice, and that the instances in which a notice by an acceptor has been held to be good at *nisi prius, e.g.,* Rosher v. Kieran, 1814, 4 Camp. 87, are explained in Bayley on Bills on the supposition that in those cases the acceptor had a special authority to give notice.

When a bill is presented for payment through the post office (sec. 90), the acceptor is deemed to be the agent of the holder for the purpose of giving notice of dishonour. (Cf. Bailey v. Bodenham, 1864, 33 L.J. C.P. at p. 255; Prideaux v. Criddle, 1869, L.R. 4 Q.B. at p. 461; Heywood v. Pickering, 1874, L.R. 9 Q.B. 428.)

Cf. sec. 98, as to notice given by an agent.

A bill endorsed by C. and held by D. is dishonoured. E., who was at one time employed by the drawer to get the bill discounted, but who is not in any way acting on D.'s behalf, informs C. that the bill has been dishonoured. This is not sufficient; C. is discharged. (Stewart v. Kennett, 1809, 2 Camp. 177; cf. East v. Smith, 1847, 16 L.J. Q.B. 292.)

C. is the first endorser of a dishonoured bill held by D. D. gives notice to C. one day late. C. on the *same* day gives notice to the drawer; thus, as it were, making up the lost day. This notice is ineffectual; for C., having been discharged by the holder's delay, is a mere stranger. (Turner v. Leech, 1821, 4 B. & Ald. 451.)

Death of drawer or endorser.

Clause (c) is probably declaratory, although there is no English decision in point. Chalmers, p. 163.

But notice of dishonour of a ·bill payable in Canada is not invalid by reason only of the fact that the party to whom it is addressed is dead, provided it has been addressed and posted as provided in sec. 103. *Quære*, therefore, what is the operation of clause (*c*) of sec. 97, since if a bill is not payable in Canada, notice of its dishonour is governed by the law of the place where it is dishonoured (sec. 162) and not by this Act?

98. Notice of dishonour may be given,— Notice.

(*a*) as soon as the bill is dishonoured; Earliest time.

(*b*) to the party to whom the same is required to be given, or to his agent in that behalf; To whom.

(*c*) by an agent either in his own name or in the name of any party entitled to give notice whether that party is his principal or not; By agent.

(*d*) in writing or by personal communication and in any terms which identify the bill and intimate that the bill has been dishonoured by non-acceptance or non-payment. Manner.

2. A misdescription of the bill shall not vitiate the notice unless the party to whom the notice is given is in fact misled thereby. 53 V., c. 33, s. 49. Eng. s. 49, (2), (5), (7), (8), (12). Misdescription.

As soon as the bill is dishonoured.

Notice must be given not later than the juridical or business day next following the dishonour of the bill (sec. 97).

To the party or to his agent.

It is the duty of the drawer or endorser of a bill, if he be absent from his place of business or residence, to see that there is some person there to receive notice on his behalf. (Cf. Allen v. Edmundson, 1848, 2 Ex. at p. 723.)

A. and his wife endorse a note given as one of a series of renewals during some years under an agreement of which the husband had knowledge. A.'s wife has no personal knowledge of the transaction, and leaves the matter entirely to A., simply endorsing as she is directed. A notice of dishonour given to A. is a good notice to his wife. (Counsell v. Livingstone, 1902, 4 O.L.R. 340.)

C. is the endorser of a bill which is dishonoured. Verbal notice to his solicitor is not sufficient. (Crosse v. Smith, 1813, 1 M. & S. at p. 554.)

D., who has authority to endorse for C., endorses a bill in C.'s name. Notice of dishonour given to D. is (perhaps) sufficient. (Cf. Firth v. Thrush, 1828, 8 B. & C. at p. 391.)

The drawer of a bill is a non-trader. Verbal notice of dishonour given to his wife at his house, in his absence, may be sufficient. (Housego v. Cowne, 1837, 2 M. & W. 348; cf. Wharton v. Wright, 1844, 1 C. & K. 585.) But delivery of notice to a man cutting wood in the yard is insufficient, there being no evidence that the man was an inmate of the family. (Commercial Bank v. Weller, 1848, 5 U.C.R. 543.)

The endorser of a bill is a merchant. Notice of dishonour, verbal or written, given to or left with a clerk at his office is sufficient. (Allen v. Edmundson, 1848, 2 Ex. at p. 724; cf. Viale v. Michael, 1874, 30 L.T. N.S. 453.)

C. endorses a bill "in need at Messrs. D. & Co." Notice of dishonour given to D. & Co. is not sufficient to charge C. (Ex parte Prange, 1865, L.R. 1 Eq. at p. 5.)

By an agent, etc.

See Harrison v. Ruscoe, cited under sec. 97.

Where a note endorsed in blank is left at a bank for collection, notice of dishonour may be given by the bank, although it has no interest in the note. (Howard v. Goddard, 1860, 4 Allen (N.B.) 452; cf. Wilson v. Pringle, 1856, 14 U.C.R. 230.)

C. the endorser of a bill, holds it as agent for the endorsee. C. presents it for payment, and it is dishonoured. Notice of dishonour given by C. in his own name is sufficient. (Lysaght v. Bryant, 1850, 19 L.J. C.P. 160.)

Clause (d)—form of notice.

As to form, see also sec. 99.

Notices of dishonour are now construed very liberally. In 1834 the House of Lords, in Solarte v. Palmer, 1834, 1 Bing. N.C. 194, decided that the notice must inform the holder, either in terms or by necessary implication, that the bill had been presented and dishonoured. This inconvenient decision was frequently regretted (see *e.g.*, Everard v. Watson, 1853, 1 E. & B. at p. 804), and was eventually got rid of by considering it merely as a finding on the particular facts (Paul v. Joel, 1858, 27 L.J. Ex. at p. 384). Since 1841 (see Furse v. Sharwood, 1841,

2 Q.B. 388) it does not appear that any written notice of dishonour has been held bad on the ground of insufficiency in form.
See Counsell v. Livingstone, 1902, 2 O.L.R. 582, 4 O.L.R. 340,
where some of the authorities are reviewed. In that case the
following notice was held to be sufficient: "I beg to advise you
that Mr. L.'s note for $3,500 in your favour and endorsed by
yourself and wife and held by our estate was due yesterday.
As I have not received renewal, will you kindly see that same
is forwarded with cheque for discount, as there is no surplus
on hand."

The following written notices have been held to be sufficient:

1. I give notice that a bill. etc. (described), endorsed by you,
lies at 1 B. Street, dishonoured. (King v. Bickley, 1842, 2
Q.B. 419.)

2. B.'s acceptance due to-day is unpaid and your immediate
attention to it is requested. (Cf. Bailey v. Porter, 1845, 14
M. & W. 44; Paul v. Joel, 1858, 27 L.J. Ex. 380, 1859, 28 L.J.
Ex. 143.)

3. Your draft which became due yesterday is unpaid. Unless the same is paid immediately I shall take proceedings.
Noting 5 s. (Armstrong v. Christiani, 1848, 5 C.B. 687; Everard
v. Watson, 1853, 1 E. & B. 801.)

4. Express notice that a bill has been protested, if protest
be necessary, is not required. (Ex parte Lowenthal, 1874, L.R.
9 Ch. 591.)

An insufficient written notice may be supplemented and
validated by oral communication and a written notice need not be
signed (sec. 99).

Personal communication.

The holder's clerk goes to the drawer and tells him that his
bill has been presented, and that the acceptor cannot pay it.
The drawer replies that he will see the holder about it. This
may be sufficient. (Metcalfe v. Richardson, 1852, 11 C.B. 1011;
cf. Housego v. Cowne, 1837, 2 M. & W. 348, notice to drawer's
wife.)

Misdescription of bill.

A notice may be sufficient although it misdescribes the bill
in the following respects, namely, one which describes the bill

as payable at the A. Bank, when in fact it was payable at the
B. Bank (Bromage v. Vaughan, 1846, 16 L.J. Q.B. 10), or
which describes a bill as a note (Stockman v. Parr, 1843, 11
M. & W. 809; Bain v. Gregory, 1866, 14 L.T. N.S. 601), or which
transposes the names of drawer and acceptor (Mellersh v. Rippen, 1852, 7 Ex. 578), or which describes the acceptor by a
wrong name (Harpham v. Child, 1859, 1 F. & F. 652), or which
contains an error as to the amount of the bill (Thompson v.
Cotterell, 1854, 11 U.C.R. 185), or its due date. (Cassidy v.
Mansfield, 1874, 24 C.P. 383.)

99. In point of form,—

(*a*) the return of a dishonoured bill to the drawer or an
             endorser is a sufficient notice of dishonour;

(*b*) a written notice need not be signed.

2. An insufficient written notice may be supplemented and
validated by verbal communication. 53 V., c. 33, s. 49. Eng.
s. 49 (6), (7).

As to form of notice, cf. sec. 98.

Clause (*a*) approves a common practice of collecting bankers
which was previously of doubtful validity. Chalmers, p. 161.

A written notice need not be signed, but it must come from
a person entitled to give notice (secs. 97 and 98).

Supplementing written notice.

The sufficiency or insufficiency of the notice is a question of
fact. (Houlditch v. Carty, 1838, 4 Bing. N.C. 411.)

A notice may be by personal communication (sec. 98).

A notary's clerk takes a bill, with the notary's ticket attached, to the drawer's office, and shews it to a clerk there. The
clerk looks at it, says the drawer is out and has left no orders.
The notary then leaves the usual notice that the bill is due at
his office. This may be sufficient. (Viale v. Michael, 1874, 30
L.T. N.S. 453; cf. East v. Smith, 1847, 16 L.J. Q.B. 292; Chard
v. Fox, 1849, 14 Q.B. 200; Jennings v. Roberts, 1855, 24 L.J.
Q.B. 102.)

100. Where a bill when dishonoured is in the hands of an
agent he may himself give notice to the parties liable on the bill,

or he may give notice to his principal, in which case the principal upon receipt of the notice shall have the same time for
giving notice as if the agent had been an independent holder.

2. If the agent gives notice to his principal he must do so
within the same time as if he were an independent holder. 53
V., c. 33, s. 49. Cf. Eng. s. 49 (13).

This section has not been improved in the revision of 1906.
In addition to a re-arrangement of the sub-clauses, the phrase
"in which case" has been—not very happily—substituted· for
"if he gives notice to his principal."

Chalmers (p. 165) gives the following illustrations:

1. A bill payable in London is endorsed in blank by the
holder, and deposited with a country banker for collection.
The country banker's London agent presents it for payment and
gives him due notice of its dishonour. The country banker on
the day after the receipt of such notice gives notice to his customer, who in turn gives similar notice to his endorser. The
endorser has received due notice. (Bray v. Hadwen, 1816, 5 M.
& S. 68; cf. Firth v. Thrush, 1828, 8 B. & C. 387.)

2. C. endorses a bill to the Liverpool branch of the D. Bank.
The Liverpool branch sends it to the Manchester branch, and
the latter endorses it to the head office in London, which presents it for payment. The head office sends notice of dishonour
to the M. branch, the M. branch sends notice to the L. branch,
which gives notice to C. Each branch as regards time is to be
considered a distinct party. (Clode v. Bayley, 1843, 12 M. &
W. 51, approved Prince v. Oriental Bank, 1878, 3 App. Cas. at
p. 332; cf. Steinhoff v. Merchants Bank, 1881, 46 U.C.R. 25, 35.)

3. B. at London pays a bill *supra* protest for the honour of
C., an endorser, who resides at Bruges, and the same day posts
the bill to C. C. by return of post sends the bill back to B., who
at once gives notice of dishonour to the drawer. Although six
days have elapsed since the dishonour, the notice is in time, and
B. can sue the drawer. (Goodall v. Polhill, 1845, 14 L. J. C.P.
146.)

4. A bill bearing several endorsements is sent to a branch
bank for collection. The branch bank forwards it to a London
bank, which on the day of the dishonour of the bill gives notice

Sec. 100. by error to another branch of the forwarding bank. Next day
notice is sent to the right branch by wire, and the subsequent
notices of dishonour are given in due time. The first endorser
of the bill cannot rely on the defence that the first notice of
dishonour was out of time. (Fielding v. Corry, [1898] 1 Q.B.
268.)

Notice to
antecedent
parties.
        101. Where a party to a bill receives due notice of dishon-
our he has, after the receipt of such notice, the same period of
time for giving notice to antecedent parties that a holder has
after dishonour. 53 V., c. 33, s. 49. Eng. s. 49 (14).

Cf. notes to sec. 100.

The holder must give notice not later than the juridical or
business day next following the dishonour of the bill (sec. 97).

As to persons for whose benefit the notice accrues, see sec.
102.

The judgment of Brett, L.J. in Horne v. Rouquette, 1878,
3 Q.B.D. 514 (quoted in part in the notes to sec. 102) contains
an exposition of the duties of successive endorsers according to
the law of England in regard to giving notice of dishonour. This
must be read with due regard to the difference between the English and Canadian Acts in regard to the time which the holder
has for giving notice (see notes to sec. 97). It has been laid
down, as a rule of practice in England, that each party should
be allowed one entire day for the purpose of giving notice (Bray
v. Hadwen, 1816, 5 M. & S. 68, 17 R.R. 277). In Canada each
party would be allowed until the end of the juridical or business
day next following the receipt by him of due notice of dishonour.

If the holder, according to the usual custom in Canada, gives
notice to all parties, he must give notice to a remote party within the same time as is limited for giving notice to an immediate
party: cf. notes to sec. 97.

Benefit
enures.
        102. A notice of dishonour enures for the benefit,—

        (a) of all subsequent holders and of all prior endorsers who
            have a right of recourse against the party to whom it is
            given, where given on behalf of the holder;

(*b*) of the holder and of all endorsers subsequent to the
party to whom notice is given, where given, by or on behalf
of an endorser entitled under this Part to give notice. 53
V., c. 33, s. 49. Eng. s. 49 (3), (4).

A notice of dishonour may be given by or on behalf of the
holder, or by or on behalf of an endorser who, at the time of
giving it, is himself liable on the bill (sec. 97).

The holder of a bill is entitled to avail himself of notice of
dishonour given by any party to a bill (Chapman v. Keane, 1835,
3 A. & E. 193, 4 R.C. 490), provided such party is himself liable
on the bill. (Harrison v. Ruscoe, 1846, 15 M. & W. 234, 236;
Lysaght v. Bryant, 1850, 9 C.B. 46.)

If there are several endorsements and the bill is dishonoured in
the hands of the last endorsee, such last endorsee, the holder,
must give notice of dishonour. He may give it either only to his
immediate endorser, or only to the drawer, or to these and to all
the intermediate endorsers. Whatever notice he gives he must
give at once, *i.e.*, within the time limited for giving notice to his
immediate endorsee (sec. 97). Each endorser, as he receives
notice, must, if he would preserve his remedy over, give notice
to his endorser, or to all above him, within a similar period after
he has himself received notice (sec. 101). If all give due
notice, each can recover against his immediate endorser
or against any endorser whose name is before his on
the bill. But if any one fails to give due notice, no one whose
name is before his on the bill is liable to pay him, nor are prior
parties liable to pay each other. If those below him, who have
failed to give due notice, have given notice only to him, or to
each in succession up to him, they cannot recover from any one
above him: otherwise if they have given a direct notice to those
above him. Horne v. Rouquette, 1878, 3 Q.B.D. at p. 517.

103. Notice of the dishonour of any bill payable in Canada
shall, notwithstanding anything in this Act contained be sufficiently given if it is addressed in due time to any party to such
bill entitled to such notice, at his customary address or place of
residence or at the place at which such bill is dated, unless any
such party has, under his signature, designated another place,

Sec. 103. ir which case such notice shall be sufficiently given if addressed to him in due time at such other place.

Sufficiency of notice. 2. Such notice so addressed shall be sufficient, although the place of residence of such party is other than either of the places aforesaid, and shall be deemed to have been duly served and given for all purposes if it is deposited in any post office, with the postage paid thereon, at any time during the day on which presentment has been made, or on the next following juridical or business day.

Death of party. 3. Such notice shall not be invalid by reason only of the fact that the party to whom it is addressed is dead. 53 V., c. 33, s. 49.

This section is not in the English Act. Cf. R.S.C., 1886, c. 123, secs. 5 and 23, and C.C. Lower Canada, Art. 2328.

Address of notice of dishonour. Notice of dishonour in Canada must be given not later than the juridical or business day next following the dishonour of the bill (sec. 97), whereas in England notice need be given only within a reasonable time thereafter (see notes to sec. 97 where the English provision is set out in full). Sec. 103 provides a safe and comparatively easy method of giving notice by post of the dishonour of any bill payable in Canada. If a party to a bill does not take the precaution of designating under his signature a sufficient address, the notice may never reach him, but will be good nevertheless, although it is addressed to him only at the place where the bill is dated or at such party's customary address or place of residence.

Under the English Act, where the holder does not know the endorser's address, he must exercise due diligence in searching for him (cf. notes to sec. 106). If the endorser has held out a place of business as his own, notice may be addressed to him there (Berridge v. Fitzgerald, 1869, L.R. 4 Q.B. 639, 4 R.C. 494), and where a person drew a bill dating it generally "London," it was held that proof of a letter containing the notice of dishonour having been put into the post office addressed to the drawer at "London" was evidence of notice, on the ground that he must be taken to have said, "London is the place where I shall be found." (Clarke v. Sharpe,

1838, 3 M. & W. 166; cf. Burmester v. Barron, 1852, 17 Q.B. 828.)

In Canada if the bill is not dated at any place, and the actual or customary address or place of business of the endorser or person to receive notice, is not known to the holder, or other person who has to give notice, the latter must exercise due diligence to find the endorser. If by due diligence the holder cannot give notice within the time limited by sec. 97, the delay in giving notice is excused (see notes to sec. 106).

A notice addressed to an endorser at his place of residence and posted in due time in accordance with the Act is sufficiently given, although there is no local delivery by letter carriers in the town. (Merchants Bank v. McNutt, 1883, 11 S.C.R. 126.)

"Under his signature" in the section does not mean "below his signature," but means that the address shall be written so that the signature covers it. If a wrong address of an endorser is written in pencil under his name, and no proof is given as to who wrote it, a notice sent to such address, not being the place where the instrument is dated, is insufficient. (Banque Jacques Cartier v. Gagnon, 1894, Q.R. 5 S.C. 499.)

Nor does "under his signature" mean that the name of the place must be written by the party's own hand; it may be written by another person if that other person has in any way any kind of authority from the party to write it. Where a place has been so designated by any party, a notice sent to the party at such place is sufficient, even if the person giving the notice knows or has reason to think that such place is not the party's place of residence or place of business. (Hay v. Burke, 1889, 16 A.R. 463.)

In Baillie v. Dickson, 1882, 7 A.R. 749, the signature of an endorser was so peculiar that no one unacquainted with it could decipher it, although the holder of the instrument was well-acquainted with the signature, but omitted to communicate the name to the notary. The notary made, as near as might be, a *facsimile* of the signature, and so addressed the notice to the endorser's correct address, but the endorser swore that the notice never reached him. It was held that the endorser was discharged.

The statute declares the notice to be sufficient if it is deposited in the post office "at any time during the day,". A notice mailed in the post office between eight and nine in the evening

Sec. 103.
Address of
notice of
dishonour.

of the day after dishonour is sufficient, although it is stamped by the postmaster only on the following day and with the post mark of that day. (Wilson v. Pringle, 1856, 14 U.C.R. 230; cf. Union Bank v. McKilligan, 1887, 4 Man. L.R. 29.)

A notice addressed and posted as provided in this section is good notwithstanding any miscarriage by the post office (sec. 104.)

A notice so addressed and posted is also good, although the party to whom it is addressed is dead.

Quære whether sub-sec. 3 is to be read subject to clause (*d*) of sec. 97. If the death of the drawer or an endorser is known to the person giving notice of dishonour, it would be prudent to give notice to a personal representative, if such there is and with the exercise of reasonable diligence he can be found. Cf. Cosgrave v. Boyle, 1881, 6 S.C.R. 165.

This section applies only to bills payable in Canada. The case of the dishonour of a bill payable out of Canada will be governed by the law of the place where the bill is dishonoured (see sec. 162).

Miscarriage
in post
service.

104. Where a notice of dishonour is duly addressed and posted, as provided in the last preceding section, the sender is deemed to have given due notice of dishonour, notwithstanding any miscarriage by the post office. 53 V., c. 33, s. 49. Eng. s. 49 (15).

The corresponding section of the English Act omits the words "as in the last preceding section provided." These words were substituted in the revision of 1906 for the words "as above provided," which were inserted in the Canadian bill of 1890 by the Senate and were intended to refer to the provision of sec. 103 with regard to depositing the notice of dishonour in the post office "with the postage paid thereon" (see Debates House of Commons, 1890, p. 4263).

It is not clear however that the words "as provided in the last preceding section" do not qualify "addressed" as well as "posted." If they do, then sec. 104 must be confined to a notice which falls within the provisions of sec. 103, and does not apply to a case where a notice is addressed to the endorser at the place where he is in fact, but not being an address expressly authorized by sec. 103, and is lost in the post office. Such a case, if the words in question are to be so construed, is not provided for by the Act, and would have to be decided according to the common law of England (sec. 10). The English section appears, however, to be declaratory of the common law. (Woodcock v. Houldsworth, 1846, 16 M. & W. 124, delay; Mackay v. Judkins, 1858, 1 F. & F. 208, loss; Renwick v. Tighe, 1860, 8 W.R. 391, loss; Chalmers, p. 158.)

105. Delay in giving notice of dishonour is excused where the delay is caused by circumstances beyond the control of the party giving notice, and not imputable to his default, misconduct or negligence. Excuse for delay.

2. When the cause of delay ceases to operate the notice must be given with reasonable diligence. 53 V., c. 33, s. 50. Eng. s. 50. Diligence.

The old rule was that notice must be given (1) before action brought and (2) within a reasonable time after dishonour. The English Act has simply codified the law in this respect. (See notes to sec. 97; Studdy v. Beesty, 1889, 60 L.T. N.S. 647, 4 R.C. 498.)

If the cause of delay arises from circumstances beyond the control of the party giving notice and not imputable to his default, misconduct or negligence he is excused for not giving it within what in other circumstances is held to be reasonable time. But if the cause of delay ceases to operate before action brought the notice must then be given with reasonable diligence. Causes which excuse delay do not dispense with notice.

The cause of delay only excuses the delay, it does not dispense with notice altogether, because under sec. 106, unless notice is waived, it is dispensed with only when after the exercise of reasonable diligence, notice as required by the Act, (*i.e.*, notice before action brought), cannot be given to, or does not reach, the drawer or endorser sought to be charged. So, where the holder attempted to give notice at the time of the dishonour, but had not been able to find the drawer, it was held that the delay was excused, but that, having subsequently, before action brought, learned the drawer's address, he was bound to give him notice with reasonable diligence and was not entitled to sue

Sec. 105. him before giving notice. This was also the law before the passing of the Act. (Studdy v. Beesty, *supra*.)

Excuse for delay in giving notice of dishonour.   In applying this state of law to a bill dishonoured in Canada, it must be borne in mind that, as a consequence of the provisions of sec. 103, it will rarely happen that there can be any excuse for not giving notice within the time limited by sec. 97, on the ground that the person to receive notice cannot be found. But even on that ground, delay in giving notice may be excused in a case which does not fall within sec. 103, and in that event the English common law rule may apply. If delay is excused, due notice must still be given, *i.e.*, it must be given with reasonable diligence, after the cause of delay ceases to operate and before action brought.

Delay may also be excused on other grounds than inability to ascertain the address of the person to receive notice, *e.g.*, an accident to the person making out the notice, or taking it to the post office, or the death or sudden illness of the holder or his agent who has the bill. (Cf. Rothschild v. Currie, 1841, 1 Q.B. at p. 47.)

As to causes excusing delay, cf. sec. 91 (presentment for payment), sec. 111 (protest).

Delay caused by miscarriage by the post office is excused (sec. 104).

When the delay is caused by the negligence of the party to whom notice is sent, it is conceived that, though that party is liable, he cannot give an effectual notice to antecedent parties (Chalmers, p. 167; cf. Shelton v. Braithwaite, 1841, 8 M. & W. at pp. 254, 255.)

Dispensed with. Reasonable diligence.   **106.** Notice of dishonour is dispensed with,—

(*a*) when after the exercise of reasonable diligence, notice as required by this Act cannot be given to or does not reach the drawer or endorser sought to be charged;

Waiver.   (*b*) by waiver express or implied.

Time of.   2. Notice of dishonour may be waived before the time of giving notice has arrived, or after the omission to give due notice. 53 V., c. 33, s. 50. Eng. s. 50.

As to the necessity for notice of dishonour if not dispensed Sec. 106. with, see sec. 96.

Dispensation with notice of dishonour must be distinguished from excuse for delay in giving notice (sec. 105).

Under clause (*a*), it must be shewn that notice could not Notice of dishonour dispensed with. have been given or did not reach the drawer, etc., by the exercise of due diligence at any time prior to action brought (see notes to sec. 105).

This section deals with dispensation with notice from causes arising subsequently to the negotiation of the bill. Notice may also be dispensed with, by the circumstances arising from the relation of the parties to the bill or otherwise existing at the time the contracts on the bill are made (secs. 107 and 108).

Notice of dishonour is dispensed with in some cases where presentment for payment is not (cf. sec. 92).

Waiver.

Cf. notes to sec. 92(*e*).

The drawer of a bill and any endorser may insert therein an express stipulation waiving as regards himself some or all of the holder's duties (sec. 34).

Waiver of notice of dishonour in favour of the holder enures for the benefit of parties prior to such holder as well as subsequent holders (Rabey v. Gilbert, 1861, 30 L.J. Ex. 170), but waiver of notice by an endorser does not affect parties prior to such endorser. (Turner v. Leach, 1821, 4 B. & Ald. 451, 4 R.C. 523.)

Waiver of notice of dishonour may not include a waiver of presentment for payment. (Keith v. Burke, 1885, 1 C. & E. 551.)

Waiver of notice may be implied from an admission of liability or from a promise to pay.

An acknowledgment of liability must be made with full knowledge of the facts in order to operate as a waiver of notice. (Goodall v. Dolley, 1787, 1 T.R. 712.)

An admission of liability may be evidence of due notice having been given or evidence of waiver of notice. So with a promise to pay. "A promise to pay may operate either as evidence of notice of dishonour, or as a prior dispensation, or as a subsequent waiver of notice. Whether made after, or even before, the time for giving notice has expired (inasmuch as notice may be given at any time within the limits prescribed by law), a

Sec. 106.
Waiver of
notice.

promise to pay is always evidence from which a jury may infer due notice. But even where the other evidence is conclusive to shew that the notice has not been given, or when a jury refuses to draw the inference that it was given, yet a promise to pay made within the time for giving notice is a dispensing with notice, and made after that time is a waiver of notice. . . . The practical consequence is, that in almost every case proof of a promise to pay cures the want of notice of dishonour.'' (Cordery v. Colville, 1863, 14 C.B. N.S. 374; cf. Britton v. Milsom, 1892, 19 A.R. 96, and cases cited; McLaurin v. Seguin, 1897, Q.R. 12 S.C. 63.

The drawer of a bill tells the holder before it is due that he has no fixed residence, and that he will call in a few days to see if the acceptor has paid the bill. This waives notice. (Phipson v. Kellner, 1815, 4 Camp. 285; cf. Burgh v. Legge, 1839, 5 M. & W. 418.)

The drawer of a bill informs the holder that it will not be paid on presentment. This (probably) waives notice (Brett v. Levett, 1811, 13 East, at p. 214), but the fact that the drawer or endorser sought to be charged has reason to believe that the bill will, on presentment, be dishonoured, does not dispense with the necessity for giving him notice of dishonour. Carew v. Duckworth, 1869, L.R. 4 Ex. at p. 319.)

Dispensed
with.

Same person.

Fictitious
person.

Presented to
drawer.

No obliga-
tion.

Counter-
mand.

107. Notice of dishonour is dispensed with as regards the drawer where,—

(a) the drawer and drawee are the same person;

(b) the drawee is a fictitious person or a person not having capacity to contract;

(c) the drawer is the person to whom the bill is presented for payment;

(d) the drawee or acceptor is, as between himself and the drawer, under no obligation to accept or pay the bill;

(e) the drawer has countermanded payment. 53 V., c. 33, s. 50. Eng. s. 50.

See notes to sec. 106.
As to the meaning of fictitious person, cf. notes to sec. 21.
As to clauses (a) and (b), cf. sec. 26.

Clause (*d*) in the English bill of 1882 had the additional
words "and the drawer has no reason to expect that it will be
honoured on presentment," but these words were struck out in
committee. Chalmers, p. 171. Cf. sec. 92(*c*).

Primâ facie the acceptor, as between himself and the drawer,
is the person bound to pay the bill, but evidence is admissible
to shew that he is in reality a mere surety for the drawer or some
other party. (Cook v. Lister, 1863, 32 L.J. C.P. at p. 127.)

Bill is made payable at the drawer's house. It is accepted
and dishonoured. *Primâ facie* this is a bill accepted for the accommodation of the drawer, and he is not entitled to notice.
(Sharp v. Bailey, 1829, 9 B. & C. 44; cf. Carter v. Flower, 1847,
16 M. & W. 743.)

A bill is signed by the drawer in order to accommodate the
acceptor. The drawer is entitled to notice. (Sleigh v. Sleigh,
1850, 5 Ex. 514.)

A. having the balance of £10 at his bankers, and having no
authority to overdraw, draws a cheque for £50. A. is not entitled
to notice. (Carew v. Duckworth, 1869, L.R. 4 Ex. 313; cf. Wirth
v. Austin, 1875, L.R. 10 C.P. 689; Stayner v. Howatt, 1882, 15
N.S.R. 267.)

A bill is drawn and accepted to accommodate D., who is not
a party to it, but who is to provide for it. The drawer is entitled
to notice of dishonour. (Lafitte v. Slatter, 1830, 6 Bing. 623;
cf. Turner v. Samson, 1876, 2 Q.B.D. 23.)

A bill is drawn, accepted and endorsed by three persons in
order to raise money for their joint benefit. The drawer and
endorser are entitled to notice. Foster v. Parker, 1876, 2 C.
P.D. 18.)

108. Notice of dishonour is dispensed with as regards the
endorser where,—

    (*a*) the drawee is a fictitious person or a person not having
    capacity to contract, and the endorser was aware of the
    fact at the time he endorsed the bill;

    (*b*) the endorser is the person to whom the bill is presented
    for payment;

    (*c*) the bill was accepted or made for his accommodation.
    53 V., c. 33, s. 50. Eng. s. 50.

Sec. 108.   See notes to secs. 106 and 107.

As to the meaning of fictitious person, cf. notes to sec. 21.

Notice of dishonour dispensed with.   Clause (c) in the English bill of 1882, had the additional words "and he has no reason to expect that it will be honoured on presentment," but these words were struck out in committee. Chalmers, p. 172. Cf. sec. 92(d).

The endorser of a bill becomes the executor of the acceptor. It is presented to him and he dishonours it. He is not entitled to notice. (Caunt v. Thompson, 1849, 18 L.J. C.P. 125.)

CHAPTER XLIV.

PROTEST.

Protest is, in certain cases, one of the duties of the holder of a bill. As to such duties generally, see notes at the beginning of Chapter XLI., *supra*.

Protest.

109. In order to render the acceptor of a bill liable it is not Necessity of. necessary to protest it. 53 V., c. 33, s. 52. Eng. s. 52.

Prior to 1906 this section and sub-sec. 2 of sec. 96 formed one sub-section in a section which included the provisions of sec. 93 and sub-sec. 3 of sec. 85.

The acceptor of a bill is not entitled to notice of dishonour (sec. 96). The same rule in regard to protest and notice of dishonour applies to the maker of a note (sec. 186) as to the acceptor of a bill.

As to drawer and endorsers, see secs. 112 to 114.

110. Protest is dispensed with by any circumstances which Dispensed would dispense with notice of dishonour. 53 V., c. 33, s. 51. with. Eng. s. 51.

As to dispensing with notice of dishonour, see secs. 106 to 108.

111. Delay in noting or protesting is excused by circum- Delay stances beyond the control of the holder, and not imputable to excused. his default, misconduct or negligence.

2. When the cause of delay ceases to operate, the bill must be Diligence. noted or protested with reasonable diligence. 53 V., c. 33, s. 51. Eng. s. 51.

Sec. 111.   As to excuse for delay, cf. sec. 91 (presentment for payment) and sec. 105 (notice of dishonour).

Foreign bill, non-acceptance.   112. Where a foreign bill appearing on the face of it to be such has been dishonoured by non-acceptance it must be duly protested for non-acceptance.

Non-payment.   2. Where a foreign bill which has not been previously dishonoured by non-acceptance is dishonoured by non-payment, it must be duly protested for non-payment.

Balance.   3. Where a foreign bill has been accepted only as to part it must be protested as to the balance.

Discharge.   4. If a foreign bill is not protested as by this section required the drawer and endorsers are discharged. 53 V., c. 33, ss. 44 and 51. Eng. ss. 44 and 51.

Prior to the revision of 1906, sub-sec. 3 formed part of one section with secs. 83 and 84. See notes to sec. 84. Sub-secs. 1, 2 and 4 formed one sub-section prior to 1906.

Protest is necessary in the case of a foreign bill by the custom of merchants. (Gale v. Walsh, 1793, 5 T.R. 239, 2 R.R. 580.)

An inland bill is a bill which is, or on the face of it purports to be, (a) both drawn and payable within Canada, or (b) drawn within Canada upon some person resident therein. Any other bill is a foreign bill. Unless the contrary appears on the face of the bill, the holder may treat it as an inland bill (sec. 25).

The notice of dishonour is not bad because it omits to state that the bill has been protested. (Ex parte Lowenthal, 1874, L.R. 9 Ch. 591.) Cf. notes to sec. 98.

If a foreign bill is dishonoured and is not protested, the drawer and endorsers are discharged. Noting for protest is sufficient (sec. 118). As against the acceptor, no protest is necessary.

An inland bill, except in the Province of Quebec, need not be protested (sec. 113). Protest of a note is unnecessary except for the preservation of the liabilities of endorsers of a foreign note (sec. 187).

A bill must be protested before it is presented for payment to the acceptor for honour or referee in case of need and must be protested for non-payment by the acceptor for honour (sec. 117).

113. Where an inland bill has been dishonoured, it may, if Sec. 113. the holder thinks fit, be noted and protested for non-acceptance Protest of or non-payment as the case may be; but it shall not, except in inland bill. the province of Quebec, be necessary to note or protest an in- Quebec. land bill in order to have recourse against the drawer or endorsers. 53 V., c. 33, s. 51. Cf. Eng. s. 51.

The corresponding section of the English Act omits the words "and protested" and the words "except in the Province of Quebec."

Secs. 113 and 114 were formerly parts of one section.

By "noting" is meant the minute made by a notary on a dishonoured bill at the time of its dishonour. The formal notarial certificate or protest is based upon the noting.

The section recognizes the propriety of the usual practice Propriety of of protesting an inland bill. No legal consequence is attached to protest of noting such a bill. The protest is *primâ facie* evidence of pre- inland bill recognized. sentation and dishonour and also of service of notice of such presentation and dishonour as stated in such protest (sec. 11). The expense of noting and protesting any bill and the postages thereby incurred are to be allowed and paid to the holder in addition to any interest thereon (sec. 124).

Noting or protest is a necessary preliminary to acceptance for honour (sec. 147) and to presentment for payment to the acceptor for honour or the referee in 'case of need (sec. 117).

As to the necessity for protest in case of the dishonour of a bill which appears on its face to be a foreign bill, see sec. 112. A bill drawn upon any person in Quebec or payable or accepted at any place in that province must be protested (unless in cases in which notice of dishonour would be dispensed with: secs. 106 to 108) in order to preserve the liability of parties, other than the acceptor, liable on the bill. In other cases protest in case of dishonour is unnecessary (sec. 114).

Prior to the revision of 1906 the provisions of this section were expressly made "subject to the provisions of this Act with respect to notice of dishonour." Notice of dishonour to the drawer and endorsers is provided for by sec. 96, the provisions of which are not in any case affected by provisions as to the necessity or non-necessity of protest.

114. In the case of an inland bill drawn upon any person in
the province of Quebec or payable or accepted at any place in
the said province the parties liable on the said bill other than
the acceptor are, in default of protest for non-acceptance or non-
payment as the case may be, and of notice thereof, discharged,
except in cases where the circumstances are such as would dispense with notice of dishonour.

2. Except as in this section provided, where a bill does not
on the face of it appear to be a foreign bill, protest thereof in
case of dishonour is unnecessary. 53 V., c. 33, s. 51. Cf. Eng.
s. 51.

Sub-sec. 1 and the words "except as in this section provided"
in sub-sec. 2 do not appear in the corresponding section of the
English Act.

Sub-sec. 1 is declaratory of the law of Quebec as it existed
at the passing of the Act.

In Quebec, as in the other provinces and in England, it is
not necessary to protest a bill in order to render the acceptor
liable (sec. 109).

As against other parties, there must in Quebec be protest and
notice of protest unless these are dispensed with (cf. secs. 106
to 108 as to dispensing with notice of dishonour).

In the other provinces, the English rule prevails and any bill
which does not appear on its face to be a foreign bill need not
be protested. The Canadian Act, unlike the English Act, expressly recognizes the propriety of the protest of any dishonoured
bill (sec. 113).

Prior to 1906, secs. 113 and 114 were parts of one sub-section.
Some alteration in the wording was effected in the revision.
The provisions of sub-sec. 1 of sec. 114 which require protest
and notice of protest were made "subject, nevertheless, to the
exceptions in this section hereinafter contained." Among the
subsequent provisions of the old section were the provisions now
contained in secs. 110 and 111, 120 and 121. The revisers
(probably correctly) have selected the provisions as to dispensing as being the only ones constituting an "exception" to the
provisions requiring protest and notice.

115. A bill which has been protested for non-acceptance, Sec. 115.
or a bill of which protest for non-acceptance has been waived, Subsequent
may be subsequently protested for non-payment. 53 V., c. 33, protest for non-pay-
s. 51. Eng. s. 51. ment.

The words ''or a bill of which protest for non-acceptance has
been waived'' are not in the English Act.

As to waiver of protest, see secs. 110 and 106.

Protest in the cases provided for in this section might be necessary for the purpose of charging a foreign drawer or endorser
in his own country. Generally, however, the duties of the holder
would be regarded as regulated by the law of the place where
they are to be performed (cf. sec. 162; Chalmers, p. 175.)

Subject to the provisions of the Act, when a bill is dishonoured
by non-acceptance an immediate right of recourse against the
drawer and endorsers accrues to the holder, and no presentment
for payment is necessary (sec. 82).

116. Where the acceptor of a bill suspends payment before Protest for
it matures, the holder may cause the bill to be protested for better security
better security against the drawer and endorsers. 53 V., s. 33,
s. 51; 54-55 V., c. 17, s. 7. Eng. s. 51.

The corresponding section of the English Act reads ''Where
the acceptor of a bill becomes bankrupt or insolvent or suspends
payment,'' etc. Cf. notes to sec. 78. The words ''or insolvent''
were omitted from the Canadian Act of 1890, and the words
''becomes bankrupt or'' were struck out by amendment in 1891.

Under some of the continental codes, when the acceptor fails
during the currency of a bill, security can be demanded from
the drawer and endorsers. English law provides no such remedy,
and the only effect of such a protest in England is that the bill
may be accepted for honour (cf. sec. 147). In France, if the acceptor fails, the bill may at once be treated as dishonoured and
protested for non-payment. Chalmers, p. 176.

In Quebec a bill becomes immediately exigible upon the insolvency of the acceptor before maturity. The provisions of the
Act in regard to presentment for payment, protest and notice

Sec. 116. then become applicable and must be observed in order to bind an endorser. (Banque Nationale v. Martel, 1899, Q.R. 17 S.C. 97.)

Acceptance for honour.

117. Where a dishonoured bill has been accepted for honour *supra* protest, or contains a reference in case of need, it must be protested for non-payment before it is presented for payment to the acceptor for honour, or referee in case of need.

Protest for non-pay-ment.

2. When a bill of exchange is dishonoured by the acceptor for honour, it must be protested for non-payment by him. 53 V., c. 33, s. 66. Eng. s. 67.

Prior to 1906 this section and sec. 94 (as to presentment to acceptor for honour) formed one section.

It is in the option of the holder to resort to the referee in case of need or not, as he may think fit (sec. 33).

It is sufficient if the bill has been noted for protest before it is presented for payment (sec. 118).

As to the nature and effect of acceptance for honour, see secs. 147 to 152.

Noting equivalent to protest.

118. For the purposes of this Act, where a bill is required to be protested within a specified time or before some further proceeding is taken, it is sufficient that the bill has been noted for protest before the expiration of the specified time or the taking of the proceeding. 53 V., c. 33, s. 92. Eng. s. 93.

As to form of noting, see sec. 125, cf. notes to sec. 113. Any memorandum shewing that the bill has been duly presented and the answer given would be a sufficient noting.

Where a bill is paid *supra* protest for the honour of a party to the bill, it is not necessary, in order to give the person paying a right of action against the party for whose honour it is paid, that the protest shall have been formally drawn up or extended before the payment. (Geralopulo v. Wieler, 1851, 4 R.C. 654.)

The corresponding section of the English Act concludes, "and the formal protest may be extended at any time thereafter as of the date of the noting. These words are now part of sec. 119.

119. Subject to the provisions of this Act, when a bill is protested the protest must be made or noted on the day of its Noting or dishonour. protest.

2. When a bill has been duly noted, the formal protest may Extending be extended thereafter at any time as of the date of the noting. protest. 53 V., c. 33, ss. 51 and 92. Eng. ss. 51 and 93.

The corresponding section of the English Act reads as follows:

"Subject to the provisions of this Act, when a bill is noted or protested, it must be noted on the day of its dishonour. When a bill has been duly noted, the protest may be subsequently extended as of the date of the noting." Cf. notes to sec. 118.

As to the time of noting or protest, see sec. 121 (bill returned by post dishonoured). Delay may be excused (sec. 111), or protest dispensed with (sec. 110).

Before the Act it was not clear that a bill could not be lawfully noted for protest on the day after its dishonour; but the business members of the select committee were unanimous in thinking that noting on the day of dishonour should be made obligatory. Chalmers, p. 176.

As to the extension of the protest, cf. sec. 118.

Although the protest may be extended "thereafter at anytime," notice of dishonour or, where protest is necessary, notice of protest, must be sent within the time limited by sec. 97 or sec. 126 (as the case may be).

Notice of protest is governed by the same rules as notice of dishonour in regard to time and manner of giving notice (sec. 126).

120. Where a bill is lost or destroyed, or is wrongly or ac- Protest on cidentally detained from the person entitled to hold it, or is copy or particulars. accidentally retained in a place other than where payable, protest may be made on a copy or written particulars thereof. 53 V., c. 33, s. 51. Eng. s. 51.

The English Act omits the word "accidentally" (where it first occurs) and the clause "accidentally retained in a place other than where payable."

Sec. 120.   As to lost bills, see further sec. 156 (holder's right to duplicate of lost bill), and sec. 157 (action on lost bill).

A copy means an ordinary copy or transcript of the bill.
Cf. sec. 62 as to endorsement of a bill issued or negotiated in a
country where "copies" are recognized.

Place of protest.   **121.** A bill must be protested at the place where it is dishonoured, or at some other place in Canada situate within five
miles of the place of presentment and dishonour of such bill:
Provided that,—

Where bill returned.   (a) when a bill is presented through the post office and returned by post dishonoured, it may be protested at the
place to which it is returned, not later than on the day of
its return or the next juridical day;

Time when.   (b) every protest for dishonour, either for non-acceptance or
non-payment may be made on the day of such dishonour,
and in case of non-acceptance at any time after non-
acceptance, and in case of non-payment at any time after
three o'clock in the afternoon. 53 V., c. 33, s. 51. Cf.
Eng. s. 51.

The corresponding section of the English Act reads as follows:

"A bill must be protested at the place where it is dishonoured.
Provided that,—

(a) where a bill is presented through the post office, and
returned by post dishonoured, it may be protested at the place
to which it is returned and on the day of its return if received
during business hours, and if not received during business
hours, then not later than the next business day.

(b) when a bill drawn payable at the place of business or
residence of some person other than the drawee, has been dishonoured by non-acceptance, it must be protested for non-payment at the place where it is expressed to be payable, and no
further presentment for payment to, or demand on, the drawee
is necessary.

Clause (a) of the English section was inserted in committee
to protect a common practice of the Liverpool notaries with

regard to bills drawn on cotton-spinners in Lancashire. Clause (*b*) reproduces the effect of 2 and 3 Will. 4, c. 98. Suppose a; bill is drawn on B. in Liverpool, "payable at the A. Bank in London." It is dishonoured by non-acceptance. It is to be protested for non-payment in London without any further demand on B. Chalmers, p. 177.

In the Canadian bill as first brought down the wording was the same as the English section, but it was amended by striking out clause (*b*), by inserting the clause which allows protest to be made at any place in Canada within five miles of the place of presentment and dishonour, and by altering the wording of' clause (*a*).

The intention in striking out clause (*b*) of the English Act was to make it optional whether in the case there provided for the holder should, after dishonour by non-acceptance, protest the bill again for non-payment. (Debates House of Commons, 1890, p. 4264, cf. sec. 115.)

There is no provision in the English Act corresponding to clause (*b*) of sec. 121. Cf. sec. 119, and notes to sec. 95.

As to juridical days, see sec. 43.

122. A protest must contain a copy of the bill, or the ori- Contents of ginal bill may be annexed thereto, and the protest must be protest. signed by the notary making it, and must specify,—

    (*a*) the person at whose request the bill is protested;   Person.

    (*b*) the place and date of protest;   Place.

    (*c*) the cause or reason for protesting the bill;   Reason.

    (*d*) the demand made and the answer given, if any; or,   Proceeding.

    (*e*) the fact that the drawee or acceptor could not be found. Excuse.

    53 V., c. 33, s. 51. Eng. s. 51.

The words "or the original bill may be annexed thereto" are not in the English Act.

As to form of protest, cf. sec. 125 and schedule, Chapter LIV., *infra.*

As to protest by a justice of the peace, when the services of a notary cannot be obtained at the place where the bill is dis-honoured, see sec. 123.

Words requiring a protest to be under seal were struck out in committee. Chalmers, p. 178.

Sec. 123.   **123.** Where a dishonoured bill is authorized or required to
Official when be protested, and the services of a notary cannot be obtained at
notary is not
accessible.   the place where the bill is dishonoured, any justice of the peace
resident in the place may present and protest such bill and give
all necessary notices and shall have all the necessary powers of
a notary in respect thereto. 53 V., c. 33, s. 93. Cf. Eng. s. 94.

The corresponding section of the English Act omits the words
after "dishonoured" (where it secondly occurs) and provides
that "any householder or substantial resident of the place may,
in the presence of two witnesses, give a certificate, signed by
them, attesting the dishonour of the bill, and the certificate shall
in all respects operate as if it were a formal protest of the bill,"
and also in a schedule provides a form which may be used. The
English section also contains the words "or note" after the
word "bill" in the first line.

No clerk, teller or agent of any bank shall act as a notary
in the protesting of any bill or note payable at the bank or at
any of the branches of the bank in which he is employed (sec.
13). A notary who is one of the endorsers of a bill is not entitled to act as notary in protesting the bill. (Pelletier v. Brosseau, 1890, M.L.R. 6 S.C. 331.)

Expenses.   **124.** The expense of noting and protesting any bill and the
postages thereby incurred, shall be allowed and paid to the
holder in addition to any interest thereon.

Fees.   2. Notaries may charge the fees in each province heretofore
allowed them. 53 V., c. 33, s. 93.

The expenses of noting and protest are part of the measure
of damages allowed by sec. 134 where a bill is dishonoured.

R.S.C., 1886, c. 123 (repealed by the Bills of Exchange Act,
1890) contains provisions relating to notary's fees: sec. 7 (Nova
Scotia); sec. 8 (Prince Edward Island); sec. 25 (Ontario);
schedule B. (Quebec).

In the other parts of Canada, the changes appear to be regulated by usage, although in New Brunswick a provincial statute
(46 Vict., c. 11) purports to prescribe a tariff.

125. The forms in the schedule to this Act may be used in Sec. 125.
noting or protesting any bill and in giving notice thereof.   Forms.

2. A copy of the bill and endorsement may be included in Contents.
the forms, or the original bill may be annexed and the necessary changes in that behalf made in the forms. 53 V., c. 33, s.
93. Cf. Eng. s. 94.

The English Act provides a form only for the case of the
protest of a bill by a householder or substantial resident.   Cf.
notes to sec. 123.

As to sub-sec. 2, cf. sec. 122.

The forms in the schedule are not obligatory.   As to form of
notice of dishonour, see notes to sec. 96.

126. Notice of the protest of any bill payable in Canada When notice
shall be sufficiently given and shall be sufficient and deemed to shall be
have been duly given and served, if given during the day on given.
which protest has been made or on the next following juridical
or business day, to the same parties and in the same manner
and addressed in the same way as is provided by this Part for
notice of dishonour. 53 V., c. 33, s. 49.

Subject to the provisions of the Act, protest must be made
or noted on the day of the dishonour of a bill (sec. 119).   Notice
of protest may be given on that day or on the next following
juridical day.

As to the persons to whom notice must be given, see sec.
96 and notes. As to the manner, see secs. 98 and 99. As to the
manner in which the notice is to be addressed, see secs. 103 and
104 and notes.

CHAPTER XLV.

LIABILITIES OF PARTIES.

The sections comprised in this chapter provide for the obligations of the various contracts which are entered into by parties to a bill. A person signing a bill may be liable as acceptor (secs. 128 and 129) or as drawer (sec. 130). When a person signs a bill otherwise than as acceptor or drawer he thereby incurs the liabilities of an endorser to a holder in due course (sec. 131). The obligations of an endorser are provided for by sec. 133. A transferrer by delivery is not liable on the bill (sec. 137), but by virtue of negotiating it, enters into a contract with his immediate transferee, being a holder for value (sec. 138).

The measure of damages for dishonour of a bill and the recovery of such damages is provided for by secs. 134 to 136.

Equitable assignment

127. A bill, of itself, does not operate as an assignment of funds in the hands of the drawee available for the payment thereof, and the drawee of a bill who does not accept as required by this Act is not liable on the instrument. 53 V., c. 33, s. 53. Eng. s. 53.

The corresponding section of the English Act provides that it shall not extend to Scotland, and further, by sub-sec. 2, that "in Scotland, where the drawee of a bill has in hands funds available for the payment thereof, the bill operates as an assignment of the sum for which it is drawn in favour of the holder, from the time when the bill is presented to the drawee." The law of France is similar to that of Scotland.

A bill of exchange is an unconditional order in writing, but an order to pay out of a particular fund is not unconditional, and therefore such an order is not a bill (sec. 17).

A bill not an equitable assignment.

A bill of itself does not operate as an assignment of funds in the hands of the drawee available for the payment thereof. The drawee, as such, incurs no liability to the holder, and there is no privity of contract between them. (Hopkinson v. Forster, 1874, L.R. 19 Eq. 74, 3 R.C. 755.)

This was the law before the Act. A. having an account against B. gives C. an order upon B. In the absence of acceptance by B., B. is not liable to C. (Hall v. Prittie, 1890, 17 A.R. 306, and cases cited; Percival v. Dunn, 1885, 29 Ch. D. 128.)

One of the very incidents which makes the instrument a valid bill of exchange, namely, that it is not drawn against or payable out of any particular fund, prevents it from operating as an equitable assignment. (Hall v. Prittie, *supra*.)

An order invalid as a bill may be valid as an equitable assignment. (Buck v. Robson, 1878, 3 Q.B.D. 686; Chalmers, p. 13; see the English and American cases reviewed in Munger v. Shannon, 1874, 61 N.Y. 251.)

But where the evidence shewed that there was only one fund out of which the drawee could be expected to pay the order; that the nature of the fund and its origin were well known to all the parties; that when the drawer promised to give the persons with whom he dealt orders upon the drawee, he intended to give and these persons expected to get, orders which were to be paid out of the particular fund; and that the drawee understood the order as intended to deal with portions of the fund and to be payable only out of the fund; it was held that the court should look to the real intention of the parties to the transaction and should give effect to such intention by declaring that the drawer did make an equitable assignment to the order-holder of a portion of the fund. (Lane v. Dungannon, 1892, 22 O.R. 264.)

Where there is a specific appropriation of funds with the assent, express or implied, of the drawee there is privity between the drawer and the holder. De Bernales v. Fuller, 1810, 14 East. 590n. 13 R.R. 321n, was a case where money was expressly paid into the defendant bank for the specific purpose of taking up a bill, the purpose being declared by the payer at the time, and not being repudiated by the bank until afterwards. The case is referred to in Prince v. Oriental Bank, 1878, 3 App. Cas. 325, 334, as a case which has never been overruled; the bank so receiving the money must be held to have received it for the use of the holder of the bill, and cannot apply the money to the general indebtedness of the acceptor who paid in the money. Cf. *supra*, p. 132.

A. draws a bill on B. in favour of C., and remits funds to meet it. B. does not accept the bill, but he tells C. that he has received the funds and promises to pay the bill. B. does not pay

Sec. 127. the bill. No action on the bill can be maintained against B., but
A bill not an C. can sue B. for money received to his use. (Griffin v. Weather-
equitable   by 1868, L.R. 3 Q.B. 753; cf. Torrance v. Bank of B.N.A., 1873,
assignment. L.R. 5 P.C. 246.)

Privity may be created by agreement external to the bill,
and the relations of the parties are then regulated by the terms
of the agreement. (Robey v. Ollier, 1872, L.R. 7 Ch. 695;
Ranken v. Alfaro, 1877, 5 Ch. D. 786; cf. Bank of Montreal v.
Thomas, 1888, O.R. 503.

What Chalmers (p. 183) calls a *quasi*-privity is created by
sec. 166, which provides that when the holder of a cheque omits
to present it within a reasonable time, whereby the drawer has
been damnified (*i.e.*, by the failure of the bank), the drawer
is *pro tanto* discharged, and the holder is substituted as a creditor of the bank. As to the applicability of sec. 127 to a cheque,
see notes to sec. 165.

Subject to the rule that a customer is entitled to draw cheques on his bank, a creditor, as such, is not entitled to draw on
his debtor in respect to his debt; and the drawee of an unaccepted
bill is under no obligation to accept or pay it unless he has for
valuable consideration expressly or impliedly agreed to do so.
(Cf. Goodwin v. Robarts, 1875, L.R. 10 Ex. at p. 351.)

When the drawee breaks his contract with the drawer by dishonouring his bill, the drawee is liable to the drawer for the
damages reasonably resulting from the breach.

A customer having a balance of $200 at his banker's draws
a cheque for $100 or accepts a bill for $100 payable at his banker's. If this cheque or bill is dishonoured he may recover substantial damages for the injury to his credit, without proving
any actual loss. (Rolin v. Steward, 1854, 23 L.J.C.P. 148; cf.
Chapter XVIII, *supra*, p. 211.)

A. in a foreign country draws on B. in England under a
letter of credit. B. dishonours the draft. A. may recover the
re-exchange and notarial expenses which he has had to pay to
the holder (Walker v. Hamilton, 1860, 1 De G. F. & J. 602; Re
General South American Co., 1877, 7 Ch. D. 637), and also the
cost of telegrams, etc., consequent on the dishonour. (Prehn v.
Royal Bank, 1870, L.R. 5 Ex. 92.)

Whether the authority or obligation to accept is or is not re- voked by the death of the drawer does not appear to be well set- Effect of tled in England. Chalmers (p. 185) says, "Apart from some- drawer's thing special in the contract, it seems that the authority or ob- death on authority or ligation to accept is not revoked by the death of the drawer obligation to (Chitty (1878), p. 202; Story (1860), s. 250; Cutts v. Perkins, accept. 1815, 12 Mass. 206; cf. Billing v. Devaux, 1841, 3 M. & Gr. at p. 574; Att.-Gen. v. Pratt, 1874, L.R. 9 Ex. 140), while it is by notice of his bankruptcy; for this renders funds in the hands of the drawee no longer available for the payment of the bill, and incapacitates the drawer from fulfilling his part of the contract (Pothier, No. 96; cf. Citizens Bank v. New Orleans, 1873, L.R. 6 H.L. 352)." Chitty, at p. 202, says, "If the drawing of a bill is to be considered as a bare authority that is revocable, then the death of the drawer would determine the authority of the drawee to accept or pay; but if it is an authority coupled with an interest in favour of a payee or indorsee, then death would be no countermand." Cf. Trunkfield v. Proctor, 1901, 2 O.L.R. at p. 332. In the case of a cheque notice of the customer's death determines the duty and authority of the bank to pay the amount of the cheque.

A. and D. are indebted to C. on a mortgage. A. has funds in B.'s hands. A. addresses to B. a bill payable on demand to C. and hands the bill to B. B. tells C. that A. has left money with him (B.) to pay on the mortgage. C. states that he does not want the money till the first of the following month. B. also shews the bill to D., who acts upon it by paying to B. for A. an annuity instalment which he has been withholding until A. should pay C. the amount due by him on the mortgage, D. having previously agreed to pay the balance of the mortgage. There is either a valid equitable assignment of the fund in B.'s hands to the amount of the bill, or a trust in respect to the fund for the payment of the amount of the bill to C. in discharge of that part of the mortgage indebtedness which A. had undertaken to pay, so that C. is entitled to payment, notwithstanding A.'s death before B. has paid over the money. (Trunkfield v. Proctor, 1901, 2 O.L.R. 326.)

128. The acceptor of a bill, by accepting it, engages that he Engagement will pay it according to the tenor of his acceptance. 53 V., c. by accep-tance. 33, s. 54. Eng. s. 54.

The simple meaning of an acceptance is "I will pay" (Smith v. Vertue: cf. notes to sec. 38). The primary, and, in general, absolute, liability of an acceptor must be distinguished from the secondary and conditional liability of a drawer or endorser. (Rowe v. Young, 1820, 2 Bligh H.L. at p. 467; Jones v. Broadhurst, 1850, 9 C.B. at p. 181.)

The drawee by accepting a bill, becomes the party primarily liable thereon to the holder. (Philpot v. Briant, 1828, 4 Bing. at p. 720.)

As to presentment for payment to charge the acceptor, see sec. 93.

An acceptance may be either general or qualified (sec. 38).

As to the relations *inter se* of joint acceptors who are not partners, see Harmer v. Steele, 1849, 4 Ex. at p. 13.

As to the measure of damages for the dishonour of a bill, see sec. 134.

If a bill is negotiated back to the acceptor, he may, subject to the provisions of the Act, re-issue and further negotiate the bill, but he is not entitled to enforce payment of the bill against any intervening party to whom he was previously liable (sec. 73).

Estoppel.

129. The acceptor of a bill by accepting it is precluded from denying to a holder in due course,—

Genuineness
and author-
ity.

(a) the existence of the drawer, the genuineness of his signature, and his capacity and authority to draw the bill;

Capacity of
drawer.

(b) in the case of a bill payable to drawer's order, the then capacity of the drawer to endorse, but not the genuineness or validity of his endorsement;

Payee and
capacity.

(c) in the case of a bill payable to the order of a third person, the existence of the payee and his then capacity to endorse, but not the genuineness or validity of his endorsement. 53 V., c. 33, s. 54. Eng. s. 54.

In addition to the estoppels arising on the bill by the act of acceptance, as provided in this section, there may be an estoppel arising from other facts (cf. notes to sec. 49).

As to a holder in due course, see sec. 56.

Capacity must be distinguished from authority (see Chapter XXXVIII., *supra*, p. 428). Capacity to draw must be identical with capacity to endorse, but authority to draw on behalf of another does not necessarily include authority to endorse on his behalf. (Cf. Prescott v. Flinn, 1832, 9 Bing. at p. 22.)

This distinction reconciles cases which otherwise seem to be inconsistent with each other. The acceptor is precluded from denying to a holder in due course the existence, or the capacity to draw or endorse, of the drawer (Braithwaite v. Gardiner, 1846, 8 Q.B. 473), or the existence or capacity to endorse of the payee. He is also precluded from denying to a holder in due course the genuineness of the drawing or the authority to draw of the drawer, because the acceptance amounts to a representation of the validity of the drawing by which the acceptor is estopped as against a person who has acted upon it. (Cf. Pickard v. Sears, 1837, 6 A. & E. 469; Phillips v. im Thurn, 1866, L.R. 1 C.P. at p. 472, 4 R.C. at p. 633.)

But the acceptor makes no representation as to the genuineness or validity of the signature of the payee, whether it be that of the drawer of a bill payable to the drawer's order, or of a third person to whom the bill is payable, if the payee in each case is a real person.

The acceptor may decline to pay on the ground that the payee's signature is forged or written without authority, unless, apart from the mere act of acceptance, he is precluded from setting up the forgery or want of authority (sec. 49).

If, however, the drawer of a bill payable to the drawer's order is fictitious, the bill may be treated as payable to bearer (sec. 21) and the acceptor is liable.

The acceptor's liability in such a case has been based, in some instances, on a different ground, namely, that the acceptor undertakes to pay in pursuance of an endorsement in the same handwriting as the drawer's signature. (Cooper v. Meyer, 1830, 10 B. & C. 468; Beeman v. Duck, 1843, 11 M. & W. at p. 256, 4 R.C. at p. 625; Phillips v. im Thurn, 1866, L.R. 1 C.P. at p. 471, 4 R.C. at p. 632.)

Even if the endorsement of the drawer-payee, being a real person, is upon the bill at the time of the acceptance and the handwriting of the drawing is the same as that of the endorsement, the acceptor is not estopped from setting up that

Sec. 129.
Acceptor
estopped by
the act of
acceptance.

the endorsement is forged or made without authority, provided he did not know of the forgery or want of authority. (Beeman v. Duck, 1843, 11 M. & W. 251, 4 R.C. 622; Phillips v. im Thurn, 1866, L.R. 1 C.P. 463, 4 R.C. 626; cf. Ryan v. Bank of Montreal, 1887, 14 A.R. 533, 536, and cases cited.)

Many of the authorities are discussed in London & S. W. Bank v. Wentworth, 1880, 5 Ex. D. 96. In that case, however, the defendant accepted a bill of exchange in blank and delivered it for the purpose of negotiation, and the person who received it forged the drawing and the drawer's endorsement. It was held that the acceptor was liable and that the case must be governed, not by the rules of law applicable to cases in which the acceptor has signed his name after that of the drawer has been inserted, but by those which ought to prevail where the acceptor has signed his name upon a blank piece of paper or on a paper upon which a drawing in blank has been written (cf. secs. 31 and 32).

Where a bill or acceptance is materially altered, the acceptor is not precluded by this section from setting up such alteration (cf. sec. 145).

Drawer.

130. The drawer of a bill, by drawing it,—

Engages
acceptance
and compen-
sation.

(*a*) engages that on due presentment it shall be accepted and paid according to its tenor, and that if it is dishonoured he will compensate the holder or any endorser who is compelled to pay it, if the requisite proceedings on dishonour are duly taken;

Estoppel or
to payee.
Sic qy.
For 'or' read
'*as.*'

(*b*) is precluded from denying to a holder in due course the existence of the payee and his then capacity to endorse. 53 V., c. 33, s. 55. Eng. s. 55.

As to due presentment, see sec. 78 (for acceptance) and sec. 86 (for payment).

As to dishonour, see secs. 81 and 95.

As to the requisite proceedings on dishonour, see sec. 96 (notice of dishonour) and secs. 112 to 114 (protest).

As to a holder in due course, see sec. 56.

As to measure of damages, see sec. 135.

The drawer and any endorser may insert in the bill an express stipulation negativing or limiting his own liability to the holder (sec. 34).

Subject to any express stipulation to the contrary and subject to the necessity for due presentment and for the requisite proceedings on dishonour, the drawer and endorsers are jointly and severally responsible to the holder for the due acceptance and payment of the bill. If it be dishonoured the holder may enforce payment from the drawer, or an endorser, or the acceptor, or any or all of them at his option. (Rouquette v Overmann, 1875, L.R. 10 Q.B. 525, at pp. 536-7, 4 R.C. 287, at p. 298; cf. sec. 135.)

The drawer or endorser is not strictly a surety for the acceptor, or co-surety with those who are sureties for the acceptor, yet he stands in a position sufficiently analogous to that of a surety to entitle him to the equities of a surety when the bill has been dishonoured, though not before. (Duncan Fox & Co. v. N. & S. Wales Bank, 1880, 6 App. Cas. 1, at p. 19, where the relations *inter se* of drawer or endorser, acceptor and holder are discussed.)

If a bill is dishonoured and the requisite proceedings on dishonour are taken, *primâ facie* the drawer or an endorser of a bill (sec. 133) is liable to the holder or to any endorser who is compelled to pay the bill.

Where a bill is negotiated back to the drawer, or to a prior endorser, or to the acceptor, such party may, subject to the provisions of the Act, re-issue and further negotiate the bill, but he is not entitled to enforce the payment of the bill against any intervening party to whom he was previously liable (sec. 73).

The presumption that the drawer is liable to an endorser who has been compelled to pay the bill may be rebutted by shewing that both drawer and endorser became parties to the bill to accommodate some third party, and that the one who pays the bill is therefore only entitled to contribution as a co-surety, or by proving an express agreement, properly evidenced, that the relations of the parties to the bill are other than those which are *primâ facie* presumed (see notes to sec. 133).

Subject to the provisions of sec. 21, as to a fictitious or non-existing payee, the drawer is not estopped from denying the genuineness or validity of the payee's signature. Cf. notes to sec. 129.

Sec. 130. *Discharge of surety by dealings of creditor with principal or other surety.*

Where a relation in the nature of principal and surety exists between the parties to a bill, or the parties to a bill transaction, and the holder has notice of the relation, the ordinary consequences which flow from that relation ensue. Any such dealing by the creditor with the principal or other sureties as would ordinarily discharge a surety discharges the party to a bill transaction who is in the position of surety. For the present purpose *primâ facie* the acceptor is the principal debtor, and the drawer and endorsers are, as regards him sureties, and the drawer of a bill is the principal as regards the endorsers, and the first endorser is the principal as regards the second and subsequent endorsers, and so on in order; but evidence for the present purpose is admissible to shew the real relation of the parties, and it is immaterial that the holder was ignorant of the relation when he took the bill, provided he had notice thereof at the time of his dealing with the principal. (Ewin v. Lancaster, 1865, 6 B. & S. at p. 577; Oriental v. Overend, 1871, L.R. 7 Ch. 142; 1874, L.R.7 H.L. 348.) Even if two or more are originally indebted as principals, and it is afterwards agreed between them that as between themselves one shall be surety only, and this agreement is made known to the creditor, the rule as to the discharge of a surety by dealings with the principal applies. (Rouse v. Bradford, [1894] A.C. 586; Allison v. McDonald, 1894, 23 S.C.R. 635.)

As to the circumstances under which a surety is discharged there is nothing peculiar to bills or bill transactions, and the reader is referred to De Colyar on Guarantees or other standard works on Principal and Surety. See also Chalmers, at pp. 224 *et seq.*, where the salient points are noted.

Liability by signature.

Irregular endorsement.

131. No person is liable as drawer, endorser or acceptor of a bill who has not signed it as such: Provided that when a person signs a bill otherwise than as a drawer or acceptor he thereby incurs the liabilities of an endorser to a holder in due course and is subject to all the provisions of this Act respecting endorsers. 53 V., c. 33, ss. 23 and 56. Eng. ss. 23 and 56.

Who has not signed it as such.

Prior to 1906 the first clause of this section formed one section with sec. 132, which contains provisions with regard to a signature of a firm.

By sec. 4 the signature to a bill may be written by the hand of an agent, but it must be the principal's signature, not the agent's. In the case of a corporation, a bill is sufficiently signed if it is sealed with the corporate seal (sec. 5).

Bills and notes form an exception to the ordinary rule that when a contract is made by an agent in his own name, evidence is admissible to charge the undisclosed principal, though it is not admissible to discharge the agent.

A. draws a bill, signing it "J. A., agent." ·A. is liable. His ·principal is not. (Pentz v. Stanton, 1833, 10 Wend. (N.Y.) 271.)

A., who is agent for B., draws a bill in his own name. The payee knows that A. is only an agent. A. is liable as drawer. B. is not. (Cf. Leadbitter v. Farrow, 1816, 5 M. & S. at p. 350; Ex parte Rayner, 1868, 17 W.R. 64.)

Conversely a clerk who draws a bill in the name of a firm whose affairs he is winding up, two of the partners being dead, is not liable on· the bill. (Wilson v. Barthrop, 1837, 2 M. & W. 863.)

A. and B. are jointly liable to C. B. alone makes a note in favour of C. for the amount of the debt. B. alone is liable on the note (Siffkin v. Walker, 1809, 2 Camp. 308). But A. would be liable on the original consideration. The distinction is that B.'s liability is transferable by negotiation of the note while A.'s is not, and the onus of proof is different in the two cases.

A person who converts a blank endorsement into a special endorsement by writing above the endorser's signature a direction to pay the bill to the order of another person (sec. 67) to whom he delivers the bill, is not liable as an endorser. (Vincent v. Horlock, 1808, 1 Camp. 442.)

Signs a bill otherwise than as drawer or acceptor.

The words "and is subject to all the provisions of this Act respecting endorsers" are not in the English Act, but it is not apparent what, if any, effect their insertion in the Canadian Act has.

As to the liabilities of an endorser, see sec. 133 and notes. Under sec. 131 a person who signs a bill otherwise than as drawer or acceptor, if he is not an endorser properly so-called, is liable as an endorser only to a holder in due course.

An endorsement, properly so-called, must be made by the holder; but when a person who is not the holder of a bill or note backs it with his signature, he is not an endorser, but a *quasi*-endorser. The law annexes to his acts consequences similar to those which follow the endorsement of a bill by the holder. Formerly, when a stranger to the bill backed it with his signature, a pleading difficulty arose, as to whether he was to be described as an endorser or as a new drawer. The difficulty was, it is submitted, simply technical, for the consequences are identical. Now, it would be sufficient to state the facts or describe the person signing as an endorser. Chalmers, p. 192.

Lord Blackburn in Steele v. McKinley, 1880, 5 App. Cas. at p. 772, 4 R.C. at p. 227, says: "An endorsement in general is a transfer in writing by the holder of the bill to a new holder on whom the property is thereby conferred; and it is quite clear that J. McKinley is not such an endorser." [See notes to sec. 35, *supra*, where the facts of this case are briefly stated.] "But I quite agree that by the custom of merchants, as modified by English law, there may also be an endorsement by a person, not a holder of a bill, who puts his name on the bill to facilitate the transfer to a holder. By the old foreign law, not in this respect entirely adopted by the English law, this might be done by what was called an *aval* (said to be an antiquated word signifying "underwriting"), either on the bill itself or on a separate paper; and if such an *aval* was given by any one, his obligation to all subsequent holders of the bill was precisely the same as that of the person to facilitate whose transfer the *aval* was given. It appears from Pothier, that the *aval* might be given by one who gave his name, either by way of incurring responsibility for the drawer, placing the signature under the name of the drawer, or for the endorser, placing it under the endorsement, or for the acceptor, placing it under that of the acceptance. An *aval* for the honour of the acceptor, even if on the bill, is not effectual in English law, as appears by Jackson v. Hudson, 1810, 2 Camp. 447. [See notes to sec. 35, *supra*.] But the endorsement by a stranger to the bill on it to one who is about to take it is efficacious in English law, and has the same effect as an *aval*. The effect, according to English law, of such an endorsement is re- cognized by Lord Holt, in Hill v. Lewis, 1 Salk. at p. 133, and again in Penny v. Innes, 1 C.M. & R. 439; 4 L.J. Ex. 12; such an endorsement creates no obligation to those who previously were parties to the bill; it is solely for the benefit of those who take subsequently. It is not a collateral engagement, but one on the bill.''

The section says that ''where a person signs a bill otherwise than as a drawer or acceptor, he thereby incurs the liability of an endorser to a holder in due course, and is subject to all the provisions of this Act respecting endorsers.'' The section is also applicable to promissory notes, and for that purpose (sec. 186), the maker of a note is deemed to correspond with the acceptor of a bill, and the first endorser of a note with the drawer of an accepted bill payable to drawer's order. Therefore when we wish to apply this section to a note payable to order we must read ''where a person signs a note otherwise than as a maker or payee,'' etc., for according to the terms of the note the first endorser must be the payee.

It has been said that the section does not establish any new law and, as stated by one of the judges in Ex parte Yates, 1858, 2 DeG. & J. 191, it has been settled for more than a century that it makes no difference where the signature is placed if the intention is proved. In that case the intention was proved that a person was to sign a note in the character of endorser, and the note when produced shewed his signature not below that of the maker's, but in a different part of the note, although on its face. He was held liable. In Carrique v. Beatty, 1897, 24 A.R. 302, a person signed his name below the maker's names. There was no evidence that he intended to sign as endorser nor was there anything on the face of the note to throw doubt upon or qualify the character in which it purported to be signed by him, which was that of maker. It was held therefore that the section did not apply and that the note was voided, by reason of material alteration, as against an accommodation maker who had not assented to the addition of the name.

Since the Act, there has been considerable difference of judicial opinion as to the liability of a stranger to an instrument who signs his name on the back before the payee has endorsed.

In Duthie v. Essery, 1895, 22 A.R. 191, E. made two notes in favour of D. & Sons or order. K. endorsed them before de-

Sec. 131.
Signs a bill otherwise than as drawer or acceptor.

Signature by a stranger before payee's endorsement.

Sec. 131.

Signature by
a stranger
before
payee's en-
dorsement.
livery to the payees, who afterwards endorsed them for value to
the plaintiff. In an action against K. it was held that the plaintiff as holder in due course was entitled to recover, the majority
of the court basing their decision on sec. 131 of the Act. The
third member of the court expressed the opinion that the payees
themselves could not have recovered upon the note, but decided
in favour of the plaintiff, as a holder in due course, apart from
the Act. It is pointed out in this case (22 A.R. at p. 192) that,
in order to render a note backed by a third party's signature
capable of being sued upon by the payee, the old practice was for
the payee to endorse without recourse to such party: See notes
to sec. 73.

In Jenkins v. Coomber, [1898] 2 Q.B. 168 the plaintiffs
addressed to C. a bill payable to their own order. C. accepted,
and procured the defendant to write his name on the back
of the bill in order to guarantee payment. C. then delivered the
bill to the plaintiffs who endorsed it. Held by a Divisional
Court that the drawers could not recover from the defendant.
This decision was based on the fact that in the view of the court
the plaintiffs were not holders in due course, in that they did
not take a bill "complete and regular on the face of it" (sec. 56).
The bill in question was not on the face of it complete and regular, since when the defendant endorsed it, the bill had not been
endorsed by the payees. Sec. 131 therefore did not apply. It
was also urged that the defendant was liable as an endorser
under sec. 133, but the court held that the plaintiff was met by
the same difficulty as that which defeated the claim of the plaintiff in Steele v. McKinley, namely that the bill was never made
complete so far as he was concerned by the necessary endorsement of the drawer. If the bill had been made complete by the
endorsement of the drawers before the defendant wrote his name
upon the back of it, then it would have been competent for the
drawers to shew that by the agreement between the parties, they
were not subject to the ordinary liability of drawers to compensate the endorser (sec. 130) and therefore there was no obstacle
by reason of circuity of action to suit by them against the
endorser (cf. notes to sec. 73). But the bill not being complete
it was necessary for the plaintiffs, in order to succeed, to prove
a contract of suretyship independently of the bill, and in this
they failed because they could not satisfy the Statute of Frauds.

In Canadian Bank of Commerce v. Perram, 1899, 31 O.R.
116, the defendant put his name on the back of a promissory

note before it was endorsed by the plaintiffs, the payees. The
payees afterwards endorsed the note. A divisional court held
that the defendant was not liable, following Jenkins v. Coomber,
supra. The case of Small v. Henderson, 1899, 27 A.R. 492 was
decided prior to Canadian Bank of Commerce v. Perram, but
the judgments were not handed out until later. The facts relevant to the present subject were very similar, and the Court of
Appeal for Ontario followed Jenkins v. Coomber and Steele v.
McKinley.

Sec. 131.
Signature by
a stranger
before
payee's en-
dorsement.

In 1901 the question of the endorsement of an incomplete
note again came before the Court of Appeal. The defendant put
his name on the back of a note before its endorsement by the
payee, intending thereby to become surety for the maker. The
maker subsequently executed a chattel mortgage to the defendant
to indemnify him against the payment of the note. The note
was discounted by the payee, and upon the maker's failure to
pay it at maturity, the defendant paid it. The maker afterwards made an assignment for the benefit of his creditors, and
an action was brought by the assignee to set aside the mortgage
as fraudulent and void as against creditors. The Court of Appeal, while adhering to the view that a person in the position of
the defendant would not be liable on the note, held that the mortgage ought not to be set aside (Robinson v. Mann, 2 O.L.R. 63).
On appeal to the Supreme Court of Canada, however, it was held
that the payee was a holder in due course and that the defendant
was liable under sec. 131 (31 S.C.R. 484). The judgment of the
court was an oral one, delivered by Strong, C.J. Neither the
English case of Jenkins v. Coomber, nor any of the Ontario
cases above mentioned were cited in the judgment, or, so far
as appears by the official report, in argument. In Ayr v. Wallace,
1892, 21 S.C.R. 256, the same judge had expressed a strong opinion that under the Act a person signing his name on the back of
a note before endorsement by the payee would be liable as an endorser, but in that case the plaintiff failed for want of notice
of dishonour.

The decision in Robinson v. Mann is probably satisfactory
to the mercantile community, as it gives effect to the clear intention of the parties, and being an express and the latest decision
on the point raised, it must be followed by all courts in Canada.
They cannot call in question a decision of the highest court in
Canada as not being in accordance with the previous cases.
(Slater v. Laboree, 1905, 10 O.L.R. 648.)

Sec. 131.   In some of the provinces of Canada other than Ontario the
Signature by cases since the Act have been in accord with the decision in
a stranger Robinson v. Mann. See, for instance, Watson v. Harvey, 1894,
before
payee's en- 10 Man. R. 641; Wells v. McCarthy, 1895, 10 Man. R. 639;
dorsement. Fraser v. McLeod, 1895, 2 Terr. L.R. 154.

In Quebec a person signing a note as guarantor or *aval* before the payee had signed is liable as endorser. Since the passing
of the Act he is entitled to notice of protest (Emard v. Marcille,
1892, Q.R. 2 S.C. 525; Banque Jacques Cartier v. Gagnon, 1894,
Q.R. 5 S.C. 499). Prior to the Act he was not entitled to notice.
(Cf. Pratt v. MacDougall, 1868, 12 L.C.J. 515, 17 R.J.R.Q. 493;
Merchants Bank v. Cunningham, 1892, Q.R. 1 Q.B. 33.)

Trade or as-   **132.** Where a person signs a bill in a trade or assumed name
sumed name. he is liable thereon as if he had signed it in his own name.

Firm name.   2. The signature of the name of a firm is equivalent to the
signature by the person so signing, of the names of all persons
liable as partners in that firm. 53 V., c. 33, s. 23. Eng. s. 23.

In the English Act the provisions of this section read as a
proviso to the clause "no person is liable as drawer, endorser or
acceptor of a bill who has not signed it as such," which is now
part of sec. 131 in the Canadian Act.

Trade or assumed name.

John Smith carries on business under the name of "John
Brown," or "Brown & Co.," or the "London Iron Co." He is
liable on a bill drawn, endorsed, or accepted by him in any of
these names. (Cf. Wilde v. Keep, 1834, 6 C. & P. 235; Forman
v. Jacob, 1815, 1 Stark. 47; Lindus v. Bradwell, 1848, 5 C.B., at
p. 591; and Trueman v. Loder, 1840, 11 A. & E. at p. 594.)

Firm signature.

The signature of a firm is deemed to be the signature of all
persons who are liable as partners in the firm, whether working, .
dormant (Yorkshire Banking Co. v. Beatson, 1880, 5 C.P.D.
109), or secret (Pooley v. Driver, 1876, 5 Ch. D. 458), or who,
by holding themselves out as partners, are liable as such to third
parties. (Gurney v. Evans, 1858, 27 L.J. Ex. 166.)

Where the name of a firm and the name of one of the partners in it is the same, and that partner draws, endorses, or accepts a bill in the common name, the signature is *primâ facie*
deemed to be the signature of the firm; but the presumption may
be rebutted by shewing that the bill was not given for partnership purposes or under the authority of the firm. (Yorkshire
Banking Co. v. Beatson, *supra,* in which the English and American cases are reviewed.)

If a partner or other person signs his own name and not that
of the firm, he alone is liable: cf. notes to sec. 35. In order to
bind the firm, the signature must be that of the name of the firm.

B., a partner in a firm which trades as C.D. makes a note in
respect of a partnership transaction, signing it D. & Co. If he
has no authority from his partners to vary the firm style, the
firm is not liable, but B. is liable. (Faith v. Richmond, 1840, 11
A. & E. 339; Royal Canadian Bank v. Wilson, 1874, 24 C.P.
362; but as to an accidental mis-spelling or an immaterial and
unintentional variation in the name, see Kirk v. Blurton, 1841,
9 M. & W. at p. 289; Forbes v. Marshall, 1855, 11 Ex. 166.)

A principal trades in the name of one of his agents (a clerk).
He is liable on a bill accepted by the clerk in his own name in
respect of the business, although the clerk in accepting it acted
contrary to his private instructions. (Edmunds v. Bushell, 1865,
L.R. 1 Q.B. 97; cf. Alliance Bank v. Kearsley, 1871, L.R. 6 C.P.
at p. 438.)

In order to bind the firm the person signing must have
authority to bind his partners, unless the partners sought to
be charged have afterwards ratified the signing, or are precluded
from setting up the want of authority (sec. 49).

The authority may be actual or it may be implied by law.
A partner has implied authority to do any act necessarily incidental to the proper conduct of the partnership business and
there the presumption of authority ends. This general rule, so
far as concerns the firm's liability upon a bill signed in the firm's
name, gives rise to two distinct rules as applied to trading partnerships and non-trading partnerships respectively.

A partner in a trading firm has *primâ facie* authority to bind
the firm by drawing, endorsing or accepting bills in the firm
name for partnership purposes; and if the bill gets into the
hands of a holder in due course, the presumption of authority
becomes absolute, and it is immaterial whether it was given for

partnership purposes or not. (Bank of Australasia v. Breillat, 1847, 9 Moo. P.C. 152, at p. 194; Wiseman v. Easton, 1863, 8 L.T.N.S. 637; McLeod v. Carman, 1869, 1 Han. (N.B.) 602.)

A partner in a non-trading firm has *primâ facie* no authority to render his co-partners liable by signing bills in the firm name. The holder must shew authority, actual or ostensible. (Dickinson v. Valpy, 1829, 10 B. & C. at p. 137; Thicknesse v. Bromilow, 1832, 2 Cr. & J. 425.)

The following have been held to be non-trading partnerships: professional firms (*e.g.*, solicitors, Garland v. Jacomb, 1873, L.R. 8 Ex. at p. 219; Wilson v. Brown, 1881, 6 A.R. 411), agricultural firms (Kimbro v. Bullit, 1859, 20 Howard 256), commission agencies (Yates v. Dalton, 1858, 28 L. J. Ex. 69) and auctioneers (Wheatley v. Smithers, [1906] 2 K.B. 321; trading implies a buying and selling; an auctioneer does not buy—he does sell, but only the goods of other persons).

If a person takes a note signed in a firm name knowing that it was not made or endorsed for partnership purposes, or if the circumstances or the nature of the transaction indicate that the making or endorsing of the note is not for the benefit of the firm or is in fraud of the partners other than the one who signs, the onus is cast upon the person so taking the note of proving that the partnership signature was authorized or assented to by the other partners. (Union Bank v. Bulmer, 1885, 2 Man. R. 380; Federal Bank v. Northwood, 1884, 7 O.R. 389; McConnell v. Wilkins, 1885, 12 A.R. 438; Creighton v. Halifax Banking Co., 1890, 18 S.C.R. 140.

Where a bill is payable to the order of a firm, a partner who cannot by his endorsement render his co-partners liable may transfer the property in the bill by negotiating it in the firm name to an endorsee without notice. (Cf. Smith v. Johnson, 1858, 3 H. & N. 222; Heilbut v. Nevill, 1870, L.R. 5 C.P. 478.)

When a bill is payable to the order of a firm and the partnership is subsequently dissolved, the endorsement of an ex-partner in the late firm name transfers the property in the bill and authorizes its payment. (King v. Smith, 1829, 4 C. & P. 108; Lewis v. Reilly, 1841, 1 Q.B. 349: the latter case may be open to question in so far as it lays down that an ex-partner, by endorsing a bill in the late firm name, renders his former partners liable as endorsers to a holder with notice of the dissolution: Chalmers, p. 72.)

It was formerly thought that where two distinct firms, hav- <small>Sec 132.</small>
ing one or more partners in common, carried on business under <small>Firm signa-</small>
the same name, each firm was liable on the acceptance of the <small>ture.</small>
other to a holder for value without notice, but since the case of
Yorkshire Banking Co. v. Beatson, 1880, 5 C.P.D. 109, it seems
clear that this hard rule is no longer law. (Chalmers, p. 69;
Standard Bank v. Dunham, 1887, 14 O.R. 67.)

133. The endorser of a bill, by endorsing it, subject to the <small>Endorser.</small>
effect of any express stipulation hereinbefore authorized,—

> (a) engages that on due presentment it shall be accepted and <small>Engages</small>
> paid according to its tenor, and that if it is dishonoured <small>acceptance or compen-</small>
> he will compensate the holder or a subsequent endorser <small>sation.</small>
> who is compelled to pay it, if the requisite proceedings on
> dishonour are duly taken;
>
> (b) is precluded from denying to a holder in due course the <small>Genuineness</small>
> genuineness and regularity in all respects of the drawer's <small>and regu- larity.</small>
> signature and all previous endorsements;
>
> (c) is precluded from denying to his immediate or a subse- <small>Validity.</small>
> quent endorser that the bill was, at the time of his endorse-
> ment, a valid and subsisting bill, and that he had then a
> good title thereto. 53 V., c. 33, s. 55. Eng. s. 55.

As to the liabilities and rights of successive endorsers of a
bill in regard to notice of dishonour, see secs. 101 and 102 and
notes.

It is conceived that the words "according to its tenor" mean
the tenor of the bill at the time of its endorsement, and not its
tenor at the time it was drawn, if its effect has been varied, e.g.,
by a qualified acceptance or by an alteration of the sum payable.
(Chalmers, p. 190; cf., however, Lebel v. Tucker, 1867, L.R.
3 Q.B. at p. 81 with Gibbs v. Fremont, 1853, 9 Ex. at p. 31.)

As to the re-issue and further negotiation of a bill by a endorser to whom the bill is negotiated back, see sec. 73.

The provisions of clauses (b) and (c) may usefully be com- <small>Endorser</small>
pared with sec. 129. In each case the party who signs a bill by <small>how</small>
the act of signing represents to a holder in due course that all <small>estopped.</small>
the signatures on the bill at the time of his so signing are

Sec. 133. genuine and valid. The endorser in addition is estopped from denying to his immediate or a subsequent endorser that the bill was, at the time of his endorsement, a valid and subsisting bill, and that he had then a good title to it.

The endorser of a bill is in the nature of a new drawer, that is, his relations with the holder resemble those of a drawer (cf. sec. 130).

The endorser of a promissory note, purporting to be made by a corporation, is estopped from alleging that the making of the note was *ultra vires* of the corporation. (Merchants Bank v. United Empire Club, 1879, 44 U.C.R. 468.)

Primâ facie contract of endorser.

The rule laid down in this section is probably intended to be a mere statement of the contract which *primâ facie* is the contract of the endorser, and is doubtless conclusively the contract as between the endorser and a subsequent holder in due course (cf. Elder v. Kelly, 1850, 8 U.C.R. 240). The section adopts the statement of Byles, J., in Susé v. Pompe, 1860, 8 C.B. N.S. 538, with the qualification as to due notice of dishonour observed upon by Lord Blackburn in Duncan Fox v. North & S.W. Bank, 1880, 6 App. Cas. 1 at p. 18, 4 R.C. 491 at p. 606.

The nature of the contract as between the endorser and his immediate endorsee is stated in Castrique v. Buttigieg, 1855, 10 Moo. P.C. 94 at p. 108, as follows: "The liability of an endorser to his immediate endorsee arises out of a contract between them, and this contract in no case consists exclusively in the writing popularly called an endorsement, and which is indeed necessary to the existence of the contract in question; but that contract arises out of the written instrument itself, the delivery of the bill to the endorsee, and the intention with which that delivery was made and accepted, as evinced by the words, either spoken or written, of the parties, and the circumstances (such as the usage at the place, the course of dealing between the parties, and their relative situations) under which the delivery takes place."

The Act has always been construed with certain exceptions, as a declaratory Act, to be interpreted with due regard to the principles more fully explained by existing authoritative decisions. It cannot therefore have been the intention of sec. 133 to overrule the weight of authority above cited and to say that the contract of the endorser is to all intents and purposes the same as if he had made an express contract in writing in the

terms of the clause of the Act. To maintain the consistency
of the view here put forward with the words of clause (*a*), we
must read the clause with the implied addition "*primâ facie* as
between the immediate parties to the act of endorsement, and
conclusively as to a subsequent holder in due course." (4 Ruling Cases at p. 547, where the editor states the law substantially
as above.)

The liabilities *inter· se* of the successive endorsers of a bill
must, in the absence of all evidence to the contrary, be determined according to the ordinary principles of the law merchant.
He who is proved or admitted to have made a prior endorsement
must, according to these principles, indemnify subsequent endorsers. But it is a well established rule of law that the whole
facts and circumstances attendant upon the making, issue, and
transference of a bill may be legitimately referred to for the
purpose of ascertaining the true relation to each other of the
parties who put their signatures upon it; and that reasonable
inferences, derived from these facts and circumstances
are admitted to the effect of qualifying, altering, or
even inverting the relative liabilities which the law merchant
would otherwise assign to them. It is in accordance with that
rule that the drawer of a bill is made liable in relief to the acceptor when the facts and circumstances connected with the making and issue of the bill sustain the inference that it was accepted solely for the accommodation of the drawer. Even where
the liability of the party according to the law merchant is not
altered or affected by reference to such facts and circumstances,
he may still obtain relief by shewing that the party from whom
he claims indemnity agreed to give it to him; but in that case
he sets up an independent and collateral guarantee, which he can
prove only by means of a writing which will satisfy the Statute
of Frauds. Macdonald v. Whitfield, 1883, 8 App. Cas. at pp.
744-745, 4 R.C. at p. 541.

Where two or more parties become parties to a bill to accommodate some third party, their rights and liabilities between
themselves are those of co-sureties, and must be determined irrespective of the position of their names on the bill. (*Ibid.*)

A bill is drawn by one person and endorsed by another for
the accommodation of the acceptor. The drawer is compelled
to pay the bill. He can sue the endorser for contribution as a

Sec. 133.
Primâ facie
contract of
endorser.

co-surety (Reynolds v. Wheeler, 1861, 10 C.B.N.S. 561), although he could not sue him on the bill. (Steele v. McKinley, 1880, 5 App. Cas. 754, 4 R.C. 218.)

Where the directors of a company mutually agree to become sureties to a bank for certain debts, and in pursuance of the agreement successively endorse certain notes of the company, the presumption is that they are entitled and liable to equal contribution *inter se*, and are not liable to indemnify each other successively according to the priority of their endorsements. (Macdonald v. Whitfield, 1883, 8 App. Cas. 733, 4 R.C. 530, overruling Ianson v. Paxton, 1873, 23 C.P. 439, and Fisher v. Meehan, 1876, 40 U.C.R. 146; cf. Steacy v. Stayner, 1904, 7 O.L.R. 684; Vallée v. Talbot, 1892, Q.R. 1 S.C. 223; Clipperton v. Spettigue, 1868, 15 Gr. 269; Cockburn v. Jóhnston, 1869, 15 Gr. 577.)

An accommodation party and his liability on the bill to a holder for value are defined by sec. 55. As to what is an accommodation bill, see notes to that section.

When a person draws, endorses, or accepts a bill for the accommodation of another, the person accommodated impliedly engages (a) that he will provide funds for the payment of the bill at maturity, and (b) that if, owing to this omission so to do, the accommodation party is compelled to pay the bill, he will indemnify such party (Reynolds v. Doyle, 1840, 1 M. & Gr. 753; Sleigh v. Sleigh, 1850, 5 Ex. at pp. 516-7; cf. Hawley v. Beverley, 1843, 6 M. & Gr. at p. 227; Asprey v. Levy, 1847, 16 M. & W. 851.)

The endorser of a bill, like the drawer, stands in a position analogous to that of a surety for the principal debtor. See notes to sec. 130 as to the equities of a surety, and the discharge of a surety by dealings between the creditor and the principal debtor or other sureties.

Measure
of damages.

Amount of
bill.
Interest.

134. Where a bill is dishonoured, the measure of damages which shall be deemed to be liquidated damages shall be,—

(a) the amount of the bill;

(b) interest thereon from the time of presentment for payment, if the bill is payable on demand, and from the maturity of the bill in any other case;

(c) the expenses of noting and protest. 53 V., c. 33, s. 57. Sec. 134.
Expense.
Eng. s. 57.

The recovery of the damages mentioned in this section is provided for by sec. 135.

In addition to the damages mentioned in this section, in the case of a bill dishonoured abroad, re-exchange, with interest thereon until payment, can be recovered (sec. 136 and notes to that section).

It is still the law, as laid down before the Act in Walker v. Damages in Hamilton, 1860, 1 De G.F. & J. 602, and In re General South the nature American Co., 1877, 7 Ch. D. 637, 4 R.C. 565, that the drawer of of re-ex-
change. a bill of exchange in a foreign country accepted in Canada is entitled, upon the bill being dishonoured and protested, to recover from the acceptor, not only the amount of the bill with interest, but also all such reasonable expenses, including damages in the nature of re-exchange, as the drawer is by the foreign law liable to pay to the holder of the bill. The liability of the drawer in such a case depends on the foreign law, and sec. 10 preserves the former liability of the acceptor to indemnify the drawer against his liability. Sec. 134 is not addressed to this point at all (In re Gillespie, Ex parte Robarts, 1886, 18 Q.B.D. 286; cf. R.S.C. 1886, c. 123, sec. 6, now repealed). In the court below (16 Q.B.D. 702), Cave, J. expressed the opinion that sec. 134 is intended to describe the damages which may be treated as liquidated damages for the purpose of the special endorsement of a writ so as to permit of motion for judgment, and does not deprive the drawer of the right to recover from the acceptor any special damage of an unliquidated character which he can shew that he has sustained.

Amount of the bill.

The amount of the bill includes interest until maturity and exchange, if these are provided for in the bill (sec. 28).

Interest.

As to interest proper, payable by the terms of a bill, see sec. Interest as 28. Until the maturity of the bill, the interest is debt; after damages. maturity, the interest is given as damages.

The agreement between the parties for payment of interest after maturity at a certain rate fixes the rate of interest recoverable as damages, however exorbitant it may be. (Young v. Fluke, 1865, 15 C.P. 360, cf. McKay v. Fee, 1860, 20 U.C.R. 268; Popple v. Sylvester, 1882, 22 Ch. D. 98.)

But a note providing for interest at a certain rate "until paid" or "until the payment thereof" means that interest at such rate is to be paid until the day fixed for payment, and the words do not constitute an agreement that such rate shall be paid after maturity. (St. John v. Rykert, 1884, 10 S.C.R. 278; People's Loan v. Grant, 1890, 18 S.C.R. 262; and cases cited.)

In the absence of agreement, the rate of interest payable is 5%. Prior to 1900, the rate was 6%. See notes to secs. 91 and 92 of the Bank Act, supra.

The English Act contains the following provision which is omitted from the Canadian Act: "Where by this Act interest may be recovered as damages, such interest may, if justice require it, be withheld wholly or in part, and where a bill is expressed to be payable with interest at a given rate, interest as damages may or may not be given at the same rate as interest proper."

Since the Act, when a bill is dishonoured by non-acceptance, interest can be recovered only from the date of maturity, and not from the date of dishonour. This perhaps does not accord with the practice before the Act. (Harrison v. Dickson, 1811, 3 Camp. 52n.; cf. Susé v. Pompe, 1860, 8 C.B.N.S. at p. 566; Chalmers, p. 195.)

Expenses of noting and protest.

The English Act reads, "The expenses of noting, or, when protest is necessary, and the protest has been extended, the expenses of protest."

It has been held in England that where a bill which had been protested for better security (sec. 116) has been accepted by a bank for the honour of the drawer (sec. 147), the bank cannot recover the expenses of the protest for non-payment or the commission for so accepting (In re English Bank. Ex parte Bank of Brazil, [1893] 2 Ch. 438). This decision is criticized by Chalmers (p. 195). So far as the expenses of protest are concerned, the case is put upon the ground that such protest was not "necessary" (sec. 114) and it is inapplicable to the Canadian

Act. Under our Act, it is always proper to protest a dishonoured bill (sec. 113) and by sec. 134 the damages include "the expenses of noting and protesting."

In Banque Populaire v. Cavé, 1895, 1 Com. Ca. 67, it was held that the holder of a bill drawn abroad and dishonoured in England is entitled to recover no other charges than those provided by this section.

135. In case of the dishonour of a bill the holder may recover from any party liable on the bill, the drawer who has been compelled to pay the bill may recover from the acceptor, and an endorser who has been compelled to pay the bill may recover from the acceptor or from the drawer, or from a prior endorser, the damages aforesaid. 53 V., c. 33, s. 57. Eng. s. 57.

As to the parties liable on a bill, see sec. 128 (acceptor), sec. 130 (drawer), secs. 131 and 133 (endorser).

The "damages aforesaid" are provided for by sec. 134. Prior to 1906, the provisions of secs. 134, 135 and 136 were parts of one section.

136. In the case of a bill which has been dishonoured abroad in addition to the damages aforesaid, the holder may recover from the drawer or any endorser, and the drawer or an endorser who has been compelled to pay the bill may recover from any party liable to him, the amount of the re-exchange with interest thereon until the time of payment. 53 V., c. 33, s. 57. Eng. s. 57.

The corresponding provision of the English Act provides for the recovery of re-exchange only "in lieu of the above damages," whereas under the Canadian Act re-exchange may be recovered "in addition" to the damages provided for by sec. 134.

Apparently in the Canadian Act the word re-exchange is used to signify, not the whole amount of the damages (exclusive of interest) as used in the English Act and as explained by Byles, J., in Susé v. Pompe, 1860, 8 C.B.N.S. 538, 565, but the excess of those damages over the amount of the bill and the expenses of noting and protest. (Cf. Willans v. Ayres, 1877, 3 App. Cas. 133, 144, and judgments in In re Gillespie, Ex parte Robarts, 1886, 16 Q.B.D. 702, 18 Q.B.D. 286.)

The wording of the Canadian Act renders inapplicable the decision in In re Commercial Bank, 1887, 36 Ch. D. 522, in which it was held that the only damages which the holder of a bill dishonoured abroad can recover are the amount of the re-exchange, with interest thereon, as provided by sub-sec. 2 of sec. 57 of the South Australian Act [sec. 136], and that he has no option to sue for interest under sub-sec. 1 [sec. 134].

This re-exchange must be distinguished from the expenses or damages in the nature of re-exchange which the person suing may have had to pay under the foreign law to the holder of a foreign bill drawn upon an acceptor in Canada. (Cf. In re Gillespie, in notes to sec. 134.)

The re-exchange in the sense used in the English Act, is ascertained by proof of the sum for which a sight bill (drawn at the time and place of dishonour at the then rate of exchange on the place where the drawer or endorser sought to be charged resides) must be drawn in order to realize at the place of dishonour the amount of the dishonoured bill and the expenses consequent on its dishonour. (De Tastet v. Baring, 1809, 11 East, at p. 269; Susé v. Pompe, *supra*.) The expenses consequent on dishonour are the expenses of protest, postage, customary commission and brokerage, and, when a re-exchange bill is drawn, the price of the stamp. Chalmers, p. 196.

The holder is entitled to draw a re-exchange bill upon the party liable. If the drawee accepts and pays such bill, he fulfils his contract of indemnity. According to English practice the re-exchange bill is now seldom drawn, but the right of the holder to draw it is settled by the law merchant, and it is only by a reference to this supposed bill that the re-exchange, in other words, the true damages in an action on the original bill, can be scientifically understood and computed. (In re Commercial Bank, 1887, 36 Ch. D. at p. 528.)

137. Where the holder of a bill payable to bearer negotiates it by delivery without endorsing it, he is called a 'transferrer by delivery.'

2. A transferrer by delivery is not liable on the instrument.   Sec. 137.
53 V., c. 33, s. 58. Eng. s. 58.   Liability of.

No person is liable as endorser who has not signed the bill   Transferor
(sec. 131), but the transferor by delivery, by the act of negotiat-   by delivery.
ing it gives a warranty to his immediate transferee, being a
holder for value, in the terms mentioned in sec. 138.

See sec. 2 as to "holder" and "delivery," and sec. 21 as to
"bill payable to bearer."

As to negotiation, see sec. 60.

A transfer by delivery is frequently spoken of as a sale of
the bill. This is of course a different transaction from the sale
of a bill or draft payable in another place as a means of enabling
the buyer to remit money. Cf. *supra*, pp. 135, 141.

138. A transferrer by delivery who negotiates a bill thereby   Warranty
warrants to his immediate transferee, being a holder for   by.
value,—

     (*a*) that the bill is what it purports to be;   Genuineness.

     (*b*) that he has a right to transfer it; and,   Right to
                                                       transfer.

     (*c*) that at the time of transfer he is not aware of any fact   Bona fides.
        which renders it valueless. 53 V., c. 33, s. 58. Eng. s. 58.

A transferor by delivery is not liable on the instrument
(sec. 137), but as an incident of the contract of sale he warrants
the genuineness of the instrument, like an ordinary vendor of a
chattel.

When the transferee discovers the defect in the bill, he must
repudiate the transaction with reasonable diligence. (Pooley
v. Brown, 1862, 31 L.J.C.P. 134.)

Chalmers (p. 199) gives the following illustrations of this   Liability of
section: transferor
                                                                                   by delivery.

1. C. discounts with D. a bill payable to bearer without endorsing it. It turns out that, unknown to C., the amount of the
bill had been fraudulently altered by a previous holder. D. can
recover from C. the money paid. (Jones v. Ryde, 1814, 5 Taunt.
488; cf. Burchfield v. Moore, 1854, 23 L.J.Q.B. 261.)

2. A bill broker discounts with a bank a bill endorsed in blank by the payee. The endorser absconds, and the signatures of the drawer and acceptor turn out to be forgeries. The bank can recover the money paid from the broker. (Fuller v. Smith, 1824, R. & M. 49.)

3. An agent gets a bank to discount a bill drawn and endorsed in blank by his principal, and then pays over the money to his principal. The signature of the acceptor was a forgery, but the agent did not know it. The drawer fails. The bank cannot recover from the agent. (Ex parte Bird, 1851, 4 De G. & S. 273.)

4. The *bonâ fide* holder of a bill purporting to be drawn by A., accepted by B., and endorsed in blank by C., discounts it with a banker. It turns out that the signatures of A. and B. were forgeries, and that C., whose endorsement was genuine, is insolvent. The banker can recover from the holder the money he paid. (Gurney v. Womersley, 1854, 24 L.J.Q.B. 46; Merriam v. Wolcott, 1861, 85 Mass. 258.)

CHAPTER XLVI.

DISCHARGE OF BILL.

A bill is discharged when all rights of action on it are extinguished. The bill then ceases to be negotiable. (Cf. Harmer v. Steele, 1849, 4 Ex. 1, 4 R.C. 515.)

A bill may be discharged by payment in due course (sec. 139), by renunciation (sec. 142), by cancellation (secs. 143 and 144), by material alteration (secs. 145 and 146). It is also discharged when the acceptor is or becomes the holder of the bill, at or after its maturity, in his own right (sec. 141).

The discharge of a bill must be distinguished from the discharge of one or more of the parties thereto, *e.g.*, a particular endorser may be discharged by want of notice of dishonour, while the drawer and other endorsers remain liable on the bill; or an endorser may be discharged as regards a particular party but not as against subsequent parties (cf. sec. 96). <!-- margin: Discharge of bill distinguished from discharge of party. -->

Again, liabilities arising out of the bill transaction, as distinguished from liabilities on the bill itself, may or may not be extinguished by the discharge of the bill. For instance, if one of three joint acceptors pays a bill, it is discharged, but he personally has a right of contribution from his co-acceptors (Harmer v. Steele, *supra*). If an accommodation acceptor pays a bill it is discharged, but he has a personal right of action for indemnity. If an acceptance be given for a debt, and the acceptance is paid, both the bill and the debt are discharged. Chalmers, p. 202.

The discharge of a party from his liability on a bill, as distinguished from the discharge of the bill, is also subject to the general rules of the provincial law of property and civil rights. The liability may, in the province of Quebec, be extinguished by payment, by novation, by release, by compensation, by confusion, by prescription, etc.

Discharge of Bill.

139. A bill is discharged by payment in due course by or on behalf of the drawee or acceptor. <!-- margin: Payment. -->

2. Payment in due course means payment made at or after
the maturity of the bill to the holder thereof in good faith and
without notice that his title to the bill is defective.

3. Where an accommodation bill is paid in due course by the
party accommodated, the bill is discharged. 53 V., c. 33, s. 59.
Eng. s. 59.

The holder is entitled to receive payment in money, but may
elect to receive satisfaction in any other form. For the ·pur-
pose of the discharge of a bill, payment includes any satisfaction
which would be sufficient to discharge an ordinary contract.
See, for instance, Cripps v. Davis, 1843, 12 M. & W. 159 (agreement to set off another debt); Sibree v. Tripp, 1846, 15 M. &
W. 23 (negotiable bill for less amount); Ford v. Beech, 1848,
11 Q.B. 852 (agreement to suspend); Arsell v. Baker, 1850, 15
Q.B. 20 (merger); Belshaw v. Bush, 1851, 11 C.B. 207 (bill of
third party); Woodward v. Pell, 1868, L.R. 4 Q.B. 55 (debtor
taken in execution); Schroder's case, 1870, L.R. 11 Eq. 131
(payment in bonds).

But, inasmuch as the holder may, at or after maturity, re-
nounce his rights against any party (sec. 142), the law as to
accord and satisfaction (strictly so-called) is perhaps inapplicable to bills of exchange. (Cook v. Lister, 1863, 13 C.B.N.S.
at p. 593, 4 R.C. at p. 561.)

Part payment of a bill in due course operates as a discharge
pro tanto. (Graves v. Key, 1832, 3 B. & Ad. 313, cf. Pinder v.
Cronkhite, 1898, 34 N.B.R. 498.)

As to payment of a smaller sum in satisfaction of a larger
sum, see Foakes v. Beer, 1884, 9 App. Cas. 605, 1 R.C. 370; but
provincial law governs the meaning of payment. In Ontario,
for instance, by statute a smaller sum may be accepted in satisfaction of a larger sum. (R.S.O., 1897, c. 51, sec. 58(8).)

As to payment between banks through the clearing house.
see Chapter XXVIII., *supra*, at p. 297.

As to when payment by a bank to an individual is complete,
cf. Chapter XVIII., *supra*, at p. 212.

The payee of a note payable on demand takes also a mortgage
to secure the debt. He then transfers the mortgage, receiving
the amount of the note. This does not constitute payment of
the note, and the payee may afterwards negotiate it to a holder
in due course. (Glasscock v. Balls, 1889, 24 Q.B.D. 13.)

By or on behalf of drawee or acceptor.

This provision applies also to the maker of a note (sec. 186).

As to the effect of payment by the drawer or an endorser, see sec. 140.

Although a bill is discharged by payment, the acceptor paying may have his right of contribution from his co-acceptors, independently of the bill.

A bill is accepted by three joint acceptors (not partners). One of them pays it at maturity. The bill is discharged and cannot be again negotiated. It is immaterial that the acceptor who paid accepted the bill for the accommodation of the other two. (Harmer v. Steele, 1849, 4 Ex. at pp. 13, 14; cf. Bartrum v. Caddy, 1838, 9 A. & E. 275.)

A joint and several note is paid at maturity by one of the makers. The note is discharged. (Beaumont v. Greathead, 1846, 2 C.B. 494.)

Payment by a stranger does not discharge the bill according to English law.

A bill accepted payable at a bank and endorsed in blank by C. is sent to D. to collect. D. improperly discounts it. To regain possession, D. goes to the acceptor's bankers, pays in the amount of the bill and asks to have the bill given up to him, when the holder has been paid. This is done. The bill is not discharged. C. can sue the acceptor. (Deacon v. Stodhart, 1841, 2 M. & Gr. 317; Thomas v. Fenton, 1847, 5 D. & L. 28, 38; cf. Walter v. James, 1871, L.R. 6 Ex. 124, and sec. 140.)

C. is the holder of a dishonoured bill endorsed in blank. D. pays the amount and costs to C. in order to get the bill and sue on it. C. parts with the bill under the impression that D. has paid it on behalf of the acceptor. The bill is not discharged. D. can sue the drawer. (Lyon v. Maxwell, 1868, 18 L.T.N.S. 28; and sec. 140.)

At or after maturity.

Payment by the drawee or aceptor before maturity is valid between the immediate parties to the payment, but does not operate as a discharge of the bill. The drawee or acceptor becomes the purchaser of the bill, and, if the form of the bill permits, may re-issue and further negotiate it. (Morley v. Culverwell, 1840, 7 M. & W. 174, 182; Attenborough v. Mackenzie, 1856,

25 L.J. Ex. 244.) If however he holds it until maturity, the bill is discharged (sec. 141).

To the holder thereof in good faith and without notice.

Payment must be made to the holder or to some person authorized to receive payment on his behalf (cf. sec. 87).

See sec. 2, as to holder, sec. 3, as to good faith, and sec. 56, as to defective title.

A bill is endorsed payable to John Smith or order. Another person of the same name gets the bill, and presents it. The acceptor pays it. The bill is not discharged. The acceptor is still liable to the real John Smith. (Cf. sec. 49; McEntire v. Potter, 1889, 22 Q.B.D. at p. 441.)

The endorser of a bill has obtained it by fraud. He presents it at maturity to the acceptor, who pays him in good faith. The bill is discharged. (Cf. Robarts v. Tucker, 1851, 16 Q.B. at p. 576.)

By the party accommodated.

Accommodation bill is defined by sec. 55.

Primâ facie, the acceptor is the principal debtor and payment by him discharges the bill. But in the case of an accommodation bill, the person accommodated is the principal debtor, if the holder knows of the relation between the person accommodated and the acceptor, and in any case the person accommodated is the person ultimately liable. Payment by him discharges the bill and is a good defence to an action by the holder against the acceptor. (Cf. Cook v. Lister, 1863, 13 C.B.N.S. 543, 4 R.C. 552; In re Oriental Commercial Bank, Ex parte European Bank, 1871, L.R. 7 Ch. at p. 102.)

A bill is accepted for the accommodation of the drawer. The drawer negotiates the bill, and then takes it up at maturity. Subsequently he re-issues it. The holder cannot sue the acceptor, for the bill is discharged. (Cook v. Lister, *supra.*)

Renewal.

As noted under sec. 96, *supra*, a creditor who takes a bill for a pre-existing debt presumably takes it as conditional payment of the debt, the condition being that the bill so taken is paid at

maturity. If the bill is dishonoured and the requisite proceedings on dishonour are taken or waived, then the original debt
revives.

The same principles apply to the renewal of a bill. When a
bill is given in renewal of a former bill, and the holder retains the
former bill, the renewal, in the absence of special agreement operates merely as a conditional payment of the former bill. (Noad v.
Bouchard, 1860, 10 L.C.R. 476, 8 R.J.R.Q. 473; cf. Lewis v.
Lyster, 1835, 2 C.M. & R. 704; Lumley v. Musgrave, 1837, 4
Bing. N.C. at p. 15.) If the renewal bill be paid in due course or
otherwise discharged, the original bill is likewise discharged
(Dillon v. Rimmer, 1822, 1 Bing. 100); but if the renewal bill be
dishonoured, then, the liabilities of the parties to the original
bill (other than a surety who has been released by the extension
of time given to the principal) revive, and they may be sued
thereon. (Ex parte Barclay, 1802, 7 Ves. jr. 597); Norris v.
Aylett, 1809, 2 Camp. 329.) Renewing a bill or note operates
as an extension of the time for paying it. Hence if a bill be
renewed without the assent of all parties liable thereon as sureties, the parties so liable are discharged. (Cf. Oriental v. Overend, 1871, L.R. 7 Ch. 142; 1874, L.R. 7 H.L. 348; Torrance v.
Bank of B.N.A., 1873, L.R. 5 P.C. at p. 252.)

140. Subject to the provisions aforesaid as to an accommo- Payment by]
dation bill, when a bill is paid by the drawer or an endorser, it drawer or
is not discharged; but.— endorser.

  (a) where a bill payable to, or to the order of, a third party
      is paid by the drawer, the drawer may enforce payment
      thereof against the acceptor, but may not re-issue the bill;

  (b) where a bill is paid by an endorser, or where a bill pay-
      paying it is remitted to his former rights as regards the
      acceptor or antecedent parties, and he may, if he thinks fit,
      strike out his own and subsequent endorsements, and again
      negotiate the bill. 53 V., c. 33, s. 59. Eng. s. 59.

A bill is discharged by payment in due course by or on behalf
of the drawee or acceptor, or, in the case of an accommodation

bill, by the party accommodated (sec. 139). In either of these cases the payment which discharges the bill is that of the party ultimately liable. But except as aforesaid a bill is not discharged by payment by the drawer or an endorser. The endorser, or, where the bill is payable to the drawer's order, the drawer, who pays the bill, is remitted to his former rights as against the acceptor or antecedent parties. He may sue the acceptor and the parties antecedent to himself, or he may strike out his own and the subsequent endorsements and again negotiate the bill (Callow v. Lawrence, 1814, 3 M. & S. 95; cf. notes to sec. 67) and the payment by the drawer will be no answer to the holder's action against the acceptor. (Jones v. Broadhurst, 1850, 9 C.B. 173.)

The drawer's right to re-issue a bill which he has paid depends on his being payee as well as drawer. If the bill is payable to, or to the order of, a third party, the drawer paying it may enforce payment against the acceptor, but may not re-issue the bill. (Williams v. James, 1850, 15 Q.B. at p. 505.)

The C. Bank discounts a bill, which is accepted payable at the bank, and then endorses it away. At maturity it is presented to the bank and paid. It is a question of fact whether the bank paid as the agent and banker of the acceptor, or whether it took up the bill as endorser. In the latter case the bill is not discharged and the bank can sue the drawer, or, if he be a customer, debit him with the amount of the bill. (Pollard v. Ogden, 1853, 2 E. & B. 459.)

The endorser of a bill writes to the drawer promising to "retire" it, and accordingly takes it up before maturity. The bill is not discharged. (Elsam v. Denny, 1854, 15 C.B. 87; see at p. 94, as to the meaning of "retire," and cf. Ex parte Reed, 1872, L.R. 14 Eq. at p. 593.)

A drawer or endorser who pays the bill is, like a surety, entitled to the benefit of any securities deposited by the principal debtor with the holder and retained by the holder at the time of the dishonour of the bill (Duncan Fox & Co. v. N. & S. Wales Bank, 1880, 6 App. Cas. 1). *Quære* as to the rights of the endorsee to the securities if the drawer or endorser again negotiates the bill. Chalmers, p. 208.

When a bill is paid wholly or in part by the drawer or by an endorser, and the holder retains possession of the bill, the latter holds as trustee for such drawer or endorser, as regards the

amount received (Cook v. Lister, 1863, 13 C.B.N.S. at p. 596, 4
R.C. at p. 563). The holder may sue in his own name, but, in
so far as he is a trustee for the drawer or endorser, any defence
or set off available to the acceptor against such drawer or endorser will be available against the holder (see Chapter XL.,
supra, pp. 482-3.

141. When the acceptor of a bill is or becomes the holder
of it, at or after its maturity, in his own right, the bill is discharged. 53 V., c. 33, s. 60. Eng. s. 61.

It is no objection to the negotiability of a bill that it has during its currency and before it was payable become the property
of one of several joint acceptors. But if at the time of maturity it
is held by one of the acceptors,—that acceptor being entitled to
receive as well as liable to pay the amount of the bill,—the liability upon the contract of acceptance is discharged as to all the
acceptors. (Harmer v. Steele, 1849, 4 Ex. 1, 4 R.C. 515.)

In this latter case it may be that the acceptor who has paid
the bill may have a right of action against the other joint acceptors for contribution, if the state of accounts between them,
or the terms on which they agreed with one another to become
joint acceptors, should afford ground for such an action; but
that action would not be on the contract of acceptance or on the
bill, but on a different contract, arising out of the state of accounts between the joint acceptors, or the terms on which they
agreed together to accept; and the right to bring it would not be
capable of being transferred by act of the parties, by endorsement of the bill or otherwise. (*Ibid.*)

The expression "in his own right" is not used in contradistinction to a right in a representative capacity, but indicates a
right not subject to that of another person and good against
all the world. In Nash v. De Freville, [1900] 2 Q.B. 72, A. gave
three notes to cover his indebtedness to the payee, and subsequently gave two more notes in substitution for the first three
and to cover further advances. All the notes were payable on
demand and were given on the understanding that they should
not be negotiated. The payee endorsed all five notes to B.
Afterwards A. paid to the payee the amount due on the last two
notes, and at a later date the payee obtained the five notes from

Sec. 141.

Acceptor holding at maturity.

B. by fraud and handed them to A. In an action by B. against A. it was held that A., when he received back the notes, did not become holder for value, since the previous satisfaction of the notes by him was not a consideration given by him when he received back the notes, and that, as they were then overdue, he acquired no better title than the payee had, and that B. could therefore recover.

In view of the expression of opinion in Nash v. De Freville as to the meaning of the words "in his own right," it is doubtful whether these words affect the common law rule that if the acceptor or maker becomes the administrator of the holder, the bill is not discharged, but if he becomes the executor of the holder, it is discharged. (Freakley v. Fox, 1829, 9 B. & C. 130.)

The mode of discharge provided for by this section is called in the civil law *confusio,* and is recognized in the countries the law of which is founded on the civil law.

Renouncing rights.

142. When the holder of a bill, at or after its maturity, absolutely and unconditionally renounces his rights against the acceptor, the bill is discharged.

Against one party.

2. The liabilities of any party to a bill may in like manner be renounced by the holder before, at, or after its maturity.

Writing.

3. A renunciation must be in writing, unless the bill is delivered up to the acceptor.

Holder in due course.

4. Nothing in this section shall affect the rights of a holder in due course without notice of renunciation. 53 V., c. 33, s. 61. Eng. s. 62.

The words requiring the renunciation to be in writing were added in committee in amendment of the English bill. They alter the English law, and bring it into accordance with Scotch law. At common law a contract cannot be discharged by accord without satisfaction. The special rule as to bills and notes partially reproduced in this section seems to have been consciously imported into the law merchant from French law. (Foster v. Dawber, 1851, 6 Ex. at p. 852). This mode of discharge is known in France as "remise volontaire," and is recognized in countries where the civil law prevails. See Chalmers, pp. 214-5, where the following illustrations are given:

1. The holder of a bill at maturity tells the acceptor that
he renounces all claims against him, and gives up the bill to Renuncia-
him. The bill is discharged. (Whatley v. Tricker, 1807, 1 tion in
Camp. 35; Foster v. Dawber, *supra*.) writing.

2. The holder of a bill before it matures writes to the first
endorser that he renounces all claim against him. The first and
subsequent endorsers are discharged as regards such holder.
The drawer and the acceptor are not. (Cf. De la Torre v. Barclay, 1814, 1 Stark. 7.)

3. The holder of a bill verbally agrees with the drawer that
he will not exercise his right of recourse against him if a certain event takes place. The event happens. The drawer is not
discharged, for this is merely an oral agreement to vary the
effect of a bill as drawn, and not an absolute waiver of the
drawer's liabilities. (Abrey v. Crux, 1869, L.R. 5 C.P. 37.)

4. The holder of a note payable on demand, being in a dying
state, says that he wishes to forego the debt, and by his directions a memorandum is drawn up to the effect that the note is to
be destroyed as soon as it can be found. This is only the expression of an intention to cancel it, and does not operate as a renunciation. (Re George, Francis v. Bruce, 1890, 44 Ch. D. 627;
cf. Smith v. Gordon, 1883, 1 C. & E. 105, before the Act.)

5. B. makes a note in favour of C., who has lent him money.
C. afterwards hands the note to D., who is a devisee under B.'s
will, and verbally renounces his rights. This is not a discharge.
(Edwards v. Walters, [1896] 2 Ch. 157; *aliter* probably if D.
had been an executor, not a devisee.)

As to a holder in due course, see sec. 56.

143. Where a bill is intentionally cancelled by the holder or Cancellation
his agent, and the concellation is apparent thereon, the bill is of bill.
discharged.

2. In like manner, any party liable on a bill may be dis- Of any
charged by the intentional cancellation of his signature by the signature.
holder or his agent.

3. In such case, any endorser who would have had a right of Discharge of
recourse against the party whose signature is cancelled is also endorser.
discharged. 53 V., c. 33, s. 62. Eng. s. 63.

Sec. 143.
Cancellation of bill.

Cf. sec. 144.

The holder of a bill strikes out the acceptor's signature, intending to cancel it. This is a waiver of the acceptance, and discharges the bill (cf. Sweeting v. Halse, 1829, 9 B. & C. at p. 369; Yglesias v. River Plate Bank, 1877, 3 C.P.D. 60). *Aliter*, if the cancellation be not apparent, and the bill is negotiated to a holder for value before maturity. (Ingham v. Primrose, 1859, 7 C.B.N.S. 82; as to the actual decision in this case, see Baxendale v. Bennett, 1878, 3 Q.B.D. at p. 532, 4 R.C. at p. 644.)

B. accepts the first part of a foreign bill drawn in a set of two, and sends it, as directed, to a bank to be held at the disposition of the holder of the second. The drawer, who is the holder of the second part, failing to discount it, cancels it, and directs the bank to deliver up the first to B. B. gets the first part and cancels his acceptance. B. is discharged, and if the drawer subsequently issues a fresh second part, the holder cannot sue B. (Ralli v. Dennistoun, 1851, 6 Ex. 483, 4 R.C. 505.)

Unintentional cancellation.

Burden of proof.

144. A cancellation made unintentionally, or under a mistake, or without the authority of the holder, is inoperative: Provided that where a bill or any signature thereon appears to have been cancelled, the burden of proof lies on the party who alleges that the cancellation was made unintentionally, or under a mistake, or without authority. 53 V., c. 33, s. 62. Eng. s. 63.

See, for instance, Raper v. Birkbeck, 1812, 15 East. 17, acceptance cancelled by referee in case of need; Wilkinson v. Johnson, 1824, 3 B. & C. 428, endorsements cancelled by payer for honour; Novelli v. Rossi, 1831, 2 B. & Ad. 757, acceptance cancelled by bank where payable; approved Castrique v. Imrie, 1870, L.R. 4 H.L. 435; Warwick v. Rogers, 1843, 5 M. & Gr. 340, 373, acceptance cancelled by bank where payable; Prince v. Oriental Bank, 1878, 3 App. Cas. 325, note cancelled by maker's banker.

Alteration of bill.

Holder in due course.

145. Where a bill or acceptance is materially altered without the assent of all parties liable on the bill, the bill is voided, except as against a party who has himself made, authorized, or assented to the alteration and subsequent endorsers: Provided that where a bill has been materially altered, but the alteration is not apparent, and the bill is in the hands of a holder in due course, such holder may avail himself of the bill as if it had not been altered, and may enforce payment of it according to its original tenor. 53 V., c. 33, s. 63. Eng. s. 64.

As to what alterations are material, see sec. 146.

At common law a material alteration, by whomsoever made (*e.g.*, by a stranger: Davidson v. Cooper, 1843, 11 M. & W. at 799, 13 M. & W. 343), avoided and discharged the bill, except as against a party who made or assented to the alteration (Master v. Miller, 1793, 4 T.R. 320, 2 R.C. 669; Hamelin v. Bruck, 1846, 9 Q.B. 306; see Carrique v. Beaty, 1897, 24 A.R. 309, where many of the cases are reviewed). A subsequent endorsee of a bill so discharged could not sue on the bill. (Burchfield v. Moore, 1854, 23 L.J.Q.B. 261.)

The proviso was introduced into the English bill in committee to mitigate the rigour of the common law rule in favour of the holder in due course. Chalmers, p. 217.

The word "apparent" in the proviso means an alteration Apparent alteration. which can be discerned by the holder. (Cunnington v. Peterson, 1898, 29 O.R. 346, dissenting from the dictum of Denman, J., in Leeds & County Bank v. Walker, 1883, 11 Q.B.D. at p. 90 to the effect that an alteration is apparent if the person sought to be made liable can at once discover by some incongruity on the face of the bill, and point out to the holder that it is not what it was, that is to say that it has been materially and fraudulently altered, even if the alteration is not an obvious one to all mankind.)

In Cunnington v. Peterson it appeared that the name of one Holder in due course of altered bill. of the alleged makers of a note was not signed by him or with his authority but was added to the note after some and before others of the makers had signed, and before the note came to the hands of the plaintiff, a holder in due course. Held that the alteration was not apparent and the plaintiff was entitled to recover on the note as if it had not been altered.

A bill is accepted for £500. The stamp is sufficient to cover £4,000. After acceptance the drawer fraudulently alters the amount to £3,500, and the bill gets into the hands of a holder in

Sec. 145. due course. He can recover £500. (Scholfield v. Londesborough, [1895] 1 Q.B. 536; S.C. [1896] A.C. 514.)

A cheque for $5 is taken by the drawer to his bank and certified by it. The drawer afterwards fraudulently alters the cheque to one for $500, thereby largely overdrawing his account, and negotiates it to a holder in due course. The cheque is presented and paid. Next day the fraud is discovered, and the bank gives notice to the holder. The bank can recover $495 from the holder. (Imperial Bank v. Bank of Hamilton, [1903] A.C. 49; cf. notes to sec. 50.)

When holder of void bill can sue on the consider-ation. The holder of a bill which has been avoided by a material alteration cannot sue on the consideration in respect of which it was negotiated to him (Alderson v. Langdale, 1832, 3 B. & Ad. 660),

(1) unless the bill was negotiated to him after the alteration was made, and he was not privy to the alteration. (Burchfield v. Moore, 1854, 23 L.J.Q.B. 261; cf. Cundy v. Marriott, 1831, 1 B. & Ad. 696);

(2) or unless, although the bill was altered while in his custody or under his control, he did not intend to commit a fraud by the alteration, and the party sued would not have had any remedy over on the bill, if it had not been altered. (Atkinson v. Hawdon, 1835, 2 A. & E. 628; Sutton v. Toomer, 1827, 7 B. & C. 416; Alderson v. Langdale, 1832, 3 B. & Ad. 660.)

Where a bill appears to have been altered, or there are marks of erasure on it, the onus is on the party seeking to enforce the bill to shew that it is not avoided thereby. (Knight v. Clements, 1838, 8 A. & E. 215; Clifford v. Parker, 1841, 2 M. & Gr. 909; Tatum v. Catomore, 1851, 16 Q.B. at p. 746; Cariss v. Tattersall, 1841, 2 M. & Gr. 890.)

Material.
Date.
Sum.
Time.
Place.
Adding places.

146. In particular any alteration,—

(a) of the date;

(b) of the sum payable;

(c) of the time of payment;

(d) of the place of payment;

(e) by the addition of a place of payment without the acceptor's assent where a bill has been accepted generally;

is a material alteration. 53 V., c. 33, s. 63. Eng. s. 64.

As to the cases in which material alteration will make a bill void, see sec. 145.

Sec. 146.

Sec. 146 is not exhaustive.

An alteration is material which in any way alters the operation of the bill and the liabilities of the parties, whether the change be prejudicial or beneficial (Gardner v. Walsh, 1855, 5 E. & B. 83, 89; Boulton v. Langmuir, 1897, 24 A.R. 618; cf. Suffell v. Bank of England, 1882, 9 Q.B.D. 555, 568, 574-575). The materiality of an alteration is a question of law (Vance v. Lowther, 1876, 1 Ex. D. 176), and must be considered with reference to the contract itself and not with reference to the surrounding circumstances. (Re Commercial Bank, Banque d' Hochelaga's Case, 1894, 10 Man. R. 171.)

What is material alteration.

The following have been held to be material alterations in a bill:

Material alteration.

1. An alteration of the date so as to postpone (as well as one to accelerate) the time of payment. (Outhwaite v. Luntley, 1815, 4 Camp. 179; Hirschman v. Budd, 1873, L.R. 8 Ex. 171.)

2. An alteration of the date of a cheque payable on demand. (Vance v. Lowther, 1876, 1 Ex. D. 176; Beltz v. Molsons Bank, 1876, 40 U.C.R. 253; Boulton v. Langmuir, 1897, 24 A.R. 618, although the effect is to make less interest payable. The conversion of a bill payable after date into one payable after sight. (Long v. Moore, 1790, 3 Esp. 155n.)

But an alteration to correct a manifest error was held to be immaterial. (Cf. Merchants Bank v. Stirling, 1880, 1 R. & G. (N.S.) 439, an accommodation note dated "6th, 1875" changed to "8th June, 1875," the 6th of June being a Sunday.)

3. The superscription upon the face of the bill and over an endorsement of a particular rate of exchange. (Hirschfeld v. Smith, 1866, L.R. 1 C.P. 340.)

4. The addition of a new maker's name to a joint and several note. (Gardner v. Walsh, 1855, 5 E. & B. 83; Carrique v. Beaty, 1897, 24 A.R. 302.)

5. An alteration of the place of payment, or an addition of a place of payment, without the acceptor's consent. (Tidmarsh v. Grover, 1813, 1 M. & S. 735; Burchfield v. Moore, 1854, 3 E. & B. 683; McQueen v. McIntyre, 1879, 30 C.P. 426.)

Quære, if the acceptor consents: see sec. 146. See Walter v. Cubley, 1833, 2 Cr. & M. 151; Mason v. Bradley, 1843, 11 M. & W. at p. 594; Gibb v. Mather, 1832, 2 Cr. & M. at p. 262; Saul v. Jones, 1858, 28 L.J.Q.B. 37.

Sec. 146.

Material
alteration.

6. An alteration in the number of a Bank of England note. (Suffell v. Bank of England, 1882, 9 Q.B.D. 555; Leeds Bank v. Walker, 1883, 11 Q.B.D. 84.)

7. An alteration in the crossing of a cheque. (Sec. 170, overriding Simmonds v. Taylor, 1858, 27 L.J.C.P. 248.)

8. The substitution of a particular consideration for the words "value received." (Knill v. Williams, 1809, 10 East, 431.)

9. The alteration of the sum payable. (Hamelin v. Bruck, 1846, 9 Q.B. 306.)

10. The alteration of the time of payment. (Westloh v. Brown, 1878, 43 U.C.R. 402.)

11. The alteration of a specified rate of interest. (Sutton v. Toomer, 1827, 7 B. & C. 416.)

The alteration of a bill payable "with lawful interest" by adding the words "interest at six per cent." (Warrington v. Early, 1853, 23 L.J.Q.B. 47.)

The insertion of a rate of interest in a clause providing for interest but with the rate left blank would be authorized by sec. 31.

In Fitch v. Kelly, 1879, 44 U.C.R. 578, it was held that there was sufficient evidence to shew that the note was altered (by the addition of the words "with interest at seven per cent.") to conform to the original intention of the parties, and that the endorsers subsequently agreed to it.

12. The conversion of a joint note into a joint and several note. (Perring v. Hone, 1826, 4 Bing. 28; Banque Provinciale v. Arnoldi, 1901, 2 O.L.R. 624.)

13. The intentional erasure of the name of a joint and several maker. (Nicholson v. Revill, 1836, 4 A. & E. 675.)

14. The alteration of marked cheque by the drawer's making it payable to bearer instead of to order. (Re Commercial Bank, Banque d' Hochelaga's Case, 1894, 10 Man. R. 171.)

Immaterial
alteration.

The following alterations have been held to be immaterial.

1. Conversion of a bill or cheque payable to bearer into one payable to order. (Attwood v. Griffin, 1826, 2 C. & P. 368.)

2. The conversion of a blank endorsement into a special endorsement. (Hirschfeld v. Smith, 1866, L.R. 1 C.P. 340; sec. 67.)

3. The alteration in the name of the firm to which a bill is addressed so as to correspond with the name in which it is ac-

cepted, being the true name of the firm. (Farquhar v. Southey, 1826, 1 M. & M. 14.)

4. The addition to a promissory note, in which no time of payment is expressed, of the words "on demand," which are implied by law. (Aldous v. Cornwall, 1868, L.R. 3 Q.B. 573; cf. sec. 23.)

5. Striking out the word "order" in a bill payable "to order of A. B." (Decroix v. Meyer, 1890, 25 Q.B.D. 343; S.C., [1891] A.C. 520; cf. sec. 22.)

6. The alteration of the marginal figures. (Garrard v. Lewis, 1882, 10 Q.B.D. 30; cf. sec. 28.)

7. The addition of an erroneous due date. (Fanshawe v. Peet, 1857, 26 L.J. Ex. 314.)

8. The insertion of the words "pour aval" over a signature on the back of a note, the person having signed above the payee and as a guarantor. (Abbott v. Wurtele, 1894, Q.R. 6 S.C. 204.)

CHAPTER XLVII.

ACCEPTANCE AND PAYMENT FOR HONOUR.

The sections relating to acceptance *supra* protest do not apply to promissory notes: see sec. 186.

A bill may be accepted (sec. 147)), or paid (sec, 153), *supra* protest for the honour of any person liable on the bill, or for the honour of the person for whose account the bill is drawn. The last mentioned person is commonly called the "third account."

Acceptance and Payment for Honour.

Acceptance for honour *supra* protest.

147. Where a bill of exchange has been protested for dishonour by non-acceptance, or protested for better security, and is not overdue, any person, not being a party already liable thereon, may, with the consent of the holder, intervene and accept the bill *supra* protest, for the honour of any party liable thereon, or for the honour of the person for whose account the bill is drawn. 53 V., c. 33, s. 64. Eng. s. 65.

As to dishonour by non-acceptance, see sec. 81, and as to protest generally see secs. 113 and 114. As to protest for better security, see sec. 116.

As to the liability of the acceptor for honour, see sec. 152.

The holder may refuse to allow an acceptance for honour. He may desire to exercise his immediate right of recourse against the drawer and endorsers (sec. 82). If a referee in case of need is named in the bill, it is in the option of the holder to resort to him or not, as the holder may think fit (sec, 33).

As to the form of acceptance for honour, see sec. 151.

Acceptance for honour is an exception to the general rule that no one can become a party to a bill qua acceptor who is not a proper drawee, or in other words, an addressee. (Steele v. McKinlay, 1880, 5 App. Cas. 779, 4 R.C. at p. 232; cf. notes to sec. 131.)

148. A bill may be accepted for honour for part only of the Sec. 148. sum for which it is drawn. 53 V., c. 33, s. 64. Eng. s. 65. In part.

An ordinary acceptance to pay part only of the amount for which the bill is drawn is a qualified acceptance (sec. 38), which the holder may refuse to take (sec. 83).

As to the holder's option to allow an acceptance for honour, see sec. 147.

149. Where an acceptance for honour does not expressly Deemed to state for whose honour it is made, it is deemed to be an accept- be for honour of ance for the honour of the drawer. 53 V., c. 33, s. 64. Eng. s. drawer. 65.

Cf. notes to sec. 151.

150. Where a bill payable after sight is accepted for honour, Maturity of after sight its maturity is calculated from the date of protesting for non- bill. acceptance, and not from the date of the acceptance for honour. 53 V., c. 33, s. 64. Eng. s. 65.

The English Act has the word "noting" instead of the word "protesting." Cf., however, secs. 118 and 119.

The section brings the law into accordance with mercantile understanding, and gets rid of an inconvenient ruling (see Williams v. Germaine, 1827, 7 B. & C. 468 at p. 471) to the effect that maturity was to be calculated from the date of acceptance for honour. Chalmers, p. 230.

See also sec. 45, which provides that where a bill is payable at sight, or at a fixed period after sight, the time begins to run from the date of the acceptance if the bill is accepted, and from the date of noting or protest if the bill is noted or protested for non-acceptance, or for non-delivery.

151. An acceptance for honour *supra* protest, in order to be Require- valid must,— ments.

(*a*) be written on the bill, and indicate that it is an accept- Writing. ance for honour; and,

Sec. 151.
Signature.

(b) be signed by the acceptor for honour. 53 V., c. 33, s. 64.
Eng. s. 65.

It is sufficient if the acceptor for honour merely writes "accepted for honour," or "accepted S.P." on the bill and signs his name underneath; but it is usual for him to state for whose honour he accepts. Chalmers, p. 230.

If the acceptance does not expressly state for whose honour it is made, it is deemed to be an acceptance for the honour of the drawer (sec. 149).

Liability of
acceptor for
honour.

152. The acceptor for honour of a bill by accepting it engages that he will, on due presentment, pay the bill according to the tenor of his acceptance, if it is not paid by the drawee, provided it has been duly presented for payment and protested for non-payment, and that he receives notice of these facts.

To holder
as others.

2. The acceptor for honour is liable to the holder and to all parties to the bill subsequent to the party for whose honour he has accepted. 53 V., c. 33, s. 65. Eng. s. 66.

Where a dishonoured bill has been accepted for honour *supra* protest, or contains a reference in case of need, it must be protested for non-payment before it is presented for payment to the acceptor for honour, or referee in case of need (sec. 117).

Nature and
effect of ac-
ceptance for
honour.

The nature and effect of acceptance for honour is considered in the cases of Hoare v. Cazenove, 1812, 16 East 391, and Williams v. Germaine, 1827, 7 B. & C. 468. An acceptance for honour is to be considered not as absolutely such, but in the nature of a conditional acceptance. It is equivalent to saying to the holder of the bill, "keep this bill, don't return it, and when the time arrives at which it ought to be paid, if it be not paid by the party on whom it was originally drawn, come to me and you shall have the money." (7 B. & C. at p. 477). It must be duly presented for payment to the original drawee, for "effects often reach the drawee, who has refused acceptance in the first instance, out of which the bill may and would be satisfied if presented to him again when the period of payment had arrived" (16 East at p. 398). As to due presentment for payment, see sec. 86.

As to presentment for payment to the acceptor for honour, see sec. 94.

Sec. 152.

It seems an acceptor for honour is bound by the estoppels which bind an ordinary acceptor, and also by the estoppels which would bind the party for whose honour he accepted; as to which see secs. 129, 130 and 133. Chalmers, p. 232, citing Phillips v. im Thurn, 1866, L.R. 1 C.P. at p. 471.

Nature and effect of acceptance for honour.

It is sufficient if the bill has been noted for protest before the bill is presented for payment to the acceptor for honour (sec. 118). The formal protest may be extended at any time as of the date of the noting (sec. 119).

If the bill is dishonoured by the acceptor for honour, it must be protested for non-payment by him (sec. 117).

153. Where a bill has been protested for non-payment, any person may intervene and pay it *supra* protest for the honour of any party liable thereon, or for the honour of the person for whose account the bill is drawn.

Payment for honour supra protest.

2. Where two or more persons offer to pay a bill for the honour of different parties, the person whose payment will discharge most parties to the bill shall have the preference.

If more than one offer.

3. Where the holder of a bill refuses to receive payment *supra* protest, he shall lose his right of recourse against any party who would have been discharged by such payment.

Refusal to receive payment.

4. The payer for honour, on paying to the holder the amount of the bill and the notarial expenses incidental to its dishonour, is entitled to receive both the bill itself and the protest.

Entitled to bill.

5. If the holder does not on demand in such case deliver up the bill and protest, he shall be liable to the payer for honour in damages. 53 V., c. 33, s. 67. Eng. s. 68.

Liability for refusing.

Prior to 1906 the provisions now contained in this and the next two following sections were all parts of one section, as they are in the English Act. In the revision, the order of the subsections has been altered.

It is not necessary that the formal protest should have been extended. Noting for protest is sufficient (secs. 118 and 119; Geralopulo v. Wieler, 1851, 10 C.B. 690, 4 R.C. 654).

Sec. 153.
Payment for
honour
supra
protest.

As to the rights acquired by payment for honour *supra* protest, see sec. 155. The payment must be attested by a notarial act of honour (sec. 154).

The "protest" referred to in sub-sec. 4 means the protest for non-payment by the acceptor, and not protest for better security. The expense of protest for better security being a voluntary act for the benefit of the holder (sec. 116) is not chargeable against the acceptor. (In re English Bank. Ex parte Bank of Brazil, [1893] 2 Ch. 438, 444.)

Attestation
of payment
for honour.

154. Payment for honour *supra* protest, in order to operate as such and not as a mere voluntary payment, must be attested by a notarial act of honour, which may be appended to the protest or form an extension of it.

Declaration.

2. The notarial act of honour must be founded on a declaration made by the payer for honour, or his agent in that behalf, declaring his intention to pay the bill for honour, and for whose honour he pays. 53 V., c. 33, s. 67. Eng. s. 68.

This section is declaratory. (Cf. Ex parte Wyld, 1860, 2 De G. F. & J. 642.)

Discharge.

Subrogation.

155. Where a bill has been paid for honour, all parties subsequent to the party for whose honour it is paid are discharged, but the payer for honour is subrogated for, and succeeds to both the rights and duties of the holder as regards the party for whose honour he pays, and all parties liable to that party. 53 V., c. 33, s. 67. Eng. s. 68.

The most obvious and advantageous course to be pursued by a man who desires to protect the credit of any party to a dishonoured bill, is simply to pay the amount to the holder and take the bill as an ordinary transferee. But the holder may possibly object; for example, the bill may not have been endorsed in blank, and the holder may refuse to endorse even *sans recours*. In such an event a payment, *supra* protest, becomes essential. Byles, p. 273.

The payer for honour *supra* protest succeeds to the rights and duties of an endorsee from the person for whose honour he pays. He must give such person notice of dishonour, and may himself give notice to prior parties or avail himself of notice given in due time by the person for whose honour he has paid. (Goodall v. Polhill, 1845, 1 C.B. 233; cf. sec. 96 and notes.)

All parties subsequent to the party for whose honour the bill is paid are discharged. If the bill is paid for the honour of the drawer, the payer can look to the acceptor alone, as if there had been no endorsers. The payer's right of action against the acceptor, however, is not subject to any right of set off which the acceptor would have had against the drawer, this not being an equity attaching to the bill. (In re Overend, Gurney & Co. Ex parte Swan, 1868, L.R. 6 Eq. 344, 4 R.C. 375; cf. notes to sec. 70.)

Sec. 155.
Payer for honour subrogated.

Subsequent parties discharged by payment for honour.

CHAPTER XLVIII.

LOST INSTRUMENT.

Lost or destroyed instruments.   At common law when a negotiable bill has been lost or destroyed no action can be maintained either on the instrument or on the consideration for it (Crowe v. Clay, 1854, 9 Ex. 604, 4 R.C. 648), even if the instrument is lost when overdue (Hansard v. Robinson, 1827, 7 B. & C. 90), or if it is payable to order and not endorsed. (Ramuz v. Crowe, 1847, 1 Ex. 167.)

The fact that a bill has been lost or destroyed does not excuse the omission to demand payment or to give notice of dishonour (Thackray v. Blackett, 1812, 3 Camp. 164). Protest may be made on a copy or written particulars of a lost or destroyed bill (sec. 120).

But if a bill or note *not negotiable, i.e.,* an instrument payable to the payee only and with words restraining transfer, be lost, it is conceived that an action will lie either on the bill or on the consideration. Byles, 16th ed. p. 394. But the defendant may be entitled to require an indemnity under sec. 157.

Lost Instruments.

Holder to have duplicate of lost bill.   **156.** Where a bill has been lost before it is overdue, the person who was the holder of it may apply to the drawer to give him another bill of the same tenor, giving security to the drawer, if required, to indemnify him against all persons whatever, in case the bill alleged to have been lost shall be found again.

Refusal. Compulsion.   2. If the drawer, on request as aforesaid, refuses to give such duplicate bill, he may be compelled to do so. 53 V., c. 33, s. 68. Eng. s. 69.

This section reproduces the effect of 9 and 10 Will. 3, c. 17, s. 3. That act applied only to inland bills for £5 or upwards. The remedy is still very inadequate, as it gives no power to obtain an endorsement or acceptance over again. Chalmers, p. 236.

157. In any action or proceeding upon a bill, the court or
a judge may order that the loss of the instrument shall not be
set up, provided an indemnity is given to the satisfaction of the
court or judge against the claims of any other person upon the
instrument in question. 53 V., c. 33, s. 69. Eng. s. 70.

Apart from this section, the holder of a lost bill cannot sue either on the bill or on the consideration. (Tessier v. Caillé, 1902, Q.R. 25 S.C. 207; and cf. notes, *supra*.)

This section reproduces the provisions of 17 and 18 Vict., c. 125, with an extension of its provisions to all courts. Chalmers, p. 237.

It has been held that the section applies to non-negotiable instruments and gives the person liable on such instruments the right to require an indemnity. (Pillow v. Lespérance, 1902, Q. R. 22 S.C. 213.)

If no tender of an indemnity were made before suit, the court may refuse the plaintiff the costs of the suit. (King v. Zimmerman, 1871, L.R. 6 C.P. 466; Banque Jacques Cartier v. Strachan, 1869, 5 P.R. 159; Tessier v. Caillé, *supra*.)

In an action on a lost note, when the loss is pleaded, the plaintiff should, in general, tender the defendant a proper bond of indemnity with a sufficient surety or sureties before applying to set aside the plea under sec. 157, in order to avoid paying the costs of this defence and of the application. (Orton v. Brett, 1899, 12 Man. R. 448.)

Although the words of the statute are that an indemnity be given "to the satisfaction of the court or a judge," the security may be left to the master to settle. (*Ibid.*)

The defence that the bill was lost before action brought must, in the superior courts, be raised by plea, otherwise the plaintiff may recover by producing the ordinary secondary evidence. (Blackie v. Pidding, 1848, 6 C.B. 196; Charnley v. Grundy, 1854, 14 C.B. 608). And a judge had formerly no power to order a stay of proceedings until an indemnity be given. (Byles, p. 394.)

CHAPTER XLIX

BILL IN A SET.

Foreign bills are often drawn in parts called the first of exchange, the second, etc., all the parts in a set constituting one bill (sec. 158). The several parts are made on separate pieces of paper, each part being numbered and referring to the other parts (sec. 158). Each part usually contains a condition that it shall continue payable only so long as the others remain unpaid. One part may be forwarded for acceptance, while the other is delivered to an endorsee, thus relieving him from the necessity of forwarding his part for acceptance, but giving him the endorser's security immediately and diminishing the chances of losing the bill.

A part of a set (*duplicata* or *exemplaire*) must be distinguished from a "copy" (copie); cf. sec. 62.

Secs. 158 and 159 do not apply to promissory notes: see sec. 186.

Bill in a Set.

Bills in set.   **158.** Where a bill is drawn in a set, each part of the set being numbered, and containing a reference to the other parts, the whole of the parts constitute one bill.

Acceptance.   2. The acceptance may be written on any part, and it must be written on one part only. 53 V., c. 33, s. 70. Eng. s. 71.

If one part of a set omit reference to the other parts, it becomes a separate bill in the hands of a holder in good faith. Chalmers, p. 238.

It has been held that an agreement to deliver up an unaccepted bill drawn in a set is an agreement to deliver up all the parts in existence (Kearney v. West Grenada Co., 1856, 26 L.J. Ex. 15); and that a person who negotiates a bill drawn in a set is bound to deliver up all the parts in his possession, but by negotiating one part he does not warrant that he has the rest. (Pinard v. Klockman, 1863, 32 L.J.Q.B. 82.)

As to the liability of a holder who endorses two or more parts [Sec. 158. to different persons, see sec. 159.

The acceptance must be written on one part only. If the Acceptance drawee accepts more than one part, and such accepted parts get of bill in a into the hands of different holders in due course, the acceptor set. is liable on every such part as if it were a separate bill (sec. 159).

159. Where the holder of a set endorses two or more parts Endorsing to different persons, he is liable on every such part, and every more than endorser subsequent to him is liable on the part he has himself endorsed as if the said parts were separate bills.

2. Where two or more parts of a set are negotiated to differ- Negotiation ent holders in due course, the holder whose title first accures is, holders. as between such holders, deemed the true owner of the bill: Provided that nothing in this subsection shall affect the rights Acceptance of a person who in due course accepts or pays the part first pre- course. sented to him.

3. If the drawee accepts more than one part, and such More than accepted parts get into the hands of different holders in due accepted. course, he is liable on every such part as if it were a separate bill.

4. When the acceptor of a bill drawn in a set pays it without Part requiring the part bearing his acceptance to be delivered up to accepted. him, and that part at maturity is outstanding in the hands of a Payments holder in due course, he is liable to the holder thereof. delivery.

5. Subject to the provisions of this section, where any one Discharge. part of a bill drawn in a set is discharged by payment or other- wise, the whole bill is discharged. 53 V., c. 33, s. 70. Eng. s. 71.

The drawer signs all the parts of a set; an endorser does not Endorse- always sign all the parts that he holds. Inasmuch as the whole ment of bill is discharged if any one part is discharged, it is doubtful whether an endorser, before paying a dishonoured bill, can re- quire all the parts which bear his endorsement to be delivered up to him or accounted for. (Cf. Société Générale v. Metropoli- tan Bank, 1873, 27 L.T.N.S. at p. 854.)

As to holder in due course, see sec. 56.

CHAPTER L.

CONFLICT OF LAWS.

Prior to 1906 the provisions now contained in secs. 160 to 164 were all comprised in one section, as they are in the English Act, and all the clauses were governed by the words which introduced the section, namely, "where a bill drawn in one country is negotiated, accepted or payable in another, the rights duties and liabilities of the parties thereto are determined as follows":

Conflict of laws may arise between two or more provinces of the Dominion, and doubtless the word "country," as used in sec. 160, includes province.

As between different provinces, a conflict of laws may arise: (1) in regard to the provisions of the Act which create special rules for the Province of Quebec, *e.g.*, as to non-juridical days (see secs. 43 and 164) or protest (see secs. 114 and 162): and (2) in regard to matters not expressly or impliedly provided for by the Act and not governed by the law merchant within sec. 10. Such matters include the law relating to capacity, limitations and prescription, set-off and compensation, evidence, principal and surety, joint and several liability, illegality, payment and discharge.

In theory questions of conflict of laws may arise in regard to this second class of matters between any two provinces, as they may between a particular province and a foreign country, but practically the only conflict within Canada that is likely to arise is that between the Province of Quebec and one of the other provinces.

Capacity.

When laws conflict, capacity is for some purposes determined according to the *lex domicilii* of the contracting party, but for mercantile purposes it is probably determined by the *lex loci contractus.* (Chalmers, p. 62; Westlake's International Law, 4th ed., 1905, p. 43; Dicey's Conflict of Laws, pp. 546, 547.)

But the courts of Quebec make no distinction in this respect between mercantile and other contracts. Thus, although under

Quebec law a minor engaged in trade is deemed to be of age for all the purposes of his trade, a minor domiciled in a country, the law of which gives no recourse against such minor, cannot validly oblige himself in that province in the course of his trade. (Lafleur on Conflict of Laws, 1898, p. 147, citing Jones v. Dickinson, 1895, Q.R. 7 S.C. 313.)

Evidence.

Evidence is governed by the law of the place where the action is brought or proceedings are taken. (Leroux v. Brown, 1852, 12 C.B. 801; cf. notes to sec. 160.)

The general rules of the English law of evidence prevail in Quebec in regard to commercial matters (*supra*, p. 26).

Limitation and prescription.

Limitation of action, also, is governed by the *lex fori*, if the lapse of time merely bars the remedy. (Garden v. Bruce, 1868, L.R. 3 C.P. 300; Don v. Lippmann, 1837, 5 Cl. & F. 1, 5 R.C. 930; Alliance Bank v. Carey, 1880, 5 C.P.D. 429; Davis v. Isaacs, 1887, 26 N.B.R. 292.)

But if the lapse of time extinguishes the obligation according to the law which governs the contract, as *e.g.*, in Quebec, the obligation will be held to be extinguished wheresoever it is sued on. (Cf. Huber v. Steiner, 1835, 2 Bing. N.C. 202.)

Set-off and compensation.

Set-off by English law is not a modification of a party's obligation but a matter incidental to the enforcement of it, and therefore belongs to the *lex fori*. (Westlake, p. 294; Rouquette v. Overmann, 1875, L.R. 10 Q.B. at p. 541, 4 R.C. at p. 302.)

In Quebec a different rule would apply. Compensation corresponds approximately to set-off. But compensation may take place by the sole operation of law, and the effect is to extinguish the debts in so far as they correspond. Cf. Allen v. Kemble, 1848, 6 Moo. P.C. 315; Wilkinson v. Simson, 1838, 2 Moo. P.C. 275.

Matters of interpretation or modification of obligation.

The law of principal and surety, joint and several liability, illegality, payment and discharge relates to the interpretation

Matters of interpretation or modification of obligation.

and legal effect of the contracts on a bill or to the modification of the obligations of parties thereon. The question whether the law of one country or province or that of another is to govern must be determined by the rules laid down in secs. 160 to 164, or by the general rules of private international law.

These sections contain a set of rules as to the law which is applicable to cases in which the contracts on a bill are entered into, or the obligations thereon are to be performed, in different countries. For the most part the sections embody the general rules applicable to cases of conflict of laws relating to contracts. If the provisions of the Act are inconsistent with such general rules, the Act governs (cf. Embiricos v. Anglo-Austrian Bank, [1905] 1 K.B. at p. 686), but the provisions of the Act are not exhaustive and cases may frequently arise in which recourse must be had to the general rules of private international law. (Cf. S.C., [1904] 2 K.B. at pp. 875-6.)

Conflict of Laws.

Requisites of form.

160. Where a bill drawn in one country is negotiated, accepted or payable in another, the validity of the bill as regards requisites in form is determined by the law of the place of issue, and the validity as regards requisites in form of tne supervening contracts, such as acceptance, or endorsement, or acceptance *supra* protest, is determined by the law of the place where the contract was made: Provided that,—

Unstamped bills.

(*a*) where a bill is issued out of Canada, it is not invalid by reason only that it is not stamped in accordance with the law of the place of issue;

Conforming to the law of Canada.

(*b*) where a bill, issued out of Canada, conforms, as regards requisites in form, to the law of Canada, it may, for the purpose of enforcing payment thereof, be treated as valid as between all persons who negotiate, hold or become parties to it in Canada. 53 V., c. 33, s. 71. Eng. s. 72.

Cf. sec. 60, as to negotiation;
    sec. 35, as to acceptance;
    sec. 2, as to issue;

sec. 62, as to endorsement;

sec. 147, as to acceptance *supra* protest;

secs. 128 *et seq.* as to the various contracts on a bill;

sec. 17, as to form of bill;

sec. 176, as to form of note.

The general rules in regard to the form of contracts have been expressed by Westlake (4th ed., 1905, pp. 271-2) as follows: *Formalities governed by lex loci contractus.*

"207. Subject to proposition 208, the formalities required for a contract by the law of the place where it was made, the *lex loci contractus celebrati*, are sufficient for its external validity in England." (Guepratte v. Young, 1851, 4 De G. & S. 217.)

"208. But a contract, although externally perfect according to the law of the place where it was made, cannot be enforced in England unless evidenced in such manner as English law requires." (This doctrine being based on the maxim that the *lex fori* governs procedure; cf. Leroux v. Brown, 1852, 12 C.B. 801.)

"209. The formalities required for a contract by the law of the place where it was made are also necessary for its validity in England" (*e.g.*, recovery cannot be had upon a written contract, which, by reason of the absence of a stamp, is not good by the *lex loci contractus*).

Sec. 160 adopts the general rule that the formalities of a contract are governed by the law of the place where it is entered into.

It also determines a question about which the English authorities gave no clear result, namely, whether parties to a bill, so far as their liability depends on an endorsement made by a third party, contract to pay one who takes by an endorsement valid according to its own law, or one who takes by an endorsement valid according to the law of their contract. The question arises on instruments endorsed in blank in France, where such an endorsement does not transfer the property in a bill, though it does so by English law (see Trimby v. Vingnier, 1834, 1 Bing. N.C. 151; Lebel v. Tucker, 1867, L.R. 3 Q.B. 77; Bradlaugh v. De Rin, 1868, L.R. 3 C.P. 538; cf. Alcock v. Smith, [1892] 1 Ch. at p. 237, and cf. proviso to sec. 161). The section has decided the special question in favour of the forms required by the *lex actus* of the endorsement, which is in agreement with usual principles. Westlake, p. 292.

Sec. 160.

Exception to general rule.

But an exception is made to the general rule by clause (*b*) of the proviso, which allows a bill which is formally valid according to Canadian law to be validly issued out of Canada as between all persons who negotiate, hold, or become parties to it in Canada. Where a bill is drawn and endorsed out of Canada upon an acceptor in Canada, the bill would be a Canadian bill as regards the acceptor, and the endorsement would be valid, if it conforms to the law of Canada even though it does not conform to the *lex loci*. (Re Marseilles Extension Co. Smallpage's and Brandon's cases, 1885, 30 Ch. D. 598.)

Clause (*a*) of the proviso creates an exception to Westlake's proposition No. 209, *supra*.

Lex loci.

161. Subject to the provisions of this Act, the interpretation of the drawing, endorsement, acceptance or acceptance *supra* protest of a bill, drawn in one country and negotiated, accepted or payable in another, is determined by the law of the place where such contract is made: Provided that where an inland bill is endorsed in a foreign country, the endorsement shall,

Law of Canada.

as regards the payer, be interpreted according to the law of Canada. 53 V., c. 33, s. 71. Eng. s. 72.

An inland bill is a bill which is, or on the face of it purports to be, (*a*) both drawn and payable within Canada or (*b*) drawn within Canada upon some person resident therein (sec. 25).

Transfer of chattels governed by law of place of transfer.

The rule of private international law, that the validity of a transfer of movable chattels must be governed by the law of the country in which the transfer takes place, applies to the transfer of bills by endorsement (Embiricos v. Anglo-Austrian Bank, [1905] 1 K.B. 677, following Alcock v. Smith, [1892] 1 Ch. 238, as a decision to that effect).

"Interpretation."

This proposition is independent of sec. 161, unless the word "interpretation" in the section means the "legal effect" of the endorsement ([1905] 1 K.B. at p. 685).

Embiricos v. Anglo-Austrian Bank was an action by the payee of a cheque against an endorsee who claimed under a forged endorsement which was good in the country where the endorsement was made, although not good by English law (see sec. 49). In Alcock v. Smith, the bill was payable to bearer and the transfer was not by endorsement but by process of law in the shape of a judicial sale. The transfer was valid according to the *lex loci contractus* because by that law an overdue bill, as this was, could be negotiated free from any equities, but the transfer being that of a inland bill was equally valid within the proviso to sec. 161 by English law, as there was in fact no defect in title of which the endorsee could have notice.

Bill drawn by A. in Buenos Ayres on B. in New York and endorsed in blank in Buenos Ayres. It is subsequently transferred to plaintiff in Quebec and action is brought there against the endorser after dishonour. The obligations of the endorser are governed by the law of the Argentine Republic and therefore the endorser was discharged by the holder's failure to use diligence to collect the amount out of the freight, hull and cargo before applying to the endorser. Interpretation means legal effect of the endorsement including the obligation of the parties thereunder. (London, etc., Bank v. Maguire, 1895, Q.R. 8 S.C. 358, where many of the authorities are collected.)

In the case of a bill accepted in one country but payable in Is place of another, perhaps the maxim, *"contraxisse unusquisque in eo loco* payment *intelligitur in quo ut solveret se obligavit,"* would apply. But place of if not, then comes the question, what is the law of the place making? of acceptance, not as to bills accepted and payable there, but as to bills accepted there and payable in another country? Probably the *lex loci solutionis* would be regarded. Chamlers, p. 224.

Westlake (p. 293) lays down the proposition that "229. The obligation incurred by accepting a bill is measured by the law of the place where it is payable. It is a familiar example that the allowance of days of grace is regulated by the law of the place of payment" (cf. sec. 164). If "interpretation" in sec. 161 includes "obligation" as has been suggested (*e.g.*, Chalmers, p. 244, and cf. "legal effect" *supra*), this proposition is consistent with sec. 161 only on the theory that the place of payment is the true place of the making of the contract.

It is generally admitted that, on principle, the obligations of Obligations an acceptor of a bill of exchange should be interpreted by the of acceptor. law of the country where the bill is made payable, and not as sec. 161 indicates, by the law of the country where the bill is accepted. Dicey explains this anomaly by shewing that the rule expressed in the section was probably derived from Story, and

Sec. 161.

that it reproduces his words rather than his meaning. For Story really intended to lay down the rule that each contract embodied in a bill should be interpreted according to the law of the place of performance. Dicey, 606-7; Lafleur on Conflict of Laws, 182-3. Cf. Sanders v. St. Helen's Smelting Co., 1906, 1 East. L.R. 56.

Drawing
issue and
endorse-
ment.

The law governing the drawing and putting in circulation or endorsing of a bill will in general be the law of the place where the bill is signed, but if it is signed in one country and delivered in another, the contract is made in the latter. (Chapman v. Cottrell, 1865, 34 L.J. Ex. 186; Horne v. Rouquette, 1878, 3 Q.B.D. 515, 521, 532-4; as to delivery, see sec. 39.)

Damages.

As regards damages for default in payment, the place at which each party to a bill undertakes that *he himself* will pay it determines with regard to him the *lex loci contractus* according to which his liability is governed. The acceptor is liable to pay interest at the rate fixed by the law of the place where the bill is payable (Cooper v. Waldegrave, 1840, 2 Beav. 282). But the drawer and endorsers do not contract to pay the money in the place on which the bill is drawn (cf. Horne v. Rouquette, 1878, 3 Q.B.D. at p. 523), but only to guarantee its payment in that place by the acceptor, and in default of such payment they agree upon due notice to reimburse the holder in principal and damages at the places where they respectively entered into the contract. Story, sec. 315. The damages against the drawer are measured by he law of the place where the bill is drawn (Gibbs v. Fremont, 1853, 9 Ex. 25), and against each endorser by the law of the place where he endorses. Story, sec. 314. Cf., however, Hooker v. Leslie, 1868, 27 U.C.R. 295, and cases cited: North Western Bank v. Jarvis, 1883, 2 Man. R. 53).

Legality of
considera-
tion.

The legality of the consideration as regards the drawer must be determined by the law of the place where the bill was drawn. (Story v. McKay, 1888, 15 O.R. 169.)

Nevertheless the doctrine that the drawer's or endorser's obligation is to be determined by the *lex loci* of the drawing must be accepted with some qualification.

Obligation
of drawer or
endorser.

As the drawer and endorsers are in the nature of sureties for the due performance by the acceptor of his obligation, it is obvious that the law of the place where the bill is payable, which regulates such due performance, must affect their obligation by affecting that of the acceptor. Cf. Westlake, p. 393, and see

Rouquette v. Overmann, 1875, L.R. 10 Q.B. 525 at pp. 536-7, Sec. 161.
4 R.C. 287, at pp. 297-8, where it is said that, at least as regards
presentment for payment, protest and notice of dishonour, the
liability of the drawer is to be measured by that of the acceptor,
whose surety he is, and as the obligations of the acceptor are to
be determined by the *lex loci* of performance, so also must be
those of the drawer.

162. The duties of the holder with respect to presentment Law as to duties of holder.
for acceptance or payment and the necessity for or sufficiency
of a protest or notice of dishonour, are determined by the law
of the place where the act is done or the bill is dishonoured.
53 V., c. 33, s. 71. Eng. s. 72.

    Cf. sec. 75, as to presentment for acceptance;
        sec. 85, as to presentment for payment;
        secs. 81 and 85, as to dishonour;
        sec. 96, as to notice of dishonour;
        secs. 112 and 113, as to protest.

The propositions laid down by Westlake (pp. 294-5) on the
subject dealt with in this section are:

    "231. In case of (the dishonour of a bill) the necessity and *Lex loci solutionis* governs duties of last holder.
sufficiency of demand, protest or notice of dishonour, *by the last
holder*, in order to charge any other party to the bill, is determined by the law of the place where it is payable.

    (Rothschild v. Currie, 1841, 1 Q.B. 43; Hirschfeld v. Smith,
1866, L.R. 1 C.P. 340; Horne v. Rouquette, 1878, 3 Q.B.D. 514;
Rouquette v. Overmann, 1875, L.R. 10 Q.B. 525.)

    "232. But when an endorser has been made liable on a bill,
the notice which he must give to his endorser, or to the drawer
if there be no intermediate party, depends on the law governing
the contract made by the endorsement to him or by the drawing."

    Proposition 231 is a consequence of the principle of the *lex
loci actus*. Sec. 162 appears to agree with it notwithstanding
the strange wording by which Parliament is made to say that the
necessity of an act is to be determined by the law of the place
where it is done, while it is just when an act has not been done
that the question of its necessity arises. Westlake, p. 294.

Sec. 162.   As to proposition 232, the drawer of the bill, and each endorser, contracts with the next following party to pay him on due notice of dishonour being given; and such notice must be measured by the law of the contract, whenever no question arises about the formalities to be observed in a particular place. The doctrine of the proposition is asserted by the judges in Horne v. Rouquette, *supra*, and according to Westlake, is not overruled by the Act. Sec. 162 must therefore be interpreted as applying only to the *last* holder. The words "or is not done" must be understood after the word "done" in the section. Westlake, p. 295.

Special rule.   By sec. 114, in the case of an inland bill drawn upon any person in the Province of Quebec or payable or accepted at any place in the said province the parties liable on the said bill other than the acceptor are, in default of protest for non-acceptance or non-payment as the case may be, and of notice thereof, discharged, except in cases where the circumstances are such as would dispense with notice of dishonour.

Currency.   **163.** Where a bill is drawn out of but payable in Canada, and the sum payable is not expressed in the currency of Canada, the amount shall, in the absence of some express stipulation, be calculated according to the rate of exchange for sight drafts at the place of payment on the day the bill is payable. 53 V., c. 33, s. 71. Eng. s. 72.

Cf. sec. 136.

The addition to a bill by the holder of words professing to fix the rate of exchange at which the bill is payable, as "at the rate of 25 fr. 75 c. for £1 value received," is a material alteration which avoids the contract, as the rate of exchange at maturity might be lower than the rate mentioned. Hirschfeld v. Smith, 1866, L.R. 1 C.P. at p. 353.

Due date.   **164.** Where a bill is drawn in one country and is payable in another, the due date thereof is determined according to the law of the place where it is payable. 53 V., c. 33, s. 71. Eng. s. 72.

Cf. notes to sec. 161.

By English law days of grace are allowed on bills payable after date. By French law they are not. A bill drawn in Paris on London is entitled to 3 days grace, but a bill drawn in London on Paris is not entitled to grace. (Rouquette v. Overmann, 1875, L.R. 10 Q.B. 525, at pp. 535-538, 4 R.C. 287, at pp. 296-299; cf. Bank of America v. Copland, 1881, 4 L.N. 154.) *Lex loci solutionis* governs due date.

A bill is drawn in England payable in Paris 3 months after date. After the bill is drawn, but before it is due, a "moratory" law is passed in France, in consequence of war, postponing the maturity of all current bills for one month. The maturity of this bill is for all purposes to be determined by French law. (*Ibid.*)

CHAPTER LI.

CHEQUES ON A BANK.

The relation of a banker and customer in regard to cheques has been already discussed in Chapter XVIII., *supra*, especially at pp. 221 and 212. In this chapter we are concerned with a cheque in regard to its characteristics as a negotiable instrument by the law merchant or, under the Act, as a bill of exchange drawn on a bank payable on demand.

PART III.

CHEQUES ON A BANK.

Cheque defined.

165. A cheque is a bill of exchange drawn on a bank, payable on demand.

Provisions as to bills apply.

2. Except as otherwise provided in this Part, the provisions of this Act applicable to a bill of exchange payable on demand apply to a cheque. 53 V., c. 33, s. 72. Eng. s. 73.

A cheque under the Act is drawn upon a "bank" (*i.e.*, an incorporated bank or savings bank carrying on business in Canada: see sec. 2—the corresponding word in the English Act is "banker," the definition of which is pointed out in the notes to sec. 2). It has been held that an instrument in the form of a cheque drawn on a private banker is not a cheque within the meaning of the Act, but a bill of exchange. (Trunkfield v. Proctor, 1901, 2 O.L.R. 326.) *Quære*, however, whether, independently of the Act, such an instrument is not still a cheque by the law merchant.

Cheque defined.

If this section is read with sec. 17, which defines a bill of exchange, a cheque may be said to be defined by the Act as "an unconditional order in writing addressed to a bank, signed by the person giving it, requiring the bank to pay on demand a sum certain in money to or to the order of a specified person, or to bearer."

A cheque must be payable on demand (*i.e.*, expressed to be payable on demand or on presentation, or in which no time for payment is expressed: sec. 23).

As to the other elements of the definition, see notes to sec. 17.

Bill and cheque compared.

A cheque is a bill of exchange because the Act declares it to be such, and, except as otherwise provided in this part (*i.e.*, in secs. 165 to 175), the provisions of the Act applicable to a bill of exchange payable on demand are made applicable to a cheque.

For many purposes a post-dated cheque is equivalent to a bill payable after date (see notes to sec. 27).

The Act apart, there are numerous dicta to the effect that a cheque is a bill of exchange. A cheque is embraced within the definition of a bill of exchange and is analogous to it in many respects. (Cf. McLean v. Clydesdale Banking Co., 1883, 9 App. Cas. at pp. 106, 113; and cases cited in Boyd v. Nasmith, 1889, 17 O.R. at pp. 44-5.) But a cheque and a bill of exchange are in many respects different.

It has been said that a cheque is "a peculiar sort of instrument, in many respects resembling a bill of exchange, but in some entirely different. A cheque does not require acceptance; in the ordinary course it is never accepted; it is not intended for circulation, it is given for immediate payment; it is not entitled to days of grace; and though it is, strictly speaking, an order upon a debtor by a creditor to pay to a third person the whole or part of a debt, yet, in the ordinary understanding of persons, it is not so considered. It is more like an appropriation of what is treated as ready money in the hands of the banker, and in giving the order to appropriate to a creditor, the person giving the cheque must be considered as the person primarily liable to pay, who orders his debt to be paid at a particular place, and as being much in the same position as the maker of a promissory note. or the acceptor of a bill of exchange, payable at a particular place and not elsewhere, who has no right to insist on immediate presentment at that place." (Parke, B. in Ramchurn Mullick v. Luckmeechund Radakissen, 1854, 9 Moo. P.C. at pp. 69-70, 4 R.C. at pp. 465-6; cf. Serle v. Norton, 1841, 2 Moo. & Rob. 404.)

Some of the points of resemblance between a bill and a cheque are now embodied in the Act as a result of sec. 165 which makes applicable to cheques the provisions applicable to a bill payable on demand.

Some of the differences between the two instruments are expressed in the provisions referred to in the exception to sub-sec. 2 of that section. Other differences must also be noted which are only implied in the Act or which indicate a real distinction between the nature of a bill and that of a cheque.

To speak of a cheque as an "appropriation" of money in the hands of the banker is misleading. A cheque, like a bill, does not operate as an assignment of funds in the hands of the drawee available for the payment thereof (sec. 127); the holder cannot sue the bank which dishonours a cheque. (Hopkinson v. Forster, 1874, L.R. 19 Eq. at p. 76, 3 R.C. at p. 757; Boyd v. Nasmith, 1889, 17 O.R. at p. 45.)

An exception to the general rule that a cheque does not operate as an assignment of funds in the hands of the bank is made by clause (b) of sec. 166 in favour of the holder of a cheque to the extent to which the drawer has been discharged by the holder's neglect to present the cheque for payment within a reasonable time of its issue. See notes to sec. 166 where the difference in the position of the drawer of a bill and the drawer of a cheque in regard to presentment for payment is noted.

Being a bill payable on demand, a cheque is not entitled to days of grace (sec. 42).

A bank which has sufficient funds in its hands belonging to its customer is liable to him if it dishonours his cheque (supra, p. 211), whereas the drawee of a bill, in the absence of contract, is not bound to accept, or, in the case of a demand bill, to pay, a bill drawn upon him, even if he has sufficient funds of the drawer in his hands. (Cf. Goodwin v. Robarts, 1875, L.R. 10 Ex. at p. 351, quoted in Chapter II., supra, pp. 22-3.)

The holder in the case of either a bill or cheque would have his recourse against the drawer (sec. 95), subject to the necessity of giving due notice of dishonour (sec. 96).

If the drawer of a cheque had not sufficient funds at the bank to meet the cheque, notice of dishonour would be dispensed with (sec. 107). It has been held that protest in Quebec is unnecessary as against the drawer of a cheque where the cheque has not been paid by reason of the failure of the bank. (Banque

Jacques Cartier v. Limoilou, 1899, Q.B. 17 S.C. at p. 224; cf. De Serres v. Enard, 1899, Q.R. 17 S.C. 199.)

When Mr. Baron Parke stated that "a cheque is not intended for circulation, it is given for immediate payment," he pointed out what is perhaps the inherent and essential difference between a cheque and a bill. A cheque, as being a bill, may, however, be transferred by endorsement and delivery, although it is payable to a named person and not to his order, provided it does not contain words prohibiting transfer or indicating an intention that it should not be transferable (sec. 22). It is not clear, however, that under the Act a cheque payable to bearer or to order can be made not negotiable except under the provisions in secs. 168 to 175 as to crossed cheques. (National Bank v. Silke, [1891] 1 Q.B. at p. 438, 4 R.C. at p. 443.) As to crossed cheques, see next chapter, and as to the title of a person who takes a crossed cheque which bears on it the words "not negotiable," see sec. 174. See, also, a discussion of the negotiability of cheques by R. E. MacNaghten in 13 Journal C.B.A. (1906), 134, 221.

Notice of death of a customer who has drawn a cheque upon a bank, terminates the bank's authority to pay the cheque (sec. 167); the death of the drawer of a bill usually has no effect upon the duties of the parties to the bill (see notes to sec. 127).

Under the Canadian Act a cheque and a bill of exchange are in the same position as regards payment upon a forged or unauthorized endorsement, except that clause (b) of the proviso to sec. 49 contains a special provision applicable to cheques alone. The protection to a paying banker afforded by sec. 60 of the English Act is not available to a bank in Canada: see notes to secs. 49 and 50, *supra*.

Certification of cheque.

The practice of the drawee bank's certifying or "marking" a cheque is a common one in Canada and in the United States. In England the marking is recognized only as importing a promise or undertaking to pay, as between banker and banker, for the purpose of clearance. (See Paget on Banking, Chapter VII.)

In the United States there has been considerable conflict of judicial authority as to the effect of such certification. The Negotiable Instruments Law, as enacted in the State of New York and in the majority of the other States, adopts the view that the certification of a cheque is equivalent to the acceptance of a bill of exchange. For the opposite view, see article by Leslie J. Tompkins reprinted from The American Law Register in 9 Journal C.B.A. (1902) 323, and see some of the cases collected in Boyd v. Nasmith, 1889, 17 O.R. 40.

In Gaden v. Newfoundland Savings Bank [1899] A.C. 281, A, drew a cheque payable to herself or bearer, presented it to the ledger-keeper of the drawee bank, who, by direction of the manager, certified it in the usual manner by writing his initials across it and handed it back to A. At the same time the cheque was charged to A.'s account in the books of the bank, and an entry made in A.'s pass-book. A. then deposited the cheque at the Newfoundland Savings Bank, which presented it for payment within a reasonable time, but before the cheque was so presented, the drawee bank suspended payment. It was contended by A. that the initialing of the cheque had the effect of making it current as cash, but the Privy Council, in the absence of evidence of usage in favour of this contention, held that a cheque certified before delivery is subject, as regards its subsequent negotiation to all the rules applicable to uncertified cheques, and that the only effect of the certifying is to give the cheque additional currency by shewing on the face of it that it is drawn in good faith on funds sufficient to meet its payment, and by adding to the credit of the drawer that of the bank on which it is drawn. A. therefore failed to recover in an action against the Newfoundland Savings Bank. Cf. Re Commercial Bank, Banque d' Hochelaga's Case, 1894, 10 Man. R. 171.

But if a cheque is certified or marked "good" by the drawee bank at the request of the payee or holder, the amount of the cheque being charged by the bank to the drawer's account, and if the payee or holder does not there and then require payment, the drawer is discharged from all liability either on the cheque or on the original consideration for which it was given (Boyd v. Nasmith, 1889, 17 O.R. 40; Banque Jacques-Cartier v. Limoilou, 1899, Q.R. 17 S.C. 211; Re Commercial Bank, Banque d' Hochelaga's Case, supra). The true ground upon which this proposition is based, is expressed by Street, J., in the first case and by Mathieu, J., and White, J., in the second. Cf., also, foot note in 9 Journal C.B.A. at p. 323. The drawer's whole contract is that upon due presentation the cheque will be paid,

if the payee so desires. The payee's whole right is to present
the cheque and receive the money. The payee has no right as
between himself and the drawer to present the cheque for any
purpose except payment, and if, when he presents the cheque
and ascertains that the bank is prepared to pay it, he elects not
to draw the money at once, he thereby accepts in place of payment, the bank's undertaking to pay. The drawer's whole
obligation is performed, and the amount of the cheque is withdrawn from his control and charged to his account.

But in the case of a cheque certified before delivery, no presentment at the time of the certification is made by the payee
or holder who alone is entitled to present the cheque for payment, and therefore he cannot be said to have elected to accept
the bank's undertaking to pay in place of actual payment. He
it still entitled to present for payment and, if he so desires, to receive the money.

The drawer is not liable upon the original consideration,
unless the contract of the drawer of the cheque is broken, but
in the case of a cheque certified or marked at the request of the
payee-holder, the drawer's contract is fully performed. The
cheque is duly paid and therefore the payment or satisfaction
of the original consideration by the giving and taking of the
cheque becomes absolute. Cf. notes to sec. 96 as to "Payment
by bill," and see Legaré v. Arcand, 1895, Q.R. 9 S.C. 122.

The particular form of the certification seems to be immaterial. The certification may be, and often is, more formal than it
was in Gaden v. Newfoundland. Sometimes the bank stamps
upon the cheque the word "certified" or "accepted" followed
by the date and the name of the bank. In Imperial Bank v.
Bank of Hamilton, [1903] A.C. 49, the form was, "Bank of
Hamilton, Toronto. Entered January 25, 1897" (see 31 O.R.
at p. 101). In Banque Jacques-Cartier v. Limoilou the cheque
is spoken of in the judgments as having been "accepted."

In Keane v. Beard, 1860, 8 C.B.N.S. 372, it was suggested
that there is nothing to prevent a banker from accepting a
cheque, if he chooses, though in practice it is not done. Chalmers (p. 249) says "a cheque is not intended to be accepted,
but at common law there is no objection to the acceptance of a
cheque, if the holder likes to take it in lieu of payment."

But as between the payee or holder and the drawer, the
former has no right to present for any purpose other than pay-

Sec. 165.
Certification
of cheque.

ment (Boyd v. Nasmith, 1889, 17 O.R. at p. 41). Having regard to sec. 166, the Act seems to contemplate only one presentment, *i.e.*, presentment for payment. (Banque Jacques-Cartier v. Limoilou, 1899, Q.R. 17 S.C. at pp. 215 and 223.)

The fact that certification of a cheque after delivery at the instance of the holder discharges the drawer indicates that such certification is not equivalent to an acceptance, notwithstanding that the certification takes the form of an acceptance. Cf. notes, *supra*, as to certification of cheques.

In Rose-Belford Co. v. Bank of Montreal, 1886, 12 O.R. 544, the Bank of M. permitted another bank to issue a cheque upon the face of which appeared the words "payable at the Bank of M., Toronto at par." Held that the whole effect of the words was that the Bank of M. at T. would make no charge for cashing the cheque, and that the bank did not assume the risk of there being funds to meet it or lose the right to charge the amount back on ascertaining that there were no funds.

Present-
ment for
payment.

166. Subject to the provisions of this Act,—

(*a*) where a cheque is not presented for payment within a reasonable time of its issue, and the drawer or the person on whose account it is drawn had the right at the time of such presentment, as between him and the bank, to have

Measure of
damage.

the cheque paid, and suffers actual damage through the delay, he is discharged to the extent of such. damage, that is to say, to the extent to which such drawer or person is a creditor of such bank to a larger amount than he would have been had such cheque been paid;

Holder
becomes
creditor.

(*b*) the holder of such cheque, as to which such drawer or person is discharged, shall be a creditor, in lieu of such drawer or person, of such bank to the extent of such discharge, and entitled to recover the amount from it.

Reasonable
time.

2. In determining what is a reasonable time, within this section, regard shall be had to the nature of the instrument, the usage of trade and of banks, and the facts of the particular case. 53 V., c. 33, s. 73. Eng. s. 74.

By virtue of secs. 85 and 86, the endorser of a cheque, like the endorser of a bill payable on, demand, is discharged unless presentment for payment is made within a reasonable time after endorsement.

The drawer of a cheque, however, is in a very different position from the drawer of a bill in respect to presentment for payment.

The rigour of the latter part of the common law rule has been mitigated by the provisions of sec. 166—introduced in the House of Lords by Lord Bramwell when the English bill was before Parliament.

At common law the omission to present a cheque for payment did not discharge the drawer until six years had elapsed, unless some injury resulted to him from the delay, as for instance where the fund was lost by the failure of the banker (Robinson v. Hawksford, 1846, 9 Q.B. 51; Laws v. Rand, 1857, 3 C.B.N.S. 442). But if a cheque was not presented within a reasonable time and the drawer suffered actual damage by the delay, the drawer was absolutely discharged, even though the damage suffered was less than the amount of the cheque, *e.g.*, where the bank failed but ultimately paid a substantial portion of its liabilities. (Alexander v. Burchfield, 1842, 7 M. & G. 1061.)

The drawer of a bill payable on demand is discharged if it is not presented for payment within a reasonable time after its issue (sec. 86); the drawer of a cheque in such a case is discharged only if he had the right at the time of presentment as between him and the bank to have the cheque paid and suffers actual damage through the delay, and only to the extent of such damage (sec. 166).

The former part of the common law rule is impliedly preserved by the Act, namely, that if the drawer does not suffer damage by the delay, the holder may present a cheque within any period not exceeding the period of limitation of action or prescription.

Clause (*b*) of this section has adopted the principle of the civil law and modifies the general rule of sec. 127 (cf. notes to sec. 165) that a cheque does not operate as an assignment of funds in the hands of the bank. If the drawer is discharged under clause (*a*), the holder may recover from the bank, *i.e.*, out of the drawer's funds, to the extent to which the drawer is discharged (Banque Jacques-Cartier v. Limoilou, 1899, Q.R.

Sec. 166. 17 S.C. at pp. 222-3). The liability is in the alternative. The drawer and the bank are not liable jointly and severally. (*Ibid.*)

If the drawer had no funds to his credit, but was authorized to overdraw to the amount of the cheque, the drawer would probably still be discharged, but the holder could not prove against the estate of the bank.

Reasonable time.

Reasonable time for presentment if damage suffered by drawer.

Sub-sec. 2 perhaps introduces a new and less rigorous measure of reasonable time. The common law rule is stated by Chalmers (p. 251), as follows:—

(1) If the person who receives a cheque and the banker on whom it is drawn are in the same place the cheque must, in the absence of special circumstances (Firth v. Brooks, 1861, 4 L.T. N.S. 467), be presented for payment on the day after it is received. (Alexander v. Burchfield, 1842, 7 M. & Gr. 1061.)

(2) If the person who receives a cheque and the banker on whom it is drawn are in different places, the cheque must, in the absence of special circumstances, be forwarded for presentment on the day after it is received, and the agent to whom it is forwarded must, in like manner, present it or forward it on the day after he receives it. (Hare v. Henty, 1861, 30 L.J.C.P. 302; Prideaux v. Criddle, 1869, L.R. 4 Q.B. 455; Heywood v. Pickering, 1874, L.R. 9 Q.B. 428.)

(3) In computing time non-business days must be excluded (sec. 6); and when a cheque is crossed, any delay caused by presenting the cheque pursuant to the crossing is probably excused. (Cf. Alexander v. Burchfield, 1842, 7 M. & Gr. at p. 1067; since this case the crossing of cheques has received legislative sanction.)

As to unreasonable delay in presentment of cheque in view of the evidence as to the usage of trade and banks, and the facts of the particular case, see Banque Jacques-Cartier v. Limoilou, *supra,* where it was held that a cheque issued on the 11th of the month and presented on the 15th was not presented within a reasonable time. Cf. Legaré v. Arcand, 1895, Q.R. 9 S.C. 122, where one day's delay was held to be unreasonable in view of the fact that it was known that there had been a run on the bank and that suspension of payment was likely to follow.

The question of reasonable time for the purposes of sec. 166   Sec. 166.
must be distinguished from the question of reasonable time   Reasonable
under other sections of the Act. By sec. 70 a bill payable on de-   time for
mand is deemed to be overdue, so that it can be negotiated only   other pur-
subject to any defect of title affecting it at its maturity, when   poses.
it appears to have been in circulation for an unreasonable length
of time; see notes to that section as to cheques. Cf., also, sec. 77,
which is applicable only to bills payable at sight or after sight.

167. The duty and authority of a bank to pay a cheque   Authority
drawn on it by its customer, are determined by,—   to pay.

    (a) countermand of payment;   Counter-
                                                mand.
    (b) notice of the customer's death. 53 V., s. 33, s. 74. Eng.   Death.
      s. 75.

Countermand of payment.

If a bank refuses to pay an unmarked cheque the holder has
no action against the bank (see notes to sec. 165). If payment
of such a cheque is stopped, the holder may look to the drawer
(McLean v. Clydesdale Bank, 1883, 9 App. Cas. 95) and endorsers, subject to the provisions of the Act applicable to the
rights and liabilities of parties upon the dishonour of a bill.

If payment of a cheque is stopped before it is presented, it
is as if it had never been given and the debt, if any, for which
the cheque was given in payment remains subsisting. (Cohen
v. Hale, 1878, 3 Q.B.D. 371.)

If a cheque has been certified by the drawee bank at the request of the holder, it is to be considered as duly paid (see notes
to sec. 165). It would seem clear that the drawer cannot countermand payment. If the drawer assumed to stop payment of a
certified cheque and the bank refused payment, the holder could
recover from the bank, not upon the cheque, which has been discharged by payment (sec. 139), but upon the undertaking to pay
implied in the act of certification.

If the drawer of a cheque has it certified, he is entitled, before delivery of the cheque, to have the certification cancelled
and the debit entry of the amount of the cheque reversed in the
books of the bank. But if the cheque has been delivered, the
drawer cannot countermand payment so as to justify the bank

in refusing to pay the cheque to a holder otherwise entitled to present the cheque for payment.

A vendor of goods, after receiving payment, fraudulently sold them to another purchaser, who bought in good faith and gave his cheque in payment. This cheque was drawn on a bank at T., but was cashed by a bank at O. on payment being guaranteed by an endorser. The second purchaser, on being served with garnishee proceedings by the first, stopped payment of the cheque, and paid the money into court. The endorser, meanwhile, paid the bank at O., and now claimed the money in court. Held that he was entitled to it. (Wilder v. Wolf, 1902, 4 O.L.R. 451.)

Notice of death.

Clause (b) is declaratory. The bank cannot charge the customer's account with cheques presented after notice to the bank of the customer's death. (Bailey v. Jephcott, 1884, 9 A.R. 187.) Payment after the death but before notice is valid. (Rogerson v. Ladbroke, 1822, 1 Bing. 93.)

As to the effect of the death of the drawer of a bill, see notes to sec. 127.

When a firm of two partners has a banking account and one dies, the authority of the surviving partner to draw cheques on the firm account is not determined. (Backhouse v. Charlton, 1878, 8 Ch. D. 444; Usher v. Dauncey, 1814, 4 Camp. 97.) In Quebec, partnership is dissolved by the death of one of the partners, and the mandate and authority of the partners to act for the partnership cease with the dissolution, except for such acts as are a necessary consequence of business already begun. C. C., Art. 1897.

Garnishee order.

A bank is under no obligation to honour its customer's cheques if it is served with a garnishee order, even though the balance to the customer's credit exceeds the amount of the judgment. If the bank honoured cheques subsequent to notice of the order, it would do so at its own risk, for it might turn out, for instance, that a portion of the money in the bank's hands might, without the bank's knowledge, be money of which the judgment debtor was trustee. That portion could not be ordered to be paid to the judgment creditor. (Rogers v. Whiteley, 1889, 23 Q.B.D. 236, [1892] A.C. at p. 238; cf. Yates v. Terry, [1901] I Q.B. 102.)

CHAPTER LII.

CROSSED CHEQUES.

Sub-sec. 7 of sec. 169 has no corresponding provision in the English Act. In other respects secs. 168 to 175, relating to crossed cheques, are copied from the English Act with the exception of the substitution in the Canadian Act of the word "bank" throughout for the word "banker," and of "bank" in clause (a) of sub-sec. 1 of sec. 168 for "and company or any abbreviation thereof," and the verbal alterations consequential on these changes.

Although the provisions of the English Act have been adopted in the Canadian Act, the practice of using crossed cheques which is well known and frequent in England has never become usual and is in fact little understood in Canada.

The history of the English legislation in regard to crossed cheques and the meaning of the provisions of the present Act are discussed by Z. A. Lash, K.C., in an article in 6 Journal C. B.A. (1899) 166. *History of English legislation.*

Long before any legislation on the subject the custom existed in England of crossing cheques either with the name of a particular bank or simply with the words "& Co.," the popular impression being that such crossing restrained the negotiability of the cheque and made it payable, in the one case to the bank named, in the other only to some bank. It was held however in Bellamy v. Majoribanks, 1852, 4 Ex. 389, (where the origin of the custom is explained), that such was not the effect of the crossing, but that the object and effect of crossing was merely to oblige the holder to present it for payment through a banker.

A statute of 1857, (19 & 20 Vict., c. 25), declared that a crossed draft should be "payable only to or through some banker." But in Simmonds v. Taylor, 1858, 4 C.B.N.S. 463, it was held

(1) that the statute applied only where, at the time of the presentment for payment the cheque bore the crossing on its face, and not to a case where the crossing had been obliterated by a thief so completely as to make the crossing invisible except on very minute inspection;

(2) that the crossing might be put on by one holder and taken off by another;

(3) that the crossing was not part of the cheque itself, and therefore that an alteration in it would not avoid the instrument.

In consequence of this decision the statute 21 & 22 Vict., c. 79 was passed in 1858. This statute (1) made the crossing a material part of the cheque,

(2) made the obliteration of a crossing forgery,

(3) exempted a banker from liability for paying a cheque when the crossing or alteration did not plainly appear, "unless such banker shall have acted *malâ fide* or been guilty of negligence in so paying such cheque."

The statute also authorized a holder to cross a cheque which had been issued uncrossed or to cross it with the name of a banker where it had been crossed simply "& Co.," and provided that where a cheque was crossed with the name of a banker, the drawee bank should not pay the cheque to any other than the banker with whose name it was crossed.

Notwithstanding the last mentioned provision, it was held in Smith v. Union Bank, 1875, 1 Q.B.D. 31, 4 R.C. 436, that where the holder of a cheque had rendered it negotiable by endorsing it in blank, it was not rendered non-negotiable by the fact that he had also crossed it with the name of his own bank, and that, if the cheque was stolen, his bank was not liable to him in damages for paying the cheque when it was presented through another bank by a bona fide holder for value to whom the cheque had been transferred by the thief.

Each of these decisions was a great surprise to the merchants, and at their instance "The Crossed Cheques Act, 1876" was passed. That Act introduced the "not negotiable" crossing, and gave a remedy to the true owner of a crossed cheque if it should be paid contrary to the crossing. It has been embodied, with some slight modifications indicated below, in the Bills of Exchange Act (secs. 168 to 175).

Crossed Cheques.

168. Where a cheque bears across its face an addition of,—

(a) the word 'bank' between two parallel transverse lines, either with or without the words 'not negotiable'; or,

(*b*) two parallel transverse lines simply, either with or with- Sec. 168.
out the words 'not negotiable';
such addition constitutes a crossing, and the cheque is crossed General.
generally.

2. Where a cheque bears across its face an addition of the Special.
name of a bank, either with or without the words 'not negotiable,' that addition constitutes a crossing, and the cheque is
crossed specially and to that bank. 53 V., c. 33, s. 75. Eng. s.
76.

A cheque may be crossed in six ways: (1) with two parallel Various
transverse lines, (2) with the word "bank" between two parallel ways of
transverse lines, (3) with the name of a particular bank, or in cheques.
any of these three forms with the added words "not negotiable."

When a cheque bears across its face an addition of the name
of a particular bank, with or without the words "not negotiable," and either between two parallel transverse lines or not,
it is crossed specially and to the bank named. In the other cases
mentioned, the crossing is general.

The effect of adding the words "not negotiable" is that the
person taking it does not acquire and cannot give a better title
to the cheque than that which the person from whom he took it
had (sec. 174).

The crossing in any of the six ways may be made by the By whom
drawer. If the cheque is issued uncrossed, the holder may cross crossing may
it in any of the six ways. If it is crossed generally, the holder and how it
may cross it specially. If it does not bear the words "not negoti- may be
able," the holder may add them. If it is once crossed specially, allowed.
the crossing cannot be altered otherwise than by the addition
of the words "not negotiable," except in two cases: (1) the bank
to which it is crossed may again cross it specially to another
bank for collection; (2) a crossed cheque may be re-opened or
uncrossed by the drawer writing between the transverse lines the
words "Pay cash," and initialling the same. See sec. 169.

The crossing is a material part of the cheque and may not
be obliterated, or, except as above mentioned, added to or altered Payment of
by any person (sec. 170).   crossed

Where a cheque is crossed specially to more than one bank, cheque
except when crossed to another bank as agent for collection by the
(sec. 169), the drawee bank must refuse payment (sec. 171). drawee
bank.

Sec. 168.   Subject to the proviso of sec. 172 and to sec. 173, the drawee bank is liable to the true owner of the cheque for any loss he sustains by the payment of the cheque in three cases: (1) if the drawee bank pays a cheque crossed specially as in the last paragraph mentioned, (2) or pays any other specially crossed cheque otherwise than to the bank to which it is crossed, or a bank acting as the agent for collection of such last mentioned bank (3) or pays a generally crossed cheque otherwise than to some bank (sec. 172).

As to the liability of a bank which receives for a customer payment of a crossed cheque, where the customer has no title or a defective title, see sec. 175.

By drawer.   169. A cheque may be crossed generally or specially by the drawer.

By holder.   2. Where a cheque is uncrossed, the holder may cross it generally or specially.

Varying.   3. Where a cheque is crossed generally, the holder may cross it specially.

Words may added.   4. Where a cheque is crossed generally or specially, the holder may add the words *Not negotiable.*

By bank for collection.   5. Where a cheque is crossed specially the bank to which it is crossed may again cross it specially to another bank for collection.

Changing crossing.   6. Where an uncrossed cheque, or a cheque crossed generally, is sent to a bank for collection, it may cross it specially to itself.

Uncrossing.   7. A crossed cheque may be re-opened or uncrossed by the drawer writing between the transverse lines, the words *Pay cash,* and initialling the same. 53 V., c. 33, s. 76. Eng. s. 77.

See notes to sec. 168.

Sub-sec. 7 is not in the English Bills of Exchange Act. Chalmers (p. 259) says: "The drawer of a cheque sometimes strikes out a crossing at the request of the payee, and writes 'Pay cash' on it. The Act does not sanction this practice; but it is difficult to see who in such case could have any effective remedy."

A crossing may not be obliterated or, except as authorized by this section, added to or altered, by any person (sec. 170).

The English Act of 1876 (see notes *supra*) in terms only authorized the "lawful holder" to cross a cheque. The words "to another bank [banker] for collection" have been substituted for the words "to another banker, his agent for collection." Sub-sec. 6 was not in the Act of 1876.

170. A crossing authorized by this Act is a material part of the cheque. Materially.

2. It shall not be lawful for any person to obliterate or, except as authorized by this Act, to add to or alter the crossing. 53 V., c. 33, s. 77. Eng. s. 78. Altering crossing

This section reproduces the effect of sec. 6 of the English Act of 1876 (see notes, *supra*).

The various forms of crossing are provided for by sec. 168.

As to when a crossing may be added to or altered, see sec. 169.

As to an obliteration which is not apparent, see sec. 172.

As to the effect of material alterations generally, see sec. 145.

171. Where a cheque is crossed specially to more than one bank, except when crossed to another bank as agent for collection, the bank on which it is drawn shall refuse payment thereof. 53 V., c. 33, s. 78. Eng. s. 79. Crossed to more than one bank.

This section reproduces the effect of sec. 8 of the English Act of 1876 (see notes, *supra*).

Where a cheque is crossed specially the bank to which it is crossed may again cross it specially to another bank for collection (sec. 169).

As to the liability of a bank which pays a cheque in contravention of this section, see sec. 172.

As there is no privity between the holder and the drawee of a cheque, a bank incurs no liability to the holder by refusing to pay. The only liability of the bank is to its customer, the drawer.

Sec. 172.

Liability for improper payment.

172. Where the bank on which a cheque so crossed is drawn, nevertheless pays the same, or pays a cheque crossed generally otherwise than to a bank, or, if crossed specially, otherwise than to the bank to which it is crossed, or to the bank acting as its agent for collection, it is liable to the true owner of the cheque for any loss he sustains owing to the cheque having been so paid: Provided that where a cheque is presented for payment which does not at the time of presentment appear to be crossed,

Bona fides.

or to have had a crossing which has been obliterated, or to have been added to or altered otherwise than as authorized by this Act, the bank paying the cheque in good faith and without negligence shall not be responsible or incur any liability, nor shall the payment be questioned by reason of the cheque having been crossed, or of the crossing having been obliterated or having been added to or altered otherwise than as authorized by this Act, and of payment having been made otherwise than to a bank or to the bank to which the cheque is or was crossed, or to the bank acting as its agent for collection, as the case may be. 53 V., c. 33, s. 78. Eng. s. 79.

This section reproduces the effect of secs. 10 and 11 of the English Act of 1876 (see notes, *supra*).

Liability for improper payment of crossed cheque by bank.

Prior to 1906, this section and sec. 171 formed one section. "A cheque so crossed" refers to a cheque crossed specially to more than one bank, except when crossed to another bank as agent for collection (sec. 171).

As to the other forms of crossing mentioned in this section, see sec. 168.

In a case before the Act of 1876 a crossed cheque payable to order was stolen from the payee. His endorsement was forged, and the cheque was paid in contravention of the crossing to a person who gave value in good faith. The drawer gave the payee another cheque. On these facts it was held (1) that the banker had no right to debit the drawer's account with the first cheque, (2) that the payee who lost the cheque might have recovered the amount from the person who received the money for it, but (3) that the drawer, having allowed his account to be

debited with the cheque, might himself recover the amount from
the person who got the cash for it. (Bobbett v. Pinkett, 1876,
1 Ex. D. 368, at p. 372). The Act does not appear to affect this
decision, but it gives an additional remedy against the banker
to the true owner, who, in the case referred to, would have been
the payee. If the cheque had been payable to bearer, or had been
endorsed in blank by the payee before it was stolen, there would
be no remedy apart from this section. (Smith v. Union Bank,
1875, 1 Q.B.D. 31, unless the cheque was crossed "not negotiable." Chalmers, p. 261.)

It is to be noted that the bank is protected only if it pays
the cheque "in good faith and without negligence," whereas
under sec. 50 the protection of the Act extends to a payment
of a bill bearing a forged or unauthorized endorsement made
"in good faith and in the ordinary course of business." The
difference is important, as by sec. 3 a thing is deemed to be done
in good faith, within the meaning of the Act, where it is done
honestly whether it is done negligently or not.

173. Where the bank, on which a crossed cheque is drawn,
in good faith and without negligence pays it, if crossed generally to a bank, or, if crossed specially, to the bank to which it
is crossed, or to a bank acting as its agent for collection, the
bank paying the cheque, and if the cheque has come into the
hands of the payee, the drawer, shall respectively be entitled to
the same rights and be placed in the same position as if payment of the cheque had been made to the true owner thereof.
53 V., c. 33, s. 79. Eng. s. 80.

This section reproduces the effect of sec. 9 of the Act of 1876
(see notes, *supra*).

As to the forms of crossing mentioned in this section, see sec.
168.

As to the expression "in good faith and without negligence,"
see notes to sec. 172.

174. Where a person takes a crossed cheque which bears
on it the words 'not negotiable,' he shall not have and shall not
be capable of giving a better title to the cheque than that which

Sec. 174. had the person from whom he took'it. 53 V., c. 33, s. 80. Eng. s. 81.

This section reproduces the effect of the first part of sec. 12 of the English Act of 1876 (see notes, *supra*).

A crossed cheque which bears on it the words "not negotiable" is put very much on the same footing as an overdue bill (sec. 70). It is still negotiable in the sense that it is subject to negotiation, but it does not possess the quality of negotiability which confers upon a holder in due course (sec. 56) a good title to payment according to the tenor of the bill and irrespective of defects in the title of the transferor. Cf. Chapter XL., *supra*, p. 462. As to the negotiability of cheques, see also notes to sec. 165, *supra* p. 611.

A bank which pays a cheque crossed "not negotiable" takes it at its own risk, and if it obtains payment of the cheque from the drawee bank, its title to the money so obtained is as defective as its title to the cheque itself, unless it comes within the protection of sec. 175. (Great Western v. London & County Banking Co., [1901] A.C. 414, 422, 424.)

Customer without title.

Bank paying.

Bona fides.

175. Where a bank, in good faith and without negligence, receives for a customer payment of a cheque crossed generally or specially to itself, and the customer has no title, or a defective title thereto, the bank shall not incur any liability to the true owner of the cheque by reason only of having received such payment. 53 V., c. 33, s. 81. Eng. s. 82.

This section reproduces the proviso to sec. 12 of the Act of 1876 (see notes to sec. 174). It was held in Mathiessen v. London & County Bank, 1879, 5 C.P.D. 7, that the proviso protected the collecting banker whether the cheque was crossed with or without the words "not negotiable," for the proviso was to be construed as an independent section. The proviso was accordingly re-enacted in the Bills of Exchange Act as a separate section.

As to general and special crossings, see sec. 168.

As to the expression "in good faith and without negligence," see notes to sec. 172.

A thief steals a crossed cheque payable to order, and inserts his own name in the place of the endorsee's. He then takes it for collection to a Paris bank, which collects the cheque through its London agents. The endorsee can recover the amount from the Paris bank. (Kleinwort v. Comptoir d' Escompte, [1894] 2 Q.B. 147; followed in Lacave v. Crédit Lyonnais, [1897] 1 Q.B. 148.)

A bank collects a cheque for a person who has no account there, and who has had no previous dealings with it. He is not a customer, and the bank is not protected. (Matthews v. Williams, [1894] The Reports, 267.)

C., having obtained by fraud a cheque which is crossed "& Co., not negotiable," takes it to a bank, which cashes it for him. He has no account at the bank, but for many years the bank has been in the habit of cashing cheques for him. C. is not a customer of the bank, and it is not protected by the section in obtaining payment of the cheque. (Great Western Ry. v. London and County Bank, [1901] A.C. 414.)

Prior to the Act a bank in dealing with a cheque drawn on another bank, stood unprotected against the risk of a signature on a cheque being forged, and if the bank dealt with such a cheque on the strength of a forged endorsement in a manner contrary to the rights of the true owner, it was liable to an action by him (Gordon v. London City Bank, [1902] 1 K.B. at p. 262; where the scope of the present section is discussed). By the Act, the bank is now protected where, in good faith and without negligence, it receives for a customer payment of a cheque crossed generally or specially to itself. It is not protected in the case of a cheque crossed specially to another bank or a cheque which comes to it uncrossed.

As to the protection afforded by the English Act to the drawee bank in paying an uncrossed cheque on the faith of a forged endorsement, see notes to sec. 50.

A solicitor's clerk steals a crossed cheque payable to his employer, forges the endorsement, and pays it into his own account, which is overdrawn. The bank receives payment of the cheque, and then places the amount to its customer's account. The bank is protected by this section, and the fact that the customer's account is overdrawn makes no difference. (Clarke v. London and County Bank, [1897] 1 Q.B. 552, as explained in Gordon v. London & Midland Bank, [1902] 1 K.B. at p. 270.)

Sec. 175.
Protection of bank which receives payment for a customer in good faith, etc.

Sec. 175.

Protection
of bank
which re-
ceives pay-
ment for a
customer in
good faith,
etc.

In Gordon v. London City Bank, [1903] A.C. 240, a merchant's clerk stole crossed cheques payable to order, forged his employer's endorsement, and paid the cheques in to his own banking account. The banker at once credited his account with the amount of the cheques, which were duly paid by the drawee bank. It was held that the bank in collecting these cheques did not "receive payment for a customer" but received payment for itself as holder, and was not protected by the section. The true owner was therefore entitled to recover the money. The "inconvenient rule" (22 L.Q.R. 452) established by this case is law in Canada, but has been abolished in England by 6 Edw. VII., c. 17, which provides that "a banker receives payment of a crossed cheque for a customer within the meaning of section eighty-two of the Bills of Exchange Act, 1882, notwithstanding that he credits his customer's account with the amount of the cheque before receiving payment thereof."

CHAPTER LIII.

PROMISSORY NOTES.

Prior to the Statute 3 and 4 Anne, c. 9., it was the opinion of Lord Holt and the majority of the judges that no action could be maintained, even by the payee, on a promissory note as an instrument, but that it was only evidence of a debt. The statute, however, made promissory notes "assignable and indorsable over in the same manner as inland bills of exchange are or may be, according to the custom of merchants." Cf. Chapter XXXI., *supra*, p. 336.

While a promissory note continues in its original shape of a promise by one man to pay to another, it bears no similitude to a bill of exchange. When it is endorsed, the resemblance begins; for then it is an order by the endorser upon the maker of the note (his debtor by the note), to pay to the endorsee. (Heylyn v. Adamson, 1758, 2 Burr. at p. 676, 4 R.C. at p. 452.)

Secs. 176 to 187, under the heading "Promissory Notes," compose Part IV. of the Act.

It is enacted by sec. 186 that, except as in that section provided, and subject to the provisions of this Part, the provisions of the Act relating to bills of exchange apply, with the necessary modifications, to promissory notes, and that in the application of such provisions the maker of a note shall be deemed to correspond with the acceptor of a bill, and the first endorser of a note shall be deemed to correspond with the drawer of an accepted bill payable to drawer's order. *Provisions as to bills, how far applicable to notes.*

Generally speaking, the provisions of the Act relating to a bill of exchange as an *order* to pay are inapplicable to a promissory note which is a promise to pay, although, as will be noted under sec. 176, many of the other elements of a bill as defined by sec. 17 equally belong to a note.

Sec. 186 expressly provides that the provisions of the Act as to bills relating to presentment for acceptance, acceptance, acceptance *supra* protest, and bills in a set, do not apply to notes.

Other sections of Part IV. by enacting special rules for notes, impliedly make inapplicable to notes some of the earlier provisions of the Act relating to bills. See notes to secs. 180 and

!Sec. 176.

Provisions
as to bills,
how far
applicable
to notes.

181 as to time of presentment for payment of a note payable on demand, sec. 182 as to when a demand note is deemed to be overdue, secs. 183 and 184 as to the place of and necessity for presentment for payment and sec. 187 as to protest.

The contract entered into by the maker of a note is embodied in sec. 185.

A note may be made by two or more makers, and they may be liable thereon jointly, or jointly and severally, according to its tenor (sec. 179).

A bank note is a promissory note made by a bank payable to bearer on demand: see Chapter XIV., *supra*, p. 114.

As to Dominion notes, see Chapter XXIX., *supra*, p. 314.

See also sec. 9 of the Bills of Exchange Act as to the English Acts, 15 Geo. 3, c. 51, and 17 Geo. 3, c. 30, which have never been expressly repealed in Canada.

PART IV.

PROMISSORY NOTES.

Definition.

176. A promissory note is an unconditional promise in writing made by one person to another, signed by the maker, engaging to pay, on demand or at a fixed or determinable future time, a sum certain in money, to, or to the order of, a specified person, or to bearer.

Endorsed by maker.

2. An instrument in the form of a note payable to the maker's order is not a note within the meaning of this section, unless it is endorsed by the maker.

Pledge.
Invalidity.

3. A note is not invalid by reason only that it contains also a pledge of collateral security with authority to sell or dispose thereof. 53 V., c. 33, s. 82. Eng. s. 83.

Unconditional.

See notes to sec. 17 under this head.

A note cannot be made conditionally, but a bill may be accepted conditionally (sec. 38).

Cf. notes to sec. 95 of the Bank Act in regard to deposit receipts, *supra*, p. 216.

An instrument may be a promissory note although it provides   Sec. 176.
for payment by instalments, the whole to become due on de- Uncondi-
fault in payment of any one instalment, and contains in addition tional.
the following clause: "No time given to, or security taken from,
or composition or arrangement entered into with, either party
hereto shall prejudice the rights of the holder to proceed against
any other party." (Kirkwood v. Carroll, [1903] 1 K.B. 531;
quære whether the addition to the note is in any proper sense
operative.)

Promise . . . engaging to pay.

The following are valid promissory notes: Promise to
1. Received from C. £30 payable on demand. (McGubbin v. pay.
Stephen, 1856, 18 D. 1824, 28 Jurist (Sc.) 618.)

2. Due A. or bearer $482, payable in 14 days after date.
(Gray v. Worden, 1870, 29 U.C.R. 535.

3. An I.O.U. containing a promise to pay, *e.g.* "I.O.U. £20,
to be paid on the 22nd inst." (Brooks v. Elkins, 1836, 2 M. &
W. 74.)

4. In Quebec an I.O.U. or *bon* has been usually considered
as a promissory note without additional words importing a
promise to pay. See, *e.g.*, Beaudry v. Laflamme, 1862, 6 L.C.J.
307; Désy v. Daly, 1897, Q.R. 12 S.C. 183.

5. Received from A.B. $1,200 for which I am responsible
with interest at the rate of 7 p.c. per annum, upon production
of this receipt, and after 3 months notice. (La Forest v. Babineau, 1906, 37 S.C.R. 521.)

The following are not promissory notes.   Not a pro-
1. I.O.U. £20 for value received. (Gould v. Coombs, 1845, mise to pay.
1 C.B. 543.)

2. Good to A.B. for $850 on demand. (Palmer v. McLennan,
1873, 22 C.P. 565.)

3. Borrowed of C. £100 to account for on behalf of the D.
Club at — months notice, if required. (White v. North, 1849,
3 Ex. 689.)

4. A writing merely certifying that a person is indebted to
another in a certain sum of money. (Dasylva v. Dufour, 1866,
16 L.C.R. 294.)

5. Received from A.B. loan of $800 to be returned when re-
quired. (De Sola v. Ascher, 1889, 17 R.L. 315.)

176. *In writing.*

See notes to sec. 2, *supra*, p. 347.

Made by one person to another.

Cf. notes to sec. 17 under the head ''addressed by one person to another.''

An instrument addressed to A.B. undertaking to pay C.D., although it complies literally with the section, only enures to the benefit of C.D. C.D. cannot sue on it as a promissory note, although it may be evidence of a contract to pay money to C.D. (Trimble v. Miller, 1892, 22 O.R. 500.)

Where in a bill drawer and drawee are the same person, or where the drawee is a fictitious person or a person not having capacity to contract, the holder may treat the instrument, at his option, either as a bill of exchange or a promissory note (sec. 26).

Where an instrument is so ambiguously worded that it is doubtful whether it was intended for a bill or for a note, the holder may treat it at his option as either. (Edis v. Bury, 1827, 6 B. & C. 433; Fielder v. Marshall, 1861, 30 L.J.C.P. 158; Golding v. Waterhouse, 1876, 3 Pugs. (N.B.) 313; Mare v. Charles, 1856, 5 E. & B. at p. 981; Allen v. Mawson, 1814, 4 Camp. 115.)

An instrument in the form of a note with a blank left for the payee's name is not a completed note (Reg. v. Cormack, 1891, 21 O.R. 213); but see secs. 31 and 32 as to the right to fill up blanks.

Signed by the maker.

As to signature, see sec. 4 and notes.

As to a simple signature on a blank paper delivered by the signer in order that it may be converted into a note, see sec. 31.

As to the contract entered into by the maker, see sec. 185.

On demand.

As to when a note is payable on demand, see sec. 23.

At a fixed or determinable future time.

As to when a note is payable at a determinable future time, see sec. 24. Cf. notes to sec. 17 under this head.

A note must not be expressed to be payable on a contingency (sec. 18).

A sum certain in money.
Sec. 176.

Cf. notes to sec. 17 under this head.

A promise to pay out of a particular fund, is not a note (sec. 17).

Specified person or bearer.

Cf. notes to sec 17 under this head.

Payable.to the maker's order.

The provision of the English Act corresponding to sub-sec. 2 reads "unless and until it is indorsed by the maker."

B. makes a note payable to his own order, and endorses it in blank. This is a valid note payable to bearer. (Hooper v. Williams, 1848, 2 Ex. 13; Masters v. Baretto, 1849, 8 C.B. 433.)

B. makes a note payable to his own order, and endorses it to C. This is a valid note payable to C. or order. (Gay v. Lander, 1848, 17 L.J.C.P. 286.)

Pledge of collateral security.

Prior to the Act it was held that a note with the words "this note to be held as collateral security" upon it was invalid (Hall v. Merrick, 1877, 40 U.C.R. 566 and cases cited; Sutherland v. Patterson, 1884, 4 O.R. 565), but a memorandum that the maker had deposited collateral security with the payee was held not to invalidate an instrument as a note. (Chesney v. St. John, 1879, 4 A.R. at p. 156.)

177. A note which is, or on the face of it purports to be, Inland note. both made and payable within Canada, is an inland note.

2. Any other note is a foreign note. 53 V., c. 33, s. 82. Eng. Foreign s. 83. note.

Cf. sec. 25 and notes, as to inland and foreign bills.

Where a foreign note is dishonoured, protest thereof is unnecessary, except for the preservation of the liabilities of endorsers (sec. 187).

178. A promissory note is inchoate and incomplete until Delivery delivery thereof to the payee or bearer. 53 V., c. 33, s. 83. Eng. s. 84.

Sec. 178.   By sec. 2, delivery means transfer of possession, actual or
constructive, from one person to another. Cf. notes to sec. 39.

Joint and ⌐   179. A promissory note may be made by two or more
several note.   makers, and they may be liable thereon jointly, or jointly and
severally, according to its tenor.

Individual   2. Where a note runs 'I promise to pay,' and is signed by
promise.   two or more persons, it is deemed to be their joint and several
note. 53 V., c. 33, s. 84. Eng. s. 85.

A note which runs "we promise to pay," and is signed by
two or more persons, is deemed to be a joint note only. Perhaps
if a note runs "I, John Brown, promise to pay," and is signed
by Smith as well as Brown, Smith would only be liable as an endorser under sec. 131, and not as a co-maker. Chalmers, p. 271.
As to the liability of a person who signs otherwise than as maker,
see notes to sec. 131.

Joint or joint   The Act has introduced in Quebec the English rule that two
and several   or more makers of a note may be liable jointly, or jointly and sev-
liability.   erally, according to the tenor of the note. (Noble v. Forgrave,
1899, Q.R. 17 S.C. 234.) But when the question whether the
liability is joint or joint and several has been decided, then the
appropriate provincial law determines the consequences of such
liability, which may be different from the liability at common
law. (Cook v. Dodds, 1903, 6 O.L.R. 608.) Cf. notes to sec. 10.

By English law, judgment, without satisfaction, against one
of the makers of a joint note is a bar to proceedings against the
other maker (King v. Hoare, 1844, 13 M. & W. 494); not so if
the note be joint and several. (Ibid.; Re Davison, 1884, 13
Q.B.D. at p. 53). Payment or satisfaction by one of the makers
of a joint and several note discharges it (Nicholson v. Revill,
1836, 4 A. & E. 675; Beaumont v. Greathead, 1846, 2 C.B. 494;
Thorne v. Smith, 1851, 20 L.J.C.P. 71; cf. Simpson v. Henning.
1875, L.R. 10 Q.B. 406.)

A note may not be made by two persons in the alternative
(Ferris v. Bond, 1821, 4 B. & Ald. 679), but a note may be payable to persons in the alternative (sec. 19).

B.C. and D. make a joint and several note payable to C. and
D. or order. This is a valid note. C. and D. may sue B. on his
several liability. (Beecham v. Smith, 1858, E. B. & E. 442.)

.The acceptors of a bill can be liable only jointly, not jointly
and severally.

A new maker cannot be added to a joint and several note
after its issue (Gardner v. Walsh, 1855, 5 E. & B. 83), and there
cannot be two or more makers liable severally, and not jointly
and severally.

A partner, as such, cannot bind his co-partners severally, but
by a joint and several note he may bind the firm jointly (Maclae
v. Sutherland, 1854, 3 E. & B. 1), and himself severally (Penkivil v. Connell, 1850, 5 Ex. 381).

180. Where a note payable on demand has been endorsed, it
must be presented for payment within a reasonable time of the
endorsement.

2. In determining what is a reasonable time, regard shall be
had to the nature of the instrument, the usage of trade, and the
facts of the particular case. 53 V., c. 33, s. 85. Eng. s. 86.

Subject to the proviso to sec. 181, failure to present for payment within a reasonable time releases the endorser.

As to when a demand note is deemed to be overdue for the
purpose of affecting a holder with defects of title of which he
had no notice, see sec. 182.

Regard must be had to the nature of a promissory note payable on demand as a continuing security (see notes to sec. 182)
in determining what is a reasonable time. Ten months may not
be an unreasonable time (Chartered Bank v. Dickson, 1871, L.R.
3 P.C. 574, at pp. 579, 584). Cf. sec. 86, as to reasonable time in
the case of bills.

As to presentment for payment generally, see notes to secs.
183 and 184.

181. If a promissory note payable on demand, which has
been endorsed is not presented for payment within a reasonable
time the endorser is discharged: Provided that if it has, with
the assent of the endorser, been delivered as a collateral or continuing security it need not be presented for payment so long as
it is held as such security. 53 V., c. 33, s. 85. Cf. Eng. s. 86.

Sec. 179.
Joint or joint
and several
liability.

Demand
note pre-
sentment.

Reasonable
time.

Reasonable
time for pre-
sentment.

Endorser
discharged.

Security.

The proviso to this section is not in the English Act.

Before the endorsee of a note can bring an action against the endorser, he must shew a demand or due diligence to get the money from the acceptor,—just as the payee of a bill must shew a demand or due diligence to get the money from the acceptor before he brings an action against the drawer. (Heylyn v. Adamson, 1758, 2 Burr. at p. 676, 4 R.C. at p. 452.)

As to reasonable time, see sec. 180.

Not deemed overdue.

182. Where a note payable on demand is negotiated, it is not deemed to be overdue, for the purpose of affecting the holder with defects of title of which he had no notice, by reason that it appears that a reasonable time for presenting it for payment has elapsed since its issue. 53 V., c. 33, s. 85. Eng. s. 86.

A promissory note payable on demand is intended to be a continuing security. It is quite unlike the case of a bill payable on demand or cheque, which is intended to be presented speedily. (Brooks v. Mitchell, 1841, 9 M. & W. 15, 4 R.C. 398.)

Hence such a note cannot be treated as overdue, so as to affect the holder with a defect of title of which he had no notice, on the ground that an unreasonable time for presenting it for payment had elapsed since the date of its issue. (Glasscock v. Balls, 1889, 24 Q.B.D. 13, 4 R.C. 401.)

A different rule applies to bills: see sec. 70.

A different rule also applies to the presentment of a note in order to charge an endorser, and for that purpose presentment within a reasonable time must be. shewn (sec. 181).

Presentment, where.

183. Where a promissory note is in the body of it made payable at a particular place, it must be presented for payment at that place.

Liability of maker.

2. In such case the maker is not discharged by the omission to present the note for payment on the day that it matures; but if any suit or action is instituted thereon against him before presentation, the costs thereof shall be in the discretion of the court.

3. If no place of payment is specified in the body of the note, presentment for payment is not necessary in order to render the maker liable. 53 V., c. 33, s. 86. Cf. Eng. s. 87.

Sub-sec. 1 of sec. 87 of the English Act which corresponds with this section, reads: "Where a promissory note is in the body of it made payable at a particular place, it must be presented for payment at the place in order to render the maker liable. In any other case presentment for payment is not necessary in order to render the maker liable." With this it is, however, necessary to read sub-sec. 2 of sec. 52 of the English Act quoted in the notes to sec. 93. Presentment of a
note payable
at a particu-
lar place.

With sec. 183 of the Canadian Act, cf. sec. 93 which makes similar provisions for presentment of a bill in order to charge the acceptor.

The omission of the words "in order to render the maker liable" from the Canadian Act have not the effect of making it unnecessary to shew presentment. Presentment at the proper place or facts excusing such presentment must be averred and proved. The next provision of the section excuses presentment on the day of payment, but not presentment at the place of payment. (Croft v. Hamlin, 1893, 2 B.C.R. 333.)

At common law no presentment or request for payment is necessary to charge the maker of a note; he is bound to pay it at maturity, and to find out the holder for that purpose. (Walton v. Mascall, 1844, 13 M. & W. at p. 458, 4 R.C. at p. 488.)

B. makes a note payable to his own order and signs it. Below his signature are the words "Payable at the Union Bank, London." He then endorses the note in blank. The holder can sue the maker without proving presentment. (Masters v. Baretto, 1849, 8 C.B. 433.)

But if a note is payable "to the order of A. at H." it must be presented there. (Cunard v. Symon-Kaye, 1894, 27 N.S.R. 340.)

In order to charge an endorser, as such, presentment for payment is necessary, but presentment at a particular place is required only where the note is made payable at a particular place in the body of it and not by way of memorandum only (sec. 184).

Sec. 183.
Present-
ment of a
note payable
at a particu-
lar place.

A note payable at a particular place must be there presented before action brought. As against the endorser it must be presented on the day it falls due. As against the maker it may be presented at any time before action brought, but presentment at some time before action brought must be proved or the action fails. The provision as to costs means that if the maker succeeds, on the ground that no presentment is proved, the court may deprive him of costs. (Jones v. England, 1906, 5 West. L.R. 83, following Warner v. Symon-Kaye, 1894, 27 N.S.R. 340 in preference to Merchants Bank v. Henderson, 1897, 28 O.R. 360.)

In Merchants Bank v. Henderson a note payable at a particular place was presented for payment only some time after its maturity and a few days before action brought against the maker. A judgment for the plaintiff with costs was affirmed with costs, on the ground that it was the maker's duty to have the money to meet the note at the particular place and to keep it there from the maturity of the note until presentment. Armour, C.J. (28 O.R. at p. 365) expressed the opinion that an action might have been brought against the maker even without any presentment at the particular place, the plaintiff in such case running the risk of having to pay the costs of the action in case the maker should shew that he had the money at the particular place to answer the note at maturity and thereafter.

A note dated at St. John, N.B., payable at the Bank of Montreal is payable at the bank's St. John branch. (Canada Paper Co. v. Gazette, 1893, 32 N.B.R. 685, 689; Commercial Bank v. Bissett, 1891, 7 Man. R. 586.)

As to endorser.

184. Presentment for payment is necessary in order to render the endorser of a note liable.

Place where.

2. Where a note is in the body of it made payable at a particular place, presentment at that place is necessary in order to render an endorser liable.

What sufficient.

3. When a place of payment is indicated by way of memorandum only, presentment at that place is sufficient to render the endorser liable, but a presentment to the maker elsewhere, if sufficient in other respects, shall also suffice. 53 V., c. 33, s. 86. Eng. s. 87.

By virtue of sec. 186, the rules applicable to presentment for payment of a bill (see sec. 85 and notes) apply also to presentment for payment of a note, except in so far as special provision is made as to notes by secs. 180 to 184. *Sec. 184.*

185. The maker of a promissory note, by making it,— *Maker.*

(*a*) engages that he will pay it according to its tenor; *Engagement.*

(*b*) is precluded from denying to a holder in due course the existence of the payee and his then capacity to endorse. *Estoppel.*

53 V., c. 33, s. 87. Eng. s. 88.

The maker of a note, like the acceptor of a bill, is the principal debtor on the instrument (Gibb v. Mather, 1832, 2 Cr. & J. at p. 263, 4 R.C. at p. 474), and in the application to notes of the provisions of the Act relating to bills, the maker is deemed to correspond with the acceptor (sec. 186). *Maker and acceptor compared.*

As to the contract of the acceptor, see secs. 128 and 129.

The distinctions that exist between maker and acceptor arise from the fact that the acceptor is not the creator of the bill, his contract being supplementary, while the maker of a note originates the instrument. A note must be unconditional (sec. 176), while an acceptance may be conditional (sec. 38). Maker and payee are immediate parties in direct relation with each other, while acceptor and payee, except in the case of a bill payable to drawer's order, are remote parties. (Cf. Bishop v. Young, 1800, 2 B. & P. at p. 83.)

Any number of persons may become bound as promisors along with the original maker of a note, whereas there cannot be an acceptor of a bill other than the drawee or one who accepts as his agent (see notes to sec. 35, *supra*, p. 405).

186. Subject to the provisions of this Part, and except as by this section provided, the provisions of this Act relating to bills of exchange apply, with the necessary modifications, to promissory notes. *Application of Act to notes.*

2. In the application of such provisions the maker of a note shall be deemed to correspond with the acceptor of a bill, and the first endorser of a note shall be deemed to correspond with the drawer of an accepted bill payable to drawer's order. *Terms corresponding.*

Sec. 186.

Provisions
inapplicable.

3. The provisions of this Act as to bills relating to,—

(a) presentment for acceptance;

(b) acceptance;

(c) acceptance *supra* protest;

(d) bills in a set;

do not apply to notes. 53 V., c. 33, s. 88. Eng. s. 89.

The "provisions of this Part" referred to in this section are contained in sec. 176 (definition of a note), sec. 177 (inland and foreign notes), sec. 178 (delivery), sec. 179 (joint and several notes), secs. 180 and 181 (time of presentment of a demand note), sec. 182 (when demand note deemed overdue), secs. 183 and 184 (presentment for payment of a note), sec. 185 (contract of maker), sec. 187 (protest of foreign notes).

See notes at the beginning of this chapter.

Protest of
foreign
notes.

187. Where a foreign note is dishonoured, protest thereof is unnecessary, except for the preservation of the liabilities of endorsers. 53 V., c. 33, s. 88. Cf. Eng. s. 89.

The words "except for the preservation of the liabilities of endorsers" are not in the English Act.

As to the necessity for protest of inland bills and notes, see secs. 113 and 114. Cf. sec. 112, as to protest of a foreign bill.

If a note is dishonoured out of Canada the necessity for or sufficiency of a protest or notice of dishonour is determined by the law of the place where the bill is dishonoured (sec. 162).

A note which does not on the face of it purport to be both made and payable in Canada is a foreign note (sec. 177).

CHAPTER LIV.

Schedule to the Bills of Exchange Act.

The forms in this schedule may be used in noting or protesting any bill and in giving notice thereof. A copy of the bill or note and endorsement may be included in the forms, or the original bill or note may be annexed and the necessary changes in that behalf made in the forms (sec. 125).

SCHEDULE.

Form A.

NOTING FOR NON-ACCEPTANCE.

(Copy of Bill and Endorsements.)

On the   19 ,   the above bill was, by me, at
the request of   presented for acceptance to
E. F., the drawee, personally (*or*, at his residence, office or
usual place of business), in the city (town *or* village) of
                    and I received for answer: '   ';
The said bill is therefore noted for non-acceptance.

A. B.,
Notary Public.

(Date and place.)   19 .

Due notice of the above was by me served upon $\left\{ \begin{matrix} A.\ B., \\ C.\ D., \end{matrix} \right\}$

the $\left\{ \begin{matrix} \text{drawer,} \\ \text{endorser,} \end{matrix} \right\}$ personally, on the   day of
(*or*, at his residence, office or usual place of business) in
          , on the   day of   (*or*, by depositing
such notice, directed to him at   in His Majesty's
post office in the city, [town *or* village], on the   day
of   , and prepaying the postage thereon).

A. B.,
Notary Public.

(Date and place.)   19 .

53 V., c. 33, sch., form A.

41—BANK ACT.

FORM B.

PROTEST FOR NON-ACCEPTANCE OR FOR NON-PAYMENT OF A BILL PAYABLE GENERALLY.

(Copy of Bill and Endorsements.)

On this   day of   , in the year 19   , I, A. B., notary public for the province of   , dwelling at   , in the province of   , at the request of   , did exhibit the original bill of exchange, whereof a true copy is above written, unto E. F., the $\left\{\begin{array}{l}\text{drawee}\\\text{acceptor}\end{array}\right\}$ thereof personally (*or*, at his residence, office *or* usual place of business) in   , and, speaking to himself (*or* his wife, his clerk, *or* his servant, &c.,) did demand $\left\{\begin{array}{l}\text{acceptance}\\\text{payment}\end{array}\right\}$ thereof; unto which demand $\left\{\begin{array}{l}\text{he}\\\text{she}\end{array}\right\}$ answered: '   .'

Wherefore I, the said notary, at the request aforesaid, have protested, and by these presents do protest against the acceptor, drawer and endorsers (*or* drawer and endorsers) of the said bill, and other parties thereto or therein concerned, for all exchange, re-exchange, and all costs, damages and interest, present and to come, for want of $\left\{\begin{array}{l}\text{acceptance}\\\text{payment}\end{array}\right\}$ of the said bill.

All of which I attest by my signature.

(Protested in duplicate.)

A. B.,
Notary Public.

53 V , c. 33, sch., form B.

FORM C.

PROTEST FOR NON-ACCEPTANCE OR FOR NON-PAYMENT OF A BILL
PAYABLE AT A STATED PLACE.
(Copy of Bill and Endorsements.)

On this   day of   in the year 19 , I,
A. B., notary public for the province of   , dwelling
at   , in the province of   , at the request
of   , did exhibit the original bill of exchange
whereof, a true copy is above written unto E. F., the
$\left\{ \begin{array}{l} \text{drawee} \\ \text{acceptor} \end{array} \right\}$ thereof, at   , being the stated
place where the said bill is payable, and there speaking
to   did demand $\left\{ \begin{array}{l} \text{acceptance} \\ \text{payment} \end{array} \right\}$
of the said bill; unto which demand he answered: '   .'

Wherefore I, the said notary, at the request aforesaid, have
protested, and by these presents do protest against the acceptor,
drawer and endorsers (*or* drawer and endorsers) of the said bill
and all other parties thereto or therein concerned, for all exchange, re-exchange, costs, damages and interest, present and
to come for want of $\left\{ \begin{array}{l} \text{acceptance} \\ \text{payment} \end{array} \right\}$ of the said bill.

All of which I attest by my signature.
(Protested in duplicate.)

A. B.,
Notary Public.

53 V., c. 33, sch., form C.

Form D.

PROTEST FOR NON-PAYMENT OF A BILL NOTED, BUT NOT PROTESTED FOR NON-ACCEPTANCE.

If the protest is made by the same notary who noted the bill, it should immediately follow the act of noting and memorandum of service thereof, and begin with the words 'and afterwards on, etc.,' *continuing as in the last preceding form, but introducing between the words* 'did' *and* 'exhibit' *the word* 'again,' *and in a parenthesis, between the words* 'written' *and* 'unto' *the words*: 'and which bill was by me duly noted for non-acceptance on the   day of   .'

But if the protest is not made by the same notary, then it should follow a copy of the original bill and endorsements and noting marked on the bill—and then in the protest introduce, in a parenthesis, between the words 'written' *and* 'unto,' *the words*: 'and which bill was on the   day of   , by   , notary public for the province of   noted for non-acceptance, as appears by his note thereof marked on the said bill.'

53 V., c. 33, sch., form D.

Form E.

PROTEST FOR NON-PAYMENT OF A NOTE PAYABLE GENERALLY.

(Copy of Note and Endorsements.)

On this   day of   , in the year 19 , 1 A. B., notary public for the province of   , dwelling at   , in the province of   , at the request of   , did exhibit the original promissory note, whereof a true copy is above written, unto   the promisor, personally (*or*, at his residence, office *or* usual place of business,) in   , and speaking to himself (*or* his wife, his clerk *or* his servant, etc.) did demand payment thereof; unto which demand $\left\{ \begin{array}{c} \text{he} \\ \text{she} \end{array} \right\}$ answered: '   .'

Wherefore I, the said notary, at the request aforesaid, have protested, and by these presents do protest against the promisor and endorsers of the said note, and all other parties thereto or therein concerned, for all costs, damages and interest, present and to come, for want of payment of the said note.

All of which I attest by my signature.

(Protested in duplicate.)

A. B.,
Notary Public.

53 V., c. 33, sch., form E.

FORM F.

PROTEST FOR NON-PAYMENT OF A NOTE PAYABLE AT A STATED
PLACE.

(*Copy of Note and Endorsements.*)

On this   day of   , in the year 19 , I, A. B., notary public for the province of , dwelling at   , in the province of , at the request of   , did exhibit the original promissory note, whereof a true copy is above written, unto

the promisor, at   , being the stated place where the said note is payable, and there, speaking to   did demand payment of the said note, unto which demand he answered: ' .'

Wherefore I, the said notary, at the request aforesaid, have protested, and by these presents do protest against the promisor and endorsers of the said note, and all other parties thereto or therein concerned, for all costs, damages and interest, present and to come, for want of payment of the said note.

All of which I attest by my signature.

(Protested in duplicate.)

A. B.,
Notary Public.

53 V., c. 33, sch., form F.

FORM G.

NOTARIAL NOTICE OF A NOTING, OR OF A PROTEST FOR NON-ACCEPT-
ANCE, OR OF A PROTEST FOR NON-PAYMENT OF A BILL.

(*Place and Date of Noting or of Protest.*)

1st.

To P. Q. (*the drawer*)

at

Sir,

Your bill of exchange for $, dated at
the day of , upon E. F., in favour of C. D., payable days
after $\left\{ \begin{array}{l} \text{sight} \\ \text{date} \end{array} \right\}$ was this day. at the request of
duly $\left\{ \begin{array}{l} \text{noted} \\ \text{protested} \end{array} \right\}$ by me for $\left\{ \begin{array}{l} \text{non-acceptance} \\ \text{non-payment} \end{array} \right\}$

A. B.,
Notary Public.

(*Place and date of Noting or of Protest.*)

2nd.

To C. D. (*endorser*)
(*or* F. G.)

at

Sir,

Mr. P. Q.'s bill of exchange for $, dated at
the day of , upon E. F., in your favour (or in favour of
C. D.,) payable days after $\left\{ \begin{array}{l} \text{sight,} \\ \text{date,} \end{array} \right\}$ and by you endorsed,
was this day at the request of duly
$\left\{ \begin{array}{l} \text{noted} \\ \text{protested} \end{array} \right\}$ by me for $\left\{ \begin{array}{l} \text{non-acceptance} \\ \text{non-payment} \end{array} \right\}$

A. B.,
Notary Public.

53 V., c. 33, sch., form G.

FORM H.

NOTARIAL NOTICE OF PROTEST FOR NON-PAYMENT OF A NOTE.

(Place and Date of Protest.)

To   ,
                at

  Sir,

      Mr. P. Q.'s promissory note for $, dated at
, the   day of   payable $\left\{ \begin{array}{l} \text{days} \\ \text{months} \\ \text{on ——} \end{array} \right\}$ after date to
$\left\{ \begin{array}{l} \text{you} \\ \text{E. F.} \end{array} \right\}$ or order, and endorsed by you, was this day, at the
request of   , duly protested by me for
non-payment.

                        A. B.,
                         Notary Public.

53 V., c. 33, sch., form H.

FORM I.

NOTARIAL SERVICE OF NOTICE OF A PROTEST FOR NON-ACCEPTANCE
OR NON-PAYMENT OF A BILL, OR NOTE.

(to be subjoined to the Protest.)

And afterwards, I, the aforesaid protesting notary public, did serve due notice, in the form prescribed by law, of the foregoing protest for $\left\{ \begin{array}{l} \text{non-acceptance} \\ \text{non-payment} \end{array} \right\}$ of the $\left\{ \begin{array}{l} \text{bill} \\ \text{note} \end{array} \right\}$ thereby protested upon $\left\{ \begin{array}{l} \text{P.Q.,} \\ \text{C.D.,} \end{array} \right\}$ the $\left\{ \begin{array}{l} \text{drawers} \\ \text{endorsers} \end{array} \right\}$ personally, on the day of (*or*, at his residence, office *or* usual place of business) in   , on the   day of   ; (*or*, by depositing such notice, directed to the said $\left\{ \begin{array}{l} \text{P. Q.} \\ \text{C. D.} \end{array} \right\}$ at   , in His Majesty's post office in   on the   day of   , and prepaying the postage thereon).

In testimony whereof, I have, on the last mentioned day and year, at   aforesaid, signed these presents.

A. B.,
Notary Public.

53 V., c. 33, sch., form I.

FORM J.

PROTEST BY A JUSTICE OF THE PEACE (WHERE THERE IS NO NOTARY)
FOR NON-ACCEPTANCE OF A BILL, OR NON-
PAYMENT OF A BILL OR NOTE.

(Copy of Bill or Note and Endorsements.)

On this   day of   , in the year 19 , I, N. O.,
one of His Majesty's justices of the peace for the district (*or*
county, etc.), of   , in the province of   , dwelling at
(*or* near) the village of   , in the said district, there
being no practising notary public at or near the said village
(*or any other legal cause*), did, at the request of
                  and in the presence of
                  well known unto me, exhibit the original

$\begin{Bmatrix} \text{bill} \\ \text{note} \end{Bmatrix}$ whereof a true copy is above written unto P.Q., the

$\begin{Bmatrix} \text{drawer} \\ \text{acceptor} \\ \text{promisor} \end{Bmatrix}$ thereof, personally (*or* at his residence, office *or*

usual place of business) in   and speaking
to himself (his wife, his clerk *or* his servant, etc.,) did demand

$\begin{Bmatrix} \text{acceptance} \\ \text{payment} \end{Bmatrix}$ thereof, unto which demand $\begin{Bmatrix} \text{he} \\ \text{she} \end{Bmatrix}$ answered:

Wherefore I, the said justice of the peace, at the request
aforesaid, have protested, and by these presents do protest

against the $\begin{Bmatrix} \text{drawer and endorsers} \\ \text{promisor and endorsers} \\ \text{acceptor, drawer and endorsers} \end{Bmatrix}$ of the said

$\begin{Bmatrix} \text{bill} \\ \text{note} \end{Bmatrix}$ and all other parties thereto and therein concerned,

for all exchange, re-exchange, and all costs, damages and in-
interest, present and to come, for want of $\begin{Bmatrix} \text{acceptance} \\ \text{payment} \end{Bmatrix}$ of the

said $\begin{Bmatrix} \text{bill} \\ \text{note} \end{Bmatrix}$.

All which is by these presents attested by the signature of the said (*the witness*) and by my hand and seal.

(Protested in duplicate.)

(*Signature of the witness*)

(*Signature and seal of the J.P.*)

53 V., c. 33, sch., form J.

INDEX.

ACCEPTANCE,
  Definition, 343, 344, 405
  Incomplete until delivery, 415
  Requisites in form, 408
  Time of, 409, 490, 491
  Must be by drawee, 405, 406
  Drawee wrongly designated or name misspelt, 406
  Must be payable in money, 409
  Date of acceptance, 411, 490
  General and qualified acceptances, 411
  Qualified acceptance, 412, 413, 493
  Conditional, 412
  Partial, 413, 493
  Payable at particular specified place, 413
  Dishonour by non-acceptance, 491
  Bill in a set, 596, 597
  See also *Firm—Signature—Corporation—Delivery—Capacity.*

ACCEPTANCE FOR HONOUR,
  Suspends right of recourse on non-acceptance, 492
  Protest necessary before presentment to acceptor for honour, 540
  Who may accept, 588
  Acceptance for part, 589
  Presumably for honour of drawer, 589
  Maturity of after sight bill, 589
  Requisites of acceptance for honour, 589
  Liability of acceptor, 590
  Nature and effect of acceptance, 590

ACCEPTOR,
  When entitled to presentment for payment, 505-507
  Not entitled to notice of dishonour, 513
  Not entitled to protest, 536
  Contract of, 549, 550
  Estoppel of, as to drawer or payee, 550, 551
  Primâ facie principal debtor, 554
  Death of acceptor of incomplete bill, 401

ACCOMMODATION BILL,
 Defined, 452, 453
 Discharged by payment, 574

ACCOMMODATION PARTY,
 Defined, 451, 453
 Liable to holder for value, 451
 Endorsement to facilitate negotiation, 482
 Presentment for payment dispensed with, 503-504
 Contract of party accommodated, 566

ACCOUNT,
 Inspection of customer's account, 106
 Disclosure of, by bank, 107

ACTION,
 Includes counterclaim and set-off, 343
 To recover money due on call, 86
 Rule against circuity of, 482
 Action by holder in his own name, 482
 No right of action on due date, 510, 511

AGENCIES OF BANK,
 See *Branches*.

AGENT,
 Liability on bill signed for principal, 443
 When agent and when principal liable, 444-446
 Warehouse receipt by agent, 175
 Goods pledged by agent, 178
 See also *Factors Acts—Signature*.

AGENT FOR COLLECTION,
 Bank acts as, 133, 134
 Agency charges, 208
 Collection charges, 207
 Due diligence required, 133
 Liability, 133, 134
 Agent of bank not agent of customer, 139

ALLONGE, 465

ALTERATION,
    When bill discharged by material, 582
    Holder in due course where alteration not apparent, 583
    Action on consideration for altered bill, 584
    What is material alteration, 584
    Alteration of crossing of cheque, 623

ANNUAL MEETING,
    See *Shareholders.*

ANNUAL STATEMENT,
    To be made to shareholders, 104
    Additional information may be called for, 105
    See *False Statement.*

APPROPRIATION,
    See *Depositor and Bank.*

ASSOCIATION,
    Means Canadian Bankers' Association, 31

AUTHORITY,
    Distinguished from capacity, 428, 551
    Authority to deliver bill, 418, 419
    Procuration signature, 441

AVAL, 556, 560

BANK,
    Definitions, 31, 33, 131, 132, 343, 344
    Charters continued, 37, 38
    Forfeiture of charter, 46
    Trading capital, 135, 136
    Prohibited business, 145, 147, 267
    Letters of credit, 135
    Safe custody of valuables, 136, 137
    Bonds and obligations of, 129
    See also *Incorporation and Organization—Capital Stock—*
        Directors—Customer—Sale of Bank's Assets.
    Business and powers generally, 131, 137, 145
    See also *Depositor and Bank—Lending Powers—Collateral*
        Security—Agent for Collection—Bank Notes.

BANK ACT,
   Short title, 30
   Interpretation, 31   ·
   Banking legislation prior to, 1
   Not affected by Bills of Exchange Act, 354
   Application of, 36-40
   Transactions in contravention of Act, 146
   See also *Schedules—Bank.*

BANK CIRCULATION REDEMPTION FUND,
   When established, 14
   Amendments of 1900, 121
   Sum retained out of deposit of new bank, 47, 122
   Summary of provisions applicable to, 120
   Annual adjustment, 122, 123
   Purpose of fund, 123   ·
   Fund to bear interest, 123
   When notes bear interest, 124
   Payments from fund, 125, 126
   Rights of Minister, 124, 125, 126
   Rules of Treasury Board, 126

BANK NOTES,   ·
   Nature of bank note, 114, 115
   Character of note issue in Canada, 13-15, 18, 19, 114
   Conditions precedent to issue, 115
   Limit of aggregate amount, 116, 117, 119
   Penalty for over-issue, 260
   Denominations of notes, 116, 118, 119
   To be payable in Canadian currency, 309
   Issued at agency in British possessions, 118
   Pledging of notes prohibited, 119
   Penalty for pledging, 263
   Not to be issued for circulation except by bank, 260
   Notes at first charge on assets, 256
   Not to be issued after suspension, 115, 117, 262
   Fraudulent issue forbidden, 263
   To circulate at par throughout Canada, 126
   Where to be redeemed, 118, 127
   Bank's own notes to be received in payment, 127
   How signed, 129, 130
   Counterfeit to be stamped, 130

BANK NOTES—*Continued*,
Penalty for defacing, 262
No payment in torn or defaced notes, 128
See also *Bank Circulation Redemption Fund—Dominion Notes—Interest—Canadian Bankers' Association.*

BANK OF BRITISH COLUMBIA,
Application of Act to, 38

BANK OF BRITISH NORTH AMERICA,
How far Bank Act applicable to, 39, 40, 116, 117

BANKRUPT,
In Bills of Exchange Act, 347, 488
Protest for better security, 539

BEARER,
Definition, 343, 345
When bill payable to bearer, 372, 374
Such bill negotiated by delivery, 463

"BILL"
means bill of exchange, 343, 345

BILL IN A SET,
Various parts constitute one bill, 596
Acceptance, 596, 597
Endorsement, 597
Negotiation, 597
Discharge, 597

BILL OF EXCHANGE,
Definition, 362
Origin and history, 336
English and French law of exchange, 337
Sources of law in Quebec, 338
Form and interpretation, 362
Document ambiguously worded, 363
Unconditional, 364
Order in writing, 365
Addressed by one person to another, 365, 372
Signed by the person giving it, 365
The person to whom it is addressed, 365
Time of payment, 366
Sum certain in money, 366, 367, 393

BILL OF EXCHANGE—*Continued,*
>Payable to specified person or bearer, 367
>Must not be payable out of a particular fund, 367
>Nor payable on a contingency, 369
>Payable to order or bearer, 372
>Payable on demand, 383
>See also *Acceptance—Acceptor—Drawer—Maker—Negotia-tion.*

BILL OF LADING,
>What it includes, 32
>Its nature, 34
>Not a negotiable instrument, 35
>Absence of endorsement, 35
>How acquired by bank, 168
>See also *Lending Powers of Bank.*

BILLS OF EXCHANGE ACT,
>Short title, 341
>Introduction to, 382
>Construction, rule of, 342, 343
>Use of cases as illustrations, 332
>Codification in England, 332
>Codification in Canada, 333
>Differences between English and Canadian Acts, 334, 414, 437
>Rules of common law applicable, 335
>Special provisions for Quebec, 335
>Reference to sections of English Act, 341
>Interpretation of words, 343
>Not to affect Bank Act, 354
>Part I. General provisions, 348
>Part II. Bills of exchange, 362
>Part III. Cheques on a bank, 608
>Part IV. Promissory notes, 629
>Schedule, 641

BLANK,
>Authority to fill up, in bill, 397
>Inserting date in undated bill, 396
>Signature on blank paper, 397
>When completed instrument enforceable, 399

BONA FIDE,
 See *Good Faith.*

BONDS,
 See *Negotiable Instruments—Lending Powers of Banks.*

BONUS,
 See *Dividends.*

BRANCHES, AGENCIES AND OFFICES,
 Power to open, 137, 138
 Branches merely offices of one bank, 138
  but sometimes treated as distinct banks, 139
 Branch and agency distinguished, 139
 See also *Agent for Collection.*

BUSINESS AND POWERS OF BANK,
 See *Bank.*

BUSINESS DAY,
 See *Holiday.*

BY-LAWS,
 See *Directors—Shareholders—Canadian Bankers' Association.*

'CALLS,
 See *Shares.*

CANADIAN BANKERS' ASSOCIATION,
 Act of incorporation, 287
 Objects and powers, 289, 292
 Members and associates, 288
 Power to appoint curator, 237
 By-laws respecting curator, 239, 241
 By-law respecting bank notes, 241, 242
 Internal regulations, 290, 291
 See also *Clearing House.*

CANCELLATION,
 Of acceptance before delivery, 416, 417
 Of bill or signature, 581
 Unintentional cancellation, 582

CAPACITY,
Distinguished from authority, 428, 551
Co-extensive with capacity to contract, 428
Bill void or voidable by reason of incapacity, 429
Holder may recover notwithstanding incapacity of drawer
or endorser, 429
Incapacity of one party, 430
Conflict of laws, 598
See also *Corporation.*

CAPITAL STOCK,
Charters continued as to, 37
To be declared in Act of incorporation, 41
Not less than $500,000, 41
$250,000 to be paid up, 43, 44
Increase, 70
Allotment in case of increase, 71, 72
Reduction, 72
Conditions for reduction, 73
Limit of reduction, 74
Impairment, 83, 109
See also *Shares—Dividends.*

CASE OF NEED,
Referee in, 402
Option to resort to, 402
Protest necessary before presentment to, 540

CERTAINTY,
As to payee, 373
As to drawee, 372
Event which is certain to happen, 385
Sum certain, 366, 393

CHEQUE,
Definition, 608
Provisions of Act applicable to, 608
Compared with bill of exchange, 609
Dominion government cheques, 222
Bank's obligation to customer, 211
No privity between holder and bank, 610
Cheque on private banker, 608
Acceptance of cheque, 609, 611, 612, 613
Certification at drawer's instance, 612

CHEQUE—*Continued,*
Certification at holder's instance, 612
Countermand of payment, 617
Notice of customer's death, 617
Paid on forged or unauthorized endorsement, 430, 435
Negligent drawing of cheque, 440
Negotiation of stale cheque, 479
Reasonable time for presentment for payment, 496, 614, 616
When drawer discharged by omission so to present, 615
Not an equitable assignment, 610
Is given for immediate payment, 609, 611
Garnishee order, 618
See also *Crossed Cheque—Depositor and Bank.*

CIRCUITY OF ACTION,
Rule against, 481, 482

CIRCULATION,
See *Bank note—Bank Circulation Redemption Fund.*

CLEARING HOUSE,
Power to establish and regulate, 289, 292, 293
Definition, 294
Voluntary association, 294
Operation illustrated, 294, 295
Purpose, 294, 295
Objection to items, 296
Payment through clearing house provisional, 297
Objecting bank not prejudiced, 297
Presentment through clearing house, 298
Rules and regulations respecting, 299-305

COINS AND COINAGE,
See *Currency.*

COLLATERAL SECURITY,
Nature of, 141
Acquiring absolute title, 159
Pledge of bill, 141
Realization of security,
Suit upon commercial paper, 141
Bound to creditor borrower, 141
Sale of security on default, 152, 153, 154, 191
See also *Lending Powers of Bank—Discount—Trusts.*

COLLECTION,
See *Agent for Collection.*

COMMON LAW,
When applicable to bills, notes and cheques, 335, 355
Primary resort to English cases, 356
When provincial law applicable, 357
See also *Law Merchant.*

COMPANY,
See *Corporation.*

COMPLETE, COMPLETION,
Complete and regular on the face of it, 455
Completing bill by filling up blank, 401
Bill incomplete until delivery, 415
Death of acceptor of incomplete bill, 401
Acceptance of incomplete bill, 409, 410
Signature by stranger to incomplete bill, 558

COMPUTATION OF TIME,
First day excluded, day of payment included, 426
When time limited less than three days, 353
In case of acceptance or dishonour of sight bill, 426

CONFLICT OF LAWS,
Reference to provincial law, 357
Cases in which conflict may arise, 598
Capacity, 598
Evidence, 599
Limitation and prescription, 599
Set-off and compensation, 599
Interpretation, 599, 602
Modification of obligation, 599
Formalities of contract, 600, 601, 602
Procedure, 601
Place of payment true place of making, 603
Obligations of acceptor, 603
Drawing issue and endorsement, 604
Legality of consideration, 604
Duties of holder, 605, 606
Bill payable in Canada in foreign currency, 606
Due date, 606

CONSIDERATION,
  Value means valuable consideration, 343, 346
  Purchase money of patent right, 359-361
  Impeachment by oral evidence, 421, 460
  What constitutes valuable consideration, 447
  Antecedent debt or liability, 448
  Adequacy will not be enquired into, 449
  Holder for value, 449
  Illegal, making title defective, 454
  When illegality a defence, 461
  Value need not be expressed, 389
  Presumption of value, 457
  Onus may be shifted, 458
  Usurious consideration, 461
  See also *Value.*

CONSTITUTIONAL LAW,
  See *Legislative Power.*

CONTINGENCY,
  Bill must not be payable on a, 369
  Event which is certain to happen, 385, 386

COPY,
  In countries where *"copies"* are recognized, 465, 466.

CORPORATION,
  Signature of, 351
  Bill under corporate seal, 351
  Bill signed on company's behalf, 351, 352
  Liability of company on a bill, 352
  Capacity to become liable, 352, 428, 429
  Acceptance on behalf of, 407, 408
  Liability of agent, 443, 444

CROSSED CHEQUE,
  Provisions as to applicable to dividend warrant, 354
  History of English legislation, 619
  Definition, 620
  Various forms of crossing, 621
  By whom cheque may be crossed, 621, 622
  How crossing may be altered, 622, 623
  Re-opening or uncrossing, 622

CROSSED CHEQUE—*Continued.*

    Crossing a material part of cheque, 623
    Crossed to more than one bank, 623
    Liability for improper payment, 624
    Bank paying in good faith and without negligence, 625
    Crossed "not negotiable," 625, 626
    Bank receiving payment for customer, 626

CURATOR,

    Definition, 31, 34
    Appointment of, 237, 239
    Duties and powers, 238, 239
    Officers, etc., of bank to assist, 238
    By-laws, etc., must be approved by, 238
    Remuneration, 239, 240
    By-laws respecting, 239, 240

CURRENCY,

    Uniform currency for Canada, 306
    The Currency Act, 307
    Standard of value of currency, 307
    Public accounts, debts and obligations, 308
    Dominion and bank notes to be payable in Canadian currency, 309
    Gold coins, 310
    Legal tender, 310, 311, 312, 316
    Silver, copper or bronze coins, 311
    Foreign gold coins, 312
    Redemption of coins, 313
    Counterfeit or diminished coin to be broken, 313
    Bill payable in Canada in foreign currency, 606

CUSTOM,

    See *Law Merchant—Negotiability.*

CUSTOMER,

    Definition, 131
    Disclosure of customer's account, 106
    Duty to keep secret, 107
    Bank must know customer's signature, 440
    See also *Depositor and Bank—Lending Powers—Collateral Security—Agent for Collection—Lien.*

DAMAGES,
See *Dishonour.*

DATE,
Bill not dated, 389
Antedated or postdated, 389, 390
Presumption as to date, 389, 396
Undated bill payable after date, 396
Undated acceptance payable at or after sight, 396
Inserting true date, 396
Effect of inserting wrong date, 396
Month or months after date, 427
Endorsement dated after maturity, 480
Alteration of date material, 584

DAYS OF GRACE,
To be added to instalment due dates, 394
To be added to bill not payable on demand, 423
When third day a legal holiday, 423, 424
No action on third day of grace, 510, 511
Notice of dishonour may be given on third day, 510

DEALER,
Bank a dealer in coin, etc., 137
Not to deal in buying, etc., of goods, 137, 147
Purchase of bill, 141
Trade or business, 147
See also *Wholesale—Lending Powers of Bank.*

DEATH,
Of acceptor of incomplete bill, 401
Of drawer before acceptance, 549
Of drawer of cheque, 618
Presentment for acceptance, drawee dead, 488, 489
Presentment for payment, drawee or acceptor dead, 497, 498
Notice of dishonour, drawer or endorser dead, 516, 518, 526
See also *Transmission of Shares.*

DEFECTIVE TITLE, DEFECT IN TITLE,
What is, 454, 456
Negotiation of overdue bill, 477
Negotiation to holder in due course, 482
See also *Equity Attaching to Bill.*

DEBENTURE,
See *Bond.*

DEFENCE,
Includes counterclaim, 343, 346

DELIVERY,
Definition, 343, 345
Contracts incomplete until, 415
Blank paper delivered for conversion into bill, 397
Requisites of effectual delivery, 418
When delivery presumed, 418, 419
Delivery conditional or for special purpose, 418, 420
Transferor by delivery, 570, 571

DEMAND, BILL PAYABLE ON,
When so payable, 383
Accepted or endorsed when overdue, 383
Sight bills are not payable on demand, 384
Demand bill not entitled to grace, 423

DEPOSITOR AND BANK,
Bank of deposit, 132, 209
Deposits by persons unable to contract, 209
Drawee of cheques, 132
Payment of customer's acceptance, 132
Locality of deposit, 210
Bank a debtor in respect of deposit, 210, 211
Not a bailee or trustee, 210
Interest on deposits, 211
Obligation to honour cheques, 211, 212
Pass-books and vouchers, 212, 213
Appropriation and set-off in current account, 214
Rule in Clayton's case, 214
Deposit receipts, 216
Receipt of one of two joint depositors, 217, 218
Payment in event of depositor's death, 220, 221
In the event of bank's insolvency, 257-8
Bank bound to know customer's signature, 440
See also *Trusts—Limitation—Cheque.*

DESCRIPTION,
Of goods pledged by Schedule C, 188, 174, 201
Of goods in warehouse receipt, 168, 174, 201

DESTROYED BILL,
See *Lost Bill.*

DETENTION OF BILL, 409

DIRECTORS,
Provisional directors, 41
their powers, 42, 43
Branch directors, 61
Powers of directors, 53, 60
Appointment of officers, 61
Election, 45, 56, 57, 58, 59
Filling vacancies, 58
Qualification, 55, 56
Number and quorum, 42, 53, 58
Meetings, 59
Liability, generally, 53, 54, 55, 107, 109, 111
not diminished by enforcement of liability of share-
holders, 254
Remuneration, 52, 61
May inspect books, etc., 106
Removal, 65, 66
By-laws, 60, 61
Informality of internal proceedings does not affect out-
siders, 42, 43, 49, 66
Discounts or loans to, 52

DISCHARGE OF BILL,
Distinguished from discharge of party, 573
Proved by oral evidence, 421
Terminates negotiability, 477
By payment, 573, 577
By acceptor's holding at maturity, 579
Confusio, 580
Renunciation of rights, 580
Remise volontaire, 580
Intentional cancellation, 581, 582
Material alteration, 582
What is material alteration, 584
Bill in a set, 597

DISCOUNT,

    Bank of discount, 135, 137
    Discount defined, 139
    Not a form of loan, 140
    See also *Collateral Security—Lending Powers of Bank.*

DISCREPANCY,

    Between words and figures, 393, 395

DISHONOUR,

    Acceptance after dishonour, 410
    Negotiation of bill with notice of dishonour, 480
    By non-acceptance, 490, 491
    Where presentment for acceptance excused, 489, 491
    Immediate right of recourse, 492
    Holder may refuse to take qualified acceptance, 493
    By non-payment, 509
    Immediate right of recourse, 509
    No right of action on due date, 510, 511
    Measure of damages, 566
    Recovery of damages, 569
    Re-exchange in case of dishonour abroad, 569
    See also *Notice of Dishonour.*

DIVIDENDS,

    May be declared out of profits, 108
    Where payable, 75
    Not so as to impair capital, 109
    When may be paid in excess of 8%, 111
    Bonus of same nature as dividend, 108
    Receipt of one of two shareholders, 98, 101
    Declaration discretionary, 108
    Purchaser's right to, 109
    Director's liability, 109, 111
    What is profit available for dividend, 110
    See also *Limitations, Statutes of—Returns.*

DIVIDEND WARRANT, 354

DOCUMENTARY BILL, 493, 412

DOMICILED BILL, 390

DOMINION GOVERNMENT,
See *Cheques—Insolvency—Lending Powers of Bank—Minister of Finance—Treasury Board.*

DOMINION NOTES,
Provincial Notes Act, 4
Notes of late province of Canada, 318
Dominion Notes Act, 314, 315
Arrangements for delivery to banks, 112
Payment by bank in Dominion notes, 128
No payment in torn or defaced notes, 128
To be payable in Canadian currency, 309
Issue, 316
Legal tender, 316
Denominations, 316
Redemption, 112, 316, 318
Security for redemption, 317
Proceeds and expenses, 317
Monthly statement, 318
See also *Reserve.*

DRAWEE,
Two or more drawees, 369, 370
Payable to drawee's order, 370
Must be named or indicated, 372
Drawer and drawee the same person, 387
Drawee fictitious or incapable of contracting, 387
Wrongly designated or name mis-spelt, 405, 408
Not liable on the bill unless he accepts, 546
May be liable to drawer for not accepting, 548
Effect of drawer's death before acceptance, 549

DRAWER,
Bill payable to drawer's order, 370
Drawer and drawee the same person, 387
May negative his liability to holder, 403
May waive, as regards himself, duties of holder, 403
Death of drawer before acceptance, 549
Acceptor estopped as to, 550
Contract of drawer, 552
Estoppel as to payee, 552
Paying bill, rights of, 577

ENDORSEE,
Under special endorsement, 469
Right to receive payment, 472

ENDORSEMENT,
Definition, 343, 346
Forged or unauthorized, 430, 436, 438
Transfer without endorsement, 464
Endorsing so as to negative personal liability, 464, 482
Requisites of, in order to operate as negotiation, 465
Partial endorsement, 465, 466
Distinguished from assignment, 465
Simple signature of endorser sufficient, 466
Endorsement of two or more payees, 466
Of payee wrongly designated or name mis-spelt, 467
Presumption as to order of endorsements, 468
Conditional endorsement, 468
In blank or special, 469
Converting blank into special, 469, 470
Striking out endorsements, 470
Restrictive endorsement, 471, 474, 475
Conventions and rules respecting endorsements, 473
Regular and irregular endorsements, 474, 475
Guarantee of endorsements, 475, 476
Endorsement dated after maturity, 480
Signature by stranger before payee's endorsement, 557
Bill in a set, 597
See also *Signature.*

ENDORSER,
May negative his liability to holder, 403
Person signing otherwise than as drawer or acceptor, 554
Contract of endorser, 563
Estoppel of, 563
Primâ facie liability, 564
Successive endorsers, 565, 563
Paying bill, rights of, 577

ENGLISH STATUTES,
In restraint of negotiation of bills and notes under limited
    sum, 355
Construction of Colonial Act in same terms as, 511
See also *Bills of Exchange Act.*

EQUITABLE ASSIGNMENT,
Bill does not operate as, 546
How privity may be created, 547, 548

EQUITY ATTACHING TO BILL,
Negotiation of overdue bill, 477
What constitutes such equity, 477, 478
Negotiation with notice of dishonour, 480

ESTOPPEL,
And negotiability, 324
From setting up forgery or want of authority, 433
Against acceptor, 550
Against drawer, 552
Against endorser, 563
Against maker, 639

EVIDENCE,
See *Oral Evidence—Conflict of Laws.*

EXCHANGE,
Bill payable according to rate of, 393, 395
See also *Re-exchange.*

EXCHEQUER BILL, 329

EXECUTION,
See *Shares.*

FACTORS ACTS,
As affecting bills of lading, 34
Legislation prior to Bank Act, 165
Person entrusted, 175-178

FALSE NUMBER,
Selling shares by, 259

FALSE STATEMENT,
In warehouse receipt, etc., 265
In return, etc., 270
Knowledge of falsity essential, 272
Wilfully, 274
Mens rea, 274
Fraudulent intent, 275

FICTITIOUS OR NON-EXISTING,
Payee, 373, 375, 377
Fictitious distinguished from forged, 382
Drawee, 387

FIRM,
See *Partner.*

FORCE AND FEAR, 456

FOREIGN BILL OR NOTE,
What is a foreign bill, 386
Distinguished from inland bill, 386, 387
Foreign or inland note, 633

FORGERY,
Ratification of forgery, 431, 433

FORGED OR UNAUTHORIZED SIGNATURE,
Wholly inoperative, 430, 431
Unless party charged is estopped, 430, 433
Ratification, 432
Recovery back of money paid, 430, 436, 438
Notice in writing of forgery, 435, 436
English Act protecting bank, 437

FORM OF BILL,
See *Bill of Exchange—Promissory Note, etc.—Date—Place
—Value—Conflict of Laws.*

FORMS,
Act of incorporation of banks, 282
Security under sec. 88 of Bank Act, 187, 283
Monthly return to government, 284
Noting for non-acceptance, 641
Protest for non-acceptance or non-payment, 642-646
Notarial notice of noting or of protest, 647, 648
Notarial service of notice, 649
Protest by a justice of the peace, 650

FRAUD,
Making title defective, 454
When fraud is a defence, 460

FRAUDULENT PREFERENCE OF CREDITOR,
See *Offences and Penalties.*

FUTURE TIME, BILL PAYABLE AT A DETERMINABLE,
What bills are, 385
Payable after specified event, 385
See also *Sight—Date.*

GOOD FAITH,
When thing done in, 348
Presumption of good faith, 458
When onus shifted to holder, 458

GOODS, WARES AND MERCHANDISE,
Definition, 32, 34, 149
Substituted goods, 174, 175, 179, 184
Goods produced from goods pledged, 174, 191
See also *Lending Powers of Bank—Description.*

GRACE,
See *Days of Grace.*

GUARANTEE,
See *Officer of Bank.*

HOLDER,
Definition, 343, 345
Holder for value, 449
Rights and powers, 482
Negotiating to a holder in due course, 482
Right of recourse on dishonour, 492, 509, 512
Duties of, may be waived by drawer or endorser, 403
General duties of, 484

HOLDER IN DUE COURSE,
Defined, 453, 455, 456
Not prejudiced by insertion of wrong date, 393
Taking bill with blank filled up, 399
Valid delivery of bill presumed, 418, 419
Bill voidable by reason of incapacity, 429
Party deriving title from, 457
Presumption that party is holder in due course, 458
When onus shifted, 458
Holds bill free from defect of title, 482
Subsequent to dishonour by non-acceptance, 513
Acceptor estopped, 550
Drawer estopped, 552

43—BANK ACT.

HOLDER IN DUE COURSE—*Continued.*
Person signing otherwise than as acceptor or drawer, 554
Endorser estopped, 563
With notice of renunciation, 580
Of bill materially altered, 582, 583

HOLIDAY,
Legal holidays or non-juridical days, 424
Non-business day, 343, 346
Last day of grace falling on, 423, 424
When holidays excluded, 353

HONOUR,
See *Acceptance for Honour—Payment for Honour.*

IMPERIAL ACTS,
See *English Statutes.*

INCOMPLETE BILL,
See *Complete.*

INCORPORATION AND ORGANIZATION OF BANK,
Act of incorporation, 41
Opening of subscription books, 42
Meeting of subscribers, 43, 44
Commencing business, 45, 46, 259

INDORSEMENT, ETC.,
See *Endorsement, etc.*

INLAND BILL,
See *Foreign Bill.*

INSOLVENCY,
No insolvency law in Canada, 489
Effect of insolvency of acceptor, 539

INSOLVENCY OF BANK,
When constituted by suspension, 249
When company deemed insolvent, 250
Calls to be made, 251
Bank notes first charge, 256
Dominion government claim second charge, 257
Provincial government claim third charge, 257
Creditors' claims prior to penalties, 257

INSOLVENCY OF BANK—*Continued*.

Claims of depositors, 257-8
Application of Winding-up Act, 246
Double liability of shareholders, 247, 251
Proceedings under Winding-up Act, 252
Liability of transferor of shares, 255
See also *Winding-up*.

INSPECTION, RIGHT OF,

Of books, correspondence and funds, 106
Of daily list of transfers, 90
No privilege in court proceedings, 106
Customer's account, 106
Director not bound to inspect books, 107

INSTALMENTS,

Bill payable by stated, 393, 394

INTEREST,

Bank not liable for usury, 204
No higher rate than 7% recoverable by bank, 204
Bank may stipulate for any rate, 206
Debtor may recover excess charged, 206
But not if excess voluntarily paid, 207
Percentage chargeable for collection, 207
Also percentage for agency charge, 208
Interest on bank notes after suspension, 124
Interest on deposits, 204, 211
Bill payable with interest, 393
Dishonour by non-payment of interest, 510
Interest as damages on dishonour, 566
In case of dishonour abroad, 569
Usurious consideration for bill, 461

INTERNAL REGULATIONS OF BANKS,

Provisions of Bank Act, 52
Informality of internal proceedings, 42, 48, 66
Court will not interfere with internal management, 49
See also *Directors—Shareholders*.

INTERPRETATION,

See *Bank Act—Bills of Exchange Act—Conflict of Laws*.

ISSUE OF BILL,
    Definition, 343, 346
    Distinguished from negotiation, 400
    Re-issue after negotiation back, 481
    Re-issue after payment, 577, 578

LAND,
    See *Property.*

LAW MERCHANT,
    Origin and history, 21
    Usage sanctioned by the courts, 22
    Evidence of usage, 23
    Introduced into Canada, 24
    How far applicable to Quebec, 26
    Applicable to bills, notes and cheques, 335, 355
    Results of formation by custom, 336
    See also *Common Law.*

LEGAL TENDER,
    See *Currency,*

LEGISLATIVE POWER,
    Currency and coinage, 4
    Banking, banks and paper money, 4
    Warehouse receipts, etc., 180-183
    Taxation of banks, 31, 76
    Succession duty on shares, 76, 77, 78, 79
    Succession duty on deposits, 78
    Insolvency and winding-up, 246
    Bills of exchange and promissory notes, 4, 341
    Interest, 4
    Legal tender, 4
    Procedure, 86

LENDING POWERS OF BANK,
    Powers generally, 135
    What bank may lend on, 137
        bills and notes, 137
        bonds, debentures, etc., 137, 142
        other negotiable securities, 137, 142, 326
        stock and shares, 137, 142, 143, 144
        government securities, 137
        timber license and timber, 162

LENDING POWERS OF BANK—*Continued.*
What bank may not lend on, 137, 145
    bank shares, 137, 147, 148
    lands and immovable property, 138, 148
    ships, 138, 149, 162, 163
    goods, wares and merchandise, 137, 138, 149
    except as additional security, 155-158
    or except as otherwise provided in the Act, 137, 146
    penalties, 267
Warehouse receipts, bills of lading or security under sec.
    88, 167, 178
    earlier legislation, 164, 197
    title to goods vested in bank, 167, 172
    effect of security, 167, 173, 179
    priority over unpaid vendor, 191, 194
    goods produced from pledged goods, 174, 191
    substituted goods, 174, 175, 179, 184
    right of bank to take possession, 172
    right of proceeds in case of sale by receiptor, 193
    right of bank to sell on default, 191, 194, 195
    wholesale purchaser, shipper or dealer, 178
    wholesale manufacturer, 179, 185
    schedule C, 186, 187
    where previous holder is agent of owner, 175
    advance must be contemporaneous, 196, 201
    or upon written promise or agreement, 196, 200
    negotiated or contracted, 198
    debt may be renewed or extended, 196, 202
    exchange or substitution of securities, 196, 202
    penalties, 263
Transactions in violation of Act,
    are subject of penalty, 146
    contract of loan valid, 146
    but security invalid, 146
See also *Collateral Security—Factors Acts—Discount—Warehouse Receipt.*

LIABILITY OF PARTIES TO BILLS AND NOTES,
    Generally, 546
    Contract on bill incomplete until delivery, 415
    Presumption as to order of endorsements, 468
    In case of re-issue of bill after negotiation back, 481

LIABILITY OF PARTIES, ETC.—*Continued.*
. Person signing otherwise than as drawer or acceptor, 554
Signature by stranger before payee's endorsement, 557
See also *Acceptor—Drawer—Endorser—Maker—Drawee.*

LIEN,
On banker's own shares, 89, 92, 149-151
Sale and transfer of shares, 150
On customer's balance and securities, 151
Enforcement of lien, 151, 152
Holder of bill having lien, 449, 451

LIMITATIONS AND PRESCRIPTION,
Not applicable to deposits or dividends, 249
When time begins to run on bill, 512
Conflict of laws, 599

LIQUIDATION AND LIQUIDATOR,
See *Winding-up.*

LOST BILL,
Protest of, on copy or particulars, 541
No action on, at common law, 594
Right of holder to duplicate bill, 594
Action may be allowed if indemnity given, 595

LUMBER,
See *Timber.*

MAKER OF NOTE,
Contract of, 639

MANUFACTURER,
What included, 32, 35, 185, 186
See also *Wholesale.*

MARRIAGE OF FEMALE SHAREHOLDER,
See *Transmission of Shares.*

MEETINGS,
See *Incorporation and Organization — Directors — Shareholders.*

"MINISTER,"
Means Minister of Finance, 31, 33

MISTAKE,

Inserting wrong date by, 396

Recovery of money paid by, 439

MONEY,

Bill must be payable in, 363, 366

See also *Currency*.

MONTH,

Means calendar month, 427

Bill payable at a month or months after date, 427

NEGLIGENCE,

And good faith, 348

Drawing cheque with spaces, 440-441

NEGOTIABLE INSTRUMENTS,

Definition, 325, 483

Negotiability discussed, 321, 462

original and acquired meaning, 323, 325

ambulatory intent, 323

by estoppel, 324

usage of money market, 327

What instruments may be negotiable,

bills, notes and cheques, 326

bonds, 143, 327

deposit receipt, 216, 217

scrip, 328

interest coupons, 329

circular notes, 329

dividend warrants, 329

exchequer bills, 329

Instruments not negotiable,

share transfers and certificates, 143, 329

bills of lading, 35, 329

post office orders, 329

letters of credit signed by provincial secretary, 329

endorsement or receipt of, 476

See also *Negotiation*.

"NEGOTIATED OR CONTRACTED," 198-200

NEGOTIATION OF BILL,
   Defined, 462, 463
   Distinguished from issue, 400
   Distinguished from transmission or transfer by assignment,
      462
   Words in bill prohibiting transfer, 372
   Requisites of endorsement in order to operate as, 465
   Restrictive endorsement, 471, 477
   When negotiability ceases, 476
   Negotiation of overdue bill subject to the equities, 477
   Presumption of negotiation before maturity, 480
   Power to negotiate distinguished from right, 483
   Within reasonable time in case of sight bill, 486
   Liability of transferor by delivery, 570, 571
   Second negotiation after payment, 577, 578
   Bill in a set, 597

NON-ACCEPTANCE,
   See *Dishonour*.

NON-BUSINESS DAYS,
   Definition, 343, 346
   See also *Holidays*.

NON-JURIDICAL DAYS,
   See *Holidays*.

NON-NEGOTIABLE BILL, 372, 373

NON-PAYMENT,
   See *Dishonour*.

NOTARY,
   In the Province of Quebec, 28
   Clerk, teller or agent of bank,
      not to act as, 359

"NOTE,"
   means promissory note, 343, 345

NOTE ISSUE,
   See *Bank Note—Dominion Notes*.

NOTICE,
Of trusts relating to shares, 100
    to deposits, 217.
Of fraud or illegality affecting bill, 455.
Of forgery upon which cheque paid, 431, 435
By payer of bill which is dishonoured, 441.

NOTICE OF DISHONOUR,
Meaning of, 514.
Who entitled to, 513
Rights of holder in due course, 513
In case of prior notice of dishonour by non-acceptance, 513
Discharge of parties by omission to give, 514, 515
Guarantor not entitled to, 514.
Time for, 515, 516, 519
By whom, 516, 518, 519, 522
To whom, 516, 517, 519, 522
Misdescription of bill, 519, 521
Form of notice, 519, 520, 521, 522
Bill dishonoured in hands of agent, 523
Notice in case of several endorsements, 523
Notice to antecedent parties, 524
For whose benefit notice enures, 524
Duties of successive endorsers, 525
Sufficiency of address of notice by post, 525
Miscarriage by post office, 528
Delay in giving notice excused, 529
Notice dispensed with, 530, 532, 533

NOTICE OF PROTEST,
See *Protest.*

NOTING,
Delay in noting excused, 536
Noting sufficient instead of protest, 540
Formal protest may be subsequently extended, 541
Form of noting, 540, 641
Time for noting, 541
Time for notice of protest, 545
Expenses part of damages on dishonour, 567
Form of notice of noting, 647

OFFENCES AND PENALTIES,
Commencing business without certificate, 259
Sale and transfer of shares in contravention of Act, 259
Cash reserves, 260
Excess of authorized issue of notes, 260
Unauthorized issue of notes, 260, 261
Defacement of notes, 262
Issue of notes after suspension, 262
Pledging of notes, 263
Fraudulent issue of notes, 263
Acquiring warehouse receipts, etc., except as authorized by
        Act, 263, 264
Sale of security except as authorized, 265
Wilfully alienating goods pledged, 266
Omission to sell shares of bank covered by lien, 267.
Prohibited business, 267.
Failure to make returns, 268, 269
Refusing to make calls in case of suspension, 276
Undue preference to bank's creditors, 277
Using the title "bank," etc, 277
Penalty for offence against the Act, 278
Procedure to enforce penalty, 278
See also *False Statement*.

OFFICER OF BANK,
Power to appoint, 61.
President, 33, 35, 52, 58
        duties of, 59, 92
Honorary president, 33, 58
Vice-president, 52, 58, 59
General manager, 61, 62
Branch manager, 61, 63
Liability of manager, 63
Bond or security to be given, 61
Guarantee and pension fund, 52
Holding out, 48
Officer's knowledge imputed to bank, 63
See also *False Statement*.

ORAL EVIDENCE,
Delivery conditional or for special purpose, 418
Presumption of valid delivery, 418, 419

ORAL EVIDENCE—*Continued,*
Inadmissible to contradict or vary, 421
Admissible to negative existence of bill, 421
Admissible to impeach the consideration, 421
Admissible to prove discharge, 421
Evidence of true date, 396

ORDER
When bill is payable to order, 372
Negotiation of such a bill, 463
Transfer without endorsement, 464

OVERDUE BILL,
Bill accepted or endorsed when overdue, 383
Acceptance of overdue bill, 410
Negotiation subject to defect in title, 477
When demand bill overdue, 477
When other bill overdue, 424
When demand note overdue, 636

PAROL EVIDENCE,
See *Oral Evidence.*

OWNER OF BILL,
Distinguished from holder, 345

PARTICULAR FUND, 367, 368

PARTIES,
To a bill, 367
See also *Liabilities of Parties—Capacity—Authority—Signature.*

PARTNER AND PARTNERSHIP,
Acceptance by, 407
Endorsement by, 466, 467
Signature of name of firm, 560
Authority of partner, 561, 562

PASS BOOK AND VOUCHERS, 212

PATENT RIGHT,
Bill or note in consideration of purchase money of, 359-361

PAYEE,
Bill payable to drawer's or drawee's order, 370
Two or more payees, 370, 371
Payable to the holder of an office, 370, 371
Payable to order or bearer, 372, 374
Payee must be named or indicated, 373, 374
Fictitious or non-existing, 373-382
Bill, when payable to payee's order, 382
Payee wrongly designated or name misspelt, 467
Acceptor estopped as to, 550
Drawer estopped as to, 552
Signature by stranger before payee's endorsement, 557

PAYMENT,
When complete, 212
Payment of bill, 573
Terminates negotiability, 477
Delivery up of bill, 505, 507
Discharge by, 573
What is payment, 574
By or on behalf of drawee or acceptor, 575
By drawer or endorser, 577

PAYMENT BY BILL,
Presumably conditional, 515
When condition fulfilled, 515
Renewal of bill, 576

PAYMENT FOR HONOUR *SUPRA* PROTEST,
Rights of payer for honour, 591
Attested by notarial act of honour, 592
Who discharged by, 492
Payer subrogated to rights of holder, 592
Subsequent parties discharged, 593

PAYMENTS TO MINISTER UPON WINDING-UP,
Unclaimed moneys, 234
Subject to order of Governor in Council, 234
Amount of outstanding bank notes, 235-6

PENALTIES,
See *Offences and Penalties.*

PENSION FUND,
See *Officer of Bank.*

PERSON,
Defined, 347

PLACE,
Of drawing or payment need not be expressed, 389
See also *Acceptance—Presentment for Acceptance—Present-
ment for Payment.*

PLEDGE,
See *Lending Powers of Bank—Collateral Security.*

PRESCRIPTION,
See *Limitations and Prescription.*

PRESENTMENT FOR ACCEPTANCE,
Compared with presentment for payment, 484
When necessary, 484, 485
Duties of agent as to presentment, 133
Delay in presentment excused, 486
Of sight bill within reasonable time, 486
What is due presentment, 488
By whom, 489
To whom, 489
Presentment excused, 489
Time for acceptance, 490
Dishonour by non-acceptance, 491

PRESENTMENT FOR PAYMENT,
Compared with presentment for acceptance, 484
When necessary, 495
Holder must exhibit bill, 495
Due presentment, 496
Time for, 496, 498, 507
By whom, 497
To whom, 497, 498
Place of, 499, 500, 501
Through post office, 501, 502
Delay in presentment excused, 502, 508
Presentment dispensed with, 503
Promissory note, 635-638

PRESIDENT,
    See *Officers of Bank.*

PRINCIPAL AND AGENT,
    See *Agent.*

PRINCIPAL AND SURETY,
    See *Surety.*

PRIVATE INTERNATIONAL LAW,
    See *Conflict of Laws.*

PROCURATION,
    See *Signature.*

PRODUCT,
    Product of the forest, 184
    See also *Goods, Wares and Merchandise.*

PROMISSORY NOTE,
    Definition, 630
    Provisions of the Act applicable to, 629, 639, 640
    After sight, 427
    Negotiability of notes, 629
    Payable to maker's order, 630, 633
    Pledge of collateral security, 630, 633
    Promise to pay, 631
    Made by one person to another, 632
    Inland and foreign notes, 633
    Inchoate and incomplete until delivery, 633
    Joint or joint and several liability, 634
    Presentment of demand note, 635
    When demand note deemed overdue, 636
    Presentment of notes payable at particular place, 636, 637,
        638
    Present as regards endorser, 638
    Presentment as regards maker, 638
    Contract of maker, 639
    Protest of foreign note, 640
    See also *Bank Notes—Dominion Notes.*

PROPERTY,
    Real and immovable,
        for bank's use and occupation, 154

PROPERTY—*Continued.*

    purchase of realty in certain cases, 158

    acquired on debtor's default, 159, 160

    forfeiture if no sale within limited period, 160, 161

  Personal and moveable,   •

    rights with regard to mortgaged realty also apply to personalty, 155, 158

  See also *Lending Powers of Bank.*

PROTEST,

    Primâ facie evidence, 358

    Foreign protest as evidence, 358

    Not necessary in order to render acceptor liable, 536

    Protest dispensed with, 536

    Delay in noting or protesting excused, 536

    Protest of foreign bill, 536

    Protest of foreign note, 640

    Protest of inland bill, 537, 538

    For non-payment after protest for non-acceptance, 539

    Protest for better security, 539

    Protest before presentment to acceptor for honour or case of need, 540

    Noting sufficient, 540

    Formal protest may be extended later, 541

    Time for protest, 541, 542

    Time for notice of protest, 545

    Protest on copy or particulars of bill, 541

    Place of protest, 542

    Contents of, 543

    By justice of the peace, 544, 650

    Expenses of protest, 544, 567

    Fees, 544

    Forms of protest and noting, 545, 641, *et seq.*

    Forms of notice of protest, etc., 647, *et seq.*

PROVINCIAL GOVERNMENT,

  See *Insolvency—Lending Powers of Bank.*

PROVINCIAL LAW,

    Frequently applicable bills, etc., 357

  See also *Conflict of Laws.*

PROXY,
See *Shareholder.*

PUBLIC NOTICE, 33, 45, 57, 64, 108

PURCHASER,
Purchase of bill, 135, 141, 571
Purchase of property taken as security, 159
Purchase of bank's assets, 223
See also *Wholesale.*

QUEBEC,
Commercial law of, 25
General differences in law, 27
Special provisions of Bills of Exchange Act, 335
Articles of Civil Code applicable to bills, 336, 340
Sources of law of exchange, 338
Additional holidays in, 425
Protest of inland bill in, 538

REALIZATION OF SECURITY,
See *Collateral Security.*

REASONABLE HOUR, 498

REASONABLE TIME,
For filling up blank in bill, 399
For demand bill to be in circulation, 477
For presentment or negotiation of sight bill, 486, 487
For presentment for payment, 496
As regards drawer of a cheque, 614, 615, 616
For various purposes, 617
For presentment of demand note, 635
In order to affect holder of note with notice of defect, 636

RE-EXCHANGE,
In case of dishonour abroad, 569
Meaning of, 569, 570

REFEREE,
See *Case of Need.*

RE-ISSUE,
See *Issue—Bank Note.*

RENEWAL,
Presumably conditional payment, 576

RESERVE,
>Proportion of cash reserve to be held in Dominion notes, 112, 260
>Bank not obliged to keep reserve, 112
>>except when dividend of more than 8% paid, 111
>Discretionary power to form, 112

RETURNS,
>Monthly, to Government, 229
>Special, may be called for, 230
>List of shareholders, 232
>Dividends unpaid for 5 years, 231
>Other amounts and balances, 231
>Drafts issued and unpaid, 232
>Penalties for failure to make returns, 268
>See *False Statement*.

REVISED STATUTES OF CANADA, 1906, 19, 341
>And see Preface.

REVOCATION,
>Contract revocable until delivery, 415

SALE OF BANK'S ASSETS,
>Power to sell assets, 223
>Consideration may be shares of purchasing bank, 223
>Consent of shareholders, 224, 225
>Approval of Governor in Council, 224, 225, 227
>Conditions of such approval, 225, 226
>Notes of selling bank assumed, 227
>Selling bank to be wound up, 228

SALE OF BILL, 135, 141, 571

SALE OF SHARES, see *Transfer of Shares*.

SCHEDULES,
>Bank Act,
>>A. Banks to which Act applies, 36, 280
>>B. Act of incorporation, 41, 282
>>C. Form of security, 187, 283
>>D. Form of monthly return, 229, 284
>Bills of Exchange Act,
>>Forms A. to J., 641

44—BANK ACT.

SCRIP,
    See *Negotiable Instruments.*

SECURITY,
    See *Officer of Bank—Collateral Security—Lending Powers
        of Bank.*

SET-OFF AND COMPENSATION,
    In case of insolvency of bank, 248
    Not an equity attaching to bill, 477, 478
    Conflict of laws, 599

SHAREHOLDERS,
    Who are, 80
    Annual meeting, 52, 56, 57, 65, 104, 105
    Special general meeting, 64, 65, 66, 105
    Voting and proxies, 66, 67, 68, 69
    Not entitled to inspect books, etc., 106
    By-laws and powers, 50, 51, 52
    Cannot usually bring action for wrong to company, 49
    Chairman of meeting, 67, 68
    Liability not affected by reduction of stock, 73
    See also *Shares—Returns.*

SHARES,
    Subscription for, 75, 80
    Allotment of, 80, 81
    Calls on, powers and conditions as to, 82, 83
        remedy for non-payment, 82, 84, 85, 86
        on winding up of bank, 247
    Personal estate, 75
    Nature of, 76
    Assignable and transferable, 75, 79, 87
    Locality of shares, 76, 77, 78
    Sale in contravention of Act, 259
    Sale under execution, 91, 92
    Double liability, 247, 251
    Liability of transferor, 255
    Liability of trustee, 102, 103
    Par value of, 41
    Invalid share certificate, 48
    See also *Transfer of Shares—Transmission of Shares—Divi-
        dends — Capital Stock—Trusts—Negotiable Instru-
        ments—Lending Powers of Bank.*

SHIPS,
> See *Lending Powers of Bank.*

SIGNATURE,
> Person's own hand not necessary, 349
> What is sufficient signature, 349
> By agent or attorney, 349, 350
> Induced by fraud, 349, 398
> Authority to sign for another, 350
> Liability for signing without authority, 443, 444
> Signature in representative capacity, 444
> Signature by procuration, 441
> To blank paper, 397
> Mere signature sufficient acceptance, 408
> Simple signature sufficient endorsement, 466
> Party to a bill must sign it as such, 554
> Signing otherwise than as drawer or acceptor, 554
> Signature by stranger before payee's endorsement, 557
> Trade or assumed name, 560
> Firm name, 560
> See also *Corporation—Forged or Unauthorized Signature— Partner.*

SIGHT, BILL PAYABLE AT OR AFTER,
> Sight bills not payable on demand, 385
> Entitled to days of grace, 384, 424
> Undated acceptance payable at or after sight, 396
> Must be presented for acceptance, 484, 485
> Presented or negotiated within reasonable time, 486

"SPECIE" means coin current, 316

SUNDAY,
> Bill dated on, 389
> Bill for contract made on, 392

SURETY,
> Acceptor *primâ facie* principal debtor, 554
> Discharge of surety by dealings with principal or other surety, 554
> Accommodation party, 565, 566
> Endorser analogous to surety, 566

SUSPENSION OF PAYMENT,
See *Insolvency—Bank Notes—Curator.*

TIMBER,
Loans on standing timber or timber limits, 162
Receipt for timber in transit, 170
Sawn lumber not product of forest, 184

TIME,
See *Computation of Time—Reasonable Time.*

TRANSFER OF BILL,
See *Negotiation—Sale of Bill.*

TRANSFER OF SHARES,
Distinguished from transmission, 93
Method of, 87, 89
Conditions for, 87, 90
Fraction of share not assignable, 87
Without production of certificate, 89
Registration not discretionary, 79, 89
Sale under execution, 91, 92
Shares sold for shareholder's debt, 150
Forfeited shares, 85
Forged power of attorney, 89
Acceptance of transfer, 90
List of transfers, 90
Closing of transfer books, 108
Purchaser's right to dividend, 109
Penalty for transfer in violation of Act, 259
See also *Trusts.*

TRANSMISSION OF SHARES,
Distinguished from transfer, 93
Proof of, 92, 95, 96
By death of shareholder, 92, 93, 95
By marriage of female shareholder, 92, 93, 94
Succession duty, 76, 79
Registration not discretionary, 79, 93, 95
See also *Trusts.*

TREASURY BOARD,
  Act respecting, 33
  Certificate permitting bank to issue notes or commence business, 45, 46
  May approve increase of capital, 70
    reduction of capital, 72, 73

TRIMBLE v. HILL,
  Rule of Privy Council in, 511

TRUSTS,
  Bank not bound to see to execution,
    as to shares, 97, 98, 99, 100
    as to deposits, 217, 219, 220
  Personal liability of trustee-holder,
    of shares, 102, 103
  Nature of a trust, 100, 101
  Trusts relating to collateral security, 142, 143

UNAUTHORIZED SIGNATURE,
  See *Forged or Unauthorized.*

USAGE,
  See *Law Merchant—Negotiability.*

USURY,
  See *Interest.*

VALUE,
  Means valuable consideration, 343, 346
  Bill need not specify value given, 389
  See *Consideration.*

VICE-PRESIDENT,
  See *Officer of Bank.*

WAIVER,
  Of holder's duties, 403
  Of presentment for payment, 503
  Of notice of dishonour, 530, 531

WAREHOUSE RECEIPT,
    Definition, 32, 34, 169, 170
  . How acquired by bank, 168
    Receiptor must not be owner, 168
    Proof of possession as bailee, 169
    Includes receipt for logs in transit, 170
    May be to third person or direct to bank, 174
    Previous holder agent of owner, 175
    See also *Lending Powers of Bank.*

WHOLESALE,
    Meaning of wholesale, 183
    Loan to wholesale purchaser, 178, 183
        shipper, 178, 183
        dealer, 178, 183, 184
        manufacturer, 179
    See also *Lending Powers of Bank.*

WINDING-UP OF BANK,
    In case of sale of assets, 228
    In case of insolvency,
        calls to be made, 251
        proceedings under Winding-up Act, 246, 251
    Priority of charges on assets, 256-7
    Set-off, 248
    Liquidator, appointment of, 253, 254
    Limitation or prescription inapplicable, 249
    See also *Insolvency—Bank Notes—Payments to Minister*
        upon Winding-up.

WRITING DEFINED, 347

CPSIA information can be obtained
at www.ICGtesting.com
Printed in the USA
LVHW081631221022
731328LV00004B/254